Muḥammad Is Not the Father of Any of Your Men

Divinations: Rereading Late Ancient Religion
Series Editors: Daniel Boyarin, Virginia Burrus, Derek Krueger
A complete list of books in the series is available from the publisher.

Muḥammad Is Not the Father of Any of Your Men

The Making of the Last Prophet

DAVID S. POWERS

PENN
University of Pennsylvania Press
Philadelphia

Published by
University of Pennsylvania Press
Philadelphia, Pennsylvania 19104-4112

Printed in the United States of America on acid-free paper
10 9 8 7 6 5 4 3 2 1

Library of Congress Cataloging-in-Publication Data
Powers, David Stephan.
Muhammad is not the father of any of your men : the making of the last prophet / David S. Powers.
p. cm. — (Divinations : rereading late ancient religion)
Includes bibliographical references and index.
ISBN 978-0-8122-4178-5 (alk. paper)
1. Muhammad, Prophet, d. 632—Prophetic office. 2. Adoption—Religious aspects—Islam. 3. Inheritance and succession (Islamic law) I. Title.
BP166.5.P69 2009
297.6'3—dc22 2008051931

In loving memory:

David Peretz Andiman (d. October 1925)
Morris Adelman, né *Moische Josef Andiman (August 17, 1888–May 28, 1973)*

Tzum end Tzuzamen

Contents

"When I think," he said on reading or listening; "When I think of this phrase, continuing its journey through eternity, while I, perhaps, have only incompletely understood it. . . ."

— Michel Foucault, citing Pierre Janet, The Archaeology of Knowledge, *221*

Preface

Two long Medinan verses set out a complex law of inheritance (Q4:11–12) . . . a very practical matter. The second includes an account of what happens in the event that "a man is inherited by kalāla"; this word, which also occurs in Q4:176, seems to have bothered the commentators from the earliest times, and remains obscure to this day.

—*Michael Cook,* The Koran: A Very Short Introduction, *139*

The word *kalāla* occurs twice in the Qur'ān, once in Q 4:12b and again in 4:176. Although the word is little known today, even among native speakers of Arabic, it was a subject of great interest to the early Muslim community. The second caliph ʿUmar b. al-Khaṭṭāb is reported to have said that he would rather know the meaning of this word than possess an amount of money equal to the poll-tax levied on the fortresses of Byzantium. One might say that the meaning of *kalāla* was a mystery. Eventually, the word was defined as either (1) a man who dies leaving neither parent nor child or (2) a person's relatives except for parents and children, that is, collateral relatives.

Western scholarly interest in *kalāla* is barely a quarter of a century old. In 1982, I published an article in which I drew attention to the fact that the Arabic word *kalāla* is derived from the same root (*k-l-l*) as the Semitic kinship terms *kallatu* (Akk.), *kallâh* (Hebr.), and *kalltā* (Syr.), all of which signify a *daughter-in-law.* Using literary evidence—reports about ʿUmar and *kalāla* that I treated as coded narratives—I argued that the Qur'ānic term originally signified *daughter-in-law* and that the original *qirā'a* or vocalization of Q. 4:12b had been modified at three points. If so, then Q. 4:12b originally awarded fractional shares of the estate, not to exceed one-third, to the siblings of a man who had designated his daughter-in-law (or wife) as his heir in a last will and testament.[1] The novelty of my argument lay in the fact that Islamic inheritance law does not allow a person contemplating death to designate *anyone* as heir—let alone a female who is not related to him or her by ties of blood. My hypothesis about Q. 4:12b became the starting point of an attempt to explain the formation of Islamic inheritance law in historical terms. In a monograph published in 1986, I argued—against Schacht—that the *ʿilm al-farāʾiḍ* or "sciences of the shares" emerged immediately and directly out of the Qurʾānic inheritance rules, but—against the received Islamic tradition—that these rules underwent radical changes before becoming the basis of the *ʿilm al-farāʾiḍ*—changes of which the Muslim community is currently unaware. Over time, I suggested, the original meaning of *kalāla* was forgotten.[2]

Several scholars who reviewed the 1986 monograph rejected my thesis about *kalāla* and the formation of Islamic inheritance law either wholly or in part: H. Motzki[3] and F. Ziadeh[4] dismissed my central thesis, W. Madelung found it weak,[5] A. Rippin could not accept the thesis in the form presented in the monograph,[6] and J. Burton characterized it as unproven.[7] Subsequently, other scholars added their voices to the discussion, and some undertook an independent examination of the evidence: C. Gilliot found no code in the *kalāla* reports, called for an analysis of the *isnāds* attached to these reports, and offered an alternative explanation of the literary evidence that I had adduced in support of my hypothesis.[8] P. Crone acknowledged that *kalāla* is a problem but suspended judgment with regard to my argument about the original meaning of the word. According to her reading of my work, I advanced a "conspiracy theory" which she found problematic because it "cannot easily be extended to cover the parallel cases." Like Gilliot, Crone was not persuaded that there is a secret message in the reports that center on ʿUmar and she saw no obvious connection between the designation of an heir and political succession. What Crone did learn from my work is that "the meaning of *kalāla* . . . had never been known: there was nothing to remember, nothing to suppress."[9] R. Kimber accepted the traditional understanding of *kalāla* while at the same time proposing that the Qurʾānic inheritance rules were designed to modify earlier Jewish inheritance rules.[10] Y. Dutton suggested that the early Muslims were concerned with the implications of *kalāla* for inheritance law but not with the word's meaning.[11] Similarly, A. Cilardo concluded that early Muslim jurists reinterpreted the meaning of *kalāla* in order to create new inheritance rules in areas not covered by the Qurʾān.[12] Finally, W. Hallaq pronounced that the "problem associated with *kalāla* . . . may not turn out to be a problem at all"—albeit without explaining why.[13] Thus it may be said with confidence that the Western scholarly community's awareness of the word *kalāla* is greater today than it was a quarter of a century ago, even if the mystery surrounding this word has not been solved.

After completing the 1986 monograph, I spent two decades studying the Islamic judicial system in the Maghrib in the fourteenth and fifteenth centuries C.E.[14] In the summer of 2005, serendipity drew me back to the Qurʾān and the rise of Islam. In June of that year, I was looking for a monograph on Islamic law in the basement of Olin Library at Cornell University. By chance, I picked up a two-volume handbook of Near Eastern law which contains an index of ancient terms in Akkadian and other Semitic languages.[15] As expected, the index includes the Akkadian word *kallatu* ("daughter-in-law"). The references in the index led me to footnote 73 in a chapter on Nuzi by Carlo Zaccagnini in which the author states: "Note that in some documents . . . the term *martūtu* is coupled with *kallūtu* ('daughter-in-lawship')."[16] In footnote 75, Zaccagnini adds: "In these documents, the woman is adopted 'as daughter-in-law' (*ana kallūti*) or 'as daughter and daughter-in-law' (*ana martūti u kallūti*)." Eureka! In Q. 4:12b the Arabic noun *kalāla* is immediately followed by *aw imraʾa*; if the nouns *kalāla* and *imraʾa* are both read in the nominative case—which they are not—the result would be the disjunctive phrase *kalālat*^{un} *aw imraʾat*^{un}. The similarities between the Akkadian phrase (*martūti u kallūti*) and the Arabic phrase (*kalāla aw imraʾa*) are striking. But there are also important differences. Be that as it may, I asked myself: Is it possible that the Akkadian phrase passed into Arabic and resurfaced 2,000 years later, in a modified form, in the Qurʾān?

In the winter of 2005, Dr. Munther Younes drew my attention to the facsimile edition of Bibliothèque Nationale de France, Arabe 328a (hereinafter BNF 328a), a substantial fragment of a Ḥijāzī-style Qurʾān codex written in the second half of the first century AH.[17] To the best of my knowledge, this is the earliest extant Qurʾān manuscript which contains the full text of *Sūrat al-Nisāʾ*. In BNF 328a, Q. 4:12b appears on folio 10b, ll.17 ff. Although I noticed some irregularities on l. 18, at least six months would pass before I even considered the possibility that the consonantal skeleton of l. 18 on this folio page had been changed. In retrospect, my resistance to this idea is understandable. The Qurʾān teaches that God sent the Torah to Moses and that He sent the Injīl or New Testament to Jesus. The Qurʾān also teaches that the Israelites and Christians failed to preserve the original contents of their respective revelations which, over time, were subjected to *taḥrīf* or textual distortion. By contrast, it is a fundamental tenet of Islam that the Qurʾān always has been, and must remain, immune from textual distortion. From this tenet it follows that the consonantal skeleton of the Qurʾānic text, as it has come down to us in the twenty-first century, is identical in all respects to the revelations received by the Prophet Muḥammad over a period of twenty-three years between 610 and 632 C.E. The idea that the early Muslim community might have revised the consonantal skeleton of the Qurʾān is *unthinkable* not only for Muslims but also for many Islamicists—including, until recently, myself. This unthinkable proposition is one of the central concerns of the present monograph.[18]

I am now persuaded that I was wrong about *kalāla*, albeit not for the reasons put forward by respected colleagues. In fact, we were all wrong because we were all working with insufficient information. This gap in our knowledge is filled by two very different types of documentary evidence: (1) cuneiform tablets produced in Mesopotamia in the middle of the second millennium B.C.E., which contain linguistic information relating to the meaning of *kalāla*;

and (2) BNF 328a, which contains paleographic evidence relating to Q. 4:12b and codicological evidence relating to 4:176. The new evidence indicates that despite my having initially missed the mark, I nevertheless was on the right track from the outset. It also suggests that Crone was correct when she asserted that "the meaning of *kalāla* . . . had never been known," but that she was mistaken when she said that "there was nothing to remember, nothing to suppress." There was something to remember, and something was suppressed—but it was not *kalāla*.

The Akkadian phrase *martūti u kallūti* led me to the subject of adoption in the ancient Near East and from there to the subject of adoption in Islam, a topic to which I had paid little or no attention, seemingly with good reason, for adoption is forbidden in classical Islamic law. Therein lies the rub. I soon learned that the early Muslim community did at first recognize adoption as a legitimate legal institution but that this institution was abolished during the Medinese phase of the Prophet's career. I also learned that the abolition of adoption was connected to the introduction of a key theological doctrine: the assertion in Q. 33:40 that Muḥammad is the Seal of Prophets (*khātam al-nabiyyīn*). It is my contention that the introduction of this new theological doctrine necessitated adjustments to (1) the consonantal skeleton of the Qurʾān; (2) several legal doctrines; and (3) historical narratives about the rise of Islam.

In the present monograph, I reverse the direction taken by my research, beginning with the doctrine of the finality of prophecy and ending with the mystery of *kalāla*. The monograph is divided into three parts. In Part I, "Fathers and Sons," I lay the groundwork for my thesis by examining the subject of adoption in the Near East from antiquity down to the rise of Islam. In Chapter 1, I draw attention to the importance of the father-son motif in the foundation narratives of Judaism and Christianity and to the apparent absence of this motif from the Islamic foundation narrative. In Chapter 2, I demonstrate that adoption was widely practiced in the Near East in antiquity and late antiquity—especially among pagans and polytheists—and that the father-son motif was an important metaphor for the God-man relationship in both Judaism and Christianity. In Chapter 3, I summarize the standard Islamic account of the abolition of adoption according to which, after Muḥammad fell in love with his daughter-in-law Zaynab, he repudiated his adopted son Zayd; this was followed by a revelation that abolished the institution of adoption.

In Part II, "From Sacred Legend to Sacred History," I link the abolition of adoption to the introduction of the doctrine that the office of prophecy came to an end with the death of Muḥammad. The success of this new theological doctrine depended on the ability of the early Muslim community to construct its foundation narrative in such a manner as to support the new theological doctrine. In Chapter 4, I challenge the standard Islamic account of the abolition of adoption by arguing that the early Muslim community formulated the story of Muḥammad's marriage to his daughter-in-law Zaynab so as to create a plausible history-like context in which the Prophet could be said to have repudiated his adopted son Zayd. In Chapter 5, I argue that the Prophet's repudiation of Zayd did not solve the theological problem because Zayd was already a mature adult male at the time of his repudiation, for which reason it was necessary to demonstrate that he predeceased Muḥammad. This demonstration was made by first-century AH historians who found a plausible setting for Zayd's death in the Battle of Muʾta. In Chapter 6, I argue that the story of Zayd's martyrdom at Muʾta is modeled on the sacrifice of Isaac in Gen. 22 and its later narrative expansions. If this is so, then during the initial stage of Islamic history, the father-son motif was as important to Muslims as it had been and continued to be to Jews and Christians. In Chapter 7, I argue that the Qurʾānic account of Muḥammad's marriage to Zaynab is best seen as a sacred legend modeled on II Sam. 11–12 and Matt. 1:18–25; and that the narrative expansions of Q. 33:37 are best seen as creative reformulations of biblical and postbiblical narratives. Zayd's life unfolded as a series of tests. As the Beloved of the Messenger of God passed from one test to the next, he took on a new sacred persona.

In Part III, "Text and Interpretation," I return to the mystery of *kalāla*. As in Part II, I argue that the consonantal skeleton of the Qurʾān was revised. However, whereas in Part II my arguments are based on literary evidence, in Part III they are based on documentary evidence. And whereas I argue in Part II that it was the introduction of a new theological doctrine—the finality of prophecy—that required adjustments to the text of the Qurʾān, in Part III I argue that it was politics—specifically the question of who would succeed the Prophet as leader of the Muslim community—that triggered adjustments to the text of the Qurʾān. There is no direct connection between the textual revisions postulated in Parts II and III, and it is possible to treat the problems that I discuss independently. In fact, there may be an indirect connection between the two sets of revisions—a connection that I will make only at the end of Chapter 9.

In Chapter 8, I analyze documentary evidence from BNF 328a which suggests that the consonantal skeleton of Q. 4:12b was revised in such a manner as to create the word *kalāla*—a word that previously had not existed in Arabic or any other Semitic language. As a result of this revision, the meaning of the verse was turned on its head. This change, in turn, created a secondary problem that made it necessary to add supplementary legislation to the Qurʾān—hence the verse at the end of *Sūrat al-Nisāʾ* that mentions the word *kalāla* a second time. In Chapter 9, I follow the work of the first Muslim exegetes as they struggled to make sense of the new word *kalāla* over the course of the first three centuries AH. Finally, in the concluding chapter, I summarize the interplay between theology and politics, on the one hand, and the Qurʾān, law, and the writing of history, on the other.

Unless otherwise specified, translations of the Hebrew Bible follow *Tanakh, The Holy Scriptures: The New JPS Translation According to the Traditional Hebrew Text*; translations of the New Testament follow *The New Oxford Annotated Bible*, New Revised Standard Version; and translations of the Qurʾān, follow *The Qurʾān*, trans. Alan Jones.

Part I
Fathers and Sons

Your fathers and your sons—you do not know which of them is nearer to benefit for you . . . Q. 4:11

Chapter 1

The Foundation Narratives of Judaism, Christianity, and Islam

Take your son, your favored one, Isaac, whom you love, and go to the land of Moriah, and offer him there as a burnt offering on one of the heights that I will point out to you. Gen. 22:2

He who did not spare his own Son, but gave him up for all of us, will he not with him also give us everything else? Rom. 8:32

Muḥammad is not the father of any of your men. . . . Q. 33:40

The foundation narratives of Judaism, Christianity, and Islam are all formulated in the idiom of family relationships. In each case, it is the same family that is the subject of the respective foundation narrative, albeit at a different stage in history. The Jewish theological doctrine of *divine election* emerges directly from the dynamics of domestic relations within the household of Abraham, to wit, the patriarch's relationship with his wife Sarah, his concubine Hagar, and his sons Ishmael and Isaac. Similarly, the Christian theological doctrine of *Christology* emerges directly from the details of domestic relations within the household of Joseph, Mary, and Jesus. In the Jewish foundation narrative, considerable importance is attached to the initial infertility of Sarah and Rebecca as opposed to the fertility of Hagar; and in the Christian narrative great importance is attached to Mary's ability to conceive and give birth without having had sexual relations with a man. Of equal and arguably greater importance, however, is the filial relationship between Abraham and his two sons Ishmael and Isaac, and the filial relationship between God and His Son Jesus. As Jon Levenson has demonstrated, the relationship between God and Jesus in the New Testament is modeled on the relationship between Abraham and Isaac in Genesis. According to Levenson, the Christian claim to supersede Judaism cannot fully be appreciated apart from the narrative dynamics of the familial saga that is being superseded by the new religion.[1] Given the importance of Abraham in the Qur'ān, one might expect to find a variant of the father-son motif in the Islamic foundation narrative. In this respect, Islam appears to be anomalous. Appearances, however, can be deceptive.

In the Jewish foundation narrative, God singles out Abraham and some—but not all—of his descendants as the chosen people whose duty is to proclaim God's message, keep His statutes, and observe His law, thereby serving as a light unto the nations. No other nation has been thus favored; and only descendants of Abraham can lay claim to this special status (Ex. 19:5–6; Deut. 7:7–8, 14:2; Amos 3:2). This special relationship is embodied in a covenant (*berit*) established between God and Abraham. In return for faithful obedience, God promises the patriarch that he will have numerous descendants, that both he and his descendants will be blessed, and that his descendants will occupy the holy land forever. Progeny, blessing, and land *cum* polity.

It was Abraham's willingness to accept the terms of this covenant—marked by the ceremony of circumcision (*berit milah*)—that conferred the quality of chosenness on the first patriarch. This covenantal relationship was transmitted from Abraham to Isaac, from Isaac to Jacob, and from Jacob to his descendants. The collective name of this lineal descent group is not, however, the Children of Abraham but rather the Children of Israel. The latter term refers to the twelve sons of Jacob—who was renamed Israel after struggling with a mysterious being at Beth El (Gen. 32:25–29). From Jacob, the covenant was transmitted to his twelve sons and their descendants. It is important to note that *only* the twelve sons of Jacob and their descendants qualify as Children of Israel. Collateral lines were not chosen; or, to put it another way, collaterals were excluded.

The Jewish foundation narrative is both tribal and exclusive: One must be a member of the tribe in order to qualify for chosenness; and only members of the tribe qualify for inclusion.[2] But which tribe had been chosen? Abraham had two sons, Ishmael and Isaac. And Isaac, in turn, had two sons, Esau and Jacob. The biblical text identifies Ishmael as the father of the Ishmaelites and Esau as the father of the Edomites. In theory, the Ishmaelites rightly might claim to be descendants of Abraham; and the Edomites rightly might claim to be descendants of both Abraham and Isaac. Had these claims been conceded, however, chosenness would not be the exclusive privilege of the Children of Israel/Jacob.

The Ishmaelites and Edomites were tribal confederations that flourished in the area between Palmyra and Yathrib between the eighth and fifth centuries B.C.E.[3] One might say that the existence of these two tribal groups posed a threat to the integrity of the Israelite foundation narrative. This threat was successfully addressed by the Israelites who wrote, edited, and redacted the Pentateuch. With the benefit of hindsight, these men constructed their foundation narrative in such a manner as to demonstrate that neither Ishmaelites nor Edomites had been chosen by God for inclusion in the covenant. This was accomplished by the careful and artistic manipulation of the details of the Abrahamic family saga, a brief summary of which follows.

When Sarah is unable to conceive a child, she gives Abraham an Egyptian slave named Hagar in the hope that the concubine will produce a son and heir for the patriarch. Shortly thereafter, Hagar gives birth to Ishmael, who, at the age of thirteen, is circumcised by his father (Gen. 17:25). The circumcision is performed on the very day on which God promises Abraham that his wife Sarah also will give birth to a son despite her being ninety years old and well beyond the age of childbearing (Gen. 17:17). In accordance with providential design, Sarah gives birth to Isaac, with the result that Abraham, who until recently was threatened with childlessness and the extinction of his house, now has not one son but two. As the older of Abraham's two sons, Ishmael has a strong claim to be his father's heir. To avert this outcome Sarah orders her husband to expel Ishmael: "Cast out that slave-woman and her son, for the son of that slave shall not share in the inheritance with my son Isaac" (Gen. 21:10). Before carrying out his wife's instruction, Abraham implores God to save his older son: "O that Ishmael might live by your favor" (*lû Yishmaʿel yiḥyê lefaneika*; Gen. 17:18). God responds to this plea by instructing the patriarch that it is through Isaac—and only Isaac—that his offspring will be reckoned; at the same time, He assures Abraham that there is no reason to be distressed about Ishmael, who will be compensated for his pain and suffering by becoming the father of a great nation (Gen. 17:20–21). Once the matter has been decided by God, Abraham has no choice but to obey. The servant of God places Ishmael on Hagar's shoulders, gives her some bread and a skin of water, and sends mother and son off into the wilderness toward what looks like certain death. When their provisions have been exhausted, Hagar places her son on the ground and walks away from the boy, unable to bear the pain of watching him expire. Only now do we learn that God did hear Abraham's plea on behalf of his son and that He did favor Ishmael. As the boy is dying from thirst, his cries are heard by God—hence his name, Yishmaʿel, literally, *God heard*—and the Divinity directs Hagar to a well of water. Ishmael survives his ordeal—albeit only at the expense of his relationship with his father.[4] Just as Sarah procured an Egyptian concubine for her husband, Hagar now procures an Egyptian wife for her son, thereby reinforcing his detachment from the privileged line (Gen. 21:11–21). And Ishmael—in anticipation of Jacob—produces twelve sons whose names are listed in Genesis 25:12–18. Each son is the eponymous founder of a tribal group; together, these twelve tribal groups constitute the tribal confederation known as the Ishmaelites. The Ishmaelites may have been descendants of Abraham, but they were not Children of Israel.

It is only after Ishmael has been cast out by his father that Isaac can take his place as Abraham's favored son (*yaḥīd*) and heir-apparent. It should be smooth sailing from here. "Some time afterward," however, God tests Abraham by commanding him to sacrifice "your son, your favored one, the one whom you love, Isaac" (*et binka et yaḥīdka asher ahavta et yiṣḥaq*; Gen. 22:1–2). The dutiful and obedient father takes Isaac—whose age is not specified in the biblical account—to a mountain in the land of Moriah, where he constructs an altar, lays out wood for the fire, and binds his son in preparation for the sacrifice. In the biblical narrative, Isaac appears to be an innocent and naive victim. In later Jewish *midrash*, the rabbis teach that both father and son were being tested and that Isaac was a willing participant in this strange event; indeed, some rabbis go so far as to suggest that Abraham did sacrifice Isaac, who became the prototype of the Jewish martyr (see Chapter 6). After Isaac has been bound, Abraham places his son on top of the altar, takes a knife, and raises it aloft. Just as the knife is about to fall, Abraham hears a heavenly voice that instructs him not to sacrifice his son. When Abraham looks up, he sees a ram that has been caught in a thicket by its horns. Abraham takes the ram and offers it as a sacrifice in place of Isaac (Gen. 22:1–14). It is only now—after the human sacrifice has been averted—that the covenant is established. God informs Abraham that because of his willingness to sacrifice his beloved son, He will confer His blessing upon him, provide him with countless descendants, and make his descendants victorious over their enemies (Gen. 22:15–18). Abraham passes the test—although one wonders about the impact of this traumatic experience on the relationship between father and son.

The father-son motif is repeated in the next generation. When Isaac is forty years old and Abraham is advanced in years, the patriarch decides that it is time for his son to marry. Although there surely were plenty of Canaanite women available, the patriarch insists that Isaac must marry within the tribe. For this reason Abraham sends his trusted senior servant to Aram-naharaim, birthplace of the patriarch, to secure a wife for Isaac from among his relatives there. First, however, he makes the servant swear "by the Lord, the God of heaven and earth" (Gen. 24:3) that the woman he chooses must agree to leave her home and family and migrate to the Promised Land. The only condition on which the servant will be relieved of the solemn oath, Abraham explains, is if the woman does not agree (Gen. 24:5) or if her family "refuses" (Gen. 24:41). The servant travels to Aram-naharaim, where he encounters Rebecca and selects her as Isaac's bride, in part because of her generosity, hospitality, beauty, and virginity. Of equal importance, however, is her genealogy: Rebecca is the daughter of Bethuel ben Milcah, who is the wife of Nahor, the brother of Abraham.[5] Thus Isaac and Rebecca are both lineal descendants of Terah, the father of Abraham and Nahor: members of the tribe. It curious that when Rebecca brings the news of the servant's arrival to her family, it is to her mother's household that she goes. Her father, Bethuel, apparently is dead.[6] For this reason, it is Rebecca's brother Laban who serves as the guardian of her virginity and negotiates the terms of the marriage. Abraham's servant tells Laban that the marriage between Rebecca and Isaac was "decreed" by the Lord (Gen. 24:44). Laban concurs: "The matter was decreed by the Lord" (Gen. 24:50). One might say that this was a marriage made in Heaven—a point to which we shall return in Chapter 4. To seal the transaction, Abraham's servant gives Rebecca silver, gold, and garments; and he gives her brother and mother unidentified gifts (Gen. 24:42–53). Rebecca leaves her home and family and migrates to the Promised Land, where Isaac takes her as his wife, and the wedding is celebrated (Gen. 24:61–67).

Like Sarah, Rebecca has difficulty conceiving a child. Again God intervenes and Rebecca becomes pregnant with not one child but two, twin boys. Again the siblings are rivals; indeed, their mutual antagonism manifests itself already in their mother's womb. Before Rebecca gives birth, God tells her that her sons will become the leaders of two nations; and that the younger son and his descendants—the Israelites—will prevail over the older son and his—the Edomites (Gen. 25:23). The first to emerge from his mother's womb is Esau, with Jacob clutching at his heel (*ʿeqeb*, hence the latter-born son's name, Yaʿqôb, literally, *the one who follows*; Gen. 25:19–25). Whereas Esau is the favorite of his father, Jacob is the favorite of his mother. Just as Ishmael, the older and beloved son, has to be marginalized, so too Esau, the first-born and beloved son of his father. Whereas the human agent of Ishmael's marginalization is Abraham's wife Sarah, the human agent of Esau's marginalization is his brother Jacob. After persuading a famished Esau to sell him his birthright as first-born son in exchange for some food (Gen. 25:29–34), Jacob—with the assistance of his mother—tricks his dying father into giving him the covenantal blessing to which Esau is entitled as the first-born son (Gen. 27:1–40). Esau later marries Ishmael's daughter Mahalath, thereby creating a strategic political alliance between the Ishmaelites and the Edomites (Gen. 28:6–9). His descendants are listed in Genesis 36. Although the Edomites are descendants of both Abraham and Isaac, they are not Children of Israel. Once again the foundation narrative is formulated in terms of a family saga in which a first-born and favored son is marginalized.

The familial trope is repeated in the Christian foundation narrative. Just as Isaac and Rebecca are descendants of Terah, Joseph is a descendant of David; and so too is Mary—at least according to apocryphal texts. All are members of the tribe. Unlike Sarah and Rebecca, Mary has no difficulty conceiving, although the father of her child is not Joseph, the man to whom she is betrothed, but the Holy Spirit. From this claim follows the theological doctrine of the virgin birth (Matt. 1:18–25; Luke 1:26–35). Christian theology teaches that Jesus is God's son, His only son. If Jesus is the Son of God, then Joseph cannot be his natural father; conversely, if Joseph is his natural father, then Jesus is not the son of God. Whereas the Jewish foundation narrative requires the marginalization of sons and collateral branches of the tribe, the Christian narrative requires the marginalization of Jesus' apparent but not actual human father. Apart from the birth narratives, there is no mention of Joseph in the New Testament.[7]

As the beloved son of Abraham, Isaac prefigures Jesus, the Beloved Son of God (Mark 1:11). Just as Abraham is willing to sacrifice his beloved son,

God is willing to sacrifice His Beloved Son. But whereas the sacrifice of Isaac is averted by the substitution of a ram, God does sacrifice His Beloved Son, who—like the Isaac of Jewish *midrash*—willingly accepts the sacrificial role assigned to him by His Father. By sacrificing His Son, God facilitates the redemption of humanity. As John says: "For God so loved the world that He gave His only son, so that everyone who believes in him might not perish but might have eternal life" (John 3:16). The Gentiles, according to Paul, have been incorporated into the blessing of Abraham (Gal. 3:14). According to the New Covenant, divine election is no longer the exclusive possession of the Israelites but has been reinterpreted to include Christians of both Jewish and non-Jewish origin. Henceforth, membership in the Church depends on grace and election rather than genealogy.

The familial trope extends finally to the Islamic foundation narrative. As in Judaism and Christianity, the notion of covenant (*mithāq*, *ʿahd*) is an important theological concept in Islam.[8] Whereas the Jewish covenant is cut with the Children of Israel and the New Covenant includes both Jewish Christians and Gentiles, the Islamic covenant is cut with Adam and his descendants, that is to say, with all of humanity. Similarly, just as Jesus is descended from the House of David and, by extension, from Abraham, so too Muḥammad is a lineal descendant of Ishmael and Abraham. The connection between Muḥammad and Abraham is critical to the Islamic self-understanding. As a descendant of Abraham, Muḥammad is a member of the family to which the office of prophecy has been entrusted by God. Just as earlier prophets—including Abraham, Isaac, Jacob, Moses, David, Solomon, and Jesus—are all descendants of Abraham, so too is Muḥammad. But Muḥammad is not just another prophet. He is, according to Q. 33:40, the Seal of Prophets (*khātam al-nabiyyīn*), that is to say, the very last in the line of prophets that can be traced back to Abraham, a line that includes the Arab prophets Hūd, Ṣāliḥ, and Shuʿayb, all of whom are given biblical genealogies in post-Qurʾānic texts.[9] With Muḥammad's death, the office of prophecy came to an end, forever.

Muḥammad, as Renan has famously said, was born in the full light of history. Indeed, we seemingly are well informed about the Prophet's life and career, including *inter alia* details relating to his birth, childhood, marriages, children, and death. In light of the importance of Abraham and Jesus in the Qurʾān, one might expect to find in the Islamic foundation narrative a variant of the father-son *cum* sacrifice motif that plays such an important role in the Jewish and Christian narratives. If so, this expectation is disappointed. In this respect Islam is anomalous, and strikingly so. Like Jesus, Muḥammad did not have a favored son whom he might repudiate and/or sacrifice. To be precise, the Prophet did not have any natural sons who reached the age of puberty. Unlike Jesus, who never married, Muḥammad had thirteen wives and/or concubines. It is curious, however, that only his first wife Khadīja and his concubine Māriya the Copt bore him children. Like Mary, mother of Jesus, neither woman had trouble conceiving. Alas, all the sons and daughters to which these two women gave birth—with the notable exception of Fāṭima—predeceased their father at a young age. Khadīja bore Muḥammad four sons, al-Qāsim, al-Ṭayyib, al-Ṭāhir, and ʿAbdallāh, all of whom are said to have died before reaching puberty. She also gave the Prophet four daughters: Ruqayya, Umm Kulthūm, Zaynab, and Fāṭima. Of these, only Fāṭima outlived her father, albeit by less than six months: she is said to have died on 3 Ramaḍān 11/22 November 632, at the age of twenty-six. As for Māriya the Copt, her son Ibrāhīm did not survive his first year of life and died only four months before his father.[10]

The father-son motif is conspicuously absent in the Islamic foundation narrative. Because none of Muḥammad's natural sons reached puberty, there could be no competition between first-born and latter-born sons, and God could not test the Prophet by instructing him to repudiate or sacrifice any of his biological offspring. There was no exaltation, no repudiation, and no redemptive sacrifice.[11] Or perhaps there was. It is a little known fact of Islamic history that Muḥammad did have a son—and a beloved one at that; that Muḥammad did repudiate this son; and that Muḥammad did send his repudiated son to certain death on the battlefield. The existence of this son and the details of his interactions with Muḥammad are known to many if not most Muslims, although no theological significance is attached to the relationship. Similarly, Islamicists and historians of religion are familiar with this son, although I am not aware of any scholar who has ever attempted to situate Muḥammad's relationship with this son within the typology of the father-son motif that characterizes the foundation narratives of Judaism and Christianity. If this is an oversight, there is a simple explanation for it. Whereas the sons of the Jewish foundation narrative are the *natural* born offspring of their fathers, and the Son of the Christian narrative is the *supernaturally* born child of His Father, the son of the Islamic narrative is the *adopted* son of his father. This son may have been adopted, but he was nevertheless loved, repudiated, and sent to certain death by his father.

In Chapters 4–6, I will argue that in the first century AH the father-son *cum* sacrifice motif was an important component of the Islamic foundation narrative; and that at least some members of the early Muslim community understood the relationship between Muḥammad and his adopted son as a typological variant of its Jewish and Christian counterparts. As in Judaism and Christianity, so too in Islam a key theological doctrine—the finality of prophecy (*khatm al-nubūʾa*)—was linked to the father-son motif, although in the Islamic case the son was not a natural or supernatural son but an adoptee. In the narratives to be examined here, the adopted son's primary function—one might say his sole function—was to make it possible for Muḥammad to become the Last Prophet. Once this had been accomplished, the father-son motif was pushed to the margins of the Islamic tradition. But it was not forgotten. In the chapters that follow I will attempt to restore the father-son motif to its original place at the center of the Islamic foundation narrative.

Three methodological points should be kept in mind: First, many of the early Muslims had been exposed to one or another form of Judaism and/or Christianity; and Islam developed in a sectarian milieu that was characterized by dialogue and debate between and among the Children of Abraham.[12] This may explain why the early Muslim community formulated its foundation narrative in terms familiar to Jews and Christians. Second, key episodes in the *Sīra* or biography of Muḥammad that are widely treated as history are better understood as salvation history. The legendary significance of these episodes, which are based on earlier Jewish and Christian models, may have been understood by the first generations of Muslims but was forgotten by subsequent generations. As for Islamicists, with only a handful of exceptions, they prefer to treat salvation history as real history.[13] Third, adoption was not only an important legal institution in the late antique Near East but also an important theological concept. Both the legal institution and the theological concept were contested. In my view, the narrative account of the Prophet's life and the emergence of Islam cannot fully be understood without careful attention to the subject of adoption, a topic that heretofore has been virtually ignored by Islamicists. Indeed, adoption may be an important key to understanding the emergence of Islam as a historical force in the Near East.

Chapter 2

Adoption in the Near East: From Antiquity to the Rise of Islam

The rise of Islam has to be related to developments in the world of late antiquity.
—Patricia Crone, "What Do We Actually Know About Mohammed?" 5

The abstract noun *adoption* refers to the act of establishing a man or woman as parent to one who is not his or her natural child. Adoption creates a filial relationship between two individuals that is recognized as the equivalent of the natural filiation between a biological parent and his or her child. Whereas a legitimate child qualifies for certain rights (for example, inheritance) and duties (for example, support for an elderly parent) by virtue of his or her natural filiation, a male or female who does not have these rights or duties may nevertheless acquire them through the legal fiction of adoption.

Adoption practices are found in numerous human societies, and the roots of the institution can be traced back to the beginnings of recorded history. These practices are in large part a response to the problems of childlessness and parentlessness. Islamic sources indicate that the inhabitants of the Arabian peninsula practiced adoption in the last quarter of the sixth and first quarter of the seventh centuries C.E. These same sources indicate that adoption was abolished in the year 5/627 in connection with a specific episode in the life of the Prophet Muḥammad. In this chapter, I lay the groundwork for a reexamination of the traditional Islamic explanation for the abolition of adoption. To this end, I begin with an overview of adoption practices in the Near East from the middle of the second millennium B.C.E. to the middle of the first millennium C.E., treating first pagans and polytheists and then monotheists.

Adoption Among Pagans and Polytheists

Ancient Near East

In the ancient Near East, there was no abstract term for *adoption*; rather, an adult man or woman would take a male into *sonship* or a woman into *daughter-*

ship. The new relationship, recognized as the equivalent of the natural filiation between a biological parent and his or her legitimate child, was created informally without the participation of any official or representative of the state. The biological parent and the adoptor entered into an agreement with one another that was sometimes recorded in a private contract. As a consequence of this agreement, the adoptee took the name of the adoptor and became responsible for care of the new parent in his or her old age. In addition, mutual rights of inheritance were created between adoptor and adoptee.[1]

The adoption of a son served two fundamental purposes: first, to keep property in the family by securing a male heir when there was no natural son; and, second, to provide for the care of adoptive parents in their old age and to make arrangements for their proper burial. To insure that wealth would remain within the family, the adoptor might arrange for the adoptee to marry his daughter. In such cases, the adoptee—who was both a son (*mar'u*) and a son-in-law (*ḫatanu*)—became a full member of the household, and he often was given part or all of his father's inheritance.[2]

Adoptions were recorded in written contracts inscribed on clay tablets. These contracts have a stereotypical form that invariably includes a preamble, stipulations, and a penalty clause.[3] An adoption contract for a son is called *ṭuppi marūti*, that is, a document of sonship. The contract could be terminated by either party, unilaterally, by the performance of a speech act. An adoptive parent who wished to dissolve the relationship needed only to say, "You are not my son." If the adoptee wished to dissolve the relationship, he was required to say, "You are not my father" or "You are not my mother." Many adoption contracts contained a penalty clause designed to prevent unilateral dissolution. In those cases in which the adoption agreement had assigned an inheritance share to the adoptee, the party that dissolved the agreement forfeited that share. In certain cases, the adoptor was required to concede to the adoptee not only the share to which he was entitled but also the entire estate.[4]

Females were also adopted. A female adoptee became subject to the authority of her adoptive parent, who frequently would secure a husband for the girl and provide her with a dower. More than sixty matrimonial adoption contracts have been recovered from Nuzi, a Hurrian settlement located on the east bank of the Tigris River near the city of Arrapha (modern Kirkuk).[5] Matrimonial adoption falls into three categories.[6]

1. *Adoption in Daughtership.* A *ṭuppi mārtūti* is a tablet of adoption in daughtership in which a father (or mother) gives a daughter to a man (or woman) who adopts her. The adoptor pays a sum of money (usually 10–25 shekels) to the biological parent and stipulates that he (or she) will arrange for the adoptee to marry. The adopting parent usually selects a free man as the adoptee's husband, although some tablets mention marriage to a

slave. The arrangement sometimes took place between close relatives, e.g., a girl whose mother had died was given in adoption to the mother's husband or to her sister's husband or to her brother's wife's brother, while at other times it took place between people who knew each other well, e.g., a client gave his daughter in adoption to his patron in order to provide her with support for life in the patron's household.[7]

2. *Adoption in Daughter-in-Lawship.* A *ṭuppi kallatūti* is a tablet of adoption in which a father gives his daughter in daughter-in-lawship to a man who marries the girl to his son. Thus, the girl becomes the adoptive father's daughter-in-law (*kallatu*).[8]
3. *Adoption in Daughtership and Daughter-in-Lawship.* A third type of adoption combines the *ṭuppi mārtūti* and the *ṭuppi kallatūti* into a *ṭuppi mārtūti u kallatūti*, i.e., a tablet of adoption in daughtership and daughter-in-lawship. Wealthy individuals used this type of adoption to acquire the lifelong services of a female dependent. Most adoptees came from poor families and were given away in adoption because of economic hardship experienced by the biological parents. In this type of adoption, a parent gives a daughter to a free man or woman who marries the girl to a slave. If the first husband dies, the master reserves the right to marry her to a second slave, then to a third, and so on. The contract stipulates that the adopted child will remain in the adoptor's house. Any wealth acquired by the adoptee during the period of the adoption belongs to the adoptor–and not to the adoptee's children or any other heir.[9]

Ancient Greece

In ancient Greece the *oikos* or "house" of a man who died without leaving a son became extinct, even if he was survived by an uncle, nephew, or cousin. A man who had no son could avoid this misfortune by adopting one.

In Greek the abstract noun *huiothesia*, derived from *huios* ("son") and *tithemi* ("to put or place"), signifies *the act of placing or taking in of someone as a male heir.* For the Greeks, adoption served as a means to secure an heir, to provide support for an elderly parent, and to insure the continuity of one's "house" and the family cult. It was not uncommon for the adoptee to be an adult but it was uncommon—albeit not impossible—to adopt a female, who would become *epikleros* or "heiress" upon the death of her adoptive father. Over time, Attic law developed three modes of adoption.

1. *Inter vivos* adoption: A man who had no son could adopt a son during his lifetime. The adoption was marked by a ceremony in which the adoptive father introduced his son to his family, religious brotherhood, and local townsmen so that all three groups might bear witness to the new legal relationship. The adoptee took the family name, was expected to

serve and honor his father in his old age, and assumed responsibility for his burial. The adoptee was in all legal respects the son of his adoptive father so that upon the latter's death he inherited his property just like a natural son. At the same time, the adoptee ceased to be a member of his natal family and lost all inheritance rights with respect to his natural parents, siblings, and other blood relations.

2. Testamentary adoption: Solon (d. 558 B.C.E.) introduced a law that made it possible for a childless man to designate an adoptive son in a last will and testament, in which case the adoption took place immediately after the death of the testator.
3. Posthumous adoption: Eventually, it was established that even if a childless man did not leave a last will and testament, his heir nevertheless might be adopted posthumously as his son—although the details of this procedure are obscure.[10]

Pagan Rome

In pagan Rome, the only person fully recognized by the law was the *paterfamilias* or head of the household. The relationship between the *paterfamilias* and his children was regulated by the legal institution of *patria potestas*, which gave the *paterfamilias* the power of life and death over his children; he also exercised exclusive ownership of his children's wealth, even after they had become adults. Under normal circumstances, *patria potestas* was created by birth out of a Roman marriage, but it also could be created artificially by adoption.[11]

The original motive for adoption appears to have been the desire of a man who had no children to ensure the continuation of the *sacra* or family cult. Over time, the religious motive lost its force, but the desire to perpetuate the family line remained strong. Following the promulgation of the Twelve Tables in 450 B.C.E., the procedure whereby a male or female was released from the *potestas* of one person and made subject to that of another was a complicated one that involved three mancipations and two manumissions.[12]

Adoption was commonly practiced by the aristocratic families of Rome, including those with imperial ambitions. The Julio-Claudian emperors (r. 27 B.C.E.–68 C.E.) seldom produced a son, and adoption was therefore the principal means of securing a smooth succession. Of the five Julio-Claudian emperors, Augustus, Tiberius, Caligula, Claudius, and Nero, only Claudius was a blood relative of his predecessor; the other four emperors had all been adopted.[13] It may have been in response to the dynastic needs of Roman emperors that adoption procedures were simplified in later Roman law. In his *Institutes*, Gaius (130–180 C.E.) recognizes two forms of adoption, *adrogatio* and *adoptio*. (1) *Adrogatio* refers to the procedure whereby a *paterfamilias* adopted a post-pubescent male who previously had been emancipated by his biological father and was therefore *sui iuris* or master of his own affairs. In this form of adoption, which could take place only in Rome, the priestly college held a preliminary investigation during which the adopting parent was asked if he wished to adopt the male in question, and the prospective adoptee was asked to give his consent to the new relationship. If the adoption was approved, the priestly college would send a recommendation to the Roman Assembly known as the *comitia curiata*, which would make the final decision. (2) *Adoptio* or *simple adoption* refers to the procedure whereby a *paterfamilias* adopted a male or female of any age. Simple adoption differs from *adrogatio* in two respects: First, it might take place anywhere in the empire, on the condition that it was performed in the presence of a provincial governor or magistrate. Second, it involved fewer formalities. All that was needed was for the natural father to release his son from his *potestas* and for the adoptive father to affirm his acquisition of *potestas* over his adopted son. As in Greek law, an adopted son had the same rights and privileges as a legitimate natural son, including the right to inherit from his adoptive father.

Adoption Among Monotheists

Israelites

Childlessness is a universal phenomenon. Adoption is not. Some societies regard the practice of adoption as unnatural and abhorrent. In the ancient Near East, the rise of monotheism appears to have been accompanied by a turn against adoption.

The Israelites did not recognize the institution of adoption: There is no abstract word for *adoption* in biblical Hebrew, the Pentateuch contains no laws or narratives that specifically mention adoption, and neither biblical nor post-biblical law treats the institution.[14] The Israelite/Jewish attitude to adoption should come as no surprise. As we have seen, the theological doctrine of *divine election* is tribal and exclusive in nature. To qualify as a member of the group known as the Children of Israel, one had to be a lineal descendant of one of the twelve sons of Jacob. Blood lines were of critical importance. Although adoption created the appearance of filiation, the ancient Israelites regarded this tie as nothing more than a legal fiction that threatened to undermine the integrity of the Israelite tribe.

The Israelites, of course, were not immune from childlessness, a phenomenon that receives considerable attention in the biblical narratives. Adoption may have been foreclosed, but there were alternatives. A childless man, like Abraham, could take a second wife and/or concubine in the hope of producing a son and heir. Alternatively, there was the institution of *yibbûm* or levirate marriage. Under normal circumstances, it was forbidden for a man to marry his sister-in-law (Lev. 18:16), but an exception was made in the case of a man who died without leaving a son. In this instance, the importance of perpetuating the deceased man's name was so compelling that the incest taboo was waived. Indeed, the dead man's brother was *obligated* to marry his widowed sister-in-law. If the union between the widow and her brother-in-law produced a male child, the child was regarded as the son and heir of his deceased father.[15]

Even if biblical law does not recognize adoption as a legitimate institution, the biblical narratives suggest that the Israelites did in fact practice adoption.[16] The biblical practice resembled its ancient Near Eastern counterpart in three respects: there was no abstract term for *adoption*; the procedure was private and informal; and the new relationship was created by a linguistic performance in which the adopting parent took a male or female into *sonship* or *daughtership*.[17] The biblical narratives contain several references to adoption. For example, after Pharaoh's daughter discovered Moses, she paid the foundling's biological mother Leah to serve as the child's nurse (Gen. 30:9–13), and then "he became to her as a son" (*va-yehî lâ le-ben*; Ex. 2:10)—an adoption formula that resembles one used in the ancient Near East. Similarly, Jacob said to his son Joseph, "Your two sons [Manasseh and Ephraim] . . . are mine" (Gen. 48:5–6). When Hadassah/Esther was orphaned, her cousin Mordechai took her as his daughter (*lĕqaḥâh . . . le-bat*; Esth. 2:7), again using an adoption formula familiar from the ancient Near East (cf. Akkadian *ana mār(t)ūtim leqû*). In other words, he adopted her.[18]

Evidence for Jewish adoption practices is also found in the records of individual Jewish communities scattered across the Near East in late antiquity. In Egypt, adoption is mentioned in two documents in the Ananiah Family Archive composed for members of a Jewish military garrison on the island of Elephantine in the sixth century B.C.E.[19] Adoption also may have been practiced by the Bosporan Jewish community that lived on the north coast of the Black Sea in the first century C.E. Inscriptions produced by members of this community refer to the establishment of small groups made up of "adopted brothers who worship the God Most High."[20]

Adoption was not only a social practice but also a theological concept. The Israelites regarded the relationship between a father and his son as a metaphor for the relationship between God and His chosen people. The idea of *sacred adoption* is directly related to the theological principle of divine election. In Deuteronomy 14:1–2, God declares that He has chosen the Israelites as His sons out of all of mankind: "You are the sons of the Lord your God (*banîm atem le-yahweh*) . . . [who] chose you from among all other peoples on earth to be His treasured people." Within the Israelite community, it is specifically the "house" or "seed" of David that has been chosen by the divinity for sacred adoption. The key text in this regard is II Samuel 7:11–16, in which the Lord makes the following promise to David:

11 . . . The Lord declares to you that He, the Lord, will establish a house for you.
12 When your days are done and you lie with your fathers, I will raise up your offspring after you, one of your own issue, and I will establish his kingship.
13 He shall build a house for My name, and I will establish his royal throne forever.
14 I shall be a father to him, and he shall be a son to Me. When he does wrong, I shall chastise him with the rod of men and the affliction of mortals;
15 but I will never withdraw My favor from him as I withdrew it from Saul, whom I removed to make room for you.
16 Your house and your kingship shall ever be secure before you; your throne shall be established forever.

This pericope refers to a single descendant of David who, according to v. 14, will be taken into sonship by God (*anî ehyê lô le-av ve-hû yehyê lî le-ben*) and treated by Him as a father treats a son.[21] In v. 15, God promises David that He will never withdraw his favor (*ḥesed*) from this descendant. The identity of this favored descendant of David through whom the king's "house" and royal throne will be established forever subsequently would attract the attention of postbiblical Jews, Christians, and Muslims.

Sacred adoption is also mentioned by the prophet Hosea, who lived in the eighth century B.C.E. Although the Israelites appear to have broken the covenant at Sinai when they worshiped a golden calf, Hosea taught that God nevertheless would restore the covenant with His chosen people. The prophet described this new covenant in terms of divine sonship: "and in the place where it was said to them, 'You are not my people,' it shall be said to them, 'sons of the living God'" (*benei el ḥai*; Hos. 1:10). This idea is taken one step further in the Book of Jubilees, a Jewish text written in the second half of the second century B.C.E. that would become important to the Eastern Church. The author of this text took the language of Hosea ("sons of the living God") and added it to a modified version of the adoption formula in II Samuel 7:14. It is noteworthy that he changed "I shall be a father to *him*, and *he* shall be a son to Me" (II Sam. 7:14) to "I shall be a father to *them*, and *they* will be sons to me" (emphasis added), thereby producing the following formulation: "And I shall be a father to them, and they will be sons to me. And they will all be called 'sons of the living God'" (Jub. 1:24–25a). In this manner the author of Jubilees enlarged the notion of sacred adoption so that it now included all of Israel. Sacred adoption is also mentioned in the Testament of the Twelve Patriarchs, a Jewish apocryphal text written around the turn of the first century B.C.E. Here the promise of II Samuel 7:14 and Jubilees 1:24 is combined so that it applies to both the Davidic Messiah *and* the sons of God (Testament of Judah, 24:3).[22]

Christians

About Jesus it can be stated with confidence that he was born, lived, taught, and died in Palestine; the rest is historical conjecture.[23] Our earliest source for the life of Jesus is the Synoptic Gospels: Matthew, Mark, and Luke. Matthew and Luke agree that Jesus was born in Bethlehem and raised in Nazareth. Historical allusions scattered throughout the New Testament suggest that Jesus was born some time before 4 B.C.E. and died in 30 C.E. or shortly thereafter. There are two genealogies of Jesus in the Gospels, one in Matthew, the other in Luke; both suggest that Jesus was a lineal descendant of the biblical David. The genealogy found in Matthew is preceded by the assertion that Jesus is "the Messiah, the son of David, the son of Abraham." There are forty names in Matthew's list, including four women who played an important role in insuring the continuation of the Davidic line: Tamar, Rahab, Ruth, and Bathsheba. Matthew's list begins with Abraham and ends with Joseph, "the husband of Mary, of whom Jesus was born, who is called the Messiah" (Matt. 1:1–17). Luke reverses the order. His list has seventy names, all men. It begins with Jesus, "the son—as was thought—of Joseph" and ends with Adam, "the son of God" (Luke 3:23–38). Both Matthew and Luke are careful to avoid saying that Joseph was the father of Jesus.

If Joseph was not Jesus' father, then Joseph's descent from David did not make Jesus a descendant of David. In order for Jesus to be descended from David, the connection must have been through his mother, Mary. Nowhere in the Gospels, however, does it say that Mary was of the Davidic line.[24] This omission was repaired in the *Protevangelium of James*, an apocryphal text written in the second half of the second century C.E., where Mary is identified as a member of the "tribe of David."[25] If so, then both Joseph and Mary were descendants of David, which gave their marriage added theological significance. According to Matthew, Mary was impregnated by the Holy Spirit after she was betrothed to Joseph but before the marriage was consummated. When Joseph discovered that Mary was pregnant, he kept the matter to himself, intending to divorce Mary, albeit discreetly, lest she be exposed to "public disgrace." Before he could divorce her, however, an angel appeared to him in a dream and said, "Joseph, son of David, do not be afraid to take Mary as your wife, for the child conceived in her is from the Holy Spirit. She will bear a son and you are to name him Jesus" (Matt. 1:18–21; cf. Luke 2:4–5). Mary gave birth to Jesus in Bethlehem, and shortly thereafter she and her husband returned to Nazareth, where Jesus was known as "the son of Joseph" (Luke 4:22). By marrying a pregnant woman and giving the child his name, Joseph appears to have *adopted* Jesus—even if there is no explicit statement to this effect in the New Testament.[26]

Like the Israelites, the first Christians used the metaphor of sacred adoption to signify an important theological notion. As in the Hebrew Bible, so too in the Gospels the ancient Near Eastern adoption formula ("You are my son") is used to characterize God's relationship with Jesus. In II Samuel 7:14 God promised that He would take a descendant of the House of David as His son; in Mark 1:11 God fulfilled that promise by saying to Jesus, after his baptism: "You are my son, the Beloved; with you I am well pleased." Similarly, in Mark 9:7, God gave the following instruction to Peter, James, and John at the time of Jesus' transfiguration: "This is my son, the Beloved; listen to him." Just as God refers to Himself as the father (*av*) of the Messianic descendant of David (II Sam. 7:14), Jesus refers to God as his Father while praying at Gethsemane: "*Abba*, Father, for you all things are possible" (Mark 14:36).

Unlike the Evangelists, who describe the relationship between God and Jesus in terms of the relationship between a father and his son, Paul uses the Greek abstract noun *huiothesia* to refer to this relationship. This word occurs five times in the Epistles (Gal. 4:5; Rom. 8:15, 8:23, and 9:4; and Eph. 1:5), although never in the technical legal sense of *the act of placing or taking in of someone as a male heir.* Instead, Paul uses the term *huiothesia* to convey the idea of *spiritual adoption.* According to Paul, Christians have been baptized as spiritual children of God: "for in Christ you are all children of God through faith" (Gal. 3:26). Similarly, in Galatians 4:4–7 Paul explains that Christ brings freedom to those who are adopted as God's children:

4 But when the fullness of time had come, God sent his Son, born of a woman, born under the law,
5 in order to redeem those who were under the law, so that we might receive adoption as children.
6 And because you are children, God has sent the Spirit of his Son into our hearts, crying, "*Abba*! Father!"
7 So you are no longer a slave, but a child, and if a child then also an heir, through God.

As a descendant of David, Christ is the Messiah who fulfills God's promise in II Samuel 7:14. Unlike the Israelite covenant, which applies exclusively to the Children of Israel, the New Covenant includes both Christians of Jewish origin and Gentiles. The process of spiritual adoption is mediated metaphorically by the heart (a trope that resurfaces in the Qur'ān in connection with adoption—see Chapter 4). In order to become a spiritual son of God, the believer must receive the Spirit of the New Covenant into his or her heart by accepting God as father. The external sign of the believer's willingness to join with Christ in the Davidic promise of Divine redemption is the repetition of the words uttered by Jesus at Gethsemane: "Abba! Father!"[27]

The term *huiothesia* is also used in the sense of spiritual adoption in Romans 8:14–17, where Paul states that it is precisely because they have received the spirit of adoption (*huiothesia*) that God's children are entitled to refer to God as *Abba* or Father:

14 For all who are led by the spirit of God are children of God.
15 For you did not receive a spirit of slavery to fall back into fear, but you have received a spirit of adoption. When we cry, "*Abba*! Father!"
16 it is that very Spirit bearing witness with our spirit that we are children of God,
17 and if children, then heirs, heirs of God and joint heirs with Christ—if, in fact, we suffer with him so that we may also be glorified with him.

Just as, upon baptism, Jesus becomes the Son of God and receives God's Spirit, so too, upon baptism, believers become spiritual children of God by repeating the cry "*Abba*! Father!" (v. 15). Just as Jesus, at the time of His resurrection, is established as the Messianic son of God by the Holy Spirit, so too the spiritual children of God, at the end of time, will inherit God's kingdom and receive His love and grace (v. 17). Thus, in the New Testament, the Greek notion of *huiothesia* or adoption was reinterpreted by Paul as a spiritual mechanism through which God expresses love for His children.[28]

The concept of adoption played an important role in the early Church. Some early Christians—subsequently labeled as heretics—argued that Jesus was a flesh and blood human being who was the natural son of Joseph and Mary, and that it was by virtue of adoption that Jesus became the Son of God. Known as Adoptionists, adherents of this view disagreed about the moment at which the adoption took place: some early Adoptionists argued that it took place at his resurrection; by the second century C.E., most believed that it occurred at his baptism. Jewish followers of Jesus known as Ebionites held that God chose Jesus as His son because he was the most righteous man on earth. God gave His son a special mission: to sacrifice himself willingly for the sins of humanity, in fulfillment of God's promise to the Jews. The adoption occurred at the time of Jesus' resurrection, when God raised His son from the dead and took him up to Heaven. Toward the end of the second century C.E., Theodotus the Cobbler left Byzantium for Rome, where he taught that Jesus was a mere man; to this, some of his followers added that Jesus became God, either at his baptism or resurrection. Theodotus was excommunicated by Pope Victor I, who condemned Adoptionism as a heresy.[29] In the East, the Nestorians argued that Christ has two natures, one human, the other divine. In his divine nature, Christ is the son of God by generation and nature; as man, Christ is the son of God by adoption and grace—even if Jesus is nowhere specified as the *adopted* son of God in the New Testament.[30]

In some Christian communities, the theological debate over spiritual adoption appears to have collided with the practice of civil adoption. In the Latin West, the tension between the two concepts is reflected in the writings of Salvian, a fifth-century priest who lived in Marseilles. Salvian was critical of childless couples who adopted the children of others and he denounced adoptees as the "offspring of perjury" (*Ad. eccles.* III.2). Relying on Salvian, Jack Goody has argued that Church antagonism to civil adoption resulted in the disappearance of the institution from the early legislative codes of the German, Celtic, and Romanized peoples, which was followed in turn by the disappearance of civil adoption in the West.[31] In fact, the situation was not simple or clear-cut. As in Judaism, the institution of civil adoption was not recognized; and like the rabbis, the canonists developed a sophisticated and complex body of law that made it possible to incorporate illegitimate children, orphans, and foundlings into the family without formally adopting them.[32]

Byzantium

Church antagonism to civil adoption appears to have been less pronounced in the East, perhaps because the legal institution was firmly entrenched in the Near Eastern provinces of Byzantium.

The *Syro-Roman Lawbook* (hereinafter *SRL*)[33] is a compendium of Roman law composed in the Greek-speaking world that purports to record laws promulgated by the Byzantine emperors Constantine (d. 337), Theodosius II (d. 450), and Leo I (d. 474).[34] The Greek original was compiled at the end of the fifth century C.E. and the compilation was later translated into Syriac—hence, its name—although we do not know exactly when; but it is Roman law, indeed, the only work of Roman law known to have been translated into Syriac.[35] The earliest surviving manuscript in Syriac dates from the sixth century C.E.[36] Although the *SRL* has much to say about marriage, divorce, and inheritance, only two of its 157 paragraphs explicitly mention adoption: The adoption ceremony must be performed in the presence of a judge so that the biological father can release the child from his authority and transfer authority to the adopting parent (par. 89b); and if the person to be adopted exercises authority over himself, he must agree to the adoption in the presence of a judge (par. 101). A third paragraph may allude to the practice: A childless man may designate a slave as his heir in a last will and testament—presumably after adopting him (par. 3).

Adoption receives greater attention in the *Institutes* of Justinian (r. 527–65 C.E.),[37] where the essential features of the Roman *adrogratio* and simple adoption are retained, albeit with secondary but not unimportant modifications. Whereas earlier Roman law limited *adrogratio* to males, Justinian extended the scope of *adrogratio* to include females. Another imperial reform relates to the inheritance rights of an adoptee. Previously, the legal effect of adoption was to subject the adoptee to the *potestas* of the adoptor, just like a natural child. The adoptee took the name of the adoptive father and became a member of his adoptive father's agnatic group. At the same time that he acquired the right to inherit from his adoptive father, he lost all such rights with respect to his previous *potestas*.[38] This meant that if an adoptive father emancipated his adoptive son, the emancipated child no longer had *any* inheritance rights with respect to either his natural or adoptive family. To address this problem, Justinian modified the law so that an adoptee henceforth would retain the right to inherit from members of his natural family while at the same time acquiring the right to inherit from members of his adoptive family. As a consequence of this reform, an adoptee potentially had the right of inheritance in *two* families.[39]

The Sassanians

The Persians of late antiquity were familiar with the practice of adoption. As in Roman law, an adoptee did not lose all connections to his natal family and might be "returned," if necessary. Like the Israelites, however, the Persians preferred to solve the problem of childlessness in another way. Sassanian *cagar* marriage, like the levirate, was designed to address the problem of childlessness.[40] Indeed, the Persian institution can be seen as a variant of the biblical institution. According to Sassanian law, a man who failed to produce a legal heir was "nameless." The purpose of *cagar* marriage was to ensure that a man who died childless would nevertheless have a legal heir. It worked in two ways. First, if a man died childless, his widow was required to marry a male relative of her deceased husband (the obligation was not limited to the brother of the deceased, as in levirate marriage). Any child she produced with her second husband took the name of the first husband. As in Roman law, however, the "adopted" child suffered from the problem of dual loyalty and sometimes became a pawn in a struggle between two families. For the *cagar* husband himself was now threatened by "namelessness" due to the fact that *his* biological child was regarded as the heir of his wife's deceased first husband. When disputes of this nature reached the courts, judges tended to favor the interests of a living father over those of a dead one. The second way in which *cagar* marriage worked was as follows. If a wife preceded her childless husband to the grave, a woman designated *stūr* was selected to produce an heir for him (but not with him) by means of a *cagar* marriage. The *stūr* might be the man's sister or daughter. A childless man might designate a *stūr* for himself in his will. If there was no *stūr*, the priests nominated one.[41]

On the eve of the rise of Islam, civil adoption was a widely known and commonly employed social practice in the Near East, especially among pagans and polytheists; among monotheists, by contrast, adoption was avoided. The Israelites preferred to solve the problem of childlessness through the institution of the levirate, while the Persians preferred *cagar* marriage. Even if biblical law does not recognize adoption as a legal institution, the biblical narratives suggest that the Israelites did in fact practice adoption. In addition, sacred adoption was a prominent concept in both Jewish and Christian theology. In the Hebrew Bible, the relationship between a father and his son serves as a metaphor for the relationship between God and His chosen people. Early Christian Adoptionists held that Jesus was a human being, the natural son of Joseph and Mary, who became the Son of God by virtue of adoption. Thus, Muḥammad was born into a world in which adoption was an important but contested social practice and a key theological metaphor.

Chapter 3

The Abolition of Adoption in Early Islam

God has not . . . made your adopted sons your [real] sons . . . Q. 33:4

There is no adoption in Islam: the custom of the jāhiliyya *has been superseded.*
—*Prophetic* ḥadīth

In the sixth century C.E., the Arabian peninsula was inhabited by both transhumant nomads and settled people, most of whom were pagans and polytheists, although some were monotheists or had been exposed to monotheism.

The Arabs were familiar with one or another form of the ancient and late antique Near Eastern institution of adoption (and they may have been familiar with levirate and/or *cagar* marriage). Islamic sources report that in pre-Islamic Arabia, adoption served several functions: A child who had been captured and enslaved might be manumitted and adopted by a tribesman; a member of one tribe or clan who fled from his natal group might be adopted by a member of another tribe or clan; and the child of a female slave might be adopted by its mother's master. Both men and women adopted children, although only male adoptees are mentioned in the sources. If a man or woman was impressed by the talents of an orphan or a child of unknown parentage, he or she might adopt him as a son, whereupon the adoptee would take the patronymic of his adoptive father or the matronymic of his adoptive mother.[1]

The Arabic word *al-tabannī*, like the Greek *huiothesia*, is an abstract noun that signifies *to make someone a son or daughter.* Islamic sources suggest that the Arabs conferred on adopted children the same legal status as was enjoyed by full-blooded offspring.[2] As in other Near Eastern legal systems, adoption created rights of mutual inheritance (*tawāruth*) and mutual support (*tanāṣur*) between the adoptive parent and the adoptee. It was customary for an adoptive father to assign to his adopted child a share of the inheritance equal to that of a natural son.[3] Ella Landau-Tasseron has identified several instances of adoption in pre-Islamic Arabia and early Islam, including the following males who were adopted by males.

1. Abū Ḥudhayfa adopted Sālim and gave him in marriage to his niece, Fāṭima bt. al-Walīd b. ʿUqba;
2. al-Aswad b. ʿAbd Yaghūth adopted al-Miqdād b. ʿAmr (d. 33/654);[4]
3. al-Khaṭṭāb b. Nufayl adopted ʿĀmir b. Rabīʿa al-Wāʾilī (d. 35/655–56) and Wāqid b. ʿAbdallāh;
4. Maʿmar b. Ḥabīb adopted Sufyān.

Adoptions by females are also mentioned in the sources, although, according to Landau-Tasseron, much less frequently than adoptions by males. Examples include the following.

1. The mother of the *jāhilī* poet ʿĀmir b. al-Ṭufayl adopted the son of her husband's second wife. She called him *my son* and protected him from his mother's wrath.[5]
2. A woman named Ḥasana adopted the Companion Shuraḥbīl, who was henceforth called Shuraḥbīl b. Ḥasana (d. 18/639).[6]
3. A woman of Ḍubayʿa known as Umm Burthun adopted a foundling who was called ʿAbd al-Raḥmān b. Ādam. He was also known as Ibn Umm Burthun. He became a traditionist and served as an official under ʿUbaydallāh b. Ziyād (d. 67/686).[7]
4. The Prophet's wife ʿĀʾisha (d. 57/678) adopted the Kufan traditionist Masrūq b. al-Ajdaʿ (d. 63/683).[8]

The sources indicate that adoption was practiced in the Hijaz both before and after the rise of Islam, and that some adoptees continued to be known by the patronymics and matronymics of their adoptive parents as late as the middle of the first century A.H.

Muḥammad had five sons, four—al-Qāsim, al-Ṭayyib, al-Ṭāhir, and ʿAbdallāh—with his wife Khadīja, and one—Ibrāhīm—with his concubine Māriya the Copt. All five are said to have died before attaining puberty.[9] In addition to his five natural sons, Muḥammad also had an adopted son named Zayd; and Zayd in turn had a son named Usāma.

Zayd and Usāma

Ca. 605 C.E., Muḥammad acquired a slave named Zayd b. Ḥāritha al-Kalbī, who was ten years younger than his master.[10] Zayd was short, his nose was flat and wide, and his skin was either white or tawny colored. Shortly thereafter, Muḥammad manumitted Zayd and adopted him as his son, whereupon the young man's name was changed to Zayd b. Muḥammad. His nickname was Zayd al-Ḥibb (The Beloved Zayd) or Ḥibb Rasūl Allāh (The Beloved of the Messenger of God). Zayd was either the first male or the first adult male to embrace Islam after the Prophet himself.[11]

Zayd is said to have married at least five times. Shortly after receiving his first revelation, the Prophet arranged for his adopted son to marry Umm Ayman, an Ethiopian who had been Muḥammad's wet nurse and later became his client.[12] Umm Ayman must have been at least twenty years older than Zayd.[13] Between 612 and 614, eight to ten years before the hijra, Umm Ayman gave birth to a son who was called Usāma.[14] Curiously, some unnamed people claimed that the infant was not Zayd's natural son, but an expert in physiognomy confirmed that Zayd was in fact the child's father. The Prophet reportedly was delighted with the outcome.[15] Henceforth, Zayd's *kunya* was Abū Usāma (alternatively, Abū Salama). Zayd was one of the emigrants to Medina, where he married several additional women. When Umm Kulthūm bt. ʿUqba, the uterine sister of ʿUthmān b. ʿAffān, arrived in Medina, four men, including Zayd, expressed interest in marrying the female emigrant. Not knowing what to do, Umm Kulthūm asked the Prophet for his advice, and he recommended Zayd. Umm Kulthūm accepted Zayd's marriage proposal and they had two children: Zayd b. Zayd [sic], who died while a minor; and Ruqayya, who died while under the care and protection of ʿUthmān. Zayd later divorced Umm Kulthūm and married Durra bt. Abū Lahab. He divorced her too, after which he married Hind bt. al-ʿAwāmm, sister of al-Zubayr. Eventually, he would marry—and divorce—Zaynab bt. Jaḥsh al-Asadiyya—about which more below.[16]

As the Prophet's adopted son, Zayd was a member of his House, that is to say, he was one of the *ahl al-bayt*. In a letter that ʿAlī b. Abī Ṭālib is said to have written to Muʿāwiya just prior to the battle of Ṣiffīn (37/657), ʿAlī explains:

> Surely, when Muḥammad called for faith in God and for proclamation of His unity we, the people of his house (*ahl al-bayt*), were the first to have faith in him and to hold true what he brought. . . . Whenever matters got tough and the battle cry was sounded, he used to put the people of his house up in the front rank and protected his Companions from the heat of the lances and the sword. Thus ʿUbayda . . . was killed at Badr, Ḥamza on the day of Uḥud, Jaʿfar and Zayd . . . on the day of Mu'tah.[17]

Zayd was a formidable soldier and a skilled archer who participated in the battles of Badr, Uḥud, the Trench, Ḥudaybiyya, and Khaybar. Muḥammad appointed him as the commander (*amīr*) of seven or nine military expeditions.[18] Alas, Zayd was killed in 8/629 at the Battle of Muʾta—to be analyzed in Chapter 5.[19] At the time of his death he was either fifty or fifty-five years old.[20] Following his death, the Prophet's wife ʿĀʾisha is reported to have said, "The Messenger of God never sent Zayd b. Ḥāritha on a military mission without appointing him as the commander. Had [Zayd] outlived [the Prophet], he would have made him his successor" (*wa-law baqiya baʿdahu istakhlafahu*).[21]

As for Usāma, he was born a Muslim and knew no other religion. The Prophet reportedly loved his grandson dearly and regarded him as a member of his House; indeed, his love for Usāma is said to have been equal to that of his love for al-Ḥasan b. ʿAlī.[22] He gave Usāma fine clothes and jewelry to wear.[23] As a sign of his affection for his grandson, Muḥammad called him Ḥibb b. Ḥibb Rasūl Allāh, the Beloved son of the Beloved of the Messenger of God; he also called him al-Radīf or "the one who rides behind [the leader on his horse]."[24] At the time of the hijra to Medina in 1/622, Usāma would have been approximately ten years old. Upon attaining puberty at the age of fourteen, Usāma married Zaynab bt. Ḥanzala b. Qusāma but later divorced her.[25] Usāma would marry six more women: Hind bt. al-Fākiha, Durra bt. ʿAdī, Fāṭima bt. Qays, Umm al-Ḥakam b. ʿUtba, Bint Abū Ḥamdān al-Sahmī, and Barza bt. al-Ribʿī. He fathered as many as twenty children, including Muḥammad and Hind (their mother was Durra); Jubayr, Zayd, and ʿĀ'isha (their mother was Fāṭima), and Ḥasan and Ḥusayn (their mother was Barza).[26]

Muḥammad is said to have repudiated Zayd in 5/627 (see below and Chapter 4). But the Prophet did not forget the man who had been known as the Beloved of the Messenger of God. In 11/632, the Prophet appointed Usāma—who could not have been more than twenty years old at the time[27]—as the commander (*amīr*) of a military expedition whose objective was to avenge Zayd's death in southern Jordan. No sooner had the expedition set out than the Prophet died after a brief illness. Usāma returned to Medina. As a member of the Prophet's House, it was only fitting that he was one of six men who washed Muḥammad's body[28] and lowered it into the grave.[29] The expedition resumed at the beginning of the caliphate of Abū Bakr. Usāma and his men marched to Wādī al-Qurā and from there to Ubna in southern Palestine, where the Muslim forces reportedly killed anyone who approached them, took captives, set fire to houses, fields and date-palm trees, seized booty, and terrorized the local inhabitants. Usāma rode into battle on the horse that his father had ridden on the day he died, and he killed the man who had slain his father. Miraculously—or perhaps it was divine providence—the expedition returned to Medina without losing a single soldier.[30] Despite the success of the mission, this would be the last military expedition commanded by Usāma. In 20/641, the caliph ʿUmar awarded him a stipend of 4,000 dirhams, which was larger than the stipend that he awarded to his son ʿAbdallāh b. ʿUmar. When ʿAbdallāh complained to his father, the caliph told him that the Prophet had loved Zayd more than he loved ʿUmar, and that he had loved Usāma more than he loved ʿAbdallāh b. ʿUmar. It was in a house belonging to Usāma's wife that ʿUthmān was elected as caliph. The new caliph granted Usāma some land and in 34/654–55 sent him to Basra to gather information about the situation in the garrison town. Following the murder of ʿUthmān, Usāma refused to pay homage to ʿAlī, whose supporters attacked and abused him in the mosque of Medina. He died in al-Jurf ca. 54/674 and was buried in Medina.

Although his son Muḥammad was a transmitter of *ḥadīth*, Usāma's descendants played no significant role in the events of the first century A.H.[31]

The Abolition of Adoption: The Standard View

The early Muslim community practiced adoption in Mecca, and adoption continued to be practiced following the hijra to Medina in 1/622. The institution is said to have been formally abolished in 5/627. Subsequently, Muslim jurists would classify the practice as a prohibited act (*ḥarām*) and they would develop alternative legal mechanisms to regulate the care of orphans, foundlings, and children of unknown parentage.[32] Islamic sources portray the abolition of adoption as a direct result of a well-known episode in the life of Muḥammad, and most Western scholars treat this episode as an event in the life of the Prophet, that is to say, as historical fact.[33] What follows is a brief summary of the episode as it is presented in Islamic sources and understood by modern scholars.

Shortly after the hijra to Medina in 1/622, Muḥammad's adopted son Zayd married the Prophet's paternal cross-cousin Zaynab bt. Jaḥsh. One day, while Zaynab was alone in her house and in a state of dishabille, Muḥammad inadvertently caught sight of Zaynab and immediately fell in love with her. Upon learning of his father's feelings for his wife, Zayd offered to divorce Zaynab. Muḥammad rejected the offer, presumably because he knew that the Qur'ān prohibits marriage between a man and his daughter-in-law. In response to this predicament, God revealed Q. 33:37, in which He not only gave the Prophet special permission to marry Zaynab but also specified that henceforth the prohibition of marriage to a daughter-in-law would apply only to the former wife of a natural son but would no longer apply to the former wife of an adopted son. It must have been shortly after the revelation of this verse that Muḥammad informed Zayd that he was no longer his father, ostensibly to satisfy public concern about the seemingly incestuous nature of the Prophet's marriage to Zaynab. The Prophet's dissolution of his adoptive relationship with Zayd—who now reverted to his birth name of Zayd b. Ḥāritha al-Kalbī—led in turn to the abolition of adoption, as indicated by Q. 33:4–5: "God has not . . . made your adopted sons your [real] sons . . . Call them after their fathers." Although these two verses do not explicitly state that adoption had been abolished, early Muslim jurists inferred this conclusion from prophetic *ḥadīth*s in which the Prophet is reported to have said that anyone who knowingly claims as his father someone other than his biological father, or claims as his son someone other than his biological son, is an infidel who will be denied entrance to paradise.[34]

The relationship between Muḥammad's marriage to Zaynab and the abolition of adoption appears to have been that of cause-and-effect. Islamic tradition teaches that Muḥammad repudiated Zayd as his son in order to facilitate his marriage to Zaynab; and that his repudiation of Zayd triggered the abolition of adoption. The exegetes explain that adoption was abolished in order to put an end to the barbaric and unnatural *jāhilī* practice of equating the sanctity of a stranger with that of a blood relative.

By the end of the first century A.H., reports about Muḥammad's marriage to Zaynab had become grist for the mill of Christian anti-Muslim polemic. In an exchange of letters between Leo III (r. 717–41) and ʿUmar b. ʿAbd al-ʿAzīz (r. 99–101/717–20), the Byzantine emperor referred to the Prophet's "seduction" of a woman named Zeda [sic] as evidence of his "unchasteness" and duplicity. This was the worst of all the "abominations" that Leo attributed to Muḥammad because, as he knew, the Qurʾān represents the Prophet's marriage to this woman as a product of divine intervention ("of all these abominations the worst is that of accusing God of being the originator of all these filthy acts"). What greater blasphemy could there be, Leo asked rhetorically, "than . . . alleging that God is the cause of all this evil?"[35]

A similar attitude was expressed by John of Damascus (ca. 676–749) in his *Fount of Knowledge*, composed ca. 730.[36] The second section of this text, entitled *De haeresibus*, contains a chapter on Islam in which John criticizes certain "foolish" sayings attributed to Muḥammad in connection with the laws of marriage and divorce: Muslim men may marry up to four wives at a time, may engage in sexual relations with as many concubines as they can afford to maintain, and are empowered to divorce their wives freely and without cause. It is in the context of his discussion of divorce that John mentions Zayd. He begins:

> Mamed had a co-worker named Zeid. This man had a beautiful wife whom Mamed desired. When they were seated together, Mamed said, "O thou, God has commanded me to take your wife." And he replied, "Thou art an apostle; do as God has said to you; take my wife."[37]

Here, it will be noted, there is no mention of divorce. To correct this omission, John presents a longer and more detailed version of the story. "Or rather," he says, "that we may tell it from the beginning, he said to him":

> "God commanded me that you should divorce your wife." And he divorced her. After many days he said, "But God commanded that I should take her." Then when he had taken her, and when he had committed adultery with her, he made such a law: "Let him who desires it, divorce his wife. But if after the divorcement he shall return to her, let another (first) marry her. For it is not lawful (for him) to take her, unless she shall have been married by another." (Q. 2:230)[38]

In the expanded narrative, God commands Muḥammad to inform Zayd that he should divorce his (unnamed) wife. Zayd complies. Many days later—presumably after the divorcee had observed her waiting period—Muḥammad announces that God has commanded him to "take" her. He too complies with the divine order. Now, however, Muḥammad is accused of committing adultery.[39] To refute this charge, John explains, Muḥammad enacted Qur'ān 2:230, which reads as follows:

> If a man divorces her, she becomes unlawful to him until she has married another man. Then if he [the second husband] divorces her, there is no harm if the two unite again if they think they will keep within the bounds set by God and made clear for those who understand.[40]

The connection between John's version of the episode and the Qur'ānic version is not immediately apparent. If we assume that the man mentioned at the beginning of v. 230 is Zayd and that the woman is Zaynab, then the verse suggests that if Zayd divorces Zaynab, she becomes unlawful to him until after she has married another man. Subsequently Muḥammad marries Zaynab and divorces her, with the result that Zaynab is now free to remarry Zayd. Alternatively, if we assume that the man mentioned at the beginning of the verse is Muḥammad and that the woman is again Zaynab, then v. 230 suggests that if Muḥammad divorces Zaynab, she becomes unlawful to him until after she has married another man. Subsequently, Zayd marries Zaynab and divorces her, with the result that she is now free to remarry Muḥammad. Whichever assumption one makes, John's story makes little sense—except perhaps as a parody of Deut. 24:1, which prohibits the renewal of marital relations between a man and his divorced wife, if, subsequent to the divorce, she marries a second man (and is divorced or widowed). According to John, Muḥammad's marriage to Zayd's wife was the *sabab* or occasion for the revelation of Q. 2:230—and he apparently was unaware of Q. 33:37. Now John of Damascus was a Christian Arab and *De haeresibus* is a polemical text, so it is not necessarily surprising that John should have made a mistake about the identity of the verse that was revealed. It is possible, however, that John was not mistaken and that his identification of Q. 2:230 as the verse revealed to Muḥammad in connection with the Prophet's marriage to Zaynab reflects early uncertainty within the Muslim community over precisely the identity of the relevant verse, a subject to which we will return in Chapter 4. For the moment, suffice it to say that in medieval times, Christian writers regularly cited Muḥammad's marriage to Zaynab as evidence of the Prophet's promiscuity and unbridled self-interest.[41]

The contention that a specific episode in the life of the Prophet triggered the abolition of adoption is supported by a broad consensus that includes both Muslim and non-Muslim scholars alike. Even if this view is correct—and I do not think it is—one wonders about the historical factors that prepared the ground for abolition, on the one hand, and that accounted for its acceptance and ultimate success, on the other. Inasmuch as adoption is prohibited by Islamic law, the subject is not directly treated in legal texts, and it should come as no surprise that only a handful of Western scholars have paid any attention to the subject. Following in the footsteps of medieval Christian polemicists, Orientalists active at the beginning of the twentieth century suggested that Muḥammad abolished adoption out of self-interest in order to satisfy his personal sexual desires.[42] The only serious scholarly treatment of the subject with which I am familiar is a recent book chapter by Amira Sonbol in which she situates the abolition of adoption within the framework of the Qurʾān's attempt to create a new and cohesive social system in which the nuclear family was replacing tribalism.[43] In this context, Sonbol argues, adoption would have interfered with the connection between kinship (*nasab*) and the inheritance of property: Why, for example, should an adopted child inherit on a basis of equality with a natural child? At the same time, adoption threatened to make nonsense of the incest prohibitions established in Q. 4:23. Under a regime in which adoption was practiced, it is conceivable that a male adoptee unwittingly might engage in illicit sexual relations with his biological mother or sister; or that a female adoptee might do the same with her biological father or brother.

It is certainly possible that the abolition of adoption was triggered by an episode in the Prophet's career, as Islamic sources indicate; and it is also possible that the abolition of the institution was related to Qurʾānic sociolegal reforms, as Western scholarship has suggested. Be that as it may, one or the other explanation suffers from three shortcomings. First, by characterizing the Qurʾānic legislation as a response to the tribal customary law of pre-Islamic Arabia, the Islamic sources obfuscate any connection between the practice of adoption in Arabia, on the one hand, and in the greater Near East, on the other. This may explain why the handful of Western scholars who have treated the abolition of adoption focus exclusively on Arabia before and after the rise of Islam without paying any attention to the Near East in late antiquity. Second, by the beginning of the third/ninth century, Muslims appear to have forgotten that the abolition of adoption was related to the Qurʾānic pronouncement that Muḥammad is the Seal of Prophets. To the best of my knowledge, no scholar—Muslim or non-Muslim—has acknowledged or discussed the connection between the theological doctrine and the legal reform. Third, both Muslim and non-Muslim scholars treat the episode that appears to have resulted in the abolition of adoption as an actual historical event. In my view, this episode in the life of the Prophet is better seen as a sacred narrative modeled on earlier sacred narratives that were part of the Judeo-Christian tradition.

Part II
From Sacred Legend to Sacred History

In place of the mystery under which the other religious traditions have covered their origins, [Islam] was born in the full light of history; its roots are on the surface. The life of its founder is as well known to us as that of any sixteenth-century reformer. We can follow year by year the fluctuations of his thoughts, his contradictions, his weaknesses.

—Ernst Renan, "Muhammad and the Origins of Islam," 128–29

Chapter 4

The Repudiation of the Beloved of the Messenger of God

> *God has not put two hearts inside any man. . . . Call them after their fathers.*
> *Q. 33:4–5*

> *I am not your father*
> *—Muḥammad to Zayd. Muqātil,* Tafsīr, *3:49*

From antiquity down to the rise of Islam, adoption was widely practiced by Semites, Greeks, Romans, and Byzantines. Although Jews and to a lesser extent Christians rejected the civil institution, both religious communities used the concepts of *sonship* and *adoption* as metaphors for the relationship between God and man.

It is against the background of Near Eastern practices and ideas relating to adoption that I propose to reexamine Muḥammad's repudiation of his adopted son Zayd and the abolition of adoption in early Islam. According to the standard view, Muḥammad repudiated Zayd in order to facilitate his marriage to Zaynab bt. Jaḥsh. Against this view I will argue that the story of Muḥammad's marriage to Zaynab was created in order to make it possible for the Prophet to repudiate Zayd, whose name, Zayd b. Muḥammad—indeed his very existence—was incompatible with the theological doctrine of the finality of prophecy.

Q. 33:36–40

As noted in Chapter 3, Zayd married at least five women. Our concern here is with his marriage to Zaynab, to which an oblique reference is made in *Sūrat al-Aḥzāb* ("The Confederates"). This chapter of the Qur'ān takes its name from the confederation (*aḥzāb*) of Meccan forces that carried out an unsuccessful attack on Medina in the year 5/627, the same year in which Muḥammad repudiated Zayd.

In the canonical text of the Qur'ān, *Sūrat al-Aḥzāb* has seventy-three verses, although it is reported on the authority of ʿĀʾisha that it originally had 200 verses.[1] The story of the Battle of the Trench is told in vv. 1–3 and 7–27. The remainder of the *sūra* is largely taken up with domestic issues relating to Muḥammad and his family, including apparent disturbances in the Prophet's household, the status of his wives as Mothers of the Believers and duties associated with that status, the veil (*ḥijāb*), domestic privacy, and special marriage privileges accorded to Muḥammad. The allusion to Zayd's fifth marriage occurs in v. 37, which is part of a five-verse pericope that runs from v. 36 through v. 40:

36 When God and His messenger have decided a matter, it is not for any believing man or woman to have any choice in the affair. Whoever disobeys God and His Messenger has gone astray in manifest error.

37 [Recall] when you said to the one on whom God and you yourself have bestowed favor, "Keep your wife to yourself and fear God," and you hid within yourself what God would reveal, and you feared the people when God had better right to be feared by you. When Zayd had finished with her, We gave her to you in marriage, so that there should be no difficulty for the believers concerning the wives of their adopted sons, when they have finished with them. God's command was fulfilled.

38 There is no difficulty for the prophet in that which God has ordained for him: God's practice concerning those who passed away previously—God's command is a fixed decree.

39 Who conveyed God's messages and feared Him and no one else apart from God. God is sufficient as a reckoner.

40 Muḥammad is not the father of any of your men, but the messenger of God and the seal of Prophets. God is aware of everything.

As often happens, the Qurʾān assumes the familiarity of its audience with a story or event to which reference is being made. Even if the modern reader is unfamiliar with this episode, it is possible to reconstruct the skeletal frame of the underlying story based solely on what the Qurʾān says. The key to such a reconstruction is v. 37, which is considerably longer than the other four verses. The authorial voice ("We") that controls v. 37 asks a male addressee ("you") to recall a conversation between the addressee and a third party ("the one on whom"). Presumably, the addressee is Muḥammad, an inference that is reinforced by the specific mention of Muḥammad in v. 40, one of only four instances in which the Prophet's name is mentioned in the Qurʾān (cf. Q. 3:144, 47:2, and 48:29). The authorial voice invokes the memory of a verbal exchange that took place at an unspecified time in the recent past between the addressee and the third party, who is identified in the first sentence as someone who was favored by both God and the addressee ("when you said to the one on whom God and you yourself have bestowed favor"). In the continuation of v. 37, the third party is identified simply as a man named Zayd—without any further qualification, a point of some importance. Presumably this doubly favored man is the Prophet's adopted son Zayd b. Muḥammad, the Beloved of the Messenger of God. The mention of Zayd in v. 37 is significant because he is the only Muslim apart from Muḥammad whose name is mentioned in the Qurʾān. At the time of the verbal exchange, Zayd was married to a woman who, in the Qurʾān, has no name, face, identity, or personality. Compared to Zayd, she is truly a blank slate. The fact that the addressee orders Zayd to keep his wife implies that Zayd wants to divorce her. The authorial voice reminds the addressee that he is hiding something within himself, without specifying the identity of the hidden object, and—remarkably if the addressee is in fact Muḥammad—rebukes the Prophet for putting his fear of men over that of God. The authorial voice also tells the addressee that he is unaware of what God is about to bring to light, namely, special permission to marry the unidentified woman, but only on the condition that Zayd is "finished" with her. Previously, one surmises, it was prohibited to marry one's daughter-in-law. This prohibition was revised by v. 37 ("so that there should be no difficulty for the believers concerning the wives of their adopted sons"). This reinforces our assumption that the man named Zayd who is mentioned in v. 37 is the Prophet's adopted son Zayd b. Muḥammad. Henceforth, a believer is free to marry the former wife of his adopted son, and such a marriage is no longer considered sinful.

The relationship between v. 37, on the one hand, and vv. 36 and 38–40, on the other, is not immediately apparent. Verse 36 indicates that male and female believers have no choice but to obey a decision made by God and his Prophet; and that any believer who disobeys such a decision has strayed from the right path. One wonders which "decision" is being referenced. Verse 38 indicates that God has issued a decree relating to the Prophet that somehow releases him from an unspecified difficulty. This has been *sunnat allāh* or God's practice not only with the Prophet but also with "those who passed away previously"—whoever they may have been.[2] The characterization of God's command as a "fixed decree" is perhaps an allusion to the doctrine of predestination. The reference in v. 38 to "those who passed away previously" is resumed in v. 39, which indicates that the people who passed away previously feared God and no one else. Finally, in v. 40 the authorial voice that controls the Qurʾān informs His audience (presumably the Muslim community) that Muḥammad—who is identified here by name—is the Messenger of God and the Seal of Prophets.

This pericope may be cryptic but it is not incoherent. The skeletal frame of the narrative embedded in Q. 33:37 refers back to an antecedent phenomenon with which the immediate audience of the Qurʾān surely would have been familiar. The understanding of the pericope by its immediate audience would have been shaped by whatever assumptions were made about that antecedent phenomenon. There are at least two possibilities. The very formulation of v. 37—especially the reference to Zayd and the citation of a conversation between Zayd and the addressee—suggests that the pericope refers to a specific incident in the life of the Prophet. If so, then v. 37 should be read as history—which is how the verse has been read by Muslims (and most historians) for more than 1,400 years. In that case, one asks: What is the historical event to which the verse is referring? This question was answered over the course of the first two centuries A.H. by the men who laid the foundations of what would become the standard account of the origins of Islam. These popular preachers (*quṣṣāṣ*),[3] transmitters of *ḥadīth*, historians, and Qurʾān commentators taught that v. 37 refers to Muḥammad's marriage to a woman named Zaynab; and they filled in the gaps in the Qurʾānic account of the marriage by establishing—often in exquisite detail—the circumstances leading up to it. Even if the resulting narrative expansion of the Qurʾānic account was produced after the fact, Islamic tradition teaches that this narrative refers to an event in the life of the Prophet. It was this antecedent event that resulted in the revelation of v. 37, that is to say, the historical event is the *sabab al-nuzūl* or occasion on which the verse was revealed.

Alternatively, it is possible to read v. 37 of *Sūrat al-Aḥzāb* as a sacred legend or *fabula* that is derived from earlier models and designed to address an important theological issue. Viewed in this manner, it is unnecessary to ask about an event in the life of the Prophet that resulted in the revelation of v. 37. Instead one asks: What was the theological anxiety to which the verse responds? What literary models lay behind the new literary composition that appears in v. 37? How did the early Muslim community revise the earlier models in order to justify and support the new theological doctrine? It is to these questions that we now turn our attention.

The Narrative Expansion of Q. 33:36–40 and 33:4–6 in Early *Tafsīr*

The compressed version of the story embedded in Q. 33:37 is related to a larger narrative that existed outside the Qurʾān. Over the course of the first century A.H., Muslim popular preachers and transmitters of *ḥadīth* fleshed out the details of the larger narrative and connected it to the revelation of vv. 36–40. By the end of the century, these details were widely known and had been committed to writing.

Before turning to the expanded version of the narrative, I want to alert the reader to a critical linguistic issue. Verse 37 of *Sūrat al-Aḥzāb* refers to a man named Zayd without identifying him as Zayd b. Muḥammad and without mentioning his tribal affiliation (e.g., al-Qurashī). This is no coincidence. The continuation of the story that is begun in v. 37 is found in vv. 4–6 of the same *Sūra*. As we shall see, Q. 33:5 teaches that anyone who calls a man by the name of someone who is not his natural father commits a sin, crime, or act of disobedience (*junāḥ*). This Qurʾānic instruction creates a linguistic trap. The first Muslims knew that Zayd b. Ḥāritha had been renamed Zayd b. Muḥammad at the time of his adoption by the Prophet;

and that approximately twenty years later he reverted to his birth name of Zayd b. Ḥāritha. So as not to commit a sin, however, they were careful not to refer to Zayd as Zayd b. Muḥammad even with respect to the two decades during which this was in fact his legal name. On the rare occasion on which an exegete does identify Zayd as Zayd b. Muḥammad, he is careful to attribute this assertion to someone other than himself (for example, "The people say: . . . .")

We turn now to the exegetes, beginning with the earliest commentaries and working forwards in chronological order. By the middle of the second century A.H., all of the essential elements of the larger narrative with which we are concerned had been firmly established. Additional details found in sources written after the middle of the second century A.H.—some of which may be early—will be mentioned in the footnotes and/or given separate treatment in Chapter 7.

To the best of my knowledge, the first Muslim commentator to mention the name of Zayd's wife was Mujāhid b. Jabr (d. 102/720), the Meccan Successor whose *Tafsīr* is the earliest extant commentary on the Qur'ān.[4] Like John of Damascus (see Chapter 3), Mujāhid does not make this identification *ad* Q. 33:37—about which he has nothing to say. Rather, he identifies her *ad* v. 28 of this *Sūra* ("O prophet, say to your wives, 'If you want the life of this world and its ornament' ").[5] This verse, the commentator explains, was revealed "about Zaynab bt. Jaḥsh and her aversion (*karāhiyatuhā*) to marrying Zayd b. Ḥāritha [sic], when the Messenger of God ordered her to marry him."[6] Now Zaynab bt. Jaḥsh was a granddaughter of ʿAbd al-Muṭṭalib through his daughter Umayma, the wife of Jaḥsh b. Ri'āb al-Asadī, who was a client of the clan of ʿAbd Shams.[7] Zaynab and Muḥammad were paternal cross-cousins. Just as Isaac and Rebecca are both descendants of Terah, and just as Joseph and Mary are both descendants of David, so too Zaynab and Muḥammad are both descendants of ʿAbd al-Muṭṭalib and—although no commentator says so—both are lineal descendants of Ishmael and Abraham. Members of the tribe. Zaynab was one of the female Companions who left Mecca and migrated (*hājarat*) to Medina. Shortly after her arrival in the city, the Prophet reportedly ordered her to marry his adopted son Zayd.[8] As Mujāhid makes clear, she found the proposal repugnant.

To the best of my knowledge, the first Muslim commentator to connect Zaynab bt. Jaḥsh with Q. 33:37 was Muqātil b. Sulaymān (d. 150/767).[9] Whereas Mujāhid knows—or chooses to relate—only a bare bones outline of the episode relating to Muḥammad, Zayd, and Zaynab, Muqātil tells his audience—with all due respect—nearly everything that one might want to know about this episode but was afraid to ask. Muqātil's treatment of the episode takes the form of a combination of short periphrastic comments supplemented by extended narratives, none of which are accompanied by *isnāds*. Because the commentator proceeds on a verse-by-verse basis, he must break up the individual components of the story in order to link them to the relevant Qurʾānic verses. This has the effect of scrambling the chronological sequence of events. *Ad* Q. 33:4–6, to be analyzed later in this chapter, he treats Muḥammad's renunciation of Zayd and the abolition of adoption; *ad* Q. 33:36–40, he tells the story of Muḥammad's marriage to Zaynab, which is immediately followed by the Qurʾānic pronouncement that Muḥammad is the Seal of Prophets.

In the following narrative summary, based exclusively on the contents of Muqātil's *Tafsīr*, I use a different organizing principle. According to my count, there are twelve individual scenes in the larger episode: The first nine scenes are treated *ad* vv. 36–40, while the last three are treated *ad* vv. 4–6. I will discuss these twelve scenes in the order in which they would have been presented by Muqātil if he had told the story in chronological order. For convenience, it will be helpful to think of the larger episode as a play composed of five acts, with each act having anywhere from one to three scenes.

Act 1 The Beloved of the Messenger of God
- 1 Zayd's capture and acquisition by Khadīja
- 2 his adoption by Muḥammad
- 3 his marriage to Zaynab bt. Jaḥsh

Act 2 A marriage made in heaven
- 1 a sexually charged encounter between Muḥammad and Zaynab
- 2 results in Zayd's divorce of Zaynab
- 3 and her marriage to Muḥammad

Act 3 Public reaction to the marriage
- 1 was the marriage incestuous?
- 2 God's practice (*sunnat allāh*)

Act 4 Muḥammad is the Seal of Prophets

Act 5 Legal Consequences
- 1 Muḥammad's repudiation of Zayd, and
- 2 the abolition of adoption, followed by
- 3 the prohibition of marriage with the widows of the Prophet

When Muqātil and later Muslim exegetes tell the story, they begin with Act 5 (vv. 4–6) and then proceed to Acts 1–4 (vv. 36–40). It is my contention that by saving Act 5 for the end of our dramatic performance, we recover the original significance of the episode.

Act 1, Scenes 1–3: Zayd's Capture, Adoption by Muḥammad, and Marriage to Zaynab (vv. 36–38)

In pre-Islamic times, a young bedouin (*aʿrābī*) by the name of Zayd b. Ḥāritha was captured and enslaved.[10] Zayd was later acquired by Muḥammad,[11] who manumitted the youth and then adopted him as his son, declaring, "He is my son." As a result of his adoption, Zayd was renamed Zayd b. Muḥammad.[12]

Shortly after the hijra to Medina, Zayd informed his father that he wanted to marry the beautiful Zaynab bt. Jaḥsh, Muḥammad's paternal cross-cousin. Unlike the biblical Abraham, who insisted that his son Isaac marry within his tribe, Muḥammad protested that it would be inappropriate for his son to marry this noble Qurashī woman, while at the same time assuring Zayd that he would acquire a beautiful wife for him. Undeterred, Zayd pressed his father to approach Zaynab, suggesting that he say to her, "Zayd is the most noble of men in my eyes." To this Zayd added, "She is indeed a beautiful woman, and I fear that she will refuse any offer that comes [directly] from me, although I am determined to marry her." When the Prophet stood his ground, Zayd turned to his relative by adoption, ʿAlī b. Abī Ṭālib, and asked him to intercede with Muḥammad on his behalf. "Surely," Zayd said, "he shall not turn you down" (*lan yaʿṣiyaka*). The two men went to see Muḥammad, who relented and agreed to pursue the matter.[13]

Muqātil presents two independent versions of the ensuing marriage negotiations. According to the first version, the Prophet sent ʿAlī to arrange a marriage between Zaynab bt. Jaḥsh and Zayd, his son and heir. Zaynab's father Jaḥsh was nowhere to be seen and presumably was dead.[14] Technically, Zaynab was an orphan, and her brother ʿAbdallāh b. Jaḥsh therefore served as her marriage guardian.[15] Initially, neither ʿAbdallāh nor Zaynab was receptive to the marriage proposal. ʿAbdallāh was loathe to give his sister in marriage to a former slave. As for Zaynab, she protested, "I don't want him for myself, for I am the most perfect woman of Quraysh."[16] Only now did ʿAlī inform ʿAbdallāh that the Prophet had *chosen* Zayd for Zaynab and that he had *ordered* ʿAbdallāh to give his sister in marriage to the Beloved of the Messenger of God. In fact, the matter had been decided not only by the Prophet but also by God. As v. 36 states, "When God and His messenger have decided a matter, it is not for any believing man or woman to have any choice in the affair." In the face of this divine revelation, neither ʿAbdallāh nor Zaynab had any choice but to obey. Only now did ʿAbdallāh agree to marry his sister to Zayd. As compensation, Muḥammad sent them (*sāqa ilayhim*) ten *dinar*s, sixty *dirham*s, a cloth head-covering, a night gown, a house dress, a wrapper, fifty *mudd* of food, and ten *mudd* of dates.[17]

In the second version of the negotiations, there is no mention of ʿAlī's role as an intermediary. Here, ʿAbdallāh b. Jaḥsh transfers his authority over Zaynab to Muḥammad (*jaʿala . . . amrahā ilā al-nabī*), whereupon Zaynab says to the Prophet, "Authority over me has been placed in your hands, O Messenger of God (*qad juʿila amrī bi-yadika yā rasūl allāh*)."[18] Once Muḥammad has acquired this authority, he is legally empowered to marry Zaynab to his son Zayd. And he does.[19]

Act 2, Scenes 1–3: A Sexually Charged Encounter Between Muḥammad and Zaynab, Zayd Divorces Zaynab, and Muḥammad Marries Her (vv. 36–38 cont.)

Less than a year after the marriage, Muḥammad pays a visit to his son. Again Muqātil presents two versions of this visit.

In the first version, the narrator characterizes everything that happens as a function of Divine Will. After Zayd has consummated the marriage with Zaynab, he begins to complain to his father about his wife's behavior. Muḥammad goes to see Zaynab at her house with the intention of admonishing her. As he is speaking with his daughter-in-law, however, *God ordains* that he be smitten by her beauty, grace, and appearance. Muḥammad returns home, but *God causes* these feelings to linger in the Prophet's heart. Subsequently, when Muḥammad asks his son how Zaynab is treating him, Zayd repeats his complaint about his wife's behavior. Ignoring his own feelings, Muḥammad orders Zayd to "keep your wife to yourself and fear God."[20] Remarkably, these very words are reproduced verbatim in v. 37. God is all-hearing.

In the second version of the visit, the Divinity is still present, albeit offstage, and Muḥammad's response to his vision of Zaynab is formulated in the language of human passion and sexual desire. Sometime after the consummation of the marriage, Muḥammad goes to visit Zayd, who is not at home. But Zaynab is there. Somehow—the narrator leaves the details to the imagination of his audience—he catches sight of Zaynab while she is in the act of standing up (*fa-abṣara Ẓaynab qāʾimat*^{an}). Muqātil waxes eloquent:

> She was beautiful and white of skin, one of the most perfect women of Quraysh. The Prophet—may God bless him and grant him peace—immediately experienced sexual desire for her (*hawiyahā*), and he exclaimed, "Praise be to God who has the power to transform a man's heart."[21]

When Zayd returns home later that day, Zaynab tells her husband about the strange encounter with her father-in-law. Relations between the couple go from bad to worse. In a curious reversal, the man who had begged his father for permission to marry Zaynab now pleads with him for permission to divorce her on the grounds that his wife is haughty, condescending, and sharp-tongued. As in the first version, Muḥammad tells his son, "keep your wife to yourself and fear God."[22]

Now, the commentator explains, God revealed v. 37, which mentions that

Muḥammad was hiding something within himself, to wit, his desire that Zayd divorce Zaynab.[23] Presumably, the Prophet hid his feelings for Zaynab because he feared public reaction to a sexual relationship between a man and his daughter-in-law. God now rebuked the Prophet for placing his fear of men over that of God ("you feared the people when God had better right to be feared by you"). Unbeknownst to Muḥammad, God was about to reveal permission for him to marry Zaynab. This special dispensation is conveyed in the form of a divine revelation (*qurʾān*^{an})—although, curiously, the dispensation is embedded in the very verse in which God tells Muḥammad that He is about to send down a revelation. Following the revelation of v. 37, Muḥammad recited the verse to his Companions, no doubt drawing attention to two of its clauses: "When Zayd had finished with her" (*fa-lammā qaḍā Ẓayd*^{un} *minhā waṭar*^{an})—which, Muqātil explains, means when he no longer had any "need" for her—that is to say, when his sexual desire for the woman had been satisfied; and "We gave her to you in marriage," which suggests that God himself acted as Zaynab's marriage guardian. At this point in the verse, the language shifts from direct to indirect address. The next clause in v. 37 specifies that the special permission received by the Prophet applies generally to all Believers, introducing a crucial distinction between natural sons and adopted sons: "so that there should be no difficulty (*ḥaraj*) for the believers concerning the wives of their adopted sons (*azwāj adʿiyāʾihim*), when they have finished with them." This clause is glossed by Muqātil as follows: "so that it will not be a sin for a man to marry the wife of his son whom he adopted and who is not from his loins (*min ṣulbihi*)." Verse 37 concludes with the pronouncement, "God's command was fulfilled," that is to say, the marriage had been predetermined and its consummation was a fulfillment of God's command. It was in compliance with this divine command that Zayd divorced his wife and Muḥammad married her, although the narrator is careful to add that the Prophet did not consummate the marriage until after the expiration of her waiting period.[24] The ever-boastful Zaynab would later flaunt the circumstances of her marriage to the Prophet in the faces of her co-wives: "You were given in marriage to the Prophet by men, but I was given in marriage to the Prophet by God—may He be magnified and exalted."[25]

The circumstances of Muḥammad's marriage to Zaynab are extraordinary for several reasons, above and beyond the fact that it is described in the Qurʾān as having been made in Heaven. Readers familiar with the Gospel of Matthew no doubt will have noticed parallels between Muḥammad's marriage to Zaynab and Joseph's marriage to Mary: When Joseph discovered that his bride was pregnant, he kept the matter to himself, intending to divorce Mary, discretely, lest she be exposed to public disgrace. Before Joseph could divorce Mary, however, an angel appeared to him and said, "Joseph, son of

David, do not be afraid to take Mary as your wife" (Matt. 1:18–21). Similarly, readers familiar with the Hebrew Bible no doubt will have noticed parallels between the story of Muḥammad's marriage to Zaynab and the biblical account of David's marriage to Bathsheba. Although Muqātil makes no reference to Joseph and Mary, he was keenly aware of the thematic links between the biblical account of David's marriage to Bathsheba and the Qur'ānic account of Muḥammad's marriage to Zaynab. We will attend to his comparison of these two episodes in Act 3, Scene 2.

Act 3, Scene 1: Public Reaction to Muḥammad's Marriage to Zaynab: Was the Marriage Incestuous? (v. 37, cont.)

In the century that separates the revelation of the Qur'ān from the first extant commentaries, the character of the woman who is mentioned in Q. 33:37 underwent a significant development. In v. 37, this woman has no name, face, or personality. It was Mujāhid b. Jabr who identified her as Zaynab bt. Jaḥsh, and it was Muqātil b. Sulaymān who gave her a face and a personality. She was not only beautiful but also proud, vain, boastful, and sharp-tongued. She emasculated her first husband Zayd and instilled jealousy in the Prophet's other wives. Like many biblical figures, her character is an uneasy combination of positive and negative traits.

In v. 37 God gave Muḥammad special permission to marry the wife of his adopted son and extended this special dispensation to all Believers. But this did not prevent Muḥammad's contemporaries from expressing opposition to the very idea of such a marriage. What troubled them was precisely the fact that the Prophet had married his daughter-in-law. Many years later, the long-lived Companion Anas b. Mālik (d. ca. 91–93/709–11, between 97 and 107 years old)[26] would recall having uttered the following statement at the time of Muḥammad's marriage to Zaynab: "Verily Muḥammad married the wife of his son (*imra'at ibnihi*) at the same time that he has forbidden us to marry them [the wives of our sons]."[27] Unidentified Jews are reported to have made a nearly identical statement: "Muḥammad has married the wife of his son at the same time that he forbids us to do the same!"[28] What surely stung the most, however, was the inclusion of the Hypocrites in the chorus of critics, for they too are reported to have said, "Muḥammad has married the wife of his son at the same time that he forbids us to do the same!"[29] Thus, it appeared to the Prophet's contemporaries—Muslims, Jews, and Hypocrites—as if he were saying one thing and doing another. The inconsistency—indeed, the seeming hypocrisy—of the Prophet did not fail to attract the attention of both his supporters and his opponents.

The Qur'ānic prohibition of a marriage between a man and his daughter-in-law is found in v. 23 of *Sūrat al-Nisā'* ("Women"):

> Forbidden to you are: your mothers; your daughters; your sisters; your paternal aunts; your maternal aunts; brother's daughters; sister's daughters; [those who have become] your mothers by suckling you; your sisters by suckling; your wives' mothers; your step-daughters who are in your care, born to wives with whom you have consummated marriage; but if you have not consummated the marriage, it is no sin for you [to marry the daughters]; the wives of your sons who are from your own loins (*wa-ḥalāʾil abnāʾikum alladhīna min aṣlābikum*). [It is also forbidden] that you should have two sisters together, except for cases that happened in the past. God is Forgiving and Merciful.[30]

Although Q. 4:23 prohibits inter alia a marriage between a man and the former wife of his natural son ("sons who are from your own loins"), the verse clearly indicates that there is nothing improper or unlawful about a marriage between a man and the former wife of his adopted son. Accordingly, the Prophet's marriage to Zaynab was perfectly legal.[31] It is therefore odd that Anas b. Mālik, the Jews, and the Hypocrites would all say that the Prophet had forbidden the Believers from marrying the wives of their sons. There is no such prohibition in the Qurʾān: Q. 4:23 unequivocally indicates that Muḥammad's marriage to Zaynab was licit and did not violate any incest taboo whatsoever.[32] How are we to explain the discrepancy between the assertion attributed to Anas, the Jews, and the Hypocrites, on the one hand, and the language of the Qurʾān, on the other? Why did Muslims, Jews, and Hypocrites think that the Qurʾān and/or Muḥammad had prohibited marriage to a daughter-in-law? Did the Qurʾān once contain such a prohibition? To answer these questions, we interrupt our analysis of Act 3, scene 1 (v. 37) and turn to the Hebrew Bible, to Leviticus 18:5–18 and 20:12–21, known as the Holiness Code.

Excursus: Leviticus 18:5–18 and 20:12–21 Compared to Q. 4:23

The biblical Holiness Code and Q. 4:23 are structurally and thematically related to one another. Leviticus 18:5–18 forbids marriage inter alia with a man's mother, sister, paternal and maternal aunt, sister-in-law, daughter-in-law, and two sisters simultaneously. For almost every kinship bar based on affinity or consanguinity in the Holiness Code there is a corresponding prohibition in the Qurʾān. The only exceptions are the Qurʾān's prohibition of a marriage between an uncle and his niece and its prohibition of a marriage between a man and his step-daughter, for which no corresponding prohibition is found in the Holiness Code.[33] These parallels are sufficiently close to have caused two scholars writing in the first half of the twentieth century to posit a historical connection—direct or indirect—between the two sacred texts.[34]

There is also a linguistic connection between the Holiness Code and Q. 4:23. The lexicon shared by the different Semitic languages includes kinship terms. Leviticus uses the Hebrew version of these kinship terms to identify the relatives with whom one may not have sexual relations, always in the singular followed by a second person masculine singular pronoun suffix; for example, *immeka* ("your mother") or *aḥotka* ("your sister"). In the Qurʾān, the corresponding prohibition is conveyed with the Arabic equivalent of these kinship terms, always in the plural followed by a second person masculine plural pronoun suffix, as in *ummahātukum* ("your mothers"), *banātukum* ("your daughters"), or *akhawātukum* ("your sisters").[35]

Sexual relations between a man and his daughter-in-law are prohibited in Leviticus 18:15: "Do not uncover the nakedness of your daughter-in-law (*kallatka*): she is your son's wife" (*eshet binka*). The legal consequences of such a union are spelled out in Leviticus 20:12: "If a man lies with his daughter-in-law (*kallatô*), both of them shall be put to death; they have committed incest—their bloodguilt is upon them."[36] Notice, first, that neither biblical verse distinguishes between a natural son and an adopted son and, second, that Leviticus 18:15 glosses *kallâh* as *eshet ben*, "the wife of a son." The Arabic equivalent of *eshet ben* is *imraʾat ibn*.[37]

The reaction to Muḥammad's marriage to Zaynab attributed to Anas b. Mālik, Jews, and Hypocrites suggests that the Qurʾān did at one time forbid marriage with "your daughters-in-law" or "the wives of your sons," without however distinguishing between a natural son and an adopted son. In the following linguistic exercise, I shall attempt to explain how the hypothetical Qurʾānic equivalent of the biblical prohibition might have been formulated; and how the original formulation might have been revised to produce the current formulation.

Leviticus 18:15 prohibits sexual relations with *your daughter-in-law* (*kallatka*) and glosses this kinship term as *the wife of your son* (*eshet binka*). As noted, the Qurʾānic equivalents of the biblical prohibitions are formulated as plural nouns with masculine plural pronoun suffixes. In Chapter 8, I will argue that the original consonantal skeleton of 4:12b specified **kalla* rather than *kalāla* (hereinafter an asterisk [*] signifies a hypothetical word or reading); and that this word signified *daughter-in-law*. One plural of **kalla* would have been **kalāʾil*.[38] If so, then the Qurʾānic equivalent of *kallatka* in Leviticus 18:15 would have been **kalāʾilukum* ("*your daughters-in-law"). Likewise—and unproblematic—the Qurʾānic equivalent of *eshet binka* in Leviticus 18:15 would have been *nisāʾ abnāʾikum* ("the wives of your sons"). Therefore, if *4:23 originally prohibited marriage with a *daughter-in-law*, the original Qurʾānic formulation would have been "**kalāʾilukum*." If a gloss were needed for this technical kinship term, it would have been "*nisāʾ abnāʾikum*." However, once Q. 33:37 extended to all Believers the special dispensation that had been granted to Muḥammad, the prohibition of marrying "*your daughters-in-law" in a hypothetical *4:23 would have required revision. Q. 33:37, it will be recalled, uses the language of permission to extend to all Believers the special dispensation granted to Muḥammad to marry his daughter-in-law: "so that there should be no difficulty for the believers concerning the wives of their adopted sons" (*azwāj adʿiyāʾihim*). The inverse of this rule must be stated in the language of prohibition. In English, this prohibition may be formulated as follows: You are forbidden to marry the wives of your natural sons.

How might this idea be expressed in Arabic? One cannot just add *alladhīna min aṣlābikum* ("of your loins") to *kalāʾilukum*, thus saying, *kalāʾilukum alladhīna min aṣlābikum*, because *your* daughters-in-law do not emerge from *your* loins. Nor can one say *kalāʾil abnāʾikum alladhīna min aṣlābikum* ("the daughters-in-law of your sons who issued from your loins") because that would refer to your sons' daughters-in-law, not to yours.[39] The solution to this linguistic problem is found in the shift from the technical term **kalāʾilukum* ("*your daughters-in-law") to its gloss—*nisāʾ abnāʾikum* ("your sons' wives"). What was needed was the Arabic equivalent of the concept *the wives of your natural sons.* Happily, in Arabic, this may be accomplished by replacing the broken plural of **kalāʾil* (*daughters-in-law) with a broken plural of the same pattern derived from the root *ḥ-l-l*, that is to say, *ḥalāʾil* (sg. *ḥalīla*) or "licit wives." If one makes *ḥalāʾil* the first element of an *iḍāfa* construct whose second term is *abnāʾukum*, the result is "*ḥalāʾil abnāʾikum*," or "the licit wives of your sons." To this one might add the critical gloss that is suggested by the language of Muqātil's commentary on Q. 33:37 (*min ṣulbihi*), in the plural with a plural pronoun suffix: *alladhīna min aṣlābikum* ("of your own loins").

Hypothesis 4.1. The original formulation of the clause in Q. 4:23 that prohibits marriage with a daughter-in-law specified **kalāʾilukum* or *daughters-in-law. This was changed to "*ḥalāʾil abnāʾikum alladhīna min aṣlābikum*" or "the wives of your sons who are from your own loins." This hypothesis awaits scholarly confirmation, based on the evidence of early Qurʾān manuscripts.

In order to move from the language of permission in Q. 33:37 to the language of prohibition in Q. 4:23 it was necessary to replace the technical kinship term *daughters-in-law* with *licit wives*, followed by *your sons*, followed by the specification that the sons in question are *natural sons* ("of your own loins"). The resulting formulation—*ḥalāʾil abnāʾikum alladhīna min aṣlābikum*—makes it clear that the prohibition articulated in Q. 4:23 does *not* apply to Muḥammad's marriage to his daughter-in-law Zaynab. If such a change was introduced to the consonantal skeleton of *4:23, it is likely to have *followed* the revelation of Q. 33:37. It appears that some Muslims and even some non-Muslims remembered the original formulation of *4:23. Otherwise, it is difficult to make sense of the assertion attributed variously to Anas, Jews, and Hypocrites: "Muḥammad has married the wife of his son but has forbidden us from marrying them." There is no such prohibition anywhere in the Qurʾān.

Muqātil has now completed his narrative expansion of the first three acts of the sacred drama under consideration. Before proceeding to Act 4, the commentator pauses briefly to discuss v. 38, which alludes to a connection between the story of Muḥammad's marriage to Zaynab and the biblical account of David's marriage to Bathsheba. Let us attend to what he says.

Act 3, Scene 2: Public Reaction to the Marriage: *Sunnat Allāh* and the Divine Decree (v. 38)

Verse 38 of *Sūrat al-Aḥzāb* begins: "There is no difficulty for the prophet in that which God has ordained for him."

These words, Muqātil explains, were uttered by unidentified critics of Muḥammad. Unlike the Muslims, Jews, and Hypocrites who, as we have seen, are said to have been shocked by Muḥammad's marriage to his daughter-in-law, this second group of critics reportedly was troubled by the manner in which God's decree appears to have been designed to satisfy the sexual desires of the Prophet.[40] The response to this criticism is found in the continuation of the verse. The sexual life of a prophet is governed by *sunnat allāh* or God's practice. This is true not only of Muḥammad but also of "those who passed away previously," a phrase which, the commentator explains, refers to previous prophets. From the long line of prophets who preceded Muḥammad, Muqātil singles out the figure of David.

The first Muslims surely were familiar with the story of David and Bathsheba as related in II Samuel 11:6–27, and there was no need to repeat it. Indeed, the details of the biblical account are carefully avoided by Muslims because of the negative manner in which David is portrayed therein. Dā'ūd is mentioned sixteen times in the Qur'ān, where he is identified as an important link in the chain of prophets who preceded Muḥammad; in Q. 38:26 he is identified as God's "viceroy in the land" (*khalīfat*^{an} *fī'l-arḍ*).[41] In the Qur'ānic worldview, the biblical representation of David as a king who coveted another man's wife, engaged in illicit sexual relations with the woman, and was complicit in the murder of her husband, is literally unthinkable. Indeed, the negative portrayal of David in II Samuel is one of the grounds on which the Qur'ān accuses the Jews of falsifying their sacred scripture (*yuḥarrifūna al-kalima ʿan mawāḍiʿihi*).[42] This may explain why the Qur'ān does not specifically mention by name either Bathsheba or Uriah the Hittite.

The discomfiture of the early Muslim community with the negative portrayal of King David in II Samuel may have been related to Jewish discomfiture with the biblical narrative. In the Talmudic period (ca. 200–500 C.E.), some rabbis attempted to exonerate David from the charge of adultery. For example, Rabbi Samuel b. Nachman/Nahmani is reported to have said in the name of Rabbi Jonathan, "Everyone who went out in the wars of the House of David wrote a bill of divorcement for his wife."[43] From this one might infer that Uriah had written such a document. If so, then Uriah was no longer Bathsheba's husband when David lay with her. But no amount of legal casuistry could clear David of indirect culpability for the soldier's death. In II Samuel, David acknowledges his guilt to the prophet Nathan, who then informs the king that God has remitted his sin. In the Talmud, David confesses directly to God: "David prayed before the Holy One, blessed be He, 'Lord of the universe! Forgive me for that sin.' 'It is forgiven you,' He replied."[44] The rabbis teach that God was testing David; the fact that He forgave the king proves that he passed the test.[45] This argument was taken one step further by Rabbi Samuel b. Nahmani, who is reported to have said, again in the name of Rabbi Jonathan: "Whoever says that David sinned is mistaken . . . he contemplated the act, but did not go through with it."[46] Similarly, it may be said of Muḥammad that he contemplated the act but did not go through with it. Neither prophet committed a sin.

In my view, scholarly appreciation of the early Muslim community's understanding of Q. 33:37 and its narrative expansion is enhanced when we view the narrative account of Muḥammad's marriage to Zaynab against the background of the rabbinic response to the biblical portrayal of David as a man who coveted another man's wife, committed adultery, and was responsible for the death of Uriah the Hittite. *Ad* v. 38, Muqātil compares the story of Muḥammad's infatuation with, and subsequent marriage to, Zaynab—as related in his commentary on v. 37—to the biblical story of David's infatuation with, and subsequent marriage to, Bathsheba. Just as the Qur'ān does not mention the name of the woman who married first Zayd and then Muḥammad, so too Muqātil does not mention the name of the woman who married first Uriah and then David. Just as some rabbis exonerate King David by arguing inter alia that God was testing the king, who passed the test by expressing forgiveness for his sin, so too Muqātil vindicates the Prophet David by correcting the falsified biblical account. The Muslim commentator explains that the Prophet David did fall in love with (*hawiya*) the wife of Uriah b. Ḥanān [sic];[47] and that the Prophet Muḥammad did fall in love with Zaynab bt. Jaḥsh—but only because both prophets were being tested (*futina*) by God.[48] Both prophets passed the test. Similarly, Muqātil explains, it was God who united (in the sense of sexual congress) David with the (here unnamed) woman with whom he had fallen in love (*fa-jamaʿa allāh bayna Dāʾūd wa bayna al-marʾa allatī hawiyahā*); and it was God who united (in the sense of sexual congress) Muḥammad with Zaynab when he fell in love with her (*ka-dhālika jamaʿa allāh bayna Muḥammad wa bayna Zaynab idh hawiyahā*). The early Muslim community clearly had no qualms about portraying the Prophet as a man who, unlike Jesus, but like David (and Solomon), had a healthy sexual appetite. After all, Islamic tradition teaches that Muḥammad had thirteen wives and concubines and the potency of forty men.[49] It was not long, however, before a reaction set in, perhaps in response to Christian anti-Muslim polemic (see Chapter 3). The growing discomfiture of the Muslim community with the story of Muḥammad's infatuation with Zaynab is reflected in a statement attributed variously to ʿUmar b.

al-Khaṭṭāb, Anas b. Mālik, and ʿĀʾisha, all of whom are reported to have said about v. 37, "Had the Messenger of God concealed (*katama*) any part of the Qurʾān, he would have concealed this [verse]!"[50] The evidence of the *isnād*s suggests that this statement was first put into circulation in the last quarter of the first century A.H., at which time it was no longer possible to remove v. 37 from the Qurʾān (as reportedly was done with 137 other verses in *Sūrat al-Aḥzāb*). That is to say, it was too late to *conceal* anything. The only remaining alternative was to explain away the unfavorable light in which the Prophet is portrayed in the narrative expansion of v. 37.[51]

The juxtaposition of the story of David and Bathsheba and that of Muḥammad and Zaynab was important to the early Muslim community because it highlighted the Qurʾānic notion that the history of mankind unfolds according to *sunnat allāh*, or providential design, which accounts for the cyclical patterns and uncanny regularities of history. This is one reason why I have chosen to treat the Islamic narrative as a play in five acts, composed by an omniscient playwright, and featuring Muḥammad, Zayd, and Zaynab as the dramatis personae. Like David's marriage to Bathsheba, Muḥammad's marriage to Zaynab was preordained by a divine playwright who is thought to have composed the script for the play before creating the world. For this reason, resistance to the divine playwright's instructions would be sheer folly. As v. 38 teaches, "God's command is a fixed decree."[52]

Act 4: Muḥammad Is the Seal of Prophets (v. 40)

In Q. 33:37 God gave Muḥammad special permission to marry Zaynab, in Q. 33:38 He assured the Prophet that his marriage to Zaynab was a divine command and a determined act, and in Q. 4:23 He decreed that there is nothing improper or illegal about a marriage between a man and the former wife of his adopted son. Curiously, none of these divine directives—either individually or in combination—was sufficient to solve whatever problem it was that the early Muslim community was facing. We are now in a position to identify this problem.

The pericope that we have been analyzing begins with v. 36 and ends with v. 40, a short verse composed of three clauses:

a Muḥammad is not the father of any of your men,
b but the messenger of God and the seal of Prophets.
c God is aware of everything.

Verse 40 is the only verse in the Qurʾān that identifies Muḥammad as the Seal of Prophets (*khātam al-nabiyyīn*). Here the voice that controls the text addresses an unidentified audience—presumably the Muslim community—

about its leader, who is identified by name. The first clause states that Muḥammad has no adult son, the second identifies him as a messenger of God and as the Seal of Prophets, and the third asserts God's omniscience. The verse contains three key terms: messenger, prophet, and seal of prophets, to which we now turn our attention.

The term *rasūl*, or messenger, occurs 236 times in the Qurʾān, always in the sense of a human agent sent by God to guide a people in a language that they understand. A messenger delivers a book and establishes a new religious law. The term *nabī*, or prophet, occurs seventy-five times in the Qurʾān and it generally signifies a man who continues an earlier religious law without bringing a new book. Occasionally, the titles overlap and refer to one and the same person. Thus Moses and Muḥammad are both messengers and prophets. Similarly Q. 19:54–55 identifies Ishmael as both a messenger and a prophet, presumably because he ordained worship and almsgiving for his people.[53]

The Qurʾān suggests—without specifically saying so—that prophecy (*al-nubūʾa*) is the exclusive possession of a single family. Q. 57:26 establishes that God assigned prophecy and the Book to the progeny (*dhurriyya*) of Noah and Abraham. Similarly Q. 29:27 specifies that God conferred prophecy and the Book on the progeny of Abraham. Q. 4:163 identifies successive generations of prophets within a single family: "We have made revelations to you, as We made them to Noah and the prophets after him, and as We made them to Abraham and Ishmael and Isaac and Jacob and the tribes. . . ." Q. 19:58 links the progeny of Adam, Noah, Abraham, and Israel: "These are those whom God blessed among the prophets of the seed (*dhurriyya*) of Adam and of those whom We carried with Noah and of the seed of Abraham and Israel and of those whom We guided and chose. . . ." From these verses, we learn that the prophets emerged in succession and that they were all members of a single tribe or family that extended from Adam to Muḥammad. It is reasonable to infer from these verses that the office of prophecy is hereditary, that is to say, it passes from father to son within this family—even if not every male link in this genealogical chain was himself a prophet.[54]

The phrase *alladhīna anʿama allāhᵘ ʿalayhim min al-nabiyyīn* in Q. 19:58 may be translated into English either as "those on whom God bestowed favor, namely, the prophets" or as "the prophets on whom God bestowed favor" (my translation). A similar phrase occurs in Q. 33:37: *li-lladhī anʿama allāhᵘ ʿalayhi wa-anʿamta ʿalayhi* ("the one on whom God and you yourself have bestowed favor").[55] In the latter verse, the commentators explain, this phrase refers specifically to Zayd. As a man favored by God, Zayd may be compared to Solomon, the biblical king who, according to II Samuel 12:24, was favored by God (*ve-yahweh ahevô*). It is noteworthy that the same language used in Q. 19:58 to refer to prophets is used in Q. 33:37 to refer to Zayd.[56] Was Zayd also *min al-*

nabiyyīn, that is to say, a member of the family to which the office of prophecy had been entrusted—either in fact or in potential? For the moment, we leave this question unanswered.

The third key term in Q. 33:40 is *khātam al-nabiyyīn*, "Seal of Prophets," a linguistic metaphor which suggests that Muḥammad is to the class of prophets as a seal or stamp is to the object it seals. The association of a *khātam*, or *seal*, with the office of prophecy has a long history that predates Islam.[57] We find the noun *seal* or the verb *to seal* juxtaposed to the office of prophecy in Jewish,[58] Christian,[59] and Manichean texts.[60] In all of these texts, the seal metaphor is invoked to signify the *confirmation* or *fulfillment* of prophecy; conversely, in none of these texts is the metaphor used to signify the *end* of prophecy.

As noted, in the standard text of the Qur'ān, the phrase "Seal of Prophets" occurs only once, in v. 40 of *Sūrat al-Aḥzāb*. The early Muslim community may have experimented with both the placement and formulation of this figure of speech. The codex of Ubayy b. Kaʿb is said to have contained a variant of what would become the standard reading of v. 6 of *Sūrat al-Ṣaff* ("The Ranks"). In the variant, the relevant section of Q. 61:6 reads as follows: "announcing a prophet to you, whose community will be the last one among the communities (*ummatuhu ākhir al-umam*), and by means of whom God seals the messengers and the prophets (*yakhtum allāh*[u] *bihi al-anbiyā' wa'l-rusul*)."[61] Here it is clear that the new prophet's community will be the last or final one. As for the assertion that God will *seal* the earlier messengers and prophets by means of the prophet announced by Jesus, this is easily understood as signifying that the new prophet will *confirm* or *fulfill* (*yakhtum*) the mission of earlier prophets. From this statement, one may infer that Muḥammad will be the Last Prophet. This understanding of the variant attributed to Ubayy is supported by what would become the standard version of Q. 61:6, in which Jesus is quoted as saying to the Children of Israel, "I am God's messenger to you, confirming (*muṣaddiq*[an]) the Torah that was [revealed] before me, and giving you good tidings of a messenger who will come after me, whose name will be Aḥmad." Just as Jesus confirms the Torah, so too Muḥammad confirms both the Torah and the Injīl.

We turn now to the phrase *khātam al-nabiyyīn* in v. 40 of *Sūrat al-Aḥzāb*. The first word in this phrase may be read in one of three ways: (1) As a noun, *khātam*, which means *a seal*; (2) as an active participle, *khātim*, which means *the end or last part or portion*; and (3) as a verb, *khatama*, which means either *to seal, stamp*, or *impress* or *to reach the end of a thing*.[62] Let us focus our attention on the first reading (*khātam*)—which is the hardest to reconcile with the assertion that Muḥammad is the Last Prophet. The literal meaning of *khātam al-nabiyyīn* is Seal of Prophets. It is possible to understand this figure of speech by analogy to its use in the above-mentioned Jewish, Christian, and Manichean texts. As we have seen, the Qur'ān identifies Muḥammad as a link in a chain of messengers that goes back to Abraham. Previously, God delivered the Torah to Moses and the Injīl to Jesus. In this context, the metaphor in v. 40 may be read as signifying that the revelation sent to Muḥammad confirms or fulfills the earlier Jewish and Christian revelations. By bearing witness to the truth of the earlier revelations, Muḥammad placed his personal seal (*khātam*) on those texts. This is how some members of the early Muslim community understood the phrase Seal of Prophets.[63]

Other members of the early Muslim community understood the phrase *khātam al-nabiyyīn* as signifying that Muḥammad brought the office of prophecy to a close, that is to say, that he was the Last Prophet. It is the formulation of Q. 33:40 which makes it possible to interpret the phrase in this manner. Verse 40 juxtaposes the assertion that Muḥammad is *khātam al-nabiyyīn* with the fact that he "is not the father of any of your men." According to the Qur'ānic conception of prophecy, if Muḥammad had a son who reached manhood, the office of prophecy would continue. It is only the qualification of the Seal of Prophets as a man who had no adult sons that makes it possible to assert that he was the Last Prophet. Only if he is sonless can Muḥammad be the Last Prophet. Thus, the placement of v. 40 at the end of a five-verse pericope that serves as the Qur'ānic peg for Muḥammad's repudiation of Zayd is no coincidence. As we shall see, there is a direct connection between Muḥammad's repudiation of Zayd and the early Muslim community's claim that Muḥammad was the Last Prophet.

In a seminal article published in 1986, Yohanan Friedmann demonstrated that the meaning of the phrase *khātam al-nabiyyīn* was contested during the first century A.H.[64] In one tradition, for example, ʿĀ'isha is reported to have said, "Say [that the Prophet is] the Seal of Prophets (*khātam al-nabiyyīn*) but do not say that there is no prophet after him (*lā nabiyy*[a] *baʿdahu*)."[65] Here the statement attributed to ʿĀ'isha leaves open the possibility that a prophet might appear after Muḥammad, notwithstanding the latter's status as the Seal of Prophets. The statement suggests that Muḥammad is the best prophet, albeit not necessarily the last one.[66]

The shift in the understanding of *khātam al-nabiyyīn* from Seal of Prophets to Last Prophet may be related to events that took place during the course of the first century A.H.[67] Both during the Prophet's lifetime and in the years following his death, there was a significant spike in claims of prophecy. News of Muḥammad's final illness is said to have spread quickly throughout the Arabian Peninsula. In the Yemen, al-Aswad seized on the opportunity of the Prophet's imminent demise to claim the office of prophecy for himself. In al-Yamāma, Musaylima did the same.[68] During the so-called apostasy (*ridda*) wars (11–12/633–34) the rebel Sajāḥ claimed to be a prophet.[69] At least three false prophets appeared during the reign of the Umayyad caliph ʿAbd al-Malik (r. 65–86/685–705). That some followers of al-Mukhtār (d. 67/687), the leader of a pro-ʿAlid movement in Kufa, regarded him as a prophet is suggested by their claim that he was impeccable (*maʿṣūm*) and received visits from the Angels Gabriel and Michael.[70] Several years later, al-Ḥārith b. Saʿīd (d. 79/699) was put to death after claiming to be a prophet.[71] And Abū ʿĪsā al-Iṣfahānī, leader of a Jewish uprising against the Umayyads, claimed to be a prophet (*nabī*) and a Messenger of the Messiah (*rasūl al-masīḥ*), sent by God to deliver the Children of Israel.[72] It may have been in response to these "false" claims to prophecy that the phrase *khātam al-nabiyyīn* came to be accepted as signifying *the Last Prophet*, a doctrine that, in Friedmann's words, "eventually acquired an undisputed and central place in the religious thought of Islam."[73]

By the end of the first century A.H., the contention that Muḥammad was the Last Prophet had taken its place alongside the contention that he confirmed or fulfilled earlier prophecies. This new understanding required that he be sonless. Once the notion of Muḥammad's sonlessness had become firmly established, it became important—indeed, imperative—to demonstrate that absolutely no one could claim to be Muḥammad's son and, conversely, that Muḥammad could not be said to have been the father of any male who reached puberty. This imperative brings us back to Muqātil's commentary on v. 40, where he explains that the assertion that "Muḥammad is not the father of any of your men" refers specifically to Zayd b. Ḥāritha [sic]. "Muḥammad is not Zayd's father," Muqātil pronounces. Indeed, he continues, the verse indicates that Muḥammad is "*rasūl allāh wa-khātam al-nabiyyīn.*" Lest there be any doubt about the meaning of the metaphor, the commentator adds—in apparent disregard of the above-mentioned statement attributed to ʿĀʾisha—that he is "the last Prophet, there is no prophet after Muḥammad."[74]

What is the connection between Muḥammad's not being Zayd's father and his being the Last Prophet? To this question Muqātil responds in two stages. First, he poses a general counterfactual: "Had Muḥammad had a son (*walad*), he [that son] would have been a prophet [and] messenger" (*nabī rasūl*). It was because the omniscient Deity understood this, the commentator continues, that v. 40 ends with "God is aware of everything." Second, Muqātil applies to Zayd the principle that he has just established, as follows: *law kāna Zayd^un ibn^a Muḥammad^in la-kāna nabiyy^an*. There are at least two ways to understand this sentence. It may mean, "Had Zayd been Muḥammad's [biological] son, he would have been a prophet." In that case, however, one would expect to find: *law kāna Zayd^un ibn^a Muḥammad^in* ***min ṣulbi***—precisely the distinction between biological and adopted sons that one finds in v. 37. Alternatively, the sentence may mean, "Had Zayd [continued] to be the son of Muḥammad, he would have been a prophet."[75] As we shall see below (Act 5), Zayd had been, but was no longer, Muḥammad's son. It is for this reason that I find the second alternative to be the most likely meaning of Muqātil's statement. That is to say, had Zayd continued to be Muḥammad's son and had he continued to bear the name Zayd b. Muḥammad, he would have been a prophet, just like his father.[76] The fact that Zayd was Muḥammad's son—even if by adoption—was incompatible with the early Muslim community's contention that Muḥammad was the Last Prophet. Muqātil understood that just as prophecy passed from Adam to Noah to Abraham to Ishmael, and, eventually, to Muḥammad, so too it might have passed from Muḥammad to Zayd. Just as Solomon succeeded David as God's deputy (*khalīfa*), so too Zayd—also known as Abū Salama—might have succeeded Muḥammad as God's deputy. And just as Zayd might have succeeded Muḥammad, Usāma might have succeeded Zayd. Indeed, had it not been for Muḥammad's repudiation of Zayd (to be treated in Act 5) and Zayd's untimely death in the year 8 A.H. (to be treated in Chapter 5), no power on earth could have prevented Zayd from succeeding Muḥammad as either a prophet or as God's deputy—or both.

To the best of my knowledge, Muqātil is the only exegete who ever referred to Zayd's status as a potential prophet. One might object that in his commentary on v. 40, Muqātil was doing what any Qur'ān exegete would do with this verse, to wit, explain its obvious implications—even if these implications are merely hypothetical. This, after all, is what the exegetical enterprise is all about. It does not necessarily follow from a single commentator's reference to Zayd as a potential prophet that anyone in the Muslim community actually held and/or supported this theoretical position during the first 150 years of Islamic history—or at any time thereafter.

To this objection I would respond as follows: First, the Islamic tradition remembers that v. 40, which establishes Muḥammad's status as the Seal of Prophets, was revealed specifically about Zayd, that is to say, Zayd himself is the *sabab* or occasion for the revelation of the verse.[77] Second, if it is obvious that Zayd's status as Muḥammad's son made him a potential prophet, then why is it that no Muslim commentator dared to mention this possibility after the year 150 A.H.? One answer to this question has to do with Muqātil's reputation as an exegete and transmitter of *ḥadīth*. The biographers remember Muqātil as a liar who fabricated *ḥadīth* about the Prophet and whose knowledge of the Qur'ān was based on what he learned from Jews and Christians.[78] Indeed, the opprobrium heaped upon Muqātil is related directly to the verses in *Sūrat al-Aḥzāb* that are the subject of the present chapter. In his treatment of Q. 33:36–40, Muqātil is said to have been (unduly) influenced by Jewish sources, to have relied too heavily on the Isrā'īliyyāt of the People of the Book, and to have "perpetrated a falsehood against the Prophet" in his narrative expansion of the Prophet's marriage to Zaynab bt. Jaḥsh.[79] It should come as no surprise that he is largely disregarded by later Qur'ān commentators.[80] Third—and most important, Zayd was not the only one of Muḥammad's sons who threatened his status as the Last Prophet; and Muslim scholars other than Muqātil are said to have made claims about this son similar to Muqātil's claim about Zayd.

It is reported that in the year 6 or 7/627–29, Muqawqis, the governor of Alexandria, sent two female slaves to Muḥammad as a gift of honor: Sīrīn bt. Shamʿūn and her sister Māriya the Copt. The Prophet—who had no natural or adopted son at the time, gave Sīrīn to the poet Ḥassān b. Thābit and took Māriya as his concubine. Muḥammad installed Māriya in her own apartment and visited her frequently. It was not long before the Prophet's wives became jealous of the concubine. *Ad* Q. 66:1 Muqātil relates the following report:

> One day, when it was Ḥafṣa's turn to be with the Prophet, she went [instead] to visit her father ʿUmar b. al-Khaṭṭāb. When she returned to her apartment, she caught a glimpse of the Prophet (*abṣarat al-nabī*) with Māriya the Copt in her [Ḥafṣa's] apartment. Ḥafṣa waited outside until Māriya had left her apartment, at which point she said to the Prophet, "I have seen who was with you in [my] apartment, on my day and on my bed!" When the Prophet saw the jealousy and pain on Ḥafṣa's face, he issued the following order, "O Ḥafṣa, keep this a secret for me. [If you] don't tell ʿĀ'isha, I promise you that I will never touch her again."[81]

Muḥammad's Egyptian concubine Māriya became pregnant and gave birth to a son who was called Ibrāhīm. The child died in infancy. It is said that on the day he died there was a solar eclipse, in which case Ibrāhīm would have died on 28 Shawwāl 10/27 January 632. Less than five months later, on 12 Rabīʿ I 11/8 June 632, Muḥammad followed his infant son to the grave.[82]

Muḥammad's response to the death of Ibrāhīm may be compared to David's response to the death of Bathsheba's illegitimate first son. The biblical king resumed normal activities immediately following the death of his son (II Sam. 12:20–23). By contrast, Muḥammad is said to have attended the funeral ceremony, although he did not pray for Ibrāhīm during the ceremony because "one prophet does not pray for another prophet, and it is said that had he [Ibrāhīm] lived, he would have been a prophet (*law ʿāsha la-kāna nabiyy*[an])"[83]—an assertion similar to the one made about Zayd. Another report quotes the very words of Muḥammad as he placed his hand into his son's grave, "By God, he is a prophet and a son of a prophet (*nabiyy*[un] *ibn*[u] *nabiyy*[in])."[84] In another, widely circulated report, it is said that "had he lived, he would have been a righteous man [and] a prophet (*fa-law ʿāsha la-kāna ṣiddīq*[an] *nabiyy*[an])."[85] In another report it is stated, "Had it been decreed that there would be a prophet after Muḥammad . . . his son would have lived, but there is no prophet after him;"[86] that is to say, Ibrāhīm would have outlived his father but for God's pronouncement that Muḥammad is the Last Prophet. In another report, a question about Ibrāhīm's age at the time of his death is put to Anas b. Mālik, one of the Muslims who, it will be recalled, was shocked by Muḥammad's marriage to his daughter-in-law Zaynab. To this question, Anas responded, "He filled the cradle. Had he lived, he would have been a prophet, but he was not [destined] to live, because your prophet is the last of prophets."[87] A century and a half later, Ibn Ḥanbal (d. 241/855) put it bluntly, "If there were to be a prophet after Muḥammad . . . his son Ibrāhīm would not have died [viz., predeceased his father]."[88] From these reports Friedmann concludes that Ibrāhīm "had to die in order to keep the dogma of *khatm al-nubuwwa* intact."[89]

Like Ibrāhīm, Zayd had to predecease Muḥammad in order to preserve his father's status as the last prophet. The point is made clearly by Zamakhsharī (d. 538/1144) in his commentary *ad* Q. 33:40: "If he [Muḥammad] had a son who attained puberty, he [the son] would have been a prophet and he [Muḥammad] would not have been the Seal of Prophets (*khātam al-nabiyyīn*)."[90] Whereas in Ibrāhīm's case the premature demise of the Prophet's infant son was both necessary and sufficient, in Zayd's case, his death at Mu'ta was necessary but not sufficient (see Chapter 5). This is because Zayd was already a mature adult at the time of the hijra to Medina. For this reason, theological considerations demanded not only that Zayd predecease his father but also that his father repudiate him. Muḥammad's repudiation of Zayd was a theological imperative, an imperative that brings us to Act 5.

Act 5: Legal Consequences (vv. 4–6)

In Q. 33:37 God gave Muḥammad special permission to marry his daughter-in-law Zaynab, in Q. 33:38 He asserted that His command was a fixed decree that was preordained, and in Q. 4:23 He established that there is nothing improper about a marriage between a man and the former wife of his adopted son. Both individually and collectively, these three divine pronouncements failed to solve the problem that confronted the early Muslim community.

The very existence of a man named Zayd b. Muḥammad threatened the doctrine of the finality of prophecy. This threat appears to have been eliminated by Zayd's untimely—albeit theologically necessary—death in 8 A.H. But even if Zayd did in fact die in 8 A.H. (a "fact" that will be subjected to critical examination in Chapter 5), his death would not have eliminated the threat to the doctrine of *khatm al-nubū'a* because he was survived by his son Usāma b. Zayd b. Muḥammad, the Beloved Son of the Beloved of the Messenger of God. If, at the time of his death, Zayd continued to bear the name of Zayd b. Muḥammad, then the office of prophecy would have passed from Zayd to Usāma, the Prophet's grandson (just as the Imamate passed from ʿAlī to his two sons, Ḥasan and Ḥusayn, also the Prophet's grandsons). Like his father, Usāma was a potential prophet. Unlike his father, who is said to have predeceased Muḥammad, Usāma did not die until 54/674. At the time of his death, he had at least five sons.[91] Somehow, the early Muslim community had to find a way to sever the filial relationship between Muḥammad, on the one hand, and Zayd and Usāma, on the other. There were at least two options: to sever the filial connection between Zayd and Usāma, or to sever the filial connection between Muḥammad and Zayd. Let us begin with the first option. It will be recalled that immediately after Usāma was born, certain unidentified Muslims are said to have claimed that the infant did not resemble his father and therefore was not his natural and legitimate son. Alas, a physiognomist established that Usāma was in fact Zayd' son. The second option—to sever the filial relation between Muḥammad and Zayd and, transitively, that between Muḥammad and Usāma, proved more successful. To this end, the early Muslim community appropriated the biblical model of Abraham and Ishmael and applied it creatively to the Islamic foundation narrative. Just as Abraham expelled his older and beloved son Ishmael (Gen. 21:14ff.), so too Muḥammad was made to renounce Zayd, the Beloved of the Messenger of God. The uncanny similarity between the two acts is yet another manifestation of *sunnat allāh* or God's practice. Henceforth, Zayd was no longer Muḥammad's son and Usāma was no longer his grandson. The threat posed by Usāma appears to have been eliminated.

We come now to vv. 4–6 of *Sūrat al-Aḥzāb*. In terms of physical arrangement, vv. 4–6 precede vv. 36–40. In terms of dramatic unity, logic, and chronology, however, vv. 4–6 follow vv. 36–40. It is no coincidence, in my view, that the Muslims who compiled and redacted the Qurʾān and determined the sequential arrangement of its verses chose to separate these two pericopes and to place the chronological end of the episode (vv. 4–6) at the beginning of the chapter. This choice has three important consequences: First, it ruptures the narrative continuity and chronological integrity of the episode by prepositioning the end of the story (my Act 5). Second, it prepares the audience for Muḥammad's repudiation of Zayd. By the time the reader of Muqātil's commentary—or any commentary, for that matter—reaches v. 37, he or she knows that Zayd will be—indeed has been—repudiated by the Prophet, and that Zayd will recover—indeed already has recovered—his birth name: Zayd b. Ḥāritha al-Kalbī. Third, v. 5 places the early Muslim community on notice, warning that anyone who intentionally refers to Muḥammad's adopted son as Zayd b. Muḥammad thereby commits a sin (which brings to mind the rabbinic warning, "Whoever says that David sinned is mistaken").

Q. 33:4–6 read as follows.

4 God has not put two hearts inside any man, nor has He made your wives whom you declare to be as your mothers' backs your [real] mothers; nor has He made your adopted sons your [real] sons. That is what you say with your mouths, but God speaks the truth and guides to the [right] way.

5 Call them after their fathers. That is fairer with God. If you do not know their fathers, they are your brothers in religion and your clients (*mawālīkum*). There is no sin (*junāḥ*) for you in any mistakes you have made but there is in what your hearts have intended. God is forgiving and Compassionate.

6a The prophet is closer to the believers than they are themselves, and his wives are their mothers;

6b but blood relations are nearer to one another in God's decree than the believers and the emigrants, though you should act in a way recognized as proper towards your friends. That is written in the decree.

These three verses treat three independent and seemingly unrelated legal topics. Verse 4 refers to the Qur'ānic prohibition of the pre-Islamic divorce practice known as *ẓihār*,[92] vv. 4–5 treat the institution of adoption, and v. 6 refers to a change in the inheritance system that is somehow related to the fact that the wives of the Prophet are the Mothers of the Believers and that the Prophet is closer to the believers than they are to themselves. In fact, the thread that ties these three verses together is not law (divorce, adoption, and inheritance) but language, specifically the subtle and complex relationship between and among linguistic metaphors, legal fictions, and human biology. Let us now examine vv. 4–6, with special attention to the abolition of adoption. For convenience, we treat vv. 4–5 (adoption) as one unit and v. 6 (inheritance) as another.

Act 5, Scene 1: Muḥammad's Repudiation of Zayd (vv. 4–5)

The language of vv. 4–5 is formulated in general terms. Mujāhid b. Jabr knows that the phrase "nor has He made your adopted sons your [real] sons" in v. 4 "was revealed about Zayd b. Ḥāritha [sic], who had been adopted by the Prophet."[93] The commentator also knows that in v. 5 the phrase "There is no sin for you in any mistakes you have made" was revealed "prior to the prohibition of that [adoption]."[94] In an effort to avoid committing a sin, Mujāhid identifies Zayd as the son of Ḥāritha even with respect to that period of Zayd's life in which he was in fact the son of Muḥammad through adoption.

Like Mujāhid, Muqātil b. Sulaymān also connects the general language of vv. 4–5 to Muḥammad and Zayd. The commentator explains that the phrase "nor has He made your adopted sons your [real] sons" refers specifically to Muḥammad and Zayd. God did not make Zayd a true son of Muḥammad—even if Muḥammad did once say, "He is my son." Verse 5 instructs Muslims to "Call them after their fathers." This too refers to Zayd who henceforth is to be called by the name of his natural father, Ḥāritha. If some Muslims mistakenly continued to refer to Zayd as Zayd b. Muḥammad—as may have been the case—this linguistic utterance has no legal consequences, and no sin is committed—unless the utterance is made with intent ("but there is [a sin] in what your hearts have intended").[95]

Muqātil understood that the office of prophecy passes from father to son. Thus, the fact that Zayd was Muḥammad's son—even if by adoption—threatened to undermine the theological doctrine of the finality of prophecy. Logically, if Muḥammad is the Last Prophet, he cannot have a son; conversely, if Muḥammad has a son, he cannot be the Last Prophet. That Zayd was

Muḥammad's *adopted* son was of no consequence whatsoever because the act of adoption, even if it is a legal fiction, creates a filial relationship between the adoptive father and the adoptee; and this filial relationship was widely regarded as the equivalent of that between a natural father and his legitimate son. Muqātil may have been familiar with the report—even if he does not cite it—that at the time of Zayd's adoption, Muḥammad asked his fellow tribesmen to bear witness to the new filial relationship that was being established between the two men. In a narrative preserved in Ibn Saʿd (d. 230/845), Muḥammad is reported to have said: "Bear witness that Zayd is my son: I inherit from him and he inherits from me (*arithuhu wa-yarithunī*)."[96] The best way to maintain Muḥammad's status as the Last Prophet was to have him repudiate Zayd so that there no longer would be any filial ties between Muḥammad, on the one hand, and Zayd and Usāma, on the other. As Muqātil explains, this is precisely what Muḥammad did. He disinherited Zayd by uttering—or being made to utter—a formula that adoptive parents who wished to dissolve an adoptive relationship had been using for more than 2000 years: "I am not your father." To this he might have added, "You are not my son."[97] The Beloved of the Messenger of God was no longer the Prophet's son. Just as Abraham expelled Ishmael, Muḥammad repudiated Zayd. But whereas Abraham acted in order to insure that only Isaac would inherit from his father (Gen. 21:10ff.), Muḥammad's action had no connection to inheritance—at least on the surface—but rather appears to have been intended to facilitate the Prophet's marriage to Zaynab. Although Zayd had done nothing that would have justified his renunciation, the obedient son did not protest the demotion in his status. Without hesitating, he responded, "O Messenger of God, I am Zayd b. Ḥāritha, and my genealogy is well-known."[98] Indeed, the commentator adds, he was Zayd b. Ḥāritha b. Qurra b. Sharaḥīl al-Kalbī one of the Banū ʿAbd Wadd.[99] It was clear that there were no blood ties between the two men.

That the only purpose served by Muḥammad's repudiation of Zayd was a theological one can be demonstrated by the following hypothetical argument. Suppose that Muḥammad had not repudiated Zayd and that the Beloved of the Messenger of God had continued to be the Prophet's adopted son. The adoptive relationship between the two men would have posed no obstacle whatsoever to Muḥammad's marriage to Zaynab after she had been divorced by Zayd. Q. 33:37 establishes that it is permissible for a believer to marry the former wife of his adopted son. Q. 4:23 establishes the converse: it is forbidden to marry the former wife of your natural son. From a legal perspective, there was nothing objectionable about Muḥammad's marriage to Zaynab. From the perspective of Qurʾānic law, Muḥammad's repudiation of Zayd was unnecessary, irrelevant, and gratuitous.

Muḥammad was made to repudiate Zayd in order to satisfy the needs of an emerging theological doctrine. Conversely, it was the crystallization of this theological doctrine that made it necessary for the early Muslim community to create the narrative account of Muḥammad's repudiation of Zayd, which is a typological variant of Abraham's expulsion of Ishmael. Just as Abraham had to expel Ishmael in order to preserve the doctrine of divine election, Muḥammad had to repudiate Zayd in order to preserve the doctrine of the finality of prophecy. In both cases, the narrative is driven by a theological imperative; in both cases, the father's rejection of his son is presented as if it were history; in both cases, the narrative has nothing to do with events in the life of a biblical patriarch or an Arabian prophet.

Act 5, Scene 2: The Abolition of Adoption (vv. 4–5, cont.)

As noted, Muqātil goes out of his way to link the revelation of these two verses to Zayd, even though the language of vv. 4–5 is addressed to a general audience.

Verse 4 opens with a metaphor: "God has not put two hearts inside any man." This figure of speech would have triggered different reactions in different audiences. Those familiar with the institution of civil adoption may have associated this metaphor with the problem of dual loyalty among adopted children, as treated in the *Institutes* of Justinian and in the Sassanian *Book of a Thousand Judgments*. Those familiar with the New Testament may have associated the metaphor with the Christian doctrine of spiritual adoption which, according to Galatians 4:6, is mediated by the heart (see Chapter 2). Those familiar with postbiblical Jewish texts may have associated the metaphor with the rabbinic idea of the evil inclination (*yeṣer ha-raʿ*) that lies within the breast of every man.[100]

Certainly, the initial audience of v. 4 would have included Muslims familiar with the Byzantine practice of civil adoption and with the Christian doctrine of spiritual adoption. To this audience the Qur'ān proclaimed: God created only one heart in the breast of a man. A man cannot have two fathers, one natural, the other fictive or spiritual. He can have only one father. Verse 4 continues by addressing its audience in the plural: "nor has He made your (pl.) adopted sons (*adʿiyāʾakum*) your (pl.) [real] sons (*abnāʾakum*)." Similarly, v. 5 opens with a plural imperative: "Call them (*udʿūhum*; pl.) after their fathers." At the beginning of his commentary on v. 4, Muqātil explains that a man can have only one heart, from which it follows that an adopted son is not a true son. From vv. 4–5 he infers—without explicitly saying so—that the institution of adoption was abolished by the Qur'ān.

Muqātil's inference from the Qur'ān that the institution of adoption had been abolished was confirmed by the *sunna* of the Prophet, which embodies everything that Muḥammad is reported to have said, done, or condoned by his silence during those moments of his life when he was not receiving revelation.

The Prophet's adoption of Zayd constitutes one such *sunna*; his repudiation of Zayd constitutes another. These two *sunna*s, which are clearly in tension with one another, demand some form of harmonization. One might argue that the second *sunna* is specific to Muḥammad—whose repudiation of Zayd relates directly to a theological issue that does not apply to the Muslim community at large; in that case, it would be unnecessary to invoke the doctrine of abrogation or to abolish the institution of adoption. Alternatively, one might argue that the second *sunna* is general in scope and applies not only to the Prophet but also to all Muslims (just as in Q. 33:37 the special permission given to Muḥammad to marry the former wife of his adopted son was extended to all Muslims); in that case, Muḥammad's repudiation of Zayd established a new *sunna* that signaled the abolition of adoption. Lest there be any doubt about the matter, the solution chosen by the early Muslim community was put into the mouth of the Prophet himself, who was made to articulate the prohibition in clear Arabic, "There is no adoption in Islam: the custom of the *jāhiliyya* has been superseded" (*lā diʿwat*^{a} *fī al-islām dhahaba amr*^{u} *al-jāhiliyya*).[101] Henceforth, Muslim jurists treated adoption as a practice that had been prohibited.[102]

Islam's abolition of adoption was simultaneously a departure from earlier practices and the culmination of a long-term trend. With respect to the ancient Near East, the abolition of adoption was a radical break with the legal traditions of pagans and polytheists. With respect to Judaism, which never recognized civil adoption (even if individual Jews engaged in the practice), the new policy reinforced a position that is not formally articulated in biblical or rabbinic law. Similarly, with respect to the Byzantines and Sassanians, who practiced adoption but struggled with the phenomenon of dual loyalty, the new Islamic policy served to correct a flawed institution: "God has not put two hearts inside any man" (Q. 33:4). Finally, the new policy also may be seen as a conscious but indirect response to the Christian doctrine which teaches that the Holy Spirit is the true father (*Abba*) of Jesus and the spiritual father of every human being who undergoes baptism; that spiritual adoption is mediated through the heart; and that baptism is a prerequisite for salvation. By contrast, Islamic theology teaches that Muḥammad is not the father (*ab*) of any man; that the practice of civil adoption is unnatural and primitive; that God put only one heart in the breast of a man; and that a believer must earn salvation through a combination of faith in God and observance of the five pillars of Islam.

Islamic tradition compresses the historical process that culminated in the abolition of adoption into a single episode in the life of the Prophet. It stands to reason, however, that this process extended over a long period of time. A full explanation of this phenomenon would require an investigation of a host of not only theological but also political, social, and economic factors. "All societies," Patricia Crone has written, "must have a policy regarding the admission of outsiders to their ranks."[103] At the same time that v. 5 ("Call them after their fathers") closed one door relevant to the incorporation of outsiders, it opened another: "If you do not know their fathers, they are your brothers in religion and your clients (*mawālīkum*)." Contracts of brotherhood were used extensively during the Medinan period. Following the Arab conquests, however, this device was largely replaced by the institution of clientage (*walāʾ*).[104]

Act 5, Scene 3: Prohibition of Marriage with the Prophet's Widows (v. 6)

By virtue of his repudiation of Zayd (and the subsequent death in infancy of Ibrāhīm), Muḥammad was sonless, as required by the doctrine of *khatm al-nubūʾa*. Does it follow, however, from Muḥammad's sonlessness that he cannot have some kind of a paternal relationship with the Muslim community? Precisely this question was raised by the first Muslims. It is no coincidence, in my view, that vv. 4–5 of *Sūrat al-Aḥzāb*, which are said to have been revealed about Zayd, are followed by a verse which suggests—without explicitly saying so—that Muḥammad does have a paternal role to play with respect to the larger Muslim community.

Verse 6a addresses the relationship between the Prophet and the believers, on the one hand, and between his wives and the believers, on the other: "The prophet is closer to the believers than they are themselves, and his wives are their mothers . . ." (*al-nabī awlā bi'l-muʾminīn min anfusihim wa-azwājuhu ummahātuhum* . . .). The first clause suggests that there is a special relationship between the Prophet and the believers, the second that there is a special relationship between Muḥammad's wives and the believers. Let us begin with the second clause. Does it follow from the Qurʾānic proclamation that the Prophet's wives are "their mothers" that they are the true, natural mothers of the believers? Of course not, just as the wife of a man who divorces her by uttering the *ẓihār* formula ("You are to me like the back of my mother") does not become his true mother (v. 4); and just as a person taken into sonship or daughtership does not become the adoptor's true son or daughter (vv. 4–5) or, by extension, his or her heir. The subject of inheritance was of critical importance to the early Muslim community (see Appendix 3). The hijra or migration to Medina necessitated the suspension of the normal rules of inheritance because many if not most of the blood relatives of the *muhājir*s or emigrants were polytheists living in Mecca. In order to prevent the transfer of wealth and resources from Muslims to polytheists, it was necessary to suspend the normal rules of inheritance, heretofore based upon blood ties, and to institute a new system based upon common faith, the fact of migration, and compacts of brotherhood established in Medina by the Prophet. Verse 6b signals the end of this temporary state of affairs. Henceforth, inheritance is to be regulated by new rules found in "the decree" (*al-kitāb*), perhaps a reference to the inheritance verses in *Sūrat al-Nisāʾ*.[105] According to these new rules, the right to inherit is based on blood ties, affinity, and proximity to the deceased, not on a linguistic metaphor or legal fiction.

Exceptionally, the Qurʾānic pronouncement in v. 6a that the Prophet's wives are the Mothers of the Believers does have an important legal consequence. This clause indicates that the relationship between the Prophet's wives and the rest of the Muslim community is analogous to that between a mother and her children. According to Q. 4:23, it is forbidden for a Muslim to marry his biological mother. It follows from Q. 33:6a ("his wives are their mothers") that no Muslim might marry any one of the Prophet's wives subsequent to his death in 11/632.[106] Unlike the *ẓihār* and adoption formulas, which no longer have any legal consequences, in this case words do matter.[107] In the event that the implication of v. 6a was unclear, the legal rule is spelled out in Q. 33:53: "It is not for you to vex God's messenger, nor to marry his wives after him, ever. This is important with God." On the surface level, this verse highlights the sacrosanct status of Muḥammad's wives, a status that continued after the Prophet's death. As each widow died, she presumably was reunited with Muḥammad in heaven. If one of these widows had remarried during the interval between the Prophet's death and hers, the Prophet would have had good reason to be annoyed. From a theological perspective, the prohibition of marriage with the Prophet's widows makes good sense.

In this instance, one wonders if the theological motive was the primary one. Is it possible that the prohibition may have served another function, a function to which the commentators would not want to draw the attention of their audience? Muḥammad, as we know, died without leaving any male offspring—he was *abtar, a man without a tail*; and his closest surviving blood relatives were his daughter, cousin, and uncle. The fact that the Prophet did not leave any adult male issue had important implications for the survival of his *bayt* or House. How would the nascent Muslim community survive if its founder left no son and heir to carry on his name? As we have seen, sonlessness was regarded as a calamity by many inhabitants of the Near East from antiquity down to the rise of Islam. In ancient and late antique times, in Mesopotamia, Greece, Israel, Rome, and Iran, it was widely understood that the House of a man who leaves no son becomes extinct. Among pagans and polytheists, the primary response to the misfortune of sonlessness was adoption. The monotheists had another solution. According to biblical law, if a member of the community dies without leaving any male offspring, his brother is obligated to marry his widowed sister-in-law in an effort to carry on the dead man's name—even though, under normal circumstances, marriage between a man and his sister-in-law is prohibited. But Muḥammad did not have a brother. In this instance, an appropriate solution was available in the Persian institution of *cagar* marriage, according to which the widow of a man who dies without leaving a son is required to marry—not her brother-in-law, as in biblical law—but any male relative. If she produces a son with her second husband, that son is given the name of the first husband and treated as his heir. The Persian institution of *cagar* marriage—or its Arabian equivalent—would have been a viable option for the early Muslim community. Even if Muḥammad had no brothers, he was survived by his uncle and his cousin. Had the early Muslim community wanted to perpetuate the Prophet's name and prevent his House from becoming extinct, the obvious solution would have been for al-ʿAbbās or ʿAlī b. Abī Ṭālib to marry one or more of his nine surviving wives.[108] Any son produced by such a union would have taken the Prophet's name and would have qualified as his heir. In retrospect, perpetuating the Prophet's House—in the classical sense of an agnatic lineal descent group—is precisely what the early Muslim community wanted to prevent, no matter what the cost. As it happened, both the proto-Sunnīs and the proto-Shīʿīs were heavily invested—albeit for different reasons—in insuring that the Prophet's House—narrowly defined—did in fact become extinct. This is because, had one of the Prophet's sons—natural or adopted—outlived him and reached the age of maturity, that son's claim to spiritual leadership of the Muslim community would have been greater than any claim put forward by Abū Bakr, ʿUmar, or ʿUthmān, on the one hand, or by ʿAlī b. Abī Ṭālib, on the other (by extension, Usāma's credentials for spiritual leadership would have been greater than those of Ḥasan and Ḥusayn). None of the first three caliphs were related by blood to the Prophet; and ʿAlī was merely a cousin and son-in-law.[109] Thus, the Qurʾānic proclamation that "Muḥammad is not the father of any of your men" supported the interests of both the proto-Sunnīs and the proto-Shīʿīs. If there was any common ground shared by these two mutually antagonistic groups, it was that none of the Prophet's sons could be said to have attained puberty or to have outlived his father, and that there was no need to perpetuate Muḥammad's name and his House by means of a legal fiction such as adoption or *cagar* marriage. I suspect that this is why Q. 33:53 prohibits marriage with the wives of the Prophet. This prohibition is best seen as a corollary of Muḥammad's repudiation of Zayd and Islam's abolition of adoption. If I am correct, then the original function of v. 6a was to foreclose the option of *cagar* marriage or its Arabian equivalent.[110]

The elevation of the Prophet's wives to the status of Mothers of the Believers may have had unforeseen consequences. If the Prophet's wives are the Mothers of the Believers, might it not also be said that Muḥammad is the Father of the Believers? Is this perhaps what is meant by the first clause in v. 6a: "The prophet is closer to the believers than they are themselves"? In fact, Islamic tradition preserves a trace of just such a possibility. The codices of four different Companions—Ubayy b. Kaʿb (d. between 19/640 and 35/656), Ibn Masʿūd (d. 32/652–53), al-Rabīʿ b. Khuthaym (d. 64/683–84), and Ibn ʿAbbās (d. 67/686–87)—are reported to have contained the following variant of what would become the standard consonantal skeleton of v. 6a: *al-nabī awlā bi'l-muʾminīn min anfusihim* ***wa-huwa ab^{un} lahum*** *wa-azwājuhu* *ummahātuhum*.[111] Unlike the standard version of v. 6a, in which the symmetry between the Prophet and his wives is implicit, here the symmetry is explicit: Muḥammad is the Father of the Believers and his wives are the Mothers of the Believers. According to Qatāda (d. 117/735), the reading that includes the phrase *wa-huwa ab*^{un} *lahum* was "one of the readings." To this assertion, al-Ḥasan al-Baṣrī (d. 110/728) added the important specification that the reading that includes the phrase "he is their father" is not just one of the readings but rather "the first reading (*al-qirāʾa al-ūlā*)."[112] I am inclined to think that the view attributed to al-Ḥasan is correct. If so, then there is good reason to believe that the standard reading of v. 6a is not the original reading. This brings me to a second hypothesis.

Hypothesis 4.2. In its original form the consonantal skeleton of Q. *33:6a identified Muḥammad as *their father* (*wa-huwa ab*^{un} *lahum*). This phrase was removed from what became the standard version of this verse.

At present, I can do no more than speculate about how the original formulation of this sub-verse may have been revised. A scribe may have deleted the phrase *wa-huwa ab*^{un} *lahum* and rewritten the verse, now without the offending clause. Or he may have removed the folio page containing the offensive phrase from the codex and rewritten this section of the *Sūra*. It is more likely, however, that the problem was solved by destroying all of the codices that contained the offending phrase and replacing them with codices that did not. Be that as it may, the original consonantal skeleton may have been revised, but it was not forgotten: On the one hand, it continued to circulate in the codices of the four above-mentioned Companions; on the other, it was remembered as either a variant or gloss by Mujāhid (d. 102/720),[113] ʿAbd al-Razzāq (d. 211/826),[114] and some later commentators. The revision was controversial, and members of the community drew attention to it by circulating reports in which ʿUmar b. al-Khaṭṭāb is made to express his concern about a discrepancy between the original version and the revision. Writing in the last quarter of the second century A.H., Sufyān b. ʿUyayna (d. 198/813) relates the following story: One day, ʿUmar b. al-Khaṭṭāb encountered an unnamed Muslim youth (*ghulām*) who was holding a codex (*muṣḥaf*) in which Q. 33:6a began as follows: *al-nabī awlā biʾl-muʾminīn min anfusihim* ***wa-huwa ab***^{un} ***lahum***. . . . When the caliph heard the youth recite this verse, he instructed him to delete the words *wa-huwa ab*^{un} *lahum*, using the verb *ḥakkaka* which signifies *to scratch or scrape off*. The unidentified youth disobeyed the caliphal order to remove three words from this Qurʾān codex.[115] When the youth told ʿUmar that his codex was that of Ubayy b. Kaʿb, the caliph approached Ubayy and asked him to clarify the reading. Ubayy responded as follows: "Verily, I have been engaged in the study of the Qurʾān while you have been engaged in buying and selling in the market."[116] In other words, the caliph's preoccupation with worldly affairs disqualified him as an arbiter of what does or does not belong in the Qurʾān. In a variant of this report related by ʿAbd al-Razzāq in his *Tafsīr*, the caliph again instructs the youth to scratch out the words *wa-huwa ab^{un} lahum*, the youth again refuses, and the caliph again summons Ubayy. The only substantive difference between the two versions of the narrative is ʿAbd al-Razzāq's specification that when the two men came face to face, Ubayy "*raised his voice and shouted*, 'Verily, I have been occupied with the Qurʾān, while you have been occupied with buying and selling in the market'" (emphasis added). In other words, Ubayy rebuked the caliph for drawing attention to a problem with the consonantal skeleton of the Qurʾān. To this rebuke ʿUmar responded with stony silence.[117]

Islamic sources preserve the memory of an alternative reading of Q. 33:6 and at least one early authority is said to have maintained that this reading was "the first reading." Only rarely, however, do these sources openly confront the issue of what would have made the phrase *wa-huwa ab^{un} lahum* so controversial that it would have been necessary to remove these three words from the Qurʾān. I am aware of only one commentator who has addressed this issue. In his treatment of v. 6a, Fakhr al-Dīn al-Rāzī (d. 606/1209) poses the following hypothetical: Suppose someone were to ask: Why does the text of the Qurʾān not specify that "the Prophet is your father"—when that is the clear sense of the verse? To this hypothetical question al-Rāzī responds that the inclusion of the phrase *wa-huwa ab^{un} lahum* in v. 6a would have created a serious problem for Muḥammad: Just as the Qurʾānic pronouncement that Muḥammad's wives are the Mothers of the Believers created a bar to marriage between the Prophet's widows and the rest of the Muslim community, so too any Qurʾānic pronouncement stating that Muḥammad is the Father of the Believers would have created a bar to marriage between the Prophet and all female Muslims. In that case, Muḥammad would have been unable to marry any female Muslim.[118] This is surely one reason why the Muslims who collected and redacted the Qurʾān would have wanted to remove the phrase *wa-huwa ab^{un} lahum* from v. 6a.

But this is not the only explanation for the postulated removal of this phrase from the consonantal skeleton of v. 6a. If the variant of v. 6a containing the phrase "and he is their father" was in fact the original reading, as al-Ḥasan al-Baṣrī is reported to have said, then the early Muslim community could not have failed to notice a glaring contradiction between vv. 6a and 40 of *Sūrat al-Aḥzāb*. Surely they would have been compelled to ask: How is it possible that in the former verse God would say that Muḥammad is "their father," while in the latter He would say that "Muḥammad is not the father of any of your men"? As we have seen, v. 6a follows v. 40 in terms of narrative continuity and chronology. Thus, one solution to the contradiction between the two verses would have been to argue that v. 6a abrogated v. 40. In addition to the assertion that "Muḥammad is not the father of any of your men," however, v. 40 also contains the critical theological pronouncement that he is "the messenger of God and the seal of Prophets." On this theological doctrine there could be no compromise. By contrast, the assertion in v. 6a that "he is their father" could be jettisoned without sacrificing the general import of the verse. The Qurʾānic assertion that "the prophet is closer to the believers than they are themselves" does justice to the special relationship between Muḥammad and the Muslim community even without the qualifying phrase "he is their father"—which, as we have seen, would have been problematic for other reasons. I suspect that it was a calculation of this nature that motivated the Muslims who redacted the Qurʾān to modify the consonantal skeleton of v. 6a by removing the words "and he is their father" from the verse.[119]

Conclusion

In the Islamic worldview, prophecy is the exclusive possession of a single family, the House of Abraham. To qualify as a prophet, one must be a member of this family. Conversely, no person outside of this family can qualify as a prophet.[120] Muḥammad, according to the Qurʾān, is not only a prophet but also the Last Prophet. This claim has two genealogical consequences: in order to qualify as a prophet, Muḥammad must be a descendant of Abraham; and in order to bring the office of prophecy to an end, Muḥammad must be sonless.

The connection between Muḥammad's status as the Last Prophet and his sonlessness is articulated in the unique Qurʾānic witness to the theological doctrine: "Muḥammad is not the father of any of your men, but the messenger of God and the seal of Prophets. God is aware of everything." Verse 40 of *Sūrat al-Aḥzāb* is said to have been revealed about Zayd, the Prophet's adopted son, who is mentioned by name ("Zayd") in v. 37. The connection between Zayd and the theological doctrine is clear. The existence of a man whose legal name was Zayd b. Muḥammad was incompatible with Muḥammad's status as the Last Prophet. If Muḥammad is the Last Prophet, he cannot be said to have had a son who reached puberty and outlived him. To preserve the integrity of the theological doctrine, it was necessary inter alia to demonstrate that Zayd was not Muḥammad's son at the time of the Prophet's death.

Muḥammad may have had an adopted son named Zayd and a natural son named Ibrāhīm, but the statements made about these two sons in the narratives examined in this chapter are best seen as salvation history. The fact that these two individuals are represented as historical figures should not mislead us into thinking that the content of these forms corresponds to any historical reality.[121] Ibrāhīm and Zayd are best seen as figures that serve as paradigms of sonship: Ibrāhīm serves as a paradigm of the biological son; Zayd, of the adopted son. The original function of the narratives about these two individuals was to confirm the truth of the theological doctrine that Muḥammad is the Last Prophet. To this end, the early Muslim community formulated a sacred legend in which Muḥammad falls in love with Zayd's unnamed wife. Because this woman was the Prophet's daughter-in-law, he could not marry her without violating a sacred law. Fearing public reaction, Muḥammad kept his love for the woman a secret. The outcome of this episode was determined by the idea that sacred history unfolds according to divine providence. In the present instance, God intervened in history to insure that this prophet would not commit a sin (as David is said to have done in II Samuel 11). The divinity legitimized the union by introducing a distinction between an adopted son and a natural son. The biblical prohibition of marriage to a daughter-in-law was revised insofar as it applies to the former wife of an adopted son. Whereas the ostensible purpose of the Islamic sacred legend was to provide divine sanction for the Prophet's marriage to his daughter-in-law Zaynab, its true purpose was to create a narrative space into which was inserted Muḥammad's repudiation of Zayd. "I am not your father," the Prophet is reported to have said to the Beloved of the Messenger of God. By virtue of this statement, Zayd ceased to be the Prophet's son, heir, and/or potential successor.

The new sacred legend had to be situated in time and space. *Sūrat al-Aḥzāb*, the 33rd chapter of the Qur'ān, takes its name ("The Confederates") from a military encounter that took place outside of Medina in the year 5 A.H. This was the year in which a confederation of Meccan tribesmen attacked Medina but was repelled after the Muslims dug a defensive trench around the city—hence, the Battle of the Trench. The inclusion in *Sūrat al-Aḥzāb* of the five-verse pericope that begins with v. 36 and ends with v. 40 makes it possible to assign a date to Zayd's divorce of Zaynab, to Muḥammad's repudiation of Zayd, and to Muḥammad's marriage to Zaynab. All three events in the life of the Prophet took place in Medina in the year 5 A.H. Thus did a sacred legend become history.

It is curious that the celebration of Muḥammad's marriage to the unnamed woman in v. 37 should have been accompanied by the Qur'ānic pronouncement that "Muḥammad is not the father of any of your men." Presumably, one purpose of this marriage—like that of any marriage—was to produce a son and heir. The unnamed woman identified by the exegetes as Zaynab bt. Jaḥsh was Muḥammad's paternal cross-cousin. Had Zaynab become pregnant and given birth to a son, that son would have been a direct descendant of Abraham through both his father and his mother. During the approximately seven years that Zaynab was married to Muḥammad, she did not become pregnant or give birth to a son. Zaynab's failure to conceive a child was a function of theology. The Qur'ānic pronouncement that "Muḥammad is not the father of any of your men" effectively proscribed the birth of a son who would attain puberty. This theological imperative applied not only to Zaynab but also to the Prophet's other sexual partners. Two years before he died, it will be recalled, Muḥammad acquired an Egyptian concubine named Māriya the Copt with whom he is said to have engaged in sexual relations on numerous occasions. Approximately one year after the Prophet had acquired Māriya, she gave birth to a son named Ibrāhīm who died in infancy. One wonders why God caused Māriya to become pregnant with Ibrāhīm if his death in infancy was a theological imperative. Was He punishing Muḥammad for putting his fear of men above his fear of God back in the year 5/627—just as God punished David by causing Bathsheba's first son to die in infancy? Or was God merely flexing His divine muscles when, in the year 5/627, He pronounced that "Muḥammad is not the father of any of your men"?

One also wonders about the chronology assigned to vv. 36–40 of *Sūrat al-Aḥzāb*. If this pericope was in fact revealed to Muḥammad in 5 A.H., at least six years would pass before the Prophet's death in 11 A.H. During this period of time, Muḥammad reportedly visited his wives and concubines on a regular rotation. With the exception of Māriya the Copt, none of these women is said to have conceived a child.[122] In theory, the possibility that Muḥammad might father a son and heir remained open for nine months following his final sexual encounter—whenever that may have occurred. In the year 5/627, only an omniscient and omnipotent God could predict that Muḥammad would die sonless. As for the first Muslims, it was only with the advantage of hindsight that they could assert with confidence that their Prophet did in fact die sonless—or that his biography could be constructed in such a manner as to make it appear as if he had died sonless.

In Q. 33:40 the authorial voice that controls the text speaks directly to the Muslim community about a man named Muḥammad. The text objectifies the Prophet.[123] The verse begins, "Muḥammad is not the father of any of *your* men . . ." (emphasis added). Had this verse been revealed to Muḥammad, it might have begun as follows: "O Muḥammad, you are not the father of any of their men. . . ." Again, only with the advantage of hindsight would it have been possible to make this assertion with confidence.

According to Hypothesis 4.1, the prohibition of marriage to "*your daughters-in-law" in Q. 4:23 was inconsistent with Muḥammad's marriage to his daughter-in-law in Q. 33:37. According to Hypothesis 4.2, the assertion that "*he [Muḥammad] is their father" in Q. 33:6 was inconsistent with the pronouncement that Muḥammad was sonless in Q. 33:40. In both instances, the consonantal skeleton of the Qurʾān appears to have been revised to accommodate an important theological doctrine. Of course, a God who is all-knowing and all-powerful can also be inconsistent. Alternatively, it is possible to harmonize apparent inconsistencies. In this instance, however, I am inclined to another explanation. The force of the Qurʾānic pronouncement that Muḥammad brought the office of prophecy to an end surely would have been much greater in the post-conquest Near East than in pre-conquest

Arabia. The phenomena discussed in this chapter lead me to the following hypothesis:

Hypothesis 4.3. The five-verse pericope that begins with v. 36 and ends with v. 40 of *Sūrat al-Aḥzāb* was added to the Qur'ān during the generation following the Prophet's death in 11/632.

Sūrat al-Aḥzāb is said to have undergone massive editorial changes in the interval between its revelation and the production of the ʿUthmānic codex. Originally, the chapter had two hundred verses. One hundred and twenty-seven of these verses were removed, leaving seventy-three. If one hundred and twenty-seven verses could be removed, five verses surely could have been added. The addition of these five verses to the text of the Qur'ān would account for the contradictions between Q. 33:37 and 4:23, on the one hand, and between Q. 33:40 and 33:6, on the other.

Chapter 5

The Battle of Muʾta

La nation, comme l'individu, est l'aboutissant d'un long passé d'efforts, de sacrifices et de dévouements. . . . On aime en proportion des sacrifices qu'on a consentis, des maux qu'on a soufferts. . . . Oui, la souffrance en commun unit plus que la joie.

—*Ernest Renan,* Qu'est-ce que'une nation? *54*

Introduction: From *Tafsīr* to *Taʾrīkh*

In his commentary on the Qurʾān, Muqātil b. Sulaymān does not mention the date on which Zayd died or the circumstances of his demise. Later commentators likewise are silent about these matters.

The silence should come as no surprise. In their treatment of Q. 33:36–40, the commentators are interested in Zayd only insofar as he is relevant to the story of Muḥammad's marriage to Zaynab following her divorce from Zayd in the year 5 A.H., as related in v. 37. From the perspective of *tafsīr*, v. 37 has nothing to do with Zayd's death and, conversely, Zayd's death has nothing to do with v. 37. The same is not true of v. 40, which asserts that Muḥammad is not the father of any Muslim man and famously announces that he is the Messenger of God and Seal of Prophets. Although the meaning of the expression *khātam al-nabiyyīn* was initially contested, by the end of the first century A.H.—if not earlier—Muslims had come to understand this expression as signifying that Muḥammad was the Last Prophet. As the Last Prophet, Muḥammad could not have a son who reached puberty; otherwise, as Muqātil states, that son would have been a prophet. The logic of this argument applies not only to Muḥammad's natural sons, none of whom reached puberty, but also to his adopted son Zayd, who did. By virtue of his status as Muḥammad's adult son, Zayd b. Muḥammad was a member of the Abrahamic family to which the mantle of prophecy had been entrusted as an exclusive possession. Similarly, Muḥammad's grandson, Usāma b. Zayd b. Muḥammad, was also a member of this family. In theory, the mantle of prophecy might have passed from Muḥammad to Zayd, and from Zayd to Usāma. In Chapter 4, I argued that the early Muslim community had no choice but to construct its foundation narrative in such a way as to marginalize both Zayd and Usāma. However, Muḥammad's repudiation of Zayd did not fully eliminate the threat to the theological doctrine of the finality of prophecy. This is because at the time of Zayd's repudiation in 5 A.H., he was already a grown man. The fact that the Prophet had an adult son named Zayd b. Muḥammad conflicted with the assertion in v. 40 that "Muḥammad is not the father of any of your men." For the sake of theological consistency, it was important to demonstrate that the *man* who had been Muḥammad's *son* failed to outlive the Prophet. Like Muḥammad's repudiation of Zayd, the death of the Beloved of the Messenger of God some time prior to the year 11/632 was a theological imperative.

It is understandable that the early Muslim community would want to find a suitable historical context in which to situate Zayd's death—to be analyzed in this chapter—and that it would want to confer theological meaning on his death—to be analyzed in the next chapter. It is also understandable that the early Muslim community would choose to insert Zayd's death into a discursive space other than that carved out by Qur'ānic exegesis. It was not the commentators but the first Muslim historians who were responsible for the narrative account of Zayd's demise. Historical narratives formulated in the first and second centuries A.H. subsequently found their way into the biography of the Prophet (*sīra*), accounts of the Arab conquests (*maghāzī*), biographical dictionaries (*ṭabaqāt*), and general works of history (*taʾrīkh*).[1]

As befitting a man who served as the commander (*amīr*) of as many as nine military expeditions, Zayd is said to have died while leading a Muslim military expedition into the province of Balqāʾ in southern Jordan. He was killed in the village of Muʾta (alternative vocalization: Mūta), a toponym that appears to be derived from the same root (*m-w-t*) as the noun *mawt*, which means *death*; the lexicographers define *mūta* as *madness*, *insanity*, and *diabolical obsession*.[2] It is surely no coincidence that the Battle of Muʾta is presented in the Islamic sources as a suicide mission. As I shall argue, one of the primary functions of narrative accounts of the battle is to confer theological significance on the deaths of Zayd and two of his comrades. In modern times, biographers of Muḥammad and historians have long recognized that the Islamic narratives relating to the battle contain numerous theological, supernatural, and mythical elements. These scholars nevertheless attempt to extract the ahistorical elements from the seemingly historical facts and thereby to reconstruct what really happened at Muʾta.[3] In my view, it is difficult if not impossible to say what really happened at Muʾta. The historian is on firmer ground if he or she attempts to understand the significance attributed to the battle by the early Muslim community. In that case, it is precisely the theological, supernatural, and mythical elements of the Islamic narratives that merit attention.

The Battle of Muʾta

The Muslim Version

During the first three centuries A.H., the Muslim community devoted considerable attention to the Battle of Muʾta. The earliest extant account of the battle is that of al-Wāqidī (Medina and Iraq, d. 207/823) in his *Kitāb al-maghāzī*.[4] Other early accounts of the battle are found in the *Sīra* of Ibn Hishām (Iraq, d. 218/833),[5] *Kitāb al-ṭabaqāt* of Ibn Saʿd (Iraq, d. 230/845),[6] *Taʾrīkh* of al-Yaʿqūbī (d. > 292/905),[7] and *Taʾrīkh* of al-Ṭabarī (Iraq, d. 310/923).[8] The narratives preserved in these early accounts are collected and re-presented in *Taʾrīkh madīnat Dimashq* of Ibn ʿAsākir (d. 571/1176),[9] *al-Bidāya waʾl-nihāya* of Ibn Kathīr (d. 774/1373),[10] and *al-Sīra al-ḥalabiyya* of ʿAlī b. Burhān al-Dīn (d. 1044/1635).[11] These historians had access to a large number of reports about the battle, some purportedly from eyewitnesses, others from relatives and descendants of the combatants. Each historian made his own decision about how to present and arrange these sources, adding, deleting, changing, and reordering material as he saw fit. No two accounts of the battle are identical, but all share the same narrative framework and all tell more or less the same story. I have chosen to base the following summary on the account of al-Wāqidī for two reasons: First, it is the earliest extant account and, second, it contains important material relating to Zayd that is not found in most other sources. This exceptional material will be presented and discussed in Chapter 6.

Wāqidī produced his account of the Battle of Muʾta by assembling a substantial number of individual reports—twenty-nine, by my count—and arranging them in such a manner as to produce a coherent narrative, even if there is a certain amount of overlap and repetition. Each report is introduced with an *isnād*. The sources of individual reports include Abū Hurayra (d. 58/678), ʿĀʾisha (d. 58/678), Zayd b. Arqam (d. 68/787–88), ʿAwf b. Mālik al-Ashjaʿī (d. 73/692), Ibn ʿUmar (d. 74/693), Jābir b. ʿAbdallāh (d. 78/697), and Abū Bakr b. ʿAbd al-Raḥmān al-Ḥārith b. Hishām (d. 94/713). If these *isnād*s are reliable, then reports about the Battle of Muʾta may have been put into circulation as early as the first quarter of the first century A.H.; if they are not, then they may not have been put into circulation until the first quarter of the second century.

Unlike later Muslim historians, Wāqidī does not specify the month or year in which the Battle of Muʾta took place. In his *Kitāb al-maghāzī*, the narrative account of the battle immediately follows three raids that took place in Ṣafar and Rabīʿ I of the year 8, on the one hand, and it precedes the entry on the conquest of Mecca in Shaʿbān of the same year, on the other.[12] The physical placement of Wāqidī's entry on Muʾta creates a distributional chronology which suggests that the battle took place sometime between Rabīʿ I and

Shaʿbān of the year 8.[13] We will return to the date of the battle later in this chapter. What follows is a summary of Wāqidī's account.

Muḥammad instructed a Muslim named al-Ḥārith b. ʿUmayr al-Azdī to take a letter to the governor of Provincia Arabia, who resided in Buṣrā/Bostra in southern Syria.[14] Presumably, the letter contained an invitation to accept Islam. The messenger set out for Syria, but when he reached Muʾta, he was captured, incarcerated, and beheaded by Shuraḥbīl b. ʿAmr al-Ghassānī. This was the first time that a messenger of the Messenger of God had been killed by a subject of a foreign power. The decapitation of the Muslim messenger served as a casus belli. It was for the express purpose of avenging this murder that Muḥammad assembled the Army of Muʾta, which is said to have numbered 3,000 soldiers. The staging ground for the military expedition was al-Jurf, approximately three miles north of Medina. After performing the noon prayer, the Prophet issued instructions regarding the order of command.[15] He appointed Zayd b. Ḥāritha as the *amīr* or commander of the expedition; if Zayd were to be killed, then Jaʿfar b. Abī Ṭālib was to assume command of the troops; if Jaʿfar were to be killed, then ʿAbdallāh b. Rawāḥa was to assume command; and if Ibn Rawāḥa were to fall, then the surviving Muslim soldiers were to choose one of their comrades and appoint him as their commander.[16]

Each of the three commanders had outstanding leadership credentials—even if Wāqidī does not say so. Zayd was—or had been until the year 5 A.H.—the Prophet's adopted son and the first male convert to Islam. Even after his repudiation, the Beloved of the Messenger of God retained Muḥammad's confidence. Paradoxically, the Prophet's confidence in Zayd appears to have increased in the aftermath of the repudiation. In the year 6 alone, he appointed Zayd as commander of six different military expeditions.[17] As for Jaʿfar b. Abī Ṭālib, he was the Prophet's paternal cousin and the older brother of ʿAlī b. Abī Ṭālib. Like Zayd he was an early convert to Islam and, like Zayd, he was already an adult at the time of his conversion. Jaʿfar married Asmāʾ bt. ʿUmays, with whom he had three sons: ʿAwn, Muḥammad, and ʿAbdallāh.[18] In 615 C.E., the Prophet sent Jaʿfar to Abyssinia, where he served as the leader of the Muslim community-in-exile for approximately thirteen years. Jaʿfar returned to Medina in 7/628, shortly after the capture of Khaybar, at which time the Prophet is said to have embraced him, kissed him between the eyes, and exclaimed: "I do not know what gives me greater pleasure, my conquest or the return of my brother Jaʿfar." On another occasion, Muḥammad is reported to have told Jaʿfar, "You look like me and you act like I do."[19] Indeed, Jaʿfar arguably was the most distinguished Companion in the young Muslim community—apart from Zayd.[20] How unfortunate that both men should have fallen in battle at Muʾta in 8 A.H. As for ʿAbdallāh b. Rawāḥa al-Khazrajī, he was one of the twelve *naqīb*s, or representatives of the Medinese clans, at the second ʿAqaba meeting. In the years immediately following the hijra to

Medina, ʿAbdallāh distinguished himself as an energetic champion of the new religion. Like Zayd he was a soldier and like Zayd he was entrusted with important missions by Muḥammad. When the Muslims defeated the polytheists at Badr in 2/623, it was ʿAbdallāh b. Rawāḥa and Zayd who were dispatched to Medina with news of the victory. Two years later, in 4 A.H., Muḥammad appointed Ibn Rawāḥa as his *khalīfa* or deputy ruler of Medina during his absence from the city. The Medinese Companion's leadership skills no doubt were connected to his facility with the Arabic language: He was one of the Prophet's secretaries, a respected storyteller (*qāṣṣ*), and a poet whose artistry is said to have matched that of Ḥassān b. Thābit and Kaʿb b. Mālik. Fifty of his verses have survived, many of them in the *Sīra* of Ibn Hishām.[21] Thus, each of the three commanders was a recognized leader of the young Muslim community. The course of events during the first century A.H. arguably would have been much different had one or more of them outlived the Prophet. Alas, fate—or divine providence—intervened to cut short the lives of all three.

Let us return to the staging ground at al-Jurf. After specifying the order of command, the Prophet gave the Army of Muʾta clear instructions regarding the purpose of the military mission and the rules of engagement: "Wage war in the name of God [and] on the path of God, kill those who deny God; do not act treacherously or unfaithfully, and do not slay a child." The Prophet also instructed the Muslim soldiers to invite combatant polytheists to accept Islam and to treat enemy soldiers in accordance with their response to this invitation. There were three options:

1. If they accepted the invitation, then the Muslim forces should cease hostilities and do them no harm. Those who accepted Islam should be invited to transfer to the Land of the Emigrants, where they would have the same rights and obligations as the Emigrants themselves; those who chose to remain in their native abodes would acquire the same status as Bedouin Muslims; that is to say, they would be subject to God's judgment but would not be entitled to a share of the booty or spoils.
2. If they rejected the invitation to become Muslims, they were to be given the option of paying the poll tax (*jizya*). If they agreed, then the Muslim forces were to cease hostilities and do them no harm; if they refused, then the Muslim forces were to continue the fight.
3. As for the inhabitants of a fortress or town besieged by Muslim forces, if they sued for peace, they were to be given "the protection of your father and the protection of your companions" but not "the protection of God and the protection of His Prophet."[22]

After issuing the battle orders, the Prophet placed a white standard in the hands of Zayd b. Ḥāritha, whereupon the army broke camp. The Prophet and his Companions accompanied the military unit to a spot appropriately known as Thaniyyat al-Wadāʿ, or the Farewell Pass,[23] where the noncombatants took leave of the soldiers,[24] imploring God to defend the men and bring them back safe and sound. Upon hearing these pleas, ʿAbdallāh b. Rawāḥa is said to have recited a verse of poetry in which he asked God to forgive him for certain unspecified sins and to make sure that he received "a sword blow that makes a deep wound that shoots out frothing blood"—a harbinger of things to come.[25]

The Muslim army now began the march toward the village in southern Jordan where al-Ḥārith b. ʿUmayr al-Azdī had been slain. They were marching toward Muʾta, that is to say, toward *madness* or *death*—or both. Before reaching their destination, Bedouin Arabs learned of the approach of the Muslim forces. They gathered an army of their own, commanded coincidentally by another man named Shuraḥbīl, this one an Azdī, who dispatched scouts to gather intelligence on the invaders. When the Muslims reached Wādī al-Qurā, at the northern edge of the Hijaz, they set up camp for several days, after which they advanced to Maʿān in southern Jordan, south of Kerak. Here the Muslims learned that the Byzantine emperor Heraclius[26] had assembled an army of no less than 100,000 soldiers that included contingents from the tribes of Bahrāʾ, Wāʾil, Bakr, Lakhm, and Judhām, commanded by a certain Mālik from the tribe of Balī. Muslim scouts reported that the imperial army had reached Maʾāb in the province of Balqāʾ. Upon receiving this information, the Muslim army paused for two days to consider its next move. Some recommended sending a letter to Muḥammad so that the Prophet might either recall them to Medina or send reinforcements.[27] This defeatist approach was vigorously opposed by ʿAbdallāh b. Rawāḥa, who arose and delivered a stirring speech. Taking for granted his audience's familiarity with sacred revelation, Ibn Rawāḥa skillfully incorporated the language of scripture into his speech without identifying the language in question as a citation.[28] Ibn Rawāḥa urged his comrades to engage the enemy in battle, instructing them that there were only two possible outcomes: victory or martyrdom:

> By God, we have not been fighting armies on the strength of superior numbers, superior weapons, or superior horses, but rather on the strength of this religion by means of which God has honored us. Be off with you [and fight]. By God, at Badr I saw that we had only two horses and at Uḥud we had only one. There are only two possibilities, both good (*iḥdā al-ḥusnayayn*): victory over them—as God promised us (*waʿadanā*) and as His Prophet promised us, a promise that will not be broken—or martyrdom (*al-shahāda*), in which case we will join [our] brothers as their companions in the Garden.[29]

The two armies met at or near the village of Muʾta. After the Muslim soldiers had arranged themselves in rows, each of the three commanders dismounted his horse and fought on foot in hand-to-hand combat. The first to seize the standard and attack the enemy was Zayd b. Ḥāritha, who was killed by the thrust of a spear. After Zayd was slain, Jaʿfar b. Abī Ṭālib took hold of the standard, dismounted and bravely hamstrung his horse.[30] Without hesitating, Jaʿfar attacked the enemy and he too was killed, slain by a Byzantine soldier who cut his body in two. According to ostensible eyewitnesses, the lower part of Jaʿfar's body had thirty or more wounds, while the upper part of his torso had exactly seventy-two[31] sword blows and one spear wound.[32]

At the very moment that the battle was being fought in southern Jordan, the Prophet was sitting on the pulpit of the mosque in Medina. Miraculously, Muḥammad began to receive visual images of the events that were taking place on the battlefield hundreds of miles away. The identification of the Prophet as the primary witness (*shāhid*) to the martyrdom (*shahāda* or *istishhād*) of the three commanders is surely a literary device employed by the storytellers.[33] Who could contest the authenticity of an event witnessed by the Prophet himself with his very eyes in a vision that could have been granted to him only by God! As the images flashed before him, Muḥammad relayed the news to his Companions in the mosque. The Prophet reported that at the very moment that Zayd b. Ḥāritha seized the standard but before he attacked, he was approached by Satan, who attempted to entice him with the pleasures of this life and to repel his desire for death (*al-mawt*). Zayd resisted Satan's entreaties, proclaiming, "Now that belief has been firmly established in the hearts of the Believers, you are enticing me with the pleasures of this world!" After making this proclamation of his faith—the last words attributed to him—Zayd attacked the enemy and was martyred (*ustushhida*), whereupon the Prophet prayed for him, saying, "Ask [God] to forgive him, for he has entered the Garden, running." Here the Prophet makes it clear to his audience that the reward for fighting and dying in the path of God is immediate entrance to Paradise. The Prophet continued to relate the details of his vision: Jaʿfar b. Abī Ṭālib now picked up the standard, and he too was approached by Satan, who tried to arouse his desire for this life and to repel his desire for death. Like Zayd, Jaʿfar resisted Satan's entreaties, proclaiming, "Now that belief has been firmly established in the hearts of the Believers, you are stimulating my desire for this world!" Following this proclamation of faith, Jaʿfar advanced until he too was slain, whereupon the Prophet prayed for him, saying, "Ask [God] to forgive your brother, for he is now a martyr (*shahīd*)." Like Zayd, Jaʿfar immediately entered the Garden. Unlike Zayd, who entered the Garden *running*, Jaʿfar entered the Garden *flying*: miraculously he sprouted two wings made of precious stones that made it possible for him to fly at will.[34] The Prophet continued his narration: After Zayd and Jaʿfar had fallen, Ibn Rawāḥa seized the standard. In this instance there was no need for Satan to arouse the Muslim soldier's desire for life, for a reason that immediately will become apparent. Like Zayd and Jaʿfar, Ibn Rawāḥa fell as a martyr. But whereas Zayd entered the garden running and Jaʿfar entered the garden flying, Ibn Rawāḥa *stumbled* into the Garden. Upon receiving this news, the Helpers in Medina were sorely distressed. What prevented ʿAbdallāh, they no doubt asked the Prophet, from running or flying into the Garden? Muḥammad explained that when ʿAbdallāh was wounded, he could not at first give up on his desire to live. Before he could become a martyr, he had to chastise his soul and recover his courage. Eventually, he too entered the Garden, albeit neither running nor flying. Thus it was that all three of the commanders appointed by Muḥammad fell precisely in the order indicated by the Prophet; that all three of them became martyrs; and that all three of them entered the Garden—as attested by the Prophet himself in a supernatural vision.[35]

According to the Prophet's instructions at al-Jurf, in the event that all three commanders were killed, the soldiers were to select one of their comrades and to make him their commander. Al-Wāqidī now turns his attention to the last phase of the battle, in which the central figure is Khālid b. al-Walīd al-Makhzūmī (d. 21/642), a man who until recently had been one of the Prophet's inveterate enemies. Only five years earlier, in 3/625, Khālid had fought against the Muslims at the Battle of Uḥud, and it was not until Ṣafar 8/June 629—just three months prior to the Battle of Mu'ta—that he became a Muslim.[36] Khālid's conduct during the battle is the subject of widely varying assessments. Some sources are highly critical of him. According to one ostensible eyewitness, after the three commanders appointed by the Prophet had been slain, Khālid grabbed the standard and led the retreat, with the polytheists in hot pursuit. An unspecified number of Muslims were killed, and the Army of Mu'ta was routed. As the Muslims fled, Quṭba b. ʿĀmir yelled out, "O soldiers. It is better to be killed facing the enemy than to be killed with your backs turned to them." His words had no effect, however, and the Byzantines pursued Khālid and his comrades as they fled from the battlefield.[37] Another source confirms Khālid's flight from the battlefield, as a result of which the commander and his soldiers were accused of being runaways (*farrār*). This was regarded as an evil omen.[38]

Other sources portray Khālid in a more positive light. One unidentified soldier who reportedly participated in the battle refuted the charge that Khālid fled from the polytheists. This soldier explained that after Ibn Rawāḥa was slain, chaos reigned on the battlefield: Muslims and polytheists intermingled with one another, the standard was lying on the ground, and the Muslims were leaderless. It was at this critical moment that Khālid seized the standard and led the survivors to safety. The point of this report is that even if the Muslims did suffer—inexplicably—a humiliating defeat (*hazīma*), many more men would have been killed that day had it not been for Khālid.[39] According to another source, after ʿAbdallāh b. Rawāḥa was slain, the Army of Mu'ta regrouped, whereupon a Helper named Thābit b. Arqam came forward and grabbed the standard. "Gather round me, soldiers," he cried out, whereupon the Muslims came running to him from every direction. When Thābit saw Khālid b. al-Walīd, he ordered him to take hold of the standard. Khālid refused on the grounds that Thābit was older than he was and had fought at Badr. Thābit now informed Khālid that the only reason he had taken the standard was to give it to him, and he insisted that Khālid take his place as the commander of the army. Reluctantly, Khālid agreed. After he took hold of the standard, the polytheists attacked. Initially, Khālid held his ground. Indeed, when the polytheists turned around to prepare for a second attack, Khālid and his men managed to destroy one of the enemy's units. Eventually, however, the Byzantines prevailed over the Muslims by virtue of superior numbers. The Muslims lost their courage and fled from the battlefield, making their way back to Medina. This reportedly was the worst defeat that the young Muslim community had suffered to this point in its history.[40]

Muslim historians are divided about the outcome of the Battle of Muʾta. In the earliest sources, the battle is portrayed as a resounding and humiliating defeat (*hazīma*). This characterization is inconsistent with the fact that in the Qurʾān God had promised victory to the believers. The early source material was reworked by a later generation of historians, who revised the narrative account of the battle in order to bring it into line with the Islamic understanding of God's plan for mankind.[41] In these later sources, we read that God caused the Muslim forces to be victorious over the enemy (*fataḥa allāh*[u] *ʿalayhim*)—presumably by saving most of the Muslim soldiers.[42] The changing perception of the outcome of the battle is related to differing assessments of Khālid b. al-Walīd's conduct at Muʾta. Khālid is remembered by posterity as *Sayf Allāh* or "the Sword of God." There is considerable variation in the sources, however, as to where and when he acquired his nom de guerre. Muslim historians active in the second century A.H. indicate that it was the first caliph Abū Bakr who assigned the title to Khālid as a reward for his conduct during the *Ridda* wars. It was only in the third century A.H., when Muslim historians began to portray the Battle of Muʾta as a victory, that reports began to circulate in which Muḥammad—not Abū Bakr—rewarded Khālid for his efforts at Muʾta—not during the *Ridda* wars—by dubbing him the Sword of God—not a coward.[43]

It is curious that almost all the 3,000 Muslim soldiers who reportedly participated in the Battle of Muʾta are said to have survived. In fact, Wāqidī and Ibn Hishām mention the names of only eight Muslims who died at the battle, including the three commanders.[44] Both historians classify the fallen soldiers according to their tribal and clan affiliations. The dead included two men from the Banū Hāshim—Jaʿfar b. Abī Ṭālib and Zayd b. Ḥāritha; one from ʿAdī b. Kaʿb—Masʿūd b. al-Aswad b. Ḥāritha b. Naḍla; one from Banū ʿĀmir b. Luwayy—Wahb b. Saʿd b. Abī Sarḥ. The dead also included four Helpers, one from Banū Māzin—Surāqa b. ʿAmr b. ʿAṭiyya b. Khansāʾ; one from Banū al-Najjār—al-Ḥārith b. al-Nuʿmān b. Yusāf b. Naḍla b. ʿAmr b. ʿAwf b. Ghanm b. Mālik; and two from the Banū al-Ḥārith b. al-Khazraj—ʿAbdallāh b. Rawāḥa and ʿUbāda b. Qays.[45]

If there were only eight fatalities at Muʾta, then there would have been nearly 3,000 survivors who made their way back to the Hijaz. Just as the non-combatant Muslims had bid farewell to the Army of Mu'ta when the soldiers had set off on their mission, so too they were waiting at al-Jurf—the initial staging ground—to greet them upon their return, thereby closing the narrative circle. Now, however, the same people who had prayed for the safe return of the Muslim army began to throw dirt in the soldiers' faces and to taunt them: "O runaways, have you fled [while fighting] in the path of God?" In an effort to calm the mob, the Prophet intervened, explaining that these men were not runaways (*farrār*) but rather men who soon would return to the battlefield (*karrār*)—punning is another literary device used by the story-tellers.[46] But even the intervention of the Prophet himself could not at first remove the stigma of cowardice, flight and defeat. After returning to their families, many of the soldiers sequestered themselves inside their houses and refused to open the door to visitors. The shame was so great that the distinguished Companion Abū Hurayra is said to have shut himself indoors. When the Prophet learned of this, he sent each of the soldiers the following message: "You are the ones who will return to the path of God."[47]

The next topic addressed by Wāqidī is the reaction of the Prophet to the deaths of the men who were killed at Mu'ta.[48] It is curious that Wāqidī says nothing about Muḥammad's reaction to the death of either Zayd b. Ḥāritha or ʿAbdallāh b. Rawāḥa.[49] It is rather the death of Jaʿfar b. Abī Ṭālib that appears to have attracted his attention. It is related on the authority of Jaʿfar's wife, Asmāʾ bt. ʿUmays, that the Prophet informed her of her husband's death at Mu'ta *on the very day* on which he died. Since it would have taken at least a week for news of the disaster to reach Medina,[50] this information must have been based upon the Prophet's above-mentioned supernatural vision. Asmāʾ reports that the Prophet arrived at her residence just after she had finished kneading dough for 40 *mann* of seasoned bread; she also had found the time to wash the faces of her sons and to anoint them with oil. A true woman of valor—*eshet khayyil*, as is said in Hebrew.[51] After entering the apartment, the Prophet ordered Asmāʾ to summon her sons. When the boys appeared, the Prophet hugged them and smelled their bodies. Overcome with grief, his eyes welled up with tears and he began to cry. Asmāʾ asked Muḥammad if he had perhaps received news about Jaʿfar. "Yes," the Prophet replied. "He was killed *today*" (emphasis added). The widow immediately stood up and began to wail, whereupon the other women in the apartment gathered around her. After instructing Asmāʾ not to use unseemly language or to beat her chest, the Prophet left her apartment. He now went to break the bad news to his daughter, Fāṭima, the wife of ʿAlī b. Abī Ṭālib who, by virtue of the death of his older brother Jaʿfar, was now the Prophet's sole surviving male Muslim blood relative.[52] Upon hearing the grim news, Fāṭima cried out, "Woe for his [her father's] paternal cousin!" To which the Prophet responded, "Let the weepers mourn for the likes of Jaʿfar." The Prophet now instructed his daughter to prepare food for Jaʿfar's family, because they would have no time to attend to this task during their mourning.[53]

The Chronicle of Theophanes

A short summary of the battle known to Muslim historians as the Battle of Mu'ta is found in *The Chronicle of Theophanes* which is attributed to the monk Theophanes Confessor.[54] As its title suggests, the *Chronicle* establishes the order of events between *anno mundi* 5777 and 6305, which corresponds to the 528-year period between 284–85 and 812–13 C.E. Theophanes was born in 759 or 760 and died in 818. Thus, his life overlapped with many of the events mentioned in the last fifty years or so of his *Chronicle*, even if he was not an eyewitness to those events. Theophanes must have drawn on sources that are no longer extant, especially for earlier portions of his text, including what he calls the Battle of Mothous. These sources no doubt were compiled, arranged, and redacted by Theophanes. It is generally accepted that the sections of the *Chronicle* dealing with Islamic history are based in part on Eastern sources, including Syriac texts. Against the prevailing view, L. Conrad has argued that these same sections of the *Chronicle* are based in part on sources from the Arabo-Islamic historical tradition.[55] The point is of considerable importance. If Theophanes relied primarily on Greek and/or Syriac sources for his description of the Battle of Mothous, then his account is the sole independent non-Islamic witness to the battle; if, however, he relied primarily on Arabic sources—even if only indirectly—then the *Chronicle* ceases to be an independent witness to the battle.

Theophanes dates the Battle of Mothous to *anno mundi* 6123, which is the 623rd year since the incarnation of Christ. He specifies that this was the twenty-third year of the reign of the Byzantine emperor Heraclius, the first year of the reign of the leader of the Arabs, Aboubacharos (= Abū Bakr), the twenty-third year of the tenure of Sergius as Bishop of Constantinople, the first year of the tenure of Modestus as Bishop of Jerusalem, and the thirteenth year of the tenure of George as Bishop of Alexandria. In AM 6123, Theophanes reports, the Persians fought a civil war and the king of India sent valuable gifts to Heraclius on the occasion of his victory over the Persians.[56]

After establishing the chronology, Theophanes presents a short narrative that has two separate components: a description of the Battle of Mothous; and an explanation of why the Arab fighters employed by the Byzantine emperor to defend the borders of the empire would soon shift their allegiance to the Muslims. The unstated purpose of the second component is to absolve Heraclius of responsibility for the collapse of the imperial military machine in the face of the invading Muslim armies. Theophanes' account runs as follows:

> Mouamed, who had died earlier, had appointed four emirs to fight those members of the Arab nation who were Christian, and they came in front of a village called Mouchea, in which was stationed the *vicarius* Theodore, intending to fall upon the Arabs on the day when they sacrificed to their idols. The *vicarius*, on learning this from a certain Koraishite[57] called Koutabas, who was in his pay, gathered all the soldiers

of the desert guard and, after ascertaining from the Saracen the day and hour when they were intending to attack, himself attacked them at a village called Mothous, and killed three emirs and the bulk of their army. One emir, called Chaled, whom they call God's Sword, escaped. Now some of the neighboring Arabs were receiving small payments from the emperors for guarding the approaches to the desert. At that time a certain eunuch arrived to distribute the wages of the soldiers, and when the Arabs came to receive their wages according to custom, the eunuch drove them away, saying, "The emperor can barely pay his soldiers their wages, much less these dogs!" Distressed by this, the Arabs went over to their fellow-tribesmen, and it was they that led them to the rich country of Gaza, which is the gateway to the desert in the direction of Mount Sinai.[58]

A Comparison of the Muslim and Byzantine Accounts of the Battle

A comparison of Theophanes' account of the battle with that of Wāqidī reveals both similarities and differences. We begin with the similarities.

Both accounts agree that Muḥammad appointed several commanders (three according to Wāqidī—all identified by name; four according to Theophanes—who mentions the name of only the fourth); both accounts agree that the battle took place in a village named Mu'ta or Mothous—clearly the same place; both accounts agree that the Byzantines killed three of the emirs but that the fourth emir escaped; both accounts identify the fourth emir as Khālid b. al-Walīd/Chaled; and both accounts agree that the battle was a decisive victory for the Byzantines and a humiliating defeat for the Muslims (even if later Muslim historians would turn defeat into victory). It is largely on the basis of these correspondences that Conrad has concluded that the account preserved in the *Chronicle* is dependent on Arabo-Islamic sources. In support of this conclusion, Conrad adduces the following linguistic evidence: The term *ameraioi* (sg. *amer*) used by the Byzantine chronicler is clearly a Greek approximation of the Arabic military term *umarā'* (sg. *amīr*); similarly, Mothous is a Greek equivalent of the Arabic toponym Mu'ta; likewise, Mouchea is an equivalent of the Arabic toponym al-Miḥna (although it is difficult to follow Conrad on this point); and the proper name of Theodore's Arab informant, Koutabas, is a Greek approximation of either Quṭba or Qutayba. Theophanes identifies Koutabas as a Κορασηνός or Korasenite—understood by his translators as a member of the tribe of Quraysh. Conrad, however, suspects that this may be a scribal error for Σαρακηνοῦ *or Saracen*, even if there is no evidence for such a mistake in the surviving manuscripts.[59] In sum, Conrad's argument for dependence rests on the above-mentioned linguistic evidence, combined with correspondences relating to the number of Muslim commanders who participated in the battle, its location, the identification of Khālid b. al-Walīd as the fourth commander, and the outcome.

Conrad does not attend to the differences between Wāqidī's account of the battle and that of Theophanes. According to Wāqidī, the purpose of the expedition was to avenge the murder of Muḥammad's envoy at the hands of a Ghassānid soldier; according to Theophanes, the purpose of the expedition was to attack Arab idol worshippers. According to Wāqidī, Muḥammad appointed three commanders; according to Theophanes, Muḥammad appointed four. According to Wāqidī, an army of 100,000 or more soldiers was assembled by the emperor Heraclius; according to Theophanes, an unspecified number of Arab desert guards was assembled by the *vicarius* Theodore. According to Wāqidī, the defeat of the Muslim army was the result of superior Byzantine manpower; according to Theophanes, it was a result of superior military intelligence: Theodore's Arab informant Koutabas—in my view it makes little difference whether he was a Qurashī or a Saracen—told the *vicarius* the exact day and hour on which the Muslim forces were planning their attack. According to Wāqidī, the three commanders appointed by Muḥammad fell in the order indicated by the Prophet, whereupon Khālid was selected as the new commander and led the rest of the Muslim soldiers back to Medina—only eight men are said to have been killed; according to Theophanes, the Byzantine forces killed not only three of the four emirs but also "the bulk of their army"—in which case Chaled would have been one of a small number of survivors. Also, Wāqidī identifies the tribal affiliation of the bedouin Arabs who fought for the Byzantines without drawing attention to the fact that these tribes would later shift their allegiance to the Muslims. Theophanes, on the other hand, is interested in explaining why the bedouin Arabs would soon shift their allegiance to the Muslims: he attributes the shift to the fact that a Byzantine paymaster, who was a eunuch, refused to pay the bedouin Arabs and cursed them as "dogs."[60] Thus, Wāqidī and Theophanes disagree about the *number* of commanders appointed by Muḥammad, the casus belli, the *identity* of the Byzantine military commander, the *size* of the opposing armies, the *reason* for the Muslim defeat, and the *number* of Muslims who were killed. The discrepancies are so striking that one is justified in asking if these two historians are talking about the same battle.

The most striking discrepancy between the Arab and Byzantine accounts of the Battle of Muʾta, however, is surely the *date* on which the battle was fought.[61] In his biographical dictionary, Khalīfa b. Khayyāt al-ʿUṣfūrī (d. 240/854) has separate entries for Zayd b. Ḥāritha, Jaʿfar b. Abī Ṭālib, and Ibn Rawāḥa. Each entry contains the following sentence: "He was martyred on the day of Muʾta in the lifetime of the Prophet—may God bless him and grant him peace—in the year seven."[62] The year 7 A.H. is well within the lifetime of the Prophet, and one wonders why it was necessary to specify that all three men predeceased Muḥammad—unless of course the point was contested. Be that as it may, the year 7 would turn out to be too early for the Battle of Muʾta. As noted, Wāqidī situates his account of the battle between his accounts of other battles fought in the year 8—without specifying the month or year in which the battle was fought. Subsequently, most Muslim historians date the battle to Jumādā I of the year 8 A.H., that is to say, sometime between 26 August and 24 September 629 C.E. This was three years prior to the death of the Prophet. To the best of my knowledge, no Muslim historian says that the battle was fought after the Prophet's death. Thus, the date assigned to the Battle of Mothous by Theophanes—the first year of Abū Bakr's caliphate—is anomalous. It is certainly possible that Theophanes was relying on an Islamic source—as argued by Conrad. If so, however, that source has left no trace in the Islamic tradition.

Most modern historians either ignore the chronological discrepancy or reject the date given by Theophanes as a mistake. To the best of my knowledge, the only historian who has attended to the problem is the Byzantinist and military historian W. Kaegi, who expresses concern about the year in which the battle was fought, even if he does not openly and unequivocally question the date.[63] In his monograph on the early Islamic conquests, Kaegi begins his account of the Battle of Mu'ta by stating that the battle "occurred during the lifetime of the Prophet Muhammad."[64] As for the month and/or day on which the battle was fought, Kaegi indicates that it was either 10 Dhū al-Ḥijja 8/10 April 629[65] or Jumādā I 8/September 629; if forced to choose between these two dates, Kaegi finds the latter (and later) date more likely.[66] For Kaegi, the problem is not the month in which the battle was fought (Dhū al-Ḥijja or Jumādā I) but rather the year (8/629 or 11/632). In his view, the earlier date—8/629—is implausible for several reasons. He makes his point indirectly by posing the following question: What would the military status of the Byzantine army have been in September of 629? He answers this question by analyzing the military situation in Syria and the Near East in the years leading up to the battle.

In 603, the Persian king Chosroes II invaded the Byzantine empire. Over the next twenty-five years, Byzantine and Persian armies fought a series of battles that caused great destruction in the provinces of both empires. Between late 610 and 615 the Byzantine army collapsed, and Persian forces occupied Syria, Palestine, and Egypt. It was not until 628 that Heraclius was able to reconstitute his military machine. At the beginning of that year, the emperor invaded Iran and inflicted a decisive defeat on the Persian army. After imposing peace terms favorable to the Byzantines, Heraclius returned to Constantinople. In July 629, the emperor conducted negotiations with the Persian general Shahrbaraz. According to the terms of the peace agreement, the Persian commander agreed to withdraw his forces from Egypt, Syria, Palestine, and Mesopotamia, provinces that had been occupied by the Persians for fifteen years. Only in July of 629 did the Byzantines initiate the task of reestablishing their military presence in these provinces, no doubt beginning with major cities and towns and proceeding to less densely populated areas. It would have taken several months to move men, animals, equipment, and supplies into their new positions. By September of 629, a mere two months after the peace agreement, the Byzantines could not have been certain that the Persian forces had in fact withdrawn from southern Jordan and would not have had time to repair damaged roads and bridges or to build new warehouses and watchtowers. For these reasons Byzantine control of southern Jordan would have been only indirect. Effective control of the district of Balqāʾ would have been exercised by the local bedouin Arabs who were paid to prevent incursions from the south. According to Kaegi, it is "inconceivable" that the emperor would have sent substantial numbers of Byzantine soldiers to this remote and thinly populated desert region; although he does not say so, it is also inconceivable that Heraclius himself would have traveled to Balqāʾ and directed the battle, as Wāqidī and other Muslim sources indicate.[67] Kaegi concludes that in September of 629, any Byzantine forces in Balqāʾ would have been vulnerable to attack by Muslim forces approaching from the south. If this was the situation, how are we to explain the large number of imperial troops and the decisive Byzantine victory over the Muslims?[68]

The chronological and strategic problems disappear if we follow Theophanes' account of the military encounter: A small Muslim raiding party was wiped out by a Christian Arab military squadron employed by the Byzantines; the encounter took place in the first year of Abū Bakr's caliphate near the village of Mothous in southern Jordan. The date assigned to this encounter by Theophanes has the advantage of giving the Byzantines three full years in which to reestablish military control of Syria, including the area east of the Jordan River. Be that as it may, the date of the battle specified by Theophanes has been flatly rejected by Conrad:

> Theophanes is of course wrong in stating that [the Battle of] Muʾta occurred after the death of the Prophet. This error may stem from confusion between this clash and the second battle of Muʾta, which did take place shortly after Muḥammad's death. It may also reflect the general confusion among Greek and Syriac authors in their presentations of events relating to the Arab conquests.[69]

By the second battle of Muʾta, Conrad presumably is referring to the military expedition led by Usāma b. Zayd in the year 11/632. Shortly before Muḥammad died, he appointed Usāma as the commander of Muslim forces charged with exacting vengeance from the Arabs who had killed Zayd at Muʾta (see Chapter 3). The expedition was interrupted by the Prophet's sudden and untimely death, but it resumed at the beginning of Abū Bakr's caliphate. Like the first expedition, this one numbered 3,000 men. Unlike the first expedition, this one was victorious.

At first glance, it does appear as if there were two military expeditions to Muʾta: The first expedition, in 8/629, was led by three commanders appointed by Muḥammad; the second, in 11/632, was led by one commander, Usāma b. Zayd, also appointed by Muḥammad. Both expeditions numbered 3,000 men, and both had as their primary military objective vengeance for the death of a Muslim. Whereas the first expedition was routed by the Byzantines, the second was successful. If so, then there would be ample justification for Conrad's confident assertion that it was Theophanes who mistakenly assigned the date of the second battle to the first (presumably the chronicler was either unaware of the second battle or ignored it). It is curious—albeit not impossible—that two battles would have been fought in precisely the same remote region, approximately three years apart, the first led by a father, the second by his son. Also curious is Theophanes' specification that the expedition sent to southern Jordan during the first year of Abū Bakr's caliphate included not one commander but four, all appointed by Muḥammad—a detail not found in any Islamic text. Did the Byzantine chronicler get this wrong too?

I think not. The Muslim historians do not mention a second battle at Mu'ta. Rather, they report that shortly before he died, Muḥammad appointed Usāma as the sole commander of a military expedition whose objective was to avenge the murder of Zayd. This military expedition traveled not to Mu'ta but to Ubna/Yibna/Yavneh in central Palestine.[70] In this instance, it is Conrad who is mistaken. What he calls the second Battle of Mu'ta was in fact a military expedition to Ubna.[71]

To this point we have established that there was only one battle at Mu'ta, about which Muslim and Byzantine historians tell a different story. As for the date of the battle, Ibn Khayyāt places it in the year 7 A.H., others say that it took place on 10 Dhū al-Ḥijja 8/10 April 629, and still others place it in the month of Jumādā I of 8 A.H./26 Aug.–24 Sept. 629. According to Theophanes, the battle took place during the first year of Abū Bakr's caliphate, that is, 11 A.H. At the present time, the only statement that may be made with confidence is that there may have been a military encounter between Muslim and Byzantine forces at Mu'ta, although the exact date of the battle is a matter of conjecture.[72] This is as far as the extant sources take us; and this is perhaps as far as the prudent historian should go. Beyond this point, one can only speculate. Such speculation may be worth the effort. In order to proceed, let me introduce two hypotheses.

Hypothesis 5.1. The first Muslim historians adjusted the date of the Battle of Mu'ta in order to make it appear as if Zayd predeceased Muḥammad.

In this instance, there was a compelling theological reason to adjust the historical record. As we have seen in Chapter 4, Zayd's status as Muḥammad's adopted son and heir threatened to undermine Muḥammad's status as the Last Prophet. The early Qur'ān commentators responded to this challenge by teaching that Muḥammad repudiated Zayd in 5 A.H. Repudiation was not sufficient, however, because Zayd was already an adult in that year. For this reason, the first Muslim historians adjusted the historical record in an effort to establish that Zayd did in fact predecease the Prophet. The process of fixing the chronological record proceeded by trial and error. At least two temporal considerations had to be kept in mind: First, the battle had to take place sometime after Muḥammad's repudiation of Zayd in 5 A.H. Second, the battle had to take place before the Prophet's death in 11/632. Thus, the general window during which the battle could be said to have taken place was the period between Muḥammad's repudiation of Zayd in 5 A.H. and the Prophet's death in 11 A.H. But the participation of Khālid b. al-Walīd in the battle narrowed the range of possible dates because Khālid did not convert to Islam until Ṣafar 8/June 629. This reduced the chronological window during which the battle could be said to have taken place to the period between Khālid's conversion to Islam and the Prophet's death.

Hypothesis 5.2. Muslim historians settled on the month of Jumādā I 8 A.H./26 Aug.–24 Sept. 629 as the date of the Battle of Mu'ta.

The fixing of the date is likely to have been the work of scholarly circles that flourished between 75 and 125 A.H. These circles would have included ʿUrwa b. al-Zubayr (d. 94/712–13) and his disciples, including al-Zuhrī.[73] ʿUrwa b. al-Zubayr was the younger brother of ʿAbdallāh b. al-Zubayr and the nephew of ʿĀʾisha. When ʿAbdallāh b. al-Zubayr declared himself caliph in Medina, ʿUrwa supported his brother. After ʿAbdallāh was killed in 73/692, however, it was ʿUrwa who brought the news to ʿAbd al-Malik b. Marwān (r. 65–86/685–705) in Damascus.[74] The Umayyad caliph pardoned ʿUrwa, who returned to the Hijaz and settled in Medina, where he embarked on a long period of scholarly activity during which he corresponded with the caliph about the events of early Islamic history. After ʿAbd al-Malik's death, ʿUrwa carried on a similar correspondence with al-Walīd b. ʿAbd al-Malik (r. 86–96/705–15).[75] It may have been during the reigns of these two caliphs that the theological doctrine of the finality of prophecy came to prevail within the Muslim community. The emergence of this critical theological doctrine required adjustments to the historical record. As the Last Prophet, Muḥammad could not have an adult son—natural, supernatural, or adopted. Zayd's status as Muḥammad's adult son was incompatible with the new theological doctrine.[76] This problem was solved by the early Muslim commentators and historians.

Wāqidī, it will be recalled, is silent about the date of the Battle of Mu'ta, although he places his account of the battle in a context which suggests that it occurred in the year 8 A.H. In this regard, it surely is significant that Wāqidī's sources do *not* include ʿUrwa b. al-Zubayr. To the best of my knowledge, the specification of the date of the battle as Jumādā I of 8 A.H. appears for the first time in the account of Ibn Saʿd—albeit without attribution: "Then the raid of Mu'ta, at the bottom of al-Balqāʾ, which is below Damascus, in Jumādā I of the year 8 since the hijra of the Messenger of God."[77] The earliest reference to the date of the battle that is accompanied by an *isnād* appears in the *Sīra* of Ibn Isḥāq: Muḥammad b. Jaʿfar b. al-Zubayr—ʿUrwa b. al-Zubayr, "The Messenger of God sent his expedition to Muʾta in Jumādā I of the year 8."[78] An identical report with the same *isnād* is cited by Ṭabarī.[79] Thus the assignment of the date of the Battle of Muʾta to the year 8 A.H. appears to have been the work of ʿUrwa b. al-Zubayr.[80]

To sum up: There are seven discrepancies between Wāqidī's account of the Battle of Muʾta and Theophanes' account of the Battle of Mothous: (1) the date of the battle, (2) the number of commanders appointed by Muḥammad, (3) the casus belli, (4) the identity of the Byzantine military leader, (5) the size of the two armies, (6) the reason for the Muslim defeat, and (7) the number of Muslims who were killed. These discrepancies are so striking as to suggest that the Islamic and Byzantine sources are referring to different battles. Indeed, one wonders if there were in fact two battles at Muʾta or just one: a skirmish that took place during the first year of Abū Bakr's caliphate in which a small Muslim raiding party was wiped out by Arab auxiliaries of the Byzantines. If we subtract the three commanders from the list of the dead given by Wāqidī and Ibn Hishām, five names remain. Of these five, two were Qurashīs—Masʿūd b. al-Aswad b. Ḥāritha b. Naḍla, and Wahb b. Saʿd b. Abī Sarḥ; and three were Helpers—Surāqa b. ʿAmr b. ʿAṭiyya b. Khansāʾ, al-Ḥārith b. al-Nuʿmān b. Yusāf b. Naḍla b. ʿAmr b. ʿAwf b. Ghanm b. Mālik, and ʿUbāda b. Qays. These five men may have been sent to southern Jordan during the first year of Abū Bakr's caliphate. Upon reaching the administrative district of Balqāʾ they may have been killed by Arab auxiliaries employed by the Byzantines. If so, this is the historical bedrock of the Battle of Muʾta.

The Battle of Muʾta: History or Sacred Legend?

The narrative accounts of the Battle of Muʾta preserved in the Islamic sources contain numerous theological, supernatural, and mythological elements: In Medina, Muḥammad had a vision in which he witnessed the battle as it was unfolding in southern Jordan. Immediately before Zayd and Jaʿfar were martyred, Satan appeared on the battlefield and attempted to entice these two righteous men with the pleasures of this world. Both men resisted Satan's wiles. Following the deaths of Zayd and Jaʿfar, ʿAbdallāh b. Rawāḥa fell in battle and gave up the ghost, albeit reluctantly. Thus it was that all three commanders fell precisely in the order specified by Muḥammad. No sooner did each commander die than he immediately entered the Garden, albeit by a different mode of locomotion: running, flying, or crawling on hands and knees.

The theological, supernatural, and mythological components of the traditional Islamic account of the Battle of Muʾta have long been recognized by Western scholars. Historians who seek to recover what really happened at Muʾta generally proceed by bracketing the irrational elements—leaving these for theologians and historians of religion—and focusing their attention on the rational residue, presumably a reflection of historical fact. This residue may be summarized as follows: In the year 8 A.H., one of Muḥammad's messengers was captured and beheaded in the area east of the Dead Sea. The Prophet responded to this unprecedented provocation by gathering a large military force and appointing Zayd b. Ḥāritha, Jaʿfar b. Abī Ṭālib, and Abdallāh b. Rawāḥa as the successive commanders of this army. The stated objective of the expedition was to seek vengeance for the slaying of Muḥammad's messenger. As the Muslim forces approached southern Jordan, they learned that Heraclius was waiting for them with overwhelming forces. It was now clear to the Muslims that they had been sent on a suicide mission. Some soldiers wanted to call for reinforcements, while others wanted to return to Medina without engaging the enemy. In the end, the day was won by the Muslim soldiers who advocated struggle in the path of God. After the two armies had met on the battlefield and the three commanders had fallen precisely in the order specified by Muḥammad, the survivors rallied around Khālid b. al-Walīd and made their way back to Medina, where they were denounced as cowards who had fled from the field of battle. These "facts"—or variations thereof—are found in every biography of the Prophet and in every account of early Islamic history (see note 3).

It is certainly possible that a battle took place at Muʾta, although it is likely that the dimensions of this military encounter were closer to those of a skirmish or raid than to that of a large battle. Be that as it may, it is probably fruitless to ask what really happened at Muʾta. A more productive approach is to ask the following: Why did the narrative account of the battle take the particular shape that it did in the collective memory of the Muslim community? In my view, the shape taken by the narrative accounts of the battle was driven primarily by theological concerns; and the resulting narrative has as much to do with the internal affairs of the early Muslim community as it does with political and military relations between Muslims and Byzantines.

In Chapter 4, I argued that the exegetical narratives that tell the story of Muḥammad's marriage to Zaynab bt. Jaḥsh are best read as literary compositions designed to create a plausible "historical" context in which Muḥammad might be said to have repudiated Zayd. A similar argument can be made about the historical narratives relating to the Battle of Muʾta. Zayd's death at Muʾta deprived the Muslim community of the services of a man who the early Muslims appear to have regarded as one of their most qualified and talented leaders.[81] Zayd was manumitted and adopted by Muḥammad ca. 605 C.E., and for nearly two decades he was the Prophet's son and heir. His name was Zayd b. Muḥammad and his nickname was Ḥibb Rasūl Allāh or the Beloved of the Messenger of God. Zayd was the first adult male after the Prophet to become a Muslim. Muḥammad may have repudiated Zayd in 5 A.H., but he did not lose trust in him; indeed, he appointed Zayd as the commander of as many as nine military missions, including the ill-fated expedition to Muʾta. If, at the time of the Prophet's death, he was survived by a son bearing the name Zayd b. Muḥammad, that son, according to the theory of prophecy put forward in the Qurʾān, would have been a prophet—as Muqātil b. Sulaymān indicated in an exegetical comment on Q. 33:40. Had it not been for Zayd's untimely death at Muʾta in 8 A.H., he would have been a prime candidate to succeed Muḥammad as the first *khalīfa* or caliph of the Muslim community. To ʿĀʾisha is attributed the following statement: "Had Zayd outlived Muḥammad, he would have appointed him as his successor."[82] We need not accept the historicity of this statement in order to appreciate its significance for the early Muslim community. The words attributed to ʿĀʾisha point to the threat posed by Zayd to the men who produced the narrative accounts of the formation of the Muslim community in the first century A.H.

Just as the early exegetes found a plausible site for Muḥammad's repudiation of Zayd in the narrative account of the Prophet's marriage to Zaynab, so too the first Muslim historians found a plausible site for Zayd's death in narrative accounts of the Battle of Muʾta. By placing this battle in the year 8 A.H., the historians established, after the fact, that Zayd did in fact predecease Muḥammad. The statement attributed to ʿĀʾisha ("Had Zayd outlived Muḥammad, he would have appointed him as his successor") is formulated as a counterfactual. This statement could only have been formulated after the first historians had established that Zayd did predecease Muḥammad—which would have been many years after the Battle of Muʾta had taken place—whenever that may have been. This was accomplished by placing Zayd at the center of the historical narratives about the battle and granting him a glorious and meaningful death as a martyr. When the time came, Zayd was determined and resolute. He dismounted his horse and attacked the enemy, thereby signaling his unwavering devotion to God and His Prophet. By exerting himself in the path of God, Zayd exchanged temporary life in this world for eternal life in the next (cf. Q. 9:111). The fact that he ran into the Garden points to his eagerness for death and martyrdom, a narrative detail to which we shall return in Chapter 6. How fitting that the first adult male to become a Muslim was also the first Muslim to fall in battle on enemy territory in a confrontation with Byzantine forces. In this manner, Zayd became the prototype of the fighting martyr.[83]

Zayd, it will be recalled, is the only Muslim apart from Muḥammad whose name is mentioned in the Qurʾān. The first Muslims devoted considerable time and energy to preserving his memory, producing colorful narratives about his capture and eventual acquisition by Muḥammad, his adoption as Muḥammad's son and heir, the circumstances of his marriage to and divorce from Zaynab bt. Jaḥsh, his repudiation by Muḥammad in 5 A.H., and his death as a martyr at Muʾta three years later. In Chapter 7, I will suggest that all of these narratives draw on a corpus of earlier texts and traditions that were circulating in Arabia and the Near East in the years before, during, and after the rise of Islam. In these narratives, I will argue, Zayd is a *figure* whose primary function is to make it possible for Muḥammad to become the Last Prophet.

Wāqidī's account of the Battle of Mu'ta is a collage of narratives produced by Muslims who lived in the aftermath of a series of traumatic events, beginning with the assassination of the caliph ʿUthmān in 35/656 and followed in quick succession by the Battle of Ṣiffīn (37/657), the assassination of ʿAlī (40/661), the massacre at Karbalā' (61/680), and the suppression of the caliphate of ʿAbdallāh b. al-Zubayr (73/692). By the end of the first century A.H., the Muslim *umma* had split into two major factions, Marwānids and proto-Shīʿīs. The Marwānids shrewdly offered patronage to key relatives of their enemies, including ʿAbdallāh b. Jaʿfar b. Abī Ṭālib and ʿUrwa b. al-Zubayr. In return, the recipients of Marwānid patronage formulated the narrative accounts of early Islamic history in such a manner as to support the theological and political interests of the ruling dynasty. These interests demanded the marginalization of Zayd, his son Usāma, Jaʿfar b. Abī Ṭālib and—to a lesser extent—ʿAbdallāh b. Rawāḥa.

Acting on behalf of their patrons, Marwānid historians transformed what may have been a skirmish at Mu'ta into one of the "framing" events—to use Fred Donner's term—of Islamic history.[84] They took this "bedrock" incident and used it as a platform upon which to work out the significance of five key issues. First, the murder of the messenger of the Messenger of God in southern Jordan served as a casus belli for the Islamic invasion of the Near East. Second, the battle instructions put into the mouth of the Prophet at al-Jurf defined the rules of engagement for the Arabo-Islamic conquest of the Near East and points beyond—with special attention to the conquerors' treatment of the People of the Book, on the one hand, and of pagans and polytheists, on the other. Third, an ill-fated military skirmish at Mu'ta provided historians with a plausible context in which to eliminate certain figures who posed a theological and/or political threat to the interests of the Marwānids and/or the proto-Shīʿīs: As Muḥammad's adopted son and heir, Zayd threatened the theological doctrine of the finality of prophecy; as the distinguished oldest son of Abū Ṭālib, Jaʿfar's qualifications for leadership would have been greater than those of his younger and less accomplished brother ʿAlī; and as the Prophet's deputy ruler (*khalīfa*) of Medina during Muḥammad's absences from the city, ʿAbdallāh b. Rawāḥa's claim to leadership arguably would have been as great as that of Abū Bakr, ʿUmar, or ʿUthmān. Looking back at the lifetime of the Prophet from the vantage point of the end of the first century A.H., the Marwānids and their supporters understood that it was essential to marginalize all three men—just as the authors of the Pentateuch understood that it was essential to marginalize Ishmael and Esau, and just as the authors of the New Testament understood that it was essential to marginalize Joseph, the husband of Mary and apparent father of Jesus. What better way to accomplish this objective than to send all three men to certain death at Muʾta? Finally, the historians used the Battle of Muʾta as a platform upon which to work out their understanding of the emerging doctrine of martyrdom and to assess the relative merits of different groups within the Muslim community.[85] Righteous believers like Zayd and Jaʿfar who willingly sacrificed themselves on the field of battle for the sake of God and His Messenger became models of the fighting martyr who immediately enters Paradise. By contrast, ʿAbdallāh b. Rawāḥa sought to erase his earthly sins through one dramatic supererogatory act—martyrdom on the field of battle.[86] By making ʿAbdallāh hesitate before he died, the historians were sending a signal to their Muslim audience. Whereas righteous men run or fly into the Garden, sinners stumble into the Garden and occupy a lower rung on the ladder of virtue. And then there are men like Khālid b. al-Walīd, a late convert to Islam whose devotion to this life and everything in it was greater than his devotion to God and His Prophet. Although there were differences of opinion, many of the storytellers remembered Khālid as a coward who fled the battlefield, for which reason he deserved the scorn and opprobrium of the Muslim community. Such a man serves as the antithesis of the ideal martyr.[87] Thus it was that two early converts eagerly sought martyrdom, a Helper used martyrdom as a means for gaining remission of sins, and a late convert to Islam chose life on earth over martyrdom on the battlefield.

Chapter 6

The Martyrdom of the Beloved of the Messenger of God

It has been necessary from time to time to reconstruct these disparate [midrashic] texts and put them together much as an archaeologist-pottery expert puts together the broken pieces of a vase. It is only when they have all been joined in place that the original beauty of the article emerges.

—L. I. Rabinowitz, "The Study of a Midrash," 144

In future studies, it will be important to deal with the ways that midrash has been occulted in the Jewish-Christian-Moslem polysystem, and to discern the underground channels within this system in which it was kept alive as well.

—Daniel Boyarin, Intertextuality and the Reading of Midrash, *xii*

Compared to the foundation narratives of Judaism and Christianity, in which the father-son motif plays a central role, the Islamic foundation narrative is anomalous. The fact that none of Muḥammad's natural sons reached the age of maturity makes it appear as if God could not test Muḥammad by instructing him to sacrifice a beloved son.

Appearances can be deceptive. There is reason to believe that the father-son motif was initially an important component of the Islamic foundation narrative. Until the end of the first century A.H.—if not later—the early Muslim community recognized this motif and played with it, producing a typological variant of its Jewish and Christian counterparts. Following the martyrdom of Ḥusayn at Karbala in 60/680, however, the father-son motif was overshadowed by the father-grandson motif, with the result that the earlier motif quickly lost its importance and was pushed to the margins of the Muslim community's collective memory. The key to the recovery of the Islamic component of the Abrahamic typology is the figure of Zayd, the slave who was manumitted and adopted by Muḥammad ca. 605 C.E., whereupon his name was changed to Zayd b. Muḥammad. It is only when the space occupied by the Beloved of the Messenger of God within the collective memory of the early Muslim community has been returned to its original position at the center of the Islamic foundation narrative that it is possible to see in the twenty-first century what was clearly visible in the seventh and eighth centuries: the typological affinity between the father-son motif in Judaism, Christianity, and Islam: The sons of the Jewish foundation narrative are the *natural* born children of their fathers; the son of the Christian foundation narrative is the *supernaturally* born son of the Holy Spirit; and the son of the Islamic foundation narrative is the *adopted* son of his father. In all three instances, a key theological doctrine is linked to domestic relations within the family of the founder and, specifically, to the father-son motif: In Judaism, the notion of divine election emerges from the dynamics of Abraham's relationship with Ishmael and Isaac; in Christianity, the divinity of Christ emerges from God's relationship with Jesus; and in Islam, the finality of prophecy emerges from Muḥammad's relationship with Zayd. In all three cases, the theological doctrine is linked to the filial relationship between father and son, and in all three cases the integrity of the theological doctrine necessitated the marginalization of one or more members of the founder's immediate family: In Judaism, Ishmael had to be expelled and Esau deprived of his birthright so that only the Children of Israel would qualify as the Chosen People; in Christianity, Joseph had to be marginalized so that Jesus could be the Son of God; and in Islam, Zayd had to be repudiated and made to predecease Muḥammad in order to insure that Muḥammad could take his place as the Last Prophet.

Divine election, Christology, and the finality of prophecy are not the only doctrines linked to the father-son motif. The same motif plays a critical role in the doctrine of martyrdom: the willingness to suffer or die in order to demonstrate absolute commitment to a transcendent cause. Martyrdom is both a religious practice and a discourse about the performance of that practice, "a practice of dying for God and of talking about it."[1] Both the practice and the discourse appeared in the Near East for the first time in the second, third, and fourth centuries C.E., precisely the period in which rabbinic Judaism and Christianity emerged as two distinct religious entities.[2] Whereas Bowersock attributes the origins of this new doctrine exclusively to Christian authors, Boyarin argues that it is more accurate to conceptualize the emergence of this new doctrine as the combined work of "one complex religious family" composed of Greek-speaking Jews, Jewish Christians, Roman Christians, and rabbinic Jews. Indeed, he adds, the process whereby rabbinic Judaism and Christianity emerged as distinct and separate religious entities is directly related to the entanglements of rabbinic Jews and Christians with the concept of martyrdom.[3] Their disagreements notwithstanding, Bowersock and Boyarin both recognize that the Judeo-Christian martyrdom discourse was transmitted to the Muslims, either directly or, as is more likely, indirectly, through subterranean channels that have yet to be identified with precision.[4] In the present chapter, I shall attempt to identify one of the underground channels through which the Judeo-Christian tradition relating to martyrdom was transmitted to Muslims. The identification of this channel suggests that Boyarin's "one complex religious family" included Muslims living in Arabia and the Near East during the first century A.H.

The earliest Jewish and Christian martyrdom practices revolved around the idea of dying for the law. The first martyrs were responding to some form of religious persecution; for example, a command or decree that would require a believer to violate a religious prohibition. Rather than worship pagan idols, sacrifice to pagan gods or eat pagan food, these men and women chose to die a violent death.[5] Beginning in the late second century C.E., Jews and Christians began to seek out their own deaths for the sake of religion and its mandates. By choosing death, the martyr sought to fulfill the positive commandment to love God with all one's heart and all one's soul. Typically, the last words uttered by the Christian martyr would be the *nomen Christianus sum* or affirmation of Christian identity; and the last words uttered by the Jewish martyr would be the *Shema* or Unification of the Name.[6]

When the Islamic martyrdom discourse emerged in the seventh and eighth centuries C.E., its Judeo-Christian counterparts had reached an advanced stage of development even if they had not yet attained their final form. Like the rabbinic and Christian discourses, the Islamic discourse was closely linked to the process of identity formation. The jurists who developed the Islamic martyrdom discourse produced what is arguably a variant of the earlier discourses; and the storytellers who formulated the Islamic martyrdom narratives produced what are arguably variants of Jewish and Christian martyrdom narratives. The Islamic doctrine and its accompanying narratives are simultaneously connected to but distinct from the earlier doctrines and narratives. Like the Jewish or Christian martyr, the Muslim martyr (*shahīd*) is willing to give up his life for the sake of religion (*istishhād*). Like the Jewish or Christian martyr, he typically ends his life by affirming his identity as a Muslim, for example, by uttering the *shahāda* or credo of the faith: "There is no God but God and Muḥammad is the Prophet of God." But whereas the Jewish and Christian martyr typically responds to persecution by a powerful external force, the ideal Muslim martyr is the fighting martyr, a soldier who actively seeks death in battle for the sake of God and His religion. These differences notwithstanding, the Islamic discourse draws on many of the themes, motifs, and linguistic formulations found in the martyrdom discourses produced by rabbinic Jews and early Christians. As I shall attempt to demonstrate, the Muslims who circulated the stories about the martyrdom of Zayd were familiar with the martyrdom narratives of rabbinic Judaism and Christianity.[7]

Zayd exemplifies the fighting martyr, the soldier who is eager to lay down his life for the sake of Islam. In Chapter 5, I singled out for analysis Wāqidī's account of the Battle of Mu'ta, in part because it is the earliest extant account of the battle, and in part because, as noted at the outset of that chapter, it includes important material relating to Zayd that is not found in most other sources.[8] It is to this material that I now direct my attention.

Our concern here is with the opening *khabar* or narrative report in Wāqidī's account of the Battle of Muʾta, which begins with a single-strand *isnād*: "It was related to me by Rabīʿa b. ʿUthmān, on the authority of ʿUmar b. al-Ḥakam . . ." Rabīʿa b. ʿUthmān was a minor traditionist who is said to have transmitted a small number of *ḥadīth*s. According to Ibn Saʿd, he died in Medina in 154/770–71 during the caliphate of Abū Jaʿfar. At the time of his death, he is said to have been seventy-seven years old.[9] ʿUmar b. al-Ḥakam was a traditionist who died in Medina in 117/735 at the age of eighty, during the caliphate of Hishām b. ʿAbd al-Malik.[10] Let us assume, for the sake of argument, that the attribution of this report to ʿUmar b. al-Ḥakam is reliable and that he was born in the year 37 A.H. If ʿUmar was twenty years old at the time that he first put this report into circulation, the report might have existed as early as the middle of the first century, approximately forty years after the battle took place. If ʿUmar was closer to eighty years of age at the time he first put this report into circulation, then it might have been produced around the turn of the second/eighth century A.H., approximately one hundred years after the battle took place. In all likelihood, the report was first put into circulation sometime between the middle and end of the first century.

The opening narrative in Wāqidī's account of the Battle of Muʾta begins with a reference to the slaying of the messenger of the Messenger of God, al-Ḥārith b. ʿUmayr al-Azdī. Seeking revenge for the brutal and unprecedented murder of his messenger, Muḥammad traveled to al-Jurf where he gathered the men who would form the Army of Muʾta. Upon his arrival at the military staging ground, the Prophet did not at first issue any instructions regarding the order of command or rules of engagement. It was only after he had performed the afternoon prayer that he and his Companions formed a circle and began to deliberate on military matters. Coincidentally—or perhaps it was divine providence—the circle of men who had gathered around the Prophet included a Jew by the name of al-Nuʿmān b. Funḥuṣ (Phinehas).[11] This Jew—a marginal figure—was standing next to the Prophet when he issued his fateful—indeed, lethal—instructions regarding the order of command:[12]

Zayd b. Ḥāritha is the commander of the army. If Zayd b. Ḥāritha is killed, then Jaʿfar b. Abī Ṭālib [is the commander]. If Jaʿfar is killed, then ʿAbdallāh b. Rawāḥa [is the commander]. If ʿAbdallāh b. Rawāḥa is killed, then let the Muslims choose a man from among themselves and make him their [commander].[13]

When al-Nuʿmān b. Funḥuṣ heard this statement, he turned to the Prophet and said:

[O] Abū al-Qāsim, if you are a [true] prophet, then the men whose names you have specified, however many or few, will all be killed. Verily, whenever the Israelite prophets would appoint a man as the leader of an army, and say, "If so-and-so is killed," all of them would be killed, even if he specified the names of 100 men.[14]

At first glance, one may read this narrative as another example of a Jew or Christian who confirms Muḥammad's status as a true prophet. Let me suggest another reading of this narrative in which this obscure and otherwise unknown Jew plays the role of the intimate adversary. One might say that he is Satan in the guise of a Jew. Be that as it may, the Jew appeals to Muḥammad's instincts as Zayd's former adoptive father (and Jaʿfar's uncle) in an effort to expose him as a false prophet. Words have power, and that power is sometimes lethal. In Biblical Hebrew, *dābār*—often translated as *word*—signifies a *concentrated essence* or *inner character* of its real referent. In the minds of the Israelites, the verbal utterance of a true prophet is the very essence of future history and historical reality.[15] If Muḥammad was a true prophet, then the very words he had just uttered constituted a death sentence for the three commanders—including his former son Zayd and his nephew Jaʿfar—who, it will be recalled, was the Prophet's spit-and-image. The only way to commute this death sentence would be for Muḥammad to acknowledge that he was a false prophet. Muḥammad was being tested by a Jew who sought to undermine the foundation of the true religion even before that foundation had been firmly established. Whereas God instructed Abraham to sacrifice his beloved son, al-Nuʿmān b. Funḥuṣ warned Muḥammad that he was about to sacrifice the Beloved of the Messenger of God. The validity of the test depended on Muḥammad's understanding that his battle instructions—his very words—meant that Zayd, Jaʿfar and ʿAbdallāh b. Rawāḥa were heading to certain death. Note well: Muḥammad paid no heed to the Jew's advice. By choosing not to respond, Muḥammad was affirming his status as a true prophet, even if that affirmation entailed the sacrifice of Zayd and his co-commanders. Like Abraham in Genesis 22, Muḥammad passed the test—albeit with a crucial difference. In this instance there would be no last-minute animal substitute for the human sacrifice. Zayd and his co-commanders would fall—indeed they must fall—as martyrs bearing witness to the oneness of God and prophecy of Muḥammad.

The narrative continues: Al-Nuʿmān b. Funḥuṣ turned to Zayd and told him that his fate was inextricably linked to the truth of Muḥammad's claim to be a prophet. "Prepare your last will and testament," the Jew advised, "for you will never return to Muḥammad if he is a [true] prophet!" Now Zayd was being tested. In a very real sense, Zayd's entire life had unfolded in anticipation of this moment when he would be asked to surrender his life for the sake of God and His Prophet. Even if Zayd was no longer Muḥammad's son, he remained devoted and obedient. True to form, he rose to the occasion by uttering words that are recognizable as a variant of the second half of the *shahāda* or credo of the faith, "I bear witness that he [viz., Muḥammad] is a prophet." To which he added, "He speaks the truth [and] is veracious (*bārr*)."[16] Zayd's reference to the Prophet's veraciousness is a play on words, an allusion to Q. 3:92, "You will not attain piety (*birr*) until you spend some of what you love; and whatever you spend, God is aware of it." In the present instance, Muḥammad attained piety by spending (or sacrificing) Zayd, the Beloved of the Messenger of God.[17] Note well: Zayd is portrayed here as a willing participant in the sequence of events that would result in his death and martyrdom. Zayd was fully prepared for death. Recall that he ran into the Garden (Chapter 5), a detail which suggests that he was eager to lay down his life for the sake of Islam.

Wāqidī's account of the battle may be summarized as follows: Following the brutal killing of the messenger of the Messenger of God, Muḥammad accompanied the Muslim soldiers to al-Jurf, where he did not issue the battle instructions until he had performed the noon prayer. After the Prophet specified the order of command, he was confronted by a Jew who adopted an advisory role—or perhaps it would be more accurate to say that his role was adversarial. The Jew warned Muḥammad that his very words constituted a death sentence for the three commanders. The Prophet, however, paid no heed to the Jew, refusing to dignify his assertion with a response. Seemingly oblivious to the presence of Jaʿfar and ʿAbdallāh b. Rawāḥa, the Jew turned to Zayd and warned him that if Muḥammad was in fact a true prophet, he—that is to say, Zayd—would not return from the field of battle. Unlike Muḥammad, Zayd did respond, even if his response was not what the Jew wanted to hear: Zayd bore witness that Muḥammad is the Messenger of God, thereby affirming his willingness to die for the sake of God and His religion. The Prophet and other noncombatants accompanied the Army of Muʾta to the Farewell Pass, where, after an emotional leave-taking, the soldiers marched off in the direction of Muʾta in southern Jordan. Just before the battle was engaged, Zayd was confronted by Satan, who sought to entice him with the pleasures of this world—albeit unsuccessfully (the encounter was repeated with Jaʿfar). Without a moment's hesitation and with no apparent concern for his own safety, Zayd dismounted his horse and entered the fray. At the very moment that he was slain, he entered the Garden, running. The primary witness to the martyrdom of Zayd and his fellow commanders was Muḥammad, who, although physically present in Medina, was the recipient of a miraculous vision that made it possible for him to see the events on the battlefield as they unfolded in southern Jordan.

Note well the underlying themes of the Islamic narrative: the testing of a father and his erstwhile son; prayer prior to a life-threatening event; desire for the remission of sin; leave-taking and a concern about return; the adversarial function performed first by the Jew and then by Satan; eagerness for death; ascension and eternal life; and a miraculous vision. In this chapter, I shall argue that the Islamic narrative originated as a sacred legend, a playful and creative revision of the martyrdom narratives of rabbinic Judaism and early

Christianity, crafted by Muslims who were familiar with Jewish and Christian texts. If there is merit to this argument, then it should be possible to connect the key elements of the Islamic narrative about Zayd's martyrdom to an earlier corpus of rabbinic and Christian narratives. For our purposes, it will be sufficient to focus attention on Jewish and rabbinic texts, for reasons that will soon become clear.[18] We begin with the biblical account of the binding of Isaac in Genesis 22, a narrative that plays a central role in the respective martyrdom discourses of both Judaism and Christianity. Virtually unknown is the importance of Genesis 22 to the narrative account of Zayd's martyrdom.

The Biblical Account: Genesis 22:1–19

The biblical account of the binding of Isaac is found in Genesis 22:1–19. Shortly after Abraham had sent his older son Ishmael off into the wilderness, God tested the patriarch by ordering him to take his younger son Isaac to the land of Moriah, where he was to offer him as a burnt offering on a mountaintop. Verses 1–14 read as follows.

1 Some time afterward, God put Abraham to the test. He said to him, "Abraham," and he answered, "Here I am."
2 And He said, "Take your son, your favored one, Isaac, whom you love, and go to the land of Moriah, and offer him there as a burnt offering on one of the heights that I will point out to you."
3 So early in the morning, Abraham saddled his ass and took with him two of his servants and his son Isaac. He split the wood for the burnt offering, and he set out for the place of which God had told him.
4 On the third day Abraham looked up and saw the place from afar.
5 Then Abraham said to his servants (*neʿarav*), "You stay here with the ass. The boy (*naʿar*) and I will go up there; we will worship and we will return to you."
6 Abraham took the wood for the burnt offering and put it on his son Isaac. He himself took the firestone and the knife; and the two walked off together.
7 Then Isaac said to his father Abraham, "Father!" And he answered, "Yes, my son." And he said, "Here are the firestone and the wood; but where is the sheep for the burnt offering?"
8 And Abraham said, "God will see to the sheep for His burnt offering, my son." And the two of them walked on together.
9 They arrived at the place of which God had told him. Abraham built an altar there; he laid out the wood; he bound his son Isaac; he laid him on the altar, on top of the wood.
10 And Abraham picked up the knife to slay his son.
11 Then an angel of the Lord called to him from heaven: "Abraham! Abraham!" And he answered, "Here I am."
12 And he said, "Do not raise your hand against the boy, or do anything to him. For now I know that you fear God, since you have not withheld your son, your favored one, from Me."
13 When Abraham looked up, his eye fell upon a ram, caught in the thicket by its horns. So Abraham went and took the ram and offered it up as a burnt offering in place of his son.

14 And Abraham named that site Adonai-yireh, whence the present saying, "On the mount of the Lord there is vision."

Five points merit attention, beginning with the theme of vision. Note how, in v. 2, God promises to make the site of the sacrifice visible to Abraham; in vv. 4 and 13, Abraham "looks up"; and in v. 14 Abraham renames the mountain as Adonai-yireh, which means "and God will see to," an appellation that generated the maxim, "On the mount of the Lord there is vision." Second, the biblical text identifies Abraham's son as Isaac no less than five times (vv. 2, 3, 6, 7, and 9). Third, the text repeatedly links Abraham *and* Isaac, father *and* son: In v. 3 Abraham takes "his son Isaac"; in v. 5 Abraham tells his servants, "the boy and I will go up there . . . and we will return to you"; in v. 6 "the two walked off together"; in v. 8 "the two of them walked on together"; and in v. 9 "they" arrived at the desired location. Fourth, Abraham tells the two unidentified servants that he and the boy will worship before returning. Fifth, and most important, is the annunciation of a divine test (v. 1) designed to measure Abraham's devotion to God. The biblical text suggests that, but for the last-minute intervention of the angel and the sudden appearance of the ram, Abraham would have sacrificed Isaac. Thus it was that the human sacrifice was averted and replaced by animal sacrifice. As a substitute for Isaac, Abraham slaughtered the ram and offered it as a burnt offering on the altar. Abraham passed the test. God was pleased.

Whereas it is Abraham who stands at the center of Genesis 22, one of the many questions raised by this enigmatic narrative has to do with the role played by Isaac in the dramatic episode enacted on that mountain in the land of Moriah. Alas, the biblical text does not specify Isaac's age at the time. If he was only a boy (*naʿar*), as specified in v. 5, then he may have been an innocent and unwitting victim. If he was a physically mature adult, one wonders about his state of mind and willingness to be sacrificed. On this point, the biblical text is equivocal. After father and son have trekked through the wilderness for three days, Isaac exclaims in v. 7, "Father (*avī*)! . . . Here are the firestone and the wood; but where is the sheep for the slaughter?" In his response Abraham reassures Isaac that God will provide the sacrificial offering—presumably a sheep—whereupon father and son walk on in silence. The text leaves the reader uncertain about Isaac's state of mind. It is possible that Isaac's exclamation in v. 7 signals his unwillingness to be sacrificed; but it is also possible that it signals his willing acceptance of his role as a sacrificial victim.

If the biblical account ended with v. 14, there would be no escaping the conclusion that Isaac survived his ordeal. The continuation of the pericope introduces several narrative elements that point in another direction.

15 The angel of the Lord called to Abraham a second time from heaven,
16 and said, "By Myself I swear, the Lord declares: Because you have done this and have not withheld your son, your favored one,

17 I will bestow my blessing upon you and make your descendants as numerous as the stars of the heaven and the sands of the seashore; and your descendants shall seize the gates of their foes.
18 All the nations of the earth shall bless themselves by your descendants, because you have obeyed My command."
19 Abraham then returned to his servants, and they departed together for Beer-sheba; and Abraham stayed in Beer-sheba.

It is curious that in vv. 15–19, there is no mention of Isaac and only a single reference to "your son" (v. 16). It also is curious that the covenant is established between the Lord and the descendants of Abraham. In vv. 17–18, the Lord refers to "your descendants" (*zarʿaka*, from *zeraʿ* or *seed*), on three separate occasions, without any further specification. If the biblical account included only vv. 15–19—that is to say, if vv. 1–14 did not exist—one might conclude that the son who accompanied Abraham was not Isaac but Ishmael (in v. 5, the noun *naʿar* is used to signify both the two unnamed servants and the unnamed son); and that the covenant was cut not with the Children of Israel but with the Children of Abraham, that is to say, with the Ishmaelites, the Edomites, *and* the Israelites—which is more or less how the biblical narrative has been understood by Muslim scholars since the end of the second century A.H.[19] Our concern here, however, is not with the Islamic understanding of Genesis 22 but rather with literary and thematic connections between the narrative expansions of the biblical account (on which see below) and the Islamic narrative about the martyrdom of Zayd.

A comparison of the first and second parts of the pericope raises additional questions. In vv. 3, 5, 6, 8, and 9, the text draws attention to the pairing of father and son, Abraham and Isaac. In v. 5, Abraham promises the servants, "We will return to you." In v. 19, however, it is only Abraham who returns to his servants, it is only Abraham who, together with his servants, departs for Beer-sheba; and it is only Abraham who stays in Beer-sheba. Where was Isaac? Was he still on the mountain? Had he returned by himself? Is it possible that something happened to Isaac on the mountain that prevented him from returning with his father?[20]

Narrative Expansions of the Biblical Account: Targum, Midrash, and the Syriac Tradition

The process whereby the Book of Genesis took its canonical shape has been much debated and remains a contentious issue among biblical scholars. For our purposes, it is sufficient to note that the biblical text was fixed sometime between 450 B.C.E. and the end of the first century C.E.[21]

Although the establishment of a fixed, canonical text placed certain limits on the interpretive enterprise, it did not interfere with imaginative retellings of the biblical narratives. When Aramaic and Syriac replaced Hebrew as the daily spoken language of the Jews, a need arose for vernacular translations of the Hebrew Bible that might be used in the daily liturgy. The resulting Aramaic translations are known as *targûmîm* (sg. *targûm*) and the Syriac translations are known as *peshitta*. These so-called translations often contain narrative expansions on the biblical text, material that may go back to the third and second centuries B.C.E., even if the earliest extant *targums* date only to the first century C.E.[22]

Related to but distinct from the *targums* is the genre of writing known as *midrash* (pl. *midrashîm*).[23] Like the *targums* and *peshitta*, *midrash* also was produced for liturgical purposes; in addition, however, *midrash* was a product of both scholarly examination of the biblical text (in schools and academies) and the process of storytelling. There are two primary types of *midrash*: *halakhic* or legal *midrash* focuses on the interpretation of biblical laws, and *aggadic* or narrative *midrash* focuses on nonlegal or narrative material in the Bible. One finds considerable *midrash* in the Talmud, which is composed of two components: (1) the *Mishnah* or Oral law, redacted by R. Judah ha-Nasi ca. 200 C.E., preserves the views of five generations of Tannaim or rabbinic sages who lived in Israel ca. 70–200 C.E.; (2) the *Gemara* or Written Law preserves the commentary on the *Mishnah* produced by eight generations of Amoraim or scholars who lived in Palestine and/or Babylonia ca. 200–500 C.E.

Aggadic midrash often takes the form of statements attributed to prominent rabbinic authorities who addressed difficulties in the biblical text, sought to harmonize inconsistencies, drew analogies and parallels between seemingly unrelated texts, filled in gaps, and, generally, sought to make the biblical text relevant to a contemporary audience. Our concern here is with the postbiblical treatment of Genesis 22:1–19. Although clearly based on the biblical text, the *midrashic* expansions sometimes take the understanding of the biblical story in a new and unexpected direction.

In a masterful essay, Shalom Spiegel collected and analyzed an impressive number of *targums*, *midrashim*, and other texts relating to the *aqedah* or binding of Isaac.[24] The meticulous scholarly work performed by Spiegel leads inexorably to the following discovery. Not only does a *midrashic* reading of Genesis 22:1–19 invite the assumption that something did happen to Isaac on that mountaintop in the land of Moriah, but this is how the text was read and understood by several rabbinic authorities in late antiquity and in medieval times. The *midrashic* assertion that something did happen to Isaac has been reinforced in modern times by scholars who have studied and analyzed Genesis 22:1–19. Suffice it to say that there is widespread support for the notion that this pericope is the work of a later redactor who spliced together two separate documents, each composed by a different author. Spiegel himself entertains the possibility that the older of these two documents is an archaic remnant of a period in which the Israelite community did in fact engage in the practice of sacrificing first-born sons.[25] Look again. In v. 16, the Lord declares,

"Because you have done this," and in v. 18 the Lord says, "because you have obeyed My command." What had Abraham done? Which command did the patriarch obey? In vv. 1–19, the only command attributed directly to God is that Abraham sacrifice his son Isaac as a burnt offering on a high place in the land of Moriah (v. 2). Is it conceivable—Heaven forbid—that Abraham did obey God's command to offer his beloved son as a burnt offering? Is it possible that the sacrifice of the ram was not a substitute for the human sacrifice but a supplement to it? Does this explain why it is only Abraham who returns from the mountain?

A close reading of Genesis 22:1–19 raises three interrelated questions. What role did Isaac play in the events that unfolded on that mountain in the land of Moriah? Why is it that the biblical text does not mention Isaac's return from the mountain? And is it possible that Abraham did sacrifice his beloved son? These questions were raised and answered by several postbiblical authors.

What Role Did Isaac Play?

The apocryphal text called 4 Maccabees is part homily, part philosophical discourse. It was written in Greek, perhaps in Antioch, in the last quarter of the first century B.C.E. by someone who, although influenced by Hellenism, identified as a Jew. Set during the reign of Antiochus IV Epiphanes (r. 175–64 B.C.E.), the book focuses on Jews who resisted the Seleucid emperor's efforts to force them to convert to Hellenism. In response to decrees that would have required them to violate negative prohibitions of Jewish law (*halakha*), these Jews willingly chose to suffer torture and painful death in order to demonstrate their loyalty to God and His people. The author invokes the example of these brave and heroic men (and at least one woman) to support his thesis that pious reason invariably triumphs over irrational emotions such as desire and fear.[26]

After relating how an old man named Eleazar was tortured and put to death for his refusal to comply with a royal decree that would have required the consumption of defiling food, the author tells the story of a mother and her seven sons who also refused to comply with this decree. Having witnessed the sorry fate of Eleazar, the family knew what awaited them. Before issuing the order to torture them, however, Antiochus ("the tyrant") made every possible effort to persuade the seven sons to choose life over death. In the following speech, the tyrant dangles the allure of power and the trappings of this world before the seven sons.

> Young men, with favorable feelings I admire each and every one of you, and greatly respect the beauty and the number of such brothers. Not only do I advise you not to display the same madness as that of the old man who has just been tortured, but I also exhort you to yield to me and enjoy my friendship. Just as I am able to punish those who disobey my orders, so I can be a benefactor to those who obey me. Trust me, then, and you will have positions of authority in my government if you will renounce the

ancestral tradition of your national life. Enjoy your youth by adopting the Greek way of life and by changing your manner of living. (4 Macc. 8:5–8)

The seven brothers ignored the tyrant's entreaties and each one suffered a gruesome death. As for their mother, she made no attempt to dissuade her sons from choosing death. To the contrary, she "urged each child separately and all of them together . . . on to death for religion's sake" (4 Macc. 14:12; cf. 16:14). When she herself was about to be seized and tortured, "she threw herself into the flames so that no one might touch her body" (4 Macc. 17:1). By refusing to violate Jewish law and choosing death over life, the seven children and their mother were engaging in the practice that would come to be known as *martyrdom* in the second century C.E.—even if, as Bowersock has noted, that word does not occur anywhere in this text.[27]

The author of 4 Maccabees makes explicit rhetorical use of the father-son motif in Genesis 22, linking Abraham's willingness to sacrifice Isaac to the mother's willingness to sacrifice her seven sons. The mother, he says, "was of the same mind as Abraham" (4 Macc. 14:20). Like Abraham, she was unaffected by sympathy for her children. If Abraham was willing to sacrifice his only son, she was willing to sacrifice all seven of hers; indeed, she did Abraham one better—she did sacrifice her sons, all seven of them. Conversely—and this is our concern here—if the seven sons were willing to be sacrificed, so too was Isaac—even if this detail is nowhere found in Genesis 22. When the mother urges her sons to die rather than violate the law, she herself is made to draw a connection not only with Abraham but also with Isaac.

For His sake also our father Abraham was zealous to sacrifice his son Isaac, the ancestor of our nation; and when Isaac saw his father's hand wielding a knife and descending upon him, he did not cower. (4 Macc. 16:20)

Isaac did not cower. The same point is made earlier in the narrative when one brother says to the others: "Remember whence you came and the father by whose hand Isaac would have submitted to being slain for the sake of religion" (4 Macc. 13:12). Note well: Isaac was prepared to give himself to be sacrificed for the sake of his religion. He was not a naive and unwitting victim but a conscious and willing participant who *did not cower* and who, had it not been for the sudden appearance of the ram, *would have submitted* to being sacrificed. In the mind of the author of 4 Maccabees, it was not only the father but also the son who served as a role model: Abraham is the parent who is willing to sacrifice a beloved son; Isaac is the beloved son who is willing to be sacrificed—even if, in the end, the human sacrifice is averted.

If 4 Maccabees is a retelling of Genesis 22, then the narrative account of the Battle of Muʾta may be read as a retelling of both 4 Maccabees and Genesis 22. With respect to Muḥammad's willingness to sacrifice Zayd (and Jaʿfar), it may be said that the Prophet was of the same mind as both the mother of

4 Maccabees and the Abraham of Genesis 22. Like them, Muḥammad was unaffected by sympathy for the Beloved of the Messenger of God. All three parents were willing—one might say eager—to sacrifice their sons. With respect to Zayd's willingness to be sacrificed—as evidenced by his disregard for the advice of al-Nuʿmān b. Funḥuṣ—it may be said that he was of the same mind as the seven brothers of 4 Maccabees 8 and the Isaac of Genesis 22. Zayd freely and willingly chose to die for the sake of religion, just as the seven brothers affirmed their willingness to "fight the sacred and noble battle for religion" (4 Macc. 9:24), and just as Isaac affirmed his willingness to die for the sake of his religion. Zayd faced death bravely, as did the seven sons, as did Isaac, who did not cower. That Zayd was eager for death is evidenced by his running into the Garden, just as the seven brothers "ran the course toward immortality" (4 Macc. 14:5). Finally, in all three narratives the theme of vision plays a central role. It is only by virtue of a miraculous vision that Muḥammad witnesses the martyrdom of Zayd, just as the mother personally witnesses the gruesome torture of her seven sons, just as in Genesis 22:14 God makes the site of the sacrifice visible to Abraham ("On the mount of the Lord there is a vision").

Isaac's willingness to be sacrificed is also mentioned in the *Jewish Antiquities* (*JA*) of Josephus Flavius. This text, part rewritten Bible, part historical chronicle, part apologia, was written in Greek ca. 93–94 C.E., during the last year of the reign of the emperor Flavius Domitian, the son of Vespasian. Josephus wrote the text in response to a request from his Gentile patron for a full account of Jewish culture and religion. The author argued that Jews deserved to be respected because of their long and illustrious history. *JA* is divided into two parts: Books 1–10 contain a retelling of the biblical narrative from Creation to Daniel; Books 11–20 contain a retelling of the biblical narrative from Cyrus to ca. 140 B.C.E., at which point the author runs out of biblical material and continues on his own, extending the historical narrative to the Jewish revolt against Rome which lasted from 66 to 70 C.E.[28]

The retelling of Genesis 22 is found in Book 1, chapter 13, pars. 222–36. Whereas in Genesis 22 Abraham tells Isaac that God will provide the sacrificial offering, in *JA* Abraham explicitly informs Isaac that he will be the sacrificial victim. Abraham even provides a rationale for his decision, explaining that he has chosen God over his beloved son so that both father and son might be closer to God. To this explanation, Isaac responds:

> Isaac received these words with joy. He exclaimed that he deserved never to have been born at all, were he to reject the decision of God and of his father, and not readily resign himself to what was the will of both, seeing that, were this the resolution of his father alone, it would have been impious to disobey; and with that he rushed to the altar and his doom. (*JA*, Book 1, par. 232)

Isaac understood that his selection as a sacrificial victim had been made not only by his father Abraham but also by God Himself. As a true believer, Isaac had no choice in the matter after God and his father had decided it—just as in Q. 33:36 it is said: "When God and His messenger have decided a matter, it is not for any believing man or woman to have any choice in the affair." Isaac's selection had been predetermined. It was, in the language of the Qur'ān, *sunnat allāh*, or God's practice (Q. 33:38). Isaac was compelled to accept his own sacrifice and at the same time joyful; paradoxically, he was acting in compliance with a Divine Decree and also a willing participant in the *aqedah*. It is as if the very purpose of his brief earthly existence was to signal his obedience to God. In this respect, Isaac became the paradigm of the voluntary martyr. The typological detail bears repeating: Isaac rushed to the altar (*JA*, Book 1, par. 232), the seven sons ran towards immortality (4 Macc. 14:5), and Zayd ran into the Garden (Wāqidī, *Maghāzī*, 2:762).

Isaac is also portrayed as a willing participant in the *aqedah* in the *Liber Antiquitatum Biblicarum* (*LAB*) or *Biblical Antiquities* of Pseudo-Philo. The Hebrew original was probably written between 70 and 135 C.E. and is thus roughly contemporaneous with *JA*. Its purpose was to warn Jewish laymen of the dangers to their faith and to provide them with support and encouragement in the traumatic aftermath of the destruction of the Second Temple. The *midrash*ic style of *LAB* suggests that many of the traditions preserved in the text predate the fall of Jerusalem in 70 C.E. *LAB* was translated into Greek, and the Greek translation was, in turn, translated into Latin in the fourth century. Only the Latin text is currently extant.

Originally attributed to Philo of Alexandria, the true author of *LAB* is unknown. Like *JA*, the treatise belongs to the genre of rewritten bible, and it recounts the history of the Israelites from Creation to the death of Saul. Curiously, *LAB* does not mention the *aqedah* in connection with Genesis 22, although it does refer to the *aqedah* in connection with three other biblical narratives: the divine revelation to Balaam in Numbers (*LAB* 18:5); the Song of Deborah in Judges (*LAB* 32:1–4); and the answer of Sela to Jephthah in Numbers (*LAB* 40:2). Only the second of these three narratives is relevant to the present investigation. In Judges 4, we find a retelling in prose of the Song of Deborah in Judges 5: When the Israelite general Barak refused to go to battle against the Canaanites unless accompanied by Deborah the prophetess, she agreed, but prophesized that Barak would not achieve final victory over the Canaanite general Sisera. The prophecy was fulfilled when Sisera was slain by a woman, Yael, who, after inviting Sisera into her tent and offering him hospitality, waited until the general had fallen asleep and then slew him by driving a tent peg through his head.

In Pseudo-Philo's retelling of the Song of Deborah, the prophetess links the Israelite victory over the Canaanites to God's testing of Abraham in Genesis 22:1–19. Here the testing of Abraham is said to have resulted from the anger of the angels over Sarah's conception of Isaac in her old age (*LAB* 32:1). It was because of the jealousy of the angels that God commanded Abraham to "Kill the fruit of your body for me and offer for me the sacrifice which was given you by me." In compliance with the divine command, the patriarch sets out with his unidentified son. As in *JA* so too in *LAB* Abraham tells his son that he is about to be offered as a sacrifice to "the one who gave you to me" (*LAB* 32:2). After the patriarch has informed his son that he is to be the sacrificial offering, the son responds as follows:

> Listen to me, father. If a lamb from the flock is accepted in an offering of the hands with an odor of sweetness, and if for the evil acts of men animals are set aside for slaughter while man on the contrary is appointed for the inheritance of the world, how can you say to me now, "Come and inherit a life without danger and a time without limit?" But what if I had not been born to be offered in sacrifice to him who made me? However, my blessedness will be upon all men because there will be no other sacrifice [like this]—about me generations will be instructed and through me peoples will come to see that the Lord had made the soul of a man worthy to be a sacrifice. (*LAB* 32:3)

Here Isaac freely and joyfully expresses his willingness to serve as the lamb or sacrificial victim. He links the human sacrifice to other sacrifices that are offered to God and accepted by Him as atonement for human sin. He understands that as a result of his self-sacrifice, future generations of Jews will benefit. As in Genesis 22, the human sacrifice is averted at the last minute. Whereas in Genesis 22 it is an angel of the Lord who calls out from heaven instructing Abraham not to sacrifice Isaac, here it is God who manifests Himself to Abraham in the form of a voice that says: "Do not kill your son—do not destroy the fruit of your body. For now I have made you appear to those who know you not and I have closed the mouths of those who are always speaking evil of you. I shall always remember you, and your name and his will abide from one generation to the next" (*LAB* 32:4). As a reward for his obedience, Isaac—the beloved son—was granted immortality: his name would be remembered by God for all eternity. Similarly, as a reward for his obedience, Zayd—another beloved son—was granted immortality: God uttered his name—a distinction enjoyed by no other Companion of the Prophet—and the divine utterance was recorded in Q. 33:37; thus, Zayd's name will be remembered by mankind so long as the Qur'ān continues to be recited—presumably, until God inherits the earth.

In 4 Maccabees, *JA*, and *LAB*, Isaac is portrayed as a willing and active participant in the *aqedah*. The *midrash*ic tradition reflected in these three texts surely draws on an ancient tradition embodied in Aramaic *targum*s and Syriac homilies, to which we now turn our attention. The oldest extant complete *targum* to Genesis 22 is the text known as *Codex Neofiti 1*, which in all likelihood was written in the fourth century C.E. Here the focus of attention shifts from Abraham to Isaac. The father tells his son that a lamb for the sacrifice will be prepared and, if not, then the son will be the sacrificial lamb. When Abraham lifts the knife to slay his son, Isaac asks his father to tie him well so that the sacrifice will not be spoiled by the movements of his body.[29]

Isaac's willingness to be sacrificed is also described in the *Fragmentary Targum* on Genesis 22:10:

> Abraham stretched out his hand and took the knife to kill Isaac his son. Isaac answered and said to Abraham his father: "Bind my hands properly that I may not struggle in the time of my pain and disturb you and render your offering unfit."[30]

Another reference to Isaac's willingness to participate in the *aqedah* is found in a *midrash*ic commentary on Deut. 6:5, the biblical verse which famously instructs the believer to "love the Lord your God with all your heart and all your soul and all your might." In *Sifre Deuteronomy*, redacted in the fourth century C.E., Rabbi Meir, a third generation Palestinian Tanna who lived in the middle of the second century C.E., explains that the Deuteronomic phrase "with all your soul" refers to Isaac, "who bound himself upon the altar" (*Sifre Deut.* 32).[31] As in *Codex Neofiti 1* and the *Fragmentary Targum*, so too here it is not Abraham who binds Isaac but Isaac who binds himself.

Our final reference to Isaac's willingness to participate in the *aqedah* is found in two verse homilies on Genesis 22 composed by the Syrian Orthodox poet Jacob of Serugh (d. 521 C.E.). One homily is entitled "On Abraham and his types,"[32] the other "On Abraham and Isaac."[33] As in the *midrashim* and *targumim*, Isaac understands that he is to be the sacrifice and he willingly accepts his role. At one point in the first homily, Isaac says to Abraham:

> Perform your will: if the knife is sharpened against me I will not draw back; if the fire is kindled for me, I will hold my ground; if the lamb is to go up bound, here are my hands, but if you are going to slaughter me unbound, I have no objection. (92)[34]

Later in the text, Isaac deduces that he is to be the sacrifice: "When Isaac saw that there was no lamb, he asked where it was; when he knew that he was the sacrifice, he was not perturbed" (94).[35]

Did Abraham Sacrifice Isaac?

The *targumim*, *midrashim*, and Syriac homilies teach inter alia that Isaac bound himself on the altar; 4 Maccabees teaches that Isaac was prepared to give himself to be sacrificed for the sake of religion; Josephus says that Isaac "rushed to the altar and his doom"; and *LAB* teaches that Isaac freely expressed his willingness to serve as the sacrificial victim. In none of these narratives was the sacrifice carried out. However, from the assertion that Abraham was willing to sacrifice Isaac and that Isaac was willing to be sacrificed, it was only a short step to the assertion that Abraham did in fact sacrifice Isaac.

The view that Abraham actually fulfilled God's command to sacrifice his beloved son is articulated in the *Pesikta de-Rab Kahana* (*PRK*) a collection of sermons that is thought to have been composed between 500 and 700 C.E.—precisely the period in which Islam was emerging on the stage of Near Eastern history.[36] A reference to the fulfillment of the human sacrifice on Mount Moriah is found in the *PRK* commentary on Psalm 102:20–21:

> 20 For He looks down from His holy height; the Lord beholds the earth from heaven
>
> 21 to hear the groans of the prisoner, to release those condemned to death (*lishmôʿa enqat asîr le-fateaḥ bĕnê tĕmûtâ*).

This text teaches that the reference in v. 21 to God's release of "those condemned to death" means that it is only because Isaac "offered (*hiqrîb*) himself on the altar" that God "will revive the dead." Note, first, the use of the perfect tense (*hiqrîb*), which suggests that the offering was not merely contemplated but also completed, and, second, the connection drawn between the fulfillment of the sacrifice and the notion of resurrection. According to the rabbinic doctrine of the Merit of the Fathers (*zekhût avôt*), the merit conferred upon Father Isaac as a result of his being sacrificed was transmitted to later generations of Jews who, like Isaac, enjoyed—and presumably will continue to enjoy—the blessing of bodily resurrection.[37]

The assertion in *PRK* that Isaac "offered himself" on the altar may explain why it was only Abraham who returned from the mountain. If the human sacrifice was fulfilled, then Isaac did not merely disappear. He died on the mountain. At the same time that this reading answers one of our three questions, it raises a fourth, seemingly intractable question. If Isaac died on the mountain, how are we to explain his miraculous reappearance in Genesis 24:62 ("Isaac had just come back from the vicinity of Beer-lahai-roi") at precisely the moment when the trusted servant returns from Mesopotamia with Rebecca, who had been selected as Isaac's wife? How is it—from a *midrash*ic perspective—that the sacrificial victim is now alive and well?

The response to this question points clearly to the entanglements of rabbinic Judaism and Christianity. *Pirkei de Rabbi Eliezer* (*PRE*), another retelling of the Hebrew Bible, begins with Creation and no doubt was intended to continue until the death of Moses—even if the last part of the text was not completed. This work was compiled in the eighth century C.E., shortly after the rise of Islam—at just about the time that the narrative account of Zayd's martyrdom at the Battle of Mu'ta was being formulated. In Chapter 30, the following statement is attributed to R. Judah:

> When the sword touched Isaac's throat his soul flew clean out of him. And when He let His voice be heard from between the two *cherubim*, "Lay not thy hand upon the lad," his soul returned to his body. Then he [viz. Abraham] unbound him, and he [viz.

Isaac] rose. Thus did Isaac come to know the Resurrection of the dead as taught by the Torah: all of the dead will come back to life in the future; whereupon he began to recite, "Blessed art Thou, O Lord, who revives the dead."[38]

As in *PRK*, so too in *PRE*, the text suggests that the sacrifice was completed ("the sword touched Isaac's throat"), as a result of which Isaac died ("his soul flew clean out of him"), but no sooner had his soul departed from his body than he was given a new life ("his soul returned to his body"). Abraham now loosened the ropes that he had used to bind his son to the altar, whereupon the newly reborn Isaac ascended to Heaven ("rose"), where, as we learn from other texts, he remained for three years, recovering from the wound inflicted by his father.[39] It was only after the wound had healed that he returned to earth, as it is written, "Isaac had just come back" (Gen. 24:62).

The contention that Isaac was sacrificed, given new life, rose to Heaven, and returned to earth is surely related to the Christian doctrine of the crucifixion and resurrection of Jesus. The historical relationship between the respective Jewish and Christian doctrines is a crux that has exercised the minds of biblical scholars and theologians for more than a century. For our purposes, it is sufficient to note that the rabbinic assertion that Isaac rose to Heaven is related to the absence of any explicit reference to the notion of bodily resurrection in the Hebrew Bible. This theological gap was remedied inter alia through rabbinic *midrash*. The reference to Isaac's resurrection is contained in a statement attributed to R. Judah in which the rabbi says—or is made to say—that the biblical text itself bears witness to the doctrine of resurrection ("as taught by the Torah")—which it clearly does not. The example of Isaac, who was resurrected, paves the way for the resurrection of all of the dead, as reflected in the daily prayer ("Blessed art Thou, O Lord, who revives the dead"). Again, it is only because of the merit and virtue of Father Isaac that resurrection is accessible to all.[40]

Satan and His Disguises

In Wāqidī's account of the Battle of Muʾta, Muḥammad has a vision which makes him an eyewitness to the events unfolding in southern Jordan. In Medina, the Prophet informs his Companions that just before the battle was engaged, Satan appeared to Zayd and attempted to dissuade him from participating in the upcoming battle. Zayd rejected Satan's enticements, was martyred, and ran into the Garden. Like other motifs examined in this chapter, the figure of Satan can be traced back to earlier Jewish martyrdom texts.

One of the earliest narrative expansions on Genesis 22:1–19 is found in the Book of Jubilees, which was probably written sometime after ca. 164 and before 100 B.C.E.[41] Although the Hebrew original is no longer extant, there are four complete manuscripts from the fifteenth and sixteenth centuries in

Ethiopic, as well as fragments from a Syriac translation. In addition, as many as fifteen early Jubilee scrolls, all written in Hebrew, were discovered at Qumran between 1947 and 1956.[42] Like the *targums*, *JA*, and *LAB*, the Book of Jubilees belongs to the genre of rewritten bible. The author of this text was a Jewish sectarian who rewrote the biblical account of events from Creation to the departure of the Israelites from Egypt (Ex. 12). What is distinctive about the Book of Jubilees is that the biblical narrative is retold from the perspective of an angel.

The retelling of the *aqedah* in Jub. 17:15–18:19 includes several narrative elements for which there is no basis in the biblical text, including a figure identified as Mastema.[43] The Hebrew noun *masṭema* signifies *hatred*, *hostility*, *harassment*, *enmity*, or *persecution*.[44] The word occurs only twice in the Hebrew Bible, in Hosea 9:7–8:

7 The prophet was distraught,
The inspired man driven mad
By constant harassment (*masṭema*)
8 Ephraim watches for my God
As for the prophet
Fowlers' snares are on all his paths,
Harassment (*masṭema*) in the House of his God.

Whereas in Hosea *masṭema* is a simple noun that signifies *harassment*, in Jubilees *masṭema* is personified as Mastema the prince of the demons, a figure who is identical with Satan/the Adversary. In Jubilees, God does not perform any act that might be deemed unworthy of the Divinity; all such acts are performed instead by Mastema. Thus, it is not God Himself but Mastema who, with God's permission, tests human beings, seeking to identify the wicked and destroy them; and it is Mastema who persuades God to issue the command that Abraham sacrifice Isaac:

And the prince Mastema came and said before God, "Behold, Abraham loves Isaac his son, and he delights in him above all things else; bid him offer him as a burnt-offering on the altar, and Thou wilt see if he will do this command, and Thou wilt know if he is faithful in everything wherein Thou dost try him. (Jub. 17:16)

In Jubilees 18:8 (*ad* Gen. 22:10), Abraham stretches forth his hand to take the knife to slay Isaac his son, but the Lord instructs the patriarch "not to lay a hand on the lad"—as reported by an angel who was standing in the presence of Abraham and the prince of the Mastema (Jub. 18:9). As a result of Abraham's demonstrated willingness to sacrifice his son, "the prince of the Mastema was put to shame" (Jub. 18:12).

Mastema drops out of the Jewish tradition, only to reappear as Satan, a figure whose association with the *aqedah* runs deep. In the Mishnaic period, the

Tannaim were attracted to an imaginary scene in which Satan attempted—albeit without success—to dissuade Abraham from fulfilling God's command. To one of the students of R. Akiba, the Tanna R. Simeon ben Yohai (Galilee, second century C.E.), is attributed the statement: "This is how Satan talked to Abraham—Why, this son of yours is the spit-and-image of you! What kind of man sticks a knife into himself?"[45]

One wonders if Abraham responded to this challenge and, if so, how. This gap was remedied by the Palestinian Amoraim (ca. 230–500 C.E.). To the first generation Amora, R. Yose ben Zimrah, is attributed the statement: "This is how Satan talked to Abraham—Are you not he at whose door all the grandees of the world assemble at dawn in order to benefit from your counsel? If you carry out this act, they will all forsake you ever after. Turn back! *But Abraham would pay no heed to his advice*" (emphasis added).[46] One generation later, the Palestinian Amora, R. Johanan bar Nappaha (Sepphoris, d. 279 C.E.), transmitted a narrative in which Satan attempted unsuccessfully to elicit a response from Abraham by laying a legal trap for the patriarch: "This is how Satan talked to Abraham—If you get to the point of striking the blow and then recoil, by all rights He can charge you, saying, You accepted slaughtering him from the very first moment [of my command]! What retort can you [then] make? As it is said (Job 4:5), *But now it is come unto thee, and thou art weary; it toucheth thee, and thou art affrighted.* Turn back! But Abraham would pay no heed to his advice."[47] In a third version of the exchange, attributed to the third generation Amora, R. Elazar ben Pedat (d. 279 C.E.), Satan used flattery in an unsuccessful attempt to elicit a response from Abraham: "This is how Satan talked to Abraham—Are you not he at whose presence all princes rise to their feet? And when they're riding their horses, dismount before you and bow down to you? If you carry out this act, all the bowings before you will turn into bootings—for it is said (Job 4:4), *Thy words have upholden him that was falling, and thou hast strengthened the feeble knees.* [Turn back! But Abraham would pay no heed to his advice]."[48] In these three versions of the exchange, Satan uses language, logic, and legalisms in an unsuccessful effort to dissuade Abraham from sacrificing Isaac. In all three versions, Satan is unable to elicit a response from Abraham, who pays no heed to his advice.

Just as Mastema was replaced by Satan, so too Satan was replaced in later *midrashim* by Samael, literally "Venom of God," a figure better known as the Angel of Death.[49] *Genesis Rabbah* is a collection of rabbinical interpretations of the Book of Genesis traditionally attributed to the first generation Palestinian Amora Hoshaiah the Elder (third century C.E.), although the text as we have it probably attained its present form in the fifth century. *Ad* Gen. 22:7 ("Then Isaac said to his father Abraham, 'Father!' And he answered, 'Yes, my son'"), we find the following narrative expansion of the encounter between Abraham and Samael.

Samael went to the Patriarch Abraham and reproached him, saying: What means this, old man? Have you lost your mind? Are you going to slay a son granted to you at the age of one hundred?

Abraham replied: Even this I do.

Samael asked: And if He sets you an even greater test, can you stand it, as it is written, *If a thing be put to you as a trial, will you be wearied* (Job 4:2)?

Abraham replied: Even more than this.

Samael said to Abraham: Tomorrow He will say to you, "You are a murderer and you are guilty."

Abraham replied: Still I am content.

When Samael saw that he could accomplish nothing with him, he approached Isaac and said: O son of an unhappy mother! He is going to slay you!

Isaac replied: I accept my fate.

Samael said to Isaac: If so, shall all those fine tunics which your mother made be a legacy for Ishmael, the hated one of her house?

If a word is not wholly effective, it may nevertheless avail in part; hence it is written, *And Isaac said to his father Abraham, "My father."*[50]

Here Samael poses as a close advisor who seeks to help poor Abraham by dissuading the patriarch from offering his beloved son as a sacrifice to the Lord. Whereas in the *midrashim* cited above, Satan is unable to elicit a response from Abraham, in this text Samael does elicit a series of responses from Abraham: "even this I do," "even more than this," and "still I am content." These responses clearly signal Abraham's unshakeable determination to fulfill the divine command. And whereas in the *midrashim* cited above, Satan does not exchange words with Isaac, here he does. After he realizes that he will get nowhere with the father, the intimate adversary turns to the son and informs him that his father intends to slaughter him. True to his character, the obedient son replies, "Indeed so."

Note well: the literary structure of the narrative preserved in *Genesis Rabbah* is identical to the literary structure of the opening narrative in Wāqidī's account of the Battle of Muʾta. In *Genesis Rabbah*, after Samael realizes that he will get nowhere with Abraham, he turns to Isaac and informs him that his father intends to slaughter him. True to his character, the obedient son replies, "Indeed so." If we retain the *midrashic* literary structure but substitute al-Nuʿmān b. Funḥuṣ for Samael, Muḥammad for Abraham, and Zayd for Isaac, the result is as follows: When al-Nuʿmān b. Funḥuṣ realizes that he will get nowhere with Muḥammad, he turns to Zayd and informs him that his (erstwhile) father intends to send him to certain death in battle. True to his character, the obedient (erstwhile) son responds, "I bear witness that he is the Messenger of God." The structural and thematic similarities between the Jewish and Islamic narratives may be a mere coincidence—albeit a remarkable one. Alternatively, these similarities suggest that the Jewish narrative, which appears in a text redacted in Palestine in the fifth century C.E., may have served as a literary model for the Islamic narrative, which appears in a text composed in Iraq in the first quarter of the ninth century C.E.—unless of course both narratives share a common and independent source—as sometimes happens.[51]

If someone objects: the resemblance between the two narratives is incomplete inasmuch as Samael is an angel whereas al-Nuʿmān is a human—indeed, a Jew, the reply is as follows. Consider the following variant of the *Genesis Rabbah* narrative in which Samael overtakes Abraham on his way to Mount Moriah. Here Samael appears to Abraham *in the guise of an old man.* The exchange between the old man and Abraham, as translated by Spiegel, reads as follows:

Samael asked Abraham: Where are you going?

Abraham said to him: To pray.

Samael: What's the wood, the fire, and the knife for?

Abraham realized that he would not be able to put him off; he therefore said to him, *I go in mine integrity* (Ps. 26:1) to do the will of my Father in heaven.

Samael: And what did your Father say to you?

Abraham: To offer up my son before Him as a burnt offering.

Samael: Grandfather, Grandfather, are you out of your mind! You are going to slaughter the son who was born to you when you were a hundred years old?

Abraham: Those are the terms!

Samael: An elder of your years to make such a mistake! He ordered this only to mislead and deceive you! Lo, it is written in the Torah (Gen. 9:6), *Whoever sheds the blood of man, by man shall his blood be shed*; and you are going to slaughter your son? If you say to Him, Thou Thyself didst so order me—He will say to you: What witnesses to that effect have you? Besides, even if you have witnesses, no testimony of a slave against his master is of any worth!

Abraham: I'm not listening to you. I am going ahead to do the will of my father in heaven.[52]

In *Genesis Rabbah*, Satan appears to Abraham as Samael, and in the variant, Samael appears to Abraham disguised as an old man; in Wāqidī's account of the Battle of Mu'ta, the intimate adversary appears to Muḥammad in the form of a Jew. In the *midrashim*, Satan, Samael, and the old man are clearly literary figures; similarly, in Wāqidī's account, Satan and al-Nuʿmān b. Funḥuṣ are best seen as literary figures. As figures, all of these characters fulfill the function of the intimate adversary. A similar argument may be made about Abraham and Isaac in the Jewish narratives and about Muḥammad and Zayd in the Islamic narratives. The Jewish and Muslim fathers and sons may be presented as real historical personages, but they are better seen as figures or types. The only significant difference between the Jewish and the Islamic *midrashim*—if I may use that term to refer not only to the Jewish but also to the Islamic narratives—is that within a single Jewish *midrash*, Satan appears either as Samael or disguised as an old man—but not both, whereas within the Islamic *midrash*, a Jew (who may be Satan in disguise) appears to Muḥammad at al-Jurf, whereas Satan (without any disguise) appears on the battlefield at Mu'ta. Like the Satan/old man of rabbinic *midrash*, the Jew of the Islamic *midrash* is unable to elicit a response from Muḥammad, who pays no heed to his advice. Like the Samael/old man of rabbinic *midrash*, the Jew of the Islamic *midrash* turns from father to (erstwhile) son. In both cases, the intimate adversary succeeds in eliciting a response from the son, albeit not the response he wanted. Subsequently, in southern Jordan, Satan jettisons his disguise and appears as himself, dangling unspecified worldly enticements in the faces of both Zayd and Jaʿfar, to no avail.[53]

In both rabbinic *midrash* and in Wāqidī's account of the Battle of Mu'ta, a father and his son are tested; in the rabbinic narrative, father and son worship before carrying out the sacrifice, in the Islamic narrative they pray; in both cases, the son is a willing participant in the test who is prepared to sacrifice his life for the sake of religion. After a poignant leave-taking, neither son returns. Both ascend, one to Heaven, the other to the Garden; and in both cases, the father has a miraculous vision. In all these texts, the dramatis personae are figures or types. Isaac prefigures Christ on the one hand and Zayd on the other. All three figures—Isaac, Christ, and Zayd—are variants of a single type: the sacrificial victim *cum* martyr. In the *aqedah* narratives, Isaac willingly offers himself as a sacrifice, rushes to the altar, dies, and is immediately reborn, whereupon he ascends to heaven where he remains for three years until his wounds heal. In the New Testament, Christ dies on the cross, is reborn, and rises to Heaven. In the Islamic narrative, Zayd actively seeks death on the battlefield, dies, and ascends to the Garden, where he is given new—and eternal—life as a living martyr.

There are at least three possible explanations for the parallels between the *aqedah* narratives and Wāqidī's account of the Battle of Mu'ta: Coincidence, divine providence, or literary influence—direct or indirect. I am drawn to the third explanation: The *aqedah* narratives served as a literary model for the narrative account of the Battle of Muʾta.

One of the Jewish responses to persecution and exile was to develop the practice and discourse of martyrdom. In the Talmudic period, rabbinic authorities found scriptural support for the emerging doctrine in Genesis 22. By the end of this period, the rabbis had produced the *aqedah* narratives in which Isaac is portrayed as a willing participant in the ritual and Abraham is said to have sacrificed Isaac. Beginning in the first century C.E., the early Christian community, which included Jewish Christians, developed its own doctrine of martyrdom, similarly anchored in Genesis 22. The Judeo-Christian understanding of Genesis 22 was inherited by the early Muslim community; like the Tannaim, Amoraim, and Church fathers, the first Muslims used the *aqedah* as a model for the emerging martyrdom doctrine. The thematic and linguistic parallels between the rabbinic and Christian *midrashim* on Isaac, on the one hand, and Wāqidī's account of the Battle of Muʾta, on the other, suggest that the Muslims who formulated the Islamic narrative were familiar with Judeo-Christian texts and/or ideas. It is possible that these texts and/or oral traditions were already known to the Muslim community during the lifetime of Muḥammad. Even if this were not the case, however, the Muslim community would have acquired access to this material during the period between 650 and 800 C.E. Although it is difficult to pinpoint the exact mode of transmission, Jewish and Christian converts to Islam surely played an instrumental role in the process. It was no doubt these converts who traversed the underground channel through which Jewish and Christian texts and ideas were transmitted to, and transformed by, the early Muslim community.[54]

Over a period of approximately 500 years, adherents of the three Abrahamic faiths developed the practice and discourse of martyrdom. In the postbiblical period, the rabbis taught that Isaac participated actively in the *aqedah* and that his willingness to be sacrificed facilitated the resurrection of the dead. Isaac became the prototype of the Jewish martyr who chooses to die rather than violate the law. The early Christian community understood Isaac as a typos of Christ, whose crucifixion provided the scriptural basis for the Christian martyrdom doctrine. Like Isaac and Jesus, Christian martyrs were willing to die for the sake of religion. The Judeo-Christian martyrdom doctrine was inherited and modified by the early Muslim community. Whereas the Jewish martyr is willing to die for God rather than violate the law, and the Christian martyr is prepared to die for the sake of religion, the Muslim martyr is the soldier of God who takes the fight to the enemy. The narrative account in which Muḥammad sends Zayd to certain death at Muʾta sends a clear signal to the rest of the Muslim community: Fathers must be prepared to sacrifice their sons, and sons must be prepared to be sacrificed. Unlike the Jewish or Christian martyr who seeks death in response to persecution, the ideal Muslim martyr lays down his life in the battle against the forces of infidelity, paganism, and unbelief, wherever and whenever those forces manifest themselves. In theory, true believers must be willing to sacrifice their beloved sons, and sons must be willing to be sacrificed, so long as pagans, polytheists, and infidels continue to associate other gods with God, and so long as monotheists refuse to acknowledge Muḥammad as the Messenger of God.

In the narrative accounts of the Battle of Muʾta, the primary function of the figure identified as Zayd is to represent the devoted son and servant. This literary function brings us back to the seemingly anomalous nature of the Islamic foundation narrative as compared to the foundation narratives of Judaism and Christianity. As noted in Chapter 1, the father-son motif appears to be conspicuously absent from the Islamic foundation narrative. It is my contention that this motif initially was an integral component of the Islamic foundation narrative even if it was quickly marginalized. The father-son motif clearly was on the minds of the storytellers who created the figure of Zayd in the narrative account of his martyrdom: Muḥammad's relationship with his adopted son Zayd is a typological variant of God's relationship with his supernatural son Jesus, which in turn is a typological variant of Abraham's relationship with his natural sons, Ishmael and Isaac.

The Jewish and Christian foundation narratives are based on the Pentateuch and the New Testament, respectively. In Genesis 22, Yahweh instructs Abraham to sacrifice his favored son Isaac, and the patriarch demonstrates his willingness to sacrifice his beloved son, even if the sacrifice appears to have been averted. In the New Testament, God does sacrifice his Beloved Son, who dies on the cross but is resurrected three days later as the Son of God. By contrast, the Qurʾānic basis for the sacrifice of Zayd is tenuous: There is no apparent connection between the Qurʾānic pronouncement that "Muḥammad is not the father of any of your men" and the fact that Zayd is said to have fallen as a martyr at Muʾta.

Indeed, the reader may object that Zayd's death at Muʾta has nothing to do with sacrifice. It is certainly the case that in most versions of the battle preserved in Islamic sources, Muḥammad is portrayed in a manner which suggests that when he issues the battle instructions at al-Jurf, he has no idea that he is sending the three commanders to certain death in southern Jordan. In that case, Muḥammad would have been merely an unwitting participant in the martyrdoms of Zayd and his two co-commanders—just as in Genesis 22 Isaac may have been an unwitting participant in the strange event that unfolded on a mountain-top in Moriah. If so, then the fact that the three commanders died in the order specified by the Prophet is merely a strange coincidence. It is precisely for this reason that I have highlighted Wāqidī's account of the battle, especially the opening narrative in which al-Nuʿmān b. Funḥuṣ warns Muḥammad that he is sending Zayd to *certain* death and warns Zayd that he is about to be sent on a *suicide* mission. With only a few exceptions, Muslim historians who followed Wāqidī chose—consciously or unconsciously—to omit this part of the story from their respective accounts of the battle.[55]

In my view, the correspondence between the order in which the commanders were appointed and the order in which they fell is no coincidence. The reader who has followed my argument to this point surely has noticed the structural, thematic, and linguistic parallels between the Jewish, Christian, and Islamic foundation narratives. As Jon D. Levenson has argued, the Christian claim to supersede Judaism cannot fully be appreciated apart from the dynamics of the Jewish foundation narrative.[56] Likewise, I maintain, the Islamic claim to supersede both Judaism and Christianity cannot fully be understood apart from the dynamics of the foundation narratives of its two predecessors. The Muslims who created the Islamic foundation narrative bore the burden of persuading not only their coreligionists but also Jews and Christians that Islam had come to supersede both Judaism and Christianity as the one true religion. What better way to accomplish this objective than to bring the foundation narratives of the Pentateuch and the New Testament to their logical and theological conclusion?

Chapter 7

Pretexts and Intertexts

. . . every text is constructed as a mosaic of citations; every text is an absorption and transformation of other texts.

—J. Kristeva, Sēmeiōtikē: Recherches pour une sémanalyse, *146*

Introduction

Verse 37 of *Sūrat al-Aḥzāb* is one of the few verses in the Qurʾān that appears to refer to an event in the life of the Prophet: Muḥammad's marriage to the former wife of his adopted son Zayd. The circumstances surrounding this marriage would have been familiar to the Prophet's Companions. During the course of the first and second centuries A.H., Muslims treated Q. 33:37 as referring to an event in Muḥammad's life, and the historicity of this event has been universally accepted by Muslims down to the present—an attitude shared by most if not all scholars.[1] For both Muslims and non-Muslims, v. 37 is a record of an historical incident that took place in the year 5 A.H. Conversely, this incident is the *sabab al-nuzūl* or occasion that gave rise to the revelation of v. 37.

I prefer to read v. 37 as a sacred legend modeled on earlier biblical narratives. The primary function of the new literary composition was to support a key theological doctrine: the Qurʾānic pronouncement that Muḥammad is the Seal of Prophets (*khātam al-nabiyyīn*). In the Qurʾānic worldview, prophecy is the exclusive possession of a single family, and the office of prophecy is hereditary. In order to qualify as a prophet, one must be a member of this family. The early Muslim community devoted considerable effort to establishing that Muḥammad was a lineal descendant of Abraham through Ishmael. At the same time, however, the Muslims also asserted that Muḥammad was the *last* prophet. The validity of this assertion depends on Muḥammad's sonlessness: If Muḥammad had a son who reached the age of maturity and outlived him, he would not have been the Last Prophet; if Muḥammad was the Last Prophet, he could not have had a son who attained maturity and outlived him. The reciprocal relationship between Muḥammad's sonlessness and the finality of prophecy is clearly expressed in v. 40 of *Sūrat al-Aḥzāb*, the sole Qur'ānic witness to the theological doctrine: "Muḥammad is not the father of any of your men, but the messenger of God and the seal of Prophets. God is aware of everything."

The pronouncement that Muḥammad is the Seal of Prophets closes a five-verse pericope that begins with Q. 33:36. Conceptually, however, v. 40 precedes vv. 36–39. Indeed, one might say that v. 40 is the *sabab* or cause for the revelation of the four immediately preceding verses. Let us adopt as a major premise the assertion that Muḥammad is the Last Prophet. The validity of this premise is contingent on a minor premise: the Prophet's sonlessness. The fact that Muḥammad had an adopted son named Zayd was inconsistent with both the major and minor premises. In order to prevent a collision between theology and history, the early Muslim community formulated a plausible, history-like scenario in which Muḥammad could be said to have repudiated Zayd as his son. The solution took the form of a sacred legend which, in its Islamic manifestation, runs as follows: Against her will, a beautiful woman was married to Zayd b. Muḥammad, the Prophet's adopted son. Subsequently, Muḥammad fell in love with his daughter-in-law. But a marriage between a man and his daughter-in-law was prohibited by sacred law. The legal obstacle to this marriage was removed by a divinely inspired legal reform. After Zayd had divorced his wife, the Prophet took his daughter-in-law and made her his wife—but only after he first had repudiated Zayd by uttering the words, "I am not your father."

The Qur'ānic account creates a brief narrative interval between Zayd's divorcing his wife and Muḥammad's marrying her. It was into this temporal window that the early Muslim community inserted the critical prophetic utterance that was the true *sabab* or cause of the sacred legend: "I am not your father." Viewed in this manner, v. 37 is not a record of an event in the life of the Prophet but rather a theologically inspired narrative that was formulated so as to make it appear as if it referred to an historical event. If the verse originated as a sacred legend, then one wonders about its literary antecedents. Biblical narratives were circulating in Arabia long before the birth of Muḥammad. That both Muḥammad and his Companions were familiar with these narratives is attested by the Qur'ān itself. Is it possible that one or more of these biblical narratives served as a model for Q. 33:37?

This is the question to be addressed in this chapter. The demonstration will take the form of a comparison of Islamic and non-Islamic narratives. The exercise will unfold in two stages. I begin with a close reading of Q. 33:37 and then compare the results of this reading to two well-known biblical pericopes—one from the Hebrew Bible, the other from the New Testament. Second, I turn my attention to the figure of Zayd and compare his portrayal in Islamic sources with the portrayal of several well-known figures in the Hebrew Bible. In order to carry out the following analysis, it will be necessary to collect and repeat some of the information that has been treated in Parts I and II of this monograph. In most instances this material will be examined in greater detail than before and it will be placed in a new, comparative perspective.

Q. 33:37: A Literary Analysis

I begin by drawing the reader's attention, once again, to the language of Q. 33:37, which, for purposes of analysis and convenient reference, may be divided into eight clauses:

1 [Recall] when you said
2 to the one on whom God and you yourself have bestowed favor,
3 "Keep your wife to yourself and fear God,"
4 and you hid within yourself what God would reveal,
5 and you feared the people when God had better right to be feared by you.
6 When Zayd had finished with her, We gave her to you in marriage,
7 so that there should be no difficulty for the believers concerning the wives of their adopted sons, when they have finished with them.
8 God's command was fulfilled.

The authorial voice that controls the text orders a male addressee ("you")—presumably the Prophet Muḥammad, who is mentioned by name in v. 40—to recall a statement made on an earlier occasion (37.1). The person to whom the statement was made is identified as a male upon whom both God and the addressee had bestowed favor (37.2). The authorial voice reproduces the very words uttered by the addressee to the doubly favored man: "Keep your wife to yourself and fear God" (37.3). This command implies that the doubly favored man wanted to divorce his wife. The authorial voice reminds the addressee that he was hiding something that would be the subject of an upcoming revelation (37.4). The reminder is followed by a rebuke: the addressee put his fear of men over his fear of God (37.5). The authorial voice now mentions a man named Zayd—without any further identification. The context suggests that Zayd was married to the "wife" mentioned in 37.3 and that he wanted to divorce her, but that the addressee instructed him not to divorce the woman. Using the third person plural ("We"), the authorial voice explains: "When Zayd had finished with her, We gave her to you in marriage," that is to say, God authorized, legitimized, and/or gave His blessing to the addressee's marriage to the unnamed woman who had been Zayd's wife (37.6). This marriage was an apparent violation of the biblical law which prohibits—on pain of death—sexual relations between a man and his daughter-in-law (Hebr. *kallâh*).[2] The appearance of a violation was removed by introducing a distinction between a natural son and an adopted son: it had been and continued to be forbidden to marry the former wife of a natural son, but this prohibition no longer applied to the former wife of an adopted son. The special dispensation granted to the addressee was extended to all Muslims by the formulation of a legal rule: "so that there should be no difficulty for the believers concerning the wives of their adopted sons, when they have finished with them" (37.7). The verse ends with the pronouncement that the addressee's marriage to the former wife of his adopted son fulfilled a divine command (37.8).

The underlying literary structure of v. 37 may be represented as follows:

1 invocation of a statement;
2 reference to a male favored by God and the addressee;
3 the statement: a command to keep an unnamed woman as one's wife;
4 reference to a secret that would become the subject of a divine revelation;
5 a divine rebuke;
6 a condition—Zayd must have satisfied his desire for his wife, followed by a divine dispensation—God authorized or blessed the marriage;
7 a legal rule: the special dispensation extends to all believers;
8 conclusion: the marriage was a fulfillment of a divine command.

Pretexts

II Samuel 11–12: David and Bathsheba

In Chapter 4, we saw that in his commentary on Q. 33:38, the second-century exegete Muqātil b. Sulaymān compares the Qur'ānic account of the marriage between the addressee (whom he identifies as Muḥammad) and the unnamed woman mentioned in v. 37 (whom he identifies as Zaynab bt. Jaḥsh) to the biblical account of David's marriage to Uriah the Hittite's wife (whose name he does not mention) as related in II Samuel 11–12 (to which he makes no explicit reference). The connection between these two narratives was important to the commentator because it highlighted the theological contention that history unfolds according to providential design.

According to the biblical narrative, King David fell in love with Bathsheba and, acting in secret, engaged in sexual relations with the woman despite her being married to one of the king's soldiers, a foreigner named Uriah the Hittite. When Bathsheba's pregnancy threatened to expose the king's sin, David feared public reaction. He summoned Uriah and ordered the soldier to go home where, he hoped, he would sleep with his wife. When the soldier refused, David instructed a general named Joab "to place Uriah in the front line of battle, where the fighting is fiercest" (II Sam. 11:15). In the ensuing encounter between the Israelites and the Ammonites, Uriah was killed outside the walls of Rabbat Ammon. The soldier's death ended his marriage to Bathsheba. After the widow had completed the period of mourning for her husband, David married her. Because the king did not understand that he had sinned, the Lord sent the prophet Nathan to rebuke the king, who eventually repented, whereupon his sins were forgiven. Bathsheba gave birth to two sons. The first died in infancy. When a second son was born, she named him Solomon. This son was favored by the Lord (*ve-yahweh ahevô*), who let it be known through the prophet Nathan that the child's true name was Yedidiah or "Friend of God." Subsequently, Bathsheba would play an instrumental role in securing the throne for Solomon, who succeeded his father as King of Israel, thereby insuring the continuation of the Davidic line (I Kings 1:11–31) (see Appendix 3).[3]

Several elements of the biblical narrative are echoed in Q. 33:37: Just as Solomon was favored by the Lord, so too Zayd was favored by God—and His Prophet (37.2). Both David and Muḥammad fell in love with the wife of a foreign convert. Just as David could not marry Bathsheba until her marriage to Uriah had ended (through death), Muḥammad could not marry the unnamed woman until her marriage to Zayd had ended (through divorce). Whereas David ordered Uriah the Hittite to go to his home in the hope that he would sleep with his wife and thereby hide David's sin, Muḥammad ordered Zayd to keep his wife so that he, the Prophet, would not commit a sin (37.3). Just as David acted in secret, Muḥammad kept his love for the unnamed woman a secret (37.4). Just as David feared public reaction and was rebuked by the prophet Nathan, Muḥammad feared public reaction and was rebuked by God (37.5). Just as Bathsheba was married to David after observing the period of mourning for her dead husband, so too the unnamed woman was married to Muḥammad after Zayd had satisfied his sexual desire for her—and, presumably, after she had observed her waiting period (37.6).

Matthew 1:18–25: Joseph and Mary

In Chapter 1, I mentioned Joseph's marriage to Mary, as related in Matthew 1:18–25, in connection with the doctrine of Christology. To the best of my knowledge, no Muslim commentator has ever compared this marriage to Muḥammad's marriage to the unnamed woman in Q. 33:37. Matthew 1:18–25 reads as follows:

18 Now the birth of Jesus the Messiah took place in this way. When his mother Mary had been engaged to Joseph, but before they lived together, she was found to be with child from the Holy Spirit.

19 Her husband Joseph, being a righteous man and unwilling to expose her to public disgrace, planned to dismiss her quietly.

20 But just when he had resolved to do this, an angel of the Lord appeared to him in a dream and said, "Joseph, son of David, do not be afraid to take Mary as your wife, for the child conceived in her is from the Holy Spirit.

21 She will bear a son, and you are to name him Jesus, for he will save his people from their sins."
22 All this took place to fulfill what had been spoken by the Lord through the prophet:
23 "Look, the virgin shall conceive and bear a son,
and they shall name him Emmanuel,"
which means, "God is with us."
24 When Joseph awoke from sleep, he did as the angel of the Lord commanded him; he took her as his wife,
25 but had no marital relations with her until she had borne a son; and he named him Jesus.

After Joseph was engaged to Mary but before the marriage was consummated, the righteous man discovered that his bride was pregnant. Joseph knew that he was not the father of Mary's child, and it appeared to him as if she had engaged in illicit sexual relations with another man. Joseph decided to divorce Mary, albeit quietly, so that she would not suffer public disgrace. Joseph's dilemma was resolved by divine intervention: He had a dream in which an angel spoke to him. The very words uttered by the angel are quoted in vv. 20–21. Critically, the angel refers to Joseph as "Joseph, son of David," thereby establishing his Davidic credentials. From the angel's remarks, we learn that Joseph was "afraid" to take Mary as his wife. The angel dispels Joseph's fear by explaining that the child conceived by Mary is "from" the Holy Spirit. The dream concludes with the angel's announcement that Mary will give birth to a son; and with the angel's instruction that Joseph is to name the child Jesus (Yehoshua in Hebrew means "may he be saved"). When Joseph awoke, he took Mary as his wife but did not consummate the marriage until after she had given birth to Jesus. The miraculous birth of Jesus sealed or fulfilled the prediction of the biblical prophet Isaiah, "the virgin shall conceive and bear a son, and they shall name him Emmanuel" (Isaiah 7:14).[4]

Matthew 1:18–25 looks back at, and modifies, II Samuel 11–12. Whereas David did engage in illicit sexual relations with Bathsheba, Mary only appears to have engaged in illicit sexual relations with someone other than Joseph. Both women became pregnant. Both men were afraid, albeit for different reasons: David feared public reaction to the disclosure of his sin, while Joseph feared public reaction to the disclosure of Mary's sin. In both cases, a potential scandal was avoided through an act of divine providence. The Lord sent the prophet Nathan to rebuke David and induce him to repent; the prophet's very words are quoted in II Samuel 12:1–12. An angel appeared to Joseph in a dream and explained the true meaning of Mary's pregnancy; the angel's very words are quoted in Matthew 1:20–21. Just as David married Bathsheba, Joseph married Mary. Both women gave birth to a son and both sons were named by God. The New Testament episode sealed, confirmed, or fulfilled the prediction made by Isaiah in the Hebrew Bible.

Let us now extend the exercise to include Q. 33:37, which looks back at, and modifies, both Matthew 1:18–25 and II Samuel 11–12. Whereas David did engage in illicit sexual relations, and Mary appeared to have engaged in illicit sexual relations, Muḥammad was brought to the brink of engaging in illicit sexual relations. Whereas David coveted the wife of one of his soldiers, Muḥammad coveted the wife of his adopted son Zayd (there is no parallel in Matthew 1). Just as David initially acted in secret, Joseph planned to act in secret, and Muḥammad kept his love for the unnamed woman a secret. Whereas both Bathsheba and Mary became pregnant, the unnamed woman in the Qur'ān did not—albeit for a very good reason. David feared public reaction if his sin were exposed, Joseph feared that Mary would be exposed to public disgrace if he divorced her, and Muḥammad feared public reaction if he were to marry his daughter-in-law. In all three cases, scandal was averted by means of divine intervention: The Lord sent the prophet Nathan to speak to David; an angel of the Lord spoke to Joseph in a dream; and God spoke to Muḥammad. Just as David married Bathsheba and Joseph married Mary, Muḥammad married the unnamed woman. Whereas Bathsheba gave birth to two natural sons (the first of which died in infancy) and Mary gave birth to one supernatural son, the marriage between Muḥammad and the unnamed woman did not produce any offspring. The birth of Solomon insured the continuity of the Davidic line, the birth of Jesus facilitated the salvation of mankind, and the failure of the unnamed woman to produce a male heir for Muḥammad made it possible for him to become the Last Prophet. By giving birth to Jesus/Emmanuel, the virgin Mary fulfilled the word of the Lord as transmitted by the prophet Isaiah (Is. 7:14); similarly, by marrying the unnamed woman in Q. 33:37, Muḥammad fulfilled a divine command. These outcomes were all a product of providential design.

The three narratives are variations on a common theme: A key figure either engages in illicit sexual relations, appears to engage in illicit sexual relations, or is brought to the verge of engaging in illicit sexual relations. Each episode is a defining moment in the history of biblical Judaism, Christianity, or Islam. In all three cases God intervened in history to insure that His master plan for mankind would proceed exactly as He had determined: David's repentance for the sin he committed with Bathsheba paved the way for the birth of a natural son and legitimate heir who would continue the Davidic line. The impregnation of Mary by the Holy Spirit facilitated the birth of the Son of God. By contrast, no son was born of the marriage between Muḥammad and the unnamed woman in Q. 33:37—as required by the Qur'ānic pronouncement that Muḥammad is not the father of any man but the Messenger of God and the Seal of Prophets.

There are at least two ways to read Q. 33:37. If one reads the verse as history, then one or more of the following conclusions may be drawn: God spoke to Muḥammad; Zayd was favored by both God and the Prophet; Zayd wanted to divorce his wife; Muḥammad kept his feelings for this woman a secret, feared public reaction, and received a special revelation from God legitimizing his marriage to the woman—after Zayd had satisfied his desire for her; this special dispensation was extended to the entire Muslim community; and the marriage was a fulfillment of God's command. Alternatively, it is possible to read Q. 33:37 as a sacred narrative that was formulated to support the Qur'ānic pronouncement that Muḥammad is the Last Prophet. Just as Muḥammad seals the line of prophets that began with Adam, v. 37 seals a narrative sequence that looks back to Matthew 1:18–25 and II Samuel 11–12. All three sacred narratives are literary compositions that tell the same story, albeit with differences that reflect changing ideas about revelation, prophecy, and history. All three narratives are based on an illicit, extraordinary, or seemingly illicit sexual encounter between a key male-female pair. And in all three narratives, this underlying literary structure is supported by a common set of motifs: a man favored or loved by God; an extraordinary marriage; fear of public reaction; a divine rebuke; divine intervention in the personal life of a key figure; and the fulfillment of a divine command.

Intertextuality

Whether one reads Q. 33:37 as a record of an historical event or as a sacred narrative modeled on earlier biblical pretexts, the fact remains that v. 37 is a cryptic text that leaves out a number of significant details. The following are some of the questions that might have arisen in the minds of the Muslims who heard or read this verse for the first time: Who was the man named Zayd mentioned in this verse? Why is he identified only as Zayd? How did he come to be adopted by Muḥammad? How did he come to be favored by both God and His Prophet? Who was the unnamed woman and what were the circumstances of her marriage to Zayd? Why did Zayd want to divorce her? Why did the Prophet instruct him not to do so? What was the Prophet's relationship with this woman? What was Muḥammad hiding within himself? Why did he fear the people? What were the circumstances of the Prophet's marriage to the unnamed woman? What happened to Zayd after he divorced his wife?

The early Muslim community raised and responded to these very questions during the first two centuries A.H. The answers were provided by the men and women who laid the foundations for what would become the classical Islamic tradition: Companions, Followers, and Successors, popular preachers, transmitters of *ḥadīth*, and Qur'ān commentators. These Muslims filled in the gaps in the Qur'ānic narrative. The sources in which their answers have been preserved include Qur'ān commentaries, collections of *ḥadīth*, biographical dictionaries, and historical chronicles. These sources contain reports (*akhbār*) in which one learns about Zayd's origins (including his birth name), enslavement, acquisition by Muḥammad, adoption, marriage to and divorce from a woman named Zaynab bt. Jaḥsh, repudiation by his adoptive father, military career, and martyrdom. Some of these reports are accompanied by *isnād*s; others are not. Generally speaking, the *isnād*s take us back to ca. 75 A.H. Between the event itself and its first recorded source there intervened a period of approximately fifty years during which this story and others circulated orally within the Muslim community.

Just as there are at least two ways to read Q. 33:37, so too there are at least two ways to read narrative expansions of this verse. The first is to read the narratives as history, that is to say, as more or less accurate representations of the life of Muḥammad. The ultimate source of these reports would have been the Muslims who witnessed the events in question and transmitted their recollections of these events to subsequent generations of Muslims. In the last quarter of the first century A.H., the Muslim community began to record these oral traditions in writing, a process that continued for hundreds of years. Alternatively, it is possible to read the narrative expansions of Q. 33:37 as literary compositions. If so, then one wonders about literary antecedents. The exercise that is about to commence is similar to the exercise that has just been completed. Again, I shall attempt to identify earlier texts that served as models for the Islamic narratives, although in this instance I focus my attention not on Q. 33:37 itself but on its narrative expansions. Again, I shall compare the literary structures, themes, motifs, and linguistic forms found in these texts with their counterparts in Islamic sources. Again, I shall attempt to demonstrate that the earlier narratives were reimagined, recycled, and re-presented by the Muslims for a new and different purpose; and that the resulting narratives embody specifically Islamic assumptions about revelation, prophecy, and history.

The new exercise differs from the earlier one in three ways. First, I place Zayd at the center of my attention. Second, I treat the Zayd of these narratives as a figure and attempt to show how the Muslims who formulated the narrative expansions of Q. 33:37 transformed this figure into a spectacular religious symbol. Third, I am concerned not with the pretexts themselves but with specific roles and functions performed by one or more literary figures in one narrative context which subsequently are transposed into another narrative context, where they take on new and different meanings. For convenience, I refer to this phenomenon as *intertextuality.*[5] Consciously or unconsciously, the Muslims who formulated and transmitted the narratives about Zayd were engaging in a conversation or dialogue with earlier texts. Drawing on a large repertoire of biblical and postbiblical narratives, they created the figure of Zayd by modeling his persona on that of biblical figures with whom many if not most Muslims would have been familiar. As the Zayd figure passes from one stage of life to the next, he takes on the characteristics of another biblical figure. In the end, Zayd is the sum total of all of these figures.

Zayd = Joseph

In Chapter 4, I suggested that it is helpful to think of Zayd's life as a play that unfolds in five acts, beginning with his capture and ending with his martyrdom. In Act 1, Scenes 1–2, Zayd is captured, acquired by Khadīja, and gifted to Muḥammad. These two scenes are modeled on the story of Joseph in Genesis 37–45. In the Islamic narrative, Zayd is Joseph, Muḥammad is alternately Potiphar and Pharaoh, and Khadīja is Potiphar's wife.

The Islamic Narrative: Zayd's Capture, Acquisition by Muḥammad, and Rejection of His Birth Family

Narrative accounts of Zayd's capture, acquisition by Muḥammad, and adoption are found in both historical chronicles and Qur'ān commentaries. The following summary is based primarily on the narrative preserved in the *Kitāb al-ṭabaqāt al-kabīr* of Ibn Saʿd (d. 230/845).[6]

As noted in Chapter 3, Zayd was born in Syria ca. 580 C.E., the son of Ḥāritha b. Sharāḥīl al-Kalbī and Suʿdā bt. Thaʿlab. The Kalbīs were camel breeders who grazed their animals on the steppes between Syria and Iraq. Many of them were Christians. Around 605, Zayd's mother took him to visit her relatives, the Banū al-Maʿn of Ṭayy. Suddenly, horsemen of the Banū al-Qayn b. Jasr descended upon the tribal campground. The Arab raiders seized Zayd and carried him off to the Hijaz. In the market of ʿUkāẓ southeast of Mecca he was sold for 400 *dirhams* to Ḥakīm b. Ḥizām b. Khuwaylid, who was acting on behalf of his paternal aunt, Khadīja bt. Khuwaylid. Shortly thereafter, when Khadīja married Muḥammad b. ʿAbdallāh al-Qurashī, she gave the slave to her husband as a gift. Thus did Zayd find himself in a strange land in the household of a master who was about to become a powerful and influential man.[7]

Back in Syria Zayd's father was disconsolate. He is said to have formulated a poem which begins with the following line: "I weep for Zayd not knowing what has become of him // Is he alive, is there hope, or has death overcome him?"[8] By a stroke of good fortune—or perhaps it was divine providence—Kalbī pilgrims spotted Zayd near the Sacred House in Mecca. The Kalbīs shared with Zayd news about his family and his father's distress. Curiously, Zayd told his fellow tribesmen that he was *not* interested in being reunited with his family.[9] He too expressed his feelings in poetry, asking the Kalbīs to convey the following lines to his tribe:

Bear a message from me to my tribe, for I am far away.
I reside near the Kaʿba, the place of pilgrimage.
Let go of the grief that has overtaken you;
don't send camels running all over the land.
Praise be to Allāh, I live with the best family,
Maʿadd, from father to son they are the noblest.[10]

The Kalbī pilgrims returned to Syria, where they told Ḥāritha b. Sharāḥīl everything they had learned about Zayd, including his whereabouts and the identity of his master (who, it should be kept in mind, had not yet emerged as the Messenger of God). Upon hearing that Zayd was alive and well, Ḥāritha exclaimed, "My son, by the Lord of the Kaʿba!" Determined to recover Zayd, Ḥāritha traveled to Mecca, accompanied by his brother Kaʿb—an Arabic equivalent of the Hebrew Yaʿkôb or Jacob.[11]

A longer version of the encounter between Zayd and the Kalbīs is found in Qurṭubī's commentary on Q. 33:37, where it is not unidentified Kalbī pilgrims who find Zayd in Mecca but rather his uncle, Kaʿb, who was in Mecca on business. When Kaʿb encountered a young man who bore a striking resemblance to his missing nephew, he interrogated him in an effort to determine his identity:

He asked: "What is your name, O young man (*ghulām*)?"

He replied: "Zayd."

He asked: "The son of whom?"

He replied: "The son of Ḥāritha."

He asked: "The son of whom?"

He replied: "The son of Sharāḥīl al-Kalbī."

He asked: "What is your mother's name?"

He replied: "Suʿdā—and I was among my maternal aunts of Ṭayy [when I was captured]."

He embraced him and summoned his brother and his clan, and they came [to Mecca]. They wanted him to live with them.

They asked, "To whom do you belong?"

He replied: "To Muḥammad b. ʿAbdallāh."[12]

Back to Ibn Saʿd: Following the reunion, Zayd's relatives sought out Muḥammad and were told that he could be found in the *masjid* or house of prayer. The Kalbīs entered the *masjid* and introduced themselves to Muḥammad, addressing him deferentially, as follows:

O son of ʿAbdallāh, O son of ʿAbd al-Muṭṭalib, O son of Hāshim, O son of the Lord of his tribe, you (pl.) are the people of the Ḥaram and you are protected by it. In the name of the [Lord of the] House, you free the captives and feed the prisoners. We have come to you in the matter of our son who is in your possession. Trust us and be kind to us in the matter of his ransom, for surely we will pay you a large ransom.[13]

In this carefully formulated speech, the Kalbīs honor their Arabian host by identifying his noble lineage and acknowledging his membership in the tribe of Quraysh. As guardians of the Sacred Precinct, the Qurashīs have both rights and obligations. One of their obligations is to "free the captives and feed the prisoners." The language attributed to the Kalbīs echoes Ps. 102:21 ("to hear the groans of the prisoner, to release those condemned to death"),[14] while at the same time anticipating the language of Q. 90:13–14 ("the freeing of a slave or the feeding on a day of hunger"). Only after the Kalbīs have acknowledged Muḥammad's authoritative status do they mention an unnamed "son" who is a slave in his possession. Appealing to Muḥammad's sense of justice and fairness, they ask for his trust and implore him to accept a large sum of money in return for the youth. Feigning ignorance, Muḥammad inquires, "Who is he?" To which they respond, "Zayd b. Ḥāritha."

Zayd b. Ḥāritha was the slave who had been purchased by Khadīja for 400 (or 700) *dirhams* and gifted to Muḥammad. Miraculously, Zayd's father and uncle had tracked him down, and they wanted to take him back to Syria. How could anyone criticize Muḥammad for facilitating Zayd's reunification with his birth family? Surely this was the proper course of action—indeed, one might argue that it was the only ethical and humane thing to do. Not in this instance. Muḥammad informed the Kalbīs that he would summon Zayd and let the youth make the decision himself of his own free will. If Zayd chose to return to Syria with his father and uncle, he was free to do so, and no ransom would be collected; if, however, he chose to remain with Muḥammad, "then by God the decision will have been his alone and I will have had no part in it." It was inconceivable to the Kalbīs that Zayd would choose to remain in servitude. Anticipating a favorable outcome, they agreed to the proposal.[15]

Muḥammad summoned Zayd and asked the young man if he recognized the two strangers. "Yes," Zayd said, gesturing with his hand, "this one is my father and that one is my paternal uncle." Stung by Zayd's identification of Ḥāritha as his *father*, Muḥammad exclaimed, "But I am the one whom you have known, and you know what kind of a master I have been to you" (*raʾayta ṣuḥbatī laka*)—alluding no doubt to the excellent treatment that the slave had received from his master.[16] This was a decisive moment for Zayd, whose *heart* (my formulation—DSP) surely was torn between his biological father and his master. In Qurṭubī's version of the story, Muḥammad's question evokes tears from Zayd, who responds, "Why have you asked me this?"[17] To the best of my knowledge, no Muslim scholar has ever connected this particular narrative moment to the revelation of Q. 33:4 ("God has not put two hearts inside any man"), although if ever there had been an appropriate occasion for the revelation of a verse, this was it.[18]

Muḥammad explained to Zayd that the choice was his to make: He could return to Syria with his father and uncle, or he could remain in Mecca with his master—the man who, unbeknownst to Zayd or anyone else, would soon emerge as the Messenger of God and Seal of Prophets. Muḥammad was testing Zayd to determine whether or not his loyalty to his master was greater than his love for his birth family. This was Zayd's first opportunity to manifest his devotion to Muḥammad. Without a moment's hesitation, Zayd told his master, "I would not choose anyone over you." To this he added, "In my mind, you have the status of father and mother."[19] The Kalbīs were shocked. "Woe is you, O Zayd!" they exclaimed, "Would you choose slavery over freedom, and [would you choose your master] over your father, paternal uncle, and family?" To this question Zayd responded, "Yes. Having seen what I have seen in this man, I would never choose anyone over him." By freely choosing to remain with his master rather than be reunited with his birth family, Zayd had passed the test—the first of several that he would undergo over the course of the next twenty-five years.[20]

Comparison: Zayd is Joseph (Gen. 37–45)

The names Yosef (Heb.) and Zayd (Ar.) are both derived from a root that signifies *to add or increase*. The onomastic equivalence (Yosef = Zayd) is only the first of several parallels between these two figures. In the Hebrew Bible Joseph is described as *yefeh toʿar* or good looking (Gen. 39:6), while in Islamic sources Zayd is described as *ghulām yafʿa*, or an adolescent—in this instance, a beautiful one.[21] Each man was born in Syria, separated from his birth family, and sold into slavery in a strange land. In each case, the youth was captured while in the care of someone other than his father. Whereas the biblical narrative portrays Joseph as a braggart whose imperiousness fueled the jealously of his brothers, the Islamic narrative portrays Zayd as an innocent victim of circumstances. Each man was captured by nomads and taken to a foreign land where he entered the house of a powerful master: Joseph was acquired by Potiphar and subsequently entered the service of Pharaoh; Zayd was acquired by Khadīja and subsequently entered the household of Muḥammad. Whereas Potiphar's wife attempted to seduce Joseph, no such behavior is attributed to Khadīja.

Each man developed a special filial bond with his master: Joseph claimed that God had made him a father to Pharaoh (Gen. 45:8b); Zayd regarded Muḥammad as if he were his father and mother. Each man achieved high status: Joseph became the vizier of Egypt (Gen. 41:37–43); Zayd was adopted by Muḥammad as his son and heir (see further below).[22] Each man underwent a name change: Joseph was renamed Zaphenath-paneah ("creator of life"; Gen. 41:45); Zayd b. Ḥāritha al-Kalbī was renamed Zayd b. Muḥammad. Despite his servile status, each man married a woman of high station: Joseph married Asenath, the daughter of Potiphera, the priest of On (Gen. 41:45); Zayd married Zaynab bt. Jaḥsh, Muḥammad's paternal cross-cousin and a descendent of Ishmael. Whereas Pharaoh himself gave Asenath to Joseph as a wife, Muḥammad was initially opposed to Zayd's marriage to Zaynab.

The father of each man was inconsolable following the disappearance of his son: Jacob's lament in Gen. 37:35 ("No, I will go down mourning to my son in Sheol") brings to mind the opening line of the poem attributed to Ḥāritha ("I weep for Zayd not knowing what has become of him / Is he alive, is there hope, or has death overcome him?"). In both cases, the missing person and one or more of his relatives were reunited by an act of divine providence. Famine compelled Jacob to send his sons to Egypt, where Joseph was eager to acquire news of his father and younger brother (Gen. 42). Business brought Zayd's uncle Kaʿb to the Kaʿba (!) in Mecca (alternatively, pilgrimage brought Kalbī tribesmen to the town), where Zayd let it be known that he did not want to be reunited with his family and advised the Kalbīs not to grieve for him. In both cases, there is a recognition scene: In the biblical narrative, Joseph immediately recognizes his brothers although they do not at first recognize him (Gen. 42:7–8). In Qurṭubī's version of the Islamic narrative, Kaʿb recognizes Zayd although Zayd does not at first recognize his uncle. In each instance, the recognition scene is accompanied by an interrogation: In the biblical narrative it is Joseph who interrogates his brothers; in the Islamic narrative, it is Kaʿb who interrogates Zayd. In both cases, the decision about whether or not to reunite is the result of a test: In the biblical narrative, it is Joseph who tests his brothers; in the Islamic narrative, it is Muḥammad who tests Zayd. Both Joseph and Zayd shed tears, albeit a different number of times and for different reasons. Joseph cries four times: twice in private and twice in public.[23] By contrast, Zayd does not shed any tears when he is reunited with either his uncle or his father, but he does cry in public after hurting his master's feelings by identifying Ḥāritha b. Sharāḥīl as his natural father.

Joseph's status as vizier made it possible for him to bring his family to Egypt, where he reconciled with his brothers and was reunited with his father. Pharaoh was happy for Joseph and supported the family's reunification (Gen. 45–46). Thus, Joseph was able to maintain his relationship with both Pharaoh and his birth family. Zayd could not achieve this balance: If he chose to be reunited with his family and to return to Syria, he would have to abandon his master; if he chose to remain with his master in Mecca, he would have to abandon his birth family. Unlike Pharaoh, who was pleased by the arrival of Joseph's family (Gen. 45:16–20), Muḥammad was wounded by Zayd's identification of Ḥāritha as his birth father. In the biblical narrative Joseph's family joins him in Egypt, temporarily abandoning their homeland. In the Islamic narrative, Zayd's family returns to their homeland empty-handed but not dissatisfied. Presumably, they never saw Zayd again. Descendants of Joseph subsequently would conquer the Promised Land; followers of Muḥammad subsequently would conquer the Promised Land—and more. Both the Israelites and the Muslims would create a religious polity.

Zayd = Eliezer Dammesek

In Act 1, Scene 2, a sonless Muḥammad adopts his trusted servant Zayd b. Ḥāritha as his son and heir and renames him Zayd b. Muḥammad. In Act 2, Scene 3, Muḥammad repudiates Zayd and orders him to inform his ex-wife of her upcoming marriage to the Prophet. In these scenes, the figure of Zayd is modeled on that of Dammesek Eliezer in Gen. 15:1–6. In the Islamic narrative, Zayd is Dammesek Eliezer, Muḥammad is Abram, and Zaynab is Rebecca.

Abram's Trusted Servant, Dammesek Eliezer (Gen. 15:1–6)

When Abram was seventy-five years old, the Lord instructed him to leave his birthplace in Mesopotamia and to travel to a land that He would show him (Gen. 12:1). The Lord promised Abram that He would make him the father of a great nation (Gen. 12:2) and that He would assign the land of Canaan to Abram's children (Gen. 12:7).

Abram left Mesopotamia and migrated to Canaan where, after a brief stay in Shechem and Beth El, he went down to Egypt; from there he traveled to the Negev before returning to Beth El and then continuing on to Hebron. During this period of his life, Abram's closest blood relative was Lot, his paternal nephew. Due to competition over scarce resources, the two men agreed to divide the land between them: Abram settled in Canaan, while Lot occupied the cities of the plain (Gen. 13:14). Sometime after this division had taken place, a coalition of Canaanite kings invaded Sodom and Gomorrah, and they captured Lot and his family (Gen. 14:12). When Abram learned that his nephew had been taken captive, he assembled a force of 318 (!) men and pursued the Canaanites as far as Hobah, north of Damascus, where he defeated them and recovered Lot and other captives (Gen. 14:13–16).

To this point in the biblical narrative Abram had not produced a son. If Abram was to be the father of a great nation—as the Lord had promised—he had to produce a son and heir. Gen. 15:1–6 treats the subject of Abram's childlessness:

1 Some time afterward, this word of Yahweh came to Abram, in a vision:
"Fear not, Abram!
I am your shield;
Your reward shall be very great."
2 But Abram answered, "O Lord Yahweh, to what purpose are your gifts,
when I continue childless, / and the successor to my house is Dammesek Eliezer?
3 Since you have granted me no offspring," Abram continued, / "a member of my
household will become my heir."
4 Then Yahweh's word came back to him in reply, "That one shall not be your heir;
none but your own issue shall be your heir."

5 He took him outside and said, "Look up at the sky and count the stars if you can. Just so," He added, "shall be your offspring." /
6 He put his trust in Yahweh, who accounted it to his merit.[24]

The pericope takes the form of a dialogue composed of three parts: (1) The Lord appears to Abram and promises that He will protect and reward him (v. 1); (2) Abram objects to the divine promise, delivering a lament over his childlessness and its consequences (vv. 2–3); and (3) the Lord responds to Abram's objection by assuring him that he will produce a natural son who will be his heir and that his descendants will be as numerous as the stars in the sky (vv. 4–5).[25]

The Hebrew of v. 2 is difficult. The phrase *ben meshek* (translated by Speiser as "successor to my house") is a *hapax legomenon*[26] and *dammesek Eliezer* is ungrammatical.[27] All is not lost, however, because the assertion made in v. 2 is repeated in v. 3, where the meaning is clear: Because Abram has no children, a member of his household who is not a blood relative will be his heir (*ben beitî yôresh otî*). Here, the member of Abram's household is clearly the man identified in v. 2 as Dammesek Eliezer.[28] Verse 2 is the only verse in the Hebrew Bible in which Dammesek Eliezer is mentioned. Most commentators identify Dammesek Eliezer—or Eliezer of Damascus—with the nameless senior servant who, in Gen. 24 (see below), procures a bride for Isaac. Some modern scholars have suggested that Abraham adopted Dammesek Eliezer as his son, but the point is contested.[29]

Later rabbinic *midrash* fills in many of the gaps in the biblical narrative. Dammesek Eliezer is said to have been raised in the court of King Nimrod, the Mesopotamian monarch mentioned in Gen. 10:8–12. In narrative expansions of the biblical text, Nimrod is the embodiment of evil, paganism, and idolatry. After Abram begins to worship the One God, he tells Nimrod to cease the practice of idolatry. Nimrod issues an order calling for Abram to be burned at the stake, and the king prepares a large bonfire for the occasion. When Abram walks out of the fire unharmed, the king gives Eliezer to Abram (*Sefer ha-Yashar*, Noah 42). The slave enters Abram's household and eventually becomes his chief servant and heir-apparent (Gen. 15:2). Eliezer is said to have possessed all the virtues and wisdom of his master (*Yoma* 28b). He is Abram's spit-and-image; indeed, the physical resemblance between the two is so great that on one occasion Laban mistakes Eliezer for Abram (*Gen. Rabbah* 60:7). The rabbis revise the biblical account of Abram's recovery of Lot from the Canaanite kings who had captured him: Whereas in Gen. 14:14 Abram's army is said to have included exactly 318 retainers, according to *Tanḥuma B*, only one man accompanied Abram—Dammesek Eliezer, whose name in Hebrew is composed of six letters: *aleph*, *lamed*, *yod*, *ayin*, *zayin*, *resh*. By the rules of *gematria*, the combined numerical value of these six letters is 318: 1 + 30 + 10 + 70 + 7 + 200 = 318.[30]

The birth of first Ishmael and then Isaac appears to have eliminated any hopes that Dammesek Eliezer may have had to succeed Abraham. Or perhaps not. In Gen. 22, it will be recalled, Abraham and Isaac do not travel alone to the land of Moriah (see Chapter 6). They are accompanied by two unnamed servants and one donkey. According to *Gen. Rabbah* 56:2, the two servants are unable to see the vision given to Abraham and Isaac. This may explain why, in the biblical narrative, they remain at the foot of the mountain, where their only function is to watch over the donkey while father and son ascend to the site of the sacrifice. In *PRE* the two servants are identified as Ishmael and Eliezer: the former, Abraham's first-born son who was expelled by his father; the latter, Abraham's trusted servant and erstwhile heir. Both men had an interest in Isaac's demise. The following conversation is reported to have taken place while the two servants were waiting for their master and his son to descend from the mountain:

> Ishmael said to Eliezer: "Now that Abraham is proceeding to offer up his son Isaac as a burnt offering on the altar, and I am his firstborn, I will become the heir of Abraham."
>
> But Eliezer replied to Ishmael: "He has already ejected you like a woman divorced from her husband whom he has sent to the wilderness. I however am his servant and minister in his house by day and by night. I am therefore the rightful heir of Abraham." A voice came from Heaven and proclaimed: "Neither the one nor the other shall inherit!"[31]

Here Eliezer and Ishmael compete for the right to inherit from Abraham. Each man claims that, after Abraham has sacrificed Isaac, he will be the patriarch's sole heir. As we know, however, the human sacrifice is averted and it is Isaac who becomes Abraham's heir. Once Isaac's status as Abraham's heir has been established, the success of the divine promise comes to depend on Isaac's producing a natural son. In order to produce an heir, he needs a wife. In Gen. 24, Abraham sends his unnamed senior servant—presumably Dammesek Eliezer of Gen. 15:2—to Mesopotamia to secure a wife for Isaac. In the biblical account, the servant is completely devoted to his master. His personality is more complicated in *midrash*ic sources (where he is identified as Eliezer). According to *Gen. Rabbah* 59:9, Eliezer has a daughter who might become Isaac's wife if her father's mission to Mesopotamia were to fail. When Abraham learns of Eliezer's hope that his daughter will marry Isaac, he curses his servant. Eliezer's devotion to Abraham is so great that the trusted servant subordinates his own interests to those of his master. According to *PRE* 16, Abraham rewards his slave for successfully completing his mission and securing a wife for Isaac by granting him his freedom. Thereafter, Eliezer becomes the king of Bashan, ruling under the name of Og. According to *Derekh Eretz Zuta* 1:9, the Lord found Eliezer to be a worthy man—despite his having been born to the accursed Canaanite nation—for which reason he is allowed to enter Paradise before his death.

The Islamic Intertext: Muḥammad Adopts Zayd, Zayd Marries and Divorces Zaynab, and Zayd Informs Zaynab of Her Upcoming Marriage to the Prophet

After Zayd had demonstrated his absolute devotion to his master by rejecting his birth family, Muḥammad took his slave to the Kaʿba, where he manumitted him and adopted him in a formal ceremony. "O you who are present," Muḥammad said to his fellow tribesmen, "bear witness that Zayd is my son. I inherit from him and he inherits from me" (*arithuhu wa-yarithunī*).[32] The adoption ceremony created a filial relationship between the two men, including mutual rights of inheritance. To mark the new relationship, Zayd's name was changed: Zayd b. Ḥāritha became Zayd b. Muḥammad.[33]

Zayd's status as the Prophet's heir and potential successor lasted for more than twenty years. In the year 5 A.H., Muḥammad repudiated Zayd, ostensibly to facilitate his marriage to his daughter-in-law. As a result of the repudiation, Zayd forfeited his status as the Prophet's son, reverted to his birth name of Zayd b. Ḥāritha, and was no longer the Prophet's heir. Zayd accepted his demotion in status without complaint.

The Qur'ān does not indicate how Zaynab learned of the Prophet's decision to marry her. This narrative gap was filled in by Muslim storytellers. Whereas on the occasion of her marriage to Zayd, it had been Muḥammad (or ʿAlī) who informed her of the impending marriage (see Chapter 4), on the occasion of her marriage to Muḥammad it was Zayd who informed her of the impending marriage. The symmetry of the two marriage proposals is another sign of the storytellers at work—or perhaps it is a manifestation of divine providence. One might ask: Why did Muḥammad send Zayd, who had only recently divorced Zaynab, to ask for her hand in marriage on his behalf? "By my soul," the Prophet is reported to have said to Zayd, "there is no one whom I regard as more trustworthy than you."[34] Although Zayd was no longer the Prophet's son, he was still his trusted servant.

We learn more about Zayd's state of mind in a variant of the preceding report. It is related on the authority of Anas b. Mālik (d. 92/711) that after Zayd divorced Zaynab, she observed her waiting period. When it was determined that she was not pregnant, Muḥammad ordered his erstwhile son to propose to his former wife on the Prophet's behalf (*fa'dhkurhā ʿalayya*). Zayd was reluctant to carry out this instruction, but in the face of an order from the Prophet, he had no choice but to pay a visit to Zaynab in her apartment (just as previously Zaynab had no choice but to marry Zayd—see Q. 33:36). When Zayd arrived to inform his former wife of the Prophet's decision, she was kneading dough.[35]

This was another decisive moment for Zayd, who acknowledged that the very sight of Zaynab caused him great emotional distress (*ʿaẓuma fī ṣadrī*) and that he could not bear to look at her. The messenger turned his back on his former wife and walked away from her. If he failed to inform Zaynab of her upcoming marriage to Muḥammad, however, he would be disobeying a prophetic order. As he was retreating, Zayd managed to utter the following words, "O Zaynab, the Messenger of God has sent [me] to ask for your hand in marriage [on his behalf]." Whereas previously Zaynab had refused to marry Zayd until she was informed that the Prophet had chosen her for him, on this occasion she told Zayd, "I do not make any decision before consulting with my Lord." Zaynab stood up and walked to her place of prayer. And the Qurʾān—presumably Q. 33:37—was revealed [sic].[36] Then the Messenger of God came and entered without [asking for] permission" (*fa-dakhala ʿalayhā bi-ghayr idhn*).[37]

According to Qurṭubī, the Prophet was testing Zayd. The purpose of the test was to measure Zayd's patience, submissiveness, and obedience.[38] Again, Zayd passed the test. Like the earlier tests, this one was based on a biblical model.[39] The final test would be administered in the year 8 A.H., when Zayd expressed his willingness to die for the sake of God and His Prophet. The moment that he was killed, he ascended to the Garden.

Comparison: Zayd Is Dammesek Eliezer

Both Dammesek Eliezer and Zayd were born in Syria. Each man was enslaved and entered the household of a man who would soon become the founder of a new religion. Each man became his master's trusted servant. Just as Dammesek Eliezer was for a time Abram's heir, Zayd was for a time Muḥammad's heir. Dammesek Eliezer's status as Abram's heir was eliminated first by the birth of Ishmael and then by the birth of Isaac; the competition between the two natural sons was settled by Abram's expulsion of Ishmael and his decision not to sacrifice Isaac. Zayd's status as Muḥammad's heir was eliminated by his father's decision to repudiate him in 5 A.H. Just as Abram sent his trusted servant to Mesopotamia to secure a wife for Isaac, Muḥammad sent his trusted servant to inform his ex-wife Zaynab of her upcoming marriage to the Prophet. Both men were being tested, both passed the test, and both were granted eternal life in Paradise: Dammesek Eliezer ascended to heaven before he died; Zayd entered the Garden the moment he was martyred. Dammesek Eliezer's name is mentioned once in the Hebrew Bible; Zayd's name is mentioned once in the Qurʾān. Each name is a *hapax legomenon.*

Zayd Is Isaac (Gen. 24)

In Act 1, Scene 3, Muḥammad sends ʿAlī b. Abī Ṭālib to propose a marriage between the Prophet's adopted son, Zayd, and his paternal cross-cousin

Zaynab bt. Jaḥsh. The Islamic narrative is modeled on Gen. 24, in which Abraham sends his senior servant to secure a wife for Isaac. In the Islamic narrative, Zayd is Isaac, Muḥammad is Abraham, ʿAlī is the senior servant, Zaynab bt. Jaḥsh is Rebecca, and ʿAbdallāh b. Jaḥsh is Laban.

The Islamic Narrative: Muḥammad Sends ʿAlī b. Abī Ṭālib to Secure a Wife for Zayd

Shortly after the hijra, Zayd informs his father Muḥammad that he wants to marry Zaynab bt. Jaḥsh, one of the women who migrated from Mecca to Medina.[40] Zayd and Zaynab share a common ancestor: ʿAbd al-Muṭṭalib is Zayd's great-grandfather (through adoption) and Zaynab's grandfather, through her mother Umayma. In addition to her lineage, Zaynab boasts that she is the most perfect woman in the tribe of Quraysh.[41]

Initially Muḥammad opposes the marriage, protesting that it would be inappropriate for his son, a former slave, to marry a noble Qurashī woman. Undeterred, Zayd presses his father to tell Zaynab that he regards his adopted son as a nobleman. When the Prophet stands his ground, Zayd turns to his relative by adoption, ʿAlī b. Abī Ṭālib, whom he asks to intercede with Muḥammad on his behalf. "Surely," Zayd says, "he shall not turn you down" (*lan yaʿṣiyaka*). The two men go to see Muḥammad, who now relents.[42] The Prophet sends ʿAlī to propose a marriage between Zayd—his adopted son and heir—and Zaynab bt. Jaḥsh—his paternal cross-cousin.

Zaynab's father Jaḥsh b. Riʾāb al-Asadī is nowhere to be seen. Presumably, he is dead,[43] in which case Zaynab is an orphan. It is for this reason that her brother ʿAbdallāh b. Jaḥsh serves as her marriage guardian.[44] Initially, both ʿAbdallāh and Zaynab object to the marriage proposal. ʿAbdallāh is loathe to give his sister in marriage to a former slave. As for Zaynab, she protests, "I don't want him for myself, for I am the most perfect woman of Quraysh."[45] Only now does ʿAlī inform ʿAbdallāh that the Prophet has chosen Zayd for Zaynab and ordered ʿAbdallāh to give his sister in marriage to Zayd. Once the matter has been decided by the Messenger of God, neither ʿAbdallāh nor Zaynab has any choice but to obey. As Q. 33:36 states, "When God and His messenger have decided a matter, it is not for any believing man or woman to have any choice in the affair." ʿAbdallāh relents and agrees to the marriage proposal. As compensation, Muḥammad sends them ten *dinar*s, sixty *dirham*s, a cloth head-covering, a nightgown, a housedress, a wrapper, fifty *mudd* of food, and ten *mudd* of dates.[46]

Comparison: Zayd Is Isaac (in Gen. 24)

Unlike Abraham, who is determined that Isaac, his natural son and heir, marry within the family (Gen. 24:1 ff.), Muḥammad is determined that

Zayd, his adopted son and heir, not marry a member of his family—although the Prophet eventually changes his mind. Abraham sends his senior servant to Mesopotamia to secure a wife for Isaac (the servant is concerned that the woman he selects will refuse his proposal); Muḥammad sends his cousin and son-in-law, ʿAlī b. Abī Ṭālib, to secure a wife for Zayd (who fears that the woman he wants to marry will refuse a proposal that emanates directly from him). In both cases, the bride and groom are members of the same family and their respective genealogical positions are mirror images of one another. In the biblical narrative, Isaac is Terah's grandson, and Rebecca is Terah's great-granddaughter. In the Islamic narrative, Zayd is ʿAbd al-Muṭṭalib's great-grandson (through adoption), and Zaynab is ʿAbd al-Muṭṭalib's granddaughter (through her mother). In both cases, the bride's father is conspicuously absent: In Gen. 24, Rebecca's father Bethuel is nowhere to be seen and is presumably dead;[47] in the narrative expansions of Q. 33:37, Zaynab's father Jaḥsh is nowhere to be seen and is presumably dead. In both cases, the bride's brother (Laban and ʿAbdallāh b. Jaḥsh, respectively) serves as her marriage guardian. In both cases, the legitimacy of the marriage depends on the willingness of the woman to leave her birthplace and migrate to another land or city: Rebecca must agree to migrate from Mesopotamia to Canaan in order to marry Isaac (Gen. 24:57); Zaynab has already migrated from Mecca to Medina before she marries Zayd. Both women are beautiful: Rebecca is "very beautiful, a virgin whom no man had known" (Gen. 24:16); Zaynab is, by her own testimony, the most perfect woman in the tribe of Quraysh. Whereas Rebecca and her family respond favorably to the servant's proposal, Zaynab and her brother respond unfavorably to ʿAlī's proposal. In both cases, the groom's family pays handsomely for the bride: Abraham's trusted servant gives Rebecca silver, gold, and garments, and he gives her brother and mother unspecified presents; Muḥammad gives Zaynab silver, gold, and garments, and he gives her family food and dates. In both instances, God was responsible for the marriage: The marriage between Rebecca and Isaac was "decreed by the Lord" (Gen. 24:44, 50); the marriage between Zaynab and Zayd was decided by both God and His Prophet (Q. 33:36).

Zayd Is Ishmael

In Act 2, Scene 1, a visit by Muḥammad to his adopted son Zayd and daughter-in-law Zaynab results in Zayd's divorcing his wife. The Islamic narrative is related to an episode in *Pirkei de Rabbi Eliezer* (*PRE*), a Jewish *midrash* in which a visit by Abraham to Ishmael results in Ishmael's divorcing his first wife but keeping his second. In the Islamic narrative, Zayd is Ishmael, Muḥammad is Abraham, and Zaynab is Ishmael's first wife.

Abraham Visits Ishmael and His Wives: Pirkei de Rabbi Eliezer

In Gen. 21, Sarah instructs Abraham to cast out Ishmael so that the patriarch's older son will not share in the inheritance with Isaac (Gen. 21:10). After securing the Lord's promise that Ishmael will become the father of a great nation (Gen. 17:20–21), the patriarch places Ishmael on Hagar's shoulders and sends the pair into the wilderness. As the young man is about to expire, the Lord hears his cries and directs his mother to a well of water. Hagar procures an Egyptian wife for her son (Gen. 21:11–21). Eventually, Ishmael produces twelve sons and becomes the father of a great nation—as the Lord promised (Gen. 25:12–18). At this point, the biblical author loses interest in Hagar and Ishmael.

The biblical narrative raises several questions: Why does Abraham expel Ishmael? Does Abraham continue to love Ishmael even after expelling him? Does Abraham ever see Ishmael again? These questions—and more—were discussed by the rabbis of the Talmudic period, who taught that the expulsion of Hagar and Ishmael was the ninth of ten trials that Abraham underwent during his lifetime. One finds a *midrashic* account of the ninth trial in *PRE* 30. Our attention is drawn to the following paragraph in which Abraham pays a visit to Ishmael:

> After three years Abraham went to see Ishmael his son and he swore to Sarah that he would not go down from the camel at the place where Ishmael dwelt. He arrived there at midday and found Ishmael's wife. He said to her, "Where is Ishmael?" She said to him, "He and his mother went to bring fruit and dates from the desert." He said to her, "Give me a little water and bread and refreshments for I am tired from the desert journey." She said to him, "There is no bread and there is no water." He said to her, "When Ishmael returns tell him these things and say to him that an old man came from the land of Canaan to see you and said that the doorsill of the house is not good." When Ishmael returned, his wife told him what had happened. He sent her away and his mother sent and took for him a wife from her father's house and her name was Fatimah. Again after three years Abraham went to see his son Ishmael and swore to Sarah like the first time that he would not go down from the camel at the place where Ishmael dwelt. He arrived there at midday and found Ishmael's wife. He asked about Ishmael's whereabouts, to which she replied, "He and his mother went to pasture the camels in the desert." Since he was exhausted from the journey, he asked for some bread and water. She brought it out and gave it to him. Abraham stood and he prayed before the Holy One, Blessed be He for his son and as a result the house of Ishmael was filled with all the good things of blessings. When Ishmael returned, his wife told him what happened and Ishmael knew that his father still loved him, as it is said, "As a father loves his children." (Ps. 103:13)[48]

PRE expands on the biblical narrative. Yes, Abraham still loves Ishmael even after sending him into the wilderness. And Abraham does make an attempt to see Ishmael at least once before he dies. How does Abraham love Ishmael? "As a father loves his son" (Ps. 103:13). Note, however, that Abraham needs Sarah's permission to visit Hagar and Ishmael and that the matriarch makes her husband swear an oath that he will not dismount his camel. One wonders about the reason for this stipulation. Does Sarah fear that if Abraham were to dismount he might be persuaded to reverse his decision to make Isaac his heir? Or does she fear that if the patriarch were to dismount, he might have sexual relations with Ishmael's wife—his daughter-in-law?[49] Be that as it may, Ishmael and Hagar are off in the desert gathering fruit when Abraham arrives at their house, where the aged patriarch finds only Ishmael's nameless wife—presumably the Egyptian woman who, according to the biblical narrative, was chosen for Ishmael by Hagar. When Abraham asks the woman for bread and water, she refuses, whereupon the patriarch instructs her to inform her husband that an old man from the land of Canaan came to visit him and that the man recommended that he replace the doorsill of his house. This is a coded message that signifies: divorce your wife. When Ishmael returns, his wife tells him what had happened, and he divorces her. Hagar now secures a new wife for her son, a woman named Fatimah who is related to Hagar's father.

Three years later, the story is repeated. Abraham asks Sarah for permission to visit Ishmael, and Sarah makes him swear an oath that he will not dismount his camel. Again, Ishmael and Hagar are off in the desert—this time tending to the camels—when Abraham arrives at his son's house. Again, the patriarch finds only Ishmael's new wife—his daughter-in-law, Fatimah. Abraham asks the woman for bread and water, and she brings it out to him. When Ishmael returns, his wife conveys another coded message. Ishmael keeps this wife. Thus did the son who had been expelled learn that his father still loved him and that his House was blessed.

The Islamic Intertext: Muḥammad Visits Zayd and His Wife

God and His Prophet may have been responsible for Zayd's marriage to Zaynab, but the union was not a happy one. Shortly after the marriage was consummated Zayd begins to complain to his father about his wife's behavior.

Muḥammad pays a visit to Zayd and Zaynab, but only his daughter-in-law is at home (we do not know where Zayd is or what he is doing at the time). The text does not specify that the Prophet was riding a camel, but if he was, he dismounted. Muḥammad enters the house intending to admonish Zaynab. As he is speaking to his daughter-in-law, he is struck by her beauty, grace, and physical appearance (a reaction ordained by God, as Muqātil is careful to add). Muḥammad returns home, harboring within himself the amorous feelings that God wants him to have for Zaynab. Subsequently, when Muḥammad asks his son about Zaynab's behavior, Zayd repeats his complaint. In a curious reversal, the man who begged his father for permission to marry Zaynab now pleads with him for permission to divorce her. Ignoring his own feelings for the woman, Muḥammad orders Zayd to "keep your wife to yourself and fear God." These very words are reproduced in Q. 33:37.[50]

Comparison: Zayd Is Ishmael

As his father's older son, Ishmael is Abraham's heir until his father expels him; as Muḥammad's adopted son, Zayd is the Prophet's heir until his father repudiates him. Whereas Abraham pays a visit to Ishmael (and his wife) subsequent to his expulsion, Muḥammad pays a visit to Zayd (and his wife) prior to his repudiation. Sarah makes her husband swear an oath that he will not dismount his camel, perhaps for fear that he will have sexual relations with his daughter-in-law; Muḥammad is subject to no such constraint. When each man arrives at his respective destination, he finds only his daughter-in-law at home. Abraham stays on his camel; if Muḥammad was riding a camel, he dismounts and falls in love with his daughter-in-law—although he does not as yet have sexual relations with her.[51] Whereas Abraham advises Ishmael to divorce his first wife after she treats her father-in-law inappropriately, Muḥammad orders his son not to divorce his wife despite the fact that she was treating her husband inappropriately. In the rabbinic narrative one man marries two women in succession but only the second marriage is successful; in the Islamic narrative one woman marries two men in succession but only the second marriage is successful. Just as Abraham continues to love Ishmael after expelling him, Muḥammad continues to love Zayd after repudiating him.

Zayd Is Uriah the Hittite

In Acts 2 and 5, Muḥammad falls in love with Zaynab in the year 5 A.H. and marries her following her divorce from Zayd; three years later the Prophet sends Zayd to certain death in battle. The Islamic intertext draws on II Samuel 11–12 (one of the pretexts of Q. 33:37). In the Islamic narrative, Zayd is Uriah the Hittite, Muḥammad is David, and Zaynab is Bathsheba. The relationship between these two narratives was noted by Muqātil in the first half of the second century A.H. (see Chapter 4).

The Islamic Intertext: Muḥammad, Zaynab, and Zayd

One day Muḥammad catches a glimpse of his beautiful daughter-in-law while she is in the act of rising to her feet (*fa-abṣarat Zaynab qāʾimat*[an]), and he falls in love with her. Later that day, Zaynab tells Zayd about the encounter with her father-in-law. Relations between husband and wife—already strained—go from bad to worse. Zaynab insinuates that her husband suffered from a sexual dysfunction, although she is careful to add that she continued to make herself available to Zayd so long as they remained husband and wife, that is to say, she observed the rules of wifely obedience.[52] Be that as it may, the couple ceased having sexual relations—a key narrative detail.[53]

Zayd now asks his father for permission to divorce Zaynab. A compressed version of what happens next is found in Q. 33:37. Although Muḥammad is in love with Zaynab, he understands that her status as his daughter-in-law poses a legal obstacle to marriage. Fearing public disapproval, the Prophet keeps his feelings a secret and tells Zayd, "keep your wife to yourself and fear God." Just as the social obstacle to Zaynab's marriage to Zayd was removed by a combination of prophetic and divine intervention (Q. 33:36), so too the legal obstacle to Zaynab's upcoming marriage to the Prophet is removed by divine intervention. In Q. 33:37 God rebukes Muḥammad for placing his fear of men over that of God but then gives the Prophet permission to marry Zaynab—albeit on the condition that Zayd no longer has any sexual desire for Zaynab. As we have seen, this condition has already been satisfied, and Zayd proceeds to divorce Zaynab. During the short interval between Zayd's divorcing Zaynab and Muḥammad's marrying her, the Prophet approaches Zayd and announces, "I am not your father," thereby dissolving the filial relationship established two decades earlier. This is another test. The man who renounced his birth family in order to remain with his slave master now relinquishes his wife so that his father—or ex-father—might marry her. The devoted servant accepts the repudiation and the resulting demotion in status without complaint. It is only after Zayd has lost the right to call himself Zayd b. Muḥammad and has been stripped of his status as Muḥammad's son and legal heir that God arranges for Muḥammad to marry Zaynab, as indicated in Q. 33:37: "We gave her to you in marriage."[54]

Following his repudiation, Zayd retains the confidence of the Prophet, who has no misgivings about placing his former son and Zaynab's former husband in harm's way. In the year 6 A.H., Muḥammad appoints Zayd as the commander of six different military expeditions. In 8 A.H., the Prophet assembles the Army of Mu'ta and appoints Zayd as its first commander. Zayd marches to Mu'ta in southern Jordan, where he falls as a martyr.

Comparison: Zayd Is Uriah the Hittite

Several themes or motifs in II Samuel 11—one of the pretexts of Q. 33:37 (see above)—were transferred to the Islamic narratives about Zayd. Just as the beautiful wife of Uriah the Hittite is espied by King David while she is in the act of bathing (*roḥetset*; II Sam. 11:2), so too the beautiful wife of Zayd b. Muḥammad is espied by his father while she is in the act of standing up (*qā'imat^{an}*). Whereas Uriah's wife exposes herself in public, the exposure of Zayd's wife takes place within the privacy of her home. Whereas David is unable to control his sexual desires, and, acting in secret, sins by engaging in sexual relations with Uriah's wife—but only after she has purified herself

(II Sam. 11:4), Muḥammad exercises restraint, keeping his feelings for his daughter-in-law a secret until God intervenes to insure that he can have sexual relations with her within the framework of a legal marriage—but only after the expiration of her waiting period. Both men fear public disapproval. Just as Uriah the Hittite ceases to have sexual relations with Bathsheba after she has been impregnated by David (II Sam. 11:8–11), Zayd ceases to have sexual relations with Zaynab after his father falls in love with his wife. Just as David sends Uriah the Hittite to certain death at Rabbat Ammon (II Sam. 11:14ff.), Muḥammad sends Zayd to certain death at Muʾta—approximately 30 km from Rabbat Ammon.[55]

Whereas David marries Bathsheba shortly after causing Uriah's death (II Sam. 11:27), Muḥammad marries Zaynab shortly after repudiating Zayd—but three years before sending Zayd to certain death in battle. Whereas David does not understand that he has committed a sin (II Sam. 12:1 ff.), Muḥammad struggles to avoid committing a sin. Just as David is rebuked by the prophet Nathan (II Sam. 12:1–14), Muḥammad is rebuked by God. Just as David takes Uriah's wife before the very eyes of the Israelite community, Muḥammad takes Zayd's wife before the very eyes of the Muslim community (thus appearing to fulfill the Lord's threat to David in II Samuel 12:11). Whereas Bathsheba becomes pregnant with David's child, Zaynab does not become pregnant with Muḥammad's child.[56]

The following motifs are shared by II Samuel 11–12 and the narrative expansion of Q. 33:37: Illicit sexual relations, a secret, fear of public opinion, sin, and rebuke.

Zayd Is Solomon

Zayd also resembles Solomon. Just as in II Samuel 12:24–25 the second child born to Bathsheba has two names, Solomon (the name given to him by his mother) and Yedidiah, or Friend of God (the name given to him by the Lord), so too Zayd has two names, Zayd b. Muḥammad and the Beloved of the Messenger of God (both names are given to him by the Prophet). Just as Solomon/Yedidiah is favored by God, so too Zayd is favored by God and His Prophet. Just as Solomon succeeds his father as King of Israel (I Kings 1:28 ff.) or, according to the Qurʾān, as a prophet (Q. 27:16), so too Zayd would have succeeded his father as a prophet and/or as *khalīfa* had it not been for his repudiation in 5 and martyrdom in 8 A.H.

Zayd Is Isaac of the Aqedah

Islamic sources report that in the year 8 A.H. Muḥammad sent Zayd to certain death at Muʾta, where the Beloved of the Messenger of God fell in battle as a martyr. The Islamic narrative is modeled on rabbinic *midrash* in which

Abraham sacrifices his son Isaac. In the Islamic narrative, Zayd is Isaac, Muḥammad is Abraham, and al-Nuʿmān b. Funḥuṣ is Satan.

The Binding of Isaac in Rabbinic Midrash (Gen. 22)

In *midrashic* expansions of Genesis 22, the rabbis entertain the idea that Abraham did sacrifice Isaac. Such a reading is facilitated by the narrative detail that it is only Abraham who returns from the mountain in the land of Moriah, only Abraham—accompanied by his two servants—who departs for Beer-sheba, and only Abraham who stays in Beer-sheba (Gen. 22:19).

In later narrative expansions of Genesis 22, both Abraham and Isaac serve as models for the rabbinic doctrine of *qiddush ha-Shem*, or martyrdom. The rabbis taught that Abraham was eager to sacrifice his son and that Isaac was an adult who was eager to be sacrificed: "he rushed to the altar and his doom" (*JA*, Book 1, par. 232). Isaac instructed his father to bind his hands tightly so that he would not struggle and render the offering unfit (*Fragmentary Targum* on Gen. 22:10). Isaac bound himself upon the altar (*Sifre Deut.* 32) and joyfully expressed his willingness to serve as the sacrificial victim (*LAB* 32:3). When the moment arrived, "he did not cower" (4 Macc. 16:20).

Some rabbis taught that Abraham did fulfill God's command to sacrifice his son. In *PRK*'s commentary on Ps. 102:21, Isaac is said to have "offered (*hiqrîb*) himself on the altar." Any doubt about the outcome of the *aqedah* is removed in *PRE* 31, where it is specified that Abraham put the knife to Isaac's throat, whereupon Isaac died, was given new life, and ascended to Heaven, where he remained for three years while recovering from the wound inflicted by his father. It was only after the wound had healed that he returned to earth—just in time to marry Rebecca (Gen. 24:62).

The rabbis circulated short narratives in which Satan attempts to dissuade Abraham from fulfilling God's command. The narratives begin, "This is how Satan talked to Abraham," after which Satan attempts to change Abraham's mind. Invariably, Abraham ignores Satan's advice. In a longer version of these narratives, Satan is replaced by Samael, the Angel of Death. Posing as a close advisor, Samael attempts to persuade Abraham to reverse his decision to sacrifice his beloved son. The patriarch's response signals his determination to fulfill the divine command. Samael now turns to Isaac and informs him that his father intends to slaughter him. "Indeed so," Isaac replies. In a variant of this longer narrative, Samael appears to Abraham in the guise of an old man who attempts—again unsuccessfully—to persuade Abraham to reverse his decision to sacrifice his beloved son.

The Islamic Intertext: The Martyrdom of Zayd

In the year 8/629, the Prophet appoints Zayd as the first commander of a 3,000-man military force that he sends to southern Jordan with instructions to avenge the slaying of one of Muḥammad's messengers. The Prophet accompanies the Muslim soldiers to al-Jurf, where, after performing the mid-day prayer, he specifies the order of command and issues the battle instructions. One of the men gathered around the Prophet is al-Nuʿmān b. Funḥuṣ, a Jew who attempts to dissuade Muḥammad from sending Zayd into battle. The Jew warns the Prophet that his very words ("if Zayd falls, then. . . .") constitute a death sentence. When Muḥammad ignores his advice, the Jew turns to Zayd and advises him to prepare his last will and testament, warning that if Muḥammad is in fact a true prophet, he will not return from the field of battle. To this Zayd responds by affirming that Muḥammad is the Messenger of God and by announcing his willingness to die for the sake of God, His Prophet, and Islam.

Muḥammad and the other noncombatants accompany the Army of Mu'ta to the Farewell Pass, where the noncombatants take leave of the soldiers, imploring God to bring them back safe and sound. The soldiers march off in the direction of southern Jordan. Just before the battle is engaged, Zayd is confronted by Satan, who attempts to entice him with the pleasures of this world—albeit unsuccessfully. Zayd dismounts his horse and enters the battlefield, where he is the first Muslim to be killed. Immediately, he ascends to the Garden, running. The primary witness to the martyrdom of Zayd (and his fellow commanders) is Muḥammad, who, although physically located in Medina, is the recipient of a miraculous vision that makes it possible for him to see the events on the battlefield as they are unfolding in southern Jordan.

Comparison: Zayd Is Isaac of the Aqedah

Whereas Genesis 22 and later *midrashim* focus on Isaac, whose brother Ishmael recently had been expelled, the Islamic narrative focuses on Zayd, who himself recently had been repudiated.

In both cases, a father and his son are tested. In both cases, father and son worship or pray before attending to the sacrifice. In both cases, the intended sacrifice is an adult male who is a willing participant in the ritual, in both cases the intended sacrifice is eager for death, and in both cases he fails to return from the site of the sacrifice. Both Isaac and Zayd ascend—one to Heaven, the other to the Garden—and both men achieve immortality. In both narratives, the motif of vision plays a prominent role: Abraham calls the site of the sacrifice Adonai-yireh, which gave rise to the expression, "On the mount of the Lord there is vision" (Gen. 22:14); as the battle unfolds in southern Jordan, Muḥammad receives a miraculous vision of the events that are taking place several hundred miles away. In both cases, Satan plays the role of the intimate adversary: Just as Satan or Samael or an old man tries to dissuade Abraham from sacrificing Isaac, so too al-Nuʿmān b. Funḥuṣ the Jew attempts to dissuade Muḥammad from sending Zayd to certain death at Muʾta. And just as Isaac is willing to die for the sake of his religion, Zayd is willing to die for the sake of his.

The rabbinic and Islamic narratives use identical themes, motifs, literary structures, and linguistic forms: the testing of a father and his son; worship prior to a life-threatening event; leave-taking and a concern about return; an intimate adversary; eagerness for death; ascension and eternal life; and a supernatural vision.

Conclusion: The Many Faces of Zayd

Q. 33:37 is a cryptic verse that appears to refer to an event in the life of Muḥammad. The narrative gaps in this verse were filled in by Muslim storytellers during the first centuries A.H. If the verse and its narrative expansions are treated as records or traces of an episode that actually took place during the life of the Prophet, then it is possible to produce a full biography of Zayd.[57]

It is also possible to view Q. 33:37 and its narrative expansions as literary compositions that draw on and modify earlier biblical and postbiblical narratives. If v. 37 originated as a sacred legend, then there is no point in attempting to recover its underlying historical background. Rather than facts, one looks for functions. In my view, the original function of v. 37 was to support the theological doctrine of the finality of prophecy. The placement of the verse is critical. It is the second verse in a five-verse pericope that culminates in the Qurʾānic pronouncement that Muḥammad is the Seal of Prophets. The function of this pericope is to establish that at the time of his death in 11/632, Muḥammad did not have a son who had reached maturity. This was accomplished by formulating a new sacred narrative based on earlier biblical narratives. Q. 33:37 is modeled on Matthew 1:18–25, which, in turn, is modeled on II Samuel 11–12. The three episodes constitute a narrative sequence. In each instance, the relevant episode is a defining moment in Jewish, Christian, or Islamic salvation history. After David engages in illicit sexual relations with Bathsheba, God intervenes in history to insure that the king will produce a legitimate heir who continues the Davidic line. When Mary appears to engage in illicit sexual relations with someone other than the man to whom she is betrothed, an angel appears to Joseph in a dream in order to explain that the Holy Spirit is the father of the child to whom Mary will give birth. When Muḥammad is brought to the verge of engaging in illicit sexual relations with his daughter-in-law, God sends down a revelation that legitimizes the union. In the Islamic case, however, the apparent function of the sacred legend—to legitimize the Prophet's marriage to Zaynab—is not its true function. Rather, the true function of the Qur'ānic text is to create a narrative space into which Muḥammad's repudiation of his adopted son Zayd could be inserted, thereby preserving the integrity of the Islamic contention that Muḥammad is the Last Prophet.

Just as v. 37 is a sacred legend based on earlier biblical models, so too its narrative expansions are literary compositions based on earlier biblical and postbiblical models. Again, there is no point in attempting to recover the historical facts that lie behind the narratives. Again, one seeks to identify literary and/or theological functions. The Islamic narratives are modeled on Genesis 15:1–6, Genesis 24, Genesis 37–45, II Samuel 11–12, and postbiblical *midrashim*. Like v. 37, the original function of its narrative expansions was to support the doctrine of the finality of prophecy. This doctrine was incompatible with the fact that Muḥammad had an adopted son named Zayd who, in turn, had a son named Usāma. The very existence of Zayd and Usāma threatened to undermine the doctrine of the finality of prophecy—just as the existence of Ishmael and Esau threatened to undermine the Israelite doctrine of divine election; and just as the existence of Joseph threatened to undermine the Christian doctrine that Jesus is the Son of God. The uncanny parallels between these phenomena is yet another sign of God's practice, or *sunnat allāh*.

In v. 40 of *Sūrat al-Aḥzāb*, the divine pronouncement that Muḥammad is the Seal of Prophets is linked directly to his sonlessness; and Muḥammad's sonlessness is linked in turn to a man named Zayd who is the *sabab*, or cause, of the revelation of vv. 36–40. Although Zayd may have been an historical personage, the narratives about him are best seen as literary compositions. In these narratives Zayd is a sacred figure whose primary function is to make it possible for Muḥammad to become the Last Prophet. The Beloved of the Messenger of God fulfils this function by serving God and His Prophet with absolute and unwavering loyalty and devotion for nearly a quarter of a century, from the moment he enters Muḥammad's household ca. 605 C.E. until his death at Mu'ta in 8/629. The Muslims who formulated the narratives about Zayd and transmitted them from one generation to the next portrayed him as a devoted servant, son, and client. Zayd's life unfolded as a series of five tests:

1. He chose slavery with Muḥammad over freedom with his family.
2. He suffered public humiliation by divorcing his wife so that his father might marry her.
3. He suffered further discomfort when carrying out the Prophet's instruction that he inform his ex-wife of Muḥammad's decision to marry her.

4. He willingly relinquished his status as Muḥammad's son, his name (Zayd b. Muḥammad), and his right to inherit from the Prophet.
5. He laid down his life for the sake of God and His Prophet.

In the Islamic narratives, Zayd takes on a new persona as he passes from one stage of life to the next. As a youth he is Joseph, who was captured and enslaved so that he might fulfill a divine plan to insure the survival of the Children of Israel. Upon entering the household of Muḥammad, Zayd becomes Dammesek Eliezer, a trusted servant whose devotion to his master is absolute and who—so long as there is no other candidate for the position—is his heir. Zayd's status as Muḥammad's heir is reinforced by his nickname: Like Solomon/Yedidiah, who is loved by the Lord, Zayd is the Beloved of the Messenger of God and the one upon whom both God and His Prophet bestowed favor. When Muḥammad sends ʿAlī to arrange Zayd's marriage to Zaynab, Zayd becomes Isaac.

At this point, however, the Islamic narratives diverge sharply from their biblical antecedents. Whereas the purpose of the biblical narratives is to demonstrate how the divine promise to Abraham was fulfilled through biological reproduction and patrilineal continuity, the purpose of the Islamic narratives is to demonstrate the finality of prophecy. This could be accomplished only by turning the motif of biological reproduction on its head and replacing it with the motif of sonlessness. Once the early Muslim community decided to advance the notion that Muḥammad was the Last Prophet, Zayd's very existence became a threat to the new theological doctrine. This threat had to be eliminated, whatever the cost. Look now and Zayd becomes Ishmael, the son expelled by Abraham so that he will not displace Isaac as his father's heir. Look again and Zayd becomes Uriah the Hittite, the man whose wife is taken from him by King David. Look one last time and Zayd becomes Isaac of the *aqedah*, the prototype of the martyr who willingly lays down his life for the sake of God and his religion, thereby gaining immortality. At different stages of his life, Zayd's persona is modeled on that of Joseph, Dammesek Eliezer, Solomon, Isaac, Ishmael, and Uriah the Hittite. He is each one of these figures individually and all of them combined.[58] One examines his life as one peers into a kaleidoscope: With each turn of the dial, a new and different image comes into focus. The many faces of Zayd were crafted by Muslim storytellers who had access to, and drew on, a large repertory of biblical and postbiblical texts. What is remarkable about Zayd is the way in which his persona incorporates the traits and personalities of at least six different biblical figures, thereby making him a condensed religious symbol.[59]

The meaning of the phrase *khātam al-nabiyyīn* was contested within the early Muslim community. Those believers who held that revelations delivered to Muḥammad confirmed or fulfilled the revelations delivered previously to

Moses and Jesus understood the phrase as signifying that Muḥammad was the Seal of Prophets—albeit not necessarily the last one. Those believers who held that Muḥammad brought the office of prophecy to a close understood the phrase as signifying that he was the Last Prophet. By the end of the first century A.H., the finality-of-prophecy position had prevailed. The success of the new theological doctrine was dependent on Muḥammad's sonlessness, as clearly articulated in the formulation of Q. 33:40.

The new theological doctrine required adjustments not only to law (the abolition of adoption) and history (the dating of the Battle of Mu'ta), but also to the Qur'ān. In Chapter 4, I hypothesized that the consonantal skeleton of Q. 4:23 and 33:6 were revised in order to accommodate the new doctrine of the finality of prophecy. Part III is devoted to two additional instances in which the consonantal skeleton of the Qur'ān may have been revised: Q. 4:12b and 4:176. In both instances, the revision was related to the mysterious word *kalāla*. In both instances, my hypothesis is based on documentary evidence found in an early Qur'ān manuscript: Bibliothèque Nationale de France, Arabe 328a. There is no direct connection between the revision of these two sets of verses. Similarly, there is no direct connection between the revision of Q. 4:12b and 4:176 and the doctrine of the finality of prophecy. There is, however, an indirect—almost incidental—connection between all these phenomena—to which I shall draw attention in the Conclusion.

Part III
Text and Interpretation

Accordingly, in many instances of textual distortion, we may nevertheless count upon finding what has been suppressed and disavowed hidden away somewhere else, though changed and torn from its context. Only it will not always be easy to recognize it.

—*Sigmund Freud,* Moses and Monotheism, *283–84*

. . . the issue of the transmission of the Qur'ānic text immediately leads into consideration of numerous complex questions of absolutely fundamental importance to the course and character of earliest Islamic history. It seems entirely reasonable that considerable doubt should prevail until and unless the many specific and general questions raised by such theories have been addressed. And this purpose would best be served, in the present state of our knowledge, by careful and exhaustive investigation of individual verses or limited passages. This would provide the foundations necessary to focus more clearly the direction of a broader inquiry.

—*Lawrence I. Conrad, review of* Die Wiederentdeckung des Propheten Muhammad *and* Studien zur Komposition des mekkanischen Suren, *53*

Chapter 8

Paleography and Codicology: Bibliothèque Nationale de France, Arabe 328a

A cet égard [viz., l'époque précise et les conditions dans lesquelles fut rédigé le Coran], la tradition manuscrite du Coran ne nous est, pour le moment tout au moins, d'aucune aide.

—*Mohammed Ali Amir-Moezzi and Etan Kohlberg, "Révélation et falsification: Introduction à l'édition du* Kitāb al-Qirā'āt *d'al-Sayyārī," 663*

Detailed studies of these manuscripts, when combined with external evidence from related Ḥadīth and qirā'āt literature, and taken together, will add solid facts to the corpus of data necessary for better understanding the textual history of the Qur'ān . . .

—*Intisar A. Rabb, "Non-Canonical Readings of the Qur'ān: Recognition and Authenticity (The Ḥimṣī Reading)," 109*

The earlier scribes were involved not only in the copying of texts, but to a limited extent also in the creative shaping of the last stage of their content. Expressed differently, at one time scribes often took the liberty of changing the content, adding and omitting elements, sometimes on a small scale, but often substantially. . . . The nature of this creative scribal activity requires us to conceive of the persons involved as scribes-editors, who were not only active in the transmission of texts, but also in the final stage of their creative edition.

—*Emanuel Tov,* Scribal Practices, *24–25*

Islamic tradition teaches that God spoke to Muḥammad over a period of twenty-three years between 610 and 632 C.E., and that after receiving a divine communication, the Prophet would teach it to his Companions. The revelations are said to have been preserved in two ways: Some Muslims memorized the words taught to them by the Prophet; others inscribed the utterances on palm branches, animal bones, stones, cloth, parchment, papyrus, and wooden boards. Accordingly, at the time of Muḥammad's death in 11/632, the revelations would have existed in the minds of the Muslims who had memorized them and on various writing surfaces. There was as yet no codex or book. In the years immediately following the death of the Prophet, these heterogeneous and unwieldy materials were collected, placed in sequential order, divided into chapters, edited, and redacted, thereby producing the text known as the Qurʾān. The redaction of the Qurʾān is one of the fundamental cruxes of modern scholarship on the rise of Islam.[1]

One finds considerable information about the redactional process in what I shall call the standard account of the Qurʾān's collection. In the sources, this complex project is encompassed by the verb *jamaʿa* or the verbal noun *jamʿ*. The literal meaning of *jamaʿa* is *to collect*, although in the present instance it is possible that the term may signify *to gather*, that is to say, to bring together a group of sheets to form the quires of a codex. The promulgation of an official, state-sponsored codex (*muṣḥaf*) is said to have been the work of the first three caliphs, and the Qurʾān is said to have been collected or gathered on two separate occasions. The first collection was undertaken in response to conditions in Arabia following the death of the Prophet. In apparent defiance of the Qurʾānic pronouncement that Muḥammad is the Last Prophet, an erstwhile Muslim named Musaylima renounced Islam and declared himself to be a prophet. In the year 11/632, Muslim forces fought a fierce battle against Musaylima and his supporters at al-Aqrabāʾ in the district of al-Yamāma in the Najd.[2] The fighting was intense and large numbers of Qurʾān reciters (*qurrāʾ*) are said to have fallen in battle. The death of the reciters reportedly caused ʿUmar b. al-Khaṭṭāb (d. 23/644) to express concern that the record of the revelations that had been preserved in the hearts and minds of men would be lost forever.[3] For this reason, ʿUmar advised the first caliph Abū Bakr (r. 11–13/632–34) to collect all the surviving records, both written and oral. Upon hearing this proposal, the caliph expressed concern about carrying out an innovation: "How can I do something that the Messenger of God did not do?" To this, ʿUmar replied that such a collection would be a good thing (*khayr*), and he persisted in his efforts to persuade the caliph until "God set [Abū Bakr's] heart at ease just as previously He had set ʿUmar's heart at ease."[4] The decision to collect the Qurʾān may have been an innovation, but it had God's blessing.

After accepting ʿUmar's proposal, Abū Bakr summoned Zayd b. Thābit al-Anṣārī (d. 45/665) who, as a young man, had served as the Prophet's secretary.[5] Zayd's initial reaction to the proposal was identical to that of Abū Bakr: "How can the two of you do something that the Messenger of God did not do?" To this, Abū Bakr replied that it was a good thing, and the caliph and ʿUmar persisted in their efforts to persuade Zayd until "God set [Zayd's] heart at ease just as previously He had set the hearts of Abū Bakr and ʿUmar at ease."[6] Zayd now asked the Companions to bring him the revelations that had been memorized and/or recorded in writing, and he transcribed these divine utterances onto unbound sheets or folio pages (*ṣuḥuf*), taking care to accept only those revelations that could be verified by two witnesses.[7] It was a difficult task—more difficult, Zayd is reported to have said, than moving a mountain from one spot to another. As the project neared completion, Zayd realized that two verses that he remembered having heard the Prophet recite were "lost." These two verses read as follows.

A messenger has come to you from among yourselves—what you suffer is grievous to him. [He is] anxious over you, and kind and compassionate toward the believers.

If they turn away, say, "God is sufficient for me. There is no God but Him. I put my trust in Him—He is the Lord of the mighty throne."

Zayd began looking for the two lost verses, which he found in the possession of Khuzayma b. Thābit, who was the only Muslim who had them. In this instance an exception was made to the two-witness rule, and Zayd inserted the newly found verses at the end of *Sūrat al-Tawba*, where they took their place as vv. 128 and 129 in that chapter.[8] After completing his work, Zayd gave the sheets to Abū Bakr, who thus earned the distinction of being the first Muslim caliph to collect the Qurʾān between two boards.[9] Before he died, Abū Bakr conveyed the sheets to ʿUmar, his successor as caliph (r. 13–23/634–44). Prior to his death, ʿUmar gave the sheets to his daughter Ḥafṣa (d. 45/665), one of the widows of the Prophet.[10]

Abū Bakr may have been the first caliph to collect the Qurʾān between two boards, but his text competed with other texts associated with the names of one or another Companion. The free circulation of unofficial versions of the Qurʾān alongside the text sponsored by the first caliph reportedly gave rise to additional anxieties relating to the accurate preservation of the divine revelations. Whereas the first collection was triggered by fear of the loss of the memorized record, the second was triggered by disagreements over the *rasm* or consonantal skeleton. And whereas the first collection was a purely Arabian affair, the second involved the Muslim community in Kufa,[11] or, alternatively, on the frontier with Armenia and Azerbayjan.[12]

In narratives about the second collection, three Companions play a prominent role: ʿAbdallāh b. Masʿūd (d. 32/653), a well-known Qurʾān reciter;[13] Ḥudhayfa b. al-Yamān (d. 36/656), a military commander;[14] and Abū Mūsa al-Ashʿarī (d. 52/672), a military commander, governor and Qurʾān reciter.[15] Ibn Masʿūd was a Muslim of humble origins who took great pride in his mastery of the Qurʾān. He is said to have boasted that he knew the location in which every verse of the Qurʾān had been revealed and the identity of every person or persons about whom a verse had been revealed. He was careful to add, however, that were he to discover someone whose knowledge of the Qurʾān exceeded his, he would jump on his camel and ride to him.[16] One day, all three Companions were sitting in the mosque in Kufa, where Ibn Masʿūd was reciting the Qurʾān. When he finished his recitation, Ḥudhayfa exclaimed, "The reading of the son of the mother of a slave and [read: versus] the reading of Abū Mūsa al-Ashʿarī! By God, if this [situation] continues, then the next time I meet the Commander of the Believers, I will order him to establish it according to a single reading." To this insult, Ibn Masʿūd responded by uttering angry words directed at Ḥudhayfa, who now remained silent.[17]

In a variant of the preceding report, it is not the reading of the Qurʾān that is problematic but the consonantal skeleton. Sometime in the year 29/649–50, Ḥudhayfa was sitting in a prayer circle in the mosque in Kufa while the Qurʾān was being recited by two groups of men who differed over the consonantal skeleton of Q. 2:196. One group read: "Fulfill the *Ḥajj* and the *ʿUmra* for God (***lillāh***)"—which would become the standard reading. The other group read: "Fulfill the *Ḥajj* and the *ʿUmra* to the house (***lil-bayt***)." Suddenly, an unidentified Muslim called out, "Let those who follow the recitation of Abū Mūsa [al-Ashʿarī] gather in the corner by the Kinda gate, and let those who follow the recitation of ʿAbdallāh b. Masʿūd gather in the corner next to ʿAbdallāh's house." Upon hearing this statement, Ḥudhayfa's face turned red. He stood up, ripped his tunic in two, and declared, "Either he [the unidentified Muslim] will ride to the Commander of the Believers or I will. This is how those who came before you behaved"[18] (alternatively: "the Muslims will disagree about their Book just as the Jews and Christians did previously").[19] When the unidentified Muslim remained in his place, Ḥudhayfa jumped on his mount and rode to Medina, where he advised ʿUthmān (r. 23–35/644–56) about the gravity of the situation and warned that if the caliph did not take immediate action, the enemies of Islam were on the verge of striking a fatal blow to the new religion.[20]

ʿUthmān set up a commission composed of twelve men, headed by Zayd b. Thābit al-Anṣārī. Three members of the commission were prominent Qurashīs: ʿAbdallāh b. al-Zubayr (d. 73/692), Saʿīd b. al-ʿĀṣ (d. 57–9/677–79), and ʿAbd al-Raḥmān b. al-Ḥārith b. Hishām (d. ?).[21] The caliph charged the commission with the task of producing a codex that would put an end to disputes over the consonantal skeleton of the Qurʾān. To facilitate matters, ʿUthmān borrowed the sheets produced at the time of the first collection, which had passed into Ḥafṣa's possession, so that they might serve as the basis for the second collection (Ḥafṣa reportedly refused to part with the sheets until the caliph had agreed to return them to her after completing his project).[22] ʿUthmān instructed Zayd to produce his new collection in the Qurashī dialect spoken by the Prophet. In the event of disagreement over a reading, the word or phrase in question was to be written and pronounced in accordance with the conventions of Qurashī speech patterns.[23] Again, the same two "lost" verses were recovered and inserted at the end of *Sūrat al-Tawba*, although on this occasion—or in this narrative—Khuzayma b. Thābit brought them forward voluntarily, and the exception to the two-witness rule was made by the caliph himself.[24] According to ʿUthmān, the resulting Book was revealed from one source, in one consonantal skeleton, and with one meaning.[25]

The *imām* or mother codex[26] produced by Zayd on behalf of ʿUthmān served as a model for copies that were sent to four cities (presumably Mecca, Basra, Kufa, and Damascus);[27] or to six towns and regions (Mecca, Syria, Yemen, Bahrayn, Basra, and Kufa);[28] or to every region, military district, or garrison town;[29] or to the people.[30] The question now arose: What should be done with the earlier unofficial codices associated with the names of prominent Companions such as ʿAbdallāh b. Masʿūd, Ubayy b. Kaʿb, ʿAlī b. Abī Ṭālib, and Ibn ʿAbbās? In theory, it should have been possible to revise the unofficial codices so as to bring them into conformity with the new mother codex. If this option was considered, it was rejected. ʿUthmān ordered his agents to recall the unofficial codices and to destroy them through immolation in fire (*iḥrāq*), immersion in water (*gharq*), erasure (*maḥw*), and/or shredding (*tamzīq*).[31] The sight of God's words rising in flames or being immersed in water, erased, or shredded surely made a strong impression on the young Muslim community. Consider, for example, the following exchange between Ḥudhayfa b. al-Yamān and certain unidentified Muslims. "What do you think?" Ḥudhayfa asked. "Would you believe me if I were to tell you that you are going to take your codices (*maṣāḥif*), burn them and throw them into the privy?" To which the Muslims replied, "May God be praised. Don't do it O Abū ʿAbdallāh!"[32] Curiously, no one criticized the action taken by ʿUthmān, at least initially. Even ʿAlī b. Abī Ṭālib is reported to have said that if ʿUthmān had not burned the *maṣāḥif*, he would have done so himself.[33] As for the sheets in Ḥafṣa's possession, they were destroyed following her death in 45/665 by the governor of Medina (and future caliph) Marwān b. al-Ḥakam (d. 65/685).[34] Marwān participated in the funeral procession for Ḥafṣa, and he himself recited the final prayer over her body. No sooner had the Prophet's wife been laid to rest than Marwān seized the sheets and burned them, purportedly for fear that with the passage of time, doubts would arise and people would claim that some revelations included in the *ṣuḥuf* or sheets had been omitted from the *muṣḥaf* or official codex.[35]

The new ʿUthmānic codex is said to have been widely distributed and welcomed everywhere except in Kufa, where Ibn Masʿūd was outraged by the caliph's decision to entrust the collection of the Qurʾān to Zayd b. Thābit, a Jewish convert to Islam who had been only eleven years old at the time of the hijra. Ibn Masʿūd may have been of servile origins (as Ḥudhayfa took care to remind him), but he had been one of the first men to become a Muslim. Indeed, he boasted, he had recited as many as seventy *sūra*s or chapters to the Prophet's Companions while Zayd was still a Jew playing with children (alternatively: before Zayd became a Muslim; or, in an even stronger formulation, while Zayd was still an infidel in his mother's womb).[36] Ibn Masʿūd advised his supporters to resist the caliphal order to surrender their codices and to protect these texts with their lives. Indeed, he instructed them to shackle the codices to their necks in anticipation of the Day of Judgment,[37] at which time, presumably, only those Muslims who adhered to his text would attain salvation.[38]

According to the logic of the preceding narrative, it was the ʿUthmānic codex that was distributed throughout the rapidly expanding Islamic polity and it was the consonantal skeleton of this codex that took its place as the universally accepted text of the Qurʾān.

That the Qurʾān was collected or gathered on two separate occasions—first by Abū Bakr and then by ʿUthmān—is widely known and accepted by Muslim and non-Muslim scholars alike. Less well known is the redactional activity that took place during the reign of ʿAbd al-Malik b. Marwān (r. 65–86/685–705), who ruled from Damascus and, like all of the Umayyads, regarded himself as God's deputy (*khalīfat allāh*).[39] It was ʿAbd al-Malik who declared Arabic to be the official language of administration, minted the first aniconic coins, and commissioned the construction of the Dome of the Rock in Jerusalem.[40]

Whereas the first two collections of the Qurʾān were carried out in Medina by caliphs who were creating an Arabo-Islamic state, the redactional activity sponsored by ʿAbd al-Malik was carried out in Damascus by a caliph who ruled over a rapidly expanding multiconfessional empire. This activity surely was related to the caliph's efforts to unify his polity, and it would have had the full support of the powerful Umayyad army. The sources do not specifically mention a *third* collection, perhaps because the consonantal skeleton that eventually was accepted is universally regarded as a product of the collection undertaken by ʿUthmān. It is noteworthy, however, that ʿAbd al-Malik is reported to have said that he was afraid to die in the month of Ramaḍān because inter alia that was the month in which "I collected the Qurʾān (*jamaʿtu al-qurʾān*)."[41] Even if (as some have argued) the verb *jamaʿa* here signifies *to know by heart* or *to memorize* rather than *to collect*, it nevertheless remains the case that ʿAbd al-Malik was closely involved with the text of the Qurʾān and instructed his talented and powerful advisor, al-Ḥajjāj b. Yūsuf al-Thaqafī (41–95/661–714) to introduce numerous changes to the text.[42] Like Ḥudhayfa b. al-Yamān before him, al-Ḥajjāj was critical of Ibn Masʿūd, whose reading of the Qurʾān he characterized as "the *rajaz* [poetry] of Bedouin."[43] Like Ḥudhayfa, al-Ḥajjāj sought to put an end to disagreements over the consonantal skeleton of the Qurʾān. Some of these disagreements may have had a bearing on caliphal legitimacy, for al-Ḥajjāj reportedly removed from the text certain unidentified verses that threatened the interests of the Marwānids. In addition, he is said to have changed the consonantal skeleton of eleven words, established the canonical order of verses and chapters, and introduced for the first time vowels and diacritical marks.[44] Just as ʿUthmān had sent four (or six) copies of his codex to major Muslim population centers, al-Ḥajjāj sent six copies of the newly revised edition to Egypt, Syria, Medina, Mecca, Kufa, and

Basra.[45] Just as ʿUthmān had ordered the destruction of all unofficial codices, so too al-Ḥajjāj ordered the destruction of all codices other than his own and copies made from it. Presumably, this instruction applied not only to official copies of the ʿUthmānic codex but also to the mother codex itself. When the order to destroy all earlier codices reached Medina, however, members of the third caliph's family refused to produce the ʿUthmānic codex, claiming that it had been destroyed on the day on which ʿUthmān was assassinated. Be that as it may, one century later, when Ibn Wahb (d. 197/813) asked Mālik b. Anas (d. 179/795) about the ʿUthmānic codex, he replied, "It has disappeared."[46]

Islamic sources report that the Qurʾān was collected on two separate occasions, once during the caliphate of Abū Bakr and again during the caliphate of ʿUthmān; and that additional redactional activity took place during the caliphate of ʿAbd al-Malik. The sources also report that a systematic campaign to destroy nonconforming Qurʾān codices was carried out on two separate occasions, first during the caliphate of ʿUthmān and again during that of ʿAbd al-Malik; and that in 45/665, the *ṣuḥuf* or sheets collected by Zayd b. Thābit for Abū Bakr were destroyed by the governor of Medina. To the best of my knowledge, the only scholars who have paid serious attention to the redactional activity sponsored by ʿAbd al-Malik are A.-L. de Prémare and C. Robinson.[47] This is unfortunate because disregard for this activity has the effect of making it appear as if the final, definitive version of the Qurʾān was established during the short period of a quarter of a century that encompassed the first three caliphates. The inclusion in this scenario of the redactional activity undertaken by al-Ḥajjāj on behalf of ʿAbd al-Malik has the effect of allowing the reading and consonantal skeleton of the Qurʾān to remain open and fluid until the death of the caliph in 86/705, a full three-quarters of a century after the death of the Prophet.[48]

There is one striking anomaly in the standard account of the collection of the Qurʾān. Islamic sources indicate that disagreements over the reading and consonantal skeleton of the Qurʾān were of such a nature as to cause the first Muslims to accuse one another of *kufr* or infidelity;[49] that these disagreements brought Muslims to the verge of *fitna* or civil strife;[50] and that the textual problems confronted by the Muslims were so serious that they could be solved only through the systematic destruction of all codices that did not conform to the ʿUthmānic *muṣḥaf*. At the same time, however, the sources do not preserve a single example of a textual variant that would account for accusations of infidelity, civil strife, or a book-burning campaign. The surviving variants are minor. What difference does it make if one reads "Fulfill the *Ḥajj* and the *ʿUmra* for God (*lillāh*)" or "Fulfill the *Ḥajj* and the *ʿUmra* to the house (*lil-bayt*)"?[51] It is difficult to imagine that a variant of this nature would have necessitated the systematic destruction of all codices that were not in conformity with the mother codex.

The traditional explanation for the establishment of the official Qur'ānic codex appears to have been formulated in such a manner as to downplay the significance of the textual problems encountered by the Muslims who edited and redacted the text. At the same time that the standard account avoids specific references to substantive textual variants, it refers generally to differences between one reading and the next, to Muslims who struggled to preserve readings that they considered to be authentic, to three successive campaigns to destroy nonconforming texts, and to the trauma and anxiety generated by those campaigns. In this respect, the standard account may be accurate, reflecting the general contours of the process that culminated in the establishment of a canonical text. What is missing are specific details.

Such details are to be found in the early Qur'ān manuscript to be analyzed in this chapter. On the basis of paleographic and codicological evidence, I shall argue that the consonantal skeleton of one verse was modified in such a manner as to transform its meaning; and that this revision made it necessary to formulate supplementary legislation. Unlike the hypotheses that I advanced in Chapter 4, which were based on literary evidence, the hypotheses advanced here are based on documentary evidence. Examination of this evidence brings me back to the mystery of *al-kalāla* (see Preface).

The Problem

The word *kalāla* is a *dis legomenon*, a word that occurs twice in the Qur'ān, both times in *Sūrat al-Nisā'* ("Women"). The early Muslim community devoted considerable effort to explaining the meaning of this word.

The first task confronted by the Muslims who were interested in *kalāla* was to locate the two verses in which it appears in *Sūrat al-Nisā'*. In early manuscripts, the transition from one verse to the next is marked by an end-of-verse symbol, but individual verses have no number assigned to them. The first mention of *kalāla* occurs near the beginning of the *Sūra*. What are now the eleventh and twelfth verses of this chapter specify the shares of inheritance to which the heirs of the deceased are entitled: the eleventh verse awards shares of the estate to daughters, a mother, and a father; the twelfth verse awards shares of the estate to husbands, wives, and siblings. Our concern here is with the second half of the twelfth verse, which awards shares of the estate to siblings. It is here that the word *kalāla* occurs for the first time in the Qur'ān. The early exegetes treated the entirety of the eleventh and twelfth verses in *Sūrat al-Nisā'* as a single unit known collectively as *āyat al-farḍ*, or *the inheritance verse.*[52] This may explain why the second half of the twelfth verse in this *sūra* has no distinctive linguistic tag that would identify it or distinguish it from the rest of the so-called *inheritance verse.* Be that as it may, it is curious that two verses should be treated as one *āya*. For convenience, I refer to this sub-verse as Q.

4:12b (or 4:12b or simply v. 12b)—although it is important to keep in mind that the Qurʾān codices produced in the first century A.H. had no system of verse numbering.

The consonantal skeleton of 4:12b is traditionally vocalized as follows (for convenience, I divide the sub-verse into five clauses and the first sentence into three sub-clauses):

1a *wa-in kāna rajul*^{un} *yūrathu* ***kalālat***^{an} *aw imraʾat*^{un}
1b *wa-lahu akh*^{un} *aw ukht*^{un}
1c *fa-li-kull*^{i} *wāḥid*^{in} *minhumā al-sudus*^{u}
2 *fa-in kānū akthar*^{a} *min dhālik*^{a} *fa-hum shurakāʾ*^{u} *fī al-thuluth*^{i}
3 *min baʿd*^{i} *waṣiyyat*^{in} *yūṣā bihā aw dayn*^{in} *ghayr*^{a} *muḍārr*^{in}
4 *waṣiyyat*^{an} *min allāh*^{i}
5 *wa'llāh*^{u} *ʿalīm*^{un} *ḥalīm*^{un}

The word *kalāla* occurs in l. 1a, which is the opening clause of a conditional sentence. Although the grammar, syntax, and meaning of l. 1a are difficult (see further Chapter 9), on one point there is universal agreement. *Kalāla* is a kinship term—albeit an odd one: some authorities defined it as *a person who dies leaving neither parent nor child*; others defined it as *those who inherit from the deceased with the exception of parent and child*, that is, *collateral relatives*. According to the first definition, the opening line of 4:12b signifies, "If a man dies leaving neither parent nor child—or [if] a woman [dies leaving neither parent nor child], and he [or she] has a brother or sister. . . ." According to the second, it signifies, "If a man is inherited by collaterals—or [if] a woman [is inherited by collaterals], and he [or she] has a brother or a sister. . . ." In both instances, it is necessary to assume, first, that the compound subject in l. 1a is the phrase "a man . . . or a woman"—even if the two elements of this compound subject are separated from one another by the adverbial phrase *yūrathu kalālat*^{an}; and, second, that the third person masculine singular pronoun suffix *-hu* in *wa-lahu* in l. 1b refers back not only to the "man" in the bifurcated compound subject in l. 1a but also to the "woman"—as if l. 1b specified, "and he *or she* has a brother or sister" (emphasis added)—which it does not.

Although there is no unanimity among Muslim commentators as to which of the two definitions of the word *kalāla* is correct, by the fourth/tenth century the second definition had come to be the preferred one. For this reason, I adopt the following as a working translation of the sub-verse:

1a If a man is inherited by collaterals—or a woman [is inherited by collaterals]—
1b and he [or she] has a brother or sister,
1c each one of them is entitled to one-sixth.

2 If they are more than that, they are partners with respect to one-third,
3 after any legacy that is bequeathed or debt, without injury (*ghayr*^{a} *muḍārr*^{in}).
4 A commandment from God.
5 God is all-knowing, forbearing.[53]

The second Qurʾānic verse in which *kalāla* appears is easier to locate. The word is mentioned in the opening line of the last verse in *Sūrat al-Nisāʾ*. According to the Companion al-Barāʾ b. ʿĀzib (d. 72/691–92), the last verse of this chapter was also the last verse of the Qurʾān revealed to the Prophet—a detail to which we will return.[54] This verse is easily identifiable in time (last verse revealed) and space (last verse in the chapter). If this were not sufficient, it was given a special linguistic tag: *āyat al-ṣayf*, or *the summer verse*, presumably a reference to the summer of 11/632 (the Prophet is said to have died on 12 Rabīʿ I/7 June of that year). For convenience, I refer to this verse as Q. 4:176 (or 4:176 or simply v. 176)—although again it is important to keep in mind that there were no individual verse numbers in early Qurʾān codices.

Q. 4:176 awards shares of the estate to siblings in circumstances similar to those of 4:12b. Verse 176 may be translated as follows (again, I divide the verse into individual clauses):

1 When they ask you for advice, say: God advises you with regard to *al-kalāla*:
2 If a man dies without a child (*laysa lahu walad*), and he has a sister, she is entitled to half of what he leaves.
3 He is her heir if she does not have a child.
4 If they [f.] are two, they are entitled to two-thirds of what he leaves.
5 If they are brothers and sisters, a male is entitled to the share of two females.
6 God makes clear for you [lest] you go astray.
7 God is all-knowing.[55]

The inheritance rules specified in ll. 2–5 are framed by an introduction in l. 1, on the one hand, and by a theological observation in l. 6 and a characterization of God in l. 7, on the other. Unlike the opening line of v. 12b, which is linguistically difficult, the language of v. 176 is straightforward and unequivocal. In l. 1, the authorial voice that controls the text refers to certain unnamed persons ("they") who have been asking the male addressee ("you") for advice about *kalāla*. The authorial voice indicates that the words inscribed in ll. 2–5 constitute God's response to these questions: "When they ask you for advice, say: God advises you with regard to *al-kalāla*" ("*Yastaftūnaka qul allāh*^{u} *yuftīkum fī al-kalāla*"). Line 2 appears to define *al-kalāla* as *a man who dies without a child*, and awards half the estate to a sister who has no living brother. Line 3 indicates that the term *kalāla* also applies to a childless woman, and it awards the entirety of the estate to a single brother. Line 4 awards two-thirds of the estate to two sisters. Line 5 establishes that when brothers and sisters inherit jointly, a male receives twice the share of a female. The theological observation in l. 6 indicates that God revealed this verse to the community ("you," in the plural) so that it would not go astray.

The circumstances mentioned in Q. 4:176 are virtually identical to those mentioned in 4:12b: In both cases, a childless man or woman dies leaving one or more siblings. There is, however, a formal difference between the two verses: Whereas in v. 12b we find only one set of rules for a childless man or woman whose closest surviving blood relative is one or more siblings, in v. 176 we find two sets of rules, one for a childless man who dies leaving siblings and another for a childless woman who dies leaving siblings. In addition to this formal difference, there are two substantive differences between the verses: First, whereas in v. 12b brothers and sisters inherit equal shares of the estate in all circumstances, in v. 176 the share of a brother is twice as large as that of a sister who inherits together with him. Second, the size of the share awarded to siblings differs in the two verses: In v. 12b, a brother and sister receive one-sixth each and, in the event that there are more than two siblings, the award is capped at one-third; in 4:176, one sister (in the absence of a brother) inherits half the estate, two or more sisters (in the absence of a brother) inherit two-thirds, and a brother (in the absence of a sister) inherits the entire estate.

Presumably, the interlocuters mentioned in the opening line of Q. 4:176 were Companions who asked the Prophet for advice about *kalāla*. The Prophet then consulted with the Divinity, who revealed 4:176 so that the community would not go astray. As for the Prophet himself, he remained silent—and conspicuously so—about the meaning of *kalāla*. If the Prophet was silent about this word, subsequent generations of Muslims were not. Beginning in the last quarter of the first century A.H., the first exegetes scrutinized the word *kalāla* as it is used in vv. 12b and 176. These men identified eight cruxes in these two verses. The first six cruxes are internal to ll. 1a and 1b of v. 12b.

Crux 1.1 Should the verb *y-w-r-th* be read as an active verb (*yū**ri**thu*) or as a passive verb (*yū**ra**thu*)?

Crux 1.2 What does *kalāla* mean?

Crux 1.3 Why is *kalāla* in the accusative case?

Crux 1.4 Why does the text specify "a man *yūrathu kalālat*^{an} or a woman" rather than "a man or a woman *yūrathu kalālat*^{an}"? In other words, why is the compound subject bifurcated?

Crux 1.5 Does *yūrathu kalālat*^{an} refer to the "man" mentioned immediately before the phrase, to the "woman" mentioned immediately after it, or to both?

Crux 1.6 Why is there no agreement in gender or number between *wa-lahu* ("and he has") in l. 1b and its antecedent in l. 1a ("a man . . . or a woman")?

The last two cruxes emerge from a comparison of vv. 12b and 176.

Crux 2.1 Why is there a discrepancy between the meaning of the word *kalāla* in vv. 12b ("a person who dies without a parent or child") and 176 ("a person who dies without a child")?

Crux 2.2 What accounts for the discrepancy in the size of the shares awarded to siblings in these two verses?

Muslim scholars eventually would provide reasonable answers to these eight cruxes, based on the traditional vocalization of Q. 4:12b (see Chapter 9). To the best of my knowledge, however, no Muslim scholar has ever asked the question, "Why do these problems exist?" It is to this question that the remainder of this chapter is devoted. Our investigation begins in Egypt at the beginning of the nineteenth century.

Bibliothèque Nationale de France, Arabe 328a

On January 17, 1809, the German traveler Ulrich Seetzen visited the Mosque of ʿAmr b. al-ʿĀṣ in Fustat, where a young boy directed him to a small room on the north side of the building. When Seetzen entered the room, he saw ancient manuscripts lying on the floor, in no apparent order, mixed with old carpets and piled up to a height of one foot. In his journal, the German traveler noted that the manuscripts included old and rare copies of the Qurʾān; and that when he attempted to purchase some specimens, he was rebuffed by women who insisted that the manuscripts could not be bought or sold because they had been endowed as *waqf*s.[56]

Undeterred, Seetzen turned to the French Orientalist who was serving as Dragoman and Vice-Consul in Cairo, Asselin de Cherville (1772–1822). This representative of the French government succeeded where the German had failed. In a letter written in 1814, de Cherville noted that he had acquired a substantial number of Qurʾān fragments written on parchment and dating from the first centuries of Islamic history. His plans to study the manuscripts and bring the results of his research to the attention of the Orientalist scholarly community were ended by his death in 1822 at the age of fifty. Three years later, de Cherville's manuscript collection was shipped to his family in Marseille. In 1833, his heirs sold the collection to the Bibliothèque Royale. In 1851, the French Orientalist Joseph Toussaint Reinaud (1795–1867) hired one of his students, the refugee Italian Orientalist Michele Amari (1806–89), to work on the manuscripts. It was Amari who identified the contents of individual fragments, collected and brought together fragments belonging to a single manuscript, and classified the manuscripts according to format and script. One of the manuscripts classified by Amari was BNF 328a.[57]

In 1998 F. Déroche and the late S. Noja Noseda published a facsimile edition of BNF 328a, thereby making this manuscript fragment available to the wider scholarly community.[58] Three years later, Y. Dutton published the first comprehensive study of the contents of BNF 328a, with special attention to variant readings and versification.[59] Dutton compared the consonantal variants in the manuscript with variants attributed to the seven authoritative Qur'ān readers. Based on this comparison, he determined that BNF 328a contains thirteen consonantal variants, six of which are associated with the reading of Ibn ʿĀmir (d. 118/736), the principal Qur'ān reader of Damascus.[60] Dutton concluded "with considerable confidence" that BNF 328a corresponds to the reading of Ibn ʿĀmir,[61] and he suggested that the codex has a distinctive Syrian flavor and probably was written somewhere in Syria or the Jazīra.[62] As for the verse numbering system, Dutton observed that the number of verses in *Sūrat al-Nisā'* varies slightly in the different regional reading systems. According to the Hijazi and Basran systems the *Sūra* has 175 verses, according to the Kufan system it has 176 verses, and according to the Syrian system it has 177 verses. Dutton noted several anomalies in the versification of *Sūrat al-Nisā'* in BNF 328a, including one or more "erroneous" verse endings which he attributed to scribal error (and characterized as "confusion"), and inconsistencies in the placement of five- and ten-verse markers which, he wrote, "shows a general inaccuracy."[63] These variations in the verse numbering system are of direct relevance to the present inquiry.[64]

Dutton's identification of BNF 328a with the reading of Ibn ʿĀmir and his conclusion that the manuscript was written in Syria or the Jazīra await scholarly confirmation. With regard to provenance, it is possible that BNF 328a was produced in Syria (or another location outside of Egypt) and subsequently made its way to Fustat, where it was deposited in the Mosque of ʿAmr b. al-ʿĀṣ. Alternatively, it is possible that BNF 328a was produced in Fustat and remained there until it was sent to France in 1825. These are not the only possibilities, but even if they were, the hypothesis of Syrian provenance, although attractive, is not definitive.

BNF 328a is a fragment of a codex that has a vertical format. The writing surface is parchment, the skin of an animal dressed and prepared for writing. Every sheet of parchment has two sides, hair and flesh. Each of the five quires in BNF 328a is—or, as we shall see, was originally—a quaternion: a rectangular sheet of parchment folded three times to produce eight folios and sixteen folio pages. The outermost side of the first folio page of each quaternion is the flesh side. Thus, when the bound manuscript lies open, the verso of a preceding folio (e.g., 25v) lies opposite the recto of the immediately following folio (e.g., 26r). Two folio pages of this type are called a *double page*. Within a given quire, the hair sides of a double page face one another and the flesh sides of a double page face one another.

BNF 328a was written by four scribes working as a team. Of the fifty-six surviving folio leaves, forty-seven were produced by Scribe A (1a–9a, 10b–25a, 27b–28a, 30b–32a, 34b–35a, and 38b–56b), seven by Scribe B (28b–30a, 32b–34a, 35b–38a), one by Scribe D (9b–10a), one by Scribe E (25b–26a).[65]

The team of scribes wrote the manuscript using metallo-gallic ink, a liquid produced from the chemical reaction that results from the combination of tannic acid (extracted from gall nuts) and a metallic salt such as ferrous or copper sulfate, to which gum arabic is added. The scribes may have used a ruler to mark the lines of the manuscript, but there is considerable variation in the number of lines on a folio page: The normal range fluctuates between twenty-two and twenty-six lines, with twenty-three lines being the most common number; but seven folio pages have twenty-one lines, seven have twenty-seven lines, and three have twenty-eight.[66] The distance between each line is generally regular, although again there is variation.

There are occasional diacritical marks but no vowel signs.[67] The last word of a verse is followed by a space of 1–1.5 cm. This space is filled with a symbol that marks the end of a verse. Each scribe used a different symbol, for example, six dots arranged in three pairs, horizontally (:::); eight dots arranged in two pairs, vertically (⁞⁞); and four dots arranged vertically (⁞). The transition from the end of one *Sūra* to the beginning of the next is marked by an empty line.[68] Originally, the manuscript had no five- or ten-verse markers, and it was not until the second or third century A.H. that these symbols were added. At that time, the end of every fifth verse was marked by a red *alif* surrounded by dots, and the end of every tenth verse was marked by a red circle containing a letter in black that represents the number of the verse according to the *abjad* system.[69]

The four scribes wrote in what is known as the Ḥijāzī style script which, despite its name, was used not only in Arabia but also in Egypt, Syria, and the Yemen in the first and second centuries A.H.[70] The letter forms found in the oldest examples of the Ḥijāzī style script vary from one fragment to the next, and at least four substyles have been identified. BNF 328a has been classified by Déroche as Ḥijāzī 1, which is the first stage in the development of Qurʾānic calligraphy. The letters are thin and slender. The long, vertical strokes give the codex an elongated appearance and a distinctive vertical emphasis. The spacing between adjacent words as well as the spacing of letters within words is regular. When used as a conjunction, the letter *wāw* ("and") is written as an independent grapheme situated roughly equidistant between the two words that it connects and from which it is usually separated by 3–5 mm. In its initial and medial forms, *kāf* occupies less than half the height of a line and has a short extension at the top written at an oblique angle. The defining feature of the Ḥijāzī style script, however, is the oblique orientation of the vertical *alif*, which, in its independent form, has a short curved return or *serif* at the base. This oblique orientation is shared by the *lām* and three final letters: *kāf*, *ṭā'*, and *ẓā'*.[71]

The number of lines on a page, spacing of letters and words, verse endings, height of initial and medial *kāf*, and oblique orientation of the *lāms* and *alifs* of the Ḥijāzī style script are all matters of direct relevance to the present investigation.

The Revision of Q. 4:12b

The following analysis of BNF 328a is based on examination of the facsimile edition published by Déroche and Noseda; examination of the manuscript in Paris in May and November of 2007 and July of 2008; and digital images of the manuscript produced using natural, ultraviolet, and infrared light.

BNF 328a contains the entirety of *Sūrat al-Nisā'*. Q. 4:12b occurs on folio 10b (second quire), and 4:176 occurs on folio 20b (third quire). Both folio pages were written by Scribe A. Let us compare the handwriting used to produce the word *kalāla* in these two verses, beginning with v. 176, the last verse of *Sūrat al-Nisā'* (see Figure 1).

The first legible word on folio 20b, l. 1 is *wa-yazīduhum*, the eighth word of 4:173.[72] The last word on folio 20b is *uḥilla*, the eighth word of v. 3 of *Sūrat al-Mā'ida*. The transition from *Sūrat al-Nisā'* to *Sūrat al-Mā'ida* is marked by a blank line (l. 13).

Folio 20b has twenty-five lines, which is within the normal range. However, the layout of the folio page is irregular in three respects. First, the spacing of the first six lines is tighter than that of ll. 7–25.[73] Second, when Scribe A was writing ll. 1–6, he continued almost to the end of each line, leaving a margin of approximately 1 cm on the left side of the page; beginning with l. 7, however, and continuing to the bottom of the page, he used less space on each line, leaving a margin of between 1.5 and 2 cm on the left side of the page. The transition point between the more tightly spaced lines with the smaller left margin and the less tightly spaced lines with the larger left margin is precisely the last verse of *Sūrat al-Nisā'*, which occupies six lines of text, beginning on l. 7 and ending on l. 12. The third irregularity on folio 20b is the end-of-verse symbol following the word *alīm*^an^ on l. 2. As noted, Scribe A generally left 1 cm of space between the end of one verse and the beginning of the next; and he filled that space with six dots arranged in three pairs (:::). On l. 2, the final word of v. 173 is *alīm*^an^. Notice that barely 2 mm separate the last word of this verse (*alīm*^an^) from the first word of the next verse (*wa-lā*). There is not enough room between these two words for six dots arranged in three pairs. Instead, the verse ending is marked by four dots arranged vertically (⁞). One wonders why.

Our primary concern, however, is the word *al-kalāla*, the third word from the end of l. 7 on folio 20b. It is spelled *alif-lām-kāf-lām-lām-hā'* (final *hā'* would

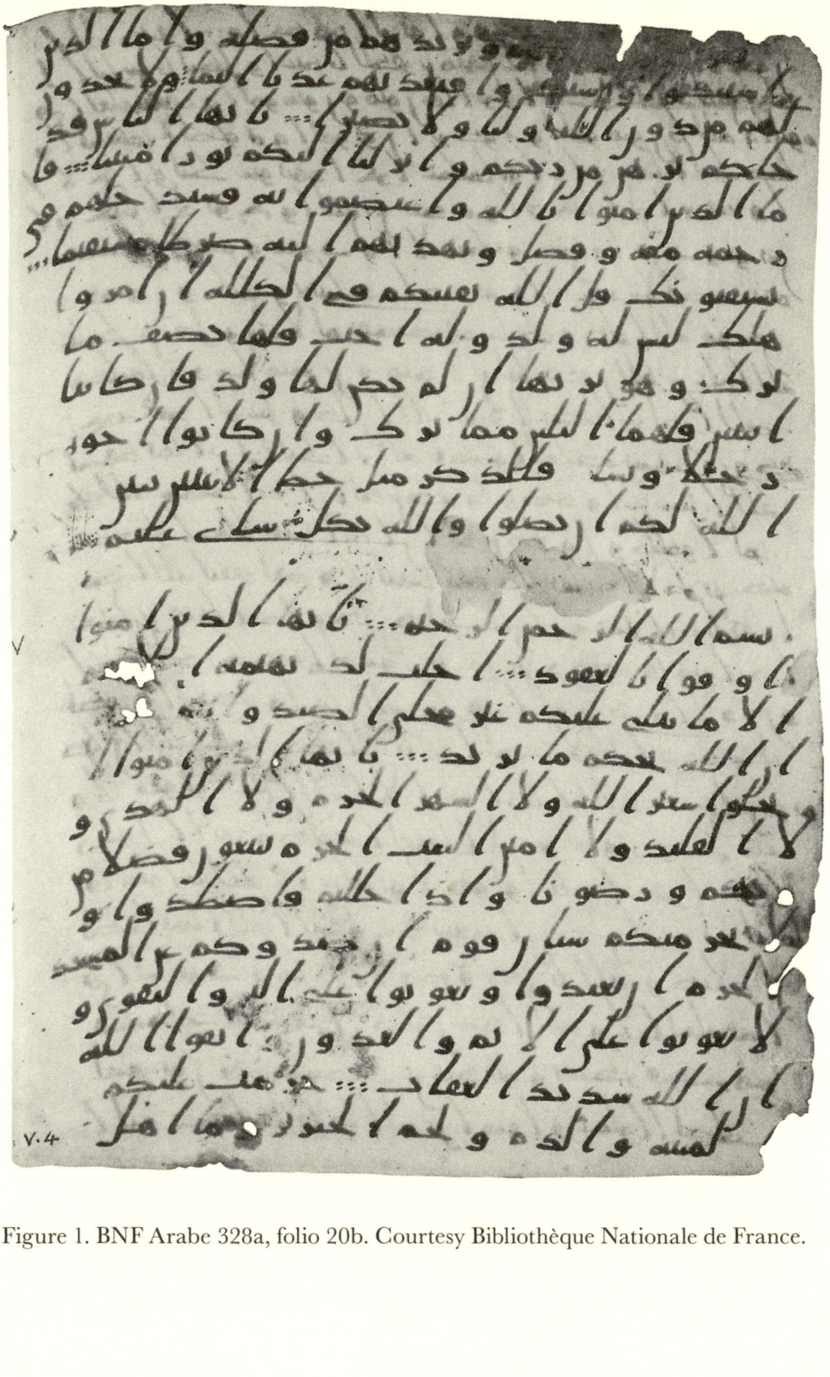

Figure 1. BNF Arabe 328a, folio 20b. Courtesy Bibliothèque Nationale de France.

become *tā᾿ marbūta* in later scripts). As expected, the medial *kāf* occupies less than half of the height of the line, and the two *lām*s occupy the full height of the line. The two *lām*s are evenly spaced and oriented on an oblique angle, leaning to the right, like the *alif* of the definite article, which has a short curved return at the base. On folio 20b, the orthography of *al-kalāla* is perfectly regular and unproblematic.

Let us turn now to folio 10b (see Figure 2), which begins with the word *khāfū* in the middle of Q. 4:9 and ends with the third word from the end of 4:12 (*allāh*). Folio 10b has twenty-one lines, which is just below the normal range of lines per page. The spacing of each line is uniform and there is a regular left margin that is approximately 2 cm wide. Like folio 20b, folio 10b was written by Scribe A, but a second hand that is clearly different from that of Scribe A is visible at numerous points on the page. I refer to this additional hand as Corrector 2. The ink used by Corrector 2 is carbon-based and he wrote in a broken cursive script that Déroche calls *ʿAbbasid book hand*. Notably, the *alif*s and *lām*s are written on a vertical axis. Examples of this ʿAbbasid book hand script are found in chancery documents produced in the second/eighth century, but this script became a book hand only in the third/ninth century, and it was first used in Qur᾿ān manuscripts only at the end of the third/ninth century. Thus, the paleographic evidence suggests that Corrector 2 lived approximately two centuries after Scribe A.[74]

Corrector 2 engaged in considerable touch-up work on folio 10b, including several letters on ll. 16–18.[75] Our concern here is with v. 12b, which begins after the midway point of l. 17 (*wa-in kāna rajul*^{un}) and continues to the first line of folio 11a (*wallāh*^{u} *ʿalīm*^{un} *ḥalīm*^{un}). On l. 18, we find the word *kalāla* (here without the definite article). The script used to produce three words on this line—the noun *kalāla*, the disjunctive particle *aw*, and the pronominal phrase *wa-lahu*—is anomalous; and the spacing between the word *kalāla* and the words that precede and follow it is unusual, albeit not necessarily irregular.

kalāla: The word *kalāla* is packed tightly between the word that precedes it and the word that follows it: Only 2 mm separate the initial *kāf* of *kalāla* from the final *thā᾿* of *y-w-r-th*; and only 1 mm separates the final *hā᾿* of *kalāla* from the base of the initial *alif* of *aw*. In addition to the tight spacing, there are three anomalies relating to the script. First, the initial *kāf* occupies the full height of the line, whereas elsewhere on folio 10b (e.g., *kāna* on l. 17 and *kānū* on l. 19), as throughout BNF 328a, initial *kāf* occupies less than half the height of the line. Note also that the oblique line that extends from the top of the *kāf* to the middle of the letter appears to be discontinuous at the point just before the hook of what might have been a Ḥijāzī *kāf*. Second, the two *lām*s are upright and vertical, unlike the *lām*s elsewhere on folio 10b and throughout BNF 328a, which are all written at an oblique angle. Third, the word *kalāla* was produced using a carbon-based ink which is darker than the metallic ink used by Scribe

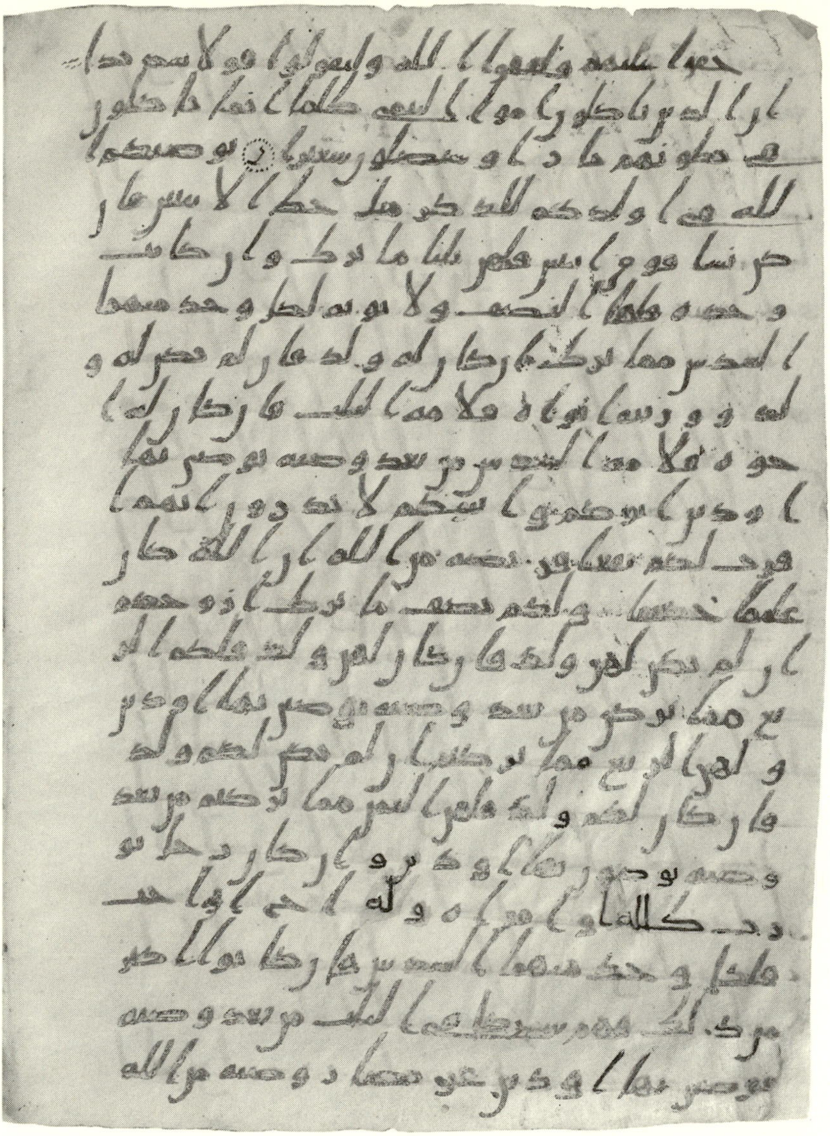

Figure 2. BNF Arabe 328a, folio 10b. Courtesy Bibliothèque Nationale de France.

A. All this is the work of Corrector 2, who scratched out the word *kalāla* and rewrote it, presumably to enhance its legibility, using the ʿAbbasid book hand script and a carbon-based ink.

aw: Again the spacing is tight. Internally, only 2 mm separate the *alif* from the *wāw* of *aw*. Compare the space between the two letters of *aw* on l. 18 with that of the same word on l. 10 (first word), l. 14 (penultimate word), l. 17 (fourth word), and l. 21 (third word). On these four lines, the space between the *alif* and the *wāw* of *aw* ranges from 3–6 mm. Also noteworthy on l. 18 is the space between the *alif* of *aw* and the final *hāʾ* of *kalāla*—barely 1 mm. To this, compare the space between *aw* and whatever word precedes it on ll. 14, 17, and 21—in each instance a healthy 4–5 mm. In addition to the tight spacing between words, the script used to produce the word *aw* is anomalous: the *alif* is vertical rather than oblique; and the base of this *alif* is flat rather than curved.[76] Again, these anomalies are the work of Corrector 2, who scratched out an earlier Ḥijāzī *alif* (visible as undertext to the immediate left of and above the final *hāʾ* of *kalāla*) and replaced it with a new *alif*, using ʿAbbasid book hand script and a carbon-based ink.

wa-lahu: Just beyond the midpoint of l. 18, the *lām* of *wa-lahu*, like the two *lām*s of *kalāla* earlier on the same line, is again oriented on a vertical axis rather than being written at an oblique angle. Notice also that the *lām* and *hāʾ* of *wa-lahu* are raised slightly above the base line. This too is the work of Corrector 2.

Corrector 2, it will be recalled, lived approximately two centuries after Scribe A. As best I can tell, the changes introduced by Corrector 2 were intended to improve the legibility of the text. He does not appear to have made any changes to the consonantal skeleton.

Examination of BNF 328a points to an earlier stage of revision carried out by a scribe-editor whom I will call Corrector 1. There is good reason to believe that Corrector 1 is Scribe A. Some of the work performed by Corrector 1 is visible to the naked eye as shadow or undertext. Access to the visual undertext can be enhanced with digital images taken with ultraviolet and infrared light (see Figure 3). On folio 10b, below the erasures and changes made by Corrector 2 (dark ink), one can see traces of some of the work done by Corrector 1 (shadow):

kalāla: To the immediate left of the irregular *kāf* and visible as undertext is a single Ḥijāzī *lām* which, as expected, is—or was, prior to its erasure—written at an oblique angle, leaning back toward the right side of the page. Notice that the anomalous extension of the *kāf* is parallel to the single Ḥijāzī *lām* which was scratched out but is still visible as shadow. Also visible as undertext approximately 6 mm to the right of the leftmost point of the irregular *kāf* is a

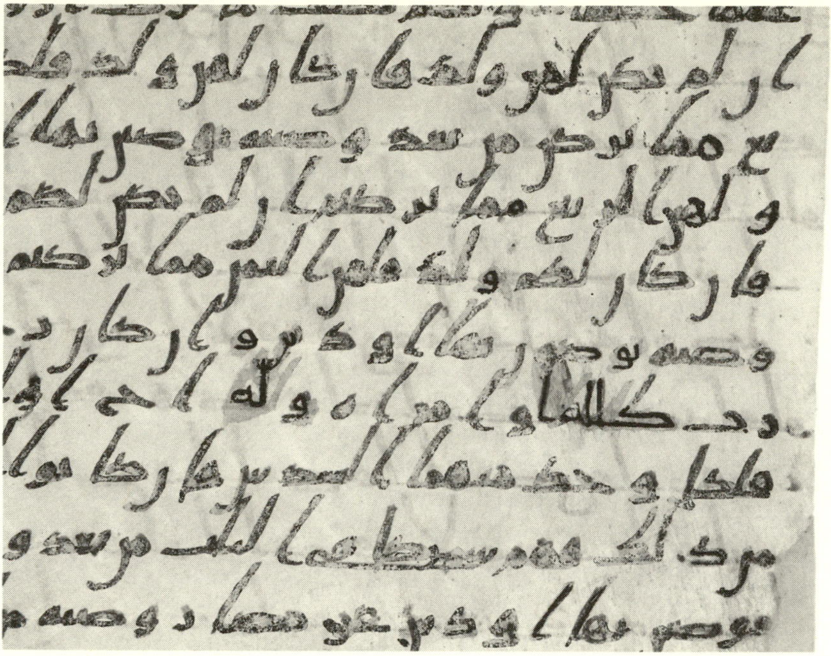

Figure 3. BNF Arabe 328a, folio 10b, detail (ultraviolet light). Courtesy Bibliothèque Nationale de France.

short stroke that was written at an oblique angle. This would have been the hook of an earlier Ḥijāzī *kāf.*

aw: no change by Corrector 1 (see above).

wa-lahu: Underneath the ʿAbbasid book hand *wa-lahu*, also the work of Corrector 2, one sees the residue of an earlier erasure. Clearly visible to the right of the ʿAbbasid *lām* is a Ḥijāzī *lām*, written at an oblique angle. Clearly visible to the left of and above the ʿAbbasid *hāʾ* is a Ḥijāzī *alif*, written at an oblique angle. These two letters would have been connected by a Ḥijāzī medial *hāʾ*. In addition, barely visible between the ʿAbbasid *lām* and *alif* is what may be a final Ḥijāzī *hāʾ*. That is to say, underneath the ʿAbbasid book hand *lahu* are *both* a Ḥijāzī *lahu* and a Ḥijāzī *lahā*. It remains to be determined which form is original and which is secondary.

Other work performed by Corrector 1 is not immediately visible to the naked eye when one examines folio 10b. But all is not lost. Parchment is translucent and metallo-gallic ink is corrosive; thus, the chemicals in the ink penetrate the surface of the parchment and remain embedded in the skin even after erasure. Some of the writing that lies beneath the erasures on folio 10b, l. 18 is still visible on the recto of folio 10, that is to say, on folio 10a. In this instance, no special camera or equipment is needed. It is necessary only to lift folio 10 to a vertical position and expose it to light. Holding the folio aloft, one can examine folio 10b from the vantage point of folio 10a, that is to say, from behind. The evidence visible (in reverse) on folio 10a is as follows:

kalāla: Viewed from the vantage point of folio 10a, the irregular extension of the initial *kāf* on folio 10b was a Ḥijāzī *lām* before it was recycled by Corrector 2 to produce an ʿAbbasid book hand *kāf*. This *lām* was produced by Corrector 1, who inserted this additional, non-original letter by manipulating the original Ḥijāzī *kāf* written by Scribe A. The original *kāf*—like all of the initial *kāf*s in BNF 328a, would have occupied less than half the line and would have had a short extension at the top written at an oblique angle (see again the initial *kāf* of *kāna* on l. 17 and of *kānū* on l. 19). Corrector 1 made this short extension the basis of a Ḥijāzī *lām* that occupied the full height of the line and leaned backwards toward the right side of the page. The new *lām* eliminated part of the original initial *kāf*, and it was therefore necessary for Corrector 1 to create a new *kāf*. He did this by inserting a new short extension, written at an oblique angle, approximately 5 cm to the right of the old one (see Figure 3). He now produced a new Ḥijāzī *kāf* which, on its right side, approached the final *thāʾ* of *y-w-r-th*, from which it is separated by only 2 mm. The tight spacing is noteworthy although not necessarily irregular.[77]

wa-lahu: Scribe A wrote *wa-lahā*, by mistake—no doubt because this word follows two nouns with feminine endings. Shortly thereafter, Corrector 1 fixed the mistake by erasing the final Ḥijāzī *alif* of *wa-lahā* and replacing it with a final Ḥijāzī *hāʾ*, thereby creating the word *wa-lahu*.

When the evidence visible on BNF 328a, folios 10a–b is combined, the result is as follows: The original spelling of *kalāla* was **kalla*—with only one *lām*. As for *wa-lahu*, this is the work of Corrector 1, who corrected Scribe A's *wa-lahā*. The original text would have looked like Figure 4.

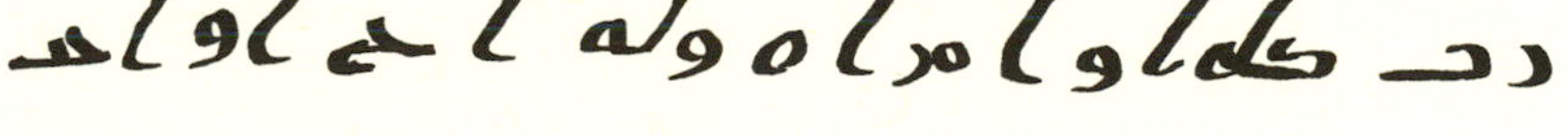

Figure 4. Folio 10b, line 18, hand reconstruction.

Before attempting to establish the meaning of this text, let me retrace the steps whereby the original consonantal skeleton was revised by Corrector 1—who, I believe, was Scribe A—after which Corrector's 1's revisions were touched up approximately two centuries later by Corrector 2. Corrector 1 changed the spelling of one word on l. 18 by adding an extra letter; and he corrected a mistake made by Scribe A by replacing a feminine pronoun suffix with a masculine pronoun suffix.

**kalla > kalāla*: Corrector 1 added a second Ḥijāzī *lām* to **kalla*, thereby creating a new word: *kalāla*.

**wa-lahā > wa-lahu*: Corrector 1 changed the consonantal skeleton of **wa-lahā* ("and she has") by scratching out the final *alif* and replacing it with a final *hā*ʾ, thereby producing *wa-lahu* ("and he has"), in Ḥijāzī script.

Corrector 2 came along approximately two centuries later. As he was touching up some of the letters on folio 10b to enhance their legibility, he noticed some serious problems on l. 18—the work of Corrector 1. In an effort to make the work of Corrector 1 less conspicuous, Corrector 2 decided to rewrite the words *kalāla* and *wa-lahu* on l. 18. He performed the following operations.

kalāla: Corrector 2 scratched out and rewrote part or all of the first three letters—*kāf*, *lām*, *lām*—all in Ḥijāzī script, replacing them with new letters, all in ʿAbbasid book hand script. He scratched out the original single Ḥijāzī *lām* of **kalla*. He also scratched out the bottom part of the Ḥijāzī *lām* that had been inserted previously by Corrector 1, and he used the top portion of this *lām* as the extension of an ʿAbbasid book hand *kāf*. To accomplish this, he also erased the short extension of Corrector 1's secondary, albeit Ḥijāzī, *kāf*.

Next, Corrector 2 reoriented the two *lām*s and the final *hā*ʾ of *kalāla*, moving all three letters to the left, in the direction of the original Ḥijāzī *alif* of *aw*. As noted, he had already erased the original Ḥijāzī *lām* of **kalla*. He continued his work by erasing the final Ḥijāzī *hā*ʾ of **kalla* and the Ḥijāzī *alif* of *aw*. Into the newly created space, he inserted two new ʿAbbasid book hand *lām*s (oriented on a vertical axis) to the left of the original single and unique Ḥijāzī *lām* (visible as undertext and written at an oblique angle); together, these two ʿAbbasid book hand *lām*s occupy the space previously occupied by the final *hā*ʾ of **kalla*.

Finally, he added a new final ʿAbbasid *hā*ʾ in the space previously occupied by the Ḥijāzī *alif* of *aw*.

aw: He replaced the original Ḥijāzī *alif* that he had just erased in order to make room for the final *hā*ʾ of *kalāla* with a vertical ʿAbbasid book hand *alif* with a flat base.

wa-lahu: He scratched out Corrector 1's Ḥijāzī *wa-lahu* and replaced it with an ʿAbbasid book hand *wa-lahu* (with a vertical *lām*). In the process, he raised *lahu* above the base line.

The original consonantal skeleton of BNF 328a, folio 10b, l. 18 differed from what would become the standard consonantal skeleton at a single point: *kalla* (with only one *lām*) instead of *kalāla* (with two *lām*s). The original consonantal skeleton and performed reading of *4:12b, l. 1a may be represented as follows, using boldface to identify a spelling that differs from the standard spelling, and a question mark to identify a performed reading that remains to be determined (inasmuch as there were as yet no vowel signs, one cannot speak of *vocalization*):

1a *wa-in kāna rajul*^{un} *yūr***?***thu ka***ll***at*^{an} *aw imraʾat*$^{?n}$

The syntax of this conditional clause suggests a performed reading that differs at two points from what would become the standard vocalization: **yūr***i***thu* (active verb) instead of *yūr***a***thu* (passive verb); and **imraʾat*$^{\mathbf{an}}$ (accusative) instead of *imraʾat*$^{\mathbf{un}}$ (nominative). Viewed in this manner, the causative verb **yūr***i***thu* is followed immediately by a compound phrase that is the direct object of the verb.[78] Thus, we have a total of three changes to v. *12b: one revision of the consonantal skeleton and two revisions of the performed reading. The original consonantal skeleton and performed reading of the opening line of *4:12b may be represented as follows:

1a *wa-in kāna rajul*^{un} *yūr***i***thu ka***ll***at*^{an} *aw imraʾat*$^{\mathbf{an}}$
1b *wa-lahu akh*^{un} *aw ukht*^{un}
1c *fa-li-kull*^{i} *wāḥid*^{in} *minhumā al-sudus*^{u}

In order to determine the meaning of l. 1 it will be necessary to establish the meaning of the word **kalla* in l. 1a. This is no simple task, as the word *kalla* does not exist in the Arabic language. Notice, however, that the Form IV active verb *yūrithu* is followed by two nouns in the accusative case: **kallat*^{an} *aw imraʾat*^{an}. This phrase brings to mind a phrase that occurs in matrimonial adoption tablets produced in ancient Nuzi in the middle of the second millennium B.C.E. (see Chapter 2).

Excursus: From Nuzi to Medina

As noted in Chapter 2, in ancient Nuzi there were three types of contracts that regulated the adoption of females for the purposes of matrimony. A woman might be adopted (1) in daughtership, (2) in daughter-in-lawship, or (3) in daughtership and daughter-in-lawship. In Akkadian, the third type of matrimonial adoption contract is referred to as *ṭuppi mārtūti u kallūti*.

The Akkadian phrase *mārtūti u kallūti* ("daughtership and daughter-in-lawship") is the abstract form of *mārtu u kallatu* ("daughter and daughter-in-law"). The Akkadian phrase is similar but not identical to the Arabic phrase **kallat^{an} aw imraʾat^{an}* in Q. *4:12b. Let us begin with the differences: The order in which the two nouns occur in the Akkadian phrase is reversed in its Arabic counterpart; and the Akkadian phrase contains the conjunctive particle *u* ("and"), whereas the Arabic phrase contains the disjunctive particle *aw* ("or"). Apart from these differences, the similarities are striking: Akkadian *mārtu* and Arabic *imraʾa* are derived from the same root (*m-r-ʾ*), share the same morphology (*faʿlat^{un}*), and have a similar meaning (the Akkadian noun signifies "daughter, girl, woman" while the Arabic noun signifies "woman, wife"). Likewise, Akkadian *kallatu* and Arabic **kalla* are derived from the same root (*k-l-l*) and share the same morphology (*faʿlat^{un}*). The homology would be complete if the Arabic noun **kalla* signified "daughter-in-law" like its Akkadian and other Semitic counterparts. Is there any reason to believe that the Arabic language once contained a kinship term **kalla* that signified "daughter-in-law"?

Linguists have long recognized that the Semitic language family, which includes Akkadian, Ugaritic, Hebrew, Aramaic, Syriac, South Arabic, Ethiopian, and Arabic, contains a shared lexicon in certain core areas, such as natural phenomena, anatomy and physiology, social organization, working methods, feeding habits, economy, and religion. Kinship terms are an important component of this common lexicon. All the Semitic languages share pairs of words that signify male and female relationships of consanguinity, for example, son/daughter, father/mother, brother/sister, and paternal uncle/maternal uncle.[79] The Semitic languages also share a common stock of terms that denote the relationship of affinity created between one spouse and the blood relatives of the other spouse. These terms also occur in pairs, for example, father-in-law/mother-in-law, bride/groom, and son-in-law/daughter-in-law.[80] Our interest here is in this last pair: son-in-law/daughter-in-law. Let us begin with the masculine term.

In the Semitic kinship lexicon, the noun that signifies *son-in-law* is invariably derived from the root *ḫ-t-n*. A noun derived from this root and signifying *son-in-law* is found in Akkadian (*ḫatanu* or *ḫatnu*), which is an East Semitic language,[81] and in *all* West Semitic languages: Ugaritic (*ḫatnu*);[82] Middle Hebrew (*ḥāṯān*); Jewish Aramaic, Syriac, Christian Palestinian Aramaic, and Samaritan (*ḥaṯnaʾ*); Nabataen (*ḥtn*);[83] Mandaic (*hatna*);[84] Old South Arabic (*ḫtn*); and Arabic (*khatan*).[85] All these words share the same root, morphology, and meaning; this particular kinship term is common to all Semitic languages, including Arabic.[86]

The feminine counterpart of *son-in-law* is *daughter-in-law*. In the Semitic kinship lexicon, the noun that signifies *daughter-in-law* is usually derived from the root *k-l-l*. The word for *daughter-in-law* in Akkadian, as we have seen, is *kallatu*.[87] A noun derived from the same root and sharing the same morphology is found in most—but not all—West Semitic languages: Ugaritic (*klt*),[88] Hebrew (*kallāh*),[89] Syriac (*kalltā*),[90] and Aramaic (*kalltā*),[91] as well as in Northwest Semitic (*klh*)[92] and South Arabic (*kela/o/un*).[93] The exception is Arabic, where one might expect to find a kinship term derived from the root *k-l-l* and sharing the same morphology as Akkadian *kallatu*, Hebrew *kallāh*, and so on. This would be our hypothetical **kalla*. In Arabic, however, the word for *daughter-in-law* is *kanna* (pl. *kanāʾin*), which the lexicographer Ibn Manẓūr (d. 711/1312) glosses as *imraʾat al-ibn*, or *the wife of one's son*.[94] Thus, the morphological and semantic pattern associated with the pair *ḥ-t-n/k-l-l*, a pattern that otherwise is common to all Semitic languages—East, Northwest, and South—breaks down in Arabic, where we encounter a linguistic shift from *k-l-l* to *k-n-n*. Conversely, in no other Semitic language do we find a kinship term derived from the root *k-l-l* that has the same meaning as the Arabic *kalāla*. Thus, the Arabic kinship term *kalāla* ("collateral relatives") is lexically unique with respect to other Semitic languages. It is also a *dis legomenon*.

	SON-IN-LAW	**DAUGHTER-IN-LAW**
Akkadian	*ḫatanu or ḫatnu*	*kallatu*
Ugaritic	*ḫatnu*	*klt*
Hebrew	*ḥāṯān*	*kallāh*
Aram., Syr., Sam.	*ḥaṯna' or ḥtn*	*kalltā*
Mandaic	*hatna*	*kalta*
Old S. Arabic	*ḫtn*	*kela/o/un*
		↙ ↘
Arabic	*khatan*	*kanna* *kalāla= collaterals*

Figure 5. *Son-in-law/daughter-in-law* in Semitic languages.

The Revision of Q. 4:12b (cont.)

We have identified two interrelated linguistic anomalies: the absence in Arabic of a hypothetical kinship term **kalla* that signifies *daughter-in-law*; and the absence in Semitic languages other than Arabic of an equivalent of the Arabic kinship term *kalāla* that signifies *collateral relatives.* On linguistic grounds there are strong reasons to make the following four assumptions about l. 1 of v. *12b:

Assumption 8.1.1. During the lifetime of the Prophet, the word for *daughter-in-law* in Arabic was **kalla*, a kinship term that was part of the shared Semitic lexicon.

Assumption 8.1.2. The noun *imraʾa* in l. 1a signifies *a wife.*[95]

Assumption 8.1.3. The man mentioned in l. 1a is childless.

Assumption 8.1.4. The siblings mentioned in ll. 1b and 1c are the closest surviving blood relatives of the deceased.

If these four assumptions are sound, we may make the following hypothesis:

Hypothesis 8.1. The original meaning of Q. *4:12b was as follows:

1a If a man designates (*yūrithu*) a daughter-in-law or wife as [his] heir,
1b and he has a brother or sister,
1c each one of them is entitled to one-sixth.
2 If they are more than that, they are partners with respect to one-third,
3 after any legacy that he bequeaths or debt, without injury.
4 A commandment from God.
5 God is all-knowing, forbearing.

In l. 1a the active verb *yūrithu*, which means *to make someone an heir*, indicates that the verse deals with testate succession. Line 1a envisages two scenarios: (1) a childless man designates his daughter-in-law as his heir or (2) a childless man designates his wife as his heir.[96] In either case, the designated heir is a female who is not a blood relative of the deceased. This was an extraordinary situation. In the absence of clear instructions from the testator, the siblings would have inherited the entire estate. The purpose of the rule formulated in v. *12b is to prevent a testator from totally disinheriting his closest surviving blood relative—in the present instance, siblings. The rule teaches that persons disinherited in this manner have a legal claim against the estate for up to one-third of its value. The law strikes a balance between the personal wishes of the deceased and the entitlement of the testamentary heir, on the one hand, and the rights of the testator's closest surviving blood relatives, on the other.[97] It does this by awarding the siblings a share of the estate not to exceed one-third. As for the testamentary heir, the size of her inheritance will vary depending on how many of the testator's siblings are alive at the time of his death. If the testator is survived by two or more siblings, the testamentary heir will inherit two-thirds of the estate; if he has only one sibling, she will inherit five-sixths of the estate; and if he has no siblings, she will inherit the entire estate.[98]

The meaning of v. *12b was transformed by the addition of an extra *lām* to the word **kalla*. The addition of the extra consonant was accompanied by two changes to the performed reading. Whereas the opening clause of v. *12b is *wa-in kāna rajul*^{un} *yūrithu ka**ll**at*^{an} *aw imraʾat*$^{\mathbf{an}}$, the opening clause of v. 12b is *wa-in kāna rajul*^{un} *yūr**a**thu ka**lāl**at*^{an} *aw imraʾat*$^{\mathbf{un}}$. It was the revised version of this verse that was accepted as canonical, that was inherited by the Muslims in the second half of the first century A.H., and that became the starting point of all future discussions of the meaning of v. 12b. At the end of the first century, the Muslim community attempted to make sense of v. 12b. As we will see in Chapter 9, the earliest exegetes made two important decisions: First, they took the phrase *yūrathu kalālat*^{an} and moved it—mentally—to a position following the word *imraʾat*^{un}; in other words, they pre-positioned this phrase in the sentence. Second, they taught that the masculine singular pronoun *-hu* in *wa-lahu* refers back to both the "man" and the "woman" mentioned earlier in the sentence. These two exegetical decisions made it possible to generate the following understanding of v. 12b.

> If a man **or a woman** is inherited by collateral relatives, and he [**or she**] has a brother or sister, each one of them is entitled to one-sixth. If they are more than that, they are partners with respect to one-third, after any legacy that is bequeathed or debt, without injury. A commandment from God. God is all-knowing, forbearing.

The standard version of v. 12b, which awards siblings a minimum of one-sixth and a maximum of one-third of the estate, was now fused together with v. 12a, which awards fractional shares of the estate to husbands (1/2 or 1/4, depending on whether there are children) and wives (1/4 or 1/8, again depending on whether there are children). Verse 12 (a–b), in turn, was fused together with v. 11, which, I believe, was the original *āyat al-farḍ* or *inheritance verse* (see Appendix 3)

Q. 4:11 awards fractional shares of the estate to one daughter (1/2) or to *three* or more daughters (2/3)—without specifying the entitlement of two daughters; to parents (1/6 each) in competition with a child; to a mother (1/3) in the absence of children and siblings; and to a mother (1/6) in the absence of a child but in competition with siblings.

The consolidation of vv. 11, 12a, and 12b into a single legal unit, referred to collectively as *āyat al-farḍ* or *the inheritance verse*, produced the following cluster of rules for the division of property:

> God commands you concerning your children: A male is entitled to the share of two females. If they are females above two, they are entitled to two-thirds of what he leaves. If there is one, she is entitled to half. Each of his parents is entitled to one-sixth of what he leaves, if he has a child. But if he does not have a child, and his parents are his heirs, his mother is entitled to one-third. If he has brothers, his mother is entitled to one-sixth, after any legacy he bequeaths or debt. Your fathers and your sons, you know not which of them is closer to you in usefulness. A commandment from God. God is knowing, wise. ::: You are entitled to half of what your wives leave, if they do not have a child; but if they have a child, you are entitled to one-fourth of what they leave, after any legacy they bequeath or debt. They are entitled to one-fourth of what you leave, if you do not have a child; but if you have a child, they are entitled to one-eighth of what you leave, after any legacy you bequeath or debt. *If a man or a woman is inherited by collateral relatives, and he [or she] has a brother or sister, each one of them is entitled to one-sixth. If they are more than that, they are partners with respect to one-third, after any legacy that is bequeathed or debt, without injury. A commandment from God. God is all-knowing, forbearing.*[99] (emphasis added)

In the revised version of 4:12b it appears as if *āyat al-farḍ* is incomplete. Verse 11 awards specific shares of the estate to (a) daughters and (b) parents. Although v. 11 mentions (c) siblings, it does not award them a specific share of the estate. It is only in v. 12b that siblings are awarded a share of the estate, not to exceed one-third. This is the only instance in *āyat al-farḍ* in which a specific share is awarded to siblings; apart from this one instance, the inheritance rights of siblings are otherwise undefined. Now, as I have argued, originally v. *12b dealt with testate succession rather than intestacy, and the share awarded to siblings in that sub-verse originally was intended to compensate the siblings who had been disinherited in favor of a woman who was not a blood relative of the testator. Following the revision of v. *12b, however, an exceptional award to one or more siblings of the testator became a compulsory share to which any and all siblings are entitled. It was only after v. *12b had been revised that the following question would have arisen: Why do the siblings in v. 12b receive no more than one-third of the estate in the case in which the deceased leaves neither parent nor child and one or more siblings are his or her closest surviving blood relatives? This question brings us to Q. 4:176.

Q. 4:176: The Standard View

The fact that the siblings in v. 12b receive no more than one-third of the estate apparently was of sufficient importance to merit a new revelation. In theory, the new verse might have been inserted immediately after vv. 11–12. In fact, it was inserted at the very end of *Sūrat al-Nisā*ʾ.

Verse 176 opens with a formulaic allusion to v. 12b and then proceeds to award fractional shares of the estate to the brothers and sisters of a childless man or woman. Let us take another look at v. 176, which reads as follows:

1 When they ask you for advice, say: God advises you with regard to *al-kalāla*:
2 If a man dies without a child, and he has a sister, she is entitled to half of what he leaves.
3 He is her heir if she does not have a child.
4 If they [f.] are two, they are entitled to two-thirds of what he leaves.
5 If they are brothers and sisters, a male is entitled to the share of two females.
6 God makes clear for you [lest] you go astray.
7 God is all-knowing.

As noted, the fact situation envisaged in v. 176 is virtually identical to the fact situation envisaged in v. 12b: Both verses refer to a childless man or woman who dies leaving one or more siblings. It will be noted, however, that v. 176 avoids the problematic language of the opening line of v. 12b (*wa-in kāna rajul*^{un} *yūrathu kalālat*^{an} *aw imraʾat*^{un}) by reformulating the fact situation. Instead of v. 12b's "if a man or a woman is inherited by collaterals," v. 176 first states the inheritance rules for a childless man who dies leaving one sister (l. 2), then for a childless woman who dies leaving one brother (l. 3), then for a childless man who dies leaving two sisters (l. 4), and finally for a childless man who dies leaving brothers and sisters (l. 5). The key difference between the two verses, however, is that v. 176 awards siblings who are the closest surviving relatives of the deceased considerably more than the third of the estate specified in v. 12b. The formulation of v. 176 also fills a textual gap in v. 12b, which states that "females above two" are entitled to two-thirds of the estate but, as noted, is silent about the entitlement of *two* daughters. Verse 176 specifies, "If they are two, they are entitled to two-thirds of what he leaves." From the fact that in v. 176 two sisters inherit two-thirds of the estate one may infer that in v. 12b two daughters inherit two-thirds of the estate.

At the same time that Q. 4:176 solved two problems, it created a third. Both 4:12b and 4:176 award shares of the estate to siblings in what appear to be identical circumstances: a childless man or woman dies leaving one or more siblings. Clearly, the shares awarded to siblings in v. 12b are not the same as the shares awarded to siblings in v. 176. This discrepancy might have been resolved by invoking the doctrine of *naskh* or abrogation.[100] As noted, al-Barāʾ b. ʿĀzib is reported to have said that v. 176 was the last verse of the Qurʾān to be revealed. If so, then v. 176 clearly was revealed after v. 12b, and it would have been easy to teach that the later verse abrogated the earlier verse. The argument for the abrogation of v. 12b, however, would have jeopardized the status of v. 12a, which awards fractional shares of the estate to husbands and wives. Indeed the argument for abrogation would have jeopardized the status of 4:11–12, which, as we have seen, had come to be treated as a single integral unit known collectively as *the inheritance verse.* This surely was undesirable. Toward the end of the first century A.H., Muslim scholars solved this problem by making a virtue out of necessity. The solution was facilitated by the fact that there are three types of sibling: uterine, consanguine, and germane. It therefore was possible for the early Qurʾān specialists to assert that when God uttered the word *brother* or *sister* in v. 12b, He was referring to uterine siblings; but that when He uttered the word *brother* or *sister* in v. 176, He was referring to consanguine and/or germane siblings.[101] This gloss or interpolation (also attested as a variant reading), not only made it possible to amend *the inheritance verse* without abrogating it, but also added greater flexibility to the newly emerging inheritance rules by distinguishing the entitlement of three different types of sibling. The added flexibility of the new version of the inheritance rules no doubt responded to pressing social and perhaps also political considerations.

Q. 4:176: An Alternative Explanation

As noted, each of the five quires in BNF 328a is a quaternion, that is to say, a quire produced by folding a rectangular sheet of parchment three times to produce eight folios and sixteen folio pages. In a normal quire, the hair sides of a double page face one another and the flesh sides of a double page face one another.

Verse 176 is found in the third quire of BNF 328a, which begins with folio 15. Thus, we should expect the following pattern (H = hair; F = flesh):

Folio #	15	16	17	18	19	20	21	22
	a:b	a:b	a:b	a:b	a:b	a:b	a:b	a:b
	F:H	H:F	F:H	H:F	F:H	H:F	F:H	H:F

Instead, we find:

Folio #	15	16	17	18	19	20	21
	a:b	a:b	a:b	a:b	a:b	a:b	a:b
	F:H	H:F	F:H	H:F	F:**H**	**F**:H	H:F

The third quire is doubly anomalous: It contains only seven folios rather than eight; and on folios 19b and 20a the hair side of the double page faces the flesh side.

Examination of the manuscript reveals the cause of these two anomalies (see Figure 6). Someone—in all likelihood Scribe A (= Corrector 1)—removed the folio that originally followed folio 19, leaving a stub, that is, the physi-

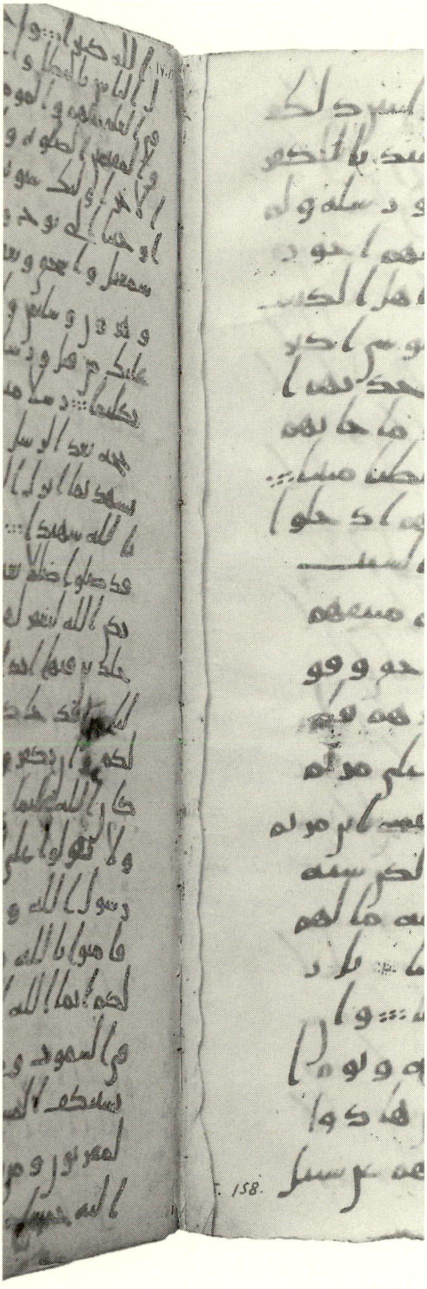

Figure 6. The stub between folios 19b and 20a. Courtesy Bibliothèque Nationale de France.

cal remains of the front and back sides of one leaf of the bifolium that was removed from the quire.[102] The stub lies in the gutter margin between the current folio 19b and folio 20a. Prior to its removal, this missing folio was located between folio 19 and what is now folio 20, but which originally was folio 21. For convenience, I refer to the missing folio as folio *20. The heuristic restoration of folio *20 to the quire eliminates both of the above-mentioned anomalies. Originally, the third quire of BNF 328a looked like this:

Folio #	15	16	17	18	19	***20**	21	22
	a:b	a:b	a:b	a:b	a:b	a:b	a:b	a:b
	F:H	H:F	F:H	H:F	F:H	H:**F**	**F**:H	H:F

This is the only stub in BNF 328a—indeed, in the *Parisino-petropolitanus codex* of which it forms a part.[103] The existence of this stub raises three questions: When was the missing folio removed, why was it removed, and what was written on it?

We begin with the first question. The team of scribes who produced the manuscript surely wrote the text before the individual quires were bound into a codex. It is conceivable that someone removed folio *20 from its quire before the scribes began their work, for instance, after discovering that the parchment surface of one side or another (or both) of folio *20 contained rough spots or glassy patches caused by marks or lesions on the animal skin.[104] Surely, however, any such defect would have been noticed before the parchment sheet had been folded to produce the quire. Alternatively, someone may have removed folio *20 from its quire after the scribes had completed their work; in that case, however, we are missing anywhere from 44 to 52 lines of text that would have been written on the recto and verso of the missing folio. Even if, for the sake of argument, the otherwise unknown contents of these two folio pages were removed from the codex, this could not have been accomplished without upsetting the continuity and sequencing of the text on folios 19b and 20a. For these reasons, both possibilities must be rejected. The only other possibility is that folio *20 was removed from its quire as the quire was being inscribed with text, or, to be more precise, after Scribe A had completed folio *20b but before he had begun work on the next folio page (currently, folio 20a). In my view, this is the only real possibility.

Second, one wonders why folio *20 was removed from the quire. It is possible—albeit unlikely, that Scribe A forgot to include one or more verses on either folio *20a or *20b. Alternatively, it is possible to envisage a scenario in which Scribe A made one or more errors on either folio *20a or b (or both), that these errors were of such magnitude that they could not be corrected through erasure and rewriting (as was done on folio 10b), and that Scribe A therefore decided to remove the flawed folio *20 from the quaternion and to begin again on the next folio page—which almost immediately became folio 20a. I am unable at the present time to rule out this possibility. As we shall see, however, there is another plausible explanation for the removal of folio *20 from the third quire in BNF 328a.

Third, one wonders about the contents of the missing folio *20 and the nature of the corrections that may have been made on its recto or verso or both. Until such time as the missing folio is discovered and examined, its contents will remain unknown. In the meantime, we can only speculate about its contents, keeping in mind that our assumptions must be consistent with the physical evidence. In the following exercise, I make three assumptions about folio *20.

Assumption 8.2.1. Scribe A completed folio *20b before he (or Corrector 1) removed it from the third quire. The last word on the missing folio page was *uhilla* of Q. 5:3. Scribe A wanted the endpoint of folio 20b to be the same as that of folio *20b.[105]

Assumption 8.2.2. Folio *20a contained only twenty-three lines—as do the eight immediately preceding folio pages (16a–19b)—all written by Scribe A.[106] Twenty-three is the second most common number of lines per page in BNF 328a.[107]

Assumption 8.2.3. On folio *20b, Scribe A followed the Syrian system of verse division, according to which v. 173 ends with *ʿadhāb*^{an} *alīm*$^{\mathbf{an}}$ and v. 174 ends with *wa-lā naṣīr*$^{\mathbf{an}}$ (boldface marks the verse ending).

In the Syrian system, the full text of these two verses is as follows:

173 *fa-ammā alladhīna āmanū wa-ʿamilū al-ṣāliḥāt*^{i} *fa-yuwaffīhim ujūrahum*
wa-yazīduhum min faḍlihi wa-ammā alladhīna ʾstankafū waʾstakbarū fa-yuʿadhdhibuhum
ʿadhāb^{an} *alīm*$^{\mathbf{an}}$.
174 *wa-lā yajidūna lahum min dūn*^{i} *allāh*^{i} *waliyy*^{an} *wa-lā naṣīr*$^{\mathbf{an}}$.

Notice that v. 173 contains two parallel clauses, each introduced by *ammā* ("as for"); and that the word *alīm*$^{\mathbf{an}}$ at the end of v. 173 rhymes with *naṣīr*$^{\mathbf{an}}$ at the end of v. 174.

These two verses would have been followed, in turn, by the two last verses in the *Sūra*:

O people, a proof has come to you from your Lord. We have sent down to you a clear light.

As for those who believe in God and hold fast to Him, He will admit them to mercy from Him and to bounty, and He will guide them to Himself along a straight road.

Thematically, the contents of these two verses are appropriate for the end of a *Sūra*.

If these three assumptions are sound, then we may make the following two hypotheses:

Hypothesis 8.2.1. The model on which BNF 328a was based did *not* include the verse that is currently the last verse in *Sūrat al-Nisāʾ* ("*Yastaftūnaka qul allāhu yuftīkum fī al-kalāla* . . ."). In the model text from which Scribe A was copying, *Sūrat al-Nisāʾ* ended with the verse, "As for those who believe in God and hold fast to Him, He will admit them to mercy from Him and to bounty, and He will guide them to Himself along a straight road." Originally, this was the last verse in the *Sūra*.

If Hypothesis 8.2.1 is correct, it may be possible to reconstruct the contents of the missing folio *20 (see Figure 7). I begin with folio *20a which, according to Assumption 8.2.2, had only twenty-three lines. If so, then this folio page would have ended close to the end of v. 171. Line 23 of folio *20a would have included the following twelve words of this verse: *lakum innamā allāhu ilāh*[un] *wāḥid*[un] *subḥānahu an yakūna lahu walad*[un] *lahu mā*. The remainder of this verse would have been written at the top of folio *20b. In that case, l. 1 of folio *20b would have begun as follows: *fī al-samawāt wa-mā fī'l-arḍ wa-kafā billāh*[i] *wakīl*[an]. This would have been followed by vv. 172–75 and, finally, v. 176 ("As for those who believe in God . . ."). Together the last words of v. 171 and vv. 172–76 would have taken up ten lines of text at the top of folio *20b. As the last verse in *Sūrat al-Nisāʾ*, "As for those who believe in God . . ." would have been followed by a blank line marking the transition between the end of this *Sūra* and the beginning of *Sūrat al-Māʾida*. The bottom half of folio *20b would have included exactly the same twelve lines of text as in the current folio 20b, which ends with the word *uhilla* in the third verse of *Sūrat al-Māʾida*. Thus, there would have been only twenty-three lines on folio *20b: the last ten lines of *Sūrat al-Nisāʾ* (ending with "and He will guide them to Himself along a straight road"), a single line for the division between the two *Sūra*s, and the first twelve lines of *Sūrat al-Māʾida* (ending with the word *uhilla* in the third verse).

Hypothesis 8.2.2. After completing folio *20 but before beginning work on the next folio page (the current folio 20), Scribe A removed folio *20 from the third quire and rewrote the contents of folio pages *20a and *20b. He took this opportunity to insert the supplementary legislation that would become the last verse of *Sūrat al-Nisāʾ* ("*Yastaftūnaka qul* . . .").

In order to perform this task, Scribe A had to know the number of lines on a folio page that would be occupied by the new verse. Using a piece of scratch writing material, he determined that the new verse would take up six lines

Folio *20a

الله كثيرا * واخذهم الربوا وقد نهوا عنه واكلهم اموا
ل الناس بالبطل واعتدنا للكفرين منهم عذبا اليما * لكن الرسخون
فى العلم منهم والمومنون يومنون بما انزل اليك وما انزل من قبلك
والمقيمين الصلوة والموتون الزكوة والمومنون بالله واليوم
الاخر اولـك سنوتيهم اجرا عظيما * انا اوحينا اليك كما
اوحينا الى نوح والنبين من بعده واوحينا الى ابرهم وا
سمعيل واسحق ويعقوب والاسبط وعيسى وايوب ويونس
وهرون وسليمن واتينا دواد زبورا * ورسلا قد قصصنهم
عليك من قبل ورسلا لم نقصصهم عليك وكلم الله موسى
تكليما * رسلا مبشرين ومنذرين لـلا يكون للناس على الله
حجة بعد الرسل وكان الله عزيزا حكيما * لكن الله
يشهد بما انزل اليك انزله بعلمه والملـكة يشهدون وكفى
بالله شهيدا * ان الذين كفروا وصدوا عن سبيل الله
قد ضلوا ضللا بعيدا * ان الذين كفروا وظلموا لم
يكن الله ليغفر لهم ولا ليهديهم طريقا * الا طريق جهنم
خلدين فيها ابدا وكان ذلك على الله يسيرا * يايها ا
لناس قد جاكم الرسول بالحق من ربكم فامنوا خيرا
لكم وان تكفروا فان لله ما فى السموت والارض و
كان الله عليما حكيما * ياهل الكتب لا تغلوا فى دينكم
ولا تقولوا على الله الا الحق انما المسيح عيسى ابن مريم
رسول الله وكلمه القـها الى مريم وروح منه
فامنوا بالله ورسله ولا تقولوا ثلثة انتهوا خيرا
لكم انما الله اله وحد سبحنه ان يكون له ولد له ما

Figure 7. Folios *20a and *20b, hypothetical reconstruction.

Folio *20b

فى السموت وما فى الارض وكفى بالله وكيلا * لن
يستنكف المسيح ان يكون عبدا لله ولا الملـكة ا
لمقربون ومن يستنكف عن عبدته ويستكبر فسيحشرهم
اليه جميعا * فاما الذين امنوا وعملوا الصلحت
فيوفيهم اجورهم ويزيدهم من فضله واما الذين
استنكفوا واستكبروا فيعذبهم عذبا اليما * ولا يجدون
لهم من دون الله وليا ولا نصيرا * يايها الناس قد
جاكم برهن من ربكم وانزلنا اليكم نورا مبينا * فا
ما الذين امنوا بالله واعتصموا به فسيدخلهم فى
رحمة منه وفضل ويهديهم اليه صرطا مستقيما *

بسم الله الرحمن الرحيم * يايها الذين امنوا
اوفوا بالعقود * احلت لكم بهيمة الانعم
الا ما يتلى عليكم غير محلى الصيد وانتم حرم
ان الله يحكم ما يريد * يايها الذين امنوا لا
تحلوا شعر الله ولا الشهر الحرم ولا الهدى و
لا القلد ولا امين البيت الحرم يبتغون فضلا من
ربهم ورضونا واذا حللتم فاصطدوا و
لا يجر منكم شنان قوم ان صدوكم عن المسجد
الحرم ان تعتدوا وتعونوا على البر والتقوى و
لا تعونوا على الاثم والعدون واتقوا الله
ان الله شديد العقاب * حرمت عليكم
الميتة والدم ولحم الخنزير وما اهل

Figure 7. Folios *20a and *20b, hypothetical reconstruction. (continued)

of text. In order to create the space needed for the new verse, Scribe A performed two operations: First, he carefully removed folio *20 from the codex by cutting along the gutter margin near the spine-fold, leaving the stub in place so as not to disturb the conjugate leaf of the bifolium (folio 17). Second, he began the task of rewriting, keeping the following three points in mind (1) an additional six lines would be needed for the new verse to be added at the end of the *Sūra*; (2) the new page, that is to say, the current folio 20b, should end with the word *uhilla* in v. 3 of *Sūrat al-Māʾida*; and (3) the number of verses in *Sūrat al-Nisāʾ* should remain unchanged.

Scribe A was able to recover four of the six lines that were needed by taking the first four lines at the top of the discarded folio *20b and placing them at the bottom of folio 20a. This is why folio 20a has twenty-seven lines, which is outside the normal range, rather than twenty-three lines, as do the preceding eight folio pages (see Figure 8).

After completing folio 20a, Scribe A turned the page and began inscribing text on folio 20b. As he began writing this page, he knew that he had to recover two additional lines for the supplementary verse. He did so by reducing the distance between the baselines of ll. 1–6 at the top of the page by approximately 1.5 mm per line and by using every possible millimeter of space on these same six lines, at the expense of the left margin. By the time that he reached l. 7, he was confident that there would be sufficient space for the new verse, which he now inserted on ll. 7–12. From l. 7 to the bottom of the folio page, the line spacing returns to normal. However, Scribe A was still concerned that on folio 20b he not go beyond the word *uhilla* (Q. 5:3), the last word on the now discarded folio *20b; this explains why he left a healthy left margin of between 1.5 and 2 cm on ll. 7–25. Thus, through the skillful and adroit manipulation of space, Scribe A was able to create room for the supplementary verse that was added at the end of *Sūrat al-Nisāʾ*.[108]

Scribe A's third concern was to keep the total number of verses in *Sūrat al-Nisāʾ* unchanged. Obviously, the addition of a supplementary verse would increase the number of verses in the *Sūra* by one. If Scribe A was using the Syrian verse-ending system (Assumption 8.2.3), then on the missing folio *20b, v. 173 would have ended with *ʿadhāb*^{an} *alīm*$^{\mathbf{an}}$ and v. 174 would have ended with *wa-lā naṣīr*$^{\mathbf{an}}$. In order to keep the number of verses in the *Sūra* unchanged, Scribe A combined these two verses into a single verse, as follows:

fa-ammā alladhīna āmanū wa-ʿamilū al-ṣāliḥāt fa-yuwaffīhim ujūrahum wa-yazīduhum min faḍlihi wa-ammā alladhīna ʾstankafū waʾstakbarū fa-yuʿadhdhibuhum ʿadhāb^{an} *alīm*$^{\mathbf{an}}$ *wa-lā yajidūna lahum min dūn*^{i} *allāh*^{i} *waliyy*^{an} *wa-lā naṣīr*$^{\mathbf{an}}$.

Notice that Scribe A did not leave the customary 1.5 cm of space between *alīm*$^{\mathbf{an}}$ and *wa-lā* (see again Figure 1). From this I infer that Scribe A regarded this block of text as a single verse.

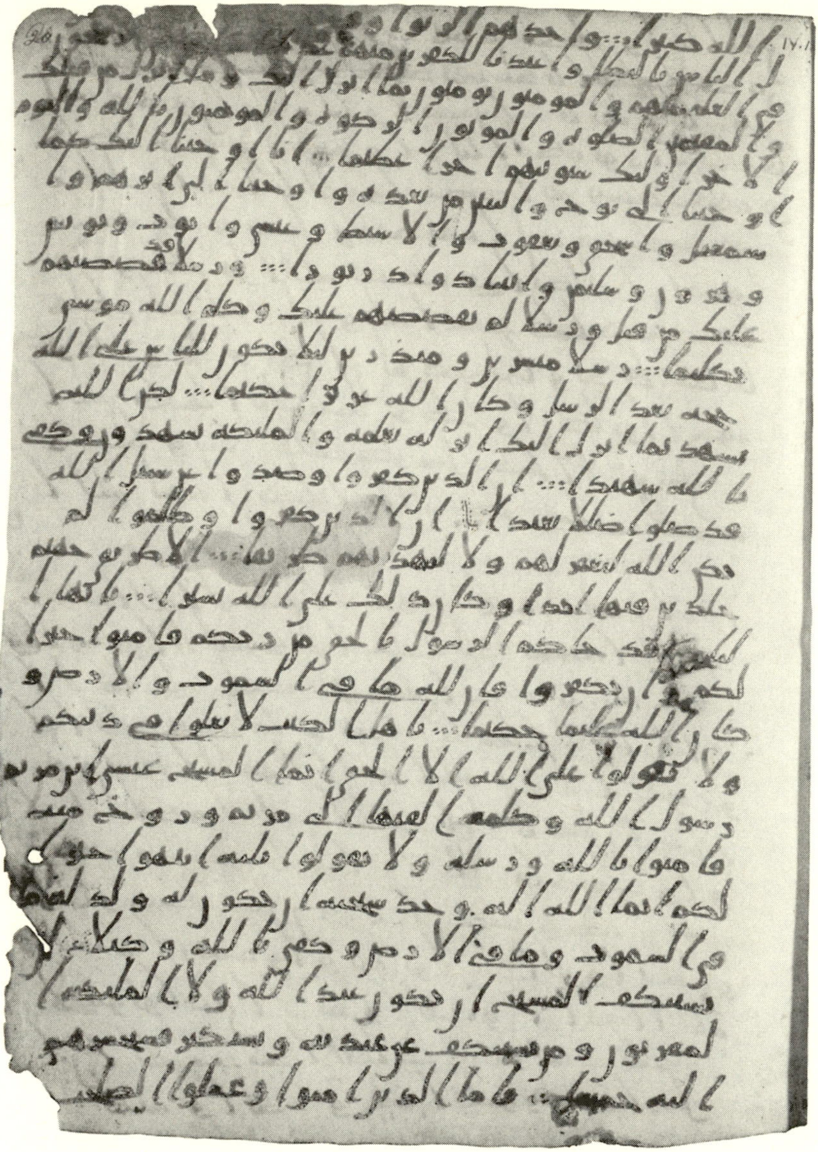

Figure 8. BNF Arabe 328a, folio 20a. Courtesy Bibliothèque Nationale de France.

Assuming that there are 176 verses in the *Sūra*, the mathematical consequence of combining two verses into one was as follows: What had been v. 175 in the *Sūra* became v. 174; what had been v. 176 became v. 175. The new, supplementary verse—reportedly the last verse to have been revealed—became the final verse (v. 176) in the *Sūra*. This is how Scribe A was able to add a verse to the end of *Sūrat al-Nisāʾ* while keeping the number of verses in the *Sūra* unchanged.

Sometime after Scribe A had completed writing this folio page, a corrector came along and restored the original Syrian system of verse division by inserting four vertical dots between the words *alīm*^{an} and *wa-lā*.

Conclusion

The evidence of BNF 328a points to two instances in which the consonantal skeleton of the Qurʾān was revised during the process of text redaction. In the first instance, the addition of a single consonant transformed the meaning of a verse dealing with inheritance. This change in turn made it necessary to add supplementary legislation at the end of a chapter. Since BNF 328a was produced in the second half of the first century A.H., it appears that the consonantal skeleton and performed reading of the Qurʾān remained open and fluid until the end of the first/seventh century. It is easy to imagine that changes like the ones discussed above would have led to disagreements, caused the first Muslims to accuse one another of infidelity, brought the community to the verge of civil strife, and justified the destruction of all codices that were not in conformity with what became the canonical text (see above).

The opening clause of Q. *4:12b originally read as follows: *wa-in kāna rajul*^{un} *yūrithu kallat*^{an} *aw imraʾat*^{an}. This clause signified, "If a man designates a daughter-in-law or wife as [his] heir." For reasons that remain to be determined (see Chapter 9), the consonantal skeleton and performed reading of this clause were revised as follows: (1) a second *lām* was added to **kalla*, thereby creating a new word, *kalāla*, which had not existed previously in Arabic and for which there is no equivalent in any Semitic language; (2) the performed reading of *y-w-r-th* was changed from active (*yūrithu*) to passive (*yūrathu*); and (3) the case ending of *imraʾa* was changed from accusative to nominative. The result was: *wa-in kāna rajul*^{un} *yūrathu kalālat*^{an} *aw imraʾat*^{un}, which came to be understood as signifying, "If a man or a woman is inherited by collaterals." The revision transforms the meaning of the opening clause by eliminating the reference to the possibility of designating an heir, the reference to a daughter-in-law, and the reference to a wife.

The revision of Q. *4:12b made it appear as if the inheritance verse (Q. 4:11–12) is incomplete. The fact that the revised text awards a maximum of one-third of the estate to siblings was of sufficient importance to merit a supplement to the inheritance rules spelled out in vv. 11–12. This supplementary legislation was added to BNF 328a by Scribe A. Just as Zayd b. Thābit inserted two "lost" verses at the end of *Sūrat al-Tawba*, so too Scribe A added a new "verse" at the end of *Sūrat al-Nisā'*.

The early exegetes and grammarians identified eight cruxes associated with Q. 4:12b and 4:176 (see above). My hypothesis disposes of all eight cruxes in one fell swoop. The first six cruxes were internal to v. 12b:

1.1 The verb *y-w-r-th* should be read as an active verb, i.e., *yūrithu*.
1.2 Verse 12b originally specified **kalla* or **daughter-in-law*.
1.3 The noun **kalla* was in the accusative case as the direct object of *yūrithu*.
1.4 Likewise, *imra'a* was in the accusative case as the second direct object of *yūrithu*. Whereas in v. 12b one finds a bifurcated compound subject ("a man . . . or a woman"), in v. *12b one finds a normal compound predicate ("daughter-in-law or wife").
1.5 The subject of *yūrithu* is the "man" mentioned immediately before the verb on l. 1a.
1.6 The masculine singular pronoun *wa-lahu* in l. 1b refers back to the "man" on l. 1a.

The last two cruxes emerged from a comparison of the two verses:

2.1 The word *kalāla* was an artificial creation and its meaning in vv. 12b and 176 is determined solely by context. In v. 12b *kalāla* is used adverbially; in v. 176 it is a simple noun. This is why *kalāla* cannot have the same meaning in the two verses.
2.1 The discrepancy in the fractional shares awarded to siblings in vv. 12b and 176 was an unavoidable consequence of the revision of v. *12b. In v. *12b, which dealt with testate succession, the siblings were awarded a maximum of one-third of the estate as compensation for their having been disinherited in favor of a woman who is not a blood relative of the testator. In v. 176, which is part of the compulsory Islamic inheritance rules, the siblings are the primary heirs of a man or woman who does not leave a last will and testament.

The consonantal skeleton of v. *12b specified **kalla*, which signified **daughter-in-law*. This word was a *hapax legomenon*. Subsequently, **kalla* was changed to *kalāla*, also a *hapax legomenon*—until its inclusion in the supplementary verse inserted at the end of *Sūrat al-Nisā'* turned it into a *dis legomenon*. Although a few key Companions surely were aware of the textual changes discussed in this chapter, the Muslim community appears to have forgotten that these revisions took place. They forgot the original consonantal skeleton and performed reading of Q. *4:12b, they forgot the meaning of the word **kalla*, and they forgot that supplementary legislation was added at the end of *Sūrat al-Nisā'*.[109]

Whoever was responsible for these changes no doubt sought to justify them. What better way to do so than to assert that God caused the Prophet and/or his community to forget them? Three verses in the Qur'ān link the phenomenon of forgetting to the divine will. Q. 87:6–7 states, "We shall cause you to recite, so that you do not forget—except that which God wills." Similarly, Q. 2:106 reads: "Whatever signs We annul or cause to be forgotten, We bring better or the like. Do you not know that God has power over everything?" Our concern here is with the latter verse, which is generally taken as the Qur'ānic peg for the doctrine of abrogation (*naskh*), according to which a later verse (*āya*) may supersede or annul an earlier one.[110] In a given pair of verses, one is *nāsikh* or *abrogating* and the other is *mansūkh* or *abrogated.*

One wonders if Q. 2:106 was originally intended to address the phenomenon of abrogation. The Arabic text reads as follows: *mā nansakh min āya aw nunsihā na'ti bi-khayr*[in] *minhā aw mithlihā a-lam ta'lam anna allāh*[a] *'alā kull*[i] *shay'*[in] *qadīr*[un]? The noun *āya*, translated above as *sign*, also signifies *verse.* And the verb *nasakha*, translated as *to annul*, also means *to copy or transcribe*, as in the sentence *nasakha al-kitāb*, which signifies *he copied or transcribed the writing or book letter-for-letter.* The active participle *nāsikh* refers to *a person who copies or transcribes a writing or writings or a book or books.* The passive participle *mansūkh* refers to *something that has been copied or transcribed.* The noun *nuskha* signifies *a copy* or *transcript.* There is a close connection between derivatives of the root *n-s-kh* and the phenomenon of producing texts in a manuscript culture. No scribe is perfect, and the production of multiple copies of a single text invariably generates variants. The association between textual reproduction and textual change is reflected in the Arabic expression, *mā nasakhahu wa-innamā masakhahu*, which signifies, *He has not copied it, but only corrupted it, by changing the diacritical points and altering its meaning.*[111]

Words derived from the root *n-s-kh* occur in Akkadian, Ge'ez, Hebrew, and Aramaic. In Hebrew, the noun *nusakh* signifies either *words arranged in a fixed form or order*, or *a version*, *a copy of a document*, *the specific form of a text.* From the Hebrew noun *nusakh* is derived the verb *nasakh* which signifies *to arrange words or ideas in writing or in one's mind* or *to fix the form of a text.*[112] The English equivalent of the Hebrew verb *nasakh* is *to formulate.* The Hebrew verb *nasakh* is clearly related to the Arabic verb *nasakha.* The similarity between these two terms brings me to the following hypothesis:

Hypothesis 8.3. In Q. 2:106, the noun *āya* originally signified *a verse* or *revelation* and the verb *nasakha* originally signified *to formulate*—like its Hebrew counterpart. If so, we may translate v. 106 into English as follows:

Whatever verses We formulate or cause to be forgotten, We bring better or the like. Do you not know that God has power over everything?

Viewed in this manner, Q. 2:106 functions as a general comment on revelation, divine power, and the human condition. The identity of any new community is forged through the complex interplay of remembrance and forgetfulness. Forgetting is an inevitable product of the human condition. As in Q. 87:6–7, the forgetting of divine revelation is openly acknowledged and said to have been subject to the control of the divine will. According to the authorial voice that controls the Qur'ān, God has the power to make Muḥammad and his community forget a revelation; and He also has the power to revise earlier revelations. In this chapter I have argued that the original meaning of *4:12b was forgotten and that a *better* version of this verse was produced: 4:12b. I also have argued that a new and improved version of 4:12b was *formulated* and inserted at the end of *Sūrat al-Nisā'*. These actions may have been performed by God. Alternatively, they may have been performed by one or more of His creatures. God knows best.

Chapter 9

Kalāla in Early Islamic Tradition

*It is He who has revealed to you the Book, with verses which are precise in meaning (*muḥkamāt*) and which are the Mother of the Book, and others which are ambiguous (*mutashābihāt*). As for those in whose hearts there is vacillation, they follow what is ambiguous in it, seeking sedition and intending to interpret it. However, no one except God knows its interpretation. Q. 3:7*

The desires of interpreters are good because without them the world and the text are tacitly declared to be impossible; perhaps they are, but we must live as if the case were otherwise.

—*Frank Kermode,* The Genesis of Secrecy: On the Interpretation of Narrative, *126*

Q. *4:12b referred to a man who designates a daughter-in-law (**kalla*) or wife as his heir. This sub-verse was revised by the early Muslim community in such a manner as to produce a text that refers to a man or a woman who is inherited by *kalāla*. The word *kalāla* was an artificial invention that was not part of the Arabic lexicon during the lifetime of the Prophet. To complicate matters, the word *kalāla* occurs only twice in the Qur'ān, and it has no equivalent in any other Semitic language. In the first half of the first century A.H., very few Muslims would have known the meaning of this word.

The fact that one finds no trace of the word **kalla* in the literary sources suggests that the Muslim community was—and remains—unaware of its existence. It was not until the consonantal skeleton of the Qur'ān had been fixed that the work of *tafsīr*, or interpretation, could begin. It was the received text that was studied by the exegetes, *ḥadīth* specialists, and grammarians. We turn now to their treatment of the word *kalāla* in Q. 4:12b and 4:176, beginning with the earliest treatises and moving forward in time until the beginning of the fourth/tenth century. The purpose of this exercise is twofold: First, to show how the successive layers of the Islamic tradition accumulated over the course of the first three centuries A.H.; and, second, to scrutinize the sources for clues that may explain why the early Muslim community revised the consonantal skeleton of the Qur'ān.

Tafsīr and *Ḥadīth*

With one notable exception, the Muslim exegetes who flourished between ca. 50 and 150 A.H. are silent about Q. 4:12b and 176.

Arguably the first extant commentary on the Qur'ān is that of Mujāhid b. Jabr (d. 102/720), a Meccan Successor associated with the school of Ibn ʿAbbās (d. 68/687).[1] Regarded as the most knowledgeable expert on the Qur'ān of his age, Mujāhid nevertheless was criticized for excessive reliance on Jews and Christians as sources of information.[2] In his discussion of 4:12b, Mujāhid has nothing to say about *kalāla*, although he does make a brief comment about the meaning of the phrase *ghayr*^a^ *muḍārr*^in^ ("without injury"), which occurs at the end of l. 3.[3] Nor does he have anything to say about 4:176. Indeed, Mujāhid's treatment of *Sūrat al-Nisā'* ends with v. 174.[4] In another early commentary, al-Ḍaḥḥāk (d. 105/723) does mention that Q. 4:8 was abrogated by *āyat al-mawārīth* or "the verse of the inheritances"—although he has nothing to say about the contents or meaning of Q. 4:11–12.[5] His treatment of *Sūrat al-Nisā'* ends with v. 172.[6] The same pattern holds in the fragmentary commentary of Sufyān al-Thawrī (d. 161/778), a *ḥadīth*-oriented legal scholar who also wrote a treatise on inheritance. Like Mujāhid, Sufyān's only comment on v. 12b relates to the expression *ghayr*^a^ *muḍārr*^in^; similarly, his treatment of *Sūrat al-Nisā'* ends with v. 174—despite the fact that we know, from his inheritance treatise, that he was familiar with v. 176.[7] Thus, neither Mujāhid, nor al-Ḍaḥḥāk, nor Sufyān al-Thawrī has anything to say about v. 176. One wonders if they were aware of the existence of this verse which, as I argued in Chapter 8 was added to the Qur'ān ca. 50 A.H.

Muqātil b. Sulaymān (d. 150/767)

Of the Muslim exegetes who flourished between ca. 50 and 150 A.H., Muqātil b. Sulaymān was the first to mention the word *kalāla* in his treatment of 4:12b and the first to mention v. 176 ("*Yastaftūnaka* . . .").[8] Like Mujāhid, Muqātil was criticized by Muslim scholars for his reliance on Jews and Christians for explanations of obscure allusions in the Qur'ān. He also was criticized for failing to attach *isnād*s to his reports.[9] Let us now attend to what Muqātil has to say about Q. 4:12b and 4:176.

Q. 4:12B

In Chapter 8, I identified eight cruxes associated with Q. 4:12b and 4:176. In his discussion of the former verse, Muqātil treats three of these eight cruxes. He begins with the bifurcated subject ("a man . . . or a woman") in l. 1a (*wa-in kāna rajul*^**un**^ *yūrathu kalālat*^an^ *aw imra'at*^**un**^)—Crux 1.4. He disposes of this problem with four words: "*fīhā taqdīm yūrathu kalālat*^an^."[10] His audience would have understood this terse remark as signifying that the phrase *yūrathu kalālat*^{an} in l. 1a does not occur in what the commentator regarded as its true syntactic position, but rather has been pre-positioned or moved forward in the sentence (*fīhā taqdīm*). Although Muqātil does not say so, he implies that in order to restore the proper sentence structure, one must move the phrase *yūrathu kalālat*^{an} backward—not physically, of course, but mentally. In other words, it is necessary to treat l. 1a as if the word order were as follows: *wa-in kāna* ***rajul***^{un} ***aw imraʾat***^{un} *yūrathu kalālat*^{an} . . . ("If a **man or a woman** *yūrathu kalālat*^{an} . . .").[11]

Second, Muqātil defines the word *kalāla* here (Crux 1.2) as *a man who dies leaving neither child nor parent nor grandfather*.[12]

Third, Muqātil addresses the discrepancy in the size of the shares awarded to siblings in 4:12b and 4:176 (Crux 2.2). He explains that the *brother* and *sister* mentioned in v. 12b are in fact uterine siblings (*al-ikhwa liʾl-umm*), that is to say, siblings who share the same mother but have different fathers.[13] In other words, the commentator was suggesting, when God used the unqualified kinship term *brother* or *sister* in v. 12b, He was referring specifically to a uterine sibling (*akh aw ukht* ***li-umm***). In addition, although Muqātil does not say so here or elsewhere in his commentary, he surely held that when God used the unqualified kinship term *brother* or *sister* in v. 176, He was referring to consanguine siblings, that is to say, siblings who share the same father but have different mothers (*akh aw ukht* ***li-ab***), and/or germane siblings, that is to say, siblings who share the same father and the same mother (*akh aw ukht* ***li-ab wa li-umm***). This solution also takes the form of a variant reading attributed to Ubayy b. Kaʿb (d. 30/651–52) and Saʿd b. Abī Waqqāṣ (d. 55/675).[14] If these attributions are accurate, then the gloss or interpolation may have been introduced before 30 A.H. Be that as it may, it has been universally accepted by the Muslim community.

Q. 4:176

Muqātil begins his discussion of 4:176 with the *sabab al-nuzūl*, or occasion, on which the verse was revealed. "*Yastaftūnaka*," he says, "was revealed about Jābir b. ʿAbdallāh al-Anṣārī, a member of the [tribe] of Banū Salama b. Jusham b. Saʿd b. ʿAlī b. Shārida b. Yazīd b. Jusham b. al-Khazraj."[15] Jābir was a long-lived Companion who died in the year 78/697, reportedly at the age of ninety-four.[16] At least sixty-eight (lunar) years prior to his death, Jābir, who would have been in his twenties at the time, is said to have had a near-death experience that prompted him to ask the Prophet about what he should do with his estate. The *sabab al-nuzūl* runs as follows (there is no *isnād*):

> Jābir b. ʿAbdallāh al-Anṣārī—may God have mercy on him—became ill in Medina, and the Messenger of God—may God bless him and grant him peace—paid him a

visit. [Jābir] said, "O Messenger of God, I am a *kalāla* who has neither father nor child (*lā ab lī wa-lā walad*). So what should I do with my wealth?" This is why God revealed [*in ʿmraʾun halaka laysa lahu waladun . . .*].[17]

In this report Jābir refers to himself as "a *kalāla*" without identifying his heirs (for example, siblings, cousins, or uncles). It is Muqātil who specifies that this verse was revealed about Jābir "and about his sisters"[18]—without identifying the sisters as uterine, consanguine, or germane siblings. The fact pattern here matches the fact pattern in 4:12b, which refers to a childless man whose closest surviving blood relatives are one or more siblings. According to this sub-verse, if Jābir had in fact died from his illness, his sisters would have inherited exactly one-third of his estate to be divided on a per capita basis. Only now was v. 176 revealed. According to the latter verse, if Jābir had in fact died from his illness, his sisters would have inherited two-thirds of his estate, again on a per capita basis. Thus, the *sabab* suggests that the revelation of v. 176 was designed to make it possible for Jābir's sisters to inherit a larger share of the estate than they would have inherited according to v. 12b. As I argued in the previous chapter, this is precisely why it was necessary to formulate the supplementary legislation that became v. 176.

Muqātil, however, expresses no interest whatsoever in the size of the shares. What does interest the commentator is the language of the *sabab*, specifically Jābir's reference to himself as "a *kalāla* who has neither father nor child." In the narrative, Jābir makes this statement prior to the revelation of v. 176, which, as noted, appears to define *al-kalāla* as *a man who dies without a child*. The fact that v. 176 was revealed about Jābir indicates that the provisions of this verse refer not only to a man who dies "without a child" but also to a man who dies "leaving neither *father* nor child" (emphasis added)—one of the two meanings attributed to the word in v. 12b. The *sabab* was important to Muqātil because it suggests that the meaning of *kalāla* in v. 12b is identical to its meaning in v. 176—even if this conclusion is not supported by the language of these two verses (Crux 2.1). It is the statement attributed to Jābir that allows Muqātil to assert that in v. 176 the word *kalāla* signifies *a person who dies without having either a child or a parent* (*laysa lahu walad wa-lā wālid*)[19]—even though this verse appears to define the word as *a man who dies without a child* (*in ʿmraʾun halaka laysa lahu walad*). The evidence for this assertion is found in a statement attributed to Jābir while he was speaking to the Prophet. The Prophet's silence with respect to the statement made by Jābir confers prophetic authority on the assertion. We will return to the language used by Jābir later in this chapter.

ʿAbd al-Razzāq al-Ṣanʿānī (d. 211/826)

Of Persian origin, ʿAbd al-Razzāq al-Ṣanʿānī was a client of Ḥimyar and the leading scholar of the Yemen. He is said to have lost his sight around the turn of the second/eighth century, and is sometimes associated with Shiʿism.[20] He was the author of an important *ḥadīth* collection known as the *Muṣannaf* and of a *Tafsīr* or Commentary on the Qurʾān. In both texts, ʿAbd al-Razzāq preserves traditions that mention the word *kalāla*. We begin with his *Muṣannaf*.

The *Muṣannaf* of ʿAbd al-Razzāq[21]

In his chapter on inheritance, ʿAbd al-Razzāq devotes a section to *al-kalāla* which contains twelve *ḥadīth*s, the *isnād*s of which are either *mursal* ("incompletely transmitted") or *munqaṭiʿ* ("interrupted").[22] A *ḥadīth* is *mursal* when the name of a Companion is missing between that of the Prophet and that of a Successor; or when a Companion narrates an event at which he could not have been present. A *ḥadīth* is *munqaṭiʿ* when a link is missing anywhere in the *isnād*.[23] The information contained in these *isnād*s makes it possible to determine when, where, and by whom these reports were first put into circulation.

Broadly speaking, these twelve reports fall into two groups: In five of them, the meaning of *kalāla* is unknown or withheld from the community at large. In the remaining seven reports, the meaning of *kalāla* is known but disputed. Curiously, there is no mention of, or reference to, 4:12b in any of these twelve reports.

We begin with the five reports in which the meaning of *kalāla* is unknown or withheld from the community at large. The central figure in these narratives is ʿUmar b. al-Khaṭṭāb, the Companion who played an instrumental role in the collection of the Qurʾān and whose ten-year reign as caliph (13–23/634–44) ended with his assassination in the mosque of Medina by a disaffected Christian slave.[24] In these five reports, ʿUmar is portrayed as a man who was obsessed with the word *kalāla* for much of his adult life, an obsession that he appears to have carried with him to his grave. In three of these reports, ʿUmar identifies *al-kalāla* as one of three critical issues about which the Prophet left no instructions. In one report, ʿUmar says, "Three things that the Prophet did not explain to us are dearer to me than the earth and its contents: *al-khilāfa*, *al-kalāla*, and *al-ribā*."[25] In a second report, the caliph expresses remorse at his failure to ask the Prophet to clarify three important matters—with *al-kalāla* now occupying the first position: "That I should have asked the Prophet about three things would be worth more to me than the finest camels: about *al-kalāla*; about *al-khalīfa* after him; and about people who say, 'We acknowledge the alms-tax with respect to our wealth but we will not pay it to you.' Is it licit to fight them or not?"[26] To this one of the tradents in the *isnād* adds, "Abū Bakr was of the opinion that fighting [them is licit]."[27] In a third report, the dying caliph instructs Ibn ʿAbbās to commit to memory three important decisions that he had made: "Remember three things about me: The Commander [of the Believers is to be selected] by a council (*shūra*); when ransoming Bedouin (*ʿarab*), one slave should be exchanged for one slave, and [when ransoming] the son of a concubine, two slaves [for one son of a concubine]; and with regard to *al-kalāla*—what did I say?" In this report, the caliph wants Ibn ʿAbbās to remember his decision about *al-kalāla* but, ironically, suffers a sudden memory lapse and cannot remember what he said about the word. This report concludes with an exchange that took place sometime before the year 131/748–49 between two of the tradents in the *isnād*: Maʿmar (d. 152–53/769–70) said: "I asked Ibn Ṭāʾūs (d. 131/748–49), 'What did he [ʿUmar] say?' But Ibn Ṭāʾūs refused to tell me."[28] One wonders why Ibn Ṭāʾūs would have withheld from Maʿmar his knowledge about what ʿUmar had said. Be that as it may, in this report ʿUmar does not divulge the meaning of *al-kalāla*.

A fourth report combines two moments in time: the first moment, unspecified, is clearly prior to ʿUmar's assassination; the second moment is the immediate aftermath of the stabbing:

> ʿUmar b. al-Khaṭṭāb wrote a document (*kitāb*) about the grandfather (*al-jadd*) and *al-kalāla*. He tarried, praying to God for assistance, saying, "O God, if You know of some goodness in it, bring it forward." Then, when he was stabbed, he called for the document, and it was erased, and no one knew its contents. He [ʿUmar] said, "Verily, I wrote a document about the grandfather and *al-kalāla*, and I asked God for guidance about it; as a result, I have decided to leave you [believing] what you already believe."[29]

This report indicates that there was a difference between ʿUmar's understanding of *al-kalāla* and the Muslim community's understanding of the word. The report appears to be pointing an accusing finger at ʿUmar, to whom responsibility is attributed for the erasure of a document relevant to the meaning of *kalāla*.

The fifth report (no. 19193) in which the meaning of *al-kalāla* is unknown is a second *sabab al-nuzūl* related to 4:176, although this *sabab* is totally independent of the Jābir-*sabab* cited by Muqātil. Like the fourth report, this one brings together two moments in time: the revelation of the verse ca. 11/632; and, at least two years later, a testy exchange between the Caliph ʿUmar and Ḥudhayfa b. al-Yamān (d. 36/656), the Companion who urged the Caliph ʿUthmān to unite the Muslim community by creating a single uniform codex.[30] The *isnād* is as follows: ʿAbd al-Razzāq (Yemen, d. 211/827)—Maʿmar (Basra, d. 152–53/769–70)—Ayyūb [al-Sakhtiyānī] (Basra, d. 131/749)—Ibn Sīrīn (Basra, d. 110/728)—ʿUmar b. al-Khaṭṭāb (d. 23/644). The *isnād* is broken: Ibn Sīrīn could not have been present at an event said to have taken place during the lifetime of the second caliph. The narrative appears to have originated in Basra and to have circulated in Basran scholarly circles for approximately a quarter of a century before Maʿmar brought it to ʿAbd al-Razzāq in the Yemen.

As the *sabab* opens the Prophet is out on a journey, riding a camel, accompanied by ʿUmar and Ḥudhayfa (hereinafter, I refer to this report as the camel-*sabab*).[31] The narrator specifies that the three men were traveling in single file. This is when the verse—ostensibly 4:176 —was revealed to Muḥammad, who turned around and relayed it to Ḥudhayfa, who turned around and relayed it to ʿUmar. Sometime after ʿUmar became caliph in 13/634, he approached Ḥudhayfa in the hope that he would explain the meaning of the verse to him (*rajā an yakūna ʿindahu tafsīruhā*). Although the beginning of the conversation between the two men is not specified in the *sabab*, we can infer from what follows that the caliph insinuated that there was a discrepancy between what the Prophet had told Ḥudhayfa and what Ḥudhayfa had told ʿUmar during the journey on which the verse was revealed. To this insinuation Ḥudhayfa responded: "By God, you are a fool (*aḥmaq*) if you think that your position as Commander [of the Believers] requires me to tell you something that I did not tell you on that day." To this ʿUmar replied, "I meant no such thing—may God have mercy on you."[32] At this point, the *sabab* ends. However, ʿAbd al-Razzāq now adds the following supplement to the *sabab* with an identical *isnād* (Maʿmar—Ayyūb—Ibn Sīrīn): Whenever ʿUmar would recite the phrase, "God makes clear for you [lest] you go astray" (*yubayyinu allāhᵘ lakum an taḍillū*)—that is, l. 6 of 4:176—he would exclaim, "O God, to whom have you made *kalāla* clear? Surely you have not made it clear to me!"[33]

From these five reports, we learn that the word *kalāla* was extremely important to ʿUmar—or to the men who first put these reports into circulation; that the Prophet died without specifically defining this word; that ʿUmar claimed that Ḥudhayfa had misrepresented the contents of Q. 4:176; that on his deathbed, ʿUmar could not remember what he himself had said about *kalāla*; and that the caliph wrote a document about *kalāla* but ordered it to be erased just before he died.

Excursus: The *Summer Verse* and the Problem of Multiple *Asbāb*

The fifth report (no. 19193) in the *Muṣannaf* of ʿAbd al-Razzāq merits attention. It is curious that a towering figure like ʿUmar b. al-Khaṭṭāb apparently did not understand the meaning of *al-kalāla*. On one level, ʿUmar's incomprehension no doubt served to comfort and reassure Muslim scholars who were struggling to make sense of the word. On another level, the report draws attention to the process whereby 4:176 became part of the Qur'ān.

The Prophet received the revelation and immediately transmitted it to Ḥudhayfa, who then transmitted it to ʿUmar: the transmission was thus from one person to one person to one person. Whoever formulated this narrative was describing the children's game known in modern times as *telephone*. Sure enough, only a few years after the verse had been revealed, the caliph ʿUmar would allege that there was in fact a discrepancy between whatever it was that the Prophet told Ḥudhayfa and whatever it was that Ḥudhayfa told him (just as, in the fourth report in the previous section—no. 19183—there is a discrepancy between ʿUmar's understanding of *al-kalāla* and the Muslim community's understanding of this word). ʿUmar's allegation elicited anger and indignation from Ḥudhayfa, who called the caliph a fool for thinking that he had misrepresented the contents of the verse. Was this perhaps one of the *mutashābihāt* or ambiguous verses mentioned in Q. 3:7, the interpretation (*taʾwīl*) of which was sought by seditious men of uncertain faith?

The word *kalāla* occurs for the first time in v. 12 of *Sūrat al-Nisāʾ*. As noted, vv. 11–12 of this *Sūra* are referred to collectively in the singular as *āyat al-farḍ* or *the inheritance verse* (v. 12b itself apparently has no specific linguistic tag). The second occurrence of *kalāla* is in v. 176, a verse that is easily identifiable: it is the last verse in *Sūrat al-Nisāʾ*, the last verse revealed to Muḥammad, and *the summer verse*. Compared to v. 12b, v. 176 has a surfeit of identifiers. This imbalance is also reflected in the *asbāb al-nuzūl*. Although there are several *sabab*s about the revelation of vv. 11–12, none specifically references v. 12b or the word *kalāla*.[34] By contrast, v. 176 has two separate and independent *sabab*s associated with it.[35] In one, the Prophet pays a sick visit to Jābir b. ʿAbdallāh, from whose statement made in the presence of the Prophet it is possible to infer the meaning of *kalāla*. In the other—the camel-*sabab*—the Prophet receives the revelation while he is riding a camel, accompanied by Ḥudhayfa and ʿUmar. It is universally assumed that the verse revealed on this occasion was v. 176. This assumption merits examination.

As noted, in the *Muṣannaf* of ʿAbd al-Razzāq the camel-*sabab* (report no. 19193) is a composite of two separate narratives with identical *isnād*s: The first and main part of the report describes the circumstances in which the verse was revealed and the subsequent encounter between ʿUmar and Ḥudhayfa in which the caliph asks for clarification of the meaning of the verse; the second part juxtaposes ʿUmar's frustration over his inability to understand *al-kalāla* with the fact that v. 176 culminates in God's assertion that He has made the revelation "clear to you lest you go astray." The language of v. 176 is cited in the supplementary narrative. Without this supplement and its citation of language clearly identifiable as belonging to v. 176, there is nothing in the main part of the camel-*sabab* that links it directly to this verse. Conversely, one might argue that the only reason why ʿAbd al-Razzāq is able to link the camel-*sabab* to the revelation of v. 176 is because of the supplement to the main narrative.

One wonders if the camel-*sabab*—without the supplement—originally may have been formulated to explain the revelation of v. 12b rather than that of v. 176. Apart from the words *brother* and *sister*—which, as we have seen, require an interpolation—the language of v. 176 is straightforward and unequivocal. It is not immediately apparent why ʿUmar would ask Ḥudhayfa to explain the meaning of this verse to him. The same is not true of v. 12b, the understanding of which requires a solid grasp of Arabic semantics, morphology, and grammar. It is easy to imagine that ʿUmar would have wanted Ḥudhayfa to explain the meaning of *this* verse to him.

The assumption that the camel-*sabab* initially was formulated to explain the revelation of v. 12b finds support in an otherwise anomalous report in which it is v. 12b rather than v. 176 that is identified as the *summer verse*:

Ibn Wakīʿ—Abū Usāma [Ḥammād b. Usāma b. Zayd al-Kūfī, d. 201/816–17]—Zakariyyāʾ b. Abī Zāʾida [Kufa, d. 147–49/764–66]—Abū Isḥāq [al-Sabīʿī; d. 127/745]—Abū Salama [b. ʿAbd al-Raḥmān b. ʿAwf al-Zuhrī; d. 94/713]. He said: A man approached the Prophet—may God bless him and grant him peace—and asked him about *al-kalāla*. [The Prophet] replied: Have you not heard the verse that was revealed in the summer (*fī al-ṣayf*): *wa-in kāna rajul^{un} yūrathu kalālat^{an}*?—to the end of the verse.[36]

In this report, which appears to have been put into circulation some time after the middle of the first century A.H., an unidentified man approaches Muḥammad and asks him about *al-kalāla*. The Prophet responds by referring the man to "the verse that was revealed in the summer," and he quotes the opening line of this verse: *wa-in kāna rajul^{un} yūrathu kalālat^{an}*. This can only be v. 12b, here dubbed *the summer verse*. This suggests that the *summer verse* linguistic tag originally was coined to identify v. 12b. If so, then the camel-*sabab* also may have been intended to explain the revelation of v. 12b. As for v. 176, its placement at the end of *Sūrat al-Nisāʾ* facilitated its identification and it had its own *sabab*—the report about Jābir and his sisters. The location and identity of v. 176 was unequivocal; it had no need for an additional linguistic tag.

The transference of the *summer verse* tag from 4:12b to 4:176 presumably occurred after the supplementary legislation was inserted at the end of *Sūrat al-Nisāʾ*. Beginning ca. 50 A.H., Muslim scholars living in Mecca, Medina, Kufa, and Basra put into circulation a series of reports in which the meaning of *kalāla* is represented as a mystery and ʿUmar is portrayed as knowing the meaning of the word but unable or unwilling to divulge his knowledge. All of these reports, including the camel-*sabab*, are directly relevant to v. 12b. However, ca. 100 A.H. the first exegetes made a strategic decision to detach these reports from their original association with v. 12b and to link them instead with v. 176. The *summer verse* tag was shifted from v. 12b to v. 176, and the camel-*sabab* was detached from its association with v. 12b and linked to v. 176 by means of a narrative supplement. This was accomplished by borrowing a detail from another report and incorporating it in what became report no. 19193 in ʿAbd al-Razzāq's *Muṣannaf*. The borrowed detail is found in report no. 19194, the very next report in ʿAbd al-Razzāq's chapter on *al-kalāla*:

ʿAbd al-Razzāq (d. 211/827)—Ibn ʿUyayna (d. 198/813)—ʿAmr b. Dīnār (d. 126/744)—Ṭāʾūs [b. Kaysān; d. 106/724): ʿUmar ordered [his daughter] Ḥafṣa [who was one of Muḥammad's wives] to ask the Prophet about *al-kalāla*. She proceeded slowly, waiting until he had put on his clothes before asking him [the question]. After dictating it [the verse] to her on a shoulder-blade (*katif*), he said, "[It was] ʿUmar who ordered you to do this. I suspect that he does not understand it. Is not the summer verse sufficient for him?" She then brought [the shoulder-blade] to ʿUmar, who read it. [Subsequently, whenever ʿUmar would recite,] "God makes clear for you lest you go astray," he would say, "O God, to whom have you made it clear? Surely you have not made it clear to me!"[37]

Several features of this report are noteworthy. The eighty-three year gap between the death of ʿUmar in 23 A.H. and that of Ṭāʾūs b. Kaysān in 106 A.H. makes it highly unlikely that Ṭāʾūs was even alive at the time of this incident; if so, he could not have been more than seven years old. It is possible that it was Ṭāʾūs who put this report into circulation—perhaps for the first time—around the turn of the second century A.H. Ṭāʾūs b. Kaysān is the father of Ibn Ṭāʾūs, the tradent who in a report cited above apparently knew what ʿUmar said about *kalāla* but refused to share this knowledge with Maʿmar. The Prophet's dictation of the verse to Ḥafṣa was recorded on a shoulder blade (*katif*), a narrative detail that will recur in another report. It is curious that Muḥammad should question ʿUmar's intelligence or ability to understand the Qurʾān. When the Prophet asks rhetorically if the *summer verse* is not sufficient for ʿUmar, one wonders if he is referring to 4:12b or 176. The rhetorical question sets up the irony and pathos of ʿUmar's plea to the Divinity. It is clear that the summer verse—whichever verse that may have been—was not sufficient for the caliph.

Our primary interest in report no. 19194, however, is the citation of the language of 4:176 and the statement attributed to ʿUmar at the end of the narrative. This part of the text was borrowed, possibly by ʿAbd al-Razzāq himself, fitted out with a new *isnād*, and attached to the end of no. 19193, the camel-*sabab*. It was the transfer of this language from report no. 19194 to report no. 19193 that made it possible for the camel-*sabab* to be identified with 4:176. Once the change had been carried out, it stuck.

ʿAbd al-Razzāq's *Muṣannaf* (cont.)

In addition to the five reports in which the meaning of *kalāla* is unknown or withheld, the *Muṣannaf* of ʿAbd al-Razzāq also contains seven reports in which the meaning of the word is known but contested.

The early Muslim community was aware of two definitions of *kalāla* in 4:12b and of a third definition of the word in 4:176 (Cruxes 1.2 and 2.1). The latter verse opens with a reference to *al-kalāla* ("God advises you with regard to *al-kalāla*"), which is immediately followed by what appears to be a definition of this word: *if a man dies without a child* (*laysa lahu walad*). This understanding is reflected in a narrative in which ʿUmar—who, on his deathbed, reportedly could not remember what he had said about *al-kalāla*—now recovers this memory with the assistance of Ibn ʿAbbās, who asks him, "And what did you say?" To this question the caliph responds that *al-kalāla* signifies *he who has no child* (*man lā walad lahu*). Here ʿUmar's definition of *al-kalāla* is consistent with the language of v. 176.[38]

In 4:12b, on the other hand, the word *kalāla* was understood as signifying either *a man who dies leaving neither parent nor child* or *all of a person's heirs with the exception of parents and children.* In two reports, one or the other definition is attributed to a Companion who died in the seventh decade of the first century A.H. ʿAmr b. Shuraḥbīl (Kufa, d. 63/682–83) is reported to have said—apparently with reference to v. 12b: "*Al-kalāla* is he who has no child and no parent" (*man laysa lahu walad wa-lā wālid*).[39] And Ibn ʿAbbās (d. 68/687) is reported to have said—again apparently with reference to v. 12b: "*Al-kalāla* is he who has no child and no parent" (*man lā walad wa-lā wālid*). The definition of *al-kalāla* attributed to Ibn ʿAbbās was heard by Ḥasan b. Muḥammad b. ʿAlī b. al-Ḥanafiyya (d. ca. 100/719),[40] who knew that in v. 176 the reference to *al-kalāla* is immediately followed by the statement: "If a man dies without a child." For this reason, Ḥasan b. Muḥammad confronted Ibn ʿAbbās, citing the opening line of v. 176 and drawing attention to the discrepancy between the two definitions. Ibn ʿAbbās was angered by this reference to a problem with God's revelation and, the narrator indicates, he rebuked Ḥasan b. Muḥammad for drawing attention to the problem (just as Ḥudhayfa rebuked ʿUmar when the caliph drew attention to an apparent discrepancy between his understanding of Q. 4:176 and that of Ḥudhayfa; and just as Ubayy b. Kaʿb rebuked ʿUmar when the caliph drew attention to an apparent discrepancy between his understanding of Q. 33:6 and that of Ubayy—see Chapter 4).[41] One wonders if Ḥasan b. Muḥammad's interest in the meaning of *al-kalāla* was somehow related to his accusation, in his *Kitāb al-irjāʾ*, that the Sabaʾiyya "falsified the Book of God" (*ḥarrafū kitāb allāh*).[42]

As we have seen, ʿUmar defined *al-kalāla* as *a person who dies without a child.* How is it possible that the caliph would say one thing but that Companions like ʿAmr b. Shuraḥbīl and Ibn ʿAbbās would say another? Who was to be believed? The apparent discrepancy was solved in one of two ways. The first solution was to modify ʿUmar's definition so as to bring it into line with the definition attributed to ʿAmr b. Shuraḥbīl and Ibn ʿAbbās. In a variant of the above-mentioned report (no. 19189) in which the dying caliph explains the meaning of the word to Ibn ʿAbbās, ʿUmar says, "*Al-kalāla* is what I said." Again it is only after Ibn ʿAbbās asks him what he said that the caliph recovers his memory, stating, "He who has no child." At this point, one of the tradents says, "I think that [ʿUmar] added, "and no parent" (*wālid*)—that is to say, the word refers to "he who has no child *and no parent*" (emphasis added).[43] This interpolation by the tradent brings the caliph's definition into line with that of ʿAmr b. Shuraḥbīl and Ibn ʿAbbās.

The second solution was to invoke an authority higher than, or as high as, that of ʿUmar. The obvious choice would have been the Prophet himself. As noted, however, no explicit definition of *kalāla* is attributed to Muḥammad. The next choice was ʿUmar's predecessor as caliph, Abū Bakr. In fact, two different definitions of *al-kalāla* are attributed to the first caliph. He is reported to have said, "*Al-kalāla* [signifies] those [heirs] except for the child and the parent" (*mā khalā al-walad wa'l-wālid*)—which is one of the two ways of understanding the meaning of the word in v. 12b.[44] Alternatively, the first caliph is reported to have said, "*Al-kalāla* is he who has no child and no parent" (*man lā walad lahu wa-lā wālid*)—which is the other way of understanding the meaning of the word in v. 12b. It did not pass unnoticed that neither of the definitions attributed to Abū Bakr is identical to the definition attributed to ʿUmar (*he who has no child*).

This made matters even worse, making it appear as if the first two caliphs disagreed over the meaning of *al-kalāla*. This second-level problem was solved by attributing to ʿUmar both an earlier and a later definition of the word. Al-Shaʿbī (d. > 100/718), one of the tradents in the *isnād* of the report in which a definition of *al-kalāla* is attributed to Abū Bakr (no. 19190), adds the following clarification: "ʿUmar used to say, '*Al-kalāla* is he who has no child'. But when he was stabbed, ʿUmar said, 'God forbid that I should disagree with Abū Bakr. I think that *al-kalāla* is those [heirs] except for the child and the parent.' "[45] Here the statement attributed to the caliph brings his definition of *al-kalāla* into conformity with one of the two definitions attributed to Abū Bakr. In this report, ʿUmar makes this statement on his deathbed. Cruxes 1.2 and 2.1 had been explained.

The *Tafsīr* of ʿAbd al-Razzāq[46]

In his *Tafsīr*, ʿAbd al-Razzāq says nothing about 4:12b, although he does devote attention to 4:176. In his treatment of the latter verse, the commentator adduces four *ḥadīth*s, all dealing with the meaning of *al-kalāla* (Crux 2.1)

In his *Muṣannaf*, it will be recalled, ʿAbd al-Razzāq cites a report in which ʿAmr b. Shuraḥbīl says with reference to 4:12b: *al-kalāla* signifies *he who has no child and no parent.* In his *Tafsīr*, ʿAbd al-Razzāq includes a report in which the same ʿAmr makes the same statement about the meaning of *al-kalāla*—but here this statement applies to v. 176. Aware of the reported gap between the views of the first two caliphs, ʿAmr was at pains to downplay the apparent disagreement, for he prefaces his definition with the disclaimer that in his view, the two men had in fact agreed on the definition of the word.[47] In a second report, Zuhrī (d. 124/742) and Qatāda (d. 117/735) define *al-kalāla* in v. 176 as "he who has no child and no parent"—despite the fact that this verse clearly says something different. Again, the purpose of this report is to reconcile the meaning of *al-kalāla* in the two verses.[48] ʿAbd al-Razzāq also cites the *sabab al-nuzūl* in which Ḥudhayfa defies the Caliph ʿUmar's insinuation that he had misrepresented the content or wording of the revelation.[49] Finally, ʿAbd al-Razzāq cites the report in which it is said that whenever ʿUmar would recite l. 6 of v. 176—"God makes clear for you [lest] you go astray"—the caliph would exclaim, "O God, to whom have you explained *al-kalāla*? Surely you have not explained [it] to me."[50] Again, this report emphasizes that even a figure of ʿUmar's towering stature did not understand the meaning of *al-kalāla*.

At just about the same time that ʿAbd al-Razzāq al-Ṣanʿānī was collecting reports about *kalāla* in the Yemen, Muslim scholars in Iraq were developing the fields of lexicography and grammar, both of which are relevant to our investigation.

Lexicography

Khalīl b. Aḥmad al-Farāhīdī (d. between 160/776 and 175/791)

Khalīl b. Aḥmad al-Farāhīdī al-Baṣrī is regarded as the founder of three disciplines relating to the Arabic language: lexicography, grammar, and metrics. Born in ʿUmān sometime between 90 and 105 A.H., as a young man Khalīl moved to Basra, where he studied *ḥadīth* and law with Ayyūb al-Sakhtiyānī (d. 131/749), and philology with ʿĪsā b. ʿUmar al-Thaqafī (d. 149/766) and Abū ʿAmr b. al-ʿAlāʾ (d. 154/770). Among his students in the field of grammar, Sībawayhi (d. 180/796), al-Layth b. al-Muẓaffar (d. <187/803) and al-Aṣmaʿī (d. 213/828) are the best-known. Khalīl is said to have been more than seventy years old at the time of his death, which is variously attributed to the year 160/776, 170/786, or 175/791.[51]

Khalīl is regarded as the author of *Kitāb al-ʿayn*, the first dictionary of the Arabic language.[52] Although he did in fact begin the text and apparently was responsible for much of the introduction (apart from later editorial interpolations), it was his student al-Layth b. al-Muẓaffar who completed, edited, and published the treatise ca. 180/796. Twenty or so years later, ca. 200/815, the treatise was revised by Abū Muʿādh ʿAbdallāh b. ʿĀʾidh. The revised text subsequently received additions and corrections.[53]

In the *Kitāb al-ʿayn*, the following words are defined in the entry on the root *k-l-l*: *al-kall* (n.), *al-kalīl* (adj.), *al-kāll* (act. part.), *al-killa* (n.), *al-iklīl* (n.), *kallala* (Form II verb), and *kalāla* (n.).[54] The noun *al-kall* (pl. *kulūl*), the lexicographer says, is derived from the Form I verb *kalla, yakillu, kalālat*[an]. The different forms of the verb (*al-fiʿl*), he explains, are used only rarely (*wa-qallamā yutakallamu bihi*). The noun *al-kall* has four meanings:

1. *An orphan*, as in the verse: One who devours the property of the orphan (*al-kall*) before he comes of age // ere the bones of the orphan (*al-kall*) have hardened.

2. *One who is dependent upon his master* or *is a burden on his master*, as in the statement, "This one is my dependent" (*kallī*).
3. *A childless man* (*al-rajul*[u] *alladhī lā walad*[a] *lahu*)—which, as we have seen, is the meaning of *kalāla* in 4:176—although the lexicographer does not mention this verse.
4. *Distant relatives* (*al-nasab al-baʿīd*), as in the expression, "This one is more distantly related (*akallu*) [to me] than that one."[55]

The first two definitions of *al-kall* (an orphan and a dependent) clearly are related to one another, and the last two definitions (*a childless man*, and a *distant relative*) clearly are related to one another. It is difficult, however, to discern any connection between *orphan/dependent*, on the one hand, and *childless man/distant relative*, on the other. As for *kalāla*, the lexicographer specifies that it is a verbal noun derived from the Form I verb *kalla*. He gives two examples of its usage: (1) *a blunt tongue* (*lisān dhū kalālat*[in]), and (2) *someone who becomes fatigued, tired, or wearied* (*yakillu kalālat*[an])—neither of which has anything to do with the usage of *kalāla* in the Qurʾān.

Grammar

Al-Farrāʾ (d. 207/822)

Abū Zakariyyāʾ Yaḥyā b. Ziyād al-Farrāʾ (lit. "furrier" but perhaps here "the one who scrutinizes [languages]") was born ca. 144/761 in Kufa, where he became a client of the tribe of Asad or Minqār. Al-Farrāʾ is regarded by some as the founder of the grammatical school of Kufa. In his *Kitāb maʿānī al-qurʾān*, written ca. 204/819, he devotes considerable attention to the syntax of the Qurʾān.[56]

To the best of my knowledge, al-Farrāʾ is the first Arab grammarian to address the agreement problem in l. 1a–b of 4:12b (Crux 1.6). The bifurcated subject ("a man . . . or a woman") in l. 1a, it will be recalled, is referenced in l. 1b by a third person masculine singular pronoun in *wa-la***hu** ("and **he** has"). Al-Farrāʾ finds this usage noteworthy.[57] He states that it would have been permissible (*jāʾiz*) to say *wa-lahumā*, in which case the dual pronoun would refer back to both nouns in the disjunctive phrase "a man . . . or a woman." He offers the following example of three possible ways in which a pronoun may refer back to a disjunctive phrase containing two nouns, one masculine, the other feminine: (1) "If someone has a brother or a sister, let him treat him with affection" (*fa'l-yaṣil***hu**)—in which case the pronoun refers back grammatically to the brother; or "let him treat her with affection" (*fa'l-yaṣil***hā**)—in which case the pronoun refers back grammatically to the sister; or "let him treat both of them with affection" (*fa'l-yaṣil***humā**)—in which case the pronoun refers back to both the brother and the sister. As support for the use of the dual, al-Farrā' cites Q. 4:135: "whether the person be rich or poor, God is closer to **both**" (*in yakun ghaniyy*[an] *aw faqīr*[an] *fa'llāh*[u] *awlā bi**himā***). He also cites Q. 5:38: "The thief, male and female, cut off **their** (dual) hands. . . ." (*al-sāriq wa'l-sāriqa fa'qṭa'ū aydiya**humā***). These examples suggest that in 4:12b the dual form *lahumā* was not only possible but also desirable.

Abū ʿUbayda (d. 207–13/822–28)

Abū ʿUbayda Maʿmar b. al-Muthannā was born ca. 110/728 in Basra, where he was a client of one of the clans of Quraysh. His father or grandfather came from Raqqa in Mesopotamia. In Basra Abū ʿUbayda studied with the leading grammarians. He is the author inter alia of *Majāz al-qur'ān*, a treatise devoted to grammar and philology that includes notes on the meaning of selected words and phrases in the Qur'ān.[58]

To the best of my knowledge, Abū ʿUbayda is the first scholar to ask why *kalāla* is in the accusative case in the phrase *yūrathu kalālat*[an] in 4:12b (Crux 1.3). He explains that in this phrase the word *kalāla* is a cognate object derived from the expression *takallalahu al-nasab*[u], which he glosses as *taʿaṭṭafa al-nasab*[u] *ʿalayhi*, that is to say, *a person who is surrounded by relatives.* Accordingly, the meaning of the Qur'ānic phrase would be, "If a man is inherited from [while relatives are surrounding him] a real surrounding." Abū ʿUbayda adds that *kalāla* here refers to the heirs of the deceased.[59]

Al-Akhfash (d. 215/830)

Abū al-Ḥasan Saʿīd b. Masʿada, known as al-Akhfash al-Awsaṭ, was born in Balkh but moved to Basra where he became a client of the Banū Tamīm. In Basra, he studied with Sībawayhi and taught the latter's *Kitāb* or *Book.*[60] Al-Akhfash is the author of a *Kitāb maʿānī al-qur'ān.*

In his treatment of 4:12b, al-Akhfash expands on Abū ʿUbayda's explanation of Crux 1.3. In l. 1a, he says, there are three different explanations for why the word *kalāla* is in the accusative case (*kalālat*[**an**]): (1) As the direct object of the active verb *yūrithu*, a reading that he categorizes as good (*jayyid*) and attributes to al-Ḥasan al-Baṣrī. (2) As the predicate of *kāna*, in which case the passive verb *yūrathu* describes or qualifies the noun *rajul*; that is, "a man who is inherited from" (*rajul*[un] *yūrathu*) "is a *kalāla*" (*kāna . . . kalālat*[**an**]). (3) As a circumstantial clause (*ḥāl*), in which case the verb *kāna* functions as *kāna tāmma*, that is to say, the *absolute kāna* that contains the attribute within itself and does not require any other; according to this explanation, the phrase *yūrathu kalālat*[an] describes a person's state or condition at the time of death, specifically, the state of dying while leaving neither parent nor child.

Like al-Farrā', al-Akhfash discusses the lack of pronoun agreement between the compound subject "a man . . . or a woman" and the prepositional phrase *wa-lahu* ("and he has")—Crux 1.6. In his view, when God said *wa-lahu*, the intended meaning was *min al-madhkūrayn*, that is to say, *either one of the two of them.*[61]

Al-Ṭabarī (d. 310/923)

Muḥammad b. Jarīr al-Ṭabarī inherited the exegetical, lexicographical, and grammatical tradition that had accumulated over the first three centuries A.H. In large part, the genius of this commentator lay in his ability to synthesize large bodies of information and to organize and arrange the massive and often inchoate tradition in a clear and logical manner. By doing so, Ṭabarī helped to establish the boundaries of what could and could not be said about the Qur'ān and its meaning.[62]

Q. 4:12B

Like Muqātil a century and a half earlier, Ṭabarī begins his treatment of 4:12b by addressing the bifurcated subject ("a man . . . or a woman") in l. 1a: "If a man *yūrathu kalālat*^{an} or a woman" (Crux 1.4). Like Muqātil, Ṭabarī draws attention to the syntax and instructs the readers of his text to treat this line as if the word order were as follows: "*wa-in kāna rajul*^{un} ***aw imra'at***^{un} *yūrathu kalālat*^{an}."[63] By moving *aw imra'at*^{un} so that it now occurs before *yūrathu kalālat*^{an}, Ṭabarī recovers what he regards as the natural syntax of the sentence. Viewed in this manner, the phrase *yūrathu kalālat*^{an} now refers back to both the "man" and the "woman": "If **a man or a woman** is inherited by collaterals." This simple and seemingly innocuous change has shaped the subsequent understanding of this verse by Muslim scholars down to the present.

Only after he has rearranged the order of the words in l. 1a does Ṭabarī move to the reading (*qirā'a*) of the primary verb in this sentence, *y-w-r-th*, derived from the root *w-r-th* ("to inherit, to be an heir")(Crux 1.1). The standard reading is the Form IV imperfect passive, *yūr**a**thu* ("to be inherited from"). Like al-Akhfash, Ṭabarī notes that it is also permissible to read this verb as a Form IV imperfect active verb, *yūr**i**thu* ("to make someone an heir, to cause someone to inherit"). The difference is merely one vowel: *fatḥa* yields a passive verb (*yūr**a**thu*) whereas *kasra* yields an active verb (*yūr**i**thu*). Ṭabarī indicates that whichever reading one chooses, the meaning of l. 1a remains constant.[64]

As noted, Ṭabarī begins his discussion of v. 12b by rearranging the word order of l. 1a. Whereas the ostensible purpose of the heuristic change was to restore what the commentators regarded as the natural syntax of the sentence, it is also possible that they took this liberty with God's speech in an effort to insure that those Qur'ān reciters who preferred to read *y-w-r-th* as an active verb would not allow the transitivity of this verb to carry over to a second direct object: *imra'a*. By restoring what they regarded as the natural syntax of the sentence, the commentators insured that even if one does read *yūrithu*, the transitivity of this active, causative verb applies only to *kalāla*; as for *imraʾa*, as a result of its mental repositioning in the clause, it is not available to receive the action of the causative verb. Most reciters, however, preferred to read *y-w-r-th* as a passive verb (*yūrathu*), and it is this reading that has been accepted by virtually all Muslim exegetes down to the present day. Reading this verb in the passive voice is the best way to preserve the traditional understanding of the verse and its place within the science of the shares. In my view, there is nothing natural or original about the traditional reading or understanding of v. 12b.

Presumably, Ṭabarī never saw BNF 328a or any other Qurʾān codex in which the consonantal skeleton of 4:12b specified **kalla* rather than *kalāla*. Let us imagine, for the sake of argument, that the commentator had seen the opening clause of our hypothetical *4:12b: *wa-in kāna rajul*[un] *y-w-r-th kallat*[?n] *aw imraʾat*[?n]. Surely he would have read *y-w-r-th* as a Form IV active verb (*yūrithu*) followed by two nouns in the accusative case (*kallat*[an] *aw imraʾat*[an]). Surely he would have seen that there is no need to change the word order of the opening clause. At the same time, however, he would have been baffled by the notion that a man might designate someone as his heir in a last will and testament—indeed, a female not related to him by ties of blood. The complexity of the *ʿilm al-farāʾiḍ* or "science of the shares" notwithstanding, one thing is clear: Under normal circumstances, Islamic inheritance law does not allow a person contemplating death to leave a last will and testament in which he or she designates one or more persons as a testamentary heir or heirs.[65] We will return to the subject of testamentary succession at the end of this chapter.

After disposing of the syntax of the sentence and the reading of the verb—*yūrathu* or *yūrithu*—Ṭabarī turns to the meaning of *kalāla* (Crux 1.2). At this juncture the commentator had to make a critical decision. He clearly had access to most if not all of the reports preserved in the *Tafsīr* of Mujāhid, the *Tafsīr* and *Muṣannaf* of ʿAbd al-Razzāq, and many other texts produced during the second and third centuries A.H. As we have seen, these reports, which center on the figure of ʿUmar b. al-Khaṭṭāb, fall into two groups: in some ʿUmar knows the meaning of *kalāla* while in others he does not. In an effort to reconcile the two sets of reports, ʿUmar is made to say, in a text cited by Ṭabarī, that his life may be divided into two periods: During the first period he did not know the meaning of *kalāla*; during the second, he did.[66]

What was Ṭabarī to do with this corpus of reports in which ʿUmar here knows the meaning of *kalāla* but there does not? Especially problematic were the statements attributed to ʿUmar in which the caliph either does not know the meaning of the word or withholds or suppresses information relating to its meaning. In their commentaries, Muqātil and ʿAbd al-Razzāq placed all of these reports in their respective discussions of v. 176. To the best of my knowledge, Ṭabarī was the first commentator to divide this corpus of reports into two groups and to distribute them between the two verses: In his treatment of v. 12b, he included only those reports in which ʿUmar or some other Companion or Successor defines the word *kalāla*. And he withheld until his treatment of v. 176 those narratives in which ʿUmar does not know the meaning of the word, keeps its meaning to himself, or suppresses its meaning. Thus, when the reader of Ṭabarī's commentary reaches v. 12b, he (or she) finds the evidence that makes it possible to define the word *kalāla*; when the same reader encounters the word *kalāla* in v. 176, the commentator reminds him that he has already presented the evidence and defined the word in his discussion of v. 12b and that there is no need to repeat the exercise. In this manner, Ṭabarī neutralized the threat to the traditional understanding of *kalāla* posed by the narratives in which ʿUmar either does not know the meaning of the word or withholds or suppresses information relating to it. All subsequent Qurʾān commentators follow Ṭabarī's decision to divide the reports into two groups and to distribute them between the two verses.

Having made the decision to place the reports in which ʿUmar knows the meaning of *kalāla* in his treatment of 4:12b, Ṭabarī, as was his custom, informs the reader that the early authorities disagreed among themselves about the meaning of the word. He divides the different reports into three categories: (1) *those [heirs] except for the parent and child*, under which he lists twenty authority statements (*shawāhid*);[67] (2) *those [heirs] except for the child*, under which he includes one authority statement;[68] and (3) *those [heirs] except for the parent*, under which he includes one authority statement.[69]

For Ṭabarī, the only relevant category was the first one. Under this rubric he includes not only reports in which *kalāla* is defined as *those [heirs] except for the parent and child* (of which there are nine) but also those reports in which *kalāla* is defined as *a person who dies leaving neither parent nor child* (of which there are eleven). The first three reports in this section are of critical importance because they establish, first, that the correct meaning of *kalāla* can be traced back to Abū Bakr and, second, that Abū Bakr and ʿUmar were in essential agreement on the definition of the word. These three reports are related on the authority of al-Shaʿbī, who died some time after the year 100/718 and therefore could not have had direct contact with either man.[70] In the first two reports, al-Shaʿbī cites a statement attributed to Abū Bakr and then adds his own clarification, which serves two purposes. First, it suggests that ʿUmar revised his understanding of *kalāla* in order to bring it into line with that of Abū Bakr. Second, it suggests that this revision took place immediately after ʿUmar became caliph—and not on his deathbed, as in ʿAbd al-Razzāq, *al-Muṣannaf*, 10:304, no. 19191. In the first report, Abū Bakr announces:

> I have [defined] *al-kalāla* on the basis of my personal opinion (*raʾy*). If it is correct, then it is from God, the One who has no partner; but if it is wrong, then it is from me and from Satan, and God is absolved of responsibility for it: *Al-kalāla* signifies those [heirs]

except for the child and parent. [Al-Shaʿbī adds:] Subsequently, when ʿUmar—may God have mercy on him—was designated as caliph, he said, "May God the Blessed and Exalted forbid that I should disagree with Abū Bakr with respect to his personal opinion" (*raʾy raʾāhu*).[71]

In the second report, al-Shaʿbī relates that Abū Bakr said with regard to *al-kalāla*: "I base my opinion on it on my personal reasoning (*raʾyī*): If it is correct, it is from God. It means, [those heirs] except for the child and the parent." To this al-Shaʿbī adds that when ʿUmar was appointed as caliph, he said, "God forbid that I should disagree with Abū Bakr."[72] In the third report, al-Shaʿbī relates that both Abū Bakr and ʿUmar b. al-Khaṭṭāb said that *al-kalāla* [signifies] "he who has no child and no parent"—without specifying when the reconciliation occurred.[73] In this manner, it was established that Abū Bakr and ʿUmar were in agreement as to the meaning of *kalāla*.

After briefly explaining why the word *kalāla* occurs in the accusative case (Crux 1.3),[74] Ṭabarī returns to the different meanings of *kalāla*, but he now reformulates the question as follows: Does this word refer to the deceased (*al-mawrūth*) or to the heirs (*al-waratha*)? The commentator reminds the reader that in nine of the twenty reports that he has just cited, *kalāla* refers to the heirs, while in the other eleven reports it refers to the deceased. Only now does Ṭabarī divulge his own opinion, which comes as a mild surprise. Had he based his decision on the number of reports adduced for either position, then the definition according to which *kalāla* refers to the deceased would have prevailed. Instead, Ṭabarī draws attention to three reports not previously mentioned in his treatment of 4:12b. The first of these three reports is familiar to us. It is the report about Jābir b. ʿAbdallāh cited by Muqātil as the *sabab al-nuzūl* of 4:176—albeit with a critical linguistic modification. In the version cited by Muqātil, it will be recalled, Jābir is reported to have addressed the Prophet, saying, "O Messenger of God, I am a *kalāla* who has neither father nor child. So what should I do with my wealth?"[75] Here, the word *kalāla* can refer only to Jābir himself—that is to say, to the person who will be inherited from (*al-mawrūth*). In the version cited by Ṭabarī, however, Jābir is now made to say, "O Messenger of God, none but *kalāla* will inherit from me (*innamā yarithunī kalālat^{un}*). How then should the inheritance [be divided]?"[76] Here the word *kalāla* can only refer to Jābir's heirs (*al-waratha*). Ṭabarī found additional support for the view that *kalāla* refers to the heirs of the deceased in the language of a report in which the Companion Saʿd b. Abī Waqqāṣ (d. 55/675) says that, like Jābir, he too suffered a near-death experience during the lifetime of the Prophet and he too received a visit from Muḥammad. "O Messenger of God," Saʿd subsequently would recall saying to Muḥammad, "I have much wealth, and I have no heir except for *kalāla* (*wa-laysa lī wārith^{un} illā kalālat^{un}*). May I bequeath all of my wealth?"[77] As in the version of the Jābir report cited by Ṭabarī, here too *kalāla* can only refer to the heirs of the deceased.[78] Finally, Ṭabarī cites a report in which an unidentified elder approaches ʿUmar b. al-Khaṭṭāb (!) and says to him, "Verily I am an old man and I have no heir except for *kalāla*—Bedouin who are distant relatives. May I bequeath one-third of my wealth [to them]?"[79] In all three reports, a Companion is made to utter the word *kalāla* in a context in which it can only refer to the heirs of the deceased. In two of these three reports, the Companion's interlocutor was the Prophet himself. On the basis of this evidence, Ṭabarī confidently concludes that the word *kalāla* can only refer to the heirs of the deceased, that is to say, a man's relatives except for his father and his child.[80] This is how the word *kalāla* came to be understood as signifying *those who inherit from the deceased with the exception of parent and child*, that is, *collateral relatives*.

Ṭabarī now turns his attention to the words *brother* and *sister* in 4:12b. The shares awarded to siblings here, it will be recalled, are different from the shares awarded to siblings in 4:176 (Crux 2.2). Without mentioning this discrepancy, the commentator asserts that the words *brother* and *sister* in v. 12b refer to a *uterine* sibling (*akh aw ukht min ummihi*). In support of this assertion, he cites six reports, in five of which this explanation is identified as a gloss attributed to either Qatāda (d. 117/735),[81] al-Suddī (d. 127/745),[82] or Saʿd b. Abī Waqqāṣ (d. 55/675).[83] In a sixth report the explanation is attributed to the same Saʿd as a variant reading of the Qurʾān.[84] Elsewhere, it is attributed as a variant reading to Ubayy b. Kaʿb (d. between 19/640 and 35/656), one of Muḥammad's secretaries in Medina and an early collector of the Qurʾān.[85]

After clarifying the meaning of the words *brother* and *sister*, Ṭabarī turns to the lack of agreement in v. 12b between the dual subject ("a man . . . or a woman") in l. 1a and the third person masculine singular pronoun suffix *-hu* in *wa-lahu* ("and he has") in l. 1b (Crux 1.6). No doubt drawing on al-Farrāʾ and al-Akhfash, albeit without acknowledgement, he explains that a masculine singular pronoun suffix referring back to a compound subject may be linked to both nouns or to only one, as in the sentence: *man kāna ʿindahu ghulām^{un} aw jāriyat^{un} fa'l-yuḥsin ilay**hi*** ("If someone has a slave-boy or slave-girl, let him treat **him** well") (emphasis added).[86]

Q. 4:176

In his treatment of 4:176 Ṭabarī cites only the reports in which ʿUmar either does not know the meaning of *kalāla* or chooses not to divulge his understanding of the word to the Muslim community.

Some of these reports are identical to those cited by Muqātil and ʿAbd al-Razzāq. For example, we encounter the report in which ʿUmar says that three things left unexplained by the Prophet were dearer to him than the earth and everything on it: *al-kalāla*, *al-khilāfa*, and access to the rules of usury (*bāb al-ribā*);[87] and the report in which the dying caliph orders the erasure of a document that he had written about the grandfather and *al-kalāla*, leaving the community to believe what it already believed.[88]

Other reports are variants of reports cited by Muqātil and ʿAbd al-Razzāq. Thus, Ṭabarī cites a modified version of the *sabab al-nuzūl* in which Ḥudhayfa angrily rejects ʿUmar's accusation that he failed to relate v. 176 exactly as he received it from the Prophet. In the variant, Ḥudhayfa responds to the caliph as follows: "You are a fool (*aḥmaq*) if you imagine that that is how the Messenger of God taught it to me. I relayed it to you as he dictated it to me. By God, I would never add anything to it for your sake."[89] From the formulation of Ḥudhayfa's response we infer that ʿUmar had suggested that something should be, or had been, added to the verse. In another variant, instead of saying that the value of the meaning of *al-kalāla* is equivalent to that of the finest camels, ʿUmar is made to say that he would rather know the meaning of *al-kalāla* than possess the equivalent of the poll tax of the fortresses of Byzantium.[90] And the same ʿUmar who, in a report preserved in the *Muṣannaf* of ʿAbd al-Razzāq, expresses remorse at his failure to ask the Prophet to clarify the meaning of *kalāla*, is now made to say that he did not question Muḥammad (or contend with him) about anything as frequently as he did about *āyat al-kalāla* [sic][91] (or that Muḥammad did not become as rough with him about anything as frequently as he did about *al-kalāla*), until the Prophet rebuked ʿUmar by poking him in the chest and instructing him to consult "the summer verse that was revealed at the end of *Sūrat al-Nisāʾ*."[92] In these reports, ʿUmar did ask the Prophet to clarify the meaning of *kalāla* and the Prophet did respond by telling him that the answer to his question may be found in the *summer verse*—clearly identified as 4:176. *Pace* ʿUmar, the Prophet did clarify the meaning of *kalāla*, even if his clarification did not put an end to ʿUmar's perplexity.

Ṭabarī also cites texts that earlier authors were either unaware of or chose to ignore. It will be recalled that in report no. 19194 in the *Muṣannaf* of ʿAbd al-Razzāq, the Prophet dictated a verse containing the word *kalāla* to his wife Ḥafṣa; and that his dictation was recorded on a shoulder blade that Ḥafṣa gave to her father, ʿUmar. In Ṭabarī's *Tafsīr*, we find a report in which ʿUmar gathered the Companions of the Prophet and, holding a shoulder blade in his hand, predicted that a decree he was about to deliver would become a topic of conversation among women in their private chambers (*fī khudūrihinna*). At that very moment a snake (*ḥayya*) appeared, causing all the people to scatter.[93] Interpreting the sudden appearance of the snake as a sign of divine intervention, ʿUmar withheld his decree.[94] In another report in which ʿUmar again claimed to know what *kalāla* means, he said, "If I live, I will issue a decree about it [*al-kalāla*] so that no one who reads (or recites) the Qurʾān will disagree about it" (*lā yakhtalifu fīhi aḥad*[un] *qaraʾa al-qurʾān*)–which suggests that the problem was not only the meaning of *kalāla* but also the performed reading or vocalization (*qirāʾa*) of the verse.[95] This narrative was formulated by someone who knew that the caliph would not live long enough to issue any such decree. One wonders if the men who formulated these narratives had seen BNF 328a or a codex like it.

In the middle of the first century A.H., very few Muslims would have known the meaning of the word *kalāla*. It was only during the second half of the first century that tentative definitions of the word were advanced by Companions of the Prophet. During the last quarter of the first century and first quarter of the second century, Successors and Followers circulated reports in which one or another definition of *kalāla* was attributed to either Abū Bakr or ʿUmar. The discrepancy between the definitions attributed to each caliph was eventually reconciled, and Abū Bakr became the ultimate authority for the meaning of the word. After the fact, the order in which events unfolded was reversed in such a way as to make it appear as if the Muslim community's understanding of *kalāla* was the product of a linear sequence that began with Abū Bakr. The transformation of early uncertainty and confusion into an image of certain knowledge is neatly encapsulated in the following statement by the fourteenth-century commentator Ibn Kathīr (d. 774/1373):

> *Al-kalāla* is derived from *al-iklīl* ("crown"), i.e., that which encloses the head from the sides. The intention here is those who inherit from him indirectly, not from above or below, as al-Shaʿbī related on the authority of Abū Bakr al-Ṣiddīq, that he was asked about *al-kalāla* and he replied, "I have my own personal opinion (*raʾy*) on this matter. If it is correct then it is from God; if it is mistaken then it is from Satan and neither God nor his Messenger is responsible. *Al-kalāla* [signifies] *he who has neither parent nor child*." When ʿUmar became the ruler, he said: "God forbid that I should go against an opinion held by Abū Bakr." This was transmitted by Ibn Jarīr [al-Ṭabarī] and others. Ibn Abī Ḥātim said in his *Commentary*: Muḥammad b. [ʿAbd Allāh] b. Yazīd related to us, on the authority of Sufyān, on the authority of Sulaymān al-Aḥwal, on the authority of Ṭāʾūs, who said: I heard ʿAbdallāh b. ʿAbbās say: "I was the last person to meet with ʿUmar [before he died] and I heard him say: 'What did I say?' and 'What did I say?' and 'What did I say?' He [ʿUmar] said: "*Al-kalāla* is *he who has neither parent nor child*." The same opinion was held by ʿAlī b. Abī Ṭālib and Ibn Masʿūd, and it was judged correct on the authority of more than one, on the authority of ʿAbdallāh b. ʿAbbās and Zayd b. Thābit. And this opinion is held by al-Shaʿbī, al-Nakhaʿī, al-Ḥasan al-Baṣrī, Qatāda, Jābir b. Zayd, and al-Ḥakam [b. ʿUtayba]. It is held by the Medinese, Kufans, and Basrans. It is the opinion of the seven jurists [of Medina], the four *imāms*, and the majority of the ancients—indeed all of them—and more than one has attributed [universal] consensus to it.[96]

Ibn Kathīr surely was correct when he said that the definition of *kalāla* attributed to Abū Bakr and ʿUmar eventually became the consensual position of Muslim scholars. He also was correct when he noted that this consensual position was established by the likes of al-Shaʿbī, al-Nakhaʿī, al-Ḥasan al-Baṣrī, Qatāda, Jābir b. Zayd, and al-Ḥakam b. ʿUtayba—that is to say, during the second half of the first century A.H. or later. But he was mistaken when he suggested that the word *kalāla* was defined by Abū Bakr and ʿUmar. Although these two caliphs may have been involved in deliberations relating to this word, the reports about those deliberations are best seen as literary texts that were formulated and put into circulation by Muslims who were trying to generate religious authority for one or another definition of the word.

Summary

The first exegetes were working with the received text of the Qur'ān. Beginning in the last quarter of the first century A.H., they struggled to make sense of the word *kalāla*. It should come as no surprise that they encountered difficulty. This word had been coined in the first half of the first century A.H. in connection with the revision of Q. *4:12b. It occurs only twice in the Qur'ān, both times in connection with inheritance. It has no cognate in any other Semitic language. The only way to determine its meaning is from the context in which it is used in Q. 4:12b and 4:176, respectively. Tentative definitions are said to have been put forward by Companions like ʿAmr b. Shuraḥbīl (d. 63/682–83) and Ibn ʿAbbās (d. 68/687). Subsequently, one or another definition of the word was attributed to Abū Bakr or ʿUmar. Eventually, the definition attributed to the first caliph would prevail.

Beginning ca. 50 A.H., Muslims began to circulate reports about the word *kalāla* centering on the figure of ʿUmar b. al-Khaṭṭāb. These reports fall into two sets: In one set of narratives—which I will refer to as Group A—ʿUmar claims to possess information relating to *kalāla* but either withholds this information from the Muslim community or suppresses it. In my view, these narratives were formulated by Muslims who feared the consequences of openly stating that the consonantal skeleton of Q. *4:12b had been revised and that supplementary legislation had been added at the end of *Sūrat al-Nisā'*. In one report, the caliph announces his intention to issue a decree about *kalāla* which, he suggests, will be of interest to women in their private quarters. In another, the dying caliph says that if he lives, he will issue a decree about the word so that those who read or recite the Qur'ān will not disagree about it. In another report, the caliph approaches Ḥudhayfa b. al-Yamān in the hope that he will explain the meaning of the summer verse; and in a variant of this report, Ḥudhayfa chastises the caliph for suggesting that he had added something to this revelation. On his deathbed, ʿUmar either forgot what he himself had said about *kalāla* or issued an instruction calling for the erasure of a document that he had written about the word.

The Group A narratives were put into circulation in the second half of the first century A.H. by Companions such as Ibn ʿUmar (Medina, d. 73/693), Ibrāhīm b. ʿAbd al-Raḥmān b. ʿAwf al-Zuhrī (d. 75 or 76 or 95 or 96), and Ṭāriq b. Shihāb al-Bajalī (Kufa, d. 82, 83, or 84/701, 702, or 703); and by Successors such as Masrūq b. al-Ajdaʿ (Kufa, d. 63/683), Murra b. Sharāḥīl al-Hamdānī (Kufa, d. 76/695–96), Saʿīd b. al-Musayyab (Medina, d. 94/713), and Maʿdān b. Abī Ṭalḥa al-Yaʿmurī (Syria, fl. first/seventh century). All of these men would have been alive for much if not all of the caliphate of Muʿāwiya (r. 41–60/661–80); and with the exception of Masrūq b. al-Ajdaʿ, all of them would have been alive during the caliphate of ʿAbd al-Malik (r. 65–86/685–705). If the reports attributed to these men are reliable—which is an open question—then the revision of Q. *4:12b would have taken place one or more decades before 63 A.H.

BNF 328a was written at the same time as the Group A narratives were being put into circulation for the first time. Any Muslim who had the opportunity to examine BNF 328a—or a similar codex—surely would have noticed the erasures and revisions on folio 10b and the stub lying in the gutter margin between folios 19 and 20. By the final decades of the first century A.H., however, a Muslim who drew attention to such an anomaly would have risked a stern rebuke. Recall Ḥudhayfa's response to ʿUmar after the caliph insinuated that the Companion had added something to v. 176: "By God, you are a fool (*aḥmaq*) (variant: powerless [*ʿājiz*]) if you think that your position as Commander [of the Believers] requires me to tell you something that I did not tell you on that day."[97] Recall also Ubayy b. Kaʿb's response to ʿUmar's request that he scratch out three words in Q. 33:6: Ubayy raised his voice and shouted, "Verily, I have been occupied with the Qurʾān, while you have been occupied with buying and selling in the market."[98] Worse yet, any Muslim who openly suggested that the consonantal skeleton of one verse had been revised and that supplementary legislation had been added to the Qurʾān after the Prophet died would have exposed himself to a punishment considerably more severe than a stern rebuke. For this reason, the best that these Muslims could do was to formulate and circulate narratives that alluded to the problem without specifically identifying it.[99]

There is a striking correspondence between the literary evidence examined in this chapter and the documentary evidence examined in the last chapter. From the Group A narratives, we learn the following: (1) The interpretation of v. 12b was problematic; (2) the meaning of *kalāla* was important; (3) the word was relevant to women; (4) the performed reading of v. 12b was an issue; (5) something may have been added to the Qurʾān; (6) someone destroyed a document written about *kalāla*;[100] and (7) something was forgotten. These seven points line up perfectly with the documentary evidence contained in BNF 328a: (1) the revision of v. *12b made it difficult to understand v. 12b; (2) *kalāla* was a new word that had to be defined by the exegetes; (3) the revision of v. *12b was relevant to the inheritance rights of women, specifically daughters-in-law and wives; (4) the performed reading of v. *12b was revised at two points; (5) an extra *lām* was added to the word **kalla* in v. *12b and supplementary legislation was added at the end of *Sūrat al-Nisāʾ*; (6) a folio was removed from BNF 328a and destroyed; and (7) the very existence of v. *12b and the word **kalla* were forgotten.

In the second set of narratives—which I will refer to as Group B—one or another definition of *kalāla* is attributed to either ʿUmar or Abū Bakr, or both. This set of reports was not put into circulation until the last quarter of the first century or first decade of the second century A.H. by Successors such as Saʿīd b. al-Musayyab (Medina, d. 94/713),[101] Abū Salama (Medina, d. 94/713), Ṭāʾūs (Yemen, d. 100/718–19), ʿAmr b. Murra (Kufa, d. 110/728–29), and Muḥammad b. Ṭalha (Hijaz, d. 111/729–30). These reports are laced with contradictions: Whereas the Prophet identified 4:12b as the summer verse, everyone else in the Muslim community identified 4:176 as the summer verse. Whereas the Prophet suspected that ʿUmar b. al-Khaṭṭāb did not understand *kalāla*, the Companion insisted that he did know the meaning of the word—although he refused, or was prevented from, divulging this knowledge. After becoming caliph, ʿUmar regretted his failure to ask the Prophet to clarify the meaning of *kalāla*—or there was nothing about which he queried the Prophet as frequently as *kalāla*. On his deathbed, ʿUmar instructed Ibn ʿAbbās to remember what he had said about *kalāla*—but the caliph himself forgot what he had said. ʿUmar and Abū Bakr disagreed over the definition of *kalāla*—or they were in agreement on its definition. There was a period in ʿUmar's life during which he did not know the meaning of *kalāla* and a period during which he did. Alternatively, ʿUmar had an earlier and a later definition of the word: He changed his mind about its meaning upon becoming caliph; or he changed his mind after he was stabbed.

Contradictions of this nature, as Crone has noted, are beyond harmonization.[102] It is only as "facts about the tradition," she argues, that such reports constitute "genuine evidence."[103] I concur. The narrative reports examined in this chapter are genuine evidence of something—but what? Let me attempt to answer this question by returning to the subject of the collection of the Qurʾān and trying to link it to the mystery of *kalāla*.

The Collection of the Qurʾān, Revisited

I began Chapter 8 by reviewing the standard account of the collection of the Qurʾān. There is a close correspondence between key figures associated with that project and key figures associated with the word *kalāla*. Let us attend to these correspondences.

Abū Bakr (r. 11–13/632–34), who is said to have been responsible for the first collection of the Qurʾān, is the final authority for what became the standard definition of *kalāla*.

ʿUmar b. al-Khaṭṭāb (r. 13–23/634–44) is said to have persuaded Abū Bakr to undertake the first collection or was himself responsible for it; in the latter case, he was still working on the project at the time of his assassination in 23/644.[104] In the Group A reports, ʿUmar is portrayed as a man who was obsessed with the word *kalāla* for much of his life, an obsession that he appears to have taken with him to his grave. In the Group B reports, his name, like that of Abū Bakr, is associated with the standard definition of the word.

Ḥudhayfa b. al-Yamān (d. 36/656) was a Jewish convert to Islam who, after learning of disagreements over the performed reading and consonantal skeleton of the Qurʾān, advised the caliph ʿUthmān to produce a single, uniform text. Ḥudhayfa was associated with the campaign to destroy nonconforming texts. He is said to have asked a group of Muslims what they would think if he were to tell them that they were going to burn their Qurʾān codices and throw them into the toilet.[105] It was Ḥudhayfa who was riding directly behind the Prophet when the *summer verse*—whichever verse that may have been—was revealed. And it was Ḥudhayfa who transmitted the new revelation to ʿUmar. When the caliph subsequently insinuated that Ḥudhayfa had made some kind of mistake in his transmission of this revelation, the Companion rebuked him.

Ḥafṣa (d. 45/665) was ʿUmar's daughter and the Prophet's wife. When her father was uncertain about *kalāla*, he instructed his daughter to ask her husband about the word. The Prophet dictated a verse that was recorded on a shoulder blade that Ḥafṣa gave to ʿUmar. Presumably, it was this shoulder blade that ʿUmar was holding aloft when he announced his intention to issue a decree about *kalāla*. It was Ḥafṣa who, following the death of her father, inherited the *ṣuḥuf* or unbound leaves produced by Zayd. When she died, the leaves were destroyed by Marwān b. al-Ḥakam.

Zayd b. Thābit (d. 45/665), another Jewish convert to Islam, was one of Muḥammad's secretaries. At the instruction of the Prophet he learned Syriac so that he might read books in that language. Zayd was charged by Abū Bakr with the task of producing the first collection (the *ṣuḥuf* or unbound leaves), and he was charged by ʿUthmān with the task of producing the second collection (the *muṣḥaf* or bound codex). On both occasions, he is reported to have recovered two lost verses and placed them at the end of *Sūrat al-Tawba*.

To the best of my knowledge, Zayd's name is nowhere mentioned in connection with *kalāla*. But he is said to have been the first Muslim to write about the shares of inheritance. If so, he would have been familiar with the word—to say the least. Sometime prior to 45/665, Zayd is said to have received a letter from Muʿāwiya (r. 41–60/661–80)[106] in which the caliph inquired about the case of a man who dies leaving a grandfather and brothers as his closest blood relatives. In his response, Zayd emphasized that the Prophet had not said anything about this issue, but that judgments on the matter had been issued by "the two [sic] caliphs before you"—referring to Abū Bakr and ʿUmar. These two caliphs reportedly awarded the grandfather a share equal to that of one or two brothers; if there were three or more brothers, the grandfather inherits one-third. In fact, the problem was more complicated than that because of the need to take into account the distinction between uterine, consanguine, and germane siblings. It was agreed that a grandfather excludes uterine siblings but there was disagreement about the inheritance rights of a grandfather in competition with consanguine and germane siblings. Whereas Abū Bakr and Ibn ʿAbbās reportedly held that the grandfather excludes all siblings, Zayd b. Thābit held that the grandfather inherits together with consanguine and germane siblings, as noted in his letter to Muʿāwiya. The issue was complex. As ʿUmar is reported to have said, "If anyone wants to rush headlong into the depths of the Fire, let him decide between a grandfather and collaterals."[107] Nearly a century later al-Zuhrī (d. 124/742) would say, "Had it not been for the fact that Zayd b. Thābit recorded the shares, you would have seen [the shares] disappear from [the minds of] the people."[108]

The correspondences between the collection of the Qurʾān and the mystery of *kalāla* suggest the following tentative conclusions. Literary evidence indicates that the revision of Q. *4:12b may have taken place as early as the caliphate of Abū Bakr or ʿUmar. The formulation of the supplementary legislation that was inserted at the end of *Sūrat al-Nisāʾ* would have followed shortly thereafter. It was only after the insertion of this verse at the end of the chapter that questions would have arisen about the apparent contradiction between vv. 12b and 176. The solution to the contradiction is attributed to Ubayy b. Kaʿb, who died in 30/651–52 and to Saʿd b. Abī Waqqāṣ, who died in 55/675.[109] If these attributions are accurate, then the revisions to the consonantal skeleton of the Qurʾān would have taken place one or more decades before these men died. Similarly, only after the insertion of the supplementary legislation at the end of the chapter would questions have arisen about the relative entitlement of siblings in combination with other heirs. The solution to these questions was advanced by Zayd b. Thābit. If this attribution is accurate, then the revisions relating to v. 12b and 176 would have taken place one or more decades before his death in 45/665.

If the literary evidence points to an early date for the revision of Q. *4:12b and the insertion of supplementary legislation at the end of *Sūrat al-Nisāʾ*, the documentary evidence points in the opposite direction. Our analysis of BNF 328a suggests that codices that were at odds with what would become the official text continued to be produced in the second half of the first century A.H.; and that it was not until the end of this century that textual uniformity was finally achieved.

One final question remains to be addressed: Why did the early Muslim community revise Q. *4:12b and insert 4:176 at the end of *Sūrat al-Nisāʾ*? In Chapter 4, I advanced hypotheses relating to the revision of the consonantal skeleton of Q. *4:23 and *33:6, respectively. In both instances, the revision was driven by the theological doctrine of the finality of prophecy. In Chapter 8, I advanced hypotheses relating to the textual revision of Q. *4:12b and 4:176, respectively. According to Hypothesis 8.1, v. *12b originally referred to a man who designates a daughter-in-law or wife as his heir in a last will and testament. There is no apparent connection between this revision and the doctrine of the finality of prophecy. In this instance, I submit, the change was driven by politics.

The existence of a mechanism for designating an heir would have been a matter of interest to the early Muslim community in connection with the question of whether or not Muḥammad designated a successor. This is precisely what the literary evidence examined in this chapter suggests. In one report, ʿUmar says that *al-kalāla* is one of three important topics left unexplained by the Prophet that were dearer to him than the finest camels; in a second report, the caliph says that *al-kalāla* is one of three important topics that he wished he had asked Muḥammad to explain; and in a third report the dying caliph asks Ibn ʿAbbās to remember three things about him, with the third item being *al-kalāla*.[110] In all three instances, *al-kalāla* is mentioned in connection with the appointment of a successor (*khilāfa*) and a third important issue. In yet another report, the dying caliph instructs Ibn ʿAbbās to remember only two things about him, "I did not appoint a successor (*lam astakhlif*) and I did not issue a decree about *al-kalāla*."[111] In my view, the juxtaposition of *khilāfa* and *kalāla* is no coincidence. Whoever formulated these four reports was signaling a connection between the word *kalāla* in v. 12b and the issue of political succession, a connection that recurs in narrative accounts of the Prophet on his deathbed (see Appendix 2).

Although there is no direct connection between the revision of Q. *4:12b and the doctrine of the finality of prophecy, there may be an indirect connection. I have argued that this verse originally referred to a man who designates his daughter-in-law or wife as his heir. There was only one woman in the early Muslim community who was simultaneously the Prophet's daughter-in-law and his wife: Zaynab bt. Jaḥsh. At the time of his death, Muḥammad had no sons, parents, or siblings. It is reasonable to assume that a man in this situation might designate the woman who was both his daughter-in-law and his wife as his testamentary heir. If that woman were to remarry, the first male to whom she gave birth might have been affiliated to Muḥammad as his son and heir. Thus, the provisions of *4:12b point directly at Zaynab. The revision of this sub-verse obliterated the link.

Chapter 10

Conclusion

Theology and Salvation History

The assertion that Islam supersedes Judaism and Christianity cannot fully be understood apart from the dynamics of the foundation narratives of the three Abrahamic faiths. All three narratives are formulated in the idiom of family and tell the story of a single family at a different stage in its history. In all three cases, the father-son motif serves as a metaphor for a key theological doctrine: divine election, Christology, and the finality of prophecy, respectively. In all three cases, the specific shape taken by the foundation narrative was conditioned by theological considerations: The Israelite claim that only the Children of Israel had been chosen by God necessitated the marginalization of collateral lines, first Ishmael and his descendants, followed by Esau and his. The Christian claim that Jesus is the Son of God necessitated the marginalization of Joseph, the man who appeared to be—but was not—Jesus' natural father. The Islamic claim that Muḥammad is the Last Prophet necessitated the marginalization of the Prophet's sons, natural and adopted.

The finality of prophecy is one of several theological premises that shaped the early Islamic worldview. For our purposes, the most important of these premises are as follows: History unfolds according to a predetermined divine plan. A merciful God sends prophets to humanity with instructions about how to attain eternal life. Prophets are human beings who, in theory, are susceptible to sin and error; in fact, because they enjoy the benefit of divine revelation, prophets do not commit sins or make errors.[1] The office of prophecy is the exclusive possession of a single family, the descendants of Abraham. Key figures mentioned in the Hebrew Bible and New Testament, including Moses, David, and Jesus, were all true prophets who received divine revelations. Over time, however, the revelations delivered to these prophets underwent *taḥrīf* or scriptural distortion. Mistakes crept into the Torah and the New Testament, and these texts ceased to be reliable sources of divine will. This is why God sent Muḥammad to the Arabs. As a lineal descendant of Ishmael, Muḥammad was a member of the family to which the office of prophecy had been entrusted. The purpose of his mission was to restore the original, uncorrupted version of the earlier revelations. Only the faithful and accurate preservation of the revelations received by Muḥammad makes it possible for the Muslim community to assert with confidence that he was the Last Prophet and that the office of prophecy terminated upon his death.

These theological premises combined to create a formula that was used by the first Muslims to assess the validity of earlier sacred texts, on the one hand, and to construct the *Sīra* or biography of Muḥammad, on the other. If the Hebrew Bible indicates that David coveted the wife of Uriah the Hittite, engaged in illicit sexual relations with Bathsheba, and was responsible for the soldier's death, or if the Gospel of Matthew suggests that Mary engaged in illicit sexual relations with someone other than the man to whom she was betrothed, the only conclusion that can be drawn from the evidence is that the biblical narrative is corrupt. The only reliable version of these stories is the one found in the relevant Qur'ānic narrative, where one learns that neither David nor Mary committed any of the sins attributed to them in the Bible. The rectification of the corrupt biblical narratives was followed by the production of Muḥammad's biography, which was formulated in such a manner as to highlight parallels between his career and those of earlier prophets. These parallels are manifestations of *sunnat allāh*, or God's practice.

The exact meaning of the linguistic metaphor *khātam al-nabiyyīn* (lit. "Seal of Prophets") is equivocal. In the first century A.H., some Muslims took the phrase as signifying that Muḥammad confirmed the revelations sent previously to Moses and Jesus. This understanding quickly gave way to the understanding that Muḥammad brought the office of prophecy to an end. The later signification was facilitated by the fact that prophecy is portrayed in the Qurʾān as the exclusive possession of Abraham's descendants. The office is hereditary and it passes from father to son—albeit with occasional intervals between one prophet and the next. From this premise, two corollaries follow: In order to be a prophet, Muḥammad must be a lineal descendant of Abraham; and in order to be the Last Prophet, he must be sonless. This is why the assertion in Q. 33:40 that Muḥammad is "the messenger of God and seal of Prophets" is preceded by the pronouncement that "Muḥammad is not the father of any of your men," this is why it was necessary for Muḥammad to repudiate Zayd, and this is why it was necessary for Zayd to predecease Muḥammad.

The assertion that the office of prophecy ended with the death of Muḥammad was not self-evident, and it encountered resistance. Once the doctrine was introduced, nothing would have been as important to the early Muslim community as the demonstration that Muḥammad died sonless. To this end, the Islamic foundation narrative was constructed so as to make it clear that all of Muḥammad's natural sons died before reaching the age of puberty. In theory, however, the doctrine also applied to Muḥammad's adopted son Zayd b. Muḥammad. It is my contention that this seemingly marginal figure was in fact the most important figure in the early Muslim community—with the exception of the Prophet himself. Zayd's importance comes into sharp focus when we view him through the lens of salvation history. Although a man named Zayd may have been adopted by Muḥammad, the narrative reports about this man's life have nothing to do with history as that term is understood today. From the perspective of salvation history, Zayd emerges as a key figure whose sole function was to make it possible for Muḥammad to become the Last Prophet. The Beloved of the Messenger of God fulfilled this function by serving God and His Prophet with unwavering loyalty and devotion from the moment he entered Muḥammad's household ca. 605 C.E. until his martyrdom in 8/629.

As a figure, Zayd is a condensed religious symbol, the sum total of several biblical models. As a youth he is Joseph, albeit with a twist. Unlike the biblical figure, who welcomes family reunification, Zayd rejects his birth family in favor of his slavemaster. As a reward for this demonstration of loyalty, Zayd is adopted by Muḥammad, whereupon his name changes to Zayd b. Muḥammad and he acquires the right to inherit from his father. As heir apparent, he is Dammesek Eliezer. Once Muḥammad emerges as a prophet, Zayd becomes the Beloved of the Messenger of God. Just as Solomon is favored by God, Zayd is "the one on whom God and you yourself have bestowed favor" (Q. 33:37)—and the only Companion whose name is mentioned in the Qur'ān. Like Ishmael, he is repudiated by his father so that he will not be his heir. When he informs Zaynab of her impending marriage to the Prophet, he becomes Abraham's trusted servant who secures a wife for Isaac. Like Uriah the Hittite, he is sent to certain death on a battlefield in southern Jordan by the man who fell in love with his wife. Like the Isaac of some Jewish *midrashim*, he is sacrificed by his father.

Zayd had to pass five tests in order to make it possible for Muḥammad to become the Last Prophet: He chose to remain with Muḥammad rather than return to Syria with his birth family; he exposed himself to public humiliation by divorcing his wife so that his father might marry her; he carried out Muḥammad's distasteful instruction that he inform his former wife that she was to be married by her father-in-law; he relinquished his status as Muḥammad's son, his name, Zayd b. Muḥammad, and the right to inherit from the Prophet; and he willingly gave up his life for the sake of Muḥammad and Islam.

The Redaction of the Qur'ān

The literary and documentary evidence examined in this monograph suggests that the consonantal skeleton of the Qur'ān remained open and fluid for three-quarters of a century between the death of the Prophet and the caliphate of ʿAbd al-Malik. The process of fixing the consonantal skeleton proceeded by trial and error. Problems were identified and solved, mistakes were made and corrected, and verses were added, revised, and/or removed from the text. As a result, earlier versions differed from later ones.

Changes Driven by Theology

As the Seal of Prophets, Muḥammad confirmed the revelations received by earlier prophets. As the Last Prophet, he brought the office of prophecy to an end. The reinterpretation of this figure of speech was accomplished by combining the notions of *seal* and *sonlessness*. The reinterpretation of the metaphor appears to have unfolded as the consonantal skeleton of the Qurʾān was being established in the years following Muḥammad's death in 11/632. Once the figure of speech had been reinterpreted, it clashed with earlier revelations. These conflicts were solved by reformulating or revising the consonantal skeleton of the earlier verses.

The initial stages of this process are difficult to recover, in part because the textual evidence for the first and second collections of the Qurʾān is no longer extant. In the absence of documentary evidence, one can only speculate, based on literary evidence. In Chapter 4, I advanced three hypotheses relating to revisions of the consonantal skeleton of the Qurʾān. Let us now review these three hypotheses, in reverse order.

Hypothesis 4.3. Q. 33:36–40 was inserted into the middle of *Sūrat al-Aḥzāb* during the generation following the Prophet's death. The formulation of this new pericope clashed with two earlier verses: Q. *4:23 and *33:6. These tensions were eliminated by revising the consonantal skeleton of these two verses—as follows:

Hypothesis 4.2. The assertion in Q. 33:40 that "Muḥammad is not the father of any of your men" clashed with Q. *33:6: "The prophet is closer to the believers than they are themselves, he is their father and his wives are their mothers." To eliminate the tension between the two verses, the phrase "he is their father" was dropped from what would become the standard version of 33:6.

Hypothesis 4.1. The permission granted to Muḥammad in Q. 33:37 to marry the woman who had been his daughter-in-law clashed with Q. *4:23, which prohibited marriage inter alia with "*your daughters-in-law" (**kalāʾilukum*). The conflict was eliminated by introducing a distinction between the wives of natural sons and the wives of adopted sons. To this end, "*your daughters-in-law" was replaced by "the wives of your sons who are from your own loins" (*ḥalāʾil abnāʾikum alladhīna min aṣlābikum*).

Changes Driven by Politics

At the same time that theologically driven revisions were being made, other verses were being revised for reasons relating to politics. Documentary evidence found in BNF 328a indicates that Q. *4:12b originally referred to a man who designates his daughter-in-law or wife as his heir in a last will and testament. This verse became problematic following the death of the Prophet, for two reasons: first, because it referred to the possibility of designating an heir in a last will and testament; second, because the anticipated heir was the testator's daughter-in-law or wife. The problem was resolved by revising v. *12b, as follows:

Hypothesis 8.1. The consonantal skeleton and performed reading of *4:12b were revised so that the opening clause came to be understood as signifying, "If a man or a woman dies leaving collateral relatives."

This revision eliminated the problematic reference to the possibility of designating an heir and, at the same time, the references to a daughter-in-law and wife.

In its revised version, Q. 4:12b indicates that the siblings of a childless man or woman inherit no more than one-third of the estate. One would think that they would inherit the bulk of the estate—if not its entirety. This leads us to our next hypothesis:

Hypothesis 8.2. The omission in Q. 4:12b was rectified by formulating a new revelation that was inserted at the end of *Sūrat al-Nisā'*: "When they ask you for advice, say: 'God advises you with regard to *al-kalāla*'" (4:176).

These five changes to the consonantal skeleton of the Qur'ān are represented in Figure 9.

The only way to produce a single, uniform consonantal skeleton was to destroy earlier drafts. At each stage in the process of redaction those codices that had been produced prior to the "current" version were burned, shredded, or immersed in water so as to insure textual consistency. Islamic sources mention three such campaigns. The result was a uniform consonantal skeleton that came to be accepted by the Muslim community as being derived from a single divine source and having a single meaning.

Legal Reform

The above-mentioned revisions to the consonantal skeleton of the Qur'ān, which were triggered by either theological or political considerations, led to changes in three legal institutions: adoption, marriage, and inheritance.

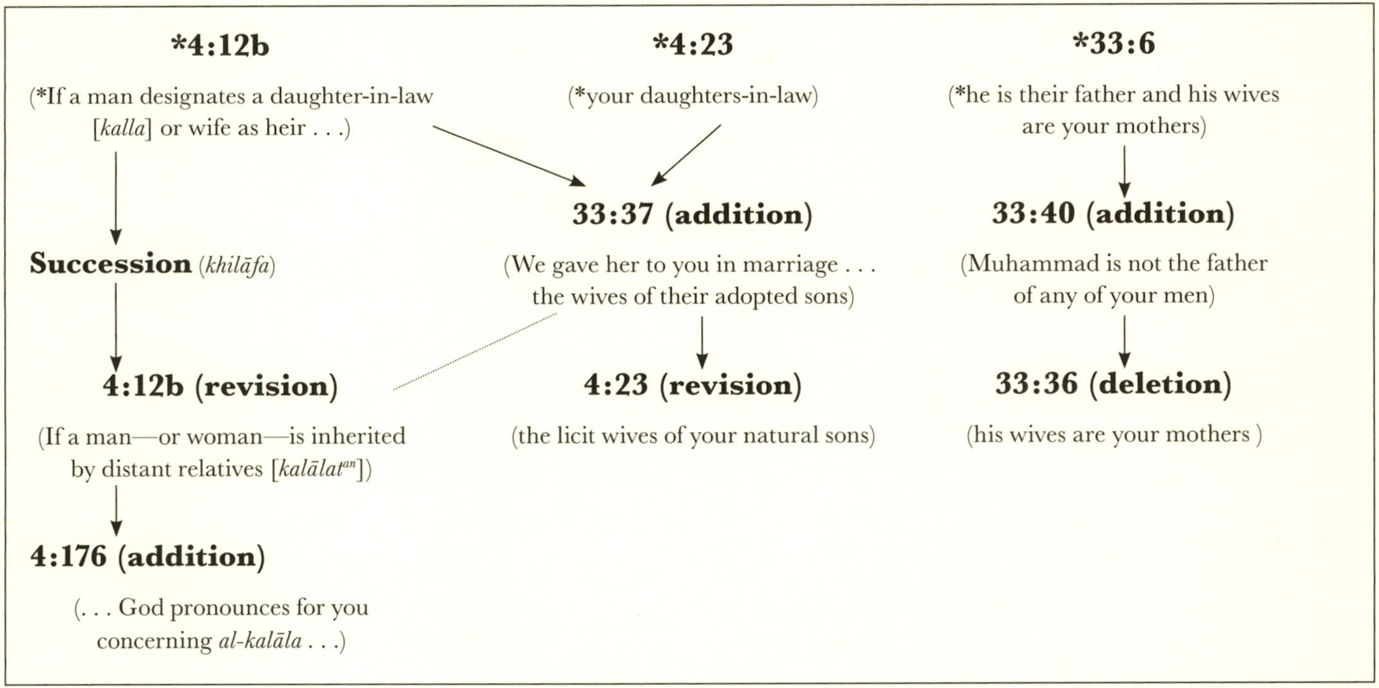

Figure 9. The redaction of the Qurʾān: hypothetical reconstructions, additions, and revisions.

Adoption

Whereas the ostensible purpose of Q. 33:37 was to facilitate Muḥammad's marriage to his daughter-in-law, its true purpose was to create a narrative space in which Muḥammad could say to Zayd, "I am not your father." Muḥammad's repudiation of Zayd served as a *sunna*ic peg on which to hang the abolition of adoption. Lest there be any doubt, the Prophet was made to say, "There is no adoption in Islam: the custom of the *jāhiliyya* has been superseded." Further support for the abolition of adoption is found in Q. 33:4–5, "God has not put two hearts inside any man . . . nor has he made your adopted sons your [real] sons. . . . Call them after their fathers." Henceforth, Muslim jurists classified adoption as a prohibited practice.

Islamic sources portray the abolition of adoption as the product of an episode in the domestic life of the Prophet. In my view, the abolition of adoption was necessitated, in the first instance, by the introduction of a new theological doctrine—the finality of prophecy—and, in the second instance, by macro level historical, legal, and social factors. Islam arose in a world in which adoption was an important, albeit contested, social practice as well as a key theological metaphor. The abolition of adoption by the early Muslim community can be seen as an extension of the Jewish rejection of adoption, on the one hand, and as a radical break with the adoption practices of pagans and polytheists in the Near East, on the other. At the same time, it can be seen as a rejection of the Jewish emphasis on Abraham's status as the spiritual father of the Israelites (*Avraham avinu*) and of the Christian doctrine that Jesus is the spiritual father (*Abba*) of every human being who undergoes baptism. Islam inverts these Judeo-Christian ideas relating to spiritual fatherhood by insisting that Muḥammad is not the father (*ab*) of any man.

Marriage

The introduction of a distinction between the wives of natural sons and adopted sons in Q. 4:23 led to a reform of marriage law. Henceforth, a marriage between a man and the former wife of his adopted son was licit, whereas a marriage between a man and the former wife of his natural son was illicit. The need to introduce a distinction between natural sons and adopted sons followed from the assertion that Muḥammad is the Last Prophet. Inasmuch as adoption was abolished, this was a distinction without a difference.

The theological doctrine of the finality of prophecy may have generated two additional revelations relating to marriage. At the time of his death, Muḥammad's closest surviving blood relatives were his uncle al-ʿAbbās, and his cousin and son-in-law (*khatan*) ʿAlī b. Abī Ṭālib. Had the early Muslim community wanted to insure the survival of Muḥammad's House, the Persian practice of *cagar* marriage offered a ready solution. If either al-ʿAbbās or ʿAlī were to have married one or more of the Prophet's widows, any son produced by these marriages would have taken Muḥammad's name and qualified as his heir. The production of a son, however, was precisely what the first Muslims wanted to prevent. By the middle of the first century A.H., if there was anything that the proto-Sunnis and proto-Shiʿis could agree on, it was that the Prophet died leaving no son or heir and that his House, in the sense of an agnatic lineal descent group, had become extinct. The sonlessness imperative may account for the revelation of Q. 33:6, which asserts that Muḥammad's wives are the Mothers of the Believers. From this assertion one may infer that it is forbidden for a Muslim to marry one of the Prophet's widows. This prohibition, which is only implicit in Q. 33:6, is spelled out in Q. 33:53: "It is not for you to vex God's messenger, nor to marry his wives after him, ever. This is important with God."

Inheritance

The revision of *4:12b set in motion a series of changes to the understanding of the Qurʾānic inheritance rules. As a consequence of these changes, what I call *proto-Islamic inheritance law* was transformed into the *ʿilm al-farāʾiḍ*, or *science of the shares.* The details of this transformation are not directly relevant to the present investigation (the interested reader is referred to Appendix 3). Suffice it to say that, as in most Near Eastern inheritance systems, so too in proto-Islamic inheritance law there was a clear distinction between testate succession and intestacy. A man contemplating death might leave a last will and testament in which he designates an heir and leaves bequests for persons other than the designated heir. In the absence of a last will and testament, simple rules of intestacy applied. By contrast, the *science of the shares* blurs the distinction between testate succession and intestacy. Freedom of testation is replaced by compulsory rules for the division of property. A Muslim contemplating death may not designate an heir in a last will and testament, bequests are limited to one-third of the estate, and they may not be made in favor of any person who receives a fractional share of the estate in accordance with the *science of the shares.*

The Mystery of *al-Kalāla*

As Michael Cook has noted, the word *kalāla* bothered the first exegetes and it has remained obscure down to the present day.[2] It is now possible to say why.

Originally, the text of Q. *4:12b referred to a man who designates a daughter-in-law (**kalla*) or wife as his heir. When the reference to a mechanism for designating an heir proved problematic, the verse was revised: **kalla* was changed to *kalāla*; the performed reading of *y-w-r-th* was changed from active to passive; and the performed reading of *imraʾa* was changed from accusative to nominative. The result was: "If a man or a woman dies leaving distant relatives. . . ."

The word *kalāla* is an artificial creation for which there is no equivalent in any other Semitic language. The word did not exist during the lifetime of the Prophet, and it only entered the Arabic language in the middle of the first/seventh century. Soon thereafter, one or another definition of the word was put forward by Companions and Successors. To augment the authority of these definitions, they were attributed to either Abū Bakr or ʿUmar. This had the unfortunate result of making it appear as if the first two caliphs disagreed over the meaning of this important word. The appearance of disagreement was eliminated by teaching that ʿUmar changed his mind about the meaning of the word so as to bring his definition into line with that of Abū Bakr. Simultaneously, Abū Bakr was made to say that the definition attributed to him was based on his personal opinion, and that if he were wrong about it, no one but Satan was responsible. As for the Prophet, in none of the early sources is a definition of *kalāla* attributed to him, perhaps because at this stage of Islamic history the prophetic *sunna* had not yet taken its place as the ultimate authority of Islamic normative practice.

Appendix 1. The Opening Line of Q. 4:12b and 4:176, Respectively, in English Translations of the Qur'ān

Ross, Alexander. *The Alcoran of Mahomet,Translated out of Arabique into French; by the Sieur Du Ryer, Lord of Malezair, and Resident for the King of France, at Alexandria. And Newly Englished, for the Satisfaction of All That Desire to Look into the Turkish Vanities.* London, 1649.

4:12b: If a man or woman be the heiress of each other, and have neither father nor mother, nor children, and have a brother or sister, each of them shall have a sixth part of the succession . . .

4:176: They will enquire of thee concerning successions; say to them, God teacheth you touching successions, as followeth.

Sale, George. *The Koran: Commonly Called the Alcoran of Mohammed/Translated into English Immediately from the Original Arabic; with Explanatory Notes, Taken from the Most Approved Commentators; to Which is Prefixed a Preliminary Discourse.* London: Virgil's Head, 1734.

4:12b: And if a man or woman's substance be inherited by a distant relation, and he or she have a brother or sister; each of them two shall have a sixth part of the estate.

4:176: They will consult thee for thy decision in certain cases; say unto them, God giveth you these determinations, concerning the more remote degrees of kindred.

Rodwell, J. M. *The Koran: Translated from the Arabic, the Suras Arranged in Chronological Order, with Notes and Index.* Edinburgh/London: Williams & Norgate, 1861.

4:12b: If a man or a woman make a distant relation their heir [sic], and he or she have a brother or a sister, each of these two shall have a sixth.

4:176: They will consult thee. SAY: God instructeth you as to distant kindred.

Palmer, Edward Henry. *The Koran.* 1880. 3rd ed. London: Oxford University Press, 1928.

4:12b: And if the man's or the woman's (property) be inherited by a kinsman who is neither parent nor child, and he have a brother or sister, then let each of these two have a sixth.

4:176: They will ask thee for a decision; say, "God will give you a decision concerning remote kinship."

Wherry, E. M. *A Comprehensive Commentary on the Qurán: Comprising Sale's Translation and Preliminary Discourse / With Additional Notes and Emendations: Together with a Complete Index to the Text, Preliminary Discourse, and Notes.* London: Trübner, 1882–86.

4:12b: And if a man or woman's *substance* be inherited by a distant relation, and he *or she* have a brother or sister; each of them two shall have a sixth part *of the estate.*

4:176: They will consult thee *for thy decision in certain cases*; say *unto them,* GOD giveth you *these* determinations concerning the more remote degrees of kindred.

Ali, Maulana Muhammad. *The Holy Qur'ān: Arabic Text, English Translation and Commentary.* 1917. 6th ed., rev. Chicago: Specialty Promotions, 1973.

4:12b: And if a man or a woman, having no children leaves property to be inherited and he (or she) has a brother or a sister, then for each of them is the sixth.

4:176: They ask thee for a decision. Say: Allāh gives you a decision concerning the person who has neither parents nor children.

Sarwar, Hafiz Ghulam. *Translation of the Holy Qur-an from the Original Arabic Text with Critical Essays, Life of Muhammad, Complete Summary of Contents.* 1928. 2nd ed. Islamabad: National Book Foundation, 1973.

4:12b: And if the deceased man whose estate is to be inherited leave neither father nor children or if a deceased woman be in the same condition, and the deceased has a brother or a sister, then for each one of them is one-sixth.

4:176: They ask thee for a decree. Say "GOD decrees to you in respect of a person who leaves neither parent nor child."

Ahmed Ali, S. V. *The Holy Qur'an; with English Translation of the Arabic Text and Commentary According to the Version of the Holy Ahlul-Bait, with Special Notes from Ayatullah Agha Haji Mirza Mahdi Pooya Yazdi on the Philosophic Aspects of Some of the Verses.* 1928. Karachi: Sterling Printing & Publishing, 1964.

4:12b: [A]nd if a man or woman leaveth (*his property*) to be inherited by (*not the lineage but*) any side relation and he or she hath a brother or a sister each of these two shall have the sixth.

4:176: They ask thee for a decree (*about the Law*): Say, (*O' Our Apostle Muhammad!*) God giveth you a decision about 'Kalala' the side kindred.

Pickthall, Mohammed Marmaduke. *The Meaning of the Glorious Koran, an Explanatory Translation.* London: Knopf, 1930.

4:12b: And if a man or a woman have a distant heir (having left neither parent nor child), and he (or she) have a brother or a sister (only on the mother's side) then to each of them twain (the brother and the sister) the sixth.

4:176: They ask thee for a pronouncement. Say: Allah hath pronounced for you concerning distant kindred.

Ali, Abdullah Yusuf. *Roman Transliteration of the Holy Quran with Full Arabic Text/English Translation.* 1934–37. Lahore: Sh. Muhammad Ashraf, 1986.

4:12b: If the man or woman whose inheritance is in question has left neither ascendants nor descendants, but has left a brother or a sister, each one of the two gets a sixth.

4:176: They ask thee for a legal decision. Say: Allah directs (thus) about those who leave no descendants or ascendants as heirs.

Bell, Richard. *The Qur'ān, Translated, with a Critical Re-arrangement of the Surahs.* Edinburgh: Clark, 1937–39.

4:12b: If a man—or a woman—whose property falls to be inherited have no direct heirs, but have a brother or a sister, each of the two receives a sixth.

4:176: They ask thee for a deliverance; say: "Allah giveth you a deliverance in regard to the person who leaves no direct heirs."

Arberry, A. J. *The Koran Interpreted.* London: Allen & Unwin, 1955.

4:12b: If a man or a woman have no heir direct, but have a brother or a sister, to each of the two a sixth.

4:176: They will ask thee for a pronouncement. Say: "God pronounces to you concerning the indirect heirs."

Dawood, N. J. *The Koran, Translated with Notes.* 1956. 4th ed., rev. New York: Penguin, 1974.

4:12b: If a man or a woman leave neither children nor parents and have a brother or a sister, they shall each inherit one-sixth.

4:176: They consult you. Say: "Thus Allah instructs you regarding those that die childless."

Hamid, S. M. Abdul. *The Divine Qur-an. It Contains the Arabic Text with a Very Lucid Translation and Short Explanatory Notes That Make the Sense Clear.* Dacca: Darul Islam, 1962–68.

4:12b: [A]nd if (the deceased leaves neither parents nor any child being) a man or a woman having a distant heir, and he (or she) has got a (step-) brother or a (step-)sister then each of them two (brother and sister) shall have the sixth.

4:176: (And to test your judgment) they ask you for a pronouncement (regarding inheritance). Say: ALLAH gives you a decision (in addition to His former decisions) concerning the person who has neither parents nor any offspring.

Asad, Muhammad. *The Message of the Qur'ān.* 1964. 2nd ed. Gibraltar: Dar al-Andalus, 1980.

4:12b: And if a man or a woman has no heir in the direct line, but has a brother or a sister, then each of these two shall inherit one-sixth.

4:176: They will ask thee to enlighten them. Say: "God enlightens you [thus] about the laws concerning [inheritance from] those who leave no heir in the direct line."

Nuri, Khadim Rahmani/Hoque, Zohurul (ed.). *The Running Commentary of the Holy Qur-an, with Underbracket Comments.* Shillong: Sufi Hamsaya-Gurudwar, 1964.

4:12b: And if the deceased man whose estate is to be inherited leave no offspring (177, but leave parents) or if a (deceased) woman (be in the same condition), and he (or she—the deceased) has a brother or a sister, then for each one of the twain (—the brother and the sister) is one-sixth.

4:176/177: They ask thee for a decree. Say: "Allāh decrees to you in respect of one who leaves no offspring (nor parents)."

Blachère, Régis. *Le Coran (al-Qor'ān).* Paris: Maisonneuve, 1966.

4:12b: Si un homme ou une femme se trouvent laisser un héritage sans avoir d'ayant droit, alors qu'ils ont un frère ou une soeur, à chacun de ceux-ci, le sixième [*de l'héritage*].

4:176: [Les Croyants] [, *Prophète!*] te demandent éclaircissement [*sur la succession sans ayant droit*]. Réponds: "Allah vous éclaire sur cette succession."

Paret, Rudi. *Der Koran.* W. Berlin: Kohlhammer, 1966.

4:12b: Und wenn ein Mann oder eine Frau von seitlicher Verwandtschaft (*kalāla*) beerbt wird und er (bzw. sie) einen (Halb)bruder oder eine (Halb) schwester hat, steht jedem von den beiden ein Sechstel zu.

4:176: Man fragt dich um Auskunft. Sag: Gott gibt euch (hiermit) über die seitliche Verwandtschaft (*kalāla*) (und deren Anteil am Erbe) Auskunft.

Maududi, Syed Abdul Aʿla. *The Holy Qur'ān: Text, Translation and Brief Notes.* 1967. Lahore: Islamic Publications, 1982. English rendering by Abdul Aziz Kamal/Muhammad Akbar Muradpuri.

4:12b: And if the deceased, whether man or woman, (whose property is to be divided as inheritance), leaves no children and no parents behind, but has one brother or one sister alive, each of the two will be entitled to one-sixth of the whole.

4:176: People seek your verdict on (the inheritance left by) a childless person. Say, "Allah gives His verdict."

Farid, Malik Ghulam (ed.). *The Holy Qur'ān: English Translation and Commentary.* Rabwah: Oriental & Religious Publication Corporation, 1969.

4:12b: And if there be a man or a woman whose heritage is to be divided and he *or she* has neither parent nor child, and he *or she* has a brother and a sister, then each one of them shall have a sixth.

4:176: They ask thee for a decision. Say, "Allāh gives His decision concerning *Kalālah.*"

Khan, Muhammad Zafrulla. *The Quran [Qur'ān Majīd]: The Eternal Revelation Vouchsafed to Muhammad, the Seal of the Prophets/Arabic Text with a New Translation.* 1971. 3rd ed., rev. Dublin: Curzon, 1981.

4:12b: If there be a man or a woman leaving property to be inherited, and there is no parent or child, but there is a uterine brother or uterine sister, then each of them shall have a sixth.

4:176: They ask thee for directions concerning the inheritance of a Kalala. Say to them: Allah gives you His directions concerning the inheritance of such a one.

Ali, Ahmed. *Al-Qur'ān, A Contemporary Translation.* Karachi: Akrash, 1984. Rev. definitive ed., Princeton, N.J.: Princeton University Press, 1988.

Q. 4:12b: If a man or woman should die without leaving either children or parents behind but have brother and sister, they shall each inherit one-sixth.

Q. 4:176: They ask you for a judgement about "Kalala" (a man who dies childless). Say: "God has given a decision in the matter of inheritance."

Irving, Thomas Ballantine. *The Qur'an/Translation and Commentary.* 1985. 3rd ed. Brattleboro, Vt.: Amana Books, 1988.

4:12b: If either a man or a woman bequeaths anything [sic] to more distant kin while he still has a brother or sister, then each one of them will have a sixth.

4:176: They will ask you for your verdict. SAY: "God advises you (all) concerning indirect heirs."

Khatib, M. M. *The Bounteous Koran: A Translation of Meaning and Commentary.* London: Macmillan, 1986.

4:12b: And if a man or a woman have no heir, but have a uterine brother or sister, then to each of the two is a sixth.

4:176: They ask your verdict, say, "God gives you His verdict concerning the Kalālah."

Abdel Haleem, M. A. S. *The Qur'ān, a New Translation.* Oxford World's Classics. Oxford: Oxford University Press, 2004.

4:12b: If a man or a woman dies leaving no children or parents, but a single brother or sister, he or she should take one-sixth of the inheritance.

4:176: They ask you [Prophet] for a ruling. Say, "God gives you a ruling about inheritance from someone who dies childless with no surviving parents."

Jones, Alan. *The Qur'ān.* Exeter: Gibb Memorial Trust, 2007.

4:12b: If a man, or a woman, has no direct heir, but has a brother or sister, each one of the two gets a sixth.

4:176: They ask you for a pronouncement. Say, "God pronounces for you concerning distant kin."

Appendix 2. Deathbed Scenes and Inheritance Disputes: A Literary Approach

The death of Muḥammad confronted the Muslim community with a crisis. Who would succeed the Prophet as the leader of the Muslim community, by what right, and what office would this person hold?

The succession crisis created tensions that led to the division of the Muslim community into Sunnis, Shiʿis, and Kharijis. The respective claims to leadership put forward by members of these three groups are preserved in reports compiled by Muslim historians. The claims advanced in these reports are tendentious, and Western scholars have questioned the reliability and usefulness of the sources for the purposes of historical investigation. Beginning with Lammens and Caetani and continuing down to the present, the prevailing view has been that reports about the succession crisis—especially those supporting the Shiʿi position—are late fabrications that were put into circulation in an effort to buttress the contention that ʿAlī had been the rightful successor of the Prophet.[1]

Two important witnesses to the succession crisis were the Prophet's wife ʿĀʾisha and his cousin Ibn ʿAbbās. Madelung recently has argued that statements attributed to these two Companions reflect sharply defined personal positions and political attitudes which, taken as a whole, are internally consistent. Thus, if the attribution of one or another assertion to ʿĀʾisha or Ibn ʿAbbās could be verified—he does not say how—then the report in question should be accepted as *authentic* until such time as the opposite can be proven. The historian is careful to add, however, that even an authentic report may not be *reliable* because ʿĀʾisha and Ibn ʿAbbās would not have hesitated to manipulate the "facts" if and when such an action had served their interests, e.g., by buttressing their own positions or discrediting their adversaries.[2] Madelung seems to think that it is possible to reconstruct history as it really happened.[3] If so, then reports preserved in Islamic sources open a window on the innermost thoughts of the Muslims who participated in the succession crisis.

Although Madelung surely has gone too far,[4] it nevertheless remains the case that some of the reports relating to the succession crisis were put into circulation long before the lead-up to the Abbasid revolution and they may preserve arguments and positions that had emerged by the end of the first century A.H. In what follows, I apply to these reports the same method that I applied to the reports about Zayd in Chapter 7. That is to say, rather than treating these narratives as records of an historical event, I treat them as literary compositions that were formulated after the fact. By analyzing selected narratives from a literary perspective, I seek to expose themes and tendencies that lie hidden beneath the smooth linguistic surface of the narratives. I shall examine two episodes: (1) Muḥammad on his deathbed; and (2) the inheritance disputes that are said to have followed his death.

The Prophet on His Deathbed

A deathbed scene is a natural setting in which to situate issues relating to inheritance and succession. It is on his deathbed that a man often makes provisions for the transmission of property from one generation to the next, and it is on his deathbed that the leader of a political or religious community nominates a successor, if he has not done so already. Narrative reports about what Muḥammad said (or did not say) on his deathbed may be compared to the deathbed scenes of biblical figures such as Jacob (Gen. 49) or David (I Kings 1), on the one hand, and to the deathbed scenes of the first caliphs, on the other. Let us examine three narratives.

> Ḥasan—Shaybān—Layth—Ṭāʾūs—Ibn ʿAbbās: When Muḥammad was on the point of death (*lammā ḥudira rasūl allāh*), he said: "Bring me a shoulder blade (*katif*) and I shall dictate for you a document (*kitāb*) on it so that no two men will disagree after me." Subsequently, Ibn ʿAbbās continued, "The people approached shouting loudly, and a woman said, 'Beware the testament (*ʿahd*) of the Messenger of God.'"[5]

In this narrative, a statement attributed to the Prophet on his deathbed is reported on the authority of Ibn ʿAbbās (d. 68/688). The *isnād* indicates that sometime before he died, Ibn ʿAbbās transmitted the Prophet's final words to his student, Ṭāʾūs (d. 100/718–19). Although Ibn ʿAbbās may have been present when Muḥammad died, one wonders if the words attributed to the Prophet were in fact uttered by him. This suspicion is reinforced by the formulation of the report. The phrase *lammā ḥudira rasūl allāh* ("when Muḥammad was on the point of death") signals a connection to Q. 2:180, which opens with *lammā ḥadara aḥadukum al-mawtᵘ* ("when death approaches one of you") and proceeds to enjoin Muslims to leave a bequest for parents and relatives. Any doubt that the reference here is to a last will and testament is removed by the enigmatic statement uttered by the unnamed woman at the end of the report: "Beware the testament of the Messenger of God." The references to a shoulder blade (*katif*) and document (*kitāb*) bring to mind three reports relating to ʿUmar. In one report, the Prophet dictated a verse of the Qurʾān containing the word *kalāla* to his wife Ḥafṣa bt. ʿUmar; and the verse was recorded on a shoulder blade. In a second report, ʿUmar held a shoulder blade in his hand while announcing his intention to issue a decree about *al-kalāla*; in a third report, the dying caliph called for a document (*kitāb*) that he had written about *al-kalāla* and ordered that it be erased.

Similarly, the Prophet's expressed desire to leave a last will and testament "so that no two men will disagree after me" brings to mind ʿUmar's desire to issue a decree about *al-kalāla* "so that no one who reads (or recites) the Qur'ān will disagree about it."[6]

Note that the identity of the woman who issues the warning as well as that of the persons who heard it is not specified. Who was this woman, to whom was she speaking, and why would anyone be afraid of what the Prophet was about to say? In Q. 33:37, it will be recalled, God gives Muḥammad special permission to marry an unnamed woman who previously had been married to his adopted son Zayd. The unnamed woman subsequently was identified by Muslim exegetes as Zaynab bt. Jaḥsh, who was not only the Prophet's daughter-in-law and wife but also his paternal cross-cousin (see Chapter 4). As the Prophet's cousin, daughter-in-law, and wife, Zaynab was one of the members of his House (*ahl al-bayt*), and one would expect to find her near Muḥammad's bed.[7] If the unnamed woman in this report was in fact Zaynab, she presumably was speaking to other members of the Prophet's House. In a report in which ʿUmar holds aloft a shoulder blade and announces that he is about to issue a decree about *al-kalāla*, he predicts that his decree will become a topic of conversation among the women in their private chambers (*fī khudūrihinna*). This statement brings to mind Joel 2:16, "Let the bridegroom go forth from his chamber (*me-ḥedrô*) and the bride (*kallâh*) from her canopy" (*ḥuppatâ*). Hebrew *ḥeder* and Arabic *khidr* are cognates (see further below). The Arabic word signifies *a curtain that is extended for a girl in a part of a house or chamber or tent*; or *a chamber or house or tent in which is a woman*.[8] Whoever formulated the report may have been drawing attention to the revision of Q. *4:12b, where **kalla*—the Arabic equivalent of Hebrew *Kallâh*—was changed to *kalāla*, in a context dealing with inheritance.[9] Note, finally, that the reports in which a shoulder blade (*katif*) or document (*kitāb*), or both, are mentioned share a common theme: In all of these reports, the central figure—Muḥammad or ʿUmar—expresses a desire to issue an important statement but is prevented from carrying out his wish.[10]

The unnamed woman who is said to have contributed to Muḥammad's decision not to leave a last will and testament on his deathbed brings to mind a named woman who interceded with her husband David on his deathbed in order to secure the succession of their son Solomon (I Kings 1). This woman—Bathsheba—entered the dying king's private chamber (*ḥeder*—see above) after hearing David's son Adonijah boast that he would succeed his father as King of Israel. David asked his wife, "What troubles you?" To which she replied:

> My lord, you yourself swore to your maidservant by the Lord your God: "Your son Solomon shall succeed me as king, and he shall sit upon my throne." Yet now Adonijah

has become king, and you, my lord the king, know nothing about it. He has prepared a sacrificial feast of a great many oxen, fatlings, and sheep, and he has invited all the king's sons and Abiathar the priest and Joab commander of the army; but he has not invited your servant Solomon. And so all of the eyes of Israel are upon you, O lord the king, to tell them who shall succeed my lord the king on the throne. Otherwise, when the lord my king lies down with his fathers, my son Solomon and I will be regarded as traitors. (1 Kings 1:17–21)

To this entreaty, David responded by swearing a solemn oath confirming his earlier oath that Solomon would succeed him, promising to fulfill the first oath that very day (vv. 28–31). After explaining how the accession ceremony was to be performed (Solomon was to be placed on the king's mule), the king said, "For he [viz., Solomon] shall succeed me as king; him I designate to be ruler of Israel and Judah" (vv. 32–35). And so it came to pass that "Solomon sat upon the throne of his father David, and his rule was firmly established" (1 Kings 2:12).

Just as the Israelites were waiting for David to tell them who would succeed him as king, so too the Companions of the Prophet were waiting for Muḥammad to tell them who would succeed him as leader of the Muslim community. In both cases, a key woman works behind the scenes to determine the outcome of the succession crisis. As expected, the Islamic narrative inverts the biblical model. Unlike David, who had several sons, Muḥammad had none. For this reason, the Prophet cannot designate a successor.

In a second version of Muḥammad's deathbed scene, it is not a woman but a man who persuades those present not to allow the Prophet to carry out his expressed intention to leave a last will and testament. This man is identified as ʿUmar b. al-Khaṭṭāb:

Wahb b. Jarīr—Ubayy—Yūnis [b. Yazīd]—al-Zuhrī—ʿUbayd Allāh b. ʿAbd Allāh—Ibn ʿAbbās: When death drew near to the Messenger of God, he said, "Come to me, and I will dictate for you a document (*kitāb*) so that you will not go astray after it." There were several men in the house, among them ʿUmar b. al-Khaṭṭāb. ʿUmar said, "The pain has overcome the Messenger of God. The Qurʾān is in your possession. Let the Book of God be sufficient for us." [Ibn ʿAbbās] said, "The people of the house (*ahl al-bayt*) disagreed and quarreled. Some of them said, 'The Messenger of God is dictating for you', or they said, 'Draw near so that the Messenger of God might dictate for you.' Others said the same thing that ʿUmar said. When the clamor and disagreement increased, causing distress to the Messenger of God, he said, 'Get out.'" Ibn ʿAbbās used to say, "The calamity—the entire calamity—is [a result of] what came between the Messenger of God and his dictating that document for them," i.e., their clamor and disagreement.[11]

The actions of Muḥammad on his deathbed may be compared to those of ʿUmar on his. As the Prophet lay dying, he summoned his Companions and expressed his desire to dictate a document, but his expressed desire was not fulfilled. As ʿUmar lay dying, he instructed unnamed Companions to destroy a document that he had written about *al-kalāla*, and the instruction was carried out. On his deathbed, the Prophet made it clear that he wanted to dictate a document "so that you will not go astray after it." The penultimate line of Q. 4:176 reads: "God makes clear for you [lest] you go astray." As the Prophet lay dying, ʿUmar intervened to prevent him from dictating a final statement to his community on the grounds that he was delirious.[12] To this the Companion added, "The Qurʾān is in your possession. Let the Book of God be sufficient for us." ʿUmar's assertion that the Qurʾān is "sufficient for us" brings to mind the report in which he says that there was nothing about which he queried the Messenger of God as frequently as *kalāla*, until the Prophet poked him in the chest and said, "Let the summer verse at the end of *Sūrat al-Nisāʾ* be sufficient for you." It also brings to mind the narrative in which the Prophet, after clarifying the meaning of *kalāla* to his wife Ḥafṣa, says to her, "[It was] ʿUmar who ordered you to do this. I suspect that he does not understand it. Is not the summer verse sufficient for him?" Clearly, the Prophet's clarification was not sufficient for ʿUmar. Notice that the same rhetorical structure is attributed to both the Prophet ("Let the summer verse at the end of *Sūrat al-Nisāʾ* be sufficient for you") and ʿUmar ("Let the Book of God be sufficient for us"). This may be a coincidence. Alternatively, it is possible that the Muslims who formulated these reports were attempting to signal a connection between Muḥammad and ʿUmar.

In a third version of Muḥammad's deathbed scene, also related on the authority of Ibn ʿAbbās, it is reported that the Prophet did manage to issue an oral testament in which he left three instructions. The first instruction was to "expel the polytheists from the Arabian peninsula." The second instruction was to "consider the [tribal] deputation lawful, as I used to do." Curiously, the tradent who transmitted this report could not remember the third instruction and the next tradent in the *isnād* suggested that his source either forgot it or omitted it intentionally.[13] The inability of the early Muslim community to remember an important statement that the Prophet is said to have made on his deathbed brings to mind ʿUmar's inability on his deathbed to remember the third item that he wanted Ibn ʿAbbās to commit to memory: the definition of *al-kalāla*. Similarly, it brings to mind a deathbed statement attributed to ʿUmar in which he instructed Ibn ʿAbbās to remember only two things about him: "I did not appoint a successor and I did not issue a decree about *al-kalāla*."[14] The formulation of this report reinforces our assumption that whoever put these reports into circulation was attempting to make a connection between political succession (*khilāfa*) and *al-kalāla*.

Inheritance Disputes Following Muḥammad's Death

Q. 4:11–12 contain detailed rules for the division of property following the death of a man or woman. Presumably, any wealth left by the Prophet would have been divided up among his heirs in accordance with these rules. In that case, the first question to arise would have been: Which of Muḥammad's relatives qualified as his heirs, and what was the entitlement of each heir?

At the time of his death in 11/632, Muḥammad's parents were no longer alive, his five natural sons had all predeceased him, he had repudiated his adopted son Zayd, and he had no siblings. The Prophet's closest surviving blood relative was his daughter Fāṭima who, according to Q. 4:11, was entitled to half the estate. In addition, nine of Muḥammad's wives, including Zaynab, are said to have outlived the Prophet. Q. 4:12a stipulates that one or more wives is entitled to either one-fourth or one-eighth of the estate, depending on whether or not there are any children. In competition with Fāṭima, the Prophet's wives were entitled to one-eighth. The remaining three-eighths of the estate would have passed to the Prophet's closest surviving blood relative, either his paternal cousin ʿAlī or his paternal uncle al-ʿAbbās, depending on how one reckons closeness.[15]

Let us attend to what the sources say about inheritance claims made by different members of the Prophet's family, beginning with his wives. Following Muḥammad's death, his wives reportedly wanted to send ʿUthmān to the first caliph, Abū Bakr, in order to demand their share of the estate. But ʿĀʾisha, who was both Muḥammad's wife and Abū Bakr's daughter, persuaded her co-wives not to press any inheritance claim. She is reported to have asked her co-wives, in a manner which points to her own uncertainty, "Did not the Messenger of God say: 'No one inherits from us; whatever we leave is charity' (*lā nūrathu mā taraknā ṣadaqat^un^*)?"[16] Here the statement attributed to the Prophet is language that ʿĀʾisha remembered him as having said. By making Muḥammad refer to himself in the first person plural ("us," "we"), ʿĀʾisha—or whoever formulated this report and put it into circulation—was suggesting that the Qurʾānic inheritance rules do not apply to prophets.[17] No one inherits from a prophet and any wealth accumulated by a prophet during his lifetime is distributed as charity after his death. It follows that there were no grounds upon which the Prophet's wives might claim a share of his estate. His co-wives reportedly conceded the point and dropped their claim.[18]

The Prophet's daughter Fāṭima reportedly was less compliant. She sent an agent to Abū Bakr demanding her inheritance from her father. To this request the caliph responded by quoting the same words that ʿĀʾisha is said to have uttered to her co-wives—albeit here as an unqualified assertion: "The Messenger of God *said*, 'No one inherits from us; whatever we leave is charity'" (emphasis added—DSP). Again, any wealth accumulated by a prophet is not subject to the normal inheritance rules. Abū Bakr explained that Muḥammad's property had become a public trust and that, although members of his family were entitled to use the proceeds of this trust for their personal needs, these resources did not belong to them. The caliph insisted that he was administering a policy that had been implemented by Muḥammad and he assured Fāṭima that he bore no enmity towards the Prophet's family. Unimpressed, Fāṭima became angry and did not speak to Abū Bakr again until her death, which followed that of the Prophet by approximately six months.[19]

The statement attributed to Muḥammad ("no one inherits from us") is inconsistent with the language of the Qurʾān. *Sūrat Maryam* relates the story of the Prophet Zakariyyāʾ, who, when his wife was unable to conceive a child, feared what his kinsmen (*mawālī*) would do after he died (Q. 19:1ff.). Zakariyyāʾ implored God to grant him a successor (*walī*) to be his heir and to inherit from *him* and from the family of Jacob (*yarithunī wa-yarithu min āl Yaʿqūb*). Similarly, Q. 27:16 begins by stating in clear Arabic, "Solomon inherited from David" (*wa-waritha Sulaymānu Dāʾūda*). Why would Muḥammad say that no one would inherit from him, viz., from a prophet, when, according to the Qurʾān, the Prophet Zakariyyāʾ implored God to give him an heir and Solomon inherited the office of prophecy from David?[20] The tension between the Qurʾān and the *sunna* was harmonized by revising the *sunna*. In the phrase "No one inherits from us; whatever we leave is charity," the first person plural "us" was glossed as referring specifically to the Prophet Muḥammad, not to prophets in general. In other words, Muḥammad is a special case within a special case, an exception to an exception.

After Fāṭima had followed her father to the grave, her husband ʿAlī asserted his right to inherit from Muḥammad on the grounds that he was the Prophet's paternal cousin (N.B. he was also his *khatan* or son-in-law). This claim brought ʿAlī into conflict with al-ʿAbbās, the Prophet's paternal uncle. Now that the Prophet's last child had died, whoever qualified as his closest surviving blood relative would inherit the estate. The dispute reportedly had not been settled at the time of ʿUmar's accession to the caliphate in 13/634. In one report, the two men approach the caliph and ask him to settle their disagreement. This narrative moment provided an opportunity to qualify the problematic prophetic statement:

> Slowly. I adjure you by God, with whose permission the heavens and earth exist, do you know that the Messenger of God said, "no one inherits from us; whatever we leave is charity"—by which [expression] the Messenger of God was *referring to himself* (emphasis added).[21]

Here the tradent clarifies that when Muḥammad said "no one inherits from us," he was referring to himself and not to all prophets. It was only after ʿAlī and al-ʿAbbās had acknowledged the truth of this assertion that ʿUmar explained the grounds of his decision. As in the earlier report, during his lifetime, Muḥammad is said to have administered on behalf of the Muslim community certain material resources ("the wealth of God") that had been entrusted to him by virtue of his prophetic office. When Muḥammad died,

Abū Bakr assumed responsibility for these resources and the first caliph continued the practice of supervising these revenues on behalf of the community, just as the Prophet had done. When ʿUmar succeeded Abū Bakr as caliph, he continued the policy.[22]

The connection between succession and inheritance was made by Goldziher more than a century ago. As the great Orientalist put it, "the tradition had to establish the principle that nothing belonging to the Prophet could be subject to inheritance" so as to "withdraw the question of the caliphate from the sphere of subtleties in the law of inheritance." He continued: "Nobody is his [viz., Muḥammad's] heir, from the point of view of civil law and therefore by extension also in regard to his office as ruler. His property goes to the treasury and in the same way the community must decide upon his successor."[23] As I argued in Chapter 9, the revision of Q. *4:12b was driven by the connection between succession and inheritance. This is the point that is being made in the narrative in which ʿUmar, on his deathbed, instructs Ibn ʿAbbās to remember two things about him, "I did not appoint a successor (*lam astakhlif*) and I did not issue a decree about *al-kalāla*."[24]

Appendix 3. Inheritance Law: From the Ancient Near East to Early Islamic Times

Inheritance in the Ancient Near East

Long before the rise of Islam, the inhabitants of the Near East had developed and refined rules and mechanisms for the intergenerational transmission of property. The general structure of Near Eastern inheritance systems displays remarkable uniformity over time and space. All Near Eastern inheritance systems make a clear distinction between rules of intestacy, on the one hand, and testate succession, on the other. In this respect, as we shall see, Islam is anomalous.[1]

Intestate Succession

In ancient Near Eastern inheritance systems, a man's primary heirs were his natural sons born of a legitimate marriage. If a man died childless, his estate passed to his brothers or nephews. In principal, husbands and wives did not inherit from one another, and the devolution of property to widows was regulated by the dower system. If a widow were indigent, she might be granted a share of her husband's estate. To facilitate the division of an estate, property was divided into individual parcels, and lots were cast to determine the share of each heir. A first-born son frequently inherited a double share.[2]

Testate Succession

Generally speaking, a last will and testament was used only in exceptional cases. If a man produced no sons, he could formulate a will in which he appointed as his heir someone who would not qualify according to the rules of intestacy, e.g., a wife, a daughter, the natural son of a concubine, or an adopted son. By means of a last will and testament, a testator might assign a specific parcel of property to an individual heir, transfer a first-born son's double share upon intestacy to another son, or award a share of the estate to a daughter. A last will and testament also could be used to disinherit a natural son, for cause. The legal instrument was revocable at any time before the testator entered his final death sickness.[3]

Arabian and Proto-Islamic Inheritance Law

Islamic sources indicate that the inheritance system practiced by the early Muslim community underwent significant changes during the course of the first century A.H. Let us examine these changes.

Mecca

There is little hard evidence on inheritance practices in Mecca.

Presumably, the Meccans followed an Arabian version of Near Eastern provincial law. If so, they would have been familiar with the distinction between intestacy and testate succession. In the absence of a last will and testament, property would have been divided among heirs who were determined on the basis of blood relationship to the deceased, that is, sons, brothers, nephews, and cousins. The emergence of Muḥammad as the leader of a small community would have made the subject of inheritance a matter of general concern, especially when blood ties conflicted with religious ties. What happened when a Muslim died and his closest blood relative was a pagan or polytheist? To strengthen communal ties and to prevent valuable economic resources from passing to non-Muslims, Muḥammad is said to have created pacts of brotherhood (*muʾākhāt*) between pairs of Muslims who were not close relatives.[4]

Medina: Stage 1

The tension between blood ties and religious ties was exacerbated by the *hijra* or migration to Medina. At first, many if not most of the *muhājir*s or emigrants would have had close blood relatives in Mecca who remained pagans or polytheists, and many if not most of the *anṣār* or Helpers in Medina would have had close relatives in that city who had not yet accepted Islam. What happened if a *muhājir* died in Medina and his or her closest blood relative was a Meccan pagan? What happened if a Medinese Helper died and his or her closest blood relative was a Christian or Jew?

Islamic sources indicate that the Prophet suspended Medinese inheritance law following his arrival in the city, presumably in an effort to prevent the transfer of wealth and property from Muslims to non-Muslims and to keep economic resources within the Muslim community. New inheritance rules were introduced, based upon the principles of common faith, migration, and, again, pacts of brotherhood. Prior to the Battle of Badr, Muḥammad is said to have created brotherhood pacts between thirteen pairs of Meccan emigrants and Medinese Helpers. These agreements were based upon the principle of "right and sharing" (*ʿalā al-ḥaqq wa'l-muʿāsāt*). Blood ties were irrelevant: When a man died, his estate passed to his metaphorical or fictive brother rather than to his closest surviving blood relatives.[5]

The suspension of Medinese inheritance law was lifted after the Muslims established themselves as the dominant group in the city. The transition from one inheritance regime to the other is said to have taken place in the year 5 A.H., the year in which *Sūrat al-Aḥzāb* was revealed to the Prophet. Q. 33:6 mentions a "decree" (*kitāb*) which establishes that the inheritance rules to be observed by Muslims once again were to be based upon blood ties (see Chapter 4, Act 5, Scene 3). Presumably, this decree specified some of the inheritance rules currently found in *Sūrat al-Nisāʾ*. Linguistic metaphors (brotherhood contracts and adoption) ceased to have any legal effect. Henceforth, the right to inherit was again based upon blood ties and proximity to the deceased.

Medina: Stage 2

Elsewhere, I have argued that the inheritance rules introduced by Muḥammad differed significantly from what came to be known as the *ʿilm al-farāʾiḍ* or *science of the shares*.[6] For convenience, I use the term *proto-Islamic law* to refer to the earlier system. Like ancient Near Eastern inheritance systems, proto-Islamic inheritance law distinguished between intestacy and testate succession.

1. Intestacy. The rules of intestacy were based upon blood ties and proximity to the deceased.[7] Unlike the later *science of the shares*, which is based on three Qurʾānic verses—Q. 4:11, 12, 176—the proto-Islamic law of intestacy was based upon only one verse—Q. 4:11 (see Chapters 8–9). This verse was the original *inheritance verse*.[8] It reads as follows:

> God commands you concerning your children: A male is entitled to the share of two females. If they are females above two, they are entitled to two-thirds of what he leaves. If there is one, she is entitled to half. Each of his parents is entitled to one-sixth of what he leaves, if he has a child. But if he does not have a child, and his parents are his heirs, his mother is entitled to one-third. If he has brothers, his mother is entitled to one-sixth, after any legacy he bequeaths or debt. Your fathers and your sons, you know not which of them is closer to you in usefulness. A commandment from God. God is knowing, wise.

Verse 11 treats several hypothetical cases: In the absence of a son, one daughter inherits half the estate and three or more daughters inherit two-thirds. Presumably, the residue passes to the closest surviving agnate (*ʿāṣib*).[9] When sons inherit together with daughters, the share of a male is equal to that of two females. For example, if a man dies leaving two sons and a daughter, the sons inherit two-fifths each and the daughter inherits one-fifth; alternatively, if a man dies leaving two daughters and a son, the daughters inherit one-fourth each and the son inherits half. Parents inherit one-sixth each in competition with one or more sons (who share two-thirds of the estate on a per capita basis). If a childless man dies leaving both parents, the father inherits two-thirds and the mother inherits one-third. If a childless man dies leaving his mother and one or more brothers, the mother inherits one-sixth and the brothers inherit five-sixths, divided on a per capita basis. The system was based upon simple mathematical rules. Compared to Near Eastern inheritance law, there were two major innovations: First, daughters inherit in competition with sons and, second, a male is entitled to the share of two females.

2. Widows. A widow is entitled to the delayed portion of her dower. If she does not receive a dower at the time of her marriage, and if she can demonstrate that she is indigent, she may be awarded either one-fourth or one-eighth of the estate, depending on whether or not she has any children.

3. Testate Succession. Like the inhabitants of the ancient Near East, the early Muslim community was familiar with the principles of testate succession, as evidenced by the Qurʾān. Q. 2:180 enjoins a Muslim who anticipates that he will predecease his parents and close relatives to leave a bequest for these individuals. Q. 2:240 encourages a man contemplating death to bequeath the equivalent of one year's maintenance to his wives, on the condition that they remain in his house. Q. 2:181–2 and 5:105–6 warn Believers not to alter a last will and testament, encourage the reconciliation of parties who disagree about the provisions of a will, and establish that a last will and testament should be drawn up in the presence of two witnesses. Under such a regime, a person contemplating death would have enjoyed a large measure of freedom to determine his or her heirs and to specify the property to be inherited. Indeed, according to Q. *4:12b, a childless man might designate a daughter-in-law or wife as his testamentary heir; the same verse awards siblings who have been disinherited one-third of the estate as compensation.[10]

Presumably, it was the proto-Islamic law of inheritance that was in force when the Prophet died in 11/632. That would soon change. As we have seen in Appendix 2, these rules are said to have been suspended for a second time insofar as they applied to the Prophet.

Islamic Inheritance Law: The Science of the Shares

The revision of *4:12b had far-reaching and no doubt unforeseen consequences, triggering a chain reaction that resulted in the transformation of the proto-Islamic law of inheritance into the *ʿilm al-farāʾiḍ* or *science of the shares*. Whereas proto-Islamic inheritance law made a clear distinction between testate succession and intestacy, the *science of the shares* imposes compulsory rules for the division of property. Like the abolition of adoption, this was a radical break with the past. The general outlines of this transformation may be summarized as follows.

1. In its revised form, the opening clause of Q. 4:12b refers to a childless man or woman who dies leaving collateral relatives. The sub-verse awards a brother or sister one-sixth each; if three or more siblings inherit jointly, they divide one-third of the estate on a per capita basis, irrespective of gender. This was a compulsory share.

2. The revision of Q. *4:12b created a secondary problem. Surely, if a childless man dies leaving siblings as his closest blood relatives, the heirs should inherit more than one-third of the estate, as specified in 4:12b. To rectify this problem, supplementary legislation was added at the end of *Sūrat al-Nisāʾ*. The new legislation specified that one sister inherits half of the estate and two or more sisters inherit two-thirds; one brother inherits the entire estate and two or more brothers divide the estate on a per capita basis. If brothers and sisters inherit jointly, the share of a male is equal to that of two females.

3. Both Q. 4:12b and 4:176 award shares of the estate to the siblings of a childless man or woman. In v. 12b, siblings inherit a maximum of one-third of the estate and males and females inherit equally. In v. 176, brothers and sisters inherit most if not all of the estate (see point 2, above), with the share of a male being equal to that of two females. The contradiction was eliminated by glossing the word *sibling* in 4:12b as *uterine* sibling and the same word in 4:176 as *consanguine and/or germane* sibling. This solution, which is attributed to Ubayy b. Kaʿb (d. 30/650–1) and Saʿd b. Abī Waqqāṣ (d. 55/675), may have been introduced during the second quarter of the first century A.H.

4. Whereas in proto-Islamic law, a husband or wife did not inherit from one another upon intestacy (it will be recalled that the award of a fractional share of the estate to a surviving spouse in *4:12a applied to the *exceptional* case of an indigent or unendowed spouse), in the *science of the shares*, the exceptional award was transformed into a compulsory share. The addition of husbands and wives to the category of *heirs* upset the mathematical system upon which proto-Islamic inheritance law was based and caused the new system to short-circuit, e.g., by awarding as much as 125 percent of the estate to certain combinations of heirs or by awarding a mother a share that is twice as large as that of a father.[11]

5. In their revised form, vv. 12a and 12b were fused together into a single verse that awards compulsory shares of the estate to husbands and wives and brothers and sisters. Q. 4:12a-b, in turn, was fused together with Q. 4:11 (the original *inheritance verse*). To these two verses was added the supplementary legislation at the end of *Sūrat al-Nisāʾ* which became Q. 4:176. Together these three verses—4:11, 12, and 176—form the basis of the *science of the shares*, which imposes compulsory rules for the division of property.[12]

6. Once the shares mentioned in Q. 4:11, 12, and 176 had become compulsory rules, it appeared as if 4:11, which awards a fractional share of the estate inter alia to a parent, contradicts 2:180, which instructs a testator to leave a bequest for parents. Similarly 4:12a, which awards a fractional share of the estate to a widow, appears to contradict 2:240, which encourages a testator to leave a bequest for his widow. The apparent contradictions were resolved by teaching that 4:11 abrogated 2:180 and that 4:12 abrogated 2:240. This solution, which is attributed to Ibn ʿAbbās (d. 68/687) and Ibn ʿUmar (d. 74/693), is likely to have been introduced by the last quarter of the first century A.H. The argument for abrogation was supported by the legal maxim, "no bequest to an heir," which circulated during the first three quarters of the second/eighth century. It was not until the end of the second/eighth century that the maxim appeared as a prophetic dictum for the first time.[13]

7. The *science of the shares* reduces but does not totally eliminate the power of testation. A person contemplating death may leave a bequest of no more than one-third of his or her estate, on the condition that no heir receives a bequest (without the permission of the other heirs). The restriction of bequests to one-third was established by a maxim attributed to the Prophet: "A bequest may not exceed one-third of the estate." This statement is mentioned in a *ḥadīth* transmitted by Saʿd b. Abī Waqqāṣ (d. 55/675) to his children approximately thirty years after the Prophet is said to have uttered it.[14]

Abbreviations

BNF	Bibliothèque Nationale de France, Arabe, 328.
BT	*The Babylonian Talmud.*
PRE	*Pirḳe de-Rabbi Eliezer.*
RPIL	Crone, Patricia. *Roman, Provincial and Islamic Law: The Origins of the Islamic Patronate.*
**EI*[2]	*Encyclopaedia of Islam.* 2nd ed.
EI[3]	*Encyclopaedia of Islam.* 3rd ed. (in progress).
EQ	*Encyclopaedia of the Qurʾān.*
SQH	Powers, David S. *Studies in Qurʾān and Ḥadīth: The Formation of the Islamic Law of Inheritance.*
SRL	*Syro-Roman Lawbook*
TDOT	*Theological Dictionary of the Old Testament.*
HANEL	Westbrook, Raymond, ed. *A History of Ancient Near Eastern Law.*

Notes

Preface

1. Powers, "The Islamic Law of Inheritance, Reconsidered."
2. Powers, *SQH.*
3. Motzki, "Review of *Studies in Qur'ān and Ḥadīth,*" 20: "Obwohl ich P[owers] in zentralen Punkt nicht folgen kann."
4. Ziadeh, "Review of *Studies in Qur'ān and Ḥadīth.*"
5. Madelung, "Review of *Studies in Qur'ān and Ḥadīth.*"
6. Rippin, "Ibn ʿAbbās's *Al-lughāt fī'l Qur'ān.*"
7. Burton, "Review of *Studies in Qur'ān and Ḥadīth.*"
8. Gilliot, "Exégèse et sémantique institutionnelle dans le commentaire de Tabari," 80ff.
9. Crone, "Two Legal Problems Bearing on the Early History of the Qur'ān," 8–9.
10. Kimber, "The Qur'anic Law of Inheritance."
11. Dutton, *The Origins of Islamic Law,* 109–12, 135.
12. Cilardo, *The Qur'ānic Term* Kalāla.
13. Wael B. Hallaq, ed., *The Formation of Islamic Law,* xxv.
14. See, for example, Powers, *Law, Society, and Culture in the Maghrib: 1300–1500.*
15. Westbrook, ed., *HANEL.*
16. Ibid., 1:588.
17. Déroche and Noseda, *Sources de la transmission manuscrite du texte coranique,* vol. 1.
18. On the unthinkable in Islamic discourse, see the many writings of Mohammed Arkoun, e.g., *Rethinking Islam: Common Questions, Uncommon Answers.*

Chapter 1. The Foundation Narratives of Judaism, Christianity, and Islam

1. Levenson, *The Death and Resurrection of the Beloved Son,* 70.
2. Unlike later Calvinist theology, the Jewish understanding of chosenness does not entail the damnation of those who have not been elected. In Gen. 9:1–17 God establishes an "everlasting covenant" with Noah and his descendants "and all living creatures." See Levenson, "The Universal Horizon of Biblical Particularism"; Kaminsky, *Yet I Loved Jacob.*
3. *The Anchor Bible Dictionary,* s.vv. Edom (J. R. Bartlett); Ishmaelites (Ernst Axel Knauf).
4. In the biblical narrative, the only subsequent contact between father and son takes place at Abraham's burial in the cave of Machpelah, at which both Isaac and Ishmael are present (Gen. 25:9). According to postbiblical *midrash,* however, Abraham did attempt to reestablish contact with Ishmael. See Chapter 7.
5. The marriage between Milcah and Nahor was a marriage between an uncle and a niece: Milcah was the daughter of Haran, whose brothers were Nahor and Abraham. Isaac was Milcah's nephew.

6. Bethuel plays no part in Gen. 24. See Chapter 7.

7. There is no specific and unequivocal statement in the Synoptic Gospels to the effect that Joseph was the natural father of Jesus. The very possibility of a sexual relationship between Joseph and Mary is excluded by the doctrine of the virgin birth. According to the *Protevangelium of James*, after Mary became pregnant, Joseph said to the High Priest Annai, "I am pure concerning her." In the *Gospel of Pseudo-Matthew*, a midwife who examined Mary after she had given birth to Jesus established that "there has been no spilling of blood in his birth, no pain in bringing him forth. A virgin has conceived, a virgin has brought forth, and a virgin she remains." See Elliot, *Apocryphal New Testament*, 62–63, 93. See further Chapter 7.

8. On covenant in the Qurʾān, see Gwynne, *Logic, Rhetoric, and Legal Reasoning in the Qurʾān*, chap. 1.

9. Both Hūd and Ṣāliḥ are said to have been descendants of Noah through his son Shem; Shuʿayb is identified as Jethro, the father-in-law of Moses. See EI^2, s.vv. Hūd (A. J. Wensinck-[Ch. Pellat]), Ṣāliḥ (A. Rippin), Shuʿayb (A. Rippin). In addition, the non-Arab prophet Dhū al-Qarnayn is said to have been a descendant of Abraham on his father's side. See *EQ*, s.v. Alexander (John Renard).

10. For details and variants, see *The History of al-Ṭabarī*, 9:127–28, note 876.

11. See again Levenson, *The Death and Resurrection of the Beloved Son*, passim.

12. See Wansbrough, *The Sectarian Milieu*.

13. In addition to Wansbrough, notable exceptions include Crone, *Meccan Trade and the Rise of Islam*; Rubin, *The Eye of the Beholder: The Life of Muhammad as Viewed by the Early Muslims*; Sizgorich, "Narrative and Community in Islamic Late Antiquity"; idem, "'Do Prophets Come with a Sword?' Conquests, Empire, and Historical Narrative in the Early Islamic World"; Maghen, "Intertwined Triangles: Remarks on the Relationship Between Two Prophetic Scandals"; idem, "Davidic Motifs in the Biography of Muḥammad." See also Reeves, ed., *Bible and Qurʾān: Essays in Scriptural Intertextuality*.

Chapter 2. Adoption in the Near East: From Antiquity to the Rise of Islam

1. The following summary of adoption practices in the ancient Near East relies on *HANEL*, 1:50–54.

2. Adoption served other functions as well. A man who wished to transfer the family gods to someone who was not a blood relative first had to incorporate the desired heir into the family through adoption. The male who was adopted often acquired the status of a legitimate heir and the right to inherit from the adoptor. Adoption also was a means by which a man could confer legitimacy on natural children born to him by a slave concubine. A slave owner could manumit a slave and then adopt him as his son. Adoption also was used to facilitate the transfer of land between people who were not blood relatives. In some ancient Near Eastern societies, ancestral property could not be alienated outside the family. A landowner who wanted to sell his property to a stranger might adopt the purchaser and convey the land to him as an inheritance, with immediate possession; in return, the adoptee/purchaser would compensate the seller/adoptor with a filial gift that was equivalent to the value of the land. Alternatively, an elderly person might adopt a nonrelative and award him his estate in return for a pension; or a creditor might adopt a man or woman who owed him money and clear the debt in return for a pension. In such cases, the adoption was a legal fiction. See *HANEL*, 1:51; Seters, "Jacob's Marriages and Ancient Near East Customs: A Reexamination," 385–86; Frymer-Kensky, "Patriarchal Family Rela-

tionships and Near Eastern Law"; Westbrook, "Care of the Elderly in the Ancient Near East: Introduction."

3. The preamble contains the names of the adoptor and the adoptee and a record of the act of adoption. This is followed by the conditions of the specific contract, e.g., a statement designating the adoptee as heir; a safety clause protecting the inheritance of the adoptee in the event that the adoptor subsequently produces a natural son; and the obligation of the adopted son to care for his adoptive father in old age. The contract ends with a penalty clause specifying the monetary consequences that follow from dissolution of the adoptive tie. See *HANEL*, 1:53–55. Cf. Seters, "Jacob's Marriages," 385–86.

4. *HANEL*, 1:53, 673–75, 711, 728–29.

5. Nuzi was destroyed by fire in the middle of the second millennium B.C.E. In 1925, an archaeological excavation was conducted on the site by Edward Chiera, who discovered more than one thousand tablets inside the ruins of an ancient house. These tablets, written in the cuneiform script and the Akkadian language, record the personal affairs and business transactions of a single family over the course of four generations. Many of the tablets deal with adoption and inheritance. See *Joint Expedition with the Iraq Museum at Nuzi*; cf. *Excavations at Nuzi conducted by the Semitic Museum and the Fogg Art Museum of Harvard University*. The practices documented at Nuzi were widespread throughout the ancient Near East.

6. On matrimonial adoption, see Grosz, "On Some Aspects of the Adoption of Women at Nuzi"; Breneman, "Nuzi Marriage Tablets."

7. Grosz, "On Some Aspects of the Adoption of Women at Nuzi," 133–41.

8. Ibid., 141–45.

9. Ibid., 145–50.

10. MacDowell, *The Law in Classical Athens*, 99–101.

11. Nicholas, *An Introduction to Roman Law*, 65ff.

12. Ibid., 77.

13. See, for example, Matyszak, *The Sons of Caesar: Imperial Rome's First Dynasty*.

14. *HANEL*, 1:737ff. Although the material record is scanty, there is no evidence of adoption practices in Canaan prior to the Israelite conquest (2000–1000 B.C.E.). The orthodox Jewish position on adoption has been articulated by Rabbi Joseph B. Soloveitchik: "Judaism did not recognize the Roman institution of adoption since the Roman concept is directed toward substituting a legal fiction for a biological fact and thus creating the illusion of a natural relationship between the foster parents and the adopted son. Judaism stated its case in no uncertain terms: . . . the natural relationship must not be altered." See Soloveitchik, *Family Redeemed: Essays on Family Relationships*, 60–61.

15. BT, *Yebamot*.

16. See, for example, Phillips, "Some Aspects of Family Law in Pre-Exilic Israel"; and Scott, *Adoption as Sons of God: An Exegetical Investigation into the Background of Υιοθεσια in the Pauline Corpus*. For a different view, which has now been refuted by Scott, see H. Donner, "Adoption oder Legitimation?"

17. If Mendelsohn is correct, Ex. 21:7–11 is a reflex of the Nuzian *ṭuppi martūti u kallūti*. See Mendelsohn, "The Conditional Sale into Slavery of Free-Born Daughters in Nuzi and the Law of Ex. 21:7–11," 190–95; cf. Paul, "Exod. 21:10: A Threefold Maintenance Clause," 48–53.

18. Additional examples: Abram's lament that his servant Dammesek Eliezer would become his heir in the absence of a son (Gen. 15:2–3) is based on the assumption that the servant would be adopted. When Abram's wife Sarai thought that she was unable to have children, she gave her husband a female slave, Hagar, so that "perhaps I shall

have a son through her" (Gen. 16:2). When Rachel bore no children to Jacob, she gave him her female slave, Bilhah. "Consort with her," she said to her husband, "that she may bear on my knees [an act that symbolizes adoption—DSP] and that through her I too may have children" (Gen. 30:3–8). Similarly, the sons of Machir were "born on his [Joseph's] knees" (again, a reference to adoption; Gen. 15:23). When Ruth gave birth to Obed, Naomi, who was Ruth's mother-in-law through her first husband, Mahlon (who died childless), "took the child and held it to her bosom." The neighbors exclaimed, "A son is born to Naomi!" In 1 Chr. 2:34–35, Sheshen, who had no sons, gave one of his daughters in marriage to Jarhah, an Egyptian slave of his (presumably after manumitting and adopting him), and she bore him Attai, who is listed as one of Sheshen's descendants. The fact that Barzilai took the name of his father-in-law points to his adoption (Ezra 2:61, Neh. 7:63). All of these examples are cited in *Anchor Bible Dictionary*, s.v. Adoption (F. W. Knobloch).

19. Porten, *The Elephantine Papyri in English*, 74, 80. These documents were drawn up between 521 and 359 B.C.E., when Egypt was controlled by Persia, and Aramaic was the lingua franca of the empire. In one document, dated 416 B.C.E., Zaccur the son of Meshullam gave up for adoption to Uriah son of Mahseiah a house-born slave of his by the name of Jedaniah. Uriah made a threefold declaration that Jedaniah was to be his son ("My son he shall be") and that Jedaniah would not subsequently be pressed into slavery, enslaved, or branded by his adoptive father, his heirs, his beneficiaries, or his representatives. The penalty for doing so was set at 30 *karsh*. Eight witnesses attested to the legal procedure. See Porten, *Elephantine Papyri*, 234–35, B42; cf. Yaron, *Aramaic Papyri*, 36, where the author observes that the adoptee in this case probably acquired a "claim to the inheritance of his adoptive father, although no mention is made of the point." In a second document, Zaccur's father, Meshullam (also son of Zaccur), has a female slave Tamet who was married to Anani and gave birth to a daughter named Jehoishma. In a last will and testament drawn up on 12 June 427 B.C.E., Meshullam declared that upon his death, Tamet and Jehoishma were to be released from slavery. In the meantime, however, mother and daughter were to become part of Meshullam's family, his adoptive children and the adoptive sisters of his son Zaccur. In return, Tamet and Jehoishma agreed to serve Meshullam "as a son or daughter supports his father, in your lifetime." Following Meshullam's death, they promised to support his son Zaccur, "like a son who supports his father." If they failed to fulfill this promise, they were liable to pay a fine of 50 *karsh*. The document was attested by four witnesses (Porten, *The Elephantine Papyri*, 220–22, B39).

20. Scott, *Adoption as Sons of God*, 81–83, citing *Corpus Inscriptionum Regni Bosporani*, nos. 1281, 1283, 1285, 1286. On the possibility that the Essenes practiced adoption, see Scott, ibid., citing Josephus, *The Wars of the Jews*, 2.120–21.

21. Verse 14, it will be noted, uses the same formula (*ve-hû yehyī lî le-ben*) as used in the adoption of Moses by Pharaoh's daughter (*va-yehî lâ le-ben*; Ex. 2:10). See also II Kings 16:7 ("Ahaz sent messengers to King Tiglath-pileser of Assyria to say, 'I am your servant and your son . . . '"); Jer. 31:9b ("For I am ever a Father to Israel, Ephraim is My first-born"); Ezek. 16; Hos. 11:1 ("I fell in love with Israel when he was still a child; and I have called [him] My son ever since Egypt"); and Ps. 2:7 ("You are My son, I have fathered you this day").

22. Par. 24 reads as follows: "And after these things shall a Star arise to you from Jacob in peace, and a Man shall rise from my seed, like the Sun of righteousness, walking with the sons of men in meekness and righteousness, and no sin shall be found in Him. And the heavens shall be opened above Him, to shed forth the blessing of the Spirit from the Holy Father; and He shall shed forth a spirit of grace upon you, and you shall be unto Him sons in truth, and you shall walk in His commandments, the

first and the last. This is the Branch of God Most High, and this the Well-spring unto life for all flesh. Then shall the scepter of my kingdom shine forth, and from your root shall arise a stem; and in it shall arise a rod of righteousness to the Gentiles, to judge and to save all that call upon the Lord." See *The Testament of the Twelve Patriarchs.*

23. Sanders, *The Historical Figure of Jesus.*

24. In Luke 1:36, 39, Mary is identified as a relative of Elizabeth and Zechariah, the parents of John the Baptist.

25. *The Apocryphal New Testament*, 61, par. 10.1. Toward the end of the seventh century C.E., Jacob of Edessa (d. 708) made the same point in a letter to John the Stylite (d. 738): "Mary the holy virgin and begetter of God is of the race of David, although this is not illustrated by the Scriptures." See F. Nau, "Lettre de Jacques d'Édesse sur la généalogie de la sainte Vierge," *Revue de l'Orient Chrétien* 6 (1901): 517–22/522–31, at 519–20, 525–26, cited in Hoyland, *Seeing Islam as Others Saw It*, 166–67.

26. For another allusion to adoption in the New Testament, see John 19, where, at the crucifixion, Jesus says to his mother, referring to his beloved disciple, "Woman, here is your son" (v. 26); after which he says to his beloved disciple, "Here is your mother" (v. 27). These two statements appear to have created an adoptive mother-son relationship between Mary Mother of Jesus and the beloved disciple. The verse concludes, "And from that hour the disciple took her into his own home" (v. 27).

27. Scott, *Adoption as Sons of God*, 267–70 and passim.

28. Ibid.

29. These Christological controversies affected the text of the New Testament. Proto-orthodox scribes of the second and third centuries C.E. modified the early manuscripts to make them conform more closely to their own Christological beliefs. For example, the scribes targeted passages that originally referred to Joseph—without qualification—as Jesus' father or parent (Luke 2:23, 43, 48). On Adoptionism and the impact of anti-Adoptionism on the New Testament textual tradition, see Ehrman, *The Orthodox Corruption of Scripture*, 47–119; idem, *Lost Christianities: The Battle for Scripture and the Faiths We Never Knew*, 101.

30. See Baum and Winkler, *The Church of the East: A Concise History.*

31. Goody, *The Development of the Family and Marriage in Europe*, 73.

32. For criticism of Goody's thesis, see Verden, "Virgins and Widows: European Kinship and Early Christianity," 497ff.; Brundage, "Adoption in the Medieval *Ius Commune*," 896–97; and Reid, *Power over the Body, Equality in the Family: Rights and Domestic Relations in Medieval Canon Law*, 179–80, 193–94.

33. See now *Das Syrisch-Römische Rechtsbuch*, new ed., ed. Selb and Kaufhold, which contains a scientific edition of the text with accompanying German translation. Previously, the *SRL* was translated into English by Arthur Vööbus as *The Syro-Roman Lawbook.* Cf. *Syrisch-Römisches Rechtsbuch aus dem fünften Jahrhundert*, ed. Bruns and Sachau.

34. The textual history of the *SRL* has been the subject of considerable discussion among classicists. Selb and Kaufhold have now established that the original Greek version was compiled in the last two decades of the fifth century C.E., approximately 150 years after the death of Constantine and approximately 50 years after the publication of the Theodosian code in 438. The compiler is likely to have been a certain Amblichus who was a professor of law in Beirut. The *SRL* is not a law code but rather a series of interpretations of key texts in collections of Imperial Constitutions. On the history of the text and the manuscript tradition, see *Das Syrisch-Römische Rechtsbuch*, vol. 1.

35. The rules and regulations of the *SRL*, which reflect the attempts of Christian emperors to regulate legal practice in the Roman empire, including Syria, may have penetrated the Hijaz. Muḥammad is reported to have had access to certain uniden-

tified writings, documents, or manuscripts (*kutub*) written in Syriac and to have instructed his secretary Zayd b. Thābit (d. 45/665) to perfect his knowledge of Syriac so that he could read, understand, and—presumably—translate these texts into Arabic. See Ibn Abī Dā'ūd, *Kitāb al-Maṣāḥif*, 3. It is conceivable that the *SRL* was one of the Syriac texts possessed by Muḥammad and his Companions. If so, the *SRL* is a possible source of Qur'ānic law. For a different view, see Crone, *RPIL*, 12, where the author argues that the *SRL* "has no bearing on the question of the sources of Islamic law."

36. See Vööbus, *Discovery of very important Manuscript Sources for the Syro-Roman Lawbook*. Writing in 1986, Crone (*RPIL*, 12) argued that the text was "almost certainly" translated into Syriac after the Arabic conquests and "very likely" in response to them; and that the purpose of the translation was to refute Muslim arguments that Christianity had no law. She also suggested that a passage in Ishoʿbokht, who wrote ca. 775 C.E., contains the first reference to the law book among the Nestorians of Iraq (ibid.). A generation later, Timothy the Patriarch (780–823) refers to the contents of the law book as "imperial laws . . . issued in accordance with the sacred synods of the fathers" and as an example of "the pure laws of Christianity" (*RPIL*, 119, note 118, citing Nallino, "Sul libro siro-romano," 558). The lawbook became a showpiece of Christian law that was widely accepted among eastern Christianity (*RPIL*, 12).

37. *Justinian's Institutes*, trans. Birks and McLeod, index, s.vv. adoption, adrogation.

38. Nicholas, *An Introduction to Roman Law*, 76–80; Reid, *Power over the Body*, 180–81, citing Gaius, *Institutes*, 1.97–1.99 (trans. F. De Zulueta).

39. Nicholas, *An Introduction to Roman Law*, 79. An adoptive relationship created the same bars to marriage as a natural one; hence the maxim "adoption imitates nature." On adoption at Dura-Europus, see Wells et al., *The Excavations at Dura-Europas*, pt. 1, *The Parchments and Papyri*. There is no mention of adoption in the Nessana archives, on which see Kraemer, *Excavations at Nessana*, vol. 3, *Non-Literary Papyri*.

40. See János, "The Four Sources of Law in Zoroastrian and Islamic Jurisprudence," 303–4, 311.

41. On adoption in Sasanian law, see *The Book of a Thousand Judgements (a Sasanian Law-book)*, **16**, 2–5; **26**, 10–12; **29**, 6–9; **42**, 1–5 and 9–14; **69**.1–**71**.7; **110**, 15–17; ***A*40**, 11–14, 15–16. Cf. *Das sasanidische Rechtsbuch "Mātakdān i hazār dātistān" (Part II)*; Macuch, *Rechtskasuistik und Gerichtspraxis zu Beginn des siebenten Jahrhunderts in Iran*.

Chapter 3. The Abolition of Adoption in Early Islam

1. See Arazi, "Les Enfants adultérins [*daʿīs*] dans la société arabe ancienne."

2. According to Ṭabarsī, *Majmaʿ al-bayān li-ʿulūm al-qur'ān*, 8:180–81, "The Arabs used to accord adoptees the same legal status as they accorded natural sons" (*inna al-ʿarab kānū yunazzilūna al-adʿiyā'a manzilat^a^ al-abnā' fī al-ḥukm*). Following Ṭabarsī, Arazi ("Les Enfants adultérins," 13–14) concludes that some adoptees were successfully integrated into their adoptive families and clans. The point has been contested by Landau-Tasseron, according to whom the legal status of an adoptee was not equal to that of a true son, and adoptees were not fully integrated into their adoptive families. See Landau-Tasseron, "Adoption, Acknowledgement of Paternity and False Genealogical Claims in Arabian and Islamic Societies," 171–73.

3. Qurṭubī, *al-Jāmiʿ li-aḥkām al-qur'ān*, 14:119.

4. Al-Miqdād, whose father was ʿAmr b. Thaʿlaba, was born ca. 585 C.E. among the tribe of Kinda but had to leave his family after he wounded a fellow tribesman.

He fled to Mecca, where he was adopted by al-Aswad b. ʿAbd Yaghūth and became a confederate of his adoptive father's tribe of Zuhra. He was called al-Miqdād b. ʿAbd Yaghūth until the institution of adoption was abolished, at which time he attempted to recover his original name, albeit unsuccessfully. See Qurṭubī, *Jāmiʿ*, 14:120; *EI*², s.v. al-Miḳdād b. ʿAmr (G. H. A. Juynboll).

5. Landau-Tasseron, "Adoption," 186, note 98, citing Santillana, *Istituzioni di diritto musulmano Malichita con riguardo anche al sistema sciafiita*, 1:196, note 29. On ʿĀmir b. al-Ṭufayl, see *EI*², s.v.

6. *EI*², s.v. Shuraḥbīl b. Ḥasana (C. E. Bosworth). His patrilineal *nasab* was . . . b. ʿAbdallāh b. al-Muṭāḥ b. Amr; cf. Ibn ʿAbd al-Barr, *al-Istīʿāb fī maʿrifat al-aṣḥāb*, on the margins of Ibn Ḥajar al-ʿAsqalānī, *al-Iṣāba fī tamyīz al-ṣaḥāba*, 2:140; Ibn Ḥajar al-ʿAsqalānī, *Tahdhīb al-tahdhīb*, 4:285.

7. Mizzī, *Tahdhīb al-kamāl fī asmāʾ al-rijāl*, 16:505, 508; Ibn ʿAsākir, *Taʾrīkh madīnat Dimashq*, 34:172.

8. Mizzī, *Tahdhīb al-kamāl*, 27:456; Dhahabī, *Siyar aʿlām al-nubalāʾ*, 4:66–67; Baghdādī, *Taʾrīkh Baghdād*, 13:234.

9. Ṭabarsī, *Majmaʿ al-bayān*, 9:183.3–8; cf. ʿAbd al-Razzāq al-Ṣanʿānī, *Tafsīr*, 3:42, note 2. For details and variants, see *The History of al-Ṭabarī*, 9:127–28, note 876.

10. On Zayd, see Ibn Saʿd, *Kitāb al-ṭabaqāt al-kabīr*, III/i, 27–32; Balādhurī, *Ansāb al-ashrāf*, 1:467–73; *The History of al-Ṭabarī*, 39:6–11; Ibn ʿAsākir, *Taʾrīkh madīnat Dimashq*, 19:342–74; *EI*², s.v. Zayd b. Ḥāritha (M. Lecker).

11. Ibn Saʿd, *Kitāb al-ṭabaqāt al-kabīr*, III/i, 30.1–10; idem, *al-Ṭabaqāt al-kubrā*, 4:61.15; Balādhurī, *Ansāb*, 1:470.17–18, 471.1–5; Ibn ʿAsākir, *Taʾrīkh madīnat Dimashq*, 19:353–54. Cf. Kister, "*Al-Taḥannuth*: An Inquiry into the Meaning of a Term," 225, end of note 13 (on the authority of al-Zuhrī).

12. On Umm Ayman, whose birth name was Baraka, see *The History of al-Ṭabarī*, 39:191–92, 199, 287.

13. In an effort to entice Zayd to marry an older woman, Muḥammad is reported to have said, "Whoever wants to experience the pleasure of marrying one of the women of Paradise, let him marry Umm Ayman." Balādhurī, *Ansāb*, 1:472.

14. On Usāma, see Ibn Saʿd, *al-Ṭabaqāt al-kubrā*, 4:61–72; Balādhurī, *Ansāb*, 1:473–76; *The History of al-Ṭabarī*, 39:65, 99, 289; *EI*², s.v. Usāma b. Zayd (V. Vacca).

15. Ibn Saʿd, *al-Ṭabaqāt al-kubrā*, 4:63.5–17; Bukhārī, *Ṣaḥīḥ*, bāb 24, Manāqib, no. 3595; bāb 31, Farāʾiḍ, nos. 6856–57; Muslim, *Ṣaḥīḥ*, bāb 11, Riḍāʿ, no. 3691; Abū Dāʾūd, *Sunan*, 31, Ṭalāq, no. 2269; Nasāʾī, *Sunan*, 51, Ṭalāq, no. 3507; Ibn Māja, *Sunan*, 21, Aḥkām, no. 2439; Ibn ʿAsākir, *Taʾrīkh madīnat Dimashq*, 19:351. Cf. Maʿjūz, *Wasāʾil al-ithbāt fī al-fiqh al-islamī*, 217.

16. Ibn Saʿd, *Kitāb al-ṭabaqāt al-kabīr*, III/i, 29.3ff., 30.18–31.1; Balādhurī, *Ansāb*, 1:471.6ff; Ibn ʿAsākir, *Taʾrīkh madīnat Dimashq*, 19:357–58.

17. Madelung, *The Succession to Muḥammad: A Study of the Early Caliphate*, 212–13. The translation is Madelung's, according to whom ʿAlī's identification of Zayd as one of the *ahl al-bayt* is "quite incompatible" with the views of later Shiʿis. He might have added: with Sunnis as well (213, note 285).

18. On Zayd's military career, see Ibn Saʿd, *Kitāb al-ṭabaqāt al-kabīr*, III/i, 31.1–16; idem, *al-Ṭabaqāt al-kubrā*, 2:36, 86–90, 128; Balādhurī, *Ansāb*, 1:473.1–3; cf. Watt, *Muhammad at Medina*, Excursus B (List of Expeditions and Dates).

19. Khalid Yahya Blankinship has suggested that the lives and careers of Zayd, Usāma, and Jaʿfar b. Abī Ṭālib merit the careful attention of historians. I could not agree more. See Blankinship, "Imārah, Khilāfah, and Imāmah: The Origin of the Succession to the Prophet Muhammad."

20. Balādhurī, *Ansāb*, 1:473.12 (fifty years old); Ibn ʿAsākir, *Taʾrīkh madīnat Dimashq*, 19:368.8–9 (fifty-five years old).

21. Ibn Saʿd, *Kitāb al-ṭabaqāt al-kabīr*, III/i, 31.9–13; Ibn ʿAsākir, *Taʾrīkh madīnat Dimashq*, 19:366.6–10. Note the variant in Balādhurī, *Ansāb*, 1:472 (bottom): *wa-in baqiya baʿdahu istakhlafahu ʿalā al-madīna* ("Had [Zayd] outlived [the Prophet], he would have made him the *khalīfa of Medina*"—emphasis added).

22. Ibn Saʿd, *al-Ṭabaqāt al-kubrā*, 4:61.16–18 and 4:62.10–20.

23. Ibid., 4:64.20–65.

24. Ibid., 4:64.1–19; Balādhurī, *Ansāb*, 1:469.19–20; Lane, *An Arabic-English Lexicon*, s.v. r-d-f.

25. N.B. Usāma's marriage to Zaynab bt. Ḥanzala would have taken place at just about the time that his father Zayd married Zaynab bt. Jaḥsh. It is curious that father and son should both marry a woman with the same name. Be that as it may, after Usāma had divorced Zaynab bt. Ḥanzala, Muḥammad was concerned to find a new husband for "the fair one who eats sparingly" (*al-waḍīʾatu ʾl-ghanīn*) and he arranged for her to marry Nuʿaym b. ʿAbdallāh al-Naḥḥām, to whom she bore a son, Ibrāhīm, who was killed at the Battle of Ḥarra in 63/683. Ibn Saʿd, *al-Ṭabaqāt al-kubrā*, 4:72.6–13.

26. Ibid., 4:71 (bottom)–72.5. The recycling of the names of key members of the Prophet's family merits attention: Usāma had sons named Muḥammad, Zayd, Ḥasan and Ḥusayn; wives named Zaynab and Fāṭima; and a daughter named ʿĀʾisha.

27. Ibid., 4:66, l. –1 (eighteen years old), 4:72.16 (twenty years old).

28. See *The History of al-Ṭabarī*, 9:202, 205, note 1407. *Isnād*: Ibn Ḥumayd—Salamah—Muḥammad b. Isḥāq (d. 150/767)—ʿAbdallāh b. Abī Bakr—Kathīr b. ʿAbdallāh and others—ʿAbdallāh b. al-ʿAbbās (d. 68/688). The list is as follows: ʿAlī b. Abī Ṭālib, al-ʿAbbās b. ʿAbd al-Muṭṭalib, al-Faḍl b. al-ʿAbbās, Quthām b. al-ʿAbbās, Usāma b. Zayd, and Shuqrān, freedman of the Messenger of God. The first four men were blood relatives of the Prophet; the last was his *mawlā*. The fact that Ibn ʿAbbās does *not* identify Usāma b. Zayd as the Prophet's *mawlā* suggests that Usāma was present in his capacity as one of the *ahl al-bayt*. Be that as it may, it is curious that Madelung would say, referring to this report, that Usāma b. Zayd and Shuqrān were "*both* clients of Muḥammad" (emphasis added). See Madelung, *The Succession to Muḥammad*, 27.

29. Ibn Saʿd, *Kitāb al-ṭabaqāt al-kabīr*, II/ii, 76–77; *The History of al-Ṭabarī*, 9:164–66, 202.

30. On the expedition to Ubna, see Wāqidī, *Kitāb al-maghāzī*, 3:1117ff.; Ibn Saʿd, *al-Ṭabaqāt al-kubrā*, 2:189–92, 4:65–68. I intend to analyze the narrative account of this battle in a future publication.

31. Ibid., 4:70–72; *EI*[2], s.v. Usāma b. Zayd (V. Vacca); Blankinship, "Imārah, Khilāfah, and Imāmah."

32. This area of the law is treated under the category of the foundling (*laqīṭ*). The legal mechanisms involved include *istilḥāq*, *kafāla* and *iqrār*. See Pollack et al., "Classical Religious Perspectives of Adoption Law," 732ff.

33. See, for example, Andrae, *Mohammed: The Man and His Faith*, 154; Watt, *Muhammad at Medina*, index, s.vv. Zayd b. Ḥārithah, Zaynab bint Jaḥsh; Stowasser, *Women in the Qurʾan, Traditions, and Interpretation*, 87–89; *EI*[2], s.vv. Zayd b. Ḥāritha (M. Lecker), Zaynab bt. Djaḥsh (C. E. Bosworth).

34. See, for example, Ṭabarī, *Tafsīr* (1373/1954), 21:117–25 and 22:11–16; Ṭabarsī, *Majmaʿ al-bayān*, 8:127–48, 176–81; Qurṭubī, *Jāmiʿ*, 14:116–22, 188–97.

35. Jeffery, "Ghevond's Text of the Correspondence between ʿUmar II and Leo III."

36. *Die Schriften des Johannes von Damaskos*, C/CI, 63–64; *Patrologiae cursus completus. Series graeca*, vol. 94, 765C–769B, cited in Hoyland, *Seeing Islam as Others Saw It*, 488.

37. Voorhis, "John of Damascus on the Muslim Heresy," 142. Cf. John of Seville's letter to Paul Albar in *Istoria de Mahomet*: "His followers say that this aforementioned wicked prophet shone out by his many miracles, such as that he took the wife of another by reason of the ardour of his lust and joined her to himself in marriage," cited in Hoyland, *Seeing Islam*, 512–13.

38. Voorhis, "John of Damascus on the Muslim Heresy," 142. This is John of Damascus's understanding of Q. 2:230, as translated into English by Voorhis.

39. Ibid., 142.

40. Again, this is John of Damascus's understanding of the verse, as translated into English by Voorhis.

41. Daniel, *Islam and the West: The Making of an Image*, index, s.v. Zaynab bint Jaḥsh.

42. Smith, *Kinship and Marriage in Early Arabia*, 51; Roberts, *The Social Laws of the Qorân*, 49–51. Cf. Stern, *Marriage in Early Arabia*, 105, where the author mentions the episode without making a value judgment.

43. Sonbol, "Adoption in Islamic Society: A Historical Survey," 45–67. Also useful is Arazi, "Les enfants adultérins [*daʿīs*]," in which the author analyzes the concept of lineage (*nasab*) and false claims of paternity through the lens of early Arabic poetry; and Landau-Tasseron, "Adoption," where the author treats the same subject from a historical perspective. See also *EI*², vol. 9 (supplement), s.v. Tabannin (E. Chaumont). A monograph by an anthropologist on the subject of abandoned children and secret adoption in contemporary Morocco contains interesting observations on adoption and its abolition; see Bargach, *Orphans of Islam: Family, Abandonment, and Secret Adoption in Morocco*, 45–71.

Chapter 4. The Repudiation of the Beloved of the Messenger of God

1. *EQ*, s.v. Collection of the Qurʾān (John Burton), 353a.

2. On this term, see Gwynne, *Logic, Rhetoric, and Legal Reasoning*, chapter 3 ("The *Sunna* of God").

3. The popular preachers included men like Abū Idrīs al-Khawlānī (d. 80/699), who would sit on the steps of the mosque of Damascus in the evening, at which time people would ask him questions and he would tell them stories and transmit *ḥadīth* reports to them. Other popular preachers were the Qurʾān commentator Mujāhid b. Jabr (d. 102/720) and the convert from Judaism Muḥammad b. Kaʿb al-Quraẓī (d. 117–20/735–38). On the *quṣṣāṣ*, see *EI*², s.v. Ḳaṣṣ (Ch. Pellat); *Ibn al-Jawzī's Kitāb al-quṣṣāṣ wa'l-mudhakkirīn*; Crone, *Meccan Trade*, 215–17; ʿAthāmina, "*al-Qasas*: Its Emergence, Religious Origin and its Socio-Political Impact on Early Muslim Society"; Lecker, "King Ibn Ubayy and the *Quṣṣāṣ*," esp. 67, note 147.

4. *EI*², s.v. Mudjāhid b. Djabr (A. Rippin).

5. Mujāhid b. Jabr, *Tafsīr*, 549–50.

6. Ibid.

7. It is reported that the father's name was originally Barra but that the Prophet later changed it to Jaḥsh. It also is reported that the daughter's name was originally Barra, but that the Prophet changed it to Zaynab. See Ibn Ḥajar al-ʿAsqalānī, *al-Iṣāba fī tamyīz al-ṣaḥāba*, 1:466, no. 1109. That both father and daughter should be said to have originally been named Barra and to have had their names changed by the Prophet merits further attention. Cf. Maghen, "Intertwined Triangles," 32, note 35. See next note.

8. *EI*², s.v. Zaynab bt. Jaḥsh (C. E. Bosworth). Zaynab bt. Jaḥsh is not to be confused with two other Zaynabs who were members of the Prophet's family: (1) Zaynab bt. Muḥammad, the Prophet's daughter by his first wife, Khadīja, reportedly died in Medina in 8/629. She had two children: ʿAlī died in infancy; and Umāma married ʿAlī b. Abī Ṭālib after the death of Fāṭima (*EI*², s.v. Zaynab bt. Muḥammad [V. Vacca]). (2) Zaynab bt. Khuzayma b. al-Ḥārith al-Hilāliyya was married to Muḥammad in 4/626 (this was her third marriage). She died eight months later in Rabīʿ II 4/October 625 and was buried in the cemetery of Baqīʿ al-Gharqad (*EI*², s.v. Zaynab bt. Khuzayma [C. E. Bosworth]). It is curious that Muḥammad should have had two wives and one daughter named Zaynab. Recall also that Usāma b. Zayd married Zaynab bt. Ḥanzala b. Qusāma (see Chapter 3).

9. Muqātil was born in Balkh and lived in Marw and Baghdād before moving to Baṣra. He was criticized by Muslim scholars for his reliance on Jews and Christians for explanations of obscure allusions in the Qurʾān. See *EI*², s.v. Muḳātil b. Sulaymān (M. Plessner-[A. Rippin]); Goldfeld, "Muqātil ibn Sulaymān"; Gilliot, "Muqātil, grand exégète, traditionniste et théologien maudit"; Ess, *Theologie und Gesellschaft im 2. und 3. Jahrhundert Hidschra*, 3:516–32; Crone, "A Note on Muqātil b. Ḥayyān and Muqātil b. Sulaymān"; Juynboll, *Encyclopedia of Canonical Ḥadīth*, 431ff.

10. In some narratives, Zayd is identified only as Zayd b. Ḥāritha; in others, he is identified as a Kalbī from the Yemen and his genealogy is traced back as many as twenty generations to a mythical Wabara or Quḍāʿa. See Ibn ʿAsākir, *Taʾrīkh madīnat Dimashq*, 19:349–50.

11. The earliest commentators drew upon an extensive oral tradition that included many stories about Zayd, some of which contain details about Zayd's identity and the manner in which he was acquired by Muḥammad. These narratives will be analyzed in Chapter 7.

12. Muqātil, *Tafsīr*, 3:34–35, 46–47.

13. Ibid., 3:46–47. Cf. the narrative account of ʿAlī's marriage to Fāṭima, cited in Klemm, "Image Formation of an Islamic Legend: Fāṭima, the Daughter of the Prophet Muḥammad," 187–88.

14. His full name was Jaḥsh b. Riʾāb al-Asadī. See *The History of al-Ṭabarī*, 39: 9 note 30, 168, 180 note 806. See also Ibn Ḥajar al-ʿAsqalānī, *al-Iṣāba fī tamyīz al-ṣaḥāba*, 1: 466, no. 1109, where al-Dāraquṭnī is quoted as saying that his birth name was Barra until the Prophet changed it to Jaḥsh ("a young ass"). One wonders if the name is intended as a criticism or as an allusion to Ishmael, about whom an angel says to Sarai that "he shall be a wild ass of a man (*perê adam*)." See Gen. 16:12 and note 7, above.

15. On ʿAbdallāh b. Jaḥsh, see *The History of al-Ṭabarī*, vol. 7, index, s.v. ʿAA b. Jaḥsh.

16. Muqātil, *Tafsīr*, 3:46–47. A marriage between a high status freewoman and a former slave clearly was not in conformity with Near Eastern law or Hijazi practice. See Bravmann, "Equality of Birth of Husband and Wife (*kafāʾah*), an Early Arab Principle." On the motif of the perfect woman, see Spellberg, *Politics, Gender, and the Islamic Past: The Legacy of ʿĀʾisha bint Abi Bakr*, chap. 5 (where Zaynab is not mentioned).

17. Muqātil, *Tafsīr*, 3:47.11–14. See further Chapter 7, where I analyze this narrative from a literary perspective.

18. Ibid., 3:47.20–21.

19. Neither version of the marriage transaction described by Muqātil conforms to the standard Islamic marriage, according to which it is the bridegroom who concludes the contract with the *walī* or legal guardian of the bride; and it is the bridegroom who undertakes to pay the *ṣadāq* or dower directly to the bride. The bride's family, on its part, contributes the trousseau.

However, version one does fit the classic model of marriage found in ancient Near Eastern law: Through his agent, ʿAlī, the Prophet negotiates the terms of a marriage between his son Zayd and his paternal cross-cousin, Zaynab bt. Jaḥsh, an orphan whose brother ʿAbdallāh b. Jaḥsh, serves as her marriage guardian. The betrothal is signaled by the payment of a *siyāq* or bridal gift (cf. Akk. *terḫatu*; Hittite *kusata*; Hebr. *mohar*; Aram. *mhr*) which, Muqātil specifies, was sent by Muḥammad "to them" (cf. Ṭabarsī, *Majmaʿ al-bayān*, 8:177.20–21: *sāqa ilayhā*. . . *mahr*[an], that is to say, Muḥammad sent it to her . . . in the form of a bridal gift). The bridal gift has three components: First, cash: 10 gold *dīnār*s and 60 silver *dirham*s. Second, a supplement in the form of a trousseau: a cloth headcover, nightgown, housedress, and wrapper which, upon receipt by the marriage guardian, will be conveyed to the bride. Third, comestibles for the wedding feast: fifty *mudd* of food and ten *mudd* of dates. Thus, the bridal gift paid by Muḥammad resembles the ancient Near Eastern *terḫatu*, which can be traced back to the Sumerian *nig-mi-us-sa* (see *HANEL*, 1:44–45). With the payment of the bridal gift the couple is legally married in the eyes of society, although the parties to the contract presumably retain the right to rescind the arrangement (albeit not without paying a penalty). During the period of betrothal, the bride is subject to the authority of her father-in-law. The marriage becomes complete only when the bride enters the groom's house and consummation occurs, at which point she becomes subject to the authority of her husband (*HANEL*, 1: 44–48). In version two, by contrast, ʿAbdallāh b. Jaḥsh transfers authority over his orphaned sister to his paternal cross-cousin, Muḥammad, who takes the girl into his house and marries her to his son, Zayd. The structure of this transaction brings to mind the ancient Near Eastern adoption procedure: *ṭuppi mārtūti u kallatūti* or adoption in daughtership and daughter-in-lawship (see Chapter 2). Recall that Zaynab was an orphan. It would have been appropriate for Muḥammad to take her into his house in daughtership and then to make her his daughter-in-law by marrying her to his son. There may be a faint echo of this dynamic in the following comment by Ṭabarsī with reference to Q. 33:37: If Zayd divorced Zaynab, Muḥammad would want to marry her because she was his orphaned paternal cross-cousin; it was customary in such circumstances for someone like Muḥammad to take the orphaned relative into his house and adopt her (*ḍammahā ilā nafsihi*). See *Majmaʿ al-bayān*, 8:179 (bottom). Be that as it may, whoever formulated the two versions of the marriage negotiations appears to have been thinking in terms of Near Eastern rather than Islamic law.

20. Muqātil, *Tafsīr*, 3:47.14–18.

21. Ibid., 3:47.20–23. For those readers who preferred to leave nothing to the imagination, a more explicit account of how Muḥammad came to catch sight of Zaynab was produced. Ṭabarī (*Jāmiʿ al-bayān* [1954–68], 22:13.9–12) transmits the following report: Yūnis—Ibn Wahb (d. 197/813)—Ibn Zayd: "One day, after the Prophet had married Zayd b. Ḥāritha [sic] to Zaynab bt. Jaḥsh, who was his paternal cross-cousin (*ibnat ʿammatihi*), the Messenger of God went out looking for [Zayd]. On the door of his house there was a curtain made of animal hair. Suddenly, the wind raised the curtain and exposed [what was behind it]. [Zaynab] was in her chamber (*ḥujra*), uncovered. Immediately, admiration for her (*iʿjābuhā*) filled the heart of the Prophet." A similar story is found in Qurṭubī (*al-Jāmiʿ*, 14:190.5–6), on the authority of a source who the commentator chose not to mention: It is said (*wa-qīla*): "God sent a wind that lifted up the curtain to reveal Zaynab wearing a single apron in her quarters (*fī manzilihā*). When [the Prophet] saw Zaynab, she sank into his heart (*waqaʿat fī nafsihi*)." As Muḥammad retreated from this vision, dumbstruck, he muttered, "Praise be to God who changes the hearts [of men]." Cf. Ṭabarsī, *Majmaʿ al-bayān*, 8:178.10–19.

22. Muqātil, *Tafsīr*, 3:47–48.

23. Other commentators offer different views on what exactly it was that Muḥammad was hiding. See, for example, Ṭabarsī, *Majmaʿ al-bayān*, 8:179.

24. Muqātil, *Tafsīr*, 3:48.1–9.

25. Ibid., 3:48.8–9. It is reported on the authority of al-Shaʿbī (d. >100/718) that Zaynab used to say to the Prophet that there were three special and unique features of their marriage: first, they were both descendants of ʿAbd al-Muṭallib, that is to say, they shared a grandfather; second, God was her marriage guardian; and, third, Gabriel was God's agent. See Ṭabarsī, *Majmaʿ al-bayān*, 8:181 (bottom).

26. See *EI*^{2}, s.v. Muʿammar (G. H. A. Juynboll).

27. Muqātil, *Tafsīr*, 3:48.14: "*inna Muḥammad*^{an} *tazawwaja ʾmraʾat ibnihi wa-huwa yanhānā ʿan tazwījihinna.*"

28. Ibid., 3:35.3–5: "*tazawwaja Muḥammad*^{un} *imraʾat ibnihi wa-huwa yanhānā ʿan dhālika.*"

29. Ibid.; cf. Balādhurī, *Ansāb*, 1:469.6–10.

30. On Q. 4:22–23 and sexual taboos, see Benkheira, "Alliance, asymétrie et différence des sexes: Un problème d'exégèse juridique."

31. According to Roman law, however, an adoptive relationship creates the same bar to marriage as a natural one; hence the maxim "adoption imitates nature." See Nicholas, *An Introduction to Roman Law*, 79.

32. Several Western scholars have been misled by Islamic tradition into thinking that the Qurʾān does in fact prohibit marriage to a daughter-in-law, irrespective of whether she had been married to the man's natural or adopted son. Roberts (*The Social Laws of the Qorân*, 50) writes that Muḥammad was reluctant to marry Zaynab "because the marriage would be contrary to his own law (Sura 4, 27 [sic])." Similarly, Smith (*Kinship and Marriage*, 51) says that "when Mohammed married Zainab, who had been Zaid's wife, it was objected that by the prophet's own law, laid down in the Coran, it was incest for a father to marry a woman who had been his son's wife." According to Watt (*Muhammad at Medina*, 330), the prohibition of marriage between a man and his daughter-in-law "was doubtless based on the Qurʾān." More recently, Landau-Tasseron ("Adoption," 169) has made the same mistake: "Muḥammad was criticized for marrying a woman who had been divorced by his own son, an act that had been prohibited by Q. 4:23."

33. Ricks, "Kinship Bars to Marriage in Jewish and Islamic Law," 130.

34. See Bialoblocki, *Materialien zum islamischen und jüdischen Eherecht mit einer Einleitung über jüdische Einflüsse auf den Ḥadīth*, 37ff.; Goitein, *Jews and Arabs: Their Contacts Through the Ages*, 50–51. Note that according to some Muslim commentators, when the Qurʾān refers to inheritance rules found in *al-kitāb* (e.g., *ad* Q. 33:6), it is referring to "the Torah" (*al-Tawrāh*). See, for example, Ṭabarsī, *Majmaʿ al-bayān*, 8:136.9.

35. See Zammit, *A Comparative Lexical Study of Qurʾānic Arabic.*

36. The biblical prohibition of sexual relations between a man and his daughter-in-law can be traced back to the second millennium B.C.E. The Code of Hammurabi envisages two scenarios: (1) if the illicit sexual union with the father-in-law takes place subsequent to betrothal but prior to consummation of the marriage by the son, the bride may leave the marriage with her bridal gift and compensation, and she is free to remarry; (2) if, however, the illicit sexual union with the father-in-law takes place subsequent to consummation by the son, the sexual act is regarded as incest and is punishable by death. See Roth, *Law Collections from Mesopotamia and Asia Minor*, 110, nos. 155–56. In Leviticus, the bride is identified as *kallâh*; in Hammurabi's Code, she is identified as *kalla.*

37. The biblical prohibition of marriage to a daughter-in-law is linked to the story of Judah and Tamar in Gen. 38:6. After the early death of her husband Er, Tamar

became the wife of his brother Onan, in accordance with the custom of levirate marriage. Realizing that his first-born son would be affiliated to his deceased brother, Onan spilled his seed so that Tamar would not become pregnant (Deut. 25:6). Like Er, Onan also died young, causing Judah to suspect that Tamar was somehow responsible for the deaths of his two sons. Judah now instructed Tamar to go and live in the house of her father, ostensibly until his third son, Shelah, reached the age of marriage. When Shelah attained manhood, Judah refrained from marrying Tamar to his son. Tamar now devised a scheme. Knowing that her father-in-law would have to pass by the gate of the city, she put aside her widow's garments and sat by the gate, covered in a veil. When Judah saw her, he mistook her for a harlot. As payment for her services, he offered her a kid, leaving with her as pledge of payment his seal, cord, and staff. When Tamar became pregnant, Judah ordered that she be burned to death on account of her harlotry. Tamar now sent the three objects to Judah, accompanied by a message that their owner was the father of her child. Only now did Judah realize that he was the father and that, unwittingly, he had had an incestuous sexual encounter with his daughter-in-law. "She is more in the right than I [am], because I did not give her to my son Shelah" (Gen. 38:26). Tamar gave birth to twin boys, Perez and Zerah. According to Ruth 4:18–22, David is a lineal descendant of Perez. In the eyes of Muslim scholars, the biblical account is an example of how the Israelites falsified their scriptures.

38. Another plural would have been **kallāt.*

39. But see BT, *Yebamot*, 21a–b, where the biblical prohibition of marrying one's daughter-in-law is extended to a son's daughter-in-law.

40. Thus, early Christian anti-Muslim polemic may have originated in a debate that was internal to the Muslim community. See Chapter 3, notes 35–41.

41. *EQ*, s.v. David (I. Hasson). On the term *khalīfa*, see Crone and Hinds, *God's Caliph: Religious authority in the first centuries of Islam*; Wadād al-Qāḍī, "The Term 'Khalīfa' in Early Exegetical Literature," 392–411.

42. As, for example, in Q. 4:46 and 5:13. See *EI*[2], s.v. Taḥrīf (Hava Lazarus-Yafeh); idem, *Intertwined Worlds: Medieval Islam and Bible Criticism*, chap. 2; Adang, *Muslim Writers on Judaism and the Hebrew Bible from Ibn Rabban to Ibn Hazm*, chap. 7.

43. BT, *Shabbat*, 56a.

44. Ibid., 30a.

45. BT, *Sanhedrin*, 107a.

46. BT, *Shabbat*, 56a. R. Samuel b. Nahmani said in R. Jonathan's name: "Whoever says that David sinned is merely erring, for it is said, 'And David behaved himself wisely in all his ways: and the Lord was with him.' Is it possible that sin came to his hand, yet the Divine Presence was with him? Then how do I interpret, 'Wherefore hast thou despised the word of the Lord, to do that which is evil in his sight?' He wished to do [evil], but did not. Rab observed: Rabbi, who is descended from David, seeks to defend him, and expounds [the verse] in David's favor. [Thus:] The *evil* [mentioned] here is unlike every other *evil* [mentioned] elsewhere in the Torah. For of every other evil [mentioned] in the Torah it is written, 'and he did,' whereas here it is written, 'to do': [this means] that he desired to do, but did not. 'Thou hast smitten Uriah the Hittite with the sword': thou should have had him tried by the Sanhedrin, but didst not. 'And hast taken his wife to be thy wife': thou hast marriage rights in her."

47. The identification of Uriah the Hittite as Uriah b. Ḥanān may be a linguistic response to David's expressed wish in II Sam. 12:22 that if he only prayed and fasted, God might have compassion on him (*yeḥanenī*) and spare the life of Bathsheba's son. In Arabic, *ḥanān* means *compassion.*

48. The use of the word *futina* here may be a double entendre. One says of a woman,

fatanathu, that is to say, *she enamored him* or *captivated his heart*. See Lane, *Arabic-English Lexicon*, s.v. f-t-n.

49. Maghen, "Davidic Motifs."

50. Muqātil, *Tafsīr*, 3:48.5. The notion of *kitmān* or *concealment* is a powerful weapon deployed in Muslim polemic against Jews and Christians, who are accused of distorting their respective sacred scriptures (Wansbrough, *The Sectarian Milieu*, 17); thus, the suggestion that Muḥammad might have concealed a verse of the Qurʾān is problematic. The use of the word *katama* also brings to mind Muḥammad's command to Ḥafṣa that she conceal (*uktumī*) the fact he had been spending extra time with Māriya the Copt.

51. If Muslims were shocked, non-Muslims were titillated. For Christians in particular, this episode exemplifies the manner in which Muslims used—or abused—the concept of divine revelation in order to satisfy their own wicked needs. See, for example, Daniel, *Islam and the West*, 97–100.

52. Muqātil, *Tafsīr*, 3:48.19–24.

53. *EQ*, s.vv. Messenger (A. H. M. Zahniser), Prophets and Prophethood (U. Rubin).

54. Bijlefeld defines prophethood in the Qurʾān as follows: "Prophethood must be understood first of all as a special gift to that part of mankind which can be indicated with the names (Adam-) Nuh—Ibrahim—Ibrahim's descendants (through Ishaq-Yaʿqub as well as through Ismaʿil), with a clear emphasis on the Ibrahim and post-Ibrahim section of this line." See Bijlefeld, "A Prophet and More Than a Prophet? Some Observations on the Qurʾanic use of the terms 'prophet' and 'apostle.'" See also Rubin, "Prophets and Caliphs: The Biblical Foundations of the Umayyad Authority." On the 600–year gap between Jesus and Muḥammad, see *EI*², s.v. Fatra (Ch. Pellat).

55. These two phrases bring to mind God's promise to David in II Sam. 7:15, "but I will never withdraw my favor from him"—referring to the messianic descendant of David who will reign as king, thereby insuring that David's House will endure forever.

56. According to Ṭabarsī, God bestowed his favor on Zayd by causing him to be loved by Muḥammad, and Muḥammad bestowed his favor on Zayd by adopting him. See *Majmaʿ al-bayān*, 8:179.2–4.

57. See Colpe, *Das Siegel der Propheten: Historische Beziehungen zwischen Judentum, Judenchristentum, Heidentum und frühem Islam*. To the best of my knowledge, this is the only sustained scholarly monograph on the subject. Cf. Stroumsa, "'Seal of Prophets': The Nature of a Manichaean Metaphor"; Simon, "Mānī and Muḥammad."

58. In the Hebrew Bible, the prophet Haggai refers to the governor of Judah, Zerubabbel, as a *ḥôtam* or seal who will confirm the truth of a divine utterance (Hag. 2:23). According to Daniel, prophetic vision will be sealed (*ve-laḥtôm ḥazôn ve-navî*) after "seventy weeks" (Dan. 9:24).

59. In the New Testament, Paul expresses the idea that his disciples confirm or validate his position by referring to them as "the seal of my apostleship" (I Cor. 9:2). According to the Church leader Tertullian, the prophets who preceded Jesus all foresaw his coming and suffering on the cross. These earlier prophecies were fulfilled by the advent of Jesus and his crucifixion. It was in this sense—as the fulfillment of earlier prophecies—that prophecy was sealed and that Jesus was the sign of all prophets (*Adversus Judaeos*, 8.12). See Dunn, *Tertullian*, 63ff., at 83 (Chapter 8.12); Colpe, *Das Siegel der Propheten*, 28–34.

60. To the best of my knowledge, the only pre-Islamic text which contains the phrase "Seal of Prophecy" is the *Xᵘāstvānīft*, a Manichean manual for the confession

of sins that appears to have been written before the second half of the sixth century C.E. Here the phrase *seal of Prophecy* is used as a metaphor for Wisdom. Note: Like Muḥammad, Mani claimed to reveal the truth in its entirety whereas the messengers who had preceded him revealed only part of the truth. See Asmussen, *Xᵘāstvānīft: Studies in Manichaeism*, 196 (text 175, ll. 173–80); commentary, 220–21; Stroumsa, "'Seal of Prophets,'" 68.

61. Jeffery, *Materials*, 170.

62. Lane, *Arabic-English Lexicon*, s.v. kh-t-m.

63. See Ess, *Theologie und Gesellschaft*, 1:29–30 and 4:593–94; idem, *The Flowering of Muslim Theology*, 23–24.

64. Friedmann, "Finality of Prophethood in Sunnī Islām"; a revised version of the article appears in idem, *Prophecy Continuous: Aspects of Aḥmadī Religious Thought and its Medieval Background*, 49–82.

65. Al-Suyūṭī, *al-Durr al-manthūr fī al-tafsīr al-maʾthūr*, 5:386. Cf. Friedmann, *Prophecy Continuous*, 63, citing Ibn Qutaybah, *Taʾwīl mukhtalif al-ḥadīth* (Cairo, 1326), 235–36.

66. Friedmann, *Prophecy Continuous*, 63.

67. Friedmann, "Finality of Prophethood in Sunnī Islām." Cf. Goldziher, *Muslim Studies*, 2:104.

68. *The History of al-Ṭabarī*, 9:164.

69. Friedmann, *Prophecy Continuous*, 65.

70. *EI*², s.v. al-Mukhtār b. Abī ʿUbayd (G. R. Hawting).

71. Friedmann, *Prophecy Continuous*, 66. Cf. Dunlop, "Al-Ḥārith b. Saʿīd al-Kadhdhāb, A Claimant to Prophecy in the Caliphate of ʿAbd al-Malik," 12–18; Ess, *Anfänge muslimischer Theologie: zwei antiqadaritische Traktate aus dem ersten Jahrhundert der Hiǧra*, 228–30.

72. According to another tradition, Abū ʿĪsā's revolt took place during the caliphate of Marwān II (r. 127–32/744–50), the last Umayyad caliph. *EI*², s.vv. Abū ʿĪsā al-Iṣfahānī (S. M. Stern), al-ʿĪsāwiyya (S. Pines).

73. Friedmann, *Prophecy Continuous*, 70.

74. Muqātil *Tafsīr*, 3:49.

75. Ibid. Cf. Friedmann, *Prophecy Continuous*, 61, note 48, citing Samarqandī, *Tafsīr* (Chester Beatty MS 3668/2 fol. 138b) *ad* Q. 33:40: Muḥammad "was not a father of men, because his sons died in infancy; if his sons had reached manhood, they would have become prophets. But there is no prophet after him, and this is expressed in the words of Allah 'and the Seal of Prophets'" (with additional references to Zamakhsharī, *al-Kashshāf ʿan ḥaqāʾiq al-tanzīl* [Calcutta, 1856], 2:1134; and Bayḍāwī, *Anwār al-tanzīl* [Leipzig, 1846], 2:130).

76. Cf. al-Thaʿlabī, *al-Kashf waʾl-bayān*, 7:50, where the author states the hypothetical ("were Muḥammad to have had a son, he would have been a prophet") without referring to Zayd's status as a potential prophet.

77. Ṭabarī, *Jāmiʿ al-bayān* (1954–68), 22:16 (*nazalat fī Zayd*); Suyūṭī, *al-Durr al-manthūr fī tafsīr al-maʾthūr*, 5:385.22–28 (*nazalat fī Zayd b. Ḥāritha*).

78. Muqātil reportedly told the ʿAbbāsid caliph Abū Jaʿfar al-Manṣūr (r. 136–58/754–75) that he would transmit anything that the caliph wanted to be transmitted about himself. And he told the caliph al-Mahdī (r. 158–69/775–85) that he was prepared to forge *ḥadīth* favorable to al-ʿAbbās.

79. See the editor's introduction to Muqātil, *Tafsīr*, 1–11, esp. 10.

80. *EI*², s.v. Muqātil b. Sulaymān (A. Rippin).

81. Muqātil, *Tafsīr*, 3:376 (text: *iktaʿī ʿalayya*; read *uktumī ʿalayya*). Muqātil has a variant of this story in which the Prophet attempts to bribe Ḥafṣa, as follows: "'O Ḥafṣa,

keep this a secret for me (again, read *uktumī ʿalayya*) so that I can give you the good tidings that Abū Bakr will succeed me and your father will succeed him.' The Prophet ordered her not to tell anyone [what she had seen]. But Ḥafṣa was angry, and she informed ʿĀʾisha—the two were close to one another—whereupon ʿĀʾisha became angry. She would not leave the Prophet alone until he swore that he would never again approach Māriya the Copt."

82. *EI*², s.v. Māriya (F. Buhl). The Islamic narrative is a creative reformulation of Gen. 17. In the Islamic narrative, Māriya is Hagar and Ibrāhīm is Ishmael. Both women were Egyptian slaves, and both were given to men who had no son. Hagar was a gift from Sarah to Abraham; Māriya was a gift from Muqawqis to Muḥammad. Both women aroused the jealousy of the wives of their respective masters; and both women produced a male child. Whereas the biblical Ishmael became the founder of a great nation—the Ishmaelites—Islam's Ibrāhīm died in infancy. In II Sam. 12 God punished King David for his sin by causing the first son borne to him by Bathsheba to die in infancy. However, Zaynab did not give Muḥammad a son. In this instance, the motif was transferred to Māriya the Copt, whose son Ibrāhīm died in infancy. See Chapter 7.

83. Friedmann, *Prophecy Continuous*, 60, citing Zaylaʿī, *Naṣb al-rāya li-aḥādīth al-hidāya* (Cairo, 1938), 2:280–81; ʿAẓīmābādī, *ʿAwn al-maʿbūd sharḥ sunan Abī Dāwūd*, 8:476.

84. Friedmann, *Prophecy Continuous*, 59–60, citing Jarrāḥī, *Kashf al-khafāʾ wa-muzīl al-ilbās* (Beirut, 1351), 2:156.

85. Friedmann, *Prophecy Continuous*, 60, citing the following sources: Ibn Māja, *Sunan*, Kitāb al-janāʾiz, 27 (1:484, no. 1511); Ibn Ḥajar al-ʿAsqalānī, *al-Iṣāba* (Cairo, 1323), 1:96; Ibn Saʿd, *Kitāb al-ṭabaqāt al-kabīr*, I/i, 90; Ibn al-Athīr, *Usd al-ghāba*, 1:40; Qasṭallānī, *Irshād al-sārī* (Cairo, A.H. 1327), 9:112–13; Suyūṭī, *Jamʿ al-jawāmiʿ* (Cairo, 1978), 1:668.

86. Friedmann, *Prophecy Continuous*, 60, note 46, citing Ibn Māja, *Sunan*, Kitāb al-janāʾiz, 27 (1:484, no. 1510); Bukhārī, *Ṣaḥīḥ*, ed. Krehl (Leiden, 1864), Kitāb al-adab, 109 (4:157–8); al-Bursawī, *Tafsīr rūḥ al-bayān* (Maṭbaʿa ʿUthmāniyya, A.H. 1330), 7:187; Ibn Ḥajar, *Iṣāba* (Cairo, 1323), 1:96; al-ʿAynī, *ʿUmdat al-qārī sharḥ Ṣaḥīḥ al-Bukhārī* (Beirut, n.d. ca. 1970), 22:210.

87. Friedmann, *Prophecy Continuous*, 61, citing Ibn ʿAbd al-Barr, *Istīʿāb* (Cairo, n.d.), 1:59–60. The use of the pronoun *your* may perhaps suggest a sectarian or polemical context.

88. Friedmann, *Prophecy Continuous*, 60, note 46, citing Ibn Ḥanbal, *Musnad* (repr. Beirut 1978), 4:353.

89. Friedmann, *Prophecy Continuous*, 62.

90. Zamakhsharī, *al-Kashshāf ʿan ḥaqāʾiq ghawāmiḍ al-tanzīl*, 5:75.18–19.

91. Ibn Saʿd, *al-Ṭabaqāt al-kubrā*, 4:71 (bottom)–72.5; *EI*², s.v. Usāma b. Zayd (V. Vacca).

92. During the *jāhiliyya*, the Arabs reportedly divorced their wives by saying, "You are to me like the back of my mother." This practice was prohibited by Q. 58:2: "Those of you who divorce your wives by calling them 'mothers', cannot (make them) their mothers. Their mothers are only those who gave birth to them. They surely utter what is unseemly and a lie." Henceforth, any Muslim who nevertheless continued to engage in this practice was required to make a gift as expiation.

93. Mujāhid, *Tafsīr*, 546.

94. Ibid.

95. Muqātil, *Tafsīr*, 3:34–35. Apparently, the transition from a regime in which adoption was a legitimate practice to one in which it was illegitimate was not a smooth one. Several members of the Muslim community had been adopted long before the

revelation of Q. 33:4–5, and their names—based on the patronymics of their adoptive fathers or mothers—were too firmly established in the minds of members of the community to be changed. Recall al-Miqdād, who was adopted during the *jāhiliyya* by al-Aswad (see Chapter 3). Everyone in the Muslim community knew him as al-Miqdād b. al-Aswad, and they continued to call him by that name, despite his protests that his real name was now—that is to say, again—al-Miqdād b. ʿAmr (Qurṭubī, *Jāmiʿ*, 14:120.4–8). The same was true of Sālim b. Abī Ḥudhayfa and other Muslims adopted during the *jāhiliyya* (ibid., ll. 9–10). In fact, Qurṭubī emphasizes that it was only Zayd who could no longer be called Zayd b. Muḥammad, and that anyone who did so with intent committed an act of rebellion for which he or she must be punished (ibid., ll. 10–11). *Rebellion* is strong language. Names were important.

96. Ibn Saʿd, *Kitāb al-ṭabaqāt al-kabīr*, III/i, 29.26–7; cf. Qurṭubī, *Jāmiʿ*, 14:193. Note: this is one instance in which I violate my policy of not citing texts later than Muqātil.

97. *HANEL*, 1:53, 673–75, 711, 728–29.

98. Muqātil, *Tafsīr*, 3:49. Cf. the parable of the lost prodigal son in Luke 15:21 ("Father I have sinned against heaven and before you; I am no longer worthy to be called your son"). From the perspective of Near Eastern law, Zayd was entitled to an indemnity as compensation for the unilateral dissolution of the adoption agreement. Just as God compensated the biblical Ishmael for his repudiation by making him the father of a great nation, so too God compensated Zayd for his willingness to relinquish the honor and distinction of being called *the son of Muḥammad*: Zayd is the only Companion whose name is mentioned in the Qurʾān. As a result, Qurṭubī explains, Zayd gained immortality, for his name will be recited forever! (Qurṭubī, *Jāmiʿ*, 14:194.8–14).

99. Muqātil, *Tafsīr*, 3:35.1. For an expanded genealogy, see *The History of al-Ṭabarī*, 9:6.

100. As suggested by Rabin, *Qumran Studies*, 122.

101. This is a rare example of what Muslim jurists call the abrogation of the *sunna* (the practice of adoption) by the Qurʾān ("Call them after their fathers"). This mode of abrogation was a point of contention between the Shāfiʿīs and Ḥanafīs. See, for example, *Islamic Jurisprudence: Shāfiʿī's Risāla*, trans. Majid Khadduri, 127–28; al-Jaṣṣāṣ, *Aḥkām al-qurʾān*, 3:361. On abrogation, see generally Powers, *SQH*, 143–88; idem, "The Exegetical Genre *nāsikh al-Qurʾān wa mansūkhuhu*," 117–38; John Burton, *The Sources of Islamic Law: Islamic Theories of Abrogation*, 39ff.

102. See Ṭabarsī, *Majmaʿ al-bayān*, 8:182.3; Ibn Kathīr, *Tafsīr al-qurʾān al-ʿaẓīm* (3rd ed., 1373/1954), 3:466; Landau-Tasseron, "Adoption"; Arazi, "Les enfants adultérins," and the sources cited there.

103. *RPIL*, 35.

104. On the origins of *walāʾ*, see *RPIL*; for a different view, see Mitter, "Unconditional Manumission of Slaves in Early Islamic Law: A *ḥadīth* Analysis."

105. According to Ṭabarsī, however, *al-kitāb* here refers to "the Torah" (*al-Tawrāh*). See *Majmaʿ al-bayān*, 8:136.9.

106. Ibid., 8:131–32.

107. Taken to its logical conclusion, the statement that the wives of the Prophets are the Mothers of the Believers entails that the Prophet's daughters are the Sisters of the Believers. This understanding, however, would have created a barrier to marriage between the Prophet's daughters and all Muslim men, e.g., ʿAlī could not have married Fāṭima. To avoid this undesirable—indeed, historically absurd—result, Ṭabarsī explains, the Qurʾānic assertion that the wives of the Prophet are the Mothers of the Believers must be understood metaphorically—as if the text read *ka'l-ummahāt*

("like the mothers")—not literally (*ʿalā al-ḥaqīqa*). See Ṭabarsī, *Majmaʿ al-bayān*, 8:135.4ff.

108. My hypothesis finds support in a tradition attributed to Qatāda (d. 117/735), according to which, while the Prophet was still alive, an unnamed Muslim said, "When the Prophet dies, I will marry So-and-So," referring to ʿĀʾisha. The unnamed individual was subsequently identified by Maʿmar (d. 153/770) as Ṭalḥa b. ʿUbayd Allāh, a kinsman of Abū Bakr and one of the ten Muslims to whom the Prophet had promised paradise. This identification came to be viewed as a calumny uttered by the ignorant Hypocrites. See ʿAbd al-Razzāq, *Tafsīr*, 3:50; Muqātil, *Tafsīr*, 3:53. For later discussions of this issue, see Ṭabarī, *Jāmiʿ al-bayān* (1954–68), 21:40; Qurṭubī, *Jāmiʿ*, 14:228–30; Ṭabarsī, *Majmaʿ al-bayān*, 8:196; *EI*², s.v. Ṭalḥa b. ʿUbayd Allāh (W. Madelung). Also interesting in this connection is the report that following the death of his wife Fāṭima, ʿAlī b. Abī Ṭālib married the Prophet's granddaughter Umāma, the daughter of Zaynab bt. Muḥammad, one of the four daughters borne to the Prophet by Khadīja. *EI*², s.v. Zaynab bt. Muḥammad (V. Vacca).

109. See Ibn ʿAsākir, *Taʾrīkh madīnat Dimashq*, 19:362.6–23, where Muḥammad says to ʿAlī, "As for you, ʿAlī, you are my son-in-law (*khatanī*) and the father of my children (*abū wuldī*).

110. As Arazi has noted, Shīʿī scholars systematically reject the idea that an adoptee (*daʿī*) is related by filiation to his or her adoptor; and they also reject the right of an adoptee to inherit from its adoptor. In this manner, they circumvent the danger posed by Zayd; and they preserve and reinforce the rights of the *ahl al-bayt*. According to the Shīʿī view, al-Ḥasan and al-Ḥusayn are the true sons of the Prophet. See Arazi, "Les enfants adultérins," 10 and note 16, citing Qummī, *Tafsīr*, 2:175.

111. Nöldeke, *Geschichte des Qorāns*, 1:252–53; Jeffery, *Materials*, 75, 156, 204, 298. Cf. Qurṭubī, *Jāmiʿ*, 14:123.15–17, where this reading is attributed to Ubayy b. Kaʿb and Ibn ʿAbbās; and al-Nasafī, *Tafsīr*, 3:294, l. -4, where it is attributed to Ibn Masʿūd.

112. Ṭabarī, *Jāmiʿ al-bayān* (1954–68), 21:122.12–18; cf. Nöldeke, *Geschichte des Qorāns*, 1:253.

113. Mujāhid (*Tafsīr*, 546) glosses the phrase "The prophet is closer to the believers than they are themselves" as "he is their father" (*huwa ab*[un] *lahum*). *Isnād*: ʿAbd al-Raḥmān—Ibrāhīm—Ādam [b. Iyās; d. 220/835]—Warqāʾ (d. 160/777)—Ibn Abī Najīḥ (d. 130/747–48)—Mujāhid. Cf. Ṭabarī, *Jāmiʿ al-bayān* (1373/1954), 21:122.5–7. Ṭabarsī reports that Mujāhid said, "Every prophet is the father of his *umma*." To this Ṭabarsī adds: "Therefore, the believers become his [viz. the Prophet's] brothers, because the Prophet is their father in religion" (*abūhum fī al-dīn*). See *Majmaʿ al-bayān*, 8:134 (bottom).

114. ʿAbd al-Razzāq, *Tafsīr*, 3:32, no. 2316: the consonantal skeleton (*ḥarf*) used by Ubayy b. Kaʿb included the words *wa-huwa ab*[un] *lahum*.

115. Similarly, Ḥudhayfa b. al-Yamān rejected ʿUmar's insinuation that something had been added to the *summer verse*. See Chapter 9.

116. Sufyān b. ʿUyayna, *Tafsīr*, 309. *Isnād*: Sufyān b. ʿUyayna—ʿAmr b. Dīnār (d. 126/744)—Bujāla [b. ʿAbda al-Tamīmī].

117. ʿAbd al-Razzāq, *Tafsīr*, 3:32, no. 2317. *Isnād*: ʿAbd al-Razzāq—Ibn Jurayj (d. 150/767)—ʿAmr b. Dīnār (d. 126/744)—Bujāla al-Tamīmī.

118. Fakhr al-Dīn al-Rāzī, *al-Tafsīr al-kabīr*, 25:195.

119. To date I have come across no classical Muslim scholar and only one modern Muslim scholar who has compared the wording of Q. 33:6a with that of 33:40. It will be recalled that *ad* v. 6 of *Sūrat al-Aḥzāb*, Sufyān b. ʿUyayna preserves one version of the testy exchange between ʿUmar b. al-Khaṭṭāb and Ubayy b. Kaʿb. In his edition of Ibn ʿUyayna's *Tafsīr*, Aḥmad Muḥammad Maḥāyirī adduces several reports that explain

the meaning of the phrase "the Prophet is closer to the believers than themselves." After summarizing these reports, Maḥāyirī asserts that they serve to refute what he identifies as the *apparent contradiction* between the variant of v. 6a containing the phrase "and he is their father," on the one hand, and God's assertion in v. 40 of the same *Sūra* that "Muḥammad is not the father of any of your men," on the other. Otherwise, Maḥāyirī—like the Caliph ʿUmar—is silent.

120. See Bijlefeld, "A Prophet and More than a Prophet?"; Rubin, "Prophets and Caliphs"; *EQ*, s.v. Prophets and Prophecy (U. Rubin).

121. See Auerbach, *Mimesis*; White, *The Content of the Form*; Assmann, *Moses the Egyptian: The Memory of Egypt in Western Monotheism*; Sizgorich, "Narrative and Community in Islamic Late Antiquity"; idem, "'Do Prophets Come with a Sword?' Conquests, Empire, and Historical Narrative in the Early Islamic World."

122. The fact that Muḥammad visited his wives on a rotational basis would have decreased the chances of his having sexual relations with any one of them during that period of her monthly cycle when she would have been fertile. Thus, there is a physiological explanation for his inability to impregnate any of his wives following the death of Khadīja.

123. On "the objectification of the Messenger," see N. Robinson, *Discovering the Qurʾān: A Contemporary Approach to a Veiled Text*, 244, 254.

Chapter 5. The Battle of Muʾta

1. See C. Robinson, *Islamic Historiography*.

2. The root *m-ʾ-t* does not exist in Arabic. The lexicographers mention the toponym Muʾta in their entries on *m-w-t*. See Khalīl b. Aḥmad al-Farāhīdī, *Kitāb al-ʿayn*, 796; Ibn Manẓūr, *Lisān al-ʿarab*, 6:4296–97. Cf. Yāqūt, *Muʿjam al-buldān*, 5:219–20.

3. Biographers: Watt, *Muhammad at Medina*, 53–56; Rodinson, *Mohammed*, 255; Lings, *Muhammad*, 287–89; Peters, *Muhammad and the Origins of Islam*, 230–33; Nagel, *Mohammed*, 375–77, 407, 465. Historians: Hitti, *History of the Arabs*, 147; Hodgson, *Venture of Islam*, 1:194; Saunders, *A History of Medieval Islam*, 332; Gabrieli, *Muhammad*, 80; Donner, *The Early Islamic Conquests*, 101, 103, 105–10; Kennedy, *Prophet*, 42; idem, *The Great Arab Conquests*, 71; Jandora, *The March from Medina*, 38, 43, 45.

4. Wāqidī, *Kitāb al-maghāzī*, 2:755–68. I am not suggesting that the individual components of Wāqidī's account are necessarily the earliest narratives about the battle. As is well known, early reports are often found in later texts.

5. *The Life of Muhammad*, trans. A. Guillaume, 531–40.

6. Ibn Saʿd, *al-Ṭabaqāt al-kubrā*, 2:128–30.

7. Al-Yaʿqūbī, *Taʾrīkh*, 2:54–55.

8. *The History of al-Ṭabarī*, 8:152–60.

9. Ibn ʿAsākir, *Taʾrīkh madīnat Dimashq*, 2:5–21.

10. Ibn Kathīr, *al-Bidāya waʾl-nihāya*, 4:241–61.

11. ʿAlī b. Burhān al-Dīn, *al-Sīra al-ḥalabiyya*, 2:787–93.

12. Wāqidī, *Kitāb al-maghāzī*, 2:752–80.

13. Wansbrough (*Sectarian Milieu*, 35) uses the term *distributional chronology* to refer to the tacit dating of events by virtue of their location in a narrative.

14. *EI*², s.v. Boṣrā (A. Abel). As a youth, Muḥammad is said to have visited Boṣrā, where a monk named Baḥīra bore witness to his forthcoming mission as a prophet.

15. On this topos—arranging the succession of command, see Noth, *Early Arabic Historical Tradition*, 120–22.

16. Wāqidī, *Kitāb al-maghāzī*, 2:755–56. Cf. *The Life of Muhammad*, trans. Guillaume,

531–32; Ibn Saʿd, *al-Ṭabaqāt al-kubrā*, 2:128; *The History of al-Ṭabarī*, 8:152; Ibn Kathīr, *al-Bidāya wa'l-nihāya*, 4:241.

17. Ibid., 4:254–55.

18. ʿAwn and Muḥammad died at Karbalāʾ fighting alongside al-Ḥusayn. As for ʿAbdallāh, he abandoned all political ambitions after the murder of ʿAlī in 40/661, at which time he made common cause with Muʿāwiya, who rewarded him with an annual stipend of one million dirhams. See Madelung, *The succession to Muḥammad*, 329.

19. On Jaʿfar, see Balādhurī, *Ansāb al-ashrāf*, 1:198; Ibn Kathīr, *al-Bidāya wa'l-nihāya*, 4:255–57; *EI*², s.v. Dja̱ʿfar b. Abī Ṭālib (L. Veccia Vaglieri); Madelung, "The Hāshimiyyāt of al-Kumayt and Hāshimī Shiʿism," 5–26.

20. Blankinship, "Imārah, Khilāfah, and Imāmah," 34.

21. On ʿAbdallāh b. Rawāḥa, see Balādhurī, *Ansāb al-ashrāf*, 1:244, 252, 340, 378, 380; Ibn al-Jawzī, *Kitāb al-quṣṣāṣ wa'l-mudhakkirīn* (trans. Swartz), 102, 107, 223 n. 2; Ibn Kathīr, *al-Bidāya wa'l-nihāya*, 4:257–59; Watt, *Muhammad at Medina*, index, s.v.; *EI*², s.v. ʿAbd Allāh b. Rawāḥa (A. Schaade).

22. Wāqidī, *Kitāb al-maghāzī*, 2:757–58. These instructions belong to the genre known as *siyar* or the Islamic law of nations. See Abū Yūsuf, *Kitāb al-kharāj*, trans. Ben Shemesh as *Taxation in Islām*, 79–93; Muslim, *Ṣaḥīḥ*, no. 4292; *The Islamic Law of Nations: Shaybānī's* Siyar, trans. Majid Khadduri; R. Peters, *Jihad in Classical and Modern Islam*, 10–12.

23. On the etiological function of toponyms which include the word Thaniyya, see Noth, *The Early Arabic Historical Tradition*, 191.

24. It is reported that when Muḥammad bade farewell to ʿAbdallāh b. Rawāḥa, the Companion asked that he assign him a special task to perform. The Prophet responded by telling ʿAbdallāh that upon arriving at his destination, he should pray frequently. Not satisfied with this, ʿAbdallāh asked the Prophet for another special task. The Prophet responded by instructing him to "remember God, for He will help you to obtain your objective." As ʿAbdallāh stood up to depart, he took one step but then turned back, intending to solicit yet another special task from the Prophet. Before he could say anything, the Prophet cut him off, advising him that if he were to perform only one good deed it would compensate for ten evil deeds that he had committed. Satisfied with this, ʿAbdallāh promised not to ask the Prophet for anything else. Wāqidī, *Kitāb al-maghāzī*, 2:758.

25. Ibid. Cf. *The Life of Muhammad*, trans. Guillaume, 532; Ibn Saʿd, *al-Ṭabaqāt al-kubrā*, 2:128; *The History of al-Ṭabarī*, 8:152–53; Ibn Kathīr, *al-Bidāya wa'l-nihāya*, 4:241–42.

26. On the image of Heraclius in Islamic sources, see Conrad, "Heraclius in Early Islamic Kerygma."

27. On letters as a topos, see Noth, *The Early Arabic Historical Tradition*, 78–86.

28. Wāqidī, *Kitāb al-maghāzī*, 2:760. Cf. *The Life of Muhammad*, trans. Guillaume, 532–33; Ibn Saʿd, *al-Ṭabaqāt al-kubrā*, 2:128–29; *The History of al-Ṭabarī*, 8:153–55; Ibn Kathīr, *al-Bidāya wa'l-nihāya*, 4:242–43. On the practice of citing Qurʾānic language in literary texts, see *EI*², s.v. Iḳtibās (D. B. MacDonald/S. A. Bonebakker); Dähne, "Context Equivalence: A Hitherto Insufficiently Studied Use of the Quran in Political Speeches from the Early Period of Islam."

29. Wāqidī, *Kitāb al-maghāzī*, 2:760. On two good outcomes (*al-ḥusnayayn*), see Q. 9:52 ("Say: 'Are you waiting for anything but one of two fairest things to befall us?' "). The word *al-ḥusnayayn* in this verse is glossed by Ibn ʿAbbās and Mujāhid as "victory or martyrdom." See Ṭabarī, *Tafsīr* (ed. Shākir), 9:291–3, no. 16796. On God's "promise," see Q. 8:7 ("God promised that one of the two parties should be yours"), and Q. 9:111 ("Who fulfils His covenant more fully than God?"). The speech delivered by Ibn Rawāḥa prior to the Battle of Muʾta may be compared to the speech delivered by

Joab prior to the military campaign against Rabat Ammon: "Let us be strong and resolute for the sake of our people and the land of our God; and the Lord will do what he deems right" (II Sam. 10:12).

30. The detail about the hamstringing of the horse would give rise to a legal discussion about animal rights. See Ibn Kathīr, *al-Bidāya wa'l-nihāya*, 4:244.

31. The number *seventy-two* brings to mind the number of names attributed to God by Jewish kabbalists, the number of Jesus' disciples, the number of men who translated the Septuagint, the number of Muslims who fought at Badr, and the number of people who were martyred with Ḥusayn at Karbala. See Conrad, "Seven and the *Tasbīʿ*: On the Implications of Numerical Symbolism for the Study of Medieval Islamic History."

32. Wāqidī, *Kitāb al-maghāzī*, 2:761. Cf. *The Life of Muhammad*, trans. Guillaume, 534–35; Ibn Saʿd, *al-Ṭabaqāt al-kubrā*, 2:129; *The History of al-Ṭabarī*, 8:156; Ibn Kathīr, *al-Bidāya wa'l-nihāya*, 4:244.

33. The Arabic verb *istashhada* means *to bear witness*; the passive form *ustushhida* means *to be slain as a martyr* (shahīd) *in the cause of God's religion* (Lane, *Arabic-English Lexicon*, s.v. sh-h-d); cf. Greek *martys*, "witness in law"; Syriac *sāhdā*, "witness" or "martyr." On martyrdom, see further Chapter 6.

34. The fact that Zayd preceded Jaʿfar into the Garden confused some Muslims. Wāqidī preserves a narrative (Wāqidī, *Kitāb al-maghāzī*, 2:762, *isnād*: ʿAbdallāh b. Muḥammad b. ʿUmar b. ʿAlī—his father) in which the Prophet said: I saw Jaʿfar transformed into an angel who flies in the Garden, with his two forearms (*qādims*) bleeding. And I saw Zayd below him. I said, "I didn't think that Zayd would be below Jaʿfar." But the angel Gabriel came and said, "Zayd is not below Jaʿfar, but we have given preference to Jaʿfar because of his relationship to you." Cf. Ibn Saʿd, *al-Ṭabaqāt al-kubrā*, 2:130; Yaʿqūbī, *Ta'rīkh*, 2:54; *The History of al-Ṭabarī*, 8:158; Ibn Kathīr, *al-Bidāya wa'l-nihāya*, 4:246.17–18.

35. Wāqidī, *Kitāb al-maghāzī*, 2:761–62. Cf. *The Life of Muhammad*, trans. Guillaume, 535, 537–40; Ibn Saʿd, *al-Ṭabaqāt al-kubrā*, 2:129–30; *The History of al-Ṭabarī*, 8:158; Ibn ʿAsākir, *Ta'rīkh madīnat Dimashq*, 19:368–69; Ibn Kathīr, *al-Bidāya wa'l-nihāya*, 4:245–47.

36. Four months after the Battle of Mu'ta, Khālid participated in the conquest of Mecca. He went on to play an important role as commander of the Muslim armies that conquered Syria and Iraq—although his role in the Iraqi campaign is disputed. He is best known for his daring march across the desert from Iraq to Syria in 12/633. In 13/634, however, he was relieved of his position as supreme military commander by the caliph ʿUmar. Despite his military achievements, many Muslims thought poorly of him. He was criticized for wrongfully attacking the Banū Jazīma and, subsequently, for killing two Muslims whom he mistook for rebels. To make matters worse, he married the widow of one of his victims. The Prophet is reported to have said in his defense, "Don't slander Khālid for verily he is the Sword of God." On Khālid, see Balādhurī, *Ansāb al-ashrāf*, 5:271–72; Conrad, "Al-Azdī's History of the Arab Conquests in Bilād al-Shām," 39–42; Klier, *Ḫālid und ʿUmar: Quellenkritische Untersuchung zur Historiographie der früislamischen Ẓeit*; *EI*[2], s.v. Khālid b. al-Walīd (P. Crone).

37. Wāqidī, *Kitāb al-maghāzī*, 2:763. Cf. Ibn Kathīr, *al-Bidāya wa'l-nihāya*, 4:245.

38. Wāqidī, *Kitāb al-maghāzī*, 2:764.

39. Ibid., 2:763. Cf. *The Life of Muhammad*, trans. Guillaume, 535; Ibn Saʿd, *al-Ṭabaqāt al-kubrā*, 2:129–30; *The History of al-Ṭabarī*, 8:158.

40. Wāqidī, *Kitāb al-maghāzī*, 2:763. Cf. *The Life of Muhammad*, trans. Guillaume, 535; Ibn Saʿd, *al-Ṭabaqāt al-kubrā*, 2:130; Ibn Kathīr, *al-Bidāya wa'l-nihāya*, 4:248.

41. This is an example of Islamic kerygma, on which, see Wansbrough, *The Sectarian Milieu*, 1–49; Conrad, "Heraclius in Early Islamic Kerygma," 113–56.

42. Ibn Kathīr, *al-Bidāya wa'l-nihāya*, 4:250 (top, citing Bayhaqī).

43. On Khālid as *Sayf Allāh*, see *The History of al-Ṭabarī*, 8:158; Balādhurī, *Ansāb al-ashrāf*, 5:272; Conrad, "Al-Azdī's History of the Arab Conquests in Bilād al-Shām," and the sources mentioned there.

44. The point was not lost on Ibn Kathīr, who qualifies the fact that only eight (or twelve) Muslims were killed as *ʿaẓīm*[un] *jidd*[an] or "very strange." See *al-Bidāya wa'l-nihāya*, 4:259.

45. Wāqidī, *Kitāb al-maghāzī*, 2:769. Cf. *The Life of Muhammad*, trans. Guillaume, 540.

46. Wāqidī, *Kitāb al-maghāzī*, 2:764–5. *Isnād*: Khālid b. Ilyās—Ṣāliḥ b. Abī al-Ḥassān—ʿUbayd b. Ḥunayn—Abū Saʿīd al-Khudrī. Cf. Ibn Kathīr, *al-Bidāya wa'l-nihāya*, 4:248.8–13, 253.17–18.

47. Wāqidī, *Kitāb al-maghāzī*, 2:765. *Isnād*: Khālid b. Ilyās—Abū Bakr b. ʿAbdallāh b. ʿUtba. Wāqidī (ibid.) has another version of this report with the *isnād*: Muṣʿab b. Thābit—ʿĀmir b. ʿAbdallāh b. al-Zubayr—Abū Bakr b. ʿAbd al-Raḥmān b. al-Ḥārith b. Hishām. Here, it is said that the wife of Salama b. Hishām b. al-Mughīra paid a visit to Umm Salama, one of the Prophet's wives. Umm Salama said to the Companion's wife, "Why have I not seen Salama b. Hishām recently? Is something the matter?" To which she responded, "No, nothing is the matter, but he is unable to come out [of the house,] for when he does, the people reproach him and his comrades, saying, 'O run-aways, have you fled in the path of God!' He therefore sits in the house." When Umm Salama informed the Prophet, he said, "No, they are the ones who will return to the path of God, so let him come out!" Only now did he emerge. In another version (*isnād*: Khālid b. Ilyās—al-Aʿraj), Abū Hurayra is reported to have said, "When we would emerge from our houses we would hear the denunciations of the people. I exchanged words with one of my paternal cousins who said, 'Except that you fled on the day of Muʾta.' I was at a loss as to how to respond to him." Cf. *The History of al-Ṭabarī*, 8:159; Ibn Kathīr, *al-Bidāya wa'l-nihāya*, 4:249.4–7.

48. On mourning practices in early Islam, see Halevi, *Muhammad's Grave: Death Rites and the Making of Islamic Society*.

49. The Prophet's response to Zayd's death is reported by Ibn Saʿd: Muḥammad paid his first condolence call to Umm Ayman, Usāma, and the rest of Zayd's family. Later that day, he returned to their house, where Zayd's daughter Zaynab, who was distraught, ran into his arms. The Prophet began to cry so hard that his body shook. This spectacle caused Saʿd b. ʿUbāda to ask the Prophet, "O Messenger of God, what is this?" To which Muḥammad responded, "This is the beloved yearning for his beloved" (*shawq al-ḥabīb ilā ḥabībihi*). Ibn Saʿd, *Kitāb al-ṭabaqāt al-kabīr*, III/i, 32; cf. Balādhurī, *Ansāb*, 1:473.4–12; Ibn ʿAsākir, *Taʾrīkh madīnat Dimashq*, 19:370–71.

50. See Silverstein, *Postal Systems in the Pre-Modern Islamic World*.

51. Like Asmāʾ, Fāṭima is portrayed in Islamic sources as a model wife and caring mother who worked herself to exhaustion for the sake of her husband and children. On this topos, see Klemm, "Image Formation of an Islamic Legend: Fāṭima, the Daughter of the Prophet Muḥammad," 200.

52. The Prophet's paternal uncle al-ʿAbbās would not become a Muslim until the conquest of Mecca later in the year 8 A.H. See *EI*[2], s.v. al-ʿAbbās b. ʿAbd al-Muṭṭalib (W. Montgomery Watt).

53. Wāqidī, *Kitāb al-maghāzī*, 2:766. *Isnād*: Mālik b. Abī al-Rajjāl—ʿAbdallāh b. Abī Bakr b. Ḥazm—Umm ʿĪsā b. al-Ḥazzār—Umm Jaʿfar bt. Muḥammad b. Jaʿfar—her grandmother Asmāʾ bt. ʿUmays. Wāqidī (ibid., 2:766–67) also has a variant of this story that is told from the perspective of Jaʿfar's son, ʿAbdallāh (*isnād*: Muḥammad b.

Muslim—Yaḥyā b. Abī Yaʿlā—ʿAbdallāh b. Jaʿfar). In this version, ʿAbdallāh recalls the moment when the Prophet visited his mother in order to inform her of Jaʿfar's death. ʿAbdallāh was looking at the Prophet, who was stroking his head and that of his brother and crying so hard that the tears were dripping off his beard. Muḥammad said, "Jaʿfar has received the best reward and, as a result, God has replaced him with the best person who could have replaced him out of all His servants." Turning to Asmāʾ, he asked her, "Have I not given you the good tidings?" When she responded that he had not, he said, "Verily, God gave Jaʿfar two wings so that he might fly in the Garden." Upon hearing this, Asmāʾ asked the Prophet to transmit the good news to the others. ʿAbdallāh reports that the Prophet now arose and took him by the hand, stroking his head until he had climbed the pulpit (*minbar*), but only after putting ʿAbdallāh in front of him on the lowest step. The grief was apparent on his face. Then he said, "Verily, a man's reputation is linked to the virtues of his siblings and cousins—and indeed Jaʿfar has been martyred. God has given him two wings so that he might use them to fly in the Garden." ʿAbdallāh continued: the Prophet now descended from the *minbar* and entered his apartment, taking me with him. He ordered that food should be prepared for my family. He sent for my brother and we had a delicious, blessed dinner with him. Cf. *The Life of Muhammad*, trans. Guillaume, 535–36; *The History of al-Ṭabarī*, 8:158; Ibn Kathīr, *al-Bidāya wa'l-nihāya*, 4:251–53 (see 252.8–9, where Muḥammad says that ʿAbdallāh looks like him and acts like him).

54. *The Chronicle of Theophanes Confessor*, trans. Mango and Scott, 466–67; cf. *The Chronicle of Theophanes*, trans. Harry Turtledove, 36 (to be used with caution).

55. Conrad, "Theophanes and the Arabic Historical Tradition."

56. *The Chronicle of Theophanes Confessor* (trans. Mango and Scott), 466.

57. Text: Κορασηνός, i.e., Korasenite. Mango and Scott translate this Arabic term as Koraishite—with no further explanation. Turtledove likewise has "man of Quraysh." See below.

58. *The Chronicle of Theophanes Confessor* (trans. Mango and Scott), 466–67; cf. *The Chronicle of Theophanes* (trans. Turtledove), 36.

59. Conrad points to the ambiguity of the phrase "intending to fall upon the Arabs on the day when they sacrificed their idols." He argues that the "idolatrous sacrifice" mentioned here "*must* refer to a festival in the *Christian* village, which on such an occasion is unlikely to have been as watchful for raiders as would normally be the case" (emphasis added). If so, Conrad concludes, Theophanes could not possibly have made such a statement, from which it follows that the chronicler must have been relying on the Arabic historical tradition. As Mango and Scott have noted, however, it is unlikely that Theophanes would have reproduced "a Muslim tradition which referred to idolatrous Christian worship." See *The Chronicle of Theophanes Confessor* (trans. Mango and Scott), 467, note 4. This rebuttal takes some of the wind out of Conrad's argument for the Byzantine chronicler's dependence on Arabic sources.

60. The alienation of Arab forces by a Byzantine paymaster may be a topos.

61. On the introduction of hijri dates to Muslim historical sources, see Noth, *The Early Arabic Historical Tradition*, 40–42; C. Robinson, *Islamic Historiography*, 20–24.

62. Khalīfa b. Khayyāṭ, *Kitāb al-ṭabaqāt*, part 1, 11, 14, 210; cf. Ibn ʿAsākir, *Taʾrīkh madīnat Dimashq*, 19:349.3–11. See *EI*², s.v. Ibn Khayyāṭ al-ʿUṣfurī (S. Zakkar).

63. Kaegi, *Byzantium and the Early Islamic Conquests*, 71–74.

64. Ibid., 71.

65. Kaegi does not give a source for the date 10 Dhū al-Ḥijja of the year 8 A.H.

66. Ibid., 72.

67. On the image of Heraclius in Islamic sources, see Conrad, "Heraclius in Early Islamic Kerygma."

68. Kaegi, *Byzantium and the early Islamic conquests*, 26–33, 71–74. Cf. Gil, *A History of Palestine, 634–1099*, 21–24.

69. Conrad, "Theophanes and the Arabic Historical Tradition," 24, note 49. Cf. de Prémare, *Les fondations de l'Islam*, 138 ("En fin de compte, la date importe peu"), 140 (the date of the expedition "fait partie des problèmes non resolus").

70. Following the destruction of the Second Temple in 70 C.E., the Sanhedrin was moved from Jerusalem to Yavneh, in central Palestine. Yavneh quickly emerged as the center of the Palestinian rabbinic academy. It is curious that Muḥammad would have sent a military expedition to Yavneh, which was hardly a strategic military site.

71. On this battle, see Wāqidī, *Kitāb al-maghāzī*, 3:1117–27; Ibn Saʿd, *al-Ṭabaqāt al-kubrā*, 2:189–92, 4:65–68, 162–64; *The History of al-Ṭabarī*, 9:163–67; *The History of al-Ṭabarī*, 10:11–18; Ibn Kathīr, *al-Bidāya wa'l-nihāya*, 6:304–5; ʿAlī b. Burhān al-Dīn, *al-Sīra al-ḥalabiyya*, 3:227–31. I intend to analyze the narrative account of the military expedition to Ubna in a future communication.

72. On the problem of chronology, see Donner, *The Early Islamic Conquests*, esp. 123–26, 142–46, 175–76, and 211–12; Kaegi, *Byzantium and the early Islamic conquests*, 1–25.

73. On ʿUrwa, see Duri, *The Rise of Historical Writing Among the Arab*s, esp. 86, 91; *EI*[2], s.v. ʿUrwa b. al-Zubayr (G. Schoeler); Schoeler, "Foundations for a New Biography of Muḥammad: the Production and Evaluation of the Corpus of Traditions from ʿUrwah b. al-Zubayr," 21–28.

74. *EI*[2], s.v. ʿAbd al-Malik b. Marwān (H. A. R. Gibb). See now also C. Robinson, *ʿAbd al-Malik*, esp. 31–48.

75. *EI*[2], s.v. al-Walīd (I) b. ʿAbd al-Malik (H. Kennedy).

76. Even if it was only hypothetical, the argument that Zayd was a potential prophet posed a threat to the legitimacy of the Marwānids, on the one hand, and to the proto-Shīʿīs, on the other. Both groups had good reason to be concerned about a man named Zayd b. Muḥammad.

77. Ibn Saʿd, *al-Ṭabaqāt al-kubrā*, 2:128.5–6.

78. *The Life of Muhammad*, trans. Guillaume, 532. This is a single-strand *isnād.*

79. *The History of al-Ṭabarī*, 8:152.

80. Changing the date of the battle to 8 A.H. did not solve the problem. Even if Zayd did in fact die in 8/629, his son Usāma—who did not die until 54/674, might have inherited the office of prophecy by virtue of the filial connection between him and his grandfather. As we have seen in Chapter 4, the threat posed by Usāma was solved by having Muḥammad repudiate the Beloved of the Messenger of God ("I am not your father") just prior to the Prophet's marriage to Zaynab in 5 A.H. Henceforth, Zayd was no longer the Prophet's son and Usāma was no longer his grandson. Once the filial tie had been severed between the adoptive father, on the one hand, and his adopted son and grandson, on the other, it could no longer be argued that either Zayd or Usāma qualified as a potential prophet. Indeed, this argument appears to have disappeared after ca. 150 A.H.

81. The same argument can be made about Jaʿfar and, to a lesser extent, about ʿAbdallāh b. Rawāḥa.

82. Ibn Saʿd, *Kitāb al-ṭabaqāt al-kabīr*, III/i, 31.10–13. *Isnād*: Muḥammad b. ʿAbīd—Wā'il b. Dā'ūd—al-Bahiyy—ʿĀ'isha. Cf. Watt, *Islamic Political Thought*, 31, where the author observes that had Zayd been alive at the time of the Prophet's death, he easily might have succeeded his father, according to "normal Arab practice."

83. On the fighting martyr, see Cook, *Martyrdom in Islam*; Bonner, *Jihad in Islamic History*, chap. 5 ("Martyrdom"). Both books are useful. Neither author mentions Zayd.

84. Donner, *Narratives of Islamic Origins: The Beginnings of Islamic Historical Writing*, 212, note 23.

85. See again Cook, *Martyrdom in Islam*.

86. In Q. 61:11–12 God says that He will forgive the sins of those who struggle in the path of God. And the Prophet is reported to have said that the remission of sins takes place at the moment that the martyr sheds his blood. See Lewinstein, "The Revaluation of Martyrdom in Early Islam," 80–81.

87. The narrative also gave Muslim scholars an opportunity to discuss issues like animal rights and mourning practices. See Ibn Kathīr, *al-Bidāya wa'l-nihāya*, 4:244, 252.

Chapter 6. The Martyrdom of the Beloved of the Messenger of God

1. Boyarin, *Dying for God: Martyrdom and the Making of Christianity and Judaism*, 94.

2. Bowersock, *Martyrdom & Rome*, 5.

3. Boyarin, *Dying for God*, 6, 20, 117.

4. Bowersock, *Martyrdom & Rome*, 74; cf. Boyarin, *Intertextuality and the Reading of Midrash*, xii (a reference to underground currents connecting Judaism and Christianity, on the one hand, with Islam, on the other—albeit without specific reference to martyrdom).

5. Boyarin first advanced an interpretation of the Talmudic understanding of *qiddush ha-shem* as martyrdom in a 1993 article entitled, "*Hamidrash Vehama'se—ʿAl Haheker Hahistori Shel Safrut Hazal.*" His understanding of this phenomenon has been criticized by A. Cohen, who argues that the Babylonian Talmud is ambivalent about the practice of voluntary martyrdom and that in the eyes of the Tannaim and Amoraim a Jew who actively seeks death rather than transgress the law is *not* performing *qiddush ha-shem*. It was only some time after the sixth century C.E. that Jewish scholars began to equate martyrdom with *qiddush ha-shem*. See Cohen, "Towards an Erotics of Martyrdom." It nevertheless remains the case that during the Talmudic period, Jews did actively seek death rather than transgress the law—even if that act did not yet qualify as *qiddush ha-shem*.

6. Bowersock, *Martyrdom & Rome*, 1–21.

7. On martyrdom in Islam, see EI^2, s.v. <u>Sh</u>ahīd (E. Kohlberg); Lewinstein, "Revaluation of Martyrdom," 78–91; Bonner, *Jihad in Islamic History*, Chapter 5; D. Cook, *Martyrdom in Islam*.

8. In addition to Wāqidī, the material in question is found in Ibn ʿAsākir, *Ta'rīkh madīnat Dimashq*, 2:8.2–9; Ibn Kathīr, *al-Bidāya wa'l-nihāya*, 4:241 (with a further reference to Bayhaqī); and ʿAlī b. Burhān al-Dīn, *al-Sīra al-ḥalabiyya*, 2:787.

9. His full name is Abū ʿUthmān Rabīʿa b. ʿUthmān b. Rabīʿa b. ʿAbdallāh b. al-Hudayr b. ʿAbd al-ʿAzīz, from the clan of Taym b. Murra. See Ibn Saʿd, *al-Ṭabaqāt al-kubrā*, 7:550. On the symbolic significance of the number seven, see Conrad, "Seven and the *Tasbīʿ*."

10. His full name is Abū Ḥafṣ ʿUmar b. al-Ḥakam b. Abī al-Ḥakam, of the Banū ʿAmr b. ʿĀmir, one of the children of al-Fiṭyawn, who were confederates of Aws. As a traditionist, he was trustworthy and in possession of numerous sound reports (*thiqa wa-lahu aḥādith ṣāliḥa*). See Ibn Saʿd, *al-Ṭabaqāt al-kabīr*, 5:207.17–21.

11. Whereas al-Nuʿmān is an Arab name, Funḥuṣ is a rendering into Arabic of a Jewish name. In the Pentateuch, Phinehas, the grandson of Aaron the priest, is a well-known figure renowned for his religious zeal. When an Israelite married a Midianite woman, Phinehas took a spear, followed them to their tent, and pierced the two of

them. For this manifestation of zeal, Phinehas was praised by Moses (Num. 25:10–15), and he later became a model for the zealots who fought against the Romans in the first century C.E. See Collins, "The Zeal of Phineas: The Bible and the Legitimation of Violence." Cf. Ibn ʿAsākir, *Taʾrīkh madīnat Dimashq*, 2:8.2, where the Jew's name is al-Nuʿmān b. Mihaḍḍ.

12. Wāqidī, *Maghāzī*, 2:756.1–5. Cf. Alī b. Burhān al-Dīn, *al-Sīra al-ḥalabiyya*, 2:787.3, where the name of the Jew is not mentioned.

13. Wāqidī, *Maghāzī*, 2:756.6–9. Cf. Ibn Kathīr, *al-Bidāya wa'l-nihāya*, 4:241.15–18 (citing Wāqidī); ʿAlī b. Burhān al-Dīn, *al-Sīra al-ḥalabiyya*, 2:787.1–2 (where the story, cited without attribution, is clearly dependent on Wāqidī).

14. Wāqidī, *Maghāzī*, 2:756.9–12. Cf. ʿAlī b. Burhān al-Dīn, *al-Sīra al-ḥalabiyya*, 2:787.4–6; Ibn Kathīr, *al-Bidāya wa'l-nihāya*, 4:241.18–20.

15. I. Rabinowitz, *Witness Forever.*

16. Wāqidī, *Maghāzī*, 2:756.12–14; cf. Alī b. Burhān al-Dīn, *al-Sīra al-ḥalabiyya*, 2:787.7–9.

17. N.B. The revelation of Q. 3:92 is said to have been followed by a verbal exchange between Muḥammad and Zayd in which Zayd dedicates his horse (named Sabal) to the path of God (*fī sabīl allāh*), after which the Prophet instructs Usāma to take the horse. See al-Fazārī (d. 186/802), *Kitāb al-siyar*, 134, no. 87.

18. Early Christian literature presents Isaac as a typos of Christ or future sacrifice (*sacramentum futuri*). In the *Epistle* of Barnabus (d. 61 C.E.), Isaac is identified as a typos of Christ. This identification would later be repeated by Clement of Alexandria (d. 211–15) ("He himself is Isaac"), Tertullian (ca. 155–230) ("And so Isaac . . . himself carried the wood for himself, and did at that early date set forth the death of Christ"), and Origen (185–ca. 254) ("Isaac prefigured the truth to come, namely, Christ's resurrection from the dead"). See Lévi, "Le Sacrifice d'Isaac et la mort de Jésus"; Schoeps, "The Sacrifice of Isaac in Paul's Theology," 385–92; Vermes, *Scripture and Tradition*, chap. 7; Swetnam, *Jesus and Isaac*; Hayward, "The Present State of Research into the Targumic Account of the Sacrifice of Isaac"; G. Stroumsa, "Christ's Laughter: Docetic Origins Reconsidered."

19. See Firestone, *Journeys in Holy Lands: The Evolution of the Abraham-Ishmael Legends in Islamic Exegesis.*

20. The suspicion that Isaac disappeared is reinforced by the fact that he is not mentioned by name in connection with the burial of his mother Sarah (Gen. 23) or in connection with Abraham's dispatch of his senior servant to Mesopotamia to secure a wife for his son. It is only when the senior servant returns with Rebecca that Isaac reappears in the flesh and blood—reportedly having just returned from the Negev (Gen. 24:62). See Chapter 7.

21. *Anchor Bible Dictionary*, s.vv. Canon (James A. Sanders), Redaction Criticism (OT) (John Barton); Leiman, *The Canonization of Hebrew Scripture: The Talmudic and Midrashic Evidence.*

22. The *targum*ic representation of Isaac may be summarized as follows: Isaac was a grown man who willingly agreed to be bound for the purpose of sacrifice; the mountain on which he was bound was Mount Zion, future site of the Temple; Isaac was fully and completely offered, even if he was not killed; and he came to be regarded as the lamb of sacrifice, the perfect victim, and the paradigmatic martyr. See Lévi, "Le Sacrifice d'Isaac"; Schoeps, "The Sacrifice of Isaac in Paul's Theology"; Vermes, *Scripture and Tradition*, chap. 7; Hayward, "Present State of Research."

23. The word *midrash* is derived from the verb *darash*, which signifies *to probe or examine.* The goal or object of *midrash* is to pierce the surface level of a sacred text in order to reveal its inner meaning. See, for example, Boyarin, *Intertextuality.* The term has been

appropriated by scholars of both the New Testament and the Qurʾān. See Kermode, *The Genesis of Secrecy: On the Interpretation of Narrative*, x, 81; Wansbrough, *Sectarian Milieu*, chap. 1.

24. Spiegel, *The Last Trial.*

25. Ibid., 127; cf. Levenson, *The Death and Resurrection of the Beloved Son*, 3–52. In a recent doctoral dissertation, Tzemach Yoreh attempts to reconstruct the Elohistic source (E) and concludes that in the original E narrative, Abraham does slaughter Isaac. Tzemach Yoreh, "The Elohistic Source" (in Hebrew).

26. Silva, *4 Maccabees.*

27. Bowersock, *Martyrdom & Rome*, 9–13.

28. *Anchor Bible Dictionary*, s.v. Josephus (Louis H. Feldman).

29. Swetnam, *Jesus and Isaac*, 58–60.

30. See Klein, *The Fragment-Targums of the Pentateuch According to their Extant Sources*, 2:16 (*ad* Gen. 22:10); Vermes, *Scripture and Tradition*, 194. Similar statements are found in *Pseudo-Jonathan*, *Genesis Rabbah*, and *Tosefta.*

31. *Sifre: A Tannaitic Commentary on the Book of Deuteronomy*, trans. Reuven Hammer, 62; cited in Levenson, *The Death and Resurrection of the Beloved Son*, 192. On *Sifre Deuteronomy*, see Strack and Stemberger, *Introduction to the Talmud and Midrash*, 294–99.

32. *Homiliae Selectae Mar-Jacobi Sarugensis IV*, 61–103, cited in Brock, "Genesis 22 in Syriac Tradition," 23 n. 11.

33. Unpublished.

34. Cited in Brock, "Genesis 22 in Syriac Tradition," 12.

35. Ibid.

36. *Pĕsiḳta dĕ-Raḇ Kahăna: R. Kahana's Compilation of Discourses for Sabbaths and Festal Days*, 613–14; cf. Strack and Stemberger, *Introduction to the Talmud and Midrash*, 95, 317–22.

37. BT, *Rosh HaShanah*, 11a; Vermes, *Scripture and Tradition*, 206–8.

38. *PRE*, chapter 31; cf. Spiegel, *The Last Trial*, 30–31.

39. Cf. *Pseudo-Jonathan*, according to which angels transported Isaac to the "school of Shem the great", where he stayed for three years.

40. Vermes, *Scripture and Tradition*, 206–8; Hayward, "The Present State of Research," 134ff.

41. On the date of this text, see VanderKam, *The Book of Jubilees*, 17–21; *The Anchor Bible Dictionary*, s.v. Jubilees, Book of (VanderKam). Some scholars suggest that Jubilees was written in the thirty-year period between 135 and 105 B.C.E., which corresponds to the tenure of John Hyrcanus as High Priest.

42. Vermes, "New Light on the Sacrifice of Isaac from 4Q225," 140–45. Paleographical evidence indicates that 4Q225 was written between 30 B.C.E. and 20 C.E.

43. On Mastema, see *The Book of Jubilees or the Little Genesis*, trans. R. H. Charles, lxxxvi; Pagels, "The Social History of Satan, the 'Intimate Enemy': A Preliminary Sketch," 108, 116, 121–23, 126; Brock, "Genesis 22 in Syriac Tradition," 5.

44. Jastrow, *Dictionary of Talmud Babli, Yerushalmi, Midrashic Literature and Targumim*, 2:1554.

45. *Midrash ha-Gadol*, 1:337.3–5; cf. Spiegel, *The Last Trial*, 106. The detail that Isaac was the spit-and-image of Abraham brings to mind the detail that Jaʿfar b. Abī Ṭālib—who also was martyred at Muʾta—was the spit-and-image of Muḥammad.

46. *Midrash ha-Gadol*, 1:336.17–18; cf. Spiegal, *The Last Trial*, 105.

47. *Midrash ha-Gadol*, 1:337.6–9; cf. Spiegal, *The Last Trial*, 106.

48. *Midrash ha-Gadol*, 1:336.19–337.3; cf. Spiegal, *The Last Trial*, 105–6.

49. On Samael, see BT, *Soṭ*, 10b.

50. *Gen. Rabbah* 56:4. The translation is based on *Midrash Rabbah*, trans. Freedman

and Simon, 1:493–94; cf. *Genesis Rabbah: The Judaic Commentary to the Book of Genesis*, trans. Jacob Neusner, 2:280–81 (to be used with caution).

51. See Silverstein, "Haman's Transition from the *Jāhiliyya* to Islam."

52. Spiegel, *The Last Trial*, 104–5, citing *Gen. Rabbah* 56:4; *Yalkut Shimʿoni*, 1:138–47, Mann, *The Bible as Read and Preached in the Old Synagogue*, 1:63ff. (Hebrew); *Midrash ha-Gadol*, 1:335–38.

53. One imagines that Satan may have uttered to Zayd (and Jaʿfar) words similar—if not identical—to those uttered by Antiochus IV to the seven sons. N.B. *Gen. Rabbah* 56:4 (Samael—or Samael disguised as an old man—challenges Abraham) also served as a model for Islamic renditions of Gen. 22 and the binding of Isaac. See Firestone, "Merit, Mimesis, and Martyrdom: Aspects of Shiʿite Meta-Historical Exegesis on Abraham's Sacrifice in Light of Jewish, Christian, and Sunni Muslim Tradition."

54. On contacts between Jews, Christians, and Muslims in the first century A.H., see Kister, "*Ḥaddithū ʿan banī isrāʾīla wa-lā ḥaraja*: A Study of an Early Tradition"; Lowin, *The Making of a Forefather: Abraham in Islamic and Jewish Exegetical Narratives*, 7–18.

55. The exceptions include Ibn Kathīr, *al-Bidāya wa'l-nihāya*, 4:241 (with a further reference to Bayhaqī); and ʿAlī b. Burhān al-Dīn, *al-Sīra al-ḥalabiyya*, 2:787.

56. Levenson, *The Death and Resurrection of the Beloved Son*, 70.

Chapter 7. Pretexts and Intertexts

1. See, for example, Andrae, *Mohammed*, 153–54; Watt, *Muhammad at Medina*, 329–30; Gabrieli, *Muhammad*, 77; Rodinson, *Mohammed*, 205–8; Haykal, *Life of Muḥammad*, 283–98; Lings, *Muhammad*, 212–14; Peters, *Muhammad and the Origins of Islam*, 197, 296 note 16; Armstrong, *Muhammad: A Biography of the Prophet*, 196–97; Nagel, *Mohammed Leben und Legende*, 786 note 361, 793 note 156, 940–41; *EI*², s.vv. Zayd b. Ḥāritha (M. Lecker), Zaynab bt. Djaḥsh (C. E. Bosworth).

2. See Lev. 18:15 and 20:12.

3. The special relationship between God and Solomon is repeated in I Kings 10:9, where the queen of Sheba says to the king: "Praised be the Lord your God, who delighted in you (*ḥafeṣ be-ka*) and set you on the throne of Israel." Although the plot of the biblical narrative bears no resemblance to Q. 33:37, several biblical motifs are echoed in the Qurʾānic narrative: Just as Zayd was favored by God and His Prophet (37.2), Solomon was loved by the Lord. Just as the name of the woman who would marry first Zayd and then Muḥammad is not mentioned anywhere in the Qurʾān, the name of the queen of Sheba is not mentioned anywhere in the Hebrew Bible (none of Solomon's foreign wives are mentioned by name). Whereas Muḥammad kept his feelings for the unnamed woman a secret (37.4), Solomon kept nothing hidden from the queen of Sheba (I Kings 10:3). Just as Muḥammad was unsure about the legality of marrying his daughter-in-law until he received a divine revelation (37.6), the queen did not believe the reports that she had received about Solomon's wealth until she had verified these reports with her own eyes (I Kings 10:4–6). And just as Muḥammad could not marry Zaynab until Zayd had satisfied his sexual desire for his wife (37.6), the queen did not return to her homeland until Solomon had satisfied all of her desires (I Kings 10:13). In v. 13, the Hebrew word for "her desire" is *ḥefṣâ*, the same word used in v. 9 to signify the Lord's love for Solomon. The desires of the queen that were satisfied by Solomon do not appear to have included sexual desires, and the encounter between this male-female pair did not result in marriage. See I Kings 10:1–10, 13 and II Chron. 9:1–9, 12.

4. For a narrative expansion of Matthew's text, see the *Protevangelium of James*, pars. 13–14, in Elliot, *The Apocryphal New Testament: Legends of the Early Church*, 61–62.

5. On intertextuality, see Kristeva, *Desire in Language: A Semiotic Approach to Literature and Art*; Boyarin, *Intertextuality and the Reading of Midrash*; Fewell, *Reading Between Texts: Intertextuality and the Hebrew Bible*; Biddle, "Ancestral Motifs in 1 Samuel 25: Intertextuality and Characterization," 617–38; Lowin, *The Making of a Forefather: Abraham in Islamic and Jewish Exegetical Narratives*.

6. Ibn Saʿd, *Kitāb al-ṭabaqāt al-kabīr*, III/i, 27–32; the narrative is related on the authority of Hishām b. Muḥammad b. al-Sāʾib al-Kalbī (d. 204–6/819–21), on the authority of his father (d. 146/763), who was an exegete and proto-Shiʿi; and on the authority of Jamīl b. Marthad al-Ṭāʾī (d. ?) and (unidentified) others. Cf. Balādhurī, *Ansāb al-ashrāf*, 1:467–69; *The History of al-Ṭabarī*, 39:6–9; Qurṭubī, *Jāmiʿ*, 14:118 (*ad* 33:4), 14:193 (*ad* 33:7).

7. Ibn Saʿd, *Kitāb al-ṭabaqāt al-kabīr*, III/i, 27.9–23. Cf. Ibn Abī Shayba, *al-Kitāb al-muṣannaf fī al-aḥādīth wa'l-āthār*, 14:321, no. 18,453: Abū Bakr [b. Abī Shayba]—Abū Usāma [Ḥammād b. Usāma b. Zayd, d. 201/816–17]—ʿAbd al-Malik [b. Abī Sulaymān al-Fazārī, d. 145/762–63]—Abū Fazāra [al-ʿAnzī?]: The Prophet—may God bless him and grant him peace—spotted Zayd b. Ḥāritha when he was a young man (*ghulām*) with a sidelock (*dhūdhuʾāba*), after his tribe had seized him in al-Baṭḥāʾ in order to sell him. [Muḥammad] approached Khadīja and said, "I saw a young man in al-Baṭḥāʾ after [his tribe] had seized him in order to sell him. If only I had the money, I would purchase him." She said, "What is his price?" He said, "700 [*dirhams*]." She said, "Take 700 and go and buy him." When he had purchased him and brought him to her, [Muḥammad] said, "Verily, if he belonged to me, I would manumit him." She said, "He is yours, so manumit him." The detail of the sidelock suggests that Zayd may have been Jewish. On early Jewish converts to Islam, see Lecker, "Zayd b. Thābit, 'A Jew with Two Sidelocks': Judaism and Literacy in Pre-Islamic Medina (Yathrib)," 259–73; idem, "Ḥudhayfa b. al-Yamān and ʿAmmār b. Yāsir, Jewish Converts to Islam." According to another early narrative, related on the authority of Anas b. Mālik (d. 91/709) and others, Zayd was a Syrian who was captured by horsemen of the tribe of Tihāma, who sold him to Ḥakīm b. Ḥizām b. Khuwaylid, who gave him to his maternal aunt, Khadīja, who gave him to the Prophet, who manumitted him and adopted him (*tabannāhu*). See Qurṭubī, *Jāmiʿ*, 14:118; Ibn ʿAsākir, *Taʾrīkh madīnat Dimashq*, 19:346.11–23. In another report, while Zayd was visiting the family of his maternal grandfather, horsemen from the tribe of Fazāra captured him and sold him, at ʿUkāẓ, not to Khadīja's paternal nephew, Ḥakīm b. Ḥizām, but to her paternal cousin, Waraqa b. Nawfal, who was a Christian. However it was that Zayd was acquired by Khadīja, following her marriage to the Prophet ca. 605 C.E., she gave the captive to her husband as a gift. See also *EI*², s.v. Zayd b. Ḥāritha (M. Lecker).

8. For the full text of the poem in Arabic, see Ibn Saʿd, *Kitāb al-ṭabaqāt al-kabīr*, III/i, 27–28; Balādhurī, *Ansāb al-ashrāf*, 1:467 (bottom)–468.7. For an English translation, see *The History of al-Ṭabarī*, 39:7.

9. Ibn Saʿd, *Kitāb al-ṭabaqāt al-kabīr*, III/i, 28.6–8. Cf. Balādhurī, *Ansāb*, 1:468.12.

10. Ibn Saʿd, *Kitāb al-ṭabaqāt al-kabīr*, III/i, 28.9–11.

11. Ibid., III/i, 28.12–13.

12. Qurṭubī, *Jāmiʿ*, 14:193.9–14.

13. Ibn Saʿd, *Kitāb al-ṭabaqāt al-kabīr*, III/i, 28.13–17; cf. Balādhurī, *Ansāb*, 1:468.15–17; Ibn ʿAsākir, *Taʾrīkh madīnat Dimashq*, 19:347–48.

14. On this verse and its relation to Jewish martyrdom doctrine, see Chapter 6.

15. Ibn Saʿd, *Kitāb al-ṭabaqāt al-kabīr*, III/i, 28.17–20; cf. Ibn ʿAsākir, *Taʾrīkh madīnat Dimashq*, 19:348.

16. Ibn Saʿd, *Kitāb al-ṭabaqāt al-kabīr*, III/i, 28.20–22.

17. Qurṭubī, *Jāmiʿ*, 14:193.14–17.

18. See the report cited in Ṭabarī, *Jāmiʿ*, 21:119 (top): *Isnād*: al-Ḥasan b. Yaḥyā—ʿAbd al-Razzāq—Maʿmar—al-Zuhrī (d. 124/742): "I have been informed that this [verse was revealed] about Zayd b. Ḥāritha [*sic*], about whom God coined a simile, which means: the son of another man is not your son." In other words, the simile at the beginning of Q. 33:4 refers to Zayd, who had been adopted by the Messenger of God. Here al-Zuhrī does connect the revelation of Q. 33:4 to Zayd, even if he does not refer to the narrative moment in which Zayd is forced to choose between his natural father and his master.

19. Zayd's rejection of his natural father and mother so that he might remain with Muḥammad brings to mind the statement attributed to Jesus in Matt. 10:37, "Whoever loves father and mother more than me is not worthy of me." This statement suggests that those individuals who chose to join the Jesus movement willy-nilly were forced to abandon their birth families. On joining the new movement, Jesus became their spiritual or surrogate father. Likewise, Muḥammad became Zayd's surrogate father, and he subsequently would become the surrogate father of the Meccan converts to Islam.

20. Ibn Saʿd, *Kitāb al-ṭabaqāt al-kabīr*, III/i, 28.22–26; Ibn ʿAsākir, *Taʾrīkh madīnat Dimashq*, 19:348.

21. See Maghen, "Intertwined Triangles," 74 note 161, citing Ibn Ḥajar al-ʿAsqalānī, *al-Iṣāba* (Cairo, 1328 A.H.), 1:563, no. 2890.

22. Zayd also was the first adult male convert, the Beloved of the Messenger of God, the only Muslim apart from Muḥammad whose name is mentioned in the Qurʾān, and a military commander.

23. Joseph weeps in private after hearing his brothers admit their guilt and regret about having mistreated him (Gen. 42:24), and again after seeing his brother Benjamin (Gen. 43:30). He weeps in public after revealing himself to his brothers (Gen. 45:14), and again at Goshen, when he is reunited with his father Jacob (Gen. 46:29).

24. Exceptionally, here I follow *The Anchor Bible: Genesis*, trans. E. A. Speiser, 110–11.

25. See Westermann, *Genesis 12–36: A Commentary*, 209ff. (Gen. 15:1–21); L. I. Rabinowitz, "The Study of a Midrash," 143–61.

26. *The Anchor Bible Dictionary*, s.v. Eliezer (William H. Propp). Cf. Bewer, "Eliezer of Damascus," 160–62; Unger, "Some Comments on the Text of Genesis 15 2, 3," 49–50; Ginsberg, "Abram's 'Damascene' Steward," 31–32.

27. Some rabbis gloss *dammesek* as "the one who draws and gives others to drink," that is, transmits to others the teachings of his master; others see an allusion to the servant's coveting of his master's possessions; others see a reference to Abraham's pursuit of the Canaanite kings to Damascus and beyond. Linguistically, *dammesek* is said to be an otherwise unattested equivalent of *damaskhqī*, that is, *of Damascus*, *Damascene*.

28. Speiser explains the biblical verse by comparing it to Nuzian law: Eliezer was the *ewuru* or indirect heir, the person who inherits in the absence of the normal, recognized heir. The *ewuru* heir might be a collateral or, as in the present case, an outsider. *The Anchor Bible: Genesis*, trans. Speiser, 111–12.

29. Westermann, *Genesis 12–36: A Commentary*, 220.

30. The number of saintly fathers who are said to have formulated the Nicene creed is 318.

31. *PRE*, Chapter 31, 151. See Bakhos, *Ishmael on the Border: Rabbinic Portrayals of the First Arab*, esp. Chapter 4 ("Ishmael in Later Midrashim"); Ben-Ari, "Stories About Abraham in Islam. A Geographical Approach."

32. Ibn Saʿd, *Kitāb al-ṭabaqāt al-kabīr*, III/i, 28.26–27. Cf. Balādhurī, *Ansāb al-ashrāf*, 1:469.3; Qurṭubī, *Jāmiʿ*, 14:193, where Muḥammad says, "Bear witness that I am [both his] heir and the one from whom [he] inherits (*al-wārith wa'l-mawrūth*)."

33. Ibn Saʿd, *Kitāb al-ṭabaqāt al-kabīr*, III/i, 28.27–28. The ceremony was witnessed by Zayd's biological father and uncle who, after consenting to the adoption, returned to Syria empty-handed, albeit not dissatisfied.

34. Qurṭubī, *Jāmiʿ*, 14:192.3–6.

35. Cf. the report in which Asmā' bt. ʿUmays was kneading dough when the Prophet arrived to break the news of Jaʿfar's death. This is a topos—another sign of the story-tellers at work. Cf. Ackerman, "'And the Women Knead Dough': The Worship of the Queen of Heaven in Sixth-Century Judah."

36. The narrative suggests that Zaynab's communication with God was followed by the revelation of Q. 33:37. Cf. Gen. 25:22 where, after discovering that she was pregnant with twins, Rebecca "went to inquire of the Lord."

37. Qurṭubī, *Jāmiʿ*, 14:192.7–13; cf. Muslim, *Ṣaḥīḥ*, Nikāḥ, bāb 15, no. 3575. *Isnād*: Muḥammad b. Ḥātim b. Maymūn—Bahz—Muḥammad b. Rāfiʿ—Abū al-Naḍr Hāshim b. al-Qāsim, the two of them said—Sulaymān b. al-Mughīra—on the authority of Thābit—on the authority of Anas–and this is the *ḥadīth* of Bahz. The fact that the Prophet entered Zaynab's apartment without permission may be related to Q. 33:53, which begins, "O you who believe, do not enter the apartment of the Prophet unless invited for a meal without waiting for the proper time." Alternatively, it may be related to Zayd's request from his father for *permission* to divorce his wife. Cf. Ṭabarsī, *Majmaʿ al-bayān*, 8:181.12–13.

38. Qurṭubī, *Jāmiʿ*, 14:192.17–18. Text: *wa-hādhā imtiḥān*[un] *li-Zayd wa'khtibār*[un] *lahu ḥattā yuẓhira ṣabrahu wa'nqiyādahu wa-ṭawʿahu.*

39. Ibid., 14:192.3–4.

40. Muqātil, *Tafsīr*, 3:47.4–5.

41. Ibid., 3:46.26, 47.1.

42. Ibid., 3:47.5–12.

43. On Jaḥsh, see Ibn Ḥajar al-ʿAsqalānī, *al-Iṣāba fī tamyīz al-ṣaḥāba*, 1:466, no. 1109.

44. On ʿAbdallāh b. Jaḥsh, see *The History of al-Ṭabarī*, 7, index, s.v. ʿAA b. Jaḥsh.

45. Muqātil, *Tafsīr*, 3:46–47.

46. Ibid., 3:46.23–47.14.

47. Bethuel plays no part in Gen. 24. In rabbinic *midrash*, Bethuel is said to have been the king of Aram-naharaim, a murderer, thief, and rapist. He would have committed incest with his virgin daughter Rebecca but for the fact that he himself was poisoned by food that he had prepared for a guest. See L. I. Rabinowitz, "The Study of a Midrash," 143–61. The assumption that Bethuel was dead is made explicit in Josephus' retelling of Gen. 24. Rebecca says, "my father was Bethuel, but he is dead; and Laban is my brother and, together with my mother, takes care of all our family affairs, and is the guardian of my virginity." See *Jewish Antiquities*, Chapter 16, 248. According to some modern scholars, Bethuel's name was added to Gen. 24:15, 24, and 44 in anticipation of the genealogy in Gen. 25:20 and 28:2, 5. See Westermann, *Genesis 12–36: A Commentary*, 86 (*ad* Gen. 24:15–16), 387 (*ad* 24:23–25), 387–88 (*ad* 24:28–32), 388–89 (*ad* 24:42–48); *Anchor Bible: Genesis* (trans. Speiser), 180–81, notes 28, 50.

48. The translation is that of Bakhos in *Ishmael on the Border*, 107. Cf. Ginzberg, *The Legends of the Jews*, 1:266–9; 5:247, note 218.

49. Cf. Gen. 24:61–67, where Rebecca arrives in Canaan riding a camel and dismounts just before Isaac takes her as his wife.

50. Muqātil, *Tafsīr*, 3:47.14–18.

51. Muḥammad is said to have been riding a camel when Q. 4:176 was revealed to him. See Chapter 9.

52. See Muqātil, *Tafsīr*, 3:47.20–23, where the text reads: *lam yastaṭiʿnī wa-lā yaqdiru ʿalayya*; for variants, see, for example, Ṭabarī, *Jāmiʿ* (1954–58), 22:13.9–12; Qurṭubī, *Jāmiʿ*, 14:190.5–6.

53. Qurṭubī, *Jāmiʿ*, 14:189.

54. Muqātil, *Tafsīr*, 3:47–49.

55. As Ze'ev Maghen has put it, "The wars that occasioned the deaths of Uriah and Zayd were fought at approximately the same location, for essentially the same reason, and after more or less the same preparations were made by both friend and foe." Maghen, "Intertwined Triangles," 69–70.

56. Because Zaynab did not bear any children, God could not punish Muḥammad by causing their first-born son to die in infancy. In this instance, the punishment motif may have been transferred to another context: God did cause Ibrāhīm, the son born to Muḥammad by Māriya the Copt, to die in infancy.

57. The following is a summary of his life as recorded in various Islamic sources: Zayd's birth name was Zayd b. Ḥāritha b. Shuraḥīl al-Kalbī. As a youth he was captured, enslaved, and acquired by Muḥammad b. ʿAbdallāh al-Qurashī. Zayd's family located him in Mecca, where Ḥāritha b. Shuraḥīl al-Kalbī attempted to ransom his son from Muḥammad. Of his own free will, Zayd chose to remain Muḥammad's slave rather than return to Syria with his father. Following this demonstration of absolute loyalty, Muḥammad adopted Zayd as his son in a formal ceremony attested by witnesses in the sacred precinct in Mecca. The act of adoption resulted in a name change—Zayd b. Ḥāritha became Zayd b. Muḥammad—and in the creation of mutual rights of inheritance between father and son. Shortly after Zayd's adoption, Muḥammad received his first revelation and emerged as a prophet. Zayd was the first adult male to become a Muslim, and his devotion to the Prophet and the new religion was absolute. Muḥammad loved Zayd and called him the Beloved of the Messenger of God. In Mecca, Zayd married Umm Ayman, who bore him a son named Usāma, the Prophet's grandson, known as the Beloved Son of the Beloved of the Messenger of God. Shortly after the hijra to Medina Zayd told his father of his desire to marry Zaynab bt. Jaḥsh, who was a descendant of ʿAbd al-Muṭṭalib, the Prophet's paternal cross-cousin and, by her own account, "the most perfect woman of Quraysh." Initially Muḥammad was opposed to the marriage but Zayd, with the assistance of ʿAlī b. Abī Ṭālib, persuaded his father to change his mind. Zayd's marriage to Zaynab was short-lived. Zayd complained to Muḥammad about Zaynab's behavior. Intending to admonish his daughter-in-law, the Prophet paid a visit to the couple. When he arrived at their residence, only Zaynab was at home. Inadvertently, Muḥammad caught sight of Zaynab in a state of dishabille and fell in love with her. When Zayd returned home later that day, Zaynab regaled him with the story of the strange encounter with her father-in-law. Zayd now was more determined than ever to divorce his wife. The Prophet, however, instructed his son not to divorce her, despite the fact that he himself was secretly in love with the woman. Muḥammad kept his love for his daughter-in-law a secret because he knew that a marriage between a man and his daughter-in-law was forbidden by law and he feared public reaction to such a union. At precisely this moment, God sent down the revelation that became v. 37 of *Sūrat al-Aḥzāb*. The revelation legitimized the union by creating a distinction between marriage with the former wife of a natural son (which continued to be forbidden), and marriage with the former wife of an adopted son (which was henceforth legitimate). Following the revelation of v. 37, Zayd divorced Zaynab so that his father could marry her. Curiously, it was Zayd whom the Prophet instructed to inform his former wife of his decision to marry her, an

assignment that Zayd carried out, albeit with difficulty. In the interval between Zayd's divorcing Zaynab and Muḥammad's marrying her, the Prophet repudiated Zayd as his son, whereupon the man who had been favored by both God and His Prophet lost the right to call himself the son of Muḥammad and forfeited his right to inherit from him. Subsequently, Zayd served as the commander of numerous military missions. In the year 8/629, Muḥammad appointed Zayd as the commander of a military expedition that was sent to southern Jordan to exact vengeance for the slaying of one of Muḥammad's messengers. A Jew failed to dissuade Muḥammad from sending Zayd to certain death; and he also failed to dissuade Zayd from participating in a suicide mission. The Muslim forces were badly outnumbered by the Byzantines, and Zayd fell as a martyr. As a reward, he gained eternal life in heaven.

58. One no doubt could expand the list of figures who served as models for Zayd. For example, the Apostle Peter was loved by Jesus, underwent a name change, became Jesus' earthly representative following the crucifixion, and suffered martyrdom.

59. On condensed symbols, see V. Turner, *Forest of Symbols*, 29–30.

Chapter 8. Paleography and Codicology: Bibliothèque Nationale de France, Arabe 328a

1. See generally EI^2, s.v. Ḳur'ān (A. Welch), *EQ*, s.vv. Codices of the Qur'ān (F. Leemhuis), The Collection of the Qur'ān (J. Burton), Manuscripts of the Qur'ān (F. Déroche), Muṣḥaf (H. Motzki); Motzki, "The Collection of the Qur'ān," 1–34; Gilliot, "Creation of a Fixed Text," 41–58.

2. EI^2, s.vv. Musaylima (W. Montgomery Watt), al-Yamāma (G.R. Smith).

3. Ibn Abī Dā'ūd, *Kitāb al-maṣāḥif*, 6.11–22, 7.1–19, 8.8–9.5, 20.10–21.2, 23.12–19. According to a variant, it was not ʿUmar but Abū Bakr who initiated the first collection (ibid., 6.7–11).

4. Ibid., 6.11–18, 23.12–19.

5. EI^2, s.v. Zayd b. Thābit al-Anṣārī (M. Lecker).

6. Ibn Abī Dā'ūd, *Kitāb al-maṣāḥif*, 6.19–7.1.

7. Alternatively, it is said that the first collection was a collective effort. See ibid., 9.5–15.

8. Ibid., 7.1–5, 31.5–8.

9. Ibid., 5.5–6.3. Alternatively, it is said that ʿUmar was the first to collect the Qur'ān, on which, see further below.

10. Ibid., 8.7–8, 9.3–5, 9.18–20, 21, l. −2.

11. Ibid., 11.20–12.12, 13.12–16, 13.22–14.10, 14.11–18.

12. Ibid., 18.15–20, 21.2–4, 23.13–18.

13. EI^2, s.v. Ibn Masʿūd (J.-C. Vadet).

14. On Ḥudhayfa, see Lecker, "Ḥudhayfa b. al-Yamān and ʿAmmār b. Yāsir, Jewish Converts to Islam," 149–62.

15. EI^2, s.v. al-Ashʿarī, Abū Mūsa (L. Veccia Vaglieri).

16. Ibn Abī Dā'ūd, *Kitāb al-maṣāḥif*, 14.11–18; cf. 16.4–7, 16.10–19.

17. Ibid., 13.12–16.

18. Ibid., 11.18–12.12.

19. Ibid., 19.1–2, 19.20–20.1, 21.4–6. According to some reports, these disagreements led to mutual accusations of *kufr* or infidelity (ibid., 22.19, 23.10, 25.8–10). According to other reports, the disagreements were so serious that the Muslim community came to the verge of *fitna* or civil strife (ibid., 21.4).

20. Ibid., 11.14–12.12.

21. Ibid., 19.2–5, 20.3–4, 25.11–12, 25.18–19, 26.4–7.

22. Ibid., 19.2–3, 20.2–3, 20.6–7, 21.7.
23. Ibid., 19.5–6, 20.4–5.
24. Ibid., 31.5–11. Cf. ibid., 30.1–31.11. In some reports, the lost verse that was recovered was the thirty-third verse of *Sūrat al-Aḥzāb* (ibid., 19.18–33, 29.5–20).
25. Ibid., 18.7–13.
26. Ibid., 21.18.
27. Ibid., 34.14.
28. Ibid., 34.17.
29. Ibid., 19.6–8, 20.6–7, 21.8, 23.7–8, 23.12, 23.18–19, 24.14.
30. Ibid., 24.6.
31. Ibid., 13.17–14.5, 19.8, 20.8–9, 22.1–2.
32. Ibid., 17.8–10.
33. Ibid., 12.12–21, 22.15–17, 23.2–5.
34. *EI*², s.vv. Ḥafṣa (L. Veccia Vaglieri), Marwān I b. al-Ḥakam (C. E. Bosworth).
35. Ibn Abī Dāʾūd, *Kitāb al-maṣāḥif*, 21.8–13, 24.20–25.5.
36. Ibid., 14.18–15.12, 16.20–17.2, 17.2–5, 17.16–17.
37. Ibid., 15.12–19. Ibn Masʿūd cited—with irony—Q. 3:161: "It is not for any prophet to deceive [the people]. Those who deceive will bring their deceit [with them] on the Day of Judgement. Then every soul will be paid in full what it has amassed, and they will not be wronged."
38. Ibid., 17.19.
39. On this term, see Crone and Hinds, *God's Caliph.*
40. *EI*², s.v. ʿAbd al-Malik b. Marwān (H.A.R. Gibb); C. Robinson, *ʿAbd al-Malik.*
41. al-Balādhurī, *Ansāb al-ashrāf*, 4:2, 586. In this same statement, the caliph is reported to have said that it was during the month of Ramaḍān that he was born, weaned, and received the oath of allegiance.
42. *EI*², s.v. al-Ḥadjdjādj b. Yūsuf (A. Dietrich).
43. de Prémare, "ʿAbd al-Malik b. Marwān et le processus de constitution du Coran," 202–3.
44. Ibn Abī Dāʾūd, *Kitāb al-maṣāḥif*, 49–50, 117–18. The verses in which the spelling of a word was changed were 2:259, 5:48, 10:22, 12:45, 23:85–89, 26:116 and 167, 43:32, 47:15, 57:7, and 81:24.
45. ʿAbd al-Masīḥ al-Kindī, *Letter to al-Hāshimī*, 137, cited in Hoyland, *Seeing Islam as Others Saw It*, 501. On al-Kindī, see *EI*², s.v.
46. Ibn Abī Dāʾūd, *Kitāb al-maṣāḥif*, 35.18–19, 49–50; cf. Ibn Wahb, *al-Ǧāmiʿ: die Koranwissenschaften*, 254.6; Ibn Shabba, *Taʾrīkh al-madīna*, 7.15.
47. de Prémare, *Les Fondations de l'Islam*; idem, "ʿAbd al-Malik b. Marwān et le processus de constitution du Coran," 179–212; C. Robinson, *ʿAbd al-Malik*, 100–104. Cp. Hoyland (*Seeing Islam as Others Saw It*, 501), who concludes that it is "almost certain" that al-Ḥajjāj undertook a revision of the Qurʾān but suggests that this project was limited to "sponsoring . . . an improved edition"—without attributing any special importance to the resulting improvements.
48. The assumption that the reading and consonantal skeleton of the Qurʾān remained open and fluid until ca. 86/705 also has the effect of bringing the literary evidence into synchrony with the surviving documentary evidence relating to the text of the Qurʾān. The earliest extant physical evidence of the Qurʾān to which a secure date can be assigned is the 240 meter long mosaic inscription that runs along the uppermost part of the octagonal arcade inside the Dome of the Rock in Jerusalem. The inscription, composed of a series of recognizable Qurʾānic verses, was addressed generally to the People of the Book and specifically to the Christians. The Dome of the Rock was commissioned by ʿAbd al-Malik and completed in the year 72/691–92. See

Grabar, *The Dome of the Rock*. The verses that make up the inscription are especially concerned with the subject of Christology.

49. Ibn Abī Dāʾūd, *Kitāb al-maṣāḥif*, 22.19, 23.10, 25.8–10

50. Ibid., 21.4.

51. This point was made nearly a century ago by Arthur Jeffery, who observed (*Materials*, 10): "when we have assembled all the variants from these earlier codices that can be gleaned from the works of the exegetes and philologers, we have only such readings as were useful for the purposes of *tafsīr* and were considered to be sufficiently near orthodoxy to be allowed to survive."

52. For ease of reference, Qurʾān scholars assigned linguistic tags to important verses, e.g. the debt verse (*āyat al-dayn*), the poll-tax verse (*āyat al-jizya*), the throne verse (*āyat al-kursī*), the light verse (*āyat al-nūr*), or the stoning verse (*āyat al-rajm*). See *EQ*, Index, 240–41. Although the second half of the twelfth verse in *Sūrat al-Nisāʾ* might have been called *āyat al-kalāla* or "the *kalāla* verse," I have found only one isolated instance of this usage—an anomaly to which we shall return in Chapter 9.

53. The variation in translations of this verse is impressive. See Appendix 1.

54. Ṭabarī, *Tafsīr* (ed. Shākir), 9:433–34, nos. 10,870–73. Other verses contend for the distinction of being the last verse revealed to Muḥammad, the best known and most widely accepted being Q. 5:3: "Today I have perfected your religion for you and completed My blessing for you and have approved Submission (*islām*) as a religion for you."

55. For English translations of 4:176, see again Appendix 1.

56. See the chapter "Les pérégrinations d'un manuscrit" in Déroche, *La transmission manuscrite du Coran aux débuts de l'islam: Le codex Parisino-petropolitanus* (forthcoming). I am grateful to Professor Déroche for sharing this chapter with me prior to publication.

57. Ibid.

58. Déroche et Noja Noseda, *Sources de la transmission manuscrite du texte coranique*, vol. 1.

59. Dutton, "An Early *Muṣḥaf*," 71–89.

60. *EI*^{2}, s.v. Ibn ʿĀmir (ed.).

61. Dutton, "An Early *Muṣḥaf*," 74, 82.

62. Ibid., 83–84.

63. Ibid., 76–77.

64. Dutton ignores 4:12b and 4:176, his interest in the meaning of *kalāla* notwithstanding. See Dutton, *The Origins of Islamic Law*, 109–12 and 135.

65. Amari speculated that BNF 328b was part of the same codex as BNF 328a, an assumption confirmed by Déroche, based on codicological evidence. The two fragments are bound together as BNF 328. Folios 57 to 70 were written by Scribe C. See Déroche, *La transmission manuscrite du Coran aux débuts de l'islam* (forthcoming).

66. Of 111 folio pages, the distribution of lines per page is as follows: 21 lines (7 pages), 22 lines (25 pages), 23 lines (23 pages), 24 lines (18 pages), 25 lines (16 pages), 26 lines (13 pages), 27 lines (7 pages), 28 lines (3 pages).

67. Like other early scripts, the Ḥijāzī style script did not have the diacritical marks that were later invented to distinguish between and among the several possible readings of a homograph: <*bāʾ/tāʾ/thāʾ/nūn/yāʾ*>, <*jīm/ḥāʾ/khāʾ*>, <*fāʾ/qāf*>; or between one of a pair of homographs: <*dāl/dhāl*>, <*ṭāʾ/ẓāʾ*>, <*ʿayn/ghayn*>, <*sīn/shīn*>.

68. See Déroche, *Islamic Codicology*, 32–43, 65–102, 114, 167–84, 205–19.

69. Déroche et Noseda, *Sources de la transmission manuscrite du texte coranique*, 1: xi ff. Cf. Déroche, *The Abbasid Tradition: Qurʾān's of the 8th to the 10th Centuries A.D.*

70. The designation of this script as *Ḥijāzī* is based on the following statement by Ibn al-Nadīm (d. 385/995) in his description of the earliest Arabic scripts: "The first of

the Arab scripts was the script of Makkah, the next of al-Madīnah, then of al-Baṣrah, and then of al-Kūfah. For the *alifs* of the scripts of Makkah and al-Madīnah there is a turning of the hand to the right and lengthening of the strokes, one form having a slight slant." *The Fihrist of al-Nadīm*, trans. Bayard Dodge, 1:10. In the middle of the nineteenth century, M. Amari coined the term *Ḥijāzī script* to refer to the style of writing practiced in Mecca and Medina. This term is misleading, however, inasmuch as most of the extant fragments and manuscripts written in this script were found in Damascus, Fustat, and Ṣanʿāʾ. For this reason, François Déroche has suggested that it is better to speak of the Ḥijāzī *style* rather than the Ḥijāzī *script*, and he uses the term *Ḥijāzī codex* to refer to manuscripts written in this style. I follow his lead. See *EQ*, s.v., Manuscripts of the Qurʾān (F. Déroche); cf. Beatrice Gruendler, *The Development of the Arabic Script*, 131–41.

71. Déroche, *The Abbasid Tradition: Qurʾān's of the 8th to the 10th centuries A.D.*, 27–33.

72. Folio 20a ends with the word *al-ṣāliḥāt* in 4:173. The verse continues at the top of folio 20b, although the first two words on l. 1 (*wa-yuwaffīhim ujūrahum*) are illegible due to damage, presumably from water.

73. In the facsimile edition, the first six lines of folio 20b occupy 58 mm (average = 9.66 mm), measured from baseline to baseline; the next six lines occupy 67 mm (average = 11.166 mm). The difference is 1.5 mm per line.

74. Déroche, *Islamic Codicology*, 217; cf. idem, *The Abbasid Tradition*, 34ff.

75. See, for example, on l. 16, the *wāw* of ***walad***; on l. 17 the *tāʾ*, *wāw*, and *ṣād* of ***tūṣūna***, the *yāʾ* and *nūn* of ***dayn***, and the *wāw* of ***wa-in***; and on l. 18 the *rāʾ* and *thāʾ* of *y-w-**r-th***.

76. On l. 21, the *alif* of *aw* is also flat. This too is the work of Corrector 2.

77. On folio 10b, one also finds an interval of only 2 mm between *al-niṣf* and *wa-lā* (l. 6) and between *in* and *kāna* (l. 7).

78. In the canonical text of the Qurʾān, it will be recalled, a bifurcated compound phrase (*rajul*^{un} . . . *aw imraʾat*^{un}) is the subject of a passive verb (*yū**ra**thu*).

79. Zammit, *A Comparative Lexical Study of Qurʾānic Arabic.*

80. *TDOT*, s.vv. *ḥāṯān*, *kallāh.*

81. *CAD*, s.v. ḫatanu.

82. Gordon, *Ugaritic Textbook.*

83. *Corpus inscriptionum semiticarum.*

84. Drower and Macuch, *Mandaic Dictionary.*

85. *Répertoire d'épigraphie sémitique*, 4878, 2.

86. *TDOT*, s.v. *ḥâṯân.*

87. *CAD*, s.v. kallatu.

88. *A Dictionary of the Ugaritic Language in the Alphabetic Tradition*, ed. Del Olmo Lete and Sanmartẓ, trans. Watson, pt. 1, 441.

89. In the Hebrew Bible, *kallâh* denotes both the relationship of a young woman to her (future) husband ("bride") and her relationship toward her husband's father or mother ("daughter-in-law"). In the first sense it can also signify a woman entering into marriage and, in the second, a woman who is already married, sometimes even a widow (Gen. 38:6–10; Ruth 1:4ff.). The abstract noun *k*^{e}*lûlôt* occurs once, in Jer. 2:2, where it signifies the "state of being a bride," just as the Akkadian abstract noun *kallūtu/kallatūtu* signifies "status as daughter-in-law or bride." *Kallâh* is used in the Hebrew Bible in three different ways. (1) *As a legal term.* Lev. 18, the so-called Holiness Code, contains a list of the women with whom a man may not have sexual relations. Lev. 18:15 states: "Do not uncover the nakedness of your daughter-in-law (*kallatkâ*): she is your son's wife; you shall not uncover her nakedness." (2) *As an identifier.* Ruth is the *kallâh* or daughter-in-law of Naomi, and Tamar is the *kallâh* or daughter-in-law of

Judah. Similarly, Gen. 11:31 reads: "Terah took his son Abram, his grandson Lot the son of Haran, and his daughter-in-law (*kallatô*) Sarai, the wife of his son Abram. . . ." (3) *As a symbol or metaphor*: *kallâh* in the sense of "bride" usually appears in tandem with *ḥâṯân* or "bridegroom"; whenever this combination occurs, the *kallâh* and *ḥâṯân* invariably appear as typical representatives of people who are especially happy. For example, the rising sun is compared to a bridegroom leaving his chamber (*ḥuppatô*) (Ps. 19:6). In Joel 2:16, the bride and bridegroom are summoned from their chambers to participate in the penitential liturgy: "Let the bridegroom go forth from his chamber (*me-ḥedrô*) and the bride from her canopy (*ḥuppatâ*). The word *kallâh* occurs thirty-four times in the Hebrew Bible, as follows (according to usage): Wife or daughter-in-law of the speaker: Gen. 11:31, Gen. 38:11, 16, and 24, Lev. 18:15, I Sam. 4:19, Micah 7:6, Ruth 1:6–8, and 22, Ruth 2:20, 22, Ruth 4:1, I Chron. 2:4. Used in parallelism with *ḥtn*: Is. 61:10, Is. 62:5, Jer. 7:34, Jer. 16:9, Jer. 25:10, Jer. 33:11. Context does not provide the meaning: Lev. 20:12, Is. 49:18 (one adorning herself, possibly bride), Jer. 2:32 (one adorning herself, possibly bride), Ezek. 22:11, Hos. 4:13–14, Song of Songs: 4:8–12, 5:1 (*TDOT*, s.v. *kallâ*, 7:165).

90. *A Compendious Syriac Dictionary*, s.v. *kalltā.*

91. Jastrow, *Dictionary of Talmud Babli, Yerushalmi, Midrashic Literature and Targumim*, s.v. *kalltā.*

92. *Dictionary of the Northwest Semitic Inscriptions*, pt. 1, 510, s.v. klh_2, citing texts from Palmyra.

93. Leslau, *Ethiopic and South Arabic Contributions to the Hebrew Lexicon*, 26: *kelán* (Soqoṭri), *kelôn* (Mehri), *kelun* (Šḫauri), *kellan* (Dhofar), *kulān* (Hadramaut).

94. Ibn Manẓūr, *Lisān al-ʿarab*, s.v. k-n-n; cf. Smith, *Kinship and Marriage in Early Arabia*, 161–62, and 209, note 1. The basic meaning of this root is *to conceal.*

95. Ibn Manẓūr, *Lisān al-ʿarab*, s.v. m-r-ʾ.

96. This is why the pronoun suffix attached to the preposition *li-* on l. 1b must be masculine, i.e., *lahu* ("and he has"). The pronoun suffix refers back to the *rajul* or "man" mentioned on l. 1a. Accordingly, the "brother" and "sister" mentioned on l. 1b must be the siblings of the *testator*; they cannot be the siblings of the designated heir.

97. The Qurʾānic rule may be compared with the *actio ad supplendam legitimam*, a reform of Roman inheritance law introduced by Justinian. See *SQH*, 44 and note 40.

98. For a similar rule in Near Eastern provincial law, see Paradise, "Nuzi Inheritance Practices," 242: if a man dies and his closest surviving blood relatives are one or more brothers, the latter customarily would succeed him—unless he previously had designated his adopted son as the *ewuru* heir, thereby sending a signal to his brothers that the *ewuru* heir would inherit not only his property but also his legal role and status as head of the household.

99. On the formation of Islamic inheritance law, see Appendix 3 and *SQH.*

100. The Qurʾān contains numerous pairs of verses that appear to contradict one another, and the early authorities often resolved this problem by invoking the doctrine of *naskh* or abrogation. On the doctrine of abrogation, see Powers, "On the Abrogation of the Bequest Verses," 246–95; idem, "The Exegetical Genre *nāsikh al-Qurʾān wa mansūkhuhu*," 117–38; Burton, *The Sources of Islamic Law: Islamic theories of abrogation.*

101. See, for example, Ṭabarī, *Tafsīr* (ed. Shakir), 8:61–62.

102. On stubs, see Déroche, *Islamic Codicology*, 67–69, 72–73, 77.

103. Déroche, *La transmission manuscrite du Coran aux débuts de l'islam* (forthcoming).

104. Déroche, *Islamic Codicology*, 39–40.

105. It is likely that Scribe A was copying from a model text. On folio 6a, l. 2, for example, he first wrote *wa'llāhu* and then corrected himself by erasing the initial *alif*,

thus producing *lillāhi.* It is unlikely that he would have made the initial mistake if he was transcribing a text that was being recited to him.

106. The number of lines on the next eight folio pages is as follows: 21a, 21b, 22a, 22b, 23a all have twenty-five lines; 23b has twenty-four lines; 24a has twenty-five lines; and 24b has twenty-four lines. All of these pages were written by Scribe A.

107. For Scribe A, the breakdown of lines per page is as follows: 21 lines (4 pages), 22 lines (20 pages), 23 lines (22 pages), 24 lines (13 pages), 25 lines (15 pages), 26 lines (12 pages), 27 lines (7 pages), 28 lines (2 pages).

108. Had Scribe A been unconcerned about making the page that he was producing identical to the model from which he was copying, he could have rewritten folio 20a–b without paying any attention to the number of lines on a folio page. After all, folio 21 was still empty.

109. Following the revision of Q. *4:12b, the word **kalla* in the sense of *daughter-in-law* disappeared from Arabic, leaving virtually no trace of its existence. Henceforth, when speakers of the Arabic language wanted to refer to a *daughter-in-law,* they used the word *kanna* (pl. *kanāʾin*) (see, e.g., Khalīl b. Aḥmad, *Kitāb al-ʿayn,* s.v. k-n-n; Ibn Manẓūr, *Lisān al-ʿarab,* s.v. k-n-n) or the *iḍāfa*-construct *imraʾat al-ibn* ("wife of a son"). As a result, the concept of *daughter-in-law* was detached from the root *k-l-l* and shifted to the root *k-n-n*—the shift from *-l-* to *-n-* is a well-known linguistic phenomenon in the Semitic language family. In this instance—which merits further study—the linguistic shift was driven by historical factors. On this consonantal shift, see Brockelmann, *Kurzgefasste vergleichende Grammatik der semitischen sprachen,* 47; Moscati, *An Introduction to the Comparative Grammar of the Semitic Languages,* 32 (par. 8.26). N.B.: The Arabic *sijīll* in Q. 11:82 and *sijjil* in 21:104 may be related to *sijjīn* in Q. 83:7–8; and both words may be related to the Latin *sigillum,* the diminutive form of *signum,* which signifies *seal.* See Selms, "*siǧǧīn* and *siǧǧīl* in the Qurʾān," 99–103. For examples of Qurʾānic terms that are rarely used in classical Arabic, see Brunschvig, "Simples remarques négatives sur le vocabulaire du Coran," 19–32.

110. On abrogation, see above, note 100.

111. Lane, *Arabic-English Lexicon,* s.v. n-s-kh; cf. al-Khalīl b. Aḥmad, *Kitāb al-ʿayn*; Ibn Manẓūr, *Lisān al-ʿarab.*

112. Even-Shoshan, *ha-Milôn he-Ḥadash,* s.v. n-s-kh.

Chapter 9. Kalāla in Early Islamic Tradition

1. On Ibn ʿAbbās, see *EI*², s.v. ʿAbd Allāh b. al-ʿAbbās (L. Veccia Vaglieri); Isaiah Goldfeld, "The *Tafsīr* of ʿAbdallāh b. ʿAbbās," 125–35; A. Rippin, "Ibn ʿAbbās's *Al-lughāt fīʾl Qurʾān,*" 15–25; idem, "Ibn ʿAbbās's *Gharīb al-Qurʾān,*" 322–23; Juynboll, *Encyclopedia of Canonical Ḥadīth,* 1–2.

2. *EI*², s.v. Mudjāhid b. Djabr (A. Rippin); Juynboll, *Encyclopedia,* 430–31.

3. Mujāhid b. Jabr, *Tafsīr,* 269.

4. Ibid., 297.

5. Q. 4:8 reads as follows: "When the kinsmen and the orphans and the destitute are present at the division, provide for them out of it and speak to them properly."

6. *Tafsīr al-Ḍaḥḥāk,* 1:277 and 314.

7. Sufyān al-Thawrī, *Tafsīr al-qurʾān al-karīm,* 49, 56. For biographical details, see *EI*², s.v. Sufyān al-Thawrī (H. P. Raddatz); Juynboll, *Encyclopedia,* 628–42.

8. It was Muqātil, it will be recalled, who identified the unnamed woman in Q. 33:37 as Zaynab bt. Jaḥsh and it was Muqātil who preserved the first full narrative expansion of that verse. See Chapter 4.

9. Muqātil b. Sulaymān, *Tafsīr.* For biographical details, see Chapter 4, note 8.

10. Ibid., 1:219.1–2.

11. Muqātil, of course, was aware of the fact that one finds examples of the splitting of a compound subject elsewhere in the Qurʾān, e.g. in Q. 9:3: "*anna **allāh**ᵃ barīʾᵘⁿ min al-mushrikīna **wa-rasūluhu***, literally, God is absolved of the polytheists and [so is] his Messenger, that is to say, both God and His Messenger are absolved of the polytheists. The point is that in Q. 4:12b, there is something unnatural about the bifurcated subject that requires explanation.

12. Muqātil, *Tafsīr,* 1:219.2. As we shall see below, one of the three definitions of *kalāla* is "a man who dies leaving neither child nor parent (*la walad wa-lā wālid*). Technically the term *wālid* may signify not only a father but also a grandfather. The question of the inheritance rights of a grandfather appears to have become acute during the caliphate of Muʿāwiya (41–60/661–80), even if the solution is attributed to Abū Bakr and ʿUmar. See Cilardo, *The Qurʾānic Term* Kalāla, 63. Cilardo's book is useful—even if I disagree with his conclusions—because, like many classical Arabic authors, he assembles information from a wide range of sources and makes it readily available. On *kalāla* and the grandfather, see also Dutton, *The Origins of Islamic Law,* 109–12, 135.

13. Muqātil, *Tafsīr,* 1:219.4.

14. See Powers, *SQH,* 29, and the sources cited there.

15. Muqātil, *Tafsīr,* 1:274.

16. *EI*[2] (supplement), s.v. D̲jābir b. ʿAbd Allāh (M. J. Kister); cf. Juynboll, *Encyclopedia,* 259–60.

17. Muqātil, *Tafsīr,* 1:274. In later versions of this report, Jābir himself specifies that he has sisters. See, for example, al-ʿAẓīmābādī, *ʿAwn al-maʿbūd: sharḥ sunan Abū Dāʾūd,* 8:93–94 (no. 2869) (*isnād*: Aḥmad b. Ḥanbal [d. 241/855]—Sufyān [b. ʿUyayna, d. 198/813]—Ibn al-Munkadir [d. 130/747–48]—Jābir); Muslim, *Ṣaḥīḥ,* 3:1234 (nos. 5 and 8); Tirmidhī, *Sunan,* 3:282 (no. 2178). Note, however, that the same report as the one cited by Muqātil is also invoked as the *sabab* of the inheritance verse, i.e., Q. 4:11–12; for references, see *SQH,* 200, note 39.

18. Muqātil, *Tafsīr,* 1:274.

19. Ibid.

20. Al-Ṣanʿānī was born in the Yemen ca. 126/744. In Ṣanʿāʾ he attended the study circle of Maʿmar b. Rāshid (d. 153/170), who settled in Ṣanʿāʾ after studying in Basra (his birthplace), Medina, and Mecca. Al-Ṣanʿānī also studied with at least three other scholars who visited Ṣanʿāʾ: Ibn Jurayj of Mecca, Sufyān b. ʿUyayna of Mecca, and Sufyān al-Thawrī of Kufa. See *EI*[3], s.v. ʿAbd al-Razzāq al-Ṣanʿānī (H. Motzki); Juynboll, *Encyclopedia,* 24–38.

21. ʿAbd al-Razzāq al-Ṣanʿānī, *Muṣannaf.*

22. The *isnād*s are conveniently collected and analyzed in Cilardo, *The Qurʾānic Term* Kalāla, 20–39 and 85–94.

23. On these terms, see *EI*[2], s.v. Mursal (G. H. A. Juynboll).

24. On ʿUmar, see *EI*[2], s.v. ʿUmar b. al-K̲h̲aṭṭāb (M. Bonner); and Hakim, "ʿUmar b. al-Ḫaṭṭāb, calife par la grâce de Dieu," 317–61. Neither Bonner nor Hakim mentions these reports.

25. ʿAbd al-Razzāq, *Muṣannaf,* 10:302, no. 19184. The *isnād,* which is broken (*munqaṭiʿ*), is Kufan: ʿAbd al-Razzāq—al-Thawrī (Kufa, d. 161/778)—ʿAmr b. Murra (Kufa, d. 110/728–29)—ʿUmar.

26. Immediately following the death of the Prophet, several of the Arab tribes that previously had joined the *umma* withdrew their support for Islam. Some of these tribes are reported to have said, "We will pray, but we refuse to pay the *zakāt*-tax." See ʿAlī b. Burhān al-Dīn, *al-Sīra al-ḥalabiyya,* 3:229.14–15.

27. ʿAbd al-Razzāq, *Muṣannaf*, 10:302, no. 19185. The *isnād*, which is broken, is Meccan: ʿAbd al-Razzāq—Ibn Jurayj (Mecca, d. 150/767) and Ibn ʿUyayna (Kufa, d. 198/813)—ʿAmr b. Dīnār (Mecca, d. 126/744)—Muḥammad b. Ṭalḥa b. Yazīd b. Rukāna (Hijaz, d. 111/729–30)—ʿUmar.

28. Ibid., 10:302, no. 19186. The *isnād* is Meccan: ʿAbd al-Razzāq—Maʿmar (Basra, d. 152–53/769–70)—Ibn Ṭāʾūs (Mecca, d. 131/748–49)—his father (Mecca, d. 100/718–19)—Ibn ʿAbbās (d. 68/687)—ʿUmar.

29. Ibid., 10:301, no. 19183. The *isnād*, which is *mursal*, is Medinese: ʿAbd al-Razzāq—Maʿmar (Basra, d. 152–53/769–70)—Zuhrī (Medina, d. 124/742)—Ibn al-Musayyab (Medina, d. 94/713)—ʿUmar. On the grandfather in Islamic inheritance law, see note 12 above.

30. On Ḥudhayfa, see Lecker, "Ḥudhayfa b. al-Yamān and ʿAmmār b. Yāsir," 149–62.

31. In this report, the fact that the Prophet was riding on a camel does not appear to have any theological significance. Elsewhere, however, the image of the Prophet as a camel rider has decisive messianic and/or apocalyptic overtones. See Bashear, "Riding Beasts on Divine Missions: An Examination of the Ass and Camel Traditions," 37–71.

32. ʿAbd al-Razzāq al-Ṣanʿānī, *Muṣannaf*, 10:304–5, no. 19193.

33. Ibid.

34. For references, see *SQH*, 193, note 14, 195, note 21, 198, notes 29 and 32, 200, note 40.

35. The phenomenon of one verse having two or more occasions for its revelation was treated by Muslim scholars under the rubric of *asbāb mutaʿaddida* ("multiple occasions"). See, for example, Suyūṭī, *Lubāb al-nuqūl fī asbāb al-nuzūl*, 8–10; cf. Qurṭubī, *Jāmiʿ*, 5:57–58; Ṭabāṭabāʾī, *al-Mīzān fī tafsīr al-qurʾān*, 4:217.

36. Ṭabarī, *Tafsīr* (ed. Shākir), 9:442, no. 10889. Cf. ibid., 9:437, no. 10877, where Q. 4:176 is identified as *āyat al-kalāla*.

37. ʿAbd al-Razzāq, *Muṣannaf*, 10:305, no. 19194. A similar report, ʿAbd al-Razzāq informs us, was transmitted with the following *isnād*: Maʿmar—Ibn Ṭāʾūs—Ṭāʾūs—ʿUmar. This is no. 19195.

38. Ibid., 10:303, no. 19187. *Isnād*: ʿAbd al-Razzāq—Ibn Jurayj (Mecca, d. 150/767)—Ibn Ṭāʾūs (Mecca, d. 131/748–49)—his father (Mecca, d. 100/718–19)—Ibn ʿAbbās (d. 68/687)—ʿUmar.

39. Ibid., 10:304, no. 19192. The *isnād* is broken: ʿAbd al-Razzāq—Maʿmar (Basra, d. 152–53/769–70)—Zuhrī (Medina, d. 124/742) and Qatāda (Basra, d. 117/735) and Abū Isḥāq [al-Hamdānī] (Kufa, d. 127/745)—ʿAmr b. Shuraḥbīl (Kufa, d. 63/682–83).

40. Ḥasan b. Muḥammad b. ʿAlī was the grandson of ʿAlī b. Abī Ṭālib and the son of Muḥammad b. al-Ḥanafiyya. To him are attributed two of the earliest treatises on *kalām*. See Ess, "Das *Kitāb al-irǧāʾ* des Ḥasan b. Muḥammad b. al-Ḥanafiyya," 20–52, at 24, 35–36; *EI*², s.vv. ʿAbd Allāh b. Sabaʾ [M. G. S. Hodgson], Muḥammad b. al-Ḥanafiyya [Fr. Buhl]; Crone and Zimmerman, *The Epistle of Sālim b. Dhakwān*.

41. ʿAbd al-Razzāq, *Muṣannaf*, 10:303, no. 19189. The *isnād* is Hijazi: ʿAbd al-Razzāq—Ibn Jurayj (Mecca, d. 150/767) and Ibn ʿUyayna (Kufa, d. 198/813)—ʿAmr b. Dīnār (Mecca, d. 126/744)—Ḥasan b. Muḥammad b. ʿAlī (Medina, d. 100/720)—Ibn ʿAbbās (d. 68/687).

42. Ess, "Das *Kitāb al-irǧāʾ*, 24.

43. ʿAbd al-Razzāq, *Muṣannaf*, 10:303, no. 19188. *Isnād*: ʿAbd al-Razzāq—Ibn ʿUyayna (Kufa, d. 198/813)—Sulaymān [b. Abī Muslim] al-Aḥwal (Basra, d. 141/758)—Ibn Ṭāʾūs (Mecca, d. 131/748–49)—Ibn ʿAbbās (d. 68/687).

44. Ibid., 10:304, no. 19190. The *isnād* is broken: ʿAbd al-Razzāq—al-Thawrī (Kufa,

d. 161/778)—Jābir [b. Yazīd] (d. 127/744–45)—al-Shaʿbī (Kufa, d. > 100/718)—Abū Bakr.

45. Ibid., 10:304, no. 19191. The *isnād* is broken: ʿAbd al-Razzāq—Ibn ʿUyayna (Kufa, d. 198/813)—ʿĀṣim b. Sulaymān [al-Aḥwal] (Basra, d. 141/758)—al-Shaʿbī (Kufa, d. > 100/718)—Abū Bakr.

46. ʿAbd al-Razzāq al-Ṣanʿānī, *Tafsīr*, 1:485–86, nos. 659–62.

47. Ibid., 1:485, no. 660. *Isnād*: ʿAbd al-Razzāq—Maʿmar (Basra, d. 152–53/769–70)—Abū Isḥāq al-Hamdānī (Kufa, d. 127/745)—ʿAmr b. Shuraḥbīl (Kufa, d. 63/682–83).

48. Ibid., 1:485, no. 659. *Isnād*: ʿAbd al-Razzāq—Maʿmar—Zuhrī (Medina, d. 124/742) and Qatāda (Basra, d. 117/745).

49. Ibid., 1:486, no. 661. The *isnād* is broken: ʿAbd al-Razzāq—Maʿmar—Ayyūb [al-Sakhtiyānī] (Basra, d. 131/749)—Ibn Sīrīn (Basra, d. 110/728)—ʿUmar.

50. Ibid., 1:486, no. 662. The *isnād* is broken: ʿAbd al-Razzāq—Maʿmar—Ayyūb [al-Sakhtiyānī]—Ibn Sīrīn—ʿUmar.

51. *EI*[2], s.v. Khalīl b. Aḥmad (R. Sellheim).

52. Khalīl b. Aḥmad al-Farāhīdī, *Kitāb al-ʿayn*.

53. *EI*[2], s.v. Khalīl b. Aḥmad (R. Sellheim).

54. Khalīl b. Aḥmad, *Kitāb al-ʿayn*, 728a–b. *Kalīl* signifies *a dull sword*; *killa* signifies *a mosquito net*; *iklīl* signifies either *a turban or crown adorned with jewels* or the *stations of the moon*. The Form II verb *kallala* signifies *to depart, leaving dependents (ʿiyāl) in a state of neglect*, as in the sentence *kallala al-rajulu*.

55. Ibid., 728a–b.

56. *EI*[2], s.v. al-Farrāʾ (R. Blachère). Cf. N. Kinberg, *A lexicon of al-Farrāʾ's Terminology in His Qurʾān commentary*.

57. Al-Farrāʾ surely understood that there are numerous cases in the Qurʾān in which the rules for pronoun agreement are violated. As with the bifurcated subject ("a man . . . or a woman"), the point is that in this instance there is something unusual about the usage that requires comment or clarification.

58. *EI*[2], s.v. Abū ʿUbayda (H.A.R. Gibb); *EI*[3], s.v. Abū ʿUbayda (R. Weipert).

59. Abū ʿUbayda, *Majāz al-qurʾān*, 118–19.

60. *EI*[2], s.v. al-Akhfash (C. Brockelmann-Ch. Pellat).

61. al-Akhfash al-Awsaṭ, *Kitāb maʿānī al-qurʾān*, 1:250–51; cf. W. Wright, *A Grammar of the Arabic Language*, 2:100.

62. Ṭabarī, *Tafsīr* (ed. Shākir). For biographical details, see *EI*[2], s.v. al-Ṭabarī; and Rosenthal, "The Life and Works of al-Ṭabarī," in *The History of al-Ṭabarī*, 1:5–134. For a comprehensive study of Ṭabarī's activity as a commentator, see Gilliot, *Exégèse, langue, et théologie en Islam: l'exégèse coranique de Ṭabarī*.

63. Ṭabarī, *Tafsīr* (ed. Shākir), 8:53.

64. Ibid.

65. N. J. Coulson, *Succession in the Muslim Family*.

66. Text: *atā ʿalayya ḥīn*[un] *wa-lastu adrī mā al-kalāla*. See Ṭabarī, *Tafsīr* (ed. Shākir), 8:54–55, no. 8748. *Isnād*: Ibn Wakīʿ—Wakīʿ (d. 197/812)—ʿImrān b. Ḥudayr—al-Sumayṭ. Alternatively, discrepancies between one or another definition of *kalāla* attributed to ʿUmar were harmonized by having his understanding of the meaning of the word change over the course of his lifetime. Some of his definitions were early, others were late.

67. Ibid., 8:54–57, nos. 8745–64.

68. Ibid., 8:57 (with a cross-reference to no. 8734).

69. Ibid., 8:57–58, no. 8765. *Isnād*: Ibn al-Muthannā—Sahl b. Yūsuf—Shuʿba (d. 160/776)—al-Ḥakam [b. ʿUtayba?, d. 115/733].

70. Al-Shaʿbī was close to the Umayyad caliph ʿAbd al-Malik and deeply involved in politics. See *EI*², s.v. al-Shaʿbī (Juynboll); cf. Juynboll, *Encyclopedia*, 463–71.

71. Ṭabarī, *Tafsīr* (ed. Shākir), 8:53–54, no. 8745. *Isnād*: al-Walīd b. Shujjāʿ al-Sakūnī—ʿAlī b. Mushir (d. 179/795)—ʿĀṣim (d. 141/758)—al-Shaʿbī (d. > 100/718). The fact that Abū Bakr referred to himself as being subject to the influence of Satan was taken by his detractors as a defect that should have disqualified him from serving as the first caliph. See ʿAbd al-Jabbār, *al-Mughnī fī abwāb al-tawḥīd wa'l-ʿadl*, vol. 20, pt. 1, 338, 352–53.

72. Ṭabarī, *Tafsīr* (ed. Shākir), 8:54, no. 8746. *Isnād*: Yaʿqūb b. Ibrāhīm (d. 208/823)—Hushaym [b. Bashīr, d. 183/799]—ʿĀṣim al-Aḥwal (d. 141/758)—al-Shaʿbī (d. > 100/718).

73. Ibid., 8:54, no. 8747. *Isnād*: [Yūnis b. ʿAbd al-Aʿlā]—Sufyān [b. ʿUyayna, d. 198/813]—ʿĀṣim al-Aḥwal—al-Shaʿbī.

74. As noted by Gilliot ("Exégèse et sémantique," 81–82), Ṭabarī, *Tafsīr* (ed. Shākir), 8:58 cites the grammatical arguments previously advanced by al-Akhfash and Abū ʿUbayda, without acknowledging his reliance on these scholars. For the two views advanced by these grammarians, see above, 211–12. Ṭabarī appears indifferent to these two explanations.

75. Muqātil, *Tafsīr*, 1:274.

76. Ṭabarī, *Tafsīr* (ed. Shākir), 8:60.9–12, with a cross-reference to no. 8730, where the *isnād* is Muḥammad b. al-Muthannā—Wahb b. Jarīr (d. 206/822)—Shuʿba (d. 160/776)—Muḥammad b. al-Munkadir (d. 130/747–48)—Jābir.

77. Ibid., 8:60, no. 8770. *Isnād*: Yaʿqūb b. Ibrāhīm (d. 208/823)—Ibn ʿUlayya (d. 193/809)—Ibn ʿAwn (d. 151/768)—ʿAmr b. Saʿīd [al-Ashdaq, d. 70/689]—Ḥumayd b. ʿAbd al-Raḥmān. The numerous variants of this *ḥadīth* have been studied extensively. See Speight, "The Will of Saʿd b. a. Waqqāṣ: The Growth of a Tradition"; Powers, "The Will of Saʿd b. Abī Waqqāṣ: A Reassessment"; I. Zaman, "The Evolution of a Hadith: Transmission, Growth and the Science of *Rijal* in a Hadith of Saʿd b. Abi Waqqas."

78. It is also possible to read: *wa-laysa lī wārith illā kalālat*ᵃⁿ, which would mean, "I have no heir except by way of collaterals." But this is not how Ṭabarī understood the sentence.

79. Ṭabarī, *Tafsīr* (ed. Shākir), 8:61, no. 8771. *Isnād*: Yaʿqūb b. Ibrāhīm (d. 208/823)—Ibn ʿUlayya (d. 193/809)—Isḥāq b. Suwayd (d. 131/749)—al-ʿAlāʾ b. Ziyād.

80. Ibid., 8:61.5–6.

81. Ibid., 8:62, no. 8776. *Isnād*: Bishr b. Muʿādh—Yazīd b. Zurayʿ (d. 182/798)—Saʿīd—Qatāda (d. 117/735).

82. Ibid., 8:62–63, no. 8778. *Isnād*: Muḥammad b. al-Ḥusayn—Aḥmad b. Mufaḍḍal—Asbāṭ—al-Suddī.

83. Ibid., 8:61–62, nos. 8772–74.

84. Ibid., 8:62, no. 8775: Al-Qāsim b. Rabīʿa said: I heard Saʿd recite: "*wa-in kāna rajul*ᵘⁿ *yūrathu kalālat*ᵃⁿ *wa-lahu akh*ᵘⁿ *aw ukht*ᵘⁿ ***min ummihi***."

85. Jeffrey, *Materials*, 126. On Ubayy, see *EI*², s.v. Ubayy b. Kaʿb (A. Rippin).

86. Ṭabarī, *Tafsīr* (ed. Shākir), 8:63.

87. Ibid., 9:438, no. 10880. *Isnād*: Ibn Wakīʿ—Wakīʿ (d. 197/812)—Sufyān [al-Thawrī (?), d. 161/787]—ʿAmr b. Murra—Murra al-Hamdānī—ʿUmar.

88. Ibid., 9:438, nos. 10878–79; cf. *SQH*, 36.

89. Ibid., 9:435–36, nos. 10874–76; cf. *SQH*, 139–40.

90. Ṭabarī, *Tafsīr* (ed. Shākir), 9:439, no. 10881. *Isnād*: Abū Kurayb (d. 248/862)—

ʿAththām (d. 194 or 195 A.H.)—al-Aʿmash (d. 148/765)—Ibrāhīm—ʿUmar. Cf. ʿAbd al-Razzāq, *Muṣannaf*, 10:302, no. 19185; *SQH*, 32.

91. To the best of my knowledge, this is the only instance in which the linguistic tag *āyat al-kalāla* is used to identify 4:12b. Cf. Ṭabarī, *Tafsīr* (ed. Shākir), 9:442, no. 10889, where "the verse that was revealed in the summer" is identified as Q. 4:12b.

92. Ibid., 9:437, no. 10877; cf. 440, nos. 10884–87; *SQH*, 33.

93. The snake is a common symbol in Jewish sources. For example, the King of Ammon who betrayed David's trust is identified as Ḥanūn ben Naḥash: He was the son of Snake (II Sam. 10:1–2). To Rav Joseph is attributed the statement, "Whoever contends against the sovereignty of the House of David deserves to be bitten by a snake" (BT, *Sanhedrin*, 110[a]). See generally *Anchor Bible Dictionary*, s.v. Serpent (Religious Symbol) (Lowell K. Handy).

94. Ṭabarī, *Tafsīr* (ed. Shākir), 9:439, no. 10882. *Isnād*: Abū Kurayb (d. 248/862)—ʿAththām (d. 194 or 195 A.H.)—al-Aʿmash (d. 148/765)—Qays b. Muslim (d. 120/738)—Ṭāriq b. Shihāb (d. ca. 83/702). Cf. *SQH*, 35. This literary structure (the sudden appearance of a snake prevents ʿUmar from making an important statement) is a topos. Cf. Bayhaqī, *al-Sunan al-kubrā*, 6:245. On the authority of Ṭāriq b. Shihāb: "ʿUmar b. al-Khaṭṭāb took a shoulder-blade and gathered the Companions of Muḥammad, with the intention of writing something about the grandfather. The Companions thought that the status of a grandfather was the same as that of a father. At that moment, a snake emerged, causing them to scatter, whereupon ʿUmar said, 'Had God wanted to see the matter through to completion, He would have done so.' " Notice that the reference to women whispering in their private chambers mentioned in Ṭabarī, *Tafsīr* (ed. Shākir), 9:439, no. 10882 is missing in Bayhaqī. Cf. Gilliot, "Exégèse et sémantique," 87–88.

95. Ṭabarī, *Tafsīr* (ed. Shākir), 9:441, nos. 10886–87; cf. 437, no. 10877 (*man yaqraʾu wa-man lā yaqraʾu*); *SQH*, 37.

96. Ibn Kathīr, *Tafsīr al-qurʾān al-ʿaẓīm* (ed. S.M. al-Salāma), 2:487.

97. ʿAbd al-Razzāq al-Ṣanʿānī, *Muṣannaf*, 10:304–5, no. 19193; Ṭabarī, *Tafsīr* (ed. Shākir), 9:435–36, nos. 10874–76.

98. Sufyān b. ʿUyayna, *Tafsīr*, 309; ʿAbd al-Razzāq, *Tafsīr*, 3:32, no. 2317.

99. On esotericism in the Arabic philosophical tradition, see Strauss, *Persecution and the Art of Writing*; Stroumsa, "Compassion for Wisdom: The Attitude of Some Medieval Arab Philosophers Towards the Codification of Philosophy," 39–55; Mahdi, "Philosophical Literature," 87ff.

100. Note that one of the grievances directed against ʿUthmān was that he "erased the book of God" (*maḥā kitāb allāh*). See Ibn Abī Dāʾūd, *Kitāb al-maṣāḥif*, 36.13–14.

101. Saʿīd b. al-Musayyab is the only authority who appears in both the Group A and Group B narratives.

102. Crone, *Meccan Trade*, 217.

103. Ibid., 223.

104. Ibn Abī Dāʾūd, *Kitāb al-maṣāḥif*, 10.12–11.6, 31, l. −4.

105. Ibid., 17.8–10.

106. *EI*[2], s.v. Muʿāwiya I b. Abī Sufyān (M. Hinds).

107. According to Cilardo, "the debate about the question of the grandfather began in the second half of the first century H. and [. . .] it was wholly concluded by the time of the Medinese Mālik and the Kūfan Abū Ḥanīfa." See Cilardo, *The Qurʾānic Term* Kalāla, 63.

108. See *SQH*, 142 and the sources cited there.

109. See above, note 14.

110. ʿAbd al-Razzāq, *Muṣannaf*, 10:302–3, nos. 19184–86.
111. Ibn Ḥanbal, *al-Musnad*, 3:286–87 (no. 1935).

Chapter 10. Conclusion

1. The term *ʿiṣma* does not occur in the Qurʾān, and the notion that prophets are by definition impeccable and immune from sin (*maʿṣūm*) appears to have emerged only during the second half of the first century A.H. See Faruki, "*Tawḥīd* and the doctrine of *ʿIṣmah*"; Hasan, "Concept of Infallibility in Islam"; Bravmann, "The Origin of the Principle of *ʿIṣmah*: Muḥammad's immunity from sin"; EI^2, s.v. ʿIṣma (W. Madelung); Bar-Asher, *Scripture and Exegesis in Early Shiism*, 162–79.
2. Cook, *The Koran: A Very Short Introduction*, 139.

Appendix 2. Deathbed Scenes and Inheritance Disputes: A Literary Approach

1. Lammens, *Fatima et les filles de Mahomet*; Caetani, *Anneli dell' Islam*.
2. Madelung, *The succession to Muḥammad*, 8ff.
3. Ibid., vii (dedication).
4. P. Crone, "In Defence of Ali," 28.
5. Ibn Ḥanbal, *Musnad*, 4:235 (no. 2676). Cf. *SQH*, 114.
6. Ṭabarī, *Tafsīr* (ed. Shākir), 9:441, nos. 10886–87; cf. 437, no. 10877 (*man yaqraʾu wa-man lāyaqraʾu*). Cf. *SQH*, 37.
7. In pre-Islamic Arabia, the word *bayt* ("house") signified the ruling family of a tribe. The phrase *ahl al-bayt* occurs twice in the Qurʾān, once in Q. 11:73, where it refers to the House of Ibrāhīm, and again in Q. 33:33, where it refers to the family of Muḥammad. Q. 33:32 opens with a direct address to the Prophet's wives ("O wives of the Prophet . . .") and Q. 33:33 concludes with, "God only wishes to turn away abomination from you and purify you fully, O People of the House (*ahl al-bayt*)." In his commentary on this verse, Muqātil (*Tafsīr*, 3:45) identifies the *ahl al-bayt* as "the wives of the Prophet, because they are in his House." Thus, the semantic range of the term *ahl al-bayt* in the Qurʾān appears to have included both the Prophet's family (*al-bayt*), and his wives (*ahl al-bayt*), as has been confirmed by Madelung (*The Succession to Muḥammad*, 15). Cf. EI^2, s.v. Ahl al-bayt (I. Goldziher, C. van Arendonk, A. S. Tritton); M. Sharon, "*Ahl al-bayt*—People of the House."
8. Lane, *Arabic-English Lexicon*, s.v. kh-d-r.
9. On bride/bridegroom symbolism in the Bible, see Frye, *The Great Code: The Bible and Literature*, index, s.v. Bride.
10. *SQH*, 115.
11. Ibid., 115–16, citing Ibn Ḥanbal, *Musnad*, 4:356 (no. 2992). Cf. Madelung, *The Succession to Muḥammad*, 23–24, and the sources cited there. N.B.: The statement attributed to Ibn ʿAbbās ("The calamity—the entire calamity . . .") brings to mind the Lord's rebuke of David in II Sam. 12: "I will make a calamity rise against you from within your own house . . .".
12. Cf. the version of Abū Bakr's deathbed scene in which the caliph, weakened by illness, begins to dictate his last will and testament to ʿUthmān b. ʿAffān. Just before reaching the substantive section of the document, the caliph faints, whereupon ʿUthmān steps aside and completes the document as if he were an extension of the caliph's consciousness: ʿUmar would succeed Abū Bakr as the next caliph. See Ṭabarī, *Taʾrīkh*, 3:429.

13. Ibn Ḥanbal, *Musnad*, 3:286–87 (no. 1935); the *isnād* is Hawdha b. Khalīfa—ʿAwf—Muḥammad—Ibn ʿAbbās. Cf. *SQH*, 116–17.

14. Ibid., 122 and the sources cited there.

15. Al-ʿAbbās did not convert to Islam until 8/630 and his connections to Islam would not have been strong in 11/632. See *EI*², s.v. al-ʿAbbās b. ʿAbd al-Muṭṭalib (W. M. Watt).

16. The statement attributed to Muḥammad on his deathbed ("no one inherits from us; whatever we leave is charity") may be compared to Bathsheba's statement to David shortly before he died: "My lord, you yourself swore to your maidservant by the Lord your God: 'Your son Solomon shall succeed me as king, and he shall sit upon my throne'" (I Kings 1:17). The prophetic utterance mimics through inversion the biblical statement attributed to Bathsheba.

17. Variants of the prophetic statement specify that Muḥammad was in fact referring to prophets, e.g., "We are the kinsmen of the prophets: no one inherits from us; that which we leave is charity" (*naḥnu maʿāshir al-anbiyāʾ lā nūrathu mā taraknāhu ṣadaqat*[un]). See ʿAbd al-Jabbār, *al-Mughnī*, vol. 20, pt. 1, 328. The notion that no one inherits from a prophet brings to mind the Christian theological doctrine of the poverty of Christ and his disciples.

18. *SQH*, 123–24.

19. *EI*², s.v. Fāṭima (L. Veccia Vaglieri). In another version of this report, Fāṭima was joined by the Prophet's paternal uncle, al-ʿAbbās, and, together, they approached Abū Bakr demanding their inheritance. Again the caliph rejected the claim, asserting that he heard the Messenger of God say, "No one inherits from us; whatever we leave is charity." See *SQH*, 123–25 and the sources cited there.

20. Cf. Madelung, *The Succession to Muḥammad*, 360–61.

21. Ibn Ḥanbal, *Musnad*, 3:213 (no. 1782). Cf. *SQH*, 125–26.

22. *SQH*, 125–26 and the sources cited there. Cf. Goldziher, *Muslim Studies*, 2:101–2; Madelung, *The Succession to Muḥammad*, 360–61.

23. Goldziher, *Muslim Studies*, 2:101. It was precisely at this point that Goldziher brought his discussion to an end. Little did he know that the subtleties of the law of inheritance—especially the provisions of Q. 4:12b—were directly relevant to the succession crisis. Nearly a century later, the subject was taken up again by Madelung, who ignored the subtleties of Islamic inheritance law despite his familiarity with them. There is no reference to Q. 4:12b or *kalāla* in *The Succession to Muḥammad*. See his review of *SQH* in *Journal of Near Eastern Studies*, 47, 4 (1988), 313–14.

24. Ibn Ḥanbal, *Musnad*, 3:286–87 (no. 1935).

Appendix 3. Inheritance Law: From the Ancient Near East to Early Islamic Times

1. See *HANEL*, 1:124–26 (Egypt: Old Kingdom), 163–65 (Mesopotamia: Early Dynastic and Sargonic Periods), 205–9 (Neo-Sumerian Period), 233–35 (Ebla), 276–79 (Egypt: Middle Kingdom), 328–31 (Egypt: New Kingdom), 393–99 (Mesopotamia: Old Babylonian Period), 457–60 (Old Assyrian Period), 505–7 (Middle Babylonian Period), 542–45 (Middle Assyrian Period), 600–603 (Nuzi), 640 (Hittite Kingdom), 676–82 (Emar), 699–700 (Alalakh), 729–31 (Ugarit); vol. 2:803–4 (Egypt: Third Intermediate Period), 839–43 (Egypt: Demotic Law), 877–80 (Egypt: Elephantine), 899–901 (Mesopotamia: Neo-Assyrian Period), 937–40 (Mesopotamia: Neo-Babylonian Period), 1015–19 (Anatolia and the Levant: Israel).

2. *HANEL*, 1:57–58.

3. Ibid., 1:58–60.

4. Adoptions in brotherhood (*aḫḫūtu*) were common in Nuzi and throughout the ancient Near East, where such arrangements were designed to regulate inheritance rights between natural heirs and outsiders who had become legal members of the family. See ibid., 1:595. For brotherhood contracts in early Islam, see *EI*[2], s.v. Muʾākhāt (W. M. Watt); Simon, *Meccan Trade and Islam*, 115–19 (Appendix 3). This institution merits further attention.

5. *EI*[2], s.v. Muʾākhāt (Watt).

6. See *SQH.*

7. Ibid., 87–109.

8. In proto-Islamic law, the shares awarded to wives in Q. 4:12a dealt with the exceptional case of an unendowed wife and the award to siblings in Q. 4:12b was part of the rules for testate succession. See ibid., 53–86. In other words, neither Q. 4:12a nor 4:12b was part of the rules of intestate succession. As for Q. 4:176, it was not added to the Qurʾān until the generation following the death of the Prophet. See Chapter 8 and *SQH.*

9. The entitlement of two daughters is not specified in Q. 4:11. This gap was filled by the specification in the supplementary verse added at the end of *Sūrat al-Nisāʾ* that two sisters are entitled to two-thirds of the estate. By analogy, in Q. 4:11, two daughters are entitled to two-thirds of the estate. See Chapter 8.

10. *SQH*, 21–52.

11. Ibid., Chapter 2.

12. Ibid., Chapter 3.

13. Ibid., Chapter 5.

14. Ibid., 50; Powers, "Will of Saʿd b. Abī Waqqāṣ"; idem, "On Bequests in Early Islam," 196.

Bibliography

Manuscript

Bibliothèque Nationale de France, Arabe, 328. [BNF]

Primary Sources

ʿAbd al-Jabbār. *al-Mughnī fī abwāb al-tawḥīd wa'l-ʿadl.* Ed. ʿAbd al-Ḥalīm Maḥmūd and Sulaymān Dunyā. 20 vols. Cairo: al-Dār al-Miṣriyya li'l-Ta'līf wa'l-Tarjama, 1959–65.

ʿAbd al-Razzāq al-Ṣanʿānī. *al-Muṣannaf.* Ed. Ḥabīb al-Raḥmān al-Aʿẓamī. 11 vols. Beirut: al-Maktab al-islāmī, 1970–72; 2nd ed. 1983.

———. *Tafsīr.* 3 vols. Beirut: Dār al-Kutub al-ʿIlmiyya, 1419/1999.

Abū ʿUbayda. *Majāz al-qur'ān.* Ed. Mehmet Fuad Sezgin. Cairo: Muḥammad Sāmī Umayn al-Khanjī, 1374/1954.

Abū Yūsuf, *Kitāb al-kharāj.* Trans. A. Ben Shemesh as *Taxation in Islām,* vol. 3. Leiden: Brill, 1969.

al-Akhfash al-Awsaṭ. *Kitāb maʿānī al-qur'ān.* Ed. Hudā Maḥmūd Qarāʿa. 2 vols. Cairo: Maktabat al-Khānjī.

ʿAlī b. Burhān al-Dīn. *al-Sīra al-ḥalabiyya fī sīrat al-amīn al-ma'mūn: insān al-ʿuyūn.* 3 vols. Beirut: Dār al-Maʿrifa li'l-Ṭibāʿa wa'l-Nashr, 1980.

The Anchor Bible: Genesis. Trans. E. A. Speiser. Garden City, N.Y.: Doubleday 1964.

The Apocryphal New Testament: A Collection of Apocryphal Christian Literature in an English Translation. Ed. J. K. Elliot. Oxford: Clarendon Press, 1993.

al-ʿAẓīmābādī. *ʿAwn al-maʿbūd: sharḥ sunan Abī Dā'ūd.* 14 vols. Medina: al-Maktaba al-Salafiyya, 1968–.

The Babylonian Talmud. Trans. with notes, glossary and indices under the editorship of I. Epstein. 18 vols. London: Soncino Press, 1978. [*BT*]

al-Baghdādī. *Ta'rīkh Baghdād.* 14 vols. Beirut: Dār al-Kutub al-ʿIlmiyya, n.d.

al-Balādhurī, *Ansāb al-ashrāf.* Vol. 1, ed. Muḥammad Ḥamīd Allāh. Cairo: Dār al-Maʿārif, 1987. Vol. 4:2, ed. ʿAbdalʿAzīz ad-Dūrī and ʿIṣām ʿUqla. Bibliotheca Islamica 28e. Beirut: Das Arabische Buch, 2001. Vol. 5, ed. Iḥsān ʿAbbās. Bibliotheca Islamica 28g. Beirut: Franz Steiner, 1996.

al-Bayhaqī. *al-Sunan al-kubrā.* 10 vols. Hayderabad, 1344–57 A. H. Repr. Beirut: Dār Ṣādir, 1968.

The Book of Jubilees or the Little Genesis. Trans. R. H. Charles. Jerusalem: Makor, 1901.

The Book of a Thousand Judgements (a Sasanian Law-book). Introduction, transcription, and translation of the Pahlavi text, notes, glossary, and indexes by Anahit Perikhanian. Trans. from Russian by Nina Garsoïan. Costa Mesa, Calif.: Mazda, 1997.

The Chronicle of Theophanes: An English translation of anni mundi *6095–6305 (A.D. 602–813).* Intro. and notes by Harry Turtledove. Philadelphia: University of Pennsylvania Press, 1982.

The Chronicle of Theophanes Confessor: Byzantine and Near Eastern History AD 284–813. Trans. Cyril Mango and Roger Scott. Oxford: Clarendon Press, 1997.

Corpus Inscriptionum Regni Bosporani. Ed. V. V. Struve. Leningrad: Nauka, 1965.

Corpus inscriptionum semiticarum. 5 vols. Paris: Reipublicae Typographeo, 1881–.

al-Ḍaḥḥāk. *Tafsīr al-Ḍaḥḥāk.* Ed. Muḥammad Shukrī Aḥmad al-Zāwīytī. 2 vols. Cairo: Dār al-Salām, 1419/1999.

al-Dhahabī. *Siyar aʿlām al-nubalāʾ.* Ed. Shuʿayb al-Arnāʾūṭ. 23 vols. Beirut: Muʾassasat al-Risāla, 1413/1993.

Excavations at Nessana. Vol. 3, *Non-Literary Papyri.* Ed. Casper J. Kraemer. Princeton, N.J.: Princeton University Press, 1958.

al-Farāhīdī, Khalīl b. Aḥmad. See Khalīl b. Aḥmad.

al-Fazārī, Abū Isḥāq. *Kitāb al-siyar.* Ed. Fārūq Ḥamāda. Beirut: Muʾassasat al-Risāla, 1408/1987.

The Fihrist of al-Nadīm: A Tenth-Century Survey of Muslim Culture. Trans. Bayard Dodge. 2 vols. New York: Columbia University Press, 1970.

Genesis Rabbah: The Judaic Commentary to the Book of Genesis, A New American Translation. Trans. Jacob Neusner. 3 vols. Atlanta: Scholars Press, 1985.

The History of al-Ṭabarī. Vol. 7, *The Foundation of the Community.* Trans. M. V. McDonald and W. Montgomery Watt. Albany: State University of New York Press, 1987. Vol. 8, *The Victory of Islam.* Trans. Michael Fishbein. Albany: State University of New York Press, 1997. Vol. 9, *The Last Years of the Prophet.* Trans. Ismail K. Poonawala. Albany: State University of New York Press, 1990. Vol. 10, *The Conquest of Arabia.* Trans. Fred M. Donner. Albany: State University of New York Press, 1993. Vol. 39, *Biographies of the Prophet's Companions and their Successors.* Trans. Ella Landau-Tasseron. Albany: State University of New York Press, 1998.

Homiliae Selectae Mar-Jacobi Sarugensis IV. Ed. Bedjan, Paris/Leipzig, 1908.

Ibn ʿAbd al-Barr. *al-Istīʿāb fī maʿrifat al-aṣḥāb.* On the margins of Ibn Ḥajar al-ʿAsqalānī, *al-Iṣāba fī tamyīz al-ṣaḥāba.* 4 vols. Cairo: Matbaʿat al-Saʿāda, 1328.

Ibn Abī Dāʾūd al-Sijistānī, Abū Bakr. *Kitāb al-maṣāḥif.* Ed. Arthur Jeffery. Cairo: al-Maṭbaʿa al-Raḥmāniyya, 1355/1936.

Ibn Abī Ḥātim. *Tafsīr al-qurʾān al-ʿaẓīm.* 14 vols. al-Riyāḍ: Maktabat Nizār Muṣṭafā al-Bāz, 1999.

Ibn Abī Shayba. *al-Kitāb al-muṣannaf fī al-aḥādīth wa'l-āthār.* Ed. Mukhtār Aḥmad al-Nadwī. 15 vols. Bombay: al-Dār al-Salafiyya, 1403/1983.

Ibn ʿAsākir. *Taʾrīkh madīnat Dimashq.* Ed. ʿUmar b. Gharāma al-ʿAmrawī. 80 vols. Beirut: Dār al-Fikr, 1415/1995.

Ibn Ḥajar al-ʿAsqalānī. *al-Iṣāba fī tamyīz al-ṣaḥāba.* Ed. ʿAlī Muḥammad al-Bajāwī. 8 vols. Cairo: Dār Nahdat Miṣr li'l-Ṭabʿ wa'l-Nashr, 1970–.

———. *Tahdhīb al-tahdhīb.* 12 vols. Hayderabad: Dāʾirat al-Maʿārif al-ʿUthmāniyya, 1325–7/1907–9; repr. Beirut: Dār Ṣādir, 1968.

Ibn Ḥanbal, Aḥmad. *al-Musnad.* Ed. Aḥmad Muḥammad Shākir. 22 vols. Cairo: Dār al-Maʿārif, 1374/1955.

Ibn al-Jawzī's Kitāb al-quṣṣāṣ wa'l-mudhakkirīn. Including a Critical Edition, Annotated Translation and Introduction by Merlin L. Swartz. Beyrouth: Dar El-Machreq Éditeurs, 1986.

Ibn Kathīr. *al-Bidāya wa'l-nihāya.* 14 vols. in 7. 1st ed. Beirut: Maktab al-Maʿārif and al-Riyāḍ: Maktab al-Naṣr, 1966.

———. *Tafsīr al-qurʾān al-ʿaẓīm.* 4 vols. 3rd ed. Cairo: Maṭbaʿat al-Istiqāma, 1373/1954.

———. *Tafsīr al-qurʾān al-ʿaẓīm.* Ed. Sāmī b. Muḥammad al-Salāma. 8 vols. Riyāḍ: Dār Ṭība li'l-Nashr wa'l-Tawzīʿ, 1418/1997.

Ibn Manẓūr. *Lisān al-ʿarab.* 6 vols. Cairo: Dār al-Maʿārif, 1981.
Ibn Saʿd. *Kitāb al-ṭabaqāt al-kabīr.* 8 vols. plus index. Ed. E. Sachau et al. Leiden: Brill, 1904–40.
———. *al-Ṭabaqāt al-kubrā.* 9 vols. Beirut: Dār Ṣādir, 1957–68.
Ibn Shabba, ʿUmar. *Kitāb taʾrīkh al-madīna.* 4 vols. Ed. F. M. Shaltūt. Beirut: Dār al-Turāth, 1990.
Ibn Wahb, *al-Ǧāmiʿ: die Koranwissenschaften.* Ed. Miklos Muranyi. Wiesbaden: Harrassowitz, 1992.
Islamic Jurisprudence: Shāfiʿī's Risāla. Trans. Majid Khadduri. Baltimore: The Johns Hopkins Press, 1961.
The Islamic Law of Nations: Shaybānī's Siyar. Trans. Majid Khadduri. Baltimore: Johns Hopkins Press, 1966.
al-Jaṣṣāṣ. *Aḥkām al-qurʾān.* 3 vols. 1335/1916. Repr. Beirut: Dār al-Kitāb al-ʿArabī, 197–.
Joint Expedition with the Iraq Museum at Nuzi. 6 vols. Paris: Geuthner, 1927–39.
Josephus, Flavius. *Jewish Antiquities.* Trans. William Whiston. Wordsworth Classics of World Literature. London: Wordsworth Editions, 2006.
Justinian's Institutes. Trans. with an introduction by Peter Birks and Grant McLeod. Ithaca, N.Y.: Cornell University Press, 1987.
Khalīfa b. Khayyāt. *Kitāb al-ṭabaqāt,* part 1. Ed. Suhayl Zakkār. Damascus: Maṭābiʿ Wizārat al-Thaqāfa, 1966.
Khalīl b. Aḥmad al-Farāhīdī. *Kitāb al-ʿayn.* Ed. Dāʾūd Salmān al-ʿAnbakī and Inʿām Dāʾūd Sallūm. Beirut: Maktabat Lubnān Nāshirūn, 2004.
The Life of Muhammad: A Translation of Ibn Ishaq's Sirat Rasul Allah. Trans. Alfred Guillaume. Oxford: Oxford University Press, 1955.
Lisān al-ʿarab. See Ibn Manẓūr.
Midrash ha-Gadol. Ed. Mordechai Margaliot et al. 5 vols. Jerusalem: Rav Kook, 1947–72.
Midrash Rabbah. Trans. H. Freedman and Maurice Simon. 10 vols. London: Soncino Press, 1939.
al-Mizzī. *Tahdhīb al-kamāl fī asmāʾ al-rijāl.* Ed. Bashshār ʿAwwād Maʿrūf. 35 vols. Beirut: Mu'assasat al-Risāla, 1400/1980.
Mujāhid b. Jabr. *Tafsīr.* Ed. Muḥammad ʿAbd al-Salām Abū al-Nīl. Cairo: Dār al-Fikr al-Islāmī al-Ḥadītha, 1410/1989.
Muqātil b. Sulaymān. *Tafsīr.* Ed. Aḥmad Farīd. 3 vols. Beirut: Dār al-Kutub al-ʿIlmiyya, 1424/2003.
Muslim. *Ṣaḥīḥ.* 5 vols. Cairo: Dār Iḥyāʾ al-Kutub al-ʿArabiyya, 1375/1955.
al-Nasafī. *Tafsīr.* 4 vols. in 2. Cairo: ʿĪsā al-Bābī al-Ḥalabī, n.d.
The New Oxford Annotated Bible. New Revised Standard Version. Ed. Bruce M. Metzger and Roland E. Murphy. New York: Oxford University Press, 1994.
Patrologiae cursus completus. Series graeca. Ed. J.-P. Migne. 161 vols. Paris: 1857–94.
Pĕsiḳta dĕ-Rab̲ Kahăna: R. Kahana's Compilation of Discourses for Sabbaths and Festal Days. Trans. William G. (Gershon Zev) Braude and Israel J. Kapstein. Philadelphia: Jewish Publication Society of America, 2002.
Pirḳe de-Rabbi Eliezer . . . im beʿûr *ha-Bayit ha-gadôl* me-et Avraham Aharôn ben ha-Rav Shalom. Bene Barak, 2005. [*PRE*]
The Qurʾān. Trans. Alan Jones. Exeter: Gibb Memorial Trust, 2007.
al-Qurṭubī. *al-Jāmiʿ li-aḥkām al-qurʾān.* Ed. ʿAbd al-Munʿim ʿAbd al-Maqṣūd. 20 vols. Cairo: Dār al-Kutub al-Miṣriyya, 1387/1967.
al-Rāzī, Fakhr al-Dīn. *al-Tafsīr al-kabīr.* 32 vols. in 16. 3rd ed. Tehran: Shirkat Ṣaḥāfī Nawīn, ca. 1980.
Répertoire d'épigraphie sémitique. Paris: Imprimerie nationale, 1900–.

Roth, Martha T. *Law Collections from Mesopotamia and Asia Minor.* Atlanta: Scholars Press, 1995.

Das sasanidische Rechtsbuch "Mātakdān i hazār dātistān." Part 2. Trans. Maria Macuch. Wiesbaden: Deutsche Morgenländische Gesellschaft, 1981. [*MHD*]

Die Schriften des Johannes von Damaskos. Ed. Bonifatius Kotter. Byzantisches Institut der Abtei Scheyern, Patristische Texte und Studien, Berlin: de Gruyter, 1969–.

Sifre: A Tannaitic Commentary on the Book of Deuteronomy. Trans. Reuven Hammer. New Haven, Conn.: Yale University Press, 1986.

Sufyān b. ʿUyayna. *Tafsīr.* Ed. Aḥmad Muḥammad Maḥāyirī. al-Riyāḍ: Maktabat Usāma, 1983.

al-Suyūṭī. *al-Durr al-manthūr fī al-tafsīr al-maʾthūr.* 6 vols. Beirut: Dār al-Kutub al-ʿIlmiyya, 1411/1990.

———. *Lubāb al-nuqūl fī asbāb al-nuzūl.* On the Margin of al-Maḥallī, *Tafsīr.* Cairo: Dār al-Qalam, 1966.

Syrisch-Römisches Rechtsbuch aus dem fünften Jahrhundert. Ed. K. G. Bruns and Eduard Sachau. Leipzig: F. A. Brockhaus, 1880; reprinted Scientia Aalen, 1961. New edition: *Das Syrisch-Römische Rechtsbuch.* Ed. and trans. Walter Selb and Hubert Kaufhold. 3 vols. Wien: Verlag der Österreichischen Akademie der Wissenschaften, 2002.

The Syro-Roman Lawbook: The Syriac Text of the Recently Discovered Manuscripts Accompanied by a Facsimile Edition and Furnished with an Introduction and Translation. Vol. 2, *A Translation with Annotations*, by Arthur Vööbus. Stockholm: Estonian Theological Society in Exile, 1983.

al-Ṭabarī, Muḥammad b. Jarīr. *Jāmiʿ al-bayān ʿan taʾwīl āy al-qurʾān.* 30 vols. in 12. 3rd ed. Cairo: Muṣṭafā al-Bābī al-Ḥalabī, 1954–68.

———. *Tafsīr al-Ṭabarī: Jāmiʿ al-bayān ʿan taʾwīl āy al-qurʾān.* Ed. M. M. Shākir and Aḥmad Muḥammad Shākir. 16 vols. Cairo: Dār al-Maʿārif, 1969.

———. *Taʾrīkh al-rusul waʾl-mulūk.* Ed. M. Abū al-Faḍl Ibrāhīm. 11 vols. Cairo: Dār al-Maʿārif, 1960–77. See also *The History of al-Ṭabarī.*

al-Ṭabarsī. *Majmaʿ al-bayān li-ʿulūm al-qurʾān.* 9 vols. Cairo: Dār al-Taqrīb bayna al-Madhāhib al-Islāmiyya, 1395/1975.

al-Ṭabāṭabāʾī. *al-Mīzān fī tafsīr al-qurʾān.* 5 vols. Beirut: al-Maṭbaʿa al-Tijāriyya, 1970–.

Tanakh, The Holy Scriptures: The New JPS Translation According to the Traditional Hebrew Text. Philadelphia: Jewish Publication Society, 1985.

The Testament of the Twelve Patriarchs: The Sons of Jacob. Trans. from the Greek by Robert Grosthead. London: Berwick, printed for W. Phorson; B. Law, 1791.

al-Thaʿlabī, Abū Isḥāq Aḥmad. *al-Kashf waʾl-bayān al-maʿrūf bi-Tafsīr al-Thaʿlabī.* Ed. Abū Muḥammad b. ʿĀshūr. 10 vols. Beirut: Dār Iḥyā al-Turāth al-ʿArabī, 1422/2002.

al-Thawrī, Sufyān b. Saʿīd b. Masrūq al-Kūfī. *Tafsīr al-qurʾān al-karīm.* Ed. Imtiyāz ʿAlī ʿArshī. Rāmbūr: Wizārat al-Maʿārif, 1385/1965.

al-Tirmidhī. *Sunan.* 5 vols. Cairo: al-Maktaba al-Salafiyya, 1965–7.

al-Wāqidī, Muḥammad b. ʿUmar. *Kitāb al-maghāzī.* Ed. Marsden Jones. 3 vols. London: Oxford University Press, 1966.

Yalkut Shimʿoni: Midrash ʿal Torah, Neviʾim u-Khetuvim. 5 vols. Jerusalem: Hotsa'at Yerid ha-sefarim, 2006.

al-Yaʿqūbī. *Taʾrīkh.* Ed. Muḥammad Ṣādiq Baḥr al-ʿUlūm. 3 vols. Najaf: al-Maktaba al-Ḥaydariyya, 1384/1964.

Yāqūt. *Muʿjam al-buldān.* 5 vols. Beirut: Dār Ṣādir, 1376/1957.

al-Zamakhsharī, Maḥmūd b. ʿUmar. *al-Kashshāf ʿan ḥaqāʾiq ghawāmiḍ al-tanzīl wa-ʿuyūn al-aqāwīl fī wujūh al-taʾwīl.* Ed. ʿĀdil Aḥmad ʿAbd al-Mawjūd and ʿAlī Muḥammad Muʿawwaḍ. 6 vols. al-Riyāḍ: Maktabat al-ʿUbaykān, 1998.

Secondary Sources

Ackerman, Susan. "'And the Women Knead Dough': The Worship of the Queen of Heaven in Sixth-Century Judah." In *Gender and Difference*, ed. Peggy Day. Minneapolis: Fortress Press, 1989, 109–24.

Adang, Camilla. *Muslim Writers on Judaism and the Hebrew Bible from Ibn Rabban to Ibn Hazm*. Leiden: Brill, 1996.

Akkadisches Handwörterbuch. Ed. Wolfram von Soden. Wiesbaden: Harrassowitz, 1972.

The Anchor Bible Dictionary. Ed. David Noel Freedman. 6 vols. New York: Doubleday, 1992.

Andrae, Tor. *Mohammed: The Man and His Faith*. 1936. Repr. New York: Harper and Row, 1955.

Arazi, Albert. "Les enfants adultérins [*daʿīs*] dans la société arabe ancienne: L'aspect littéraire." *Jerusalem Studies in Arabic and Islam* 16 (1993): 1–34.

Arazi, Albert and Salman Masalha. *Six Early Arab Poets: New Edition and Concordance*. Jerusalem: Max Schloessinger Memorial Series, 1999.

Arkoun, Mohammed. *Rethinking Islam: Common Questions, Uncommon Answers*. Trans. Robert D. Lee. Boulder, Colo.: Westview Press, 1994.

Armstrong, Karen. *Muḥammad: a Biography of the Prophet*. San Francisco: HarperSanFrancisco, 1992.

Asmussen, J. P. *Xᵘāstvānīft: Studies in Manichaeism*. Acta Theologica Danica, 7. Copenhagen: Prostant apud Munksgaard, 1965.

Assmann, Jan. *Moses the Egyptian: The Memory of Egypt in Western Monotheism*. Cambridge, Mass.: Harvard University Press, 1997.

The Assyrian Dictionary of the Oriental Institute of the University of Chicago. Chicago: Oriental Institute, 1956–. [*CAD*]

ʿAthāmina, Khalil. "*al-Qasas*: Its Emergence, Religious Origin and Its Socio-Political Impact on Early Muslim Society." *Studia Islamica* 76 (1992): 53–74.

Auerbach, Eric. *Mimesis: The Representation of Reality in Western Literature*. Trans. Willard Trask. Garden City, N.Y.: Doubleday, 1957.

Bakhos, Carol. *Ishmael on the Border: Rabbinic Portrayals of the First Arab*. Albany: State University of New York Press, 2006.

Bar-Asher, Meir M. *Scripture and Exegesis in Early Imāmī Shiism*. Leiden: Brill, 1999.

Bargach, Jamila. *Orphans of Islam: Family, Abandonment, and Secret Adoption in Morocco*. New York: Rowman & Littlefield, 2002.

Bashear, Suliman. "Riding Beasts on Divine Missions: An Examination of the Ass and Camel Traditions." *Journal of Semitic Studies* 37, 1 (1991): 37–71.

Baum, Wilhelm and Dietmar W. Winkler. *The Church of the East: A Concise History*. London: RoutledgeCurzon, 2000.

Ben-Ari, Shosh. "Stories about Abraham in Islam. A Geographical Approach." *Arabica* 54, 4 (2007): 526–53.

Ben-Barak, Zafrira. *Inheritance by Daughters in Israel and the Ancient Near East: A Social, Legal, and Ideological Revolution*. Jaffa: Archaeological Center Publications, 2006.

Benkheira, Mohammed H. "Alliance, asymétrie et différence des sexes: Un problème d'exégèse juridique: La prohibition de la belle-mere et de la belle-fille." *Islamic Law and Society* 13, 2 (2006): 153–207.

———. *L'amour de la Loi: Essai sur la normativité en islâm*. Paris: Presses Universitaires de France, 1997.

Bewer, Julius A. "Eliezer of Damascus." *Journal of Biblical Literature* 27, 2 (1908): 160–62.

Bhabha, Homi K., ed. *Nation and Narration*. London: Routledge, 1990.

Bialoblocki, Samuel. *Materialien zum islamischen und jüdischen Eherecht mit einer Einleitung über jüdische Einflüsse auf den Ḥadīth.* Gießen: Alfred Töpelmann, 1928.

Biddle, Mark E. "Ancestral Motifs in I Samuel 25: Intertextuality and Characterization." *Journal of Biblical Literature* 121, 4 (2002): 617–38.

Bijlefeld, W. A. "A Prophet and More than a Prophet? Some Observations on the Qurʾanic Use of the Terms 'Prophet' and 'Apostle'." *Muslim World* 59 (1969): 1–28. Repr. in *Koran: Critical Concepts in Islamic Studies*, ed. Colin Turner. 4 vols. London: RoutledgeCurzon, 2004, 2:295–322.

Blankinship, Khalid Yahya. "Imārah, Khilāfah, and Imāmah: The Origin of the Succession to the Prophet Muhammad." In *Shiʿite Heritage: Essays on Classical and Modern Traditions*, ed. Lynda Clarke. Binghamton, N.Y.: Global Publications, 2001, 19–44.

Bonner, Michael. *Jihad in Islamic History: Doctrines and Practice.* Princeton, N.J.: Princeton University Press, 2006.

Bowersock, G. W. *Martyrdom and Rome.* Cambridge: Cambridge University Press, 1995.

Boyarin, Daniel. *Border Lines: The Partition of Judaeo-Christianity.* Philadelphia: University of Pennsylvania Press, 2004.

———. *Dying for God: Martyrdom and the Making of Christianity and Judaism.* Stanford, Calif.: Stanford University Press, 1999.

———. "*Hamidrash Vehama'se—ʿAl Haheker Hahistori Shel Safrut Hazal.*" In *Saul Lieberman Memorial Volume*, ed. Shamma Friedmann. New York: Jewish Theological Seminary of America, 1993, 105–17.

———. *Intertextuality and the Reading of Midrash.* Bloomington: Indiana University Press, 1990.

Bravmann, M. M. "Equality of Birth of Husband and Wife (*kafāʾah*), an Early Arab Principle." In idem, *The Spiritual Background of Early Islam: Studies in Ancient Arab Concepts.* Leiden: Brill, 1972, 301–10.

———. "The Origin of the Principle of *ʿIṣmah*: Muḥammad's Immunity from Sin." *Le Muséon* 88 (1975): 221–25.

Breneman, J. Mervin. "Nuzi Marriage Tablets." Ph.D. dissertation, Brandeis University, 1971.

Brock, Sebastian. "Genesis 22 in Syriac Tradition." In *Mélanges Dominique Barthélmy*, ed. Pierre Casetti, Othmar Keel, and Adrian Schenker. Göttingen: Vandenhoeck & Ruprecht, 1981, 2–30.

Brockelmann, Carl. *Kurzgefasste vergleichende Grammatik der semitischen Sprachen: Elemente der Laut- und Formenlehre.* Berlin: Reuther & Reichard; New York: Lemcke & Buechner, 1908.

Brown, Raymond E. *The Birth of the Messiah: A Commentary on the Infancy Narratives in the Gospels of Matthew and Luke.* New updated ed. New York: Doubleday, 1993.

Brundage, James A. "Adoption in the Medieval *Ius Commune.*" In *Proceedings of the Tenth International Congress of Medieval Canon Law.* Vatican City: Bibliotheca Apostolica Vaticana, 2001, 889–905.

Brunschvig, Robert. "Simples remarques négatives sur le vocabulaire du Coran." *Studia Islamica* (1956): 19–32.

Burton, John. *The Collection of the Qurʾān.* Cambridge: Cambridge University Press, 1977.

———. Review of *Studies in Qurʾān and Ḥadīth: The Formation of the Islamic Law of Inheritance. Journal of Semitic Studies* 36 (1991): 359–62.

———. *The Sources of Islamic Law: Islamic Theories of Abrogation.* Edinburgh: Edinburgh University Press, 1990.

CAD. See *The Assyrian Dictionary of the Oriental Institute of the University of Chicago.*

Caetani, Leone. *Annali dell'Islām*. 10 vols. in 12. Milano: U. Hoepli, 1905–26.
Carter, Michael. "Foreign Vocabulary." In *The Blackwell Companion to the Qur'ān*, ed. Andrew Rippin. Oxford: Blackwell, 2006, 120–39.
Cassin, E.-M. *L'Adoption à Nuzi*. Paris: Adrien-Maisonneuve, 1938.
Cilardo, Agostino. *The Qur'ānic Term* Kalāla*: Studies in Arabic Language and Poetry, Ḥadīṯ, and Fiqh. Notes on the Origins of Islamic Law*. Edinburgh: Edinburgh University Press, 2005.
Cohen, Aryeh. "Towards an Erotics of Martyrdom." *Journal of Jewish Thought and Philosophy* 7 (1998), 227–56.
Collins, John J. "The Zeal of Phineas: The Bible and the Legitimation of Violence." *Journal of Biblical Literature* 122, 1 (2003): 3–21.
Colpe, Carsten. *Das Siegel der Propheten: Historische Beziehungen zwischen Judentum, Judenchristentum, Heidentum und frühem Islam*. Berlin: Institut Kirche und Judentum, 1989.
A Compendious Syriac Dictionary Founded upon the Thesaurus Syriacus of R. Payne Smith. Ed. J. Payne Smith. Oxford: Oxford University Press, 1902.
Conrad, Lawrence I. "Al-Azdī's History of the Arab Conquests in Bilād al-Shām: Some Historiographical Observations." In *Proceedings of the Second Symposium on the History of Bilād al-Shām During the Early Islamic Period Up to 40 A.H./640 A.D.*, vol. 1, ed. Adnan Bakhit. Amman: University of Jordan, 1987, 28–61.
———. "Heraclius in Early Islamic Kerygma." In *The Reign of Heraclius (610–641): Crisis and Confrontation*, ed. Gerrit J. Reinink and Bernard H. Stolte. Leuven: Peeters, 2002, 113–56.
———. Review of *Die Wiederentdeckung des Propheten Muhammad* and *Studien zur Komposition des mekkanischen Suren. al-Abḥāth* 33 (1985): 49–54.
———. "Seven and the *Tasbī'*: On the Implications of Numerical Symbolism for the Study of Medieval Islamic History." *Journal of the Economic and Social History of the Orient* 31 (1988): 42–73.
———. "Theophanes and the Arabic Historical Tradition: Some Indications of Intercultural Transmission." *Byzantinische Forschungen: Internationale Zeitschrift für Byzantinistik* 15 (1990): 1–44.
Cook, David. *Martyrdom in Islam*. New York: Cambridge University Press, 2007.
Cook, Michael. *The Koran: A Very Short Introduction*. Oxford: Oxford University Press, 2000.
Coulson, N. J. *Succession in the Muslim Family*. Cambridge: Cambridge University Press, 1971.
Crone, Patricia. "In defence of Ali." *Times Literary Supplement*. 7 February 1997, 28.
———. *Meccan Trade and the Rise of Islam*. Princeton, N.J.: Princeton University Press, 1987.
———. "A Note on Muqātil b. Ḥayyān and Muqātil b. Sulaymān." *Der Islam* 74 (1997): 238–49.
———. *Roman, Provincial and Islamic Law: The Origins of the Islamic Patronate*. Cambridge: Cambridge University Press, 1987. [*RPIL*]
———. "Two Legal Problems Bearing on the Early History of the Qur'ān." *Jerusalem Studies in Arabic and Islam* 18 (1994): 1–37.
———. "What do we actually know about Mohammed?" www.openDemocracy.net, 31 August 2006, 1–5.
Crone, Patricia and Martin Hinds. *God's Caliph: Religious Authority in the First Centuries of Islam*. Cambridge: Cambridge University Press, 1986.
Crone, Patricia and Fritz Zimmerman, eds. *The Epistle of Sālim b. Dhakwān*. Oxford: Oxford University Press, 2001.
Dähne, Stephan. "Context Equivalence: A Hitherto Insufficiently Studied Use of the

Quran in Political Speeches from the Early Period of Islam." In *Ideas, Images, and Methods of Portrayal: Insights into Classical Arabic Literature and Islam*, ed. Sebastian Günther. Leiden: Brill, 2005, 1–16.

Daniel, Norman. *Islam and the West: The Making of an Image.* Edinburgh: Edinburgh University Press, 1960.

Déroche, François. *The Abbasid Tradition: Qur'āns of the 8th to the 10th Centuries A.D.* Nasser D. Khalili Collection of Islamic Art, vol. 1. General editor Julian Raby. London: Nour Foundation in association with Azimuth Editions and Oxford University Press, 1992.

———. *Islamic Codicology: An Introduction to the Study of Manuscripts in Arabic Script.* Trans. Deke Dusinberre and David Radzinowicz, ed. Muhammad Isa Waley. London: Al-Furqān Islamic Heritage Foundation, 2006.

———. *La Transmission manuscrite du Coran aux débuts de l'islam: Le codex Parisino-petropolitanus.* Leiden: Brill, forthcoming.

Déroche, François and Sergio Noja Noseda. *Sources de la transmission manuscrite du texte coranique, I: Les manuscripts de style ḥiğāzī.* Vol. 1, *Le manuscript arabe 328(a) de la Bibliothèque nationale de France.* Lesa: Foundazione Ferni Noja Noseda, 1998.

Dictionary of the North-West Semitic Inscriptions, by J. Hoftijzer and K. Jongeling. Leiden: Brill, 1995.

A Dictionary of the Ugaritic Language in the Alphabetic Tradition. Ed. Gregorio Del Olmo Lete and Joaquín Sanmartí, trans. Wilfred G. E. Watson. Leiden: Brill, 2003.

Donner, Fred McGraw. *The Early Islamic Conquests.* Princeton, N.J.: Princeton University Press, 1982.

———. *Narratives of Islamic Origins: The Beginnings of Islamic Historical Writing.* Princeton, N.J.: Darwin Press, 1998.

Donner, Herbert. "Adoption oder Legitimation? Erwägungen zur Adoption im Alten Testament auf dem Hintergrund der altorientalischen Rechte." *Oriens Antiquus* 8 (1969): 87–119.

Draffkorn, Anne E. "Ilani/Elohim." *Journal of Biblical Literature* 76, 3 (1957): 216–24.

Dunlop, D. M. "Al-Ḥārith b. Saʿīd al-Kadhdhāb, A Claimant to Prophecy in the Caliphate of ʿAbd al-Malik." *Studies in Islam* 1 (1964): 12–18.

Dunn, Geoffrey D. *Tertullian.* London: Routledge, 2004.

Duri, ʿAbd al-ʿAziz. *The Rise of Historical Writing Among the Arab*s. Ed. and trans. Lawrence I. Conrad. Princeton, N.J.: Princeton University Press, 1983.

Dutton, Yasin. "An Early *Muṣḥaf* According to the Reading of Ibn ʿĀmir." *Journal of Qur'ānic Studies* 3, 1 (2001): 71–89.

———. *The Origins of Islamic Law: The Qur'ān, the Muwaṭṭa' and Madinan ʿAmal.* London: RoutledgeCurzon, 1999.

Ehrman, Bart D. *Lost Christianities: The Battle for Scripture and the Faiths We Never Knew.* Oxford: Oxford University Press, 2003.

———. *The Orthodox Corruption of Scripture: The Effect of Early Christological Controversies on the Text of the New Testament.* New York: Oxford University Press, 1993.

Encyclopaedia of Islam. 2nd ed. 11 vols. Leiden: Brill, 1954–2002. [*EI*^{2}]

Encyclopaedia of Islam. 3rd ed. (in progress). [*EI*^{3}]

Encyclopaedia of the Qur'ān. Ed. Jane Dammen McAuliffe. 5 vols. plus index. Leiden: Brill, 2001. [*EQ*]

Ess, Josef Van. *Anfänge muslimischer Theologie: zwei antiqadaritische Traktate aus dem ersten Jahrhundert der Hiğra.* Beirut: Orient-Institut; Wiesbaden: F. Steiner, 1977.

———. *The Flowering of Muslim Theology.* Cambridge, Mass.: Harvard University Press, 2006.

———. "Das *Kitāb al-irǧā'* des Ḥasan b. Muḥammad b. al-Ḥanafiyya." *Arabica* 21 (1974): 20–52.

———. *Theologie und Gesellschaft im 2. und 3. Jahrhundert Hidschra: Eine Geschichte des religiösen Denkens im frühen Islam.* 6 vols. Berlin and New York: Walter de Gruyter, 1991–97.

Even-Shoshan, Avraham. *ha-Milôn he-Ḥadash.* 5 vols. Jerusalem: Qiryat Sefer, 1963.

Excavations at Nuzi conducted by the Semitic Museum and the Fogg Art Museum of Harvard University, with the cooperation of the American School of Oriental Research at Baghdad. Ed. Edward Chiera. Cambridge, Mass.: Harvard University Press, 1929.

Faruki, Kemal. "*Tawḥīd* and the Doctrine of *ʿIṣmah.*" *Islamic Studies* 4 (1965): 31–43.

Fewell, Danna Nolan, ed. *Reading Between Texts: Intertextuality and the Hebrew Bible.* Louisville, Ky.: Westminster/John Knox Press, 1992.

Firestone, Reuven. "Abraham's Journey to Mecca in Islamic Exegesis: A Form-Critical Study of a Tradition." *Studia Islamica* 76 (1992): 5–24.

———. *Journeys in Holy Lands: The Evolution of the Abraham-Ishmael Legends in Islamic Exegesis.* Albany: State University of New York Press, 1990.

———. "Merit, Mimesis, and Martyrdom: Aspects of Shiʿite Meta-Historical Exegesis on Abraham's Sacrifice in Light of Jewish, Christian, and Sunni Muslim Tradition." *Journal of the American Academy of Religion* 66, 1 (1998): 93–116.

Foucault, Michel. *The Archaeology of Knowledge and The Discourse on Language.* Trans. A. M. Sheridan Smith. New York: Harper Colophon, 1976.

Freud, Sigmund. *Moses and Monotheism.* Trans. from the German by Katherine Jones. New York: Vintage Books, 1967.

Friedmann, Yohanan. "Finality of Prophethood in Sunnī Islam." *Jerusalem Studies in Arabic and Islam* 7 (1986): 177–215.

———. *Prophecy Continuous: Aspects of Aḥmadī Religious Thought and Its Medieval Background.* Berkeley: University of California Press, 1989.

Frye, Northrup. *The Great Code: The Bible and Literature.* New York: Harcourt Brace Jovanovich, 1982.

Frymer-Kensky, Tikva. "Patriarchal Family Relationships and Near Eastern Law." *Biblical Archaeologist* 44, 4 (1981): 209–14.

Gabrieli, Francesco. *Muhammad and the Conquests of Islam.* New York: McGraw-Hill, 1968.

Gadd, C. J. "Tablets from Kirkuk." *Revue d'assyriologie et d'archéologie orientale* 23, 2–4 (1926): 49–161.

Gil, Moshe. *A History of Palestine, 634–1099.* Cambridge: Cambridge University Press, 1992.

Gilliot, Claude. "The Beginnings of Qur'ānic Exegesis." *Revue du Monde Musulman et de la Méditerranée* 58 (1990): 82–100. Reprinted in *The Koran: Critical Concepts in Islamic Studies*, ed. Colin Turner. 4 vols. London: RoutledgeCurzon, 2004, 4: 248–70.

———. "Creation of a Fixed Text." In *The Cambridge Companion to the Qur'ān*, ed. Jane Dammen McAuliffe. Cambridge: Cambridge University Press, 2006, 41–58.

———. "Exégèse et sémantique institutionnelle dans le commentaire de Tabari." *Studia Islamica* 77 (1993): 41–94.

———. *Exégèse, langue, et théologie en Islam: L'exégèse coranique de Ṭabarī (m. 311/923).* Paris: J. Vrin, 1990.

———. "Muqātil, grand exégète, traditionniste et théologien maudit." *Journal Asiatique* 279 (1991): 39–92.

Ginsberg, H. L. "Abram's 'Damascene' Steward." *Bulletin of the American Schools of Oriental Research* 200 (1970): 31–33.

Ginzberg, Louis. *The Legends of the Jews*. 7 vols. Philadelphia: Jewish Publications Society of America, 1906–38.

Goitein, S. D. *Jews and Arabs: Their Contacts Through the Ages*. New York: Schocken Books, 1955.

Goldfeld, Isaiah. "Muqātil Ibn Sulaymān." *Arabic and Islamic Studies* 2 (1978): 1–18.

———. "The *Tafsīr* of ʿAbdallāh b. ʿAbbās." *Der Islam* 58, 1 (1981): 125–35.

Goldziher, Ignaz. *Muslim Studies*. Ed. S. M. Stern. 2 vols. Chicago: Aldine, 1971.

Goody, Jack. *The Development of the Family and Marriage in Europe*. Cambridge: Cambridge University Press, 1983.

Gordon, Cyrus H. *Ugaritic Textbook*. Rome: Pontifical Biblical Institute, 1965.

Goshen-Gottstein, Alon. *The Sinner and the Amnesiac: The Rabbinic Invention of Elisha ben Abuya and Eleazar ben Arach*. Stanford, Calif.: Stanford University Press, 2000.

Grabar, Oleg. *The Dome of the Rock*. Cambridge, Mass.: Harvard University Press, 2006.

Greenberg, J. "The Patterning of Root Morphemes in Semitic." *Word* 6 (1950): 162–81.

Grosz, Katarzyna. *The Archive of the Wullu Family*. Copenhagen: Carsten Niebuhr Institute of Ancient Near Eastern Studies, 1988.

———. "On Some Aspects of the Adoption of Women at Nuzi." In *Studies on the Civilization and Culture of Nuzi and the Hurrians*, vol. 2, ed. David I. Owen and M. A. Morrison. Winona Lake, Ind.: Eisenbrauns, 1987, 131–52.

Gruendler, Beatrice. *The Development of the Arabic Script*. Harvard Semitic Series 43. Atlanta: Scholars Press, 1993.

Gwynne, Rosalind Ward. *Logic, Rhetoric, and Legal Reasoning in the Qurʾān: God's Arguments*. London: RoutledgeCurzon, 2004.

Hakim, Avraham. "The Death of an Ideal Leader: Predictions and Premonitions." *Journal of the American Oriental Society* 126, 1 (2006): 1–16.

———. "ʿUmar b. al-Ḫaṭṭāb, calife par la grâce de Dieu." *Arabica* 54 (2007): 317–61.

Halevi, Leor. *Muhammad's Grave: Death Rites and the Making of Islamic Society*. New York: Columbia University Press, 2007.

Hallaq, Wael B., ed. *The Formation of Islamic Law*. In *The Formation of the Classical Islamic World*, vol. 27, gen. ed. Lawrence I. Conrad. Aldershot: Ashgate, 2004.

Hamidullah, Muhammad. *Le prophète de l'Islam*. 2 vols. Paris: J. Vrin, 1959/1378 H.

Hasan, Ahmad. "The concept of infallibility in Islam." *Islamic Studie*s 11 (1972): 1–11.

Haykal, Muḥammad Ḥusayn. *The Life of Muḥammad*. Trans. from 8th ed. by Ismaʿil Ragi A. al-Faruqi. Indianapolis: North American Trust Publications, 1976.

Hayward, Robert. "The Present State of Research into the Targumic Account of the Sacrifice of Isaac." *Journal of Jewish Studies* 32 (1981): 127–50.

Hendel, Ronald. *Remembering Abraham: Culture, Memory, and History in the Hebrew Bible*. Oxford: Oxford University Press, 2005.

Hirschfeld, Hartwig. *New Researches into the Composition and Exegesis of the Qoran*. Asiatic Monographs 3. London: Royal Asiatic Society, 1902.

A History of Ancient Near Eastern Law. See Westbrook, Raymond.

Hitti, Philip K. *History of the Arabs*. New York: Macmillan, 1937; 10th ed. 1970.

Hodgson, Marshall G. S. *The Venture of Islam: Conscience and History in a World Civilization*. Vol. 1, *The Classical Age of Islam*. Chicago: University of Chicago Press, 1974.

Horovitz, Josef. *The Earliest Biographies of the Prophet and Their Authors*. Ed. Lawrence I. Conrad. Studies in Late Antiquity and Early Islam 11. Princeton, N.J.: Darwin Press, 2002.

Hoyland, Robert G. *Seeing Islam as Others Saw It*. Studies in Late Antiquity and Early Islam 13. Princeton, N.J.: Darwin Press, 1997.

Jandora, John Walter. *The March from Medina: A Revisionist Study of the Arab Conquests.* Clifton, N.J.: Kingston Press, 1990.

János, Jany. "The Four Sources of Law in Zoroastrian and Islamic Jurisprudence." *Islamic Law and Society* 12:3 (2005): 291–332.

Jastrow, Marcus. *Dictionary of Talmud Babli, Yerushalmi, Midrashic Literature and Targumim.* 2 vols. New York: Pardes, 1950.

Jeffery, Arthur. *The Foreign Vocabulary of the Qur'ān.* Baroda: Oriental Institute, 1938. Reprinted Lahore: al-Biruni, 1977.

———. "Ghevond's Text of the Correspondence Between ʿUmar II and Leo III." In *The Early Christian-Muslim Dialogue: A Collection of Documents from the First Three Islamic Centuries (632–900 A.D.): Translations with Commentary*, ed. N. A. Newman. Hatfield, Pa.: Interdisciplinary Biblical Research Institute, 1993.

———. *Materials for the History of the Qur'ān.* Leiden: Brill, 1937. *See also* Ibn Abī Dā'ūd.

Juynboll, G. H. A. *Encyclopedia of Canonical Ḥadīth.* Leiden: Brill, 2007.

Kaegi, Walter. *Byzantium and the Early Islamic Conquests.* Cambridge: Cambridge University Press, 1992.

Kaminsky, Joel S. *Yet I Loved Jacob: Reclaiming the Biblical Concept of Election.* Nashville: Abingdon Press, 2007.

Kennedy, Hugh. *The Great Arab Conquests: How the Spread of Islam Changed the World We Live In.* Philadelphia: Da Capo Press, 2007.

———. *The Prophet and the Age of the Caliphates: The Islamic Near East from the Sixth to the Eleventh Century.* London: Longman, 1986.

Kermode, Frank. *The Genesis of Secrecy: On the Interpretation of Narrative.* Cambridge, MA: Harvard University Press, 1979.

Keshk, Khaled. "The Historiography of an Execution: The Killing of Ḥujr b. ʿAdī." *Journal of Islamic Studies* 19, 1 (2008): 1–35.

Kimber, Richard. "The Qur'anic Law of Inheritance." *Islamic Law and Society* 5, 3 (1998): 291–325.

Kinberg, Naphtali. *A Lexicon of al-Farrā''s Terminology in His Qur'ān Commentary: With Full Definitions, English Summaries, and Extensive Citations.* Leiden: Brill, 1996.

Kister, M. J. "*Ḥaddithū ʿan banī isrā'īla wa-lā ḥaraja*: A Study of an Early Tradition." *Israel Oriental Society* 2 (1972): 215–39.

———. "*Al-Taḥannuth*: An Inquiry into the Meaning of a Term." *Bulletin of the School of Oriental and African Studies* 31, 2 (1968): 223–36.

Klein, Michael L. *The Fragment-Targums of the Pentateuch According to their Extant Sources.* 2 vols. Rome: Biblical Institute Press, 1980.

Klemm, Verena. "Image Formation of an Islamic Legend: Fāṭima, the Daughter of the Prophet Muḥammad." In *Ideas, Images, and Methods of Portrayal: Insights into Classical Arabic Literature and Islam*, ed. Sebastian Günther. Leiden: Brill, 2005, 181–208.

Klier, Klaus. *Ḫālid und ʿUmar: Quellenkritische Untersuchung zur Historiographie der frühislamischen Zeit.* Berlin: Klaus Schwarz Verlag, 1998.

Koschaker, P. "Drei Urkunden aus Arrapha." *Zeitschrift für Assyriologie* 48 (1944): 161–221.

———. *Neue keilschriftliche Rechtsurkunden aus der El-Amarna Zeit.* Leipzig: S. Hirzel, 1928.

Kristeva, Julia. *Desire in Language: A Semiotic Approach to Literature and Art.* Ed. Leon S. Roudiez. Trans. Thomas Gora, Alice Jardine, and Leon S. Roudiez. New York: Columbia University Press, 1980.

———. *Sēmeiōtikē: Recherches pour une sémnalyse.* Paris: Éditions du Seuil, 1969.

Lammens, Henri. *Fatima et les filles de Mahomet: Notes critiques pour l'étude de la Sira.* Rome: sumptibus Ponificii instituti biblici, 1912.

Landau-Tasseron, Ella. "Adoption, Acknowledgement of Paternity and False Genealogical Claims in Arabian and Islamic Societies." *Bulletin of the School of Oriental and African Studies* 66, 2 (2003): 169–92.

Lane, Edward William. *Arabic-English Lexicon.* London: Williams and Norgate, 1863. Repr. Cambridge: Islamic Texts Society, 1984.

Lazarus-Yafeh, Hava. *Intertwined Worlds: Medieval Islam and Bible Criticism.* Princeton, N.J.: Princeton University Press, 1992.

Lecker, Michael. "Ḥudhayfa b. al-Yamān and ʿAmmār b. Yāsir, Jewish Converts to Islam." *Quaderni di Studi Arabi* 11 (1993): 149–62.

———. "King Ibn Ubayy and the *Quṣṣāṣ*." In *Method and Theory in the Study of Islamic Origins*, ed. Herbert Berg. Leiden: Brill, 2003, 29–72.

———. "Zayd b. Thābit, 'A Jew with two sidelocks': Judaism and Literacy in Pre-Islamic Medina (Yathrib)." *Journal of Near Eastern Studies* 56:4 (1997): 259–73.

Leemhuis, Fred. "Origins and Early Development of the *tafsīr* Tradition." In *Approaches to the History of the Interpretation of the Qur'ān*, ed. Andrew Rippin. Oxford: Clarendon Press, 1988, 13–30.

Leiman, Sid Z. *The Canonization of Hebrew Scripture: The Talmudic and Midrashic Evidence.* New Haven: Connecticut Academy of Arts and Sciences, 1976.

Leslau, Wolf. *Arabic Loanwords in Ethiopian Semitic.* Wiesbaden: Otto Harrassowitz, 1990.

———. *Ethiopic and South Arabic Contributions to the Hebrew Lexicon.* University of Southern California Publications in Semitic Philology 20. Berkeley: University of California Press, 1958.

———. "Vocabulary Common to Akkadian and South-East Semitic (Ethiopic and South-Arabic)." *Journal of the American Oriental Society* 64, 2 (1944): 53–58.

Levenson, Jon D. *The Death and Resurrection of the Beloved Son: The Transformation of Child Sacrifice in Judaism and Christianity.* New Haven, Conn.: Yale University Press, 1993.

———. "The Universal Horizon of Biblical Particularism." In *Ethnicity and the Bible*, ed. Mark G. Brett. Leiden: Brill, 1996, 143–69.

Lévi, Israel. "Le Sacrifice d'Isaac et la mort de Jesús." *Revue des Etudes Juives* 64 (1912): 161–84.

Lewinstein, Keith. "The Revaluation of Martyrdom in Early Islam." In *Sacrificing the Self: Perspectives on Martyrdom and Religion*, ed. Margaret Cormack. Oxford: Oxford University Press, 2001, 78–91.

Lings, Martin. *Muhammad: His Life Based on the Earliest Sources.* Cambridge: Islamic Texts Society, 1983.

Lowin, Shari I. *The Making of a Forefather: Abraham in Islamic and Jewish Exegetical Narratives.* Leiden: Brill, 2006.

MacDowell, Douglas M. *The Law in Classical Athens.* Ithaca, N.Y.: Cornell University Press, 1978.

Macuch, Maria. *Rechtskasuistik und Gerichtspraxis zu Beginn des siebenten Jahrhunderts in Iran: Die Rechtssamlung des Farroḫmard i Wahrāmān.* Wiesbaden: Harrassowitz, 1997.

Madelung, Wilfred. "The Hāshimiyyāt of al-Kumayt and Hāshimī Shiʿism." *Studia Islamica* 70 (1989): 5–26.

———. Review *of Studies in Qur'ān and Ḥadīth: The Formation of the Islamic Law of Inheritance. Journal of Near Eastern Studies* 47, 4 (1988): 313–14.

———. *The Succession to Muḥammad: A Study of the early Caliphate.* Cambridge: Cambridge University Press, 1997.

Maghen, Ze'ev. "Davidic Motifs in the Biography of Muḥammad." *Jerusalem Studies in Arabic and Islam* 34 (2008).

———. "Intertwined Triangles: Remarks on the Relationship Between Two Prophetic Scandals." *Jerusalem Studies in Arabic and Islam* 33 (2007): 17–92.

Mahdi, Muhsin. "Philosophical Literature." In *Religion, Science, and Learning in the ʿAbbasid Period*, ed. M. J. Young, J. D. Latham, and R. B. Serjeant. Cambridge: Cambridge University Press, 1990, 76–105.

Maʿjūz, Muḥammad b. *Wasāʾil al-ithbāt fī al-fiqh al-islamī.* Casablanca: Maṭbaʿat al-Najjāḥ al-Jadīda, 1984.

A Mandaic Dictionary. By E. S. Drower and R. Macuch. Oxford: Clarendon Press, 1963.

Mann, Jacob. *The Bible as Read and Preached in the Old Synagogue.* 2 vols. Cincinnati: Union of American Hebrew Congregations, 1940.

Matyszak, Philip. *The Sons of Caesar: Imperial Rome's First Dynasty.* London: Thames & Hudson, 2006.

Mendelsohn, I. "The Conditional Sale into Slavery of Free-Born Daughters in Nuzi and the Law of Ex. 21: 7–11." *Journal of the American Oriental Society* 55, 2 (1935): 190–95.

Michalowski, Peter. "The Bride of Simanum." *Journal of the American Oriental Society* 95, 4 (1975): 716–19.

Mitter, Ulrike. "Unconditional Manumission of Slaves in Early Islamic Law: A *ḥadīth* Analysis." *Der Islam* 78 (2001): 35–72.

Moscati, Sabatino, ed. *An Introduction to the Comparative Grammar of the Semitic Languages.* 3rd printing. Wiesbaden: Otto Harrassowitz, 1980.

Motzki, Harald. "The Collection of the Qurʾān: A Reconsideration of Western Views in Light of Recent Methodological Developments." *Der Islam* 78 (2001): 1–34.

———. Review of *Studies in Qurʾān and Ḥadīth: The Formation of the Islamic Law of Inheritance. Der Islam* 65 (1988): 117–20.

Nagel, Tilman. *Mohammed: Leben und Legende.* Munich: Oldenbourg, 2008.

Nicholas, Barry. *An Introduction to Roman Law.* Oxford: Clarendon Press, 1922; repr. 1975.

Nöldeke, Theodor. *Geschichte des Qorāns.* Ed. Friedrich Schwally. 3 vols. Leipzig, 1909. Repr. Hildesheim: Georg Olms, 1961.

Noth, Albrecht. *The Early Arabic Historical Tradition: A Source-Critical Study.* 2nd ed. Trans. Michael Bonner. Princeton, N.J.: Darwin Press, 1994.

Pagels, Elaine. "The Social History of Satan, the 'Intimate Enemy': A Preliminary Sketch." *Harvard Theological Review* 84, 2 (1991): 105–28.

Paradise, Jonathan S. "Nuzi Inheritance Practices." Ph.D. dissertation, University of Pennsylvania, 1972.

Paul, Shalom M. "Exod. 21:10: A Threefold Maintenance Clause." *Journal of Near Eastern Studies* 28, 1 (1969): 48–53.

Perry, Menakhem. "Counter-Stories in the Bible: Rebekah and Her Bridegroom, Abraham's Servant." *Prooftexts* 27 (2007): 275–23.

Peters, F. E. *Muhammad and the Origins of Islam.* Albany: State University of New York Press, 1994.

Peters, Rudolph. *Jihad in Classical and Modern Islam.* Princeton, N.J.: Markus Weiner, 1996.

Phillips, Anthony. "Some Aspects of Family Law in Pre-Exilic Israel." *Vetus Testamentum* 23 (1973): 349–61.

Pines, Shlomo. "'Israel, My Firstborn' and the Sonship of Jesus: A Theme of Moslem Anti-Christian Polemics." In *Studies in the History of Religions*, ed. Guy G. Stroumsa. Jerusalem: Magnes Press, 1996, 116–31.

Podany, Amanda H., Gary M. Beckman and Gudrun Colbow. "An Adoption and

Inheritance Contract from the Reign of Iggid-Lim of Hana." *Journal of Cuneiform Studies* 43 (1991–93): 39–51.

Pollack, Daniel, Moshe Bleich, Charles J. Reid, Jr., and Mohammad H. Fadel. "Classical Religious Perspectives of Adoption Law." *Notre Dame Law Review* 79 (2003–2004): 693–753.

Porten, Bezalel. *The Elephantine Papyri in English: Three Millennia of Cross-Cultural Continuity and Change.* Leiden: Brill, 1996.

Powers, David S. "Demonizing Zenobia: The Legend of al-Zabbāʾ in Islamic Sources." In *Histories of the Middle East: Studies in Middle Eastern Society, Economy, and Law in Honor of A. L. Udovitch*, ed. Roxani Margaritai, Adam Sabra, and Petra Sijpesteijn. Leiden: Brill, forthcoming.

———. "The Exegetical Genre *nāsikh al-Qurʾān wa mansūkhuhu.*" In *Approaches to the History of the Interpretation of the Qurʾān*, ed. Andrew Rippin. Oxford: Clarendon Press, 1988, 117–38.

———. "The Islamic Law of Inheritance, Reconsidered: A New Reading of Q. 4:12b." *Studia Islamica* 55 (1982): 61–94.

———. "On the Abrogation of the Bequest Verses." *Arabica* 29 (1982): 246–95.

———. "On Bequests in Early Islam." *Journal of Near Eastern Studies* 48 (1989), 185–200.

———. *Studies in Qurʾān and Ḥadīth: The Formation of the Islamic Law of Inheritance.* Berkeley: University of California Press, 1986. [*SQH*]

———. "The Will of Saʿd b. Abī Waqqāṣ: A Reassessment." *Studia Islamica* 58 (1983): 33–53.

Prémare, Alfred-Louis de. "ʿAbd al-Malik b. Marwān et le processus de constitution du Coran." In *Die dunklen Anfänge: Neue Forschungen zur Entstehung und frühen Geschichte des Islam*, ed. Karl-Heinz Ohlig and Gerd-R. Puin. Berlin: Hans Schiler, 2005, 179–212.

———. *Les Fondations de l'Islam: Entre écriture et histoire.* Paris: Seuil, 2002.

al-Qāḍī, Wadād. "The Term 'Khalīfa' in Early Exegetical Literature." *Die Welt des Islams* 28 (1988): 392–411.

Rabb, Intisar A. "Non-Canonical Readings of the Qur'an: Recognition and Authenticity (The Ḥimṣī Reading)." *Journal of Qur'anic Studies* 8, 2 (2006): 84–127.

Rabin, Chaim. *Ancient West-Arabian.* London: Taylor's Foreign Press, 1951.

———. *Qumran Studies.* New York: Schocken Books, 1957.

Rabinowitz, Isaac. *A Witness Forever: Ancient Israel's Perception of Literature and the Resultant Hebrew Bible.* Bethesda, Md.: CDL Press, 1993.

Rabinowitz, L. I. "The Study of a Midrash." *Jewish Quarterly Review* n.s. 58, 2 (1967): 143–61.

Reeves, John C., ed. *Bible and Qurʾān: Essays in Scriptural Intertextuality.* Atlanta: Society of Biblical Literature, 2003.

Reid, Charles J., Jr. *Power over the Body, Equality in the Family: Rights and Domestic Relations in Medieval Canon Law.* Grand Rapids, Mich.: Eerdmans, 2004.

Renan, Ernest. "Muhammad and the Origins of Islam." In *The Quest for the Historical Muhammad*, ed. and trans. Ibn Warraq. New York: Prometheus Books, 2000, 127–68.

———. *Qu'est-ce que'une nation?* Paris: Presses Pocket, 1992.

Ricks, Stephen D. "Kinship Bars to Marriage in Jewish and Islamic Law." In *Studies in Islamic and Judaic Traditions*, ed. William M. Brinner and Stephen D. Ricks. Atlanta: Scholars Press, 1986, 123–42.

Rippin, Andrew. "Ibn ʿAbbās's *Al-lughāt fī'l Qurʾān.*" *Bulletin of the School of Oriental and African Studies* 44, 1 (1981): 15–25.

———. "Ibn ʿAbbās's *Gharīb al-Qurʾān.*" *Bulletin of the School of Oriental and African Studies* 46, 2 (1983): 322–33.

———. Review of *Studies in Qurʾān and Ḥadīth: The Formation of the Islamic Law of Inheritance. Bulletin of the School of Oriental and African Studies* 51, 2 (1988): 323–24.

Roberts, Robert. *The Social Laws of the Qorân: Considered, and Compared with Those of the Hebrew and Other Ancient Codes.* London: Curzon Press, 1925.

Robinson, Chase F. *ʿAbd al-Malik.* Makers of the Muslim World. Oxford: Oneworld, 2006.

———. *Islamic Historiography.* Cambridge: Cambridge University Press, 2003.

Robinson, Neal. *Discovering the Qurʾān: A Contemporary Approach to a Veiled Text.* 2nd ed. Washington, D.C.: Georgetown University Press, 2003.

Rodinson, Maxime. *Mohammed.* New York: Random House, 1974.

Rosenthal, Franz. "The Life and Works of al-Ṭabarī." In *The History of al-Ṭabarī*, vol. 1, *General Introduction and From the Creation to the Flood*, trans. Franz Rosenthal. Albany: State University of New York Press, 1989, 5–134.

Rubin, Uri. *Between Bible and Qurʾān: The Children of Israel and the Islamic Self-Image.* Princeton, N.J.: Darwin Press, 1999.

———. *The Eye of the Beholder: The Life of Muhammad as Viewed by the Early Muslims.* Princeton, N.J.: Darwin Press, 1995.

———. "Prophets and Caliphs: The Biblical Foundations of the Umayyad Authority." In *Method and Theory in the Study of Islamic Origins*, ed. Herbert Berg. Leiden: Brill, 2003, 73–99.

Sachedina, Abdulaziz. "Early Muslim Traditionists and Their Familiarity with Jewish Sources." In *Studies in Islamic and Judaic Traditions: Papers Presented at the Institute for Islamic-Judaic Studies, Center for Judaic Studies, University of Denver*, vol. 2, ed. William M. Brinner and Stephen D. Ricks. Atlanta: Scholars Press, 49–59.

Sanders, E. P. *The Historical Figure of Jesus.* London: Penguin, 1993.

Santillana, David. *Istituzioni di diritto musulmano Malichita con riguardo anche al sistema sciafiita.* 2 vols. Rome: Istituto per l'Oriente, 1925.

Saunders, J. J. *A History of Medieval Islam.* London: Routledge and Kegan Paul, 1965.

Savant, Sarah Bowen. "Isaac as the Persians' Ishmael: Pride and the Pre-Islamic Past in Ninth and Tenth-Century Islam." *Comparative Islamic Studies* 2, 1 (2006): 5–25.

Schäfer, Peter. *Jesus in the Talmud.* Princeton, N.J.: Princeton University Press, 2007.

Schoeler, Gregor. "Foundations for a New Biography of Muḥammad: The Production and Evaluation of the Corpus of Traditions from ʿUrwah b. al-Zubayr." In *Method and Theory in the Study of Islamic Origins*, ed. Herbert Berg. Leiden: Brill, 2003, 21–28.

Schoeps, H. J. "The Sacrifice of Isaac in Paul's Theology." *Journal of Biblical Literature* 65 (1946): 385–92.

Scott, James M. *Adoption as Sons of God: An Exegetical Investigation into the Background of ΥΙΟΘΕΣΙΑ in the Pauline Corpus.* Wissenschaftliche Untersuchungen zum Neuen Testament 2, Reihe 48. Tübingen: J.C.B. Mohr (Paul Siebeck), 1992.

Selms, Adriaan van. "*siǧǧīn* and *siǧǧīl* in the Qurʾān." *Welt des Orients* 9, 1 (1977): 99–103.

Seters, John Van. "Jacob's Marriages and Ancient Near East Customs: A Reexamination." *Harvard Theological Review* 62, 4 (1969): 377–95.

Sezgin, Fuat. *Geschichte des arabischen Schrifttums.* 13 vols. Leiden: Brill, 1967–2007.

Sharon, Moshe. "*Ahl al-bayt*: People of the House." *Jerusalem Studies in Arabic and Islam* 8 (1986): 169–84.

Silva, David A. *4 Maccabees.* Sheffield: Sheffield Academic Press, 1998.

Silverstein, Adam J. "Haman's Transition from the *Jāhiliyya* to Islam." *Jerusalem Studies in Arabic and Islam* 34 (2008).

———. *Postal Systems in the Pre-Modern Islamic World.* Cambridge Studies in Islamic Civilization. Cambridge: Cambridge University Press, 2007.

Simon, Róbert. "Mānī and Muḥammad." *Jerusalem Studies in Arabic and Islam* 21 (1997): 118–41.

———. *Meccan Trade and Islam: Problems of Origin and Structure.* Budapest: Akadémiai Kiadó, 1989.

Sizgorich, Thomas. "'Do Prophets Come with a Sword?' Conquests, Empire, and Historical Narrative in the Early Islamic World." *American Historical Review* 112:4 (2007): 993–1015.

———. "Narrative and Community in Islamic Late Antiquity." *Past & Present* 185 (2004): 9–42.

Smith, W. Robertson. *Kinship and Marriage in Early Arabia.* Boston: Beacon Press, 1903.

Soloveitchik, Joseph B. *Family Redeemed: Essays on Family Relationships.* Ed. David Shatz and Joel Wolowelsky. New York: Meorot Harav Foundation, 2002.

Sonbol, Amira al-Azhary. "Adoption in Islamic Society: A Historical Survey." In *Children in the Middle East,* ed. Elizabeth Warnock Fernea. Austin: University of Texas Press, 1995, 45–67.

Speight, R. Marston. "The Will of Saʿd b. a. Waqqāṣ: The Growth of a Tradition." *Der Islam* 50, 2 (1973): 249–67.

Speiser, E. A. "Notes to Recently Published Nuzi Texts." *Journal of the American Oriental Society* 55, 4 (1935): 432–43.

Spellberg, D. A. *Politics, Gender, and the Islamic Past: The Legacy of ʿĀʾisha bint Abi Bakr.* New York: Columbia University Press, 1994.

Speyer, Heinrich. *Die Biblischen Erzählungen im Qoran.* Hildesheim: Georg Olms, 1931. Repr. 1961.

Spiegel, Shalom. *The Last Trial, on the Legends and Lore of the Command to Abraham to Offer Isaac as a Sacrifice: The Akedah.* Trans. Judah Goldin. New York: Schocken Books, 1969.

Stern, Gertrude. *Marriage in Early Arabia.* London: Royal Asiatic Society, 1939.

Stone, Elizabeth C. and David I. Owen. *Adoption in Old Babylonian Nippur and the Archive of Mannum-mešu-liṣṣur.* Winona Lake, Ind.: Eisenbrauns, 1991.

Stowasser, Barbara Freyer. *Women in the Qurʾan, Traditions, and Interpretation.* New York: Oxford University Press, 1994.

Strack, H. L. and G. Stemberger. *Introduction to the Talmud and Midrash.* Trans. Markus Bockmuehl. Edinburgh: T&T Clark, 1991.

Strauss, Leo. *Persecution and the Art of Writing.* Glencoe, Ill.: Free Press, 1952.

Stroumsa, Guy. "Christ's Laughter: Docetic Origins Reconsidered." *Journal of Early Christian Studies* 12, 3 (2004): 267–88.

———. "'Seal of Prophets': The Nature of a Manichaean Metaphor." *Jerusalem Studies in Arabic and Islam* 7 (1986): 61–74.

Stroumsa, Sarah. "Compassion for Wisdom: The Attitude of Some Medieval Arab Philosophers Towards the Codification of Philosophy." *Bochumer Philosophisches Jahrbuch* 1 (1997): 39–55.

Swetnam, James. *Jesus and Isaac: A Study of the Epistle to the Hebrews in Light of the Aqedah.* Rome: Biblical Institute Press, 1981.

Theological Dictionary of the Old Testament. Ed. G. Johannes Botterweck and Helmer Ringgren. Trans. David E. Green. Grand Rapids, Mich.: Eerdmans, 1974–2004. [*TDOT*]

Tov, Emanuel. *Scribal Practices and Approaches Reflected in the Texts Found in the Judean Desert.* Leiden: Brill, 2004.

Turner, Victor. *The Forest of Symbols.* Ithaca, N.Y.: Cornell University Press, 1967.

Unger, Merrill F. "Some Comments on the Text of Genesis 15 2, 3." *Journal of Biblical Literature* 72, 1 (1953): 49–50.

Van Ess, Josef. *See* Ess, Josef Van.

Van Seters, John. *See* Seters, John Van.

VanderKam, James C. *The Book of Jubilees.* Sheffield: Sheffield Academic Press, 2001.

Verden, Michel. "Virgins and Widows: European Kinship and Early Christianity." *Man* n.s. 23, 3 (1988): 488–505.

Vermes, Geza. "New Light on the Sacrifice of Isaac from 4Q225." *Journal of Jewish Studies* 32 (1981): 140–45.

———. *Scripture and Tradition.* Leiden: Brill, 1961.

Vööbus, Arthur. *Discovery of Very Important Manuscript Sources for the Syro-Roman Lawbook.* Stockholm: Estonian Theological Society in Exile, 1971.

Voorhis, John W. "John of Damascus on the Muslim Heresy." In *The Early Christian-Muslim Dialogue: A Collection of Documents from the First Three Islamic Centuries (632–900 A.D.), Translations with Commentary,* ed. N. A. Newman. Hatfield, Pa.: Interdisciplinary Biblical Research Institute, 1993, 133–62.

Wansbrough, John. *The Sectarian Milieu: Content and Composition of Islamic Salvation History.* Oxford: Oxford University Press, 1978.

Watt, W. Montgomery. *Islamic Political Thought.* Edinburgh: University Press, 1968.

———. *Muhammad at Medina.* Oxford: Clarendon Press, 1956.

Wells, Bradford et al. *The Excavations at Dura-Europas: Final Report V.* Part I, *The Parchments and Papyri.* Ed. Ann Perkins. New Haven, Conn.: Yale University Press, 1959.

Westbrook, Raymond, ed. *A History of Ancient Near Eastern Law.* 2 vols. Leiden: Brill, 2003. [*HANEL*]

———. "Legal Aspects of Care of the Elderly in the Ancient Near East: Introduction." In *The Care of the Elderly in the Ancient Near East,* ed. Marten Stol and Sven P. Fleming. Leiden: Brill, 1998, 1–20.

Westermann, Claus. *Genesis 12–36: A Commentary.* Trans. John J. Scullion, S.J. Minneapolis: Augsburg, 1981.

White, Hayden. *The Content of the Form: Narrative Discourse and Historical Representation.* Baltimore: John Hopkins University Press, 1987.

Wright, W. *A Grammar of the Arabic Language.* 3rd ed. Cambridge: Cambridge University Press, 1971.

Yaron, Reuven. *Introduction to the Law of the Aramaic Papyri.* Oxford: Clarendon Press, 1961.

al-Yāsīn, ʿIzz al-Dīn. *The Lexical Relation Between Ugaritic and Arabic.* New York: Shelton College, 1952.

Yoreh, Tzemach. "The Elohistic Source" (in Hebrew). Ph.D dissertation, Hebrew University of Jerusalem, 2003.

Zaman, Iftikhar. "The Evolution of a Hadith: Transmission, Growth and the Science of *Rijal* in a Hadith of Saʿd b. Abi Waqqas." Ph.D. dissertation, University of Chicago, 1989.

Zammit, Martin R. *A Comparative Lexical Study of Qurʾānic Arabic.* Leiden: Brill, 2002.

Ziadeh, Farhat. Review of *Studies in Qurʾān and Ḥadīth: The Formation of the Islamic Law of Inheritance. Journal of the American Oriental Society,* 108, 3 (1986): 487–88.

Zimmern, Heinrich. *Akkadische Fremdwörter als Beweis für babylonischen Kultureinfluss.* Leipzig: A. Edelmann, 1915.

Citation Index

Hebrew Bible

Apocrypha and Pseudepigrapha

Pseudo-Philo

Josephus

Babylonian Talmud

Midrash

New Testament

Apocrypha

Qur'ān

Subject Index

al-ʿAbbās b. ʿAbd al-Muṭṭalib, 65, 231, 273n78; conversion to Islam, 280n52, 303n15; and inheritance from the Prophet, 248–49, 303n19; prepares Muḥammad's body for burial, 266n28
ʿAbbāsid book hand script. *See* paleography
ʿAbdallāh, son of the Prophet Muḥammad, 9, 25
ʿAbdallāh b. ʿAbbās. *See* Ibn ʿAbbās
ʿAbdallāh b. Abī Bakr b. Ḥazm (tradent), 280n53
ʿAbdallāh b. Jaʿfar b. Abī Ṭālib, 75, 92, 278n18, 280–81n53; spit-and-image of the Prophet, 281n53. *See also* topos
ʿAbdallāh b. Jaḥsh, 41; serves as his sister Zaynab's marriage guardian, 41, 139–40, 269n19
ʿAbdallāh b. Masʿūd. *See* Ibn Masʿūd
ʿAbdallāh b. Muḥammad b. ʿUmar b. ʿAlī (tradent), 279n34
ʿAbdallāh b. Rawāḥa al-Khazrajī (Companion, d. 8/629), 75–81, 92–93, 97–99, 282n81; and Battle of Muʾta, 75, 90, 97, 278n24; death, date of, 84; *khalīfa* of Medina in Prophet's absence, 76; martyrdom of, 78–80, 89, 93; storyteller and poet, 76; speech by, prior to Battle of Muʾta, 77, 278n29
ʿAbdallāh b. ʿUmar b. al-Khaṭṭāb. *See* Ibn ʿUmar
ʿAbdallāh b. al-Zubayr (d. 73/692), 88; caliphate of, 92; and collection of the Qurʾān, 158
ʿAbd al-Malik b. Abī Sulaymān al-Fazārī (tradent, d. 145/762–63), 287n7
ʿAbd al-Malik b. Marwān (caliph, r. 65–86/685–705), 220, 227, 292n48; and false prophets, 53–54; and redaction of the Qurʾān, 160–61; and al-Shaʿbī, 300n70; and ʿUrwa b. al-Zubayr, correspondence with, 88
ʿAbd al-Muṭṭalib b. Hāshim, 130; grandfather of Zaynab and Muḥammad, 39, 139–40, 270n25, 290n57
ʿAbd al-Raḥmān b. Ādam, and adoption, 25. *See also* Ibn Umm Burthun
ʿAbd al-Raḥmān b. al-Ḥārith b. Hishām (Companion), and collection of the Qurʾān, 158
ʿAbd al-Razzāq al-Ṣanʿānī (d. 211/826), 67, 203, 206, 209, 214, 216, 218, 288n18; intellectual formation of, 297n20; on Q. 4:176, 200–203; on Q. 33:6a, 66
ʿAbd Shams (clan), 39
Abiathar (priest, OT), 246
Aboubacharos, 82. *See also* Abū Bakr
Abraham/Abram (OT), 3–8, 15, 18, 39, 41, 52, 58, 60–61, 68–69, 95, 98, 100, 120, 140–41, 143, 150, 225–26, 259n4, 260n9, 274n82, 288n27, 295n89; and the *aqedah*, 101–2, 104–5, 107–9, 110–17, 136, 146, 148, 284n20; and childlessness, 134–35, 261n18; and his daughter-in-law, 141–42; in the Qurʾān, 51, 55, 272n54; spiritual father of Israelites, 231; spit-and-image of Isaac, 285n45; undergoes ten trials, 141. *See also* Isaac
abrogation (*naskh*), 62, 67, 183–84, 195, 198, 256, 275n101, 295n100. *See also* inheritance in the Qurʾān; *nasakh*
Abū ʿAmr b. al-ʿAlāʾ (philologist, d. 154/770), 209
Abū Bakr (caliph, r. 11–13/632–34), 65, 80, 86–87, 89, 92, 201, 248–50, 274n81, 276n108, 299nn44, 45, 300n71, 302n12, 303n19; and collection of the Qurʾān, 156–57, 160–61, 221, 291n3; and inheritance rights of grandfather, 223, 297n12; and *al-kalāla*, 208, 214–15, 218–19, 221–33; sends Usāma b. Zayd to Ubna, 27
Abū Bakr b. ʿAbdallāh b. ʿUtba (tradent), 280n47
Abū Bakr b. ʿAbd al-Raḥmān b. al-Ḥārith b. Hishām (d. 94/713), 74, 280n47

warfare: and casus belli, 92; manpower versus military intelligence, 84; psychological impact of defeat, 80–81; and rules of engagement, 76, 92, 97–99, 147; standard (flag), 76. *See also* vengeance
Warqā' (tradent, d. 160/777), 276n113
wives. *See* inheritance in the Qur'ān
wives of the Prophet, 8, 36, 39, 43–44, 49, 64–65, 70; as *ahl al-bayt*, 302n7; and Māriya the Copt, 56; as Mothers of the Believers, 58–59, 63–67, 232. *See also* Mothers of the Believers

X^{u}āstvānīft, 272n60. *See also* Mani; "seal of prophecy"

Yael (OT), slays Sisera, 107
Yaḥyā b. Abī Ya'lā (tradent), 281n53
al-Yamāma, Battle of, and collection of the Qur'ān, 53, 156
Ya'qūb b. Ibrāhīm (tradent, d. 208/823), 300nn72, 77, 79
al-Ya'qūbī (historian, d. > 292/905), 74
Yathrib, 4. *See also* Medina
Yavneh. *See* Ubna
Yazīd b. Zuray' (tradent, d. 182/798), 300n81
Yedidiah. *See* Solomon (OT)
Yehoshua. *See* Jesus
Yemen, 53, 159, 168, 200, 202, 209, 268n10, 297n20
Yoreh, Tzemach, on the *aqedah*, 285n25
Yose ben Zimrah, R. (Palestinian Amora), 113
Yosef. *See* Joseph (OT)
Younes, Munther, xiii
Yūnis (tradent), 269n21
Yūnis b. 'Abd al-A'lā (tradent), 300n73
Yūnis b. Yazīd (tradent), 246
yūrathu kalālat^{an}: 163, 165, 181, 183, 193, 198–99, 205, 211–12, 300n84. See also *kalāla*
y-w-r-th: as active verb (*yūrithu*) or as passive verb (*yūrathu*), 177, 193–94, 212–13, 232. See also *kalāla*

Zaccagnini, Carlo, on adoption in the ancient Near East, xiii
Zaccur ben Meshullam, and adoption, 262n19
Zakariyyā' (prophet), 249
Zakariyyā' b. Abī Zā'ida (tradent, d. 147–49/764–66), 205
al-Zamakhsharī (exegete, d. 538/1144), on Q. 33:40, 57
Zaphenath-paneah. *See* Joseph (OT)
Zayd b. Arqam (Companion, d. 68/787–88), 74
Zayd b. Ḥāritha b. Sharāḥīl al-Kalbī (Companion, d. 8/629), xiv–xv, 25, 28, 39–41, 81, 99, 130–31, 138, 268n10, 279n34, 284n17, 290n57; acquired by Khadīja as a slave, 40–41, 91, 129, 131, 287n7; adopted by Muḥammad, 40–41, 60, 62, 91, 94, 129, 226–27, 287n7, 288n18; age at time of death, 26; chooses slavery over freedom, 131–33, 137, 144, 149, 227, 288n19; commander of military expedition to Mu'ta, 75–76, 90, 144, 147; commands numerous military expeditions, 73, 75, 144; cries, 131, 133; death of, 26, 55, 57, 73, 86–87, 90–91, 226, 280n49, 290n55; death, date of, 72, 84, 88; description of, 25; eagerness for death, 106, 116, 147–48, 150; enslavement of, 40, 91, 129; *ghulām yaf'a*, 132; given to Muḥammad, 129, 131; as literary figure, 92, 116, 118, 121; manumitted by Muḥammad, 41, 90, 94, 137, 287n7; martyrdom of, at Mu'ta, 77–78, 80, 89, 91, 93, 96, 106, 110–11, 116, 144–45, 227; name changed to Zayd b. Muḥammad, 38–39, 41, 94, 132, 137, 227; name, meaning of, 132; and al-Nu'mān b. Funḥuṣ the Jew, conversation with, 97–98, 114–15; and Q. 33:4, 288n18; and Q. 33:40, 54–55; reverts to birth name, 58, 137; runs into the Garden, 78, 89, 91, 99, 106, 111, 116, 147; and Satan, 78, 89, 99, 111, 116, 147, 286n53; and Yosef/Joseph (OT), comparison to, 132–33. *See also* Zayd b. Muḥammad
Zayd b. Muḥammad, adopted son of the Prophet, 25, 41–43, 90, 121, 143–45, 226–27, 245; Beloved of the Messenger of God (Ḥibb Rasūl Allāh), xv, 25, 27, 41, 69, 75, 90, 94, 98–99, 106, 145, 149–50, 227, 282n80, 288n22, 290n57; only Companion whose name ("Zayd") is mentioned in the Qur'ān, 35–37, 68, 91, 108, 122, 138, 227, 288n22, 290n57; divorces Zaynab so that the Prophet

Acknowledgments

This book could not have been written without the support of colleagues and the kindness of friends and strangers.

In the Near Eastern Studies Department at Cornell, David Owen gave me access to his remarkable library of Nuziana; Lance Allred, Nicole Brisch, Alhena Godotti, and Chris Monroe answered questions about Akkadian and the ancient Near East; Lauren Monroe responded to questions about the Hebrew Bible; and Kim Haines-Eitzen did the same for questions about the New Testament. Ragi Ibrahim helped me decipher a difficult Arabic text. The burdens of research were lightened by my research assistants, Ben Towbin and Esther Dorland, and by the book delivery service of Olin Library at Cornell. Special thanks to Munther Younes, who has been a steady source of support, encouragement, and expert knowledge about the Arabic language.

Quick responses to sudden and unexpected queries were sent to me by Jonathan Culler, Jany János, Geoffrey Khan, Gerd Puin, David Schapps, Keith Small, Lynn Thitchener, and Cornelia Wunsch.

I benefited from conversations with friends and colleagues, sometimes over a meal, in a corridor, or in cyberspace. I thank Khaled Abou El Fadl, Asad Ahmad, Kecia Ali, Mohammed Arkoun, Robert Ascher, Peri Bearman, Maria-Pia di Bella, Haggai Ben-Shammai, Angelica Bernal, Faik Bouhrik, Ra'anan Bustan, Vincent Cornell, Yossi David, Vivien Farhi, Richard Gauvain, Rabbi Scott Glass, Alon Goshen-Gottstein, Susannah Heschel, Gail Holst-Warhaft, Khurram Hussein, R. Kevin Jaques, Baber Johansen, Walter Kaegi, Georges Khalil, Admiel Kosman, Timur Kuran, Ella Landau-Tasseron, Michael Lecker, Gideon Libson, Moriah Libson (may her memory be for a blessing), Ghislaine Lydon, Ken and Gabi Mann-Kanovitz, Michael Marx, Brinkley Messick, Christian Müller, Angelika Neuwirth, Gordon Newby, Rhoda Posen, Peter Potter, Megan Reid, Milka Rubin, Marina Rustow, Nava Scharf, Fred Schneider, Bill and Lucy Schwartz, Roni Shaham, Shalom Shoer, Petra Sijpesteijn, Nicolai Sinai, Susan Slymovics, Guy and Sarah Stroumsa, Etty Terem, Avram Udovitch, Lucette Valensi, Michael and Peggy Wager, Phil and Amy Waldoks, Joseph Witztum, Kevin van Bladel, and Ed Zehner.

The following colleagues read one or more chapters in draft form and offered comments and criticisms that were enormously helpful: Mohammed Hocine Benkheira, Calum Carmichael, Aryeh Cohen, Michael Cook,

Patricia Crone, Yasir Kazi, Harald Motzki, Devin Stewart, Yohanan Friedmann, Aharon Layish, Jon Levenson, Scott Lucas, Ze'ev Maghen, Ghassan Masri, Maurice Pomerantz, A. Kevin Reinhart, Uri Rubin, Jens Scheiner, Ron Shaham, Adam Silverstein, Susan Spectorsky, Justin Stearns, Ray Westbrook, and Munther Younes.

Special thanks to Daniel Boyarin, Fred Donner, Frank Griffel, Steven Judd, and Andrew Rippin, who read full drafts of the typescript and offered important suggestions for improvement of the argument and its organization.

I presented drafts of individual chapters as lectures or conference papers at the following venues: American Oriental Society (2008 annual meeting), Annenberg Institute for Advanced Judaic Studies, Columbia University, Dartmouth College, Emory University, Harvard University, Hebrew University of Jerusalem, Indiana University, School of Oriental and African Studies in London, the Sorbonne, University of Southern California at Los Angeles, Washington University, Wissenschaftskolleg zu Berlin, and Yale University. Special thanks to A. Kevin Reinhart and Shawkat Toorawa, who presented my paper in my absence when an act of God made it impossible for me to attend the 2007 AOS meeting in Texas.

Three colleagues occupy a special place in my heart: Ze'ev Maghen opened my eyes to the way in which our understanding of narrative reports about the life of Muḥammad is enhanced by comparison to biblical models; François Déroche guided my first steps in the study of early Qur'ān manuscripts; and Adam Silverstein has been a delightful interlocutor, correspondent, and critic.

This project took me into areas of the academy that I never imagined entering. For assistance with multispectral imaging, I thank Virginia Cole and Tatyana Petukhova of Olin Library at Cornell University and the photographic services at Bibliothèque Nationale de France. Special thanks to Roger Easton of Rochester Institute of Technology, and to his student intern Marwah, who spent hours analyzing images of BNF 328a. For assistance with x-ray fluorescent spectroscopy, I thank Don Bilderbeck, Darren Dale, Richard Ehrlich, and Sol Gruner of Cornell University. In Paris, analysis of BNF 328a, folio 10b was carried out by Armando Solé (Grenoble) and Philippe Walter (The Louvre), with the assistance of Brice Moignard, Laurent Pichon, and Laurence de Viguerie. Special thanks also to Marie-Geneviève Guesdon, curator of Arabic manuscripts at BNF, for her many kindnesses.

Financial support for travel to Paris to work at Bibliothèque Nationale de France was provided by the Mario Einaudi Center for International Studies and by the Near Eastern Studies Department at Cornell University. The final draft of this monograph was written during my tenure as a Carnegie Scholar in 2007–8 and with a grant from the Carnegie Corporation of New

York. The statements and views expressed here are solely my responsibility. Or, to paraphrase the first caliph, Abū Bakr: "I have expressed my own personal opinion on this matter. If it is correct then it is from God; if it is mistaken, no one but I am responsible."

Last but not least, I thank my wife Jane for her love and support; and my children, Kate, Sarah, and Andy, who, as this book was being written, suffered the absences of their father with grace and understanding.